Virtual Professional Development and Informal Learning via Social Networks

Vanessa P. Dennen
Florida State University, USA

Jennifer B. Myers
Orangeburg–Calhoun Technical College, USA & Florida State University, USA

Information Science
REFERENCE

Managing Director:	Lindsay Johnston
Senior Editorial Director:	Heather A. Probst
Book Production Manager:	Sean Woznicki
Development Manager:	Joel Gamon
Development Editor:	Hannah Abelbeck
Acquisitions Editor:	Erika Gallagher
Typesetter:	Nicole Sparano
Cover Design:	Nick Newcomer

Published in the United States of America by
Information Science Reference (an imprint of IGI Global)
701 E. Chocolate Avenue
Hershey PA 17033
Tel: 717-533-8845
Fax: 717-533-8661
E-mail: cust@igi-global.com
Web site: http://www.igi-global.com

Library of Congress Cataloging-in-Publication Data

Virtual professional development and informal learning via social networks / Vanessa P. Dennen and Jennifer B. Myers, editors.
    p. cm.
  Includes bibliographical references and index.
  Summary: "This book will examine how individuals and organizations are using Web 2.0 tools to create informal learning and professional development opportunities"-- Provided by publisher.
  ISBN 978-1-4666-1815-2 (hardcover) -- ISBN 978-1-4666-1816-9 (ebook) (print) -- ISBN 978-1-4666-1817-6 (print & perpetual access) (print) 1. Internet in education. 2. Career development--Computer-assisted instruction. 3. Occupational training--Computer-assisted instruction. 4. Professional learning communities--Computer networks. 5. Web 2.0. I. Dennen, Vanessa P., 1970- II. Myers, Jennifer B., 1980-
  LB1044.87.V58 2012
  371.33'44678--dc23
                                    2012002875

British Cataloguing in Publication Data
A Cataloguing in Publication record for this book is available from the British Library.

All work contributed to this book is new, previously-unpublished material. The views expressed in this book are those of the authors, but not necessarily of the publisher.

Table of Contents

Section 1
Overview and Issues: Virtual Professional Development and Informal
Learning via Social Networks

Section 2
Lenses and Approaches

Section 3
Cases and Research in Higher Education

Section 4
Cases and Research Regarding Pre- and In-Service Teachers

Detailed Table of Contents

Section 1
Overview and Issues: Virtual Professional Development and Informal
Learning via Social Networks

This chapter presents a fresh look at collaborative applications and their use in professional development and informal learning. The chapter addresses some of the cultural challenges impacting collaborative technologies, especially given the fact that these technologies are transplanted from developed countries into regions of the world that are only beginning to understand their significance. Therefore, the chapter points to the importance of and the needs to allow cultural variation and differences in usage. The chapter acknowledge the fact that collaborative technologies possess great potential for both professional development and informal learning, but caution that external factors, such as culture and community, be taken into account to realize potential benefits.

This chapter explores the issues that can arise when professionals employ Web 2.0 social networking technologies in service of their professional development by way of informal learning. Issues around privacy, confidentiality, and compliance are discussed, and possible actions organizations and individuals can take are presented.

Chapter 3

The number of mobile devices and active users is growing. Mobile devices expand the reach of technology-mediated communication possibilities for many people. They have become a convenient, and in many instances preferred, way for people to communicate with each other as well as to access the Internet. In terms of learning, this means that people can increasingly access both content and resources from any number of locations. This chapter explores how mobile devices can be used to support informal learning practices, and it provides practical tips for researchers in conducting studies of informal mobile learning.

Section 2
Lenses and Approaches

Chapter 4

This chapter discusses the adoption of activity theory as a conceptual framework for analyzing learning processes related to professional development and informal learning via social network environments. The discussion includes an overview of professional development and informal learning via social networks, which highlights the need for a related analytical framework. Activity theory is then described and applied to an example of professional development. This operationalization of activity theory demonstrates the ability of the framework to enable viewing and analyzing learning via social networks such as Facebook communities, wiki and blog spaces, listservs, and discussion forums. The chapter ends with several key points related to implementing activity theory as a solution to investigating behaviors in social networks and potential directions for future research.

Chapter 5

Recently, researchers in the instructional technology and learning sciences arenas have started to pay attention to the concept of Personal Learning Environments (PLE). With the aim to investigate how social network theory could indicate the desired indicators for successful Personal Learning Environments, the authors address social capital theory as a conceptual framework to understand the network landscape within informal learning environments. Social capital is an inherent property of network and collaboration dynamics, along with key indicators related to personal network measurements. Personal network analysis as a means to evaluate social capital is discussed in this chapter. This chapter is not about learning what or learning as becoming, but about how people learn with whom, and with what degree of influence. It would be helpful for educators or researchers who are interested in measuring academic and psychosocial outcomes within the presence of social capital when applying personal social network analysis in personal learning networks.

This chapter discusses the role of corporate online social networks in the process of informal learning. The first part of these studies offers some introduction to the issue of online social networks used in the corporate setting. The second component of the investigation is dedicated to discussing the notion of informal learning in online social networks. To limit the scope of the research, in the subsequent sections the author concentrates on the linguistic aspect of spontaneous and unofficial education acquired online by corporate members. To discuss these issues in greater detail, the concepts of homophilous and heterophilous networks in corporate online learning are presented and discussed.

Section 3
Cases and Research in Higher Education

Chapter 7

Professionals who want to remain competitive in their fields are turning to Web 2.0 to learn the knowledge and skills they need in order to do their work more efficiently and effectively. Through a detailed description of how one instructor transformed his online graduate courses into dynamic, interactive, ongoing online learning communities that extended beyond the classroom, this chapter provides academics and practitioners a model for establishing a professional network that learners can participate in and replicate in their workplaces for their professional development and informal learning. An overview of the role of social networking in creating professional development and informal learning opportunities for cognitive apprenticeship, knowledge brokering, and ongoing online support communities, as well as the results of a survey conducted on students' perceptions of the impact of the social networking strategies and tools on their professional development and informal learning in and out of class, will also be discussed.

This chapter utilizes a peer learning community as an example to explore whether and how information exchange, learning, and knowledge creation occur when students undertake professional internships. Observation and analysis of the learners' views on their interaction are conducted by studying peer-generated blogs to determine if learners working in companies worldwide, but connected via an informal virtual community, can communicate effectively and produce a useful pool of information, thus creating meaningful knowledge and expertise to assist in future career development. The objective is to utilize the lessons learned to incorporate effective elements of the peer-learning experience into formal programs of study and so increase the employability focus of business education.

Chapter 9

Kyle Christensen, Columbus State University, USA
Iris M. Saltiel, Columbus State University, USA

This chapter describes one university-based social network created for peer mentoring, knowledge brokering, and resource sharing for faculty and students to collaborate to increase research and scholarship. First, the case study describes the process utilized to survey interests of faculty as the basis for an affiliation network of faculty research interests. The benefits of social network analysis and its applications are discussed and utilized. Next, a conversation is presented about the use of social network analysis to foster faculty collaboration through targeted programming is outlined. Finally, recommendations for practice are presented.

Chapter 10

Mariliis Vahe, Florida State University, USA
Khawaja Zain-Ul-Abdin, Florida State University, USA
Yalın Kılıç Türel, Firat University, Turkey

Social media has become one of the most dominant information phenomena of our time. As its commercial, social, activist, and informational uses multiply, questions are raised as to its efficiency as a learning tool. The authors focus this chapter on social media use in higher education, specifically in the field of medical education, and provide a modern definition of social media and its tools while elaborating on its educational uses and efficiency. Furthermore, they present a situation analysis through a review of original research published on the topic in the last five years, culminating in an identification of the gaps in literature and recommendations for future research endeavors.

Section 4
Cases and Research Regarding Pre- and In-Service Teachers

Chapter 11

Luke Rodesiler, University of Florida, USA
Lauren Tripp, University of Florida, USA

Given the potential of informal online learning via social networks for supporting the career-long professional growth of in-service teachers, research must be conducted to better understand the ways in which today's future teachers are being prepared for and experiencing such practice. This chapter presents the authors' efforts to move in that direction, a qualitative study describing six pre-service secondary English language arts teachers' perceptions of self-directed networked learning during a teaching internship. Findings suggest that participants perceived networked learning as a viable and valuable approach to supplementing professional growth despite also perceiving challenges in the form of context, identity, and time.

Chapter 12

Aline Maria de Medeiros Rodrigues Reali, Federal University of São Carlos, Brazil
Regina Maria Simões Puccinelli Tancredi, Presbyterian University Mackenzie, Brazil & Federal
University of São Carlos, Brazil
Maria da Graça Nicoletti Mizukami, Presbyterian University Mackenzie, Brazil & Federal
University of São Carlos, Brazil

This chapter examines the results of an investigation carried out by the researchers from a Brazilian public institution and experienced teachers (mentors) that aimed to produce knowledge on teacher professional development and learning, investigate educational processes of mentors interacting with novice teachers by e-mail, evaluate the continued education methodology adopted, and contribute to existing knowledge on online continued teacher education. The main sources of data were email communications between mentors and novice teachers, the mentors' and novice teachers' reflective journals, and the researchers' observations from weekly meetings between the mentors and teachers. The development of the online Mentorship Program is a much more complex enterprise than a face-to-face equivalent program would have been because it demands entirely new logistics, but it promotes the establishment of professional and affective bonds among the participants, the broadening of professional knowledge, the mastery of online adult education technologies, and the participants' professional growth.

Chapter 13

Jung Won Hur, Auburn University, USA
Thomas Brush, Indiana University, USA
Curt Bonk, Indiana University, USA

The purpose of this chapter is to discuss the findings of a research study analyzing knowledge and emotional sharing in a self-generated online teacher community. Although active informal learning occurs in online communities of teachers, scant information is available about the knowledge and emotions teachers share in these communities. The authors conducted a content analysis of 1,709 entries in a self-generated blog community and examined the types of activities teachers were engaged in. The data revealed that over 29% of entries were related to lesson plans or teaching resources. In addition, over 17% of the postings addressed teachers' positive or negative emotions. The authors argue that teacher participation in online communities should be promoted and encouraged, since online communities help teachers with informal learning and emotional sharing.

Section 5
Cases and Research in the Workplace

Chapter 14

Vanessa P. Dennen, Florida State University, USA
Wenting Jiang, Florida State University, USA

Social media provides professional organizations with a new means of distributing information and perhaps even facilitating learning among their members. This study compares Twitter use in two populations, academics and corporate professionals, and in two interaction contexts, conference and non-conference, looking at how knowledge is shared by organizations. Organizations in three fields—nursing, information technology, and educational technology—were included in the study. A content analysis showed that both types of organizations focused more on supplying original content than providing links or retweets. Conferences generated the greatest activity levels, and industry organizations were more savvy with Twitter use, although on the whole hashtags were underutilized and much room remains to maximize use of social media. Nonetheless, a wealth of knowledge sharing that can support information learning and professional development is taking place in these online networks.

Chapter 15

In this chapter, the authors describe an initiative to create a cross-organization, knowledge building communal network built from the personal workplace stories voluntarily contributed by conflict management practitioners. They identify various wiki adoption and usage issues and provide recommendations and strategies for addressing these issues based on survey data from the wiki target member population. Moreover, the authors compare and contrast their wiki design with recommended practices from the wiki literature and provide some suggestions for future research.

Chapter 16

Polymorphic innovations of Web 2.0 have both inspired and facilitated a near ubiquitous learning architecture centered on mobility, customization, and collective intelligence in a variety of fields. These reconfigurable pedagogical learning platforms have empowered participants by removing passive, standardized methods of unilateral knowledge delivery established by its Web 1.0 predecessor, and included a multitude of divergent, informal, and participant-driven social networks. These new technological devices and opportunities for self-guided, multidirectional knowledge exchange within newly established informal learning networks are affordable and flexible. The teaching and training of professional medical personnel, aligned with the flexibility and the capability of Web 2.0 platforms in the exchange of collaborative social learning, can be an authentic and productive knowledge-making andragogical approach to healthcare training. Such training must consider, study, and embrace social-constructivism, problem-based learning, andragogy, universal design for learning, media naturalness theory, divergent thinking, and the expanded rhetorical triangle in order to maximize the potential of mobile medicine through expanding the practice of telemedicine.

Foreword

The focus of this edited volume is on informal learning. As one of the authors in this volume states, more and more adults are pursuing informal learning, especially in recent years. Because of this increased prevalence of informal learning, Thomas and Brown (2011) suggest the way we think about education needs to shift. Learning does not only happen in classrooms, but also occurs by sharing stories and engaging in problem solving together.

When I was an instructional designer in a corporate setting, I realized that formal classrooms are not very effective environments for learning. Of course, people do learn something when they finish a course or training class, but the skills learned and knowledge obtained are not retained over a long period of time unless the new skills and knowledge are used immediately. Instead, I noticed that people learn and retain knowledge best when they work on a task *in situ*, share what they have experienced, and learn from each other. Later, I discovered that this concept has a name—it is called communities of practice.

Although having face-to-face communities of practice is useful, they tend to remain small and local. Organizations and professional associations are increasingly examining the potential of online communication networks to enable members to share knowledge and engage in continuous professional development without the limit of physical spaces. Lately, informal learning through participation in online communities of practice is enhanced with the advent of social networking sites such as Facebook, Google+, and Twitter. People are becoming more comfortable with connecting with others socially and professionally online than ever before. In this sense, this volume offers guidance to take advantage of informal learning happening everywhere.

The volume's lead editor, Vanessa Dennen, has been a prolific author in the field of instructional technology. Her work touches on various aspects of online learning and online communities of practice. In fact, I collaborated with her on a paper in 2000 when we were both graduate students. Since then, technologies have changed, but the importance of understanding different learning prospects has not changed.

Vanessa has studied communities of practice with blog users and, more recently, with professionals using Twitter, whereas I studied the differences between online and face-to-face communities of practice (Hara, 2009). Although our approaches differ, we are both fascinated by the opportunities to examine online informal learning to support professional development. Vanessa is one of the leading authors in this area and is most qualified to edit this collection of articles. Her co-editor, Jennifer Myers, is a doctoral candidate who studies self-regulated learning among bloggers and is a promising young scholar in this area.

This volume covers a wide range of tools that support professional development and informal learning such as pervasive e-mail, mobile devices, and video conferencing technologies, and Web 2.0 technologies such as blogs, wikis, and Twitter. Many of the contributors to this volume provide useful examples of understanding how these technologies facilitate informal learning that leads to professional development. I have noticed books like this are inclined to fall into a trap of being technologically utopian (Kling, 1994), meaning that they do not attempt to go deeper than simply advocating new technologies for learning. However, all of the contributions in this volume consist of empirically supported studies. I was especially impressed that topics such as privacy and confidentiality are explicitly addressed. For example, one of the chapters offers useful recommendations for both organizations and individuals to deal with issues related to privacy, confidentiality, and compliance when using Web 2.0 technologies.

The following chapters provide an insightful perspective on how social networks can support informal learning and professional development in classrooms, online communities, and corporate settings. This is the go-to book for those who are interested in better understanding how learning experiences in informal settings—whether it is teachers sharing their thoughts and emotions on blogs or professionals sharing contextual knowledge via Twitter—can be cultivated and will sometimes trump formal learning environments.

Noriko Hara
Indiana University – Bloomington, USA

Noriko Hara is an Associate Professor of Information Science at Indiana University Bloomington. Dr. Hara earned her Master's and Doctoral degrees in Instructional Systems Technology from Indiana University. She also worked as a National Science Foundation postdoctoral research fellow at the University of North Carolina at Chapel Hill. Her research, rooted in the social informatics perspective, examines the means by which collective behaviors—including knowledge sharing, communities of practice, and online activism—are enabled and/or impeded by information technology. She is the author of Communities of Practice: Fostering Peer-to-Peer Learning and Informal Knowledge Sharing (2009) published by Springer. In addition, her publications have been cited widely and have appeared in: Instructional Science; Journal of the American Society for Information Science and Technology; Information, Communication, and Society; and The Information Society, among others.

REFERENCES

Hara, N. (2009). *Communities of practice: Fostering peer-to-peer learning and informal knowledge sharing in the work place*. Berlin, Germany: Springer.

Kling, R. (1994). Reading "all about" computerization: How genre conventions shape non-fiction social analysis. *The Information Society, 10*(3), 147–172. doi:10.1080/01972243.1994.9960166

Thomas, D., & Brown, J. S. (2011). *A new culture of learning: Cultivating the imagination for a world of constant change*. Lexington, KY: CreateSpace.

Preface

For many people in developed countries as well as some in developing countries—and particularly those people who are involved in higher education or professional careers—the Internet has infiltrated everyday life. It has come to satisfy a wide variety of the social, information, and communication needs of these people. They carry around smartphones, tablets, and laptops. Weekly family phone calls are replaced by Skyping, and friends and family know what each other are doing based on Facebook updates rather than personal communication. Questions are answered by Google, often supported by the kindly shared knowledge and experiences of strangers.

This ubiquity of the Internet has also spread across the various sectors or activities of peoples' lives. The information that people access online helps them at home, work, and school. It facilitates making plans with other people for personal and professional purposes. It is a flexible and extending tool; and if one has an Internet-connected device constantly close at hand their range of knowledge abilities can readily be extended.

In an educational context, the Internet has become a popular platform for supporting both learning and performance. Use of the Internet to support formal learning is well known and established. As Bonk and Dennen (2003) noted, there is a continuum of Web integration in college courses that ranges from having a syllabus online or encouraging students to explore Web-based resources to teaching online as part of a larger online degree program or initiative. At that time, the continuum was being used in part to encourage instructors to think about how they could enter the online learning arena and gradually incorporate the Internet more holistically in their teaching. However, such encouragement is no longer needed. Whereas fifteen years ago the instructors who put materials online or taught online were the minority, today the minority group is comprised of instructors who have no Web integration in their courses. And according to the Babson Survey Research Group (Allen & Seaman, 2011), as of 2011 more than 1/3 of all higher education students in the United States are taking at least one online course.

At the same time, there is a tremendous amount of learning that takes place online that is not formally noted as learning. It simply occurs as people engage with each other via social networking tools and other Web 2.0 technologies. For example, a person might come up with a question in the course of a workday and send out a tweet to her personal network, seeing if anyone has an answer. Should she receive an answer, both the original questioner and people within her network may learn from the response. Another person might practice learning a new language by interacting with other people at a website like LiveMocha (livemocha.com) in anticipation of an upcoming business trip. A new teacher might blog about her experiences in the classroom, only to find at the end of her first school year that she has both generated a rich document reflecting on her own professional development and developed a network of informal mentors and supporters who leave useful comments. Concurrently, a pre-service teacher might be reading her blog with keen interest, trying to glean as much as possible about what the real first-year teaching experience is like. These are all examples of the types of informal learning that are supported by the Internet and motivated by the individual learner's desire or need to know something.

Whether learners are already actively engaged in a profession or still preparing to enter a profession, these informal learning interactions enhance their formal education and professional experiences. Granted, not everyone engages in these types of informal learning activities; these individuals represent a sub-set of their larger professional community, not all of whom have sought or may wish to seek online interaction. Still, the robust nature of these online interactions and their surrounding communities, often developed in a bottom-up fashion, indicates the value of Web 2.0-based interaction for a portion of the population.

This idea of people engaging in informal learning experiences, often facilitated by their social networks, did not originate with the Internet, but certainly has been facilitated by it. Informal, voluntary professional development activities allow people to focus on individual learning needs as they arise. These opportunities do not replace formal education and training, which should focus on core knowledge and skills within the profession. Instead, they enhance formal experiences by providing a platform through which individualization, social networking, mentoring, and knowledge brokering all may take place. Thus, the power of informal online learning and professional development is in supporting individuals as they determine their own learning needs and, typically through interaction with others, find pertinent and timely ways of meeting those needs. Ironically, these activities may not be validated by the organizations in which people work as true learning or professional development, because they are free to participants, are not typically led by "experts" (or are led by self-proclaimed experts, such as the Pro-Ams discussed by Leadbeater and Miller [2004] and Gee [2009]), are socially constructed, may include personal/off-topic chatter, are not formally assessed, and do not result in a certification or degree. Still, these activities fill an important gap in professional learning because they enable on-the-job knowledge exchange and teach what is not or what cannot be taught in formal environments.

We decided to edit this book because we felt strongly that informal learning in online environments deserves more recognition for the role that it plays in professional development. This trend is only likely to increase as time passes and more individuals are exposed to it. Because some individuals come to this form of professional development naturally, whereas others are introduced via formal learning experiences, we wanted to highlight not only online learning that clearly takes place in an informal manner, but also those experiences that may initially introduce or lead a learner to the online environments in which informal learning and virtual professional development thrive. For example, a student may first learn about using Twitter and blogs as part of a course experience, or a worker may find out about an online professional network while participating in a training session or webinar. Each may then engage with these networks independently at a later time for continued professional development.

Figure 1 demonstrates our conceptualization of the field of learning as it relates to this book. On the horizontal axis, we draw a continuum from school-based learning to workplace learning. The assumption is that a good deal of learning will occur as part of a degree program and be continued or extended in the workplace. Whereas school-based learning tends to be focused on earning a certificate or degree and provides foundational and general knowledge of a field, workplace learning tends to be more situated in the specific objectives and practices of the work context. Notably absent from this continuum is personal or hobby-related learning. While we do not mean to diminish either the importance or relevance of this type of learning, in this book we are focusing on learning that is connected to professional development.

The vertical axis is a continuum that represents degree of formality. The most formal of learning experiences typically are instructor-centered and are situated in a classroom—physical or virtual. In

Figure 1. Ranges of learning experiences

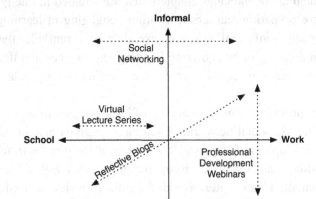

contrast, participants may not even recognize the most informal learning experiences as being about learning—as opposed to everyday life—although learning is certainly a byproduct of most interactions in everyday life.

A few examples have been placed on the figure to demonstrate a diverse, non-exhaustive range of online activities that may foster learning. Note that courses and training sessions are located directly at the formal end of the continuum, whereas other online learning activities such as professional development webinars (which some people might categorize using a third term, non-formal learning, to indicate a clearly designed learning experience with objectives that does not contribute to a degree or certificate) might represent varying levels of formality depending on the context (e.g., required by employer or voluntary). Other activities, like reflective blogging, tend to range in formality as the context shifts; most reflective blogging in higher education is done as a course requirement, whereas most workplace-based reflective bloggers engage in the activity of their own volition. Involvement in social networks, such as Facebook and LinkedIn, is placed fully at the informal end of the continuum because learning in those forums is typically a byproduct of other activities such as networking or even socializing.

The chapters contained in this book range from those that focus on more formal learning experiences that may introduce people to and lead them to participate in online professional development activities to those that represent true informal learning and professional development experiences in online environments. We have divided the book into five sections, each of which represents a different focus. The earlier chapters, appearing in Sections 1 and 2, provide many foundational and theoretical concepts, whereas the latter chapters (Sections 3, 4, and 5) represent empirical studies and cases of virtual professional development.

Throughout the book a range of contexts are addressed, from learning that is somewhat situated in formal environments to learning that is entirely informal, and from school-based to workplace-based learning. Figure 2 provides a visual reference for the diverse coverage provided by the chapters. Where appropriate, chapters are clustered together to indicate a similar position on the axes. Bi-directional arrows represent types of learning that might be included in two quadrants, depending on context (e.g., degree-seeking students using the same technology to support classroom learning and extracurricular learning). The unidirectional arrow indicates chapters that are situated in one quadrant but which represent experiences that are preparing learners to continue engaging in learning in another quadrant. These cross-quadrant (formal to informal) chapters provide a good reminder that there is a fair degree of fluidity involved when defining or categorizing learning experiences and that learning experiences set in one context or setting may impact either continued learning or other related activities in another context or setting.

The first three chapters provide a general overview of issues related to virtual professional development and informal learning via social networks. Each chapter gives insight into various factors that should be considered on this topic. In Chapter 1, "*Professional Development through Web 2.0 Collaborative Applications*," Williams and Olaniran discuss the impact that Web 2.0 has had on collaboration and professional development. This chapter provides a solid overview of tools like blogs and wikis, making it particularly helpful for any readers who are less familiar with social media. Further, the authors provide insight into cultural, financial, and policy challenges that need to be considered when using these tools.

Another challenge or concern that arises when using social media tools is privacy. The free flow of information on the Internet may be considered a double-edged sword, helping people learn through the open exchange of ideas while at the same time putting people and organizations at risk if too much or the wrong information is self-disclosed in an online environment. In Chapter 2, "*Web 2.0, the Individual, and the Organization: Privacy, Confidentiality, and Compliance*," Burner discusses the privacy and confidentiality-related complexities of using Web 2.0 technologies for informal professional development. Additionally, she provides examples of and insights into policies that might help protect both individuals and organizations from unnecessary risk while still allowing them to participate in online professional learning experiences.

Although many people will first visualize sitting at a computer when the topic of online learning is mentioned, mobile devices have entered the online learning arena and bring with them additional possibilities for professional development. In Chapter 3, "*Turn On Your Mobile Devices: Potential and Considerations of Informal Mobile Learning*," Hao provides an overview of mobile learning and discusses how it adds another layer of options for people who seek information and interactions at the tips of their fingers, even while on the go. Hao examines the strengths and drawbacks that surround informal mobile learning and discusses lessons learned from the previous research literature for educators and researchers approaching this topic.

Section 2 brings together three chapters that present different lenses and perspectives for considering informal learning and professional development in a virtual environment. In Chapter 4, "*An Activity Theoretical Approach to Examining Virtual Professional Development and Informal Learning via Social Networks*," Terantino demonstrates how activity theory can be applied in a social network setting to analyze the interactions that occur among individuals and the tools, communities, and artifacts that help them obtain their objectives.

In Chapter 5, "*Applying Social Network Analysis and Social Capital in Personal Learning Environments of Informal Learning*," Chen, Choi, and Yu explore how people build personal learning networks when using Web 2.0 technologies. With the help of social network analysis, they demonstrate how these networks might be analyzed. Through analysis of these networks, it becomes possible both to see how individuals interact with each other and with various tools as well as to document the presence and development of social capital.

Figure 2. Map of chapters in this volume

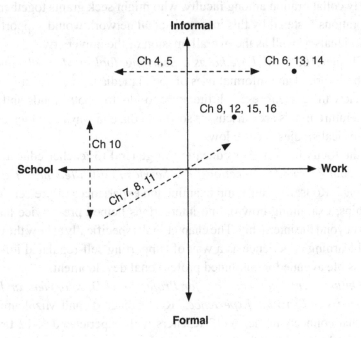

This section closes with Chapter 6, titled, *"Linguistic Aspects of Informal Learning in Corporate Online Social Networks."* In this chapter, Bielenia-Grajewska highlights the role that language plays in the development and use of social networks. Online social interactions are inherently language-based, and most frequently involve written texts. Focusing on informal corporate contexts, she demonstrates how language can bring people together or keep them apart, stressing the roles that homophily, membership, and power play in our linguistic interactions.

The last three sections of the book present empirical research and cases that examine online professional development and informal learning experiences. The three sections each are focused on a different setting or context: higher education (Section 3), pre- and in-service education (Section 4), and the workplace (Section 5).

In Chapter 7, *"Creating Ongoing Online Support Communities through Social Networks to Promote Professional Learning,"* Corbeil and Corbeil provide examples of one instructor's success as he pushed students in his online graduate courses to extend their learning experience beyond the walls of the virtual classroom. The chapter addresses how these online graduate courses were designed, how the social networking tools were used to enhance communication and interaction, and how the instructor established networks that continued after the courses had ended, providing a model for how others might do the same.

In Chapter 8, *"Developing Professional Competencies through International Peer Learning Communities,"* Yakavena discusses how blogs were used to support informal learning among students during internship experiences. These students were placed in professional positions in several different countries, and then were united via the technology. She found that overall the emergent learning community led to positive experiences for these students.

Christensen and Saltiel focus on ways of uniting faculty rather than students. In Chapter 9, *"Use of Social Network Analysis to Create and Foster Interdisciplinary Research, Projects, and Grants among Faculty,"* they describe a university-based social network designed to support peer mentoring, knowledge brokering, and resource sharing. The intended objective of their program was to increase interdisciplinary research and scholarly collaboration among faculty, who might seek grants together or co-publish. The end result of collaborations fostered by this informal social network would support both the careers of the participating individuals as well as the overall mission of the university.

The authors of Chapter 10, "*Social Media as a Learning Tool in Medical Education: A Situation Analysis*," consider both formal and informal uses of social media by medical students. Vahe, Zain-Ul-Abdin, and Türel review the current research literature to identify both trends and gaps. Surprisingly, for as much as the literature in this area discusses social media and ways in which it might be used, the actual number of empirical studies is quite low.

Section 4 shifts the focus from higher education in general to teacher education, beginning with Chapter 11, "*It's All about Personal Connections: Pre-Service English Teachers' Experiences Engaging in Networked Learning*." Rodseiler and Tripp examine the experiences of pre-service English teachers during their internships, examining how online interactions helped pre-service teachers extend their learning experiences beyond the internship. The chapter looks specifically at how the pre-service teachers perceived this social learning experience as a way of supporting self-regulated informal learning and, in the future, as a possible avenue for continued professional development.

In Chapter 12, "*Online Mentoring as a Tool for Professional Development and Change of Novice and Experienced Teachers: A Brazilian Experience*," Reali, Tancredi, and Mizukami examine an online mentoring program that connects novice K-12 teachers with experienced K-12 teachers. This online mentoring program was designed to help the novice teachers overcome some of the professional challenges that they often face and to contribute to the professional development of these teachers. The authors provide insight into the process of creating such a program and indicate how similar programs could be beneficial for others.

The last chapter in this section examines research conducted on a self-generated online teaching community. In Chapter 13, "*An Analysis of Teacher Knowledge and Emotional Sharing in a Teacher Blog Community*," Hur, Brush, and Bonk investigate a community of teachers on LiveJournal, looking for trends and patterns in teacher activity. They found that the community supports teacher professional development by offering a platform that simultaneously fosters sharing a variety of knowledge related to teaching and expressing one's feelings about the profession.

The last section of the book, Section 5, focuses on workplace learning. Chapter 14, "*Twitter-Based Knowledge Sharing in Professional Networks: The Organization Perspective*," considers how professional organizations might support ongoing professional development for their memberships by using Twitter. Dennen and Jiang analyze the Twitter feeds of six organizations, looking for trends in both content and use of Twitter features. Their findings have implications for how these organizations might act as both knowledge providers and knowledge brokers as well as how they might use the technology to bring together a learning community.

In Chapter 15, "*Story-Based Professional Development Using a Conflict Management Wiki*," Slabon and Richards discuss how learning can be supported cross-organization by sharing real world stories in a wiki environment. They present a particular case in which former students in a class that used a restorying technique were invited to join a wiki where they could share professional stories. A survey was used to learn about participants' attitudes and approaches toward using this wiki, allowing the authors to consider both the successes and the shortcomings of this medium and approach.

In Chapter 16, "*Dermatological Telemedicine Diagnoses and Andragogical Training Using Web 2.0 Mobile Medicine Video Conferencing*," Brandt and Rice share a case study about how Web 2.0-based video conferencing was used to help dermatologists engage in both diagnosis with patients and ongoing professional development with other doctors. They show how this approach supports problem-based learning and can provide learning opportunities for physicians regardless of their geographic location.

Collectively, these sixteen chapters cross over diverse territory. They represent learning from the perspectives of both people who are engaged in the process and people who are supporting the process, and in some instances individuals who may be engaged in both of those roles. They consider both emotional and knowledge-based needs and outcomes, and represent a variety of technologies and learning techniques. Still, we recognize that these chapters merely scratch the surface in terms of representing the myriad of virtual professional development and informal online learning experiences that take place these days.

In closing, we hope that this book serves as a catalyst for initiating a greater conversation about this topic among education professionals and researchers. Although virtual professional development and informal online learning in many cases are not as controlled or designed as more traditional forms of learning, they nonetheless are having a big influence on their participants. The individual learners engaged in virtual professional development will certainly keep moving forward and continue to explore the various opportunities that the Internet offers them, and those opportunities will continue to grow each day as new tools are developed and as more people with mutual interests find each other online. The roles that remain open for educators and researchers, then, are that of collaborator, investigator, instructional designer, and knowledge broker; they can learn from and with the people who are already engaged in the practice of virtual professional development, and in turn share the practice with other educators, researchers, and learners.

Vanessa P. Dennen
Florida State University, USA

Jennifer B. Myers
Orangeburg-Calhoun Technical College, USA & Florida State University, USA

REFERENCES

Allen, I. E., & Seaman, J. (2011). *Going the distance: Online education in the United States, 2011*. Babson Park, MA: Babson Survey Reearch Group.

Bonk, C. J., & Dennen, V. P. (2003). Frameworks for research, design, benchmarks, training, and pedagogy in Web-based distance education . In Moore, M. G., & Anderson, B. (Eds.), *Handbook of Distance Education* (pp. 331–348). Mahwah, NJ: Erlbaum.

Gee, J. P. (2009). Digital media and learning as an emerging field, part 1: How we got here. *International Journal of Learning and Media*, *1*(2), 13–23. doi:10.1162/ijlm.2009.0011

Leadbeater, C., & Miller, P. (2004). *The pro-am revolution: How enthusiasts are changing our economy and society*. London, UK: Demos.

Acknowledgment

In our first venture into book editing, we have learned a tremendous amount and we are grateful for the support and assistance we have received from so many sources. We would like to thank our authors, reviewers, and advisory board for their timely and detailed assistance with each task we asked them to complete. Additional thanks to Mr. Amit Chauhan, who helped us organize and format the many files that made up this book; to Ms. Hannah Abelbeck, our Editorial Assistant at IGI, who always had a quick answer to our questions; and to our families, who encouraged us and who understood when we had to work late. Finally, we would like to acknowledge the millions of people who inspired this book by engaging in virtual professional development and informal online learning every day.

Vanessa P. Dennen
Florida State University, USA

Jennifer B. Myers
Orangeburg-Calhoun Technical College & Florida State University, USA

Section 1
Overview and Issues:
Virtual Professional Development and Informal Learning via Social Networks

Chapter 1
Professional Development through Web 2.0 Collaborative Applications

Indi Marie Williams
Arizona State University, USA

Bolanie A. Olaniran
Texas Tech University, USA

ABSTRACT

This chapter presents a fresh look at collaborative applications and their use in professional development and informal learning. The chapter addresses some of the cultural challenges impacting collaborative technologies, especially given the fact that these technologies are transplanted from developed countries into regions of the world that are only beginning to understand their significance. Therefore, the chapter points to the importance of and the needs to allow cultural variation and differences in usage. The chapter acknowledges the fact that collaborative technologies possess great potential for both professional development and informal learning, but cautions that external factors, such as culture and community, be taken into account to realize potential benefits.

INTRODUCTION

The twenty-first century has marked a profound shift in how individuals, gather, evaluate, manage, and disseminate information. Many individuals do not desire to learn in isolation, but yearn for social connections that allow for sharing ideas and providing support to their colleagues. Globalization, changes in world market economies,

and information glut have challenged traditional methodologies of learning. This is especially true, as employees are becoming more computer savvy, challenging organizations to rethink the importance of professional development, and in turn, informal learning opportunities afforded to their workforce (Hanley, 2009). Some organizations have turned to the construction of online professional development learning communities (Glowacki-Dudka & Brown, 2007). Fortunately,

DOI: 10.4018/978-1-4666-1815-2.ch001

the formation of these communities is just one way in which informal learning can occur. These communities also create an arena where self-development can take place, connecting professionals with opportunities to continue cooperative and lifelong learning. This continued development is essential to organizational success because as employees strive to enhance their skills, they ultimately demonstrate improved job performance (Kukulska-Hulme & Pettit, 2008).

The emergence of Web 2.0 has brought a host of cloud-based applications, all of which create a myriad of new approaches to communication and collaboration. Yet, it is still unclear how these technologies will impact professional development. Some futurists predict that Web 2.0 applications will cause a paradigm shift comparable to the institution of the printing press (Graham, 2004; Liu, 2004). This still remains to be seen. However, if indeed 75% of learning by adults occurs informally (Hanley, 2009), then professional development models must be re-conceptualized in order to account for changes in technology and information immediacy.

Thus, areas fertile for the development of Web 2.0 collaborative applications are e-learning and distributive learning. However, an area that is often overlooked is professional development. As the growth and development of newer technologies increases, academicians, companies, and individual scholars find themselves in positions where they are constantly pushed to adopt and apply these technologies in their disciplines. Professional informal learning is also increased, and by nature, a byproduct of technology accessibility. Therefore, these learning environments and areas of knowledge dissemination, at times, may challenge the fabric of how learning can occur, and it is for this reason that adoption of Web based technologies is not always successful.

However, and despite resistance, the twenty-first century marks a profound shift in how adults regard Web 2.0 applications. For example, the Pew Internet and American Life Project (2011) discov-

ered that by 2003, 44% (i.e., 53 million) American adults had used Web 2.0 technologies to publish thoughts, share files, and interact with others. As of 2011, the current estimate of adult Internet users is 78% (i.e., 94 million). Collectively, these users contribute to the wealth of information freely available online (Lenhart, Horrigan, & Fallows, 2004), solidifying the fact that digital media are central in almost every aspect of daily life, most notably in how we learn, communicate, reflect, (co-) produce, consume, create identities, share knowledge, and understand political issues.

Unfortunately, a newer way of communicating and co-creating knowledge presents significant challenges that must be addressed before these technologies can be properly implemented into learning environments, informal or otherwise. Some of these concerns include how an individual's creation, or co-creation, of knowledge affects identity and a general sense of self in terms of socio-cultural and socio-technical underpinnings at both micro and macro levels. In other words, knowledge acquisition in the digital age extends beyond well-designed instruction, or even the simple offering of courses and curriculum via modern communication technologies (Olaniran, 2007a, 2007b). How we communicate online incorporates the essence of who we are as social beings within an information society. Therefore, communicative technologies allow an individual to actively and intentionally construct knowledge and engage in learning on his/her own terms.

Currently, there remain realistic challenges to the use and implementation of Web 2.0 technologies, even within professional development and informal learning environments. Cox (2009) states that Web 2.0 collaborative applications encourage learning and development in new and different ways. Another great advantage to their use is that they are not only cost effective but also easy to implement into learning environments. Although, Cox's analysis is based upon K-12 experiences, his observations are equally applicable to institutions of higher education and organizational programs of professional development. With the push for international collaboration and research, not to mention the financial strain that many institutions of learning and corporations have felt over the past few years in regard to budgets cuts, a cost effective method of learning and collaboration is important to encourage employee productivity and professional development in the future (Jue, Marr, & Kassotakis, 2009).

Through the investigation of current research, online resources, and corresponding case studies, it is the goal of this chapter to examine how professional development and informal learning can be achieved through Web 2.0 collaborative applications. These applications include, but are not limited to, social bookmarking, blogs, wikis, social networking, learning management systems, social media sharing, mashups, synchronous communication, conferencing, visual worlds, and gaming. We begin with a general overview of these technologies and continue to discuss their relevant technological potential within professional development and informal learning environments. However, beyond technological potential, we discuss some of the socio-cultural challenges that potential users, instructors and designers must address in the consideration, as well as in the adoption, of these technologies. The chapter will conclude with a discussion of future collaborative learning technologies, and an examination of how current advances present a positive outlook for the future. We begin this discussion with an examination of collaborative learning.

Collaborative Learning

Collaborative applications are based upon educational approaches and theories of collaborative learning. We will discuss these Web 2.0 applications in greater detail later in the chapter. However, in order to understand how these applications can be used within professional development and informal learning, it is necessary to present

a clear picture of what collaborative learning is, and why it is significant to professional development and training.

Collaborative learning is defined as "an educational approach to teaching and learning that involves groups of learners working together to solve a problem, complete a task, or create a product. Collaborative learning is based on the idea that learning is a naturally social act in which the participants talk among themselves. It is through the talk that learning occurs" (GDRC, 2011). Research has reflected that students learn best when they are actively engaged within the learning process. Therefore, when students work in small groups, they also have a tendency to retain material longer than when it is presented in other instructional formats (Beckman, 1990; Chickering & Gamson, 1991; Collier, 1980; Cooper, et al., 1990; Goodsell, et al., 1992; Johnson & Johnson, 1989; Johnson, Johnson, & Smith, 1991; Kohn, 1986; McKeachie, Pintrich, Lin, & Smith, 1986; Slavin, 1980, 1983; Smith, 1986; Whitman, 1988). This same research has also demonstrated that students who work in collaborative groups appear more satisfied with their learning experiences. Subsequently, collaborative applications are those technologies that can be utilized to create small group environments where active learning can be employed. The most successful collaborative applications are those that can be used to connect real world experience with professional development training. In this way, collaborative applications, such as blogs, can be used to see and discuss how others might handle similar job duties and responsibilities. This real world application is one of the many reasons why Web 2.0 technologies are so popular.

Konstantinidis, Tsiatsos, and Pomportsis (2009) state that collaborative learning is a term used to describe educational practices based upon "the simultaneous cognitive and mental effort of multiple students or/and educators. Students share a common goal, depend on each other and are mutually responsible for their success or failure" (p. 280). Collaboration activities that center on collaborative goals and are supported by experts not only result in meaningful and efficient knowledge acquisition, but provoke student activities, create realistic learning scenarios and motivate students to continue in the solving of complex problems. Therefore, learning becomes more student-oriented with responses being more candid, students exhibiting greater motivation and presenting more honesty in their interactions in the learning exchange (Konstantinidis, et al., 2009).

Economides (2008) states that collaborative learning "is an educational method where a group of learners collaborate to learn and improve themselves" (p. 243). This improvement occurs as learners "work together toward a common goal, exchange and share ideas, information, knowledge, resources, tools, products, work and results" (p. 243). Collaboration can consist of a team of students investigating, or exploring, an issue, solving a problem, or designing a project/product for mass consumption. Due to the need for distance based collaboration, Economides (2008) states that there is large interest in developing computer-supported collaborative environments so that users will not be limited to individuals located in the learner's immediate vicinity. Subsequently, as collaborative applications have become more popular, they have also become easier to implement and employ within learning environments (Smith & MacGregor, 1992). This creates an even greater incentive to utilize these technologies within professional development and training environments.

In general, collaboration is viewed as an essential skill. Most educational and training programs require students to engage in a collaborative project either face-to-face, or through distance learning technologies. Cox (2009) explains that collaboration is "one of the defining characteristics of the 21st century" (p. 11). However, he has observed many educators searching for ways to implement collaborative technologies within their schools and institutions of higher learning. This

reluctance may be a result of the fact that many educators believe collaborative learning to be another educational fad that given time will fade into the background (Cox, 2009). Unfortunately, and as with previous instructional techniques (i.e., personalized learning), this fear of disappearance prevents instructional designers and trainers of all ranks from taking collaborative applications seriously. Unfortunately, this is to the detriment of student learning.

Professional Development and Informal Learning

Johnson, Levine, Smith, and Stone (2010) in the *Horizon Report 2010* state that "the role of the academy – and the way we prepare students for their future lives, is changing" (p. ii). In this way, work which used to be viewed as an independent activity has become more collaborative, not to mention cross-cultural in nature. Students who graduate in the next decade will be using technologies that are not only cloud-based, but present a decentralized location where anytime, anywhere learning can occur. Consequently, a multidisciplinary approach to learning has added a need for collaboration within professional development and research.

In a similar vein, The Association of Professional Engineers, Geologists, and Geophysicists of Alberta (APEGGA) states that in order to protect health safety and welfare, it is imperative that individuals engage in a plan of lifetime learning of their profession (Apegga, 2011). However, no professional development can be complete without the incorporation of informal learning. Therefore, and for the purposes of this discussion, lifetime learning will incorporate two essential elements, professional development, and informal learning. It is within the confines of lifetime learning, simply defined as the continual re-education, renewal and refinement of professional skills necessary to improve work performance, that professional development training becomes merged with informal learning. Consequently, it is next to impossible for an individual to acquire every necessary skill through formalized training. Some skills simply require conversations by the water cooler (Grebow, 2002).

Traditionally, professional development is regarded as formal learning. This learning typically is provided by an educational or training institution, and occurs in a structured manner. Formal learning is regarded as intentional, and many times consists of learning objectives that lead to a particular outcome, such as a certification and/or a degree (Hanley, 2009). Therefore, informal learning can be defined as learning that occurs during the course of daily life, work, or leisure time. This type of learning lacks structure, as defined by learning objectives, or a defined time where learning might occur. Often times this learning is un-intentional (Hanley, 2009). However, although this type of learning does not lead to a certification as is expected in formal learning, it is important to note that improvement in job performance is at many times attributed to an employee's ability to informally acquire the skills needed for success.

Therefore, professional development can take many forms from structured training to daily reflections upon work experiences. Mentorship, observations, and simple discussions between experienced and novice employees can also lead to knowledge acquisition. Utilizing this definition of professional development means that it is not always necessary to attend a workshop to improve skills and/or knowledge about a subject (Campbell, McNamara, & Gilroy, 2004). Thus, informal learning becomes an essential component within any educational framework, and as a consequence is vital to a successful professional development program. This is why it is important to have both components (i.e., professional development and informal learning) within any organization's employee training program, especially if said organization desires an improvement in employee performance.

Therefore, we propose that with the acceptance of certain cultural challenges, lifetime learning and instruction can occur through the use of Web 2.0 collaborative applications. This approach to collaboration creates what Johnson et al. (2010) describe as being "a climate in which students, their peers, and their teachers are all working toward the same goal" (p. ii). With the birth (or rebirth) of oftentimes free collaborative online tools, this advent of learning has become not only popular, but available to more learners, many which are physically spread apart over great distances. Hence, it is encouraging that the International Society for Technology in Education (ISTE) and the partnership for 21st Century Skills both place collaboration as essential to the social nature of learning and the formation of intellectual networks of diverse learners (Cox, 2009).

Attributes of Collaborative Applications

Within Cox's (2009) discussion of 21st Century collaboration, the author states that there are five key attributes of collaborative applications and these are: ubiquitous access, authentic appearance, intuitive design, ability to share content and ability to export content to other applications. Additionally, Konstantinidis et al. (2009), state that collaborative learning environments must contain the following seven components: users are assigned roles and privileges, educational interactions enhance communication, presentation of information employs multiple modalities, users actively participate interacting between other users and the virtual environment, multiple technologies are integrated into the learning system, users are presented with multiple learning opportunities, and visual representations contain real world elements. Therefore, in order to incorporate these seven components within virtual collaborative learning, Konstantinidis et al. (2009) state that dialogue and action, workspace awareness, student's self-regulation or guidance, teacher assistance and community level management become essential for the successful creation and implementation of the learning environment. Instructors and trainers within this framework do not become obsolete; however, they take on a secondary role of facilitators of the learning environment, acting as subject matter experts who are only called upon when the learner has run into difficulty within his/her personalized learning environment.

Furthermore, Kojiri, Ogawa, and Watanabe (2009) present a conceptual view of the traditional collaborative learning environment. In a typical collaborative application, there are two types of "agents", one of which is a coordinator and the other of which is a learner. The coordinator lies at the center of the virtual environment, and according to Kojiri et al. (2009) acts as a network server monitoring interactions that occur between students. This coordinator generates advice only if it is necessary. Thus, conceptually, it is the learner that takes responsibility by personally managing the learning environment, or in this case, the interaction interface. It is through this interface that a learner controls his/her own private learning history. All of the individuals connected in this virtual environment, interact using a public communication infrastructure that surrounds and undergirds their exchanges.

Subsequently, it is also important to note that learners also have the ability to exchange information with one another through private lines of communication. These lines can be used in order to ask for help, or reorient their personal learning history to line up with the tasks in virtual learning environment. Therefore, Kojiri et al. (2009) state that Web based collaborative learning environments consist of the actions/reactions of individual participants, learners and instructors alike. These actions/reactions differ drastically from real-world (i.e., face-to-face) interactions and communication. Due to these differences, individuals who use collaborative applications are confined to a particular learning space in which different sensitive receptors are needed. These receptors allow

for new events to be detected indirectly, and in a way that is not as natural as what would occur within a face-to face environment. However, when using collaborative applications, this traditional model must adapt in order to fit the learner and the professional development context.

CHALLENGES TO COLLABORATIVE APPLICATIONS

Financial and Policy Challenges

Cox (2009) states that financial constraints continue to be one of the most common reasons cited for the lack of integration of collaborative applications into organizations. The inability to purchase, not to mention maintain, software and hardware equipment prevents many instructors from being able to implement technology-based training. This fact coupled with the challenges of reduced or non-existent access to the Internet, make using collaborative technologies next to impossible.

Despite the fact that Cox (2009) and others (i.e., Johnson, et al., 2010) perceive that the use of online collaborative tools far outweighs the policy debates (i.e., potential safety issues), Web 2.0 online collaborative tools are still not valued as a priority. However, with the push for international collaboration and research, not to mention the financial strain that many institutions have felt over the past few years in regard to budgets cuts, a cost effective method of collaboration is important to encourage the development of learning technologies in the future. The advent of Web 2.0 tools such as wikis and blogs give professionals the ability to re-conceptualize learning, making it meaningful to both themselves and their peers. Additionally, collaboration when coupled with these Web 2.0 technologies strengthen the ability for individuals to make connections between their professional development training and real world application.

Cultural Challenges

There exist many cultural challenges to the use of Web 2.0 technologies, especially when they are implemented within cross-cultural situations. Economides (2008) states that informal collaborative learning through Web 2.0 technologies draws away from teacher centered education. In this way, the teacher, or the head of authority in the classroom, no longer has the function of imparting knowledge to students. This provides the opportunity for both teachers and learners to interact freely and actively participate in the learning experience. However, it may remain unclear to some learners as to whether or not a teacher continues to possess the duty of directing the learning environment and/or activities that occur during the learning process. In fact, within most Web 2.0 environments, a teacher/instructor, in the formal sense, does not exist. Therefore, although an instructor is present within a collaborative learning environment, he/she may not have the ability to support learners in groups, or even individually (Economides, 2008). It also stands to reason that individuals who are not familiar, or comfortable, with informal learning may not benefit as greatly as learners who are comfortable, especially if the work is more independent and self directed. In other words, improper implementation of Web 2.0 professional development learning opportunities may inadvertently lead to discouragement, and eventually disassociation from the learning environment by some students (Olaniran, 2007).

Economides (2008) explains that although contemporary systems provide a framework for collaborative applications, this framework does not guarantee that it contains the ability to support diverse learner types and/or varying learner collaborative preferences or styles. One concern is that learners' lack the preparation for a different cultural approach to learning that they encounter through the use of a collaborative application. This is especially true as users transition from their native cultural environment to the new learning environment (Olaniran, 2010; Olaniran & Agnello, 2008; Ramburuth & Tani, 2009; Scovic, 2008). Therefore, culturally diverse student populations, bring to light that background (i.e., culture) of the learner has a significant effect upon communication and interaction. Culture also affects the conceptualization of collaboration as a whole. Thus, entering an exchange from an individual of another culture could affect the method of collaboration in addition to the final outcome of the project. Burnham (2005) explains that even though individual learners of all cultures find themselves in various learning situations (i.e., online distance learning) they still bring to the learning environment a sense of cultural identity which drastically affects how the instructional environment is designed, how collaboration is understood and how instruction is implemented (Rogers, Graham, & Mayes, 2007). All of these factors are based on the learner's perspective and personal experiences.

Olaniran (2010) states that since all learners have a unique way of understanding and defining concepts as dictated by their personal experiences, it is important that learning technologies possess the ability to adapt to the learner's needs. Subsequently, technologies must provide resources required by a particular learner at the appropriate juncture of the learning process. The push for the digitalization of information and quick access does not always have the end user in mind. For this reason, the use of particulars, or the presentation of information uniquely tailored to user's specific context, as opposed to universals, or standardized and uniformed information presented similarly to all users, becomes even more vital to the success of a collaborative application, especially when an application is integrated into a cross-cultural context (Olaniran, 2010). In other words, just because information is available, it does not mean the information will be universally interpreted. This is particularly true when a cross-cultural user has a perspective of knowledge acquisition that differs from the original designer or instructor. Olaniran (2007) explains that since it is clear that all cultures accept and reject varying aspects of information knowledge, then it is important to take into account the history, sources of meanings and worldview of the culture before implementing a collaborative application within a cross-cultural context (Williams, Warren, & Olaniran, 2009; Olaniran, 2007a, 2007b). To this end, some scholars have extensively explored the role of cultural variability and its impact in e-learning within international collaborative environments. One common method of evaluation involves the use of Hofstede's (1980) dimensions of cultural variability (e.g. Olaniran, Rodriguez, & Williams, 2011; Olaniran, 2007a, 2007b, 2010; Olaniran & Agnello, 2008).

Therefore, when discussing technology implementation, one particular area of concern is the application of learning models and how they are germane to the issue of culture. Nevertheless, no issue of culture and technology would be complete without looking at affordability and/or the digital divide that some of these technologies have created (Williams, Warren, & Olaniran, 2009; Olaniran, 2007a, 2007b). Additionally, there are also challenges to implementation in terms of technical literacy and competencies. These challenges occur when individuals who possess modern technology (i.e., the haves) continue to increase their accessibility while individuals who cannot afford the technology (i.e., the have-nots) are slowly left behind. As a result, the have-nots become isolated due to their lack of technological literacy. The determent lies within the fact that both groups live in a global economy that is based upon information exchange, making the appropriate technological acquisition and use essential for survival (Olaniran, 2007a, 2007b). Unfortunately, for some, this inability to "keep up" with technology could have devastating economic consequences. Therefore, the key to resolving cross-cultural issues lies within the recognition of differences and the cultural sensitivity to predominant cultural values, preferences and needs

of the target culture (Olaniran, 2010; Williams, Warren, & Olaniran, 2009). Subsequently, if there is a disjuncture between the technology and the culture, then the chances of technological acceptance will be seriously hindered and as a result, the technology can be viewed as a threat to the society as a whole (Olaniran, 2007a, 2007b)

Economides (2008) explains that when designing or implementing any collaborative learning system, it is not only essential to incorporate appropriate collaborative application guidelines (i.e., Konstantinidis et al.'s (2009) seven components discussed above), but it is imperative that the cultural values of the learner be integrated in such a way that it increases the efficiency of the interaction. This, along with providing necessary learner support, assures that the learner has the ability to accomplish the instructional task. Thus, from a cultural design and implementation perspective, the following cultural criteria should be included within collaborative learning environments. First, team communication must be supported with the understanding of cultural differences among the participants and second, student individuality in regard to culture and social development must also be taken under consideration as to provide a safe environment for interaction within a collaborative application (Economides, 2008). Finally, Michailidou and Economides (2003) explain that in order for a virtual learning environment to support individuals from diverse backgrounds, it must include four distinct dimensions: 1) pedagogical and psychological, 2) technical and functional, 3) organizational and economical, and 4) social and cultural.

COLLABORATIVE APPLICATIONS

As research has demonstrated, the purpose of utilizing collaborative applications in programs of professional development is to allow employees to experience both the complex and ambiguous nature of real world challenges commonly found in workplace situations (Samarawickrema, Benson, & Brack, 2010). Therefore, due to the varying nature of employee training needs, collaborative learning technologies can be divided into approximately eight distinct categories. These categories include, but are not limited to, social bookmarking, blogs, wikis, social networking and Learning Management Systems (LMS), social media sharing, mashups, synchronous communication and conferencing, visual worlds, and gaming (Shex, 2011; Lund, 2010). Each of these applications provides various opportunities for professional development or informal learning. Consequently, not all of these applications are appropriate for every working environment. Discretion must be used when implementing a collaborative application solution in order to achieve the best possible learning outcomes.

Social Bookmarking

Social bookmarking is the sharing of a personal collection of URL's on a Web-based server. This presents a user with the ability to organize, re-use, and re-categorize a collection of links based on a user's needs. The ability to tag various resources helps individuals develop relationships between concepts and ideas. These tags also allow users to network with other individuals in order to catalog additional Web resources and later share those resources with others.

Common examples of social bookmarking are Del.icio.us (http://delicious.com), CiteUlike (http://www.citeulike.org), Edtags (http://edtags.org), and Digg (http://www.digg.com).

Professional Development

Professional development resources that can be designed using social bookmarking sites are lists of important company websites, recommended readings, project resources for virtual teams and organizational policies and procedures. Other uses for social bookmarking include RSS feeds, shar-

ing of departmental information, lists of common organizational resources, emergency procedures and relevant local, community, and world events (Shex, 2011).

Case in Point: Motorola

Motorola encourages the use of Enterprise 2.0 (i.e., Web 2.0 for business) technologies through an initiative known as Intranet 2.0. This employee social network allows basic collaborative functionality which includes employee created wikis, blogs and social bookmarking collections (Allen & Naughton, 2011; Motorola, 2011). The success of this network is demonstrated through its daily usage by 70,000 employees who interact through 4400 blogs, 4200 wiki pages, a commonly shared social bookmarking resource, and a social network interface similar to Facebook and Twitter. Through Intranet 2.0, employees are able to connect with one another and see industry relationships in a new way. This allows individuals to utilize the group knowledge base to solve work related problems and capitalize on business opportunities in new and innovative ways (Hoover, 2007).

Challenges to Implementation

One of the greatest drawbacks to social bookmarking is that resources are constructed by individuals of diverse backgrounds and experience levels. Additionally, there is commonly little, or no, oversight to the collection of resources. To be successful, the validity of social bookmarking resource collections must frequently be reviewed to verify accuracy. Another concern is that due to the variety of perspectives involved in constructing an online bookmark collection, it becomes possible for the formation of biases and/or skewed perspectives relating to a particular topic (Educause, 2005). Therefore, the solution lies in both the organization and employees taking responsibility over network resources, along with the institution of acceptable protocols to control the resources created. The risk of unregulated or even false information being disseminated throughout an organization can have devastating effects upon employee productivity, and even moral (Walters, 2009). Therefore, if social bookmarking is implemented, then it must be done in such a way that it provides a balanced view of all resources available, with enough oversight assuring the legitimacy of the information provided.

Blogs

Blogs are public spaces that allow a user to create a dated diary entry. These entries are usually created by a single author and accompanied by a series of website links, photographs, videos, and other Web content that the user finds interesting and/or visits on a regular basis. Blogs allow for the public display of reflective writing for the ability to read the thoughts and feelings of other individuals. In instruction, blogs provide an opportunity for students to create Web content in the form of personal writings, and to receive external feedback from other employees in diverse locations (Shex, 2011). Similarly, organizations can utilize these networks in order to allow employees to take part in the organizational dialogue, expanding how they view their position in respect to the company as a whole. Individuals can also use blogs to track work assignments and inform other virtual team members about upcoming issues and concerns during the course of project development. Additionally, opportunities for RSS subscriptions to other blogs allow users to keep up to date with what others have written and/or how others have responded to an individual's approach to a particular topic.

Some common examples of blogs are Blogger (http://www.blogger.com), LiveJournal (http://www.livejournal.com), and Wordpress (http://www.wordpress.com). All of these sites allow individuals to create blogs for free. Twitter (http://www.twitter.com) is also a microblogging resource that might be helpful to professional development trainers who desire employees to send tweets about real world experiences. A network such as twitter can also help bridge the gap between formal and informal learning (i.e., professional development) such that employees can actively participate in constructing resources that assist in learning day to day on the job procedures.

Professional Development

Some professional development activities that can be designed using blogs are a critique of assigned reading materials and/or articles, a response to a case study, a self reflective journal entry, a production schedule, a discussion of acceptable on the job behaviors, a list of frequently asked questions with common solutions and a suggestion box. Another idea for blogs is to create employee virtual introductions using words and photographs. This can be done by featuring various employees or departments located in diverse locations across the globe. CEOs have used blogs to provide progress reports of organizational initiatives (i.e., Jonathan Schwartz, President and CEO Sun Microsystems and John Dragoon, CMO Novell) (Sundar, 2006; AccountingDegree.com, 2010). These leaders have used blogs to discuss the impact that current events have had on the company and upcoming changes or growth to be expected in the future (Shex, 2011).

Case in Point: Csdn.net

Csdn.net is the largest Chinese-language scientific blog community on the Internet. This community unites researchers from the disciplines of computer, information science, and technology in one location whereby they can interact, share data along with exchange information, knowledge and expertise with one another. Wang, Jiang, and Ma (2010) completed a social network analysis study on the community, and at the time there were over 14,000 active bloggers on the network. These bloggers, connected across time and space, created what is known as a professional blogging community. A professional community is formed when personal information is replaced with professional related issues regarding project based interactions, in this case scientists, who share common interests and similar research goals. It is within communities such as Csdn.net where informal learning occurs.

Challenges to Implementation

One drawback of blogs is that they lie within the realms of public opinion. Blogs, as with most Web 2.0 resources, are created by various individuals of diverse backgrounds and experience levels. Therefore, on popular blogging websites there is little or no oversight of content or biased views that are oftentimes presented. In addition, organizations must be aware that public online resources are prone to distractions from other users, possibly thwarting the original intent of the blog being used for professional development. For this reason, it would be best for an organization to utilize an internal network for company blogging, so that the opinions can remain contained and in line with acceptable company guidelines. This will help protect intellectual property and allow employees to receive credit for their ideas, assuming, of course, that the ideas are not presented anonymously. Therefore, bearing in mind the pros and cons, it is still possible for organizations to implement blogs into the workplace. However, as with most online technologies, this must be accomplished with great foresight and sense of purpose (Daniel, 2004).

Wikis

A wiki is a collection of webpages that can be accessed and edited by any authorized person, at anytime, anywhere in the world. This is an excellent resource for professional development projects, limited only by the imagination of the employees and administrators involved. In this way, wikis possess the potential to support both professional development and creative project-based teamwork (Shex, 2011). Caverly and Ward (2008) explain that collaborative wiki applications used for instruction can be placed into five stages of inquiry. These stages are:

1. **Resource Wiki**: A knowledge-based wiki (i.e., Wikipedia),
2. **Presentation Wiki**: A communication-based wiki used for creating drafts of documents that are to be shared with a group. These wikis are usually used in work environments (i.e., Google Docs).
3. **Gateway Wiki**: A wiki (i.e., forum) where data is shared amongst group members to facilitate discussion and project development. This can be easily implemented in an academic or training setting, especially when instruction is based upon the analysis of data to draw conclusions in regard to a particular sample or population.
4. **Simulation Wiki**: A wiki where a simulated environment is created through the co-construction of knowledge unfolding in a real life environment. Here, contributors create a "world" through the development of alternative solutions and multiple paths of inquiry (i.e., role playing).
5. **Illuminated Wik**: A text-based wiki where the parts of a document are divided amongst participants. The goal is for a group of individuals to construct a completed project by attending to their assigned roles (i.e., group presentation).

Some common examples of wikis are Wikipedia (http://www.wikipedia.com), Wikiversity (http://www.wikiversity.org), and Business Wiki (http://www.onbusinesswiki.com). Some wiki applications are Wikispaces (http://www.wikispaces. com) and Google Sites (http://sites.google.com).

Professional Development

Wikis can be used for constructing virtual team projects, assigning project responsibilities, tracking virtual team member contributions, constructing peer reviews of organizational reports, in addition to assisting in the construction of professional development opportunities (i.e., required company certification and training courses). Organizations can also use wikis for planning, networking, constructing knowledge databases, creating personal learning experiences, facilitating informal professional development, and encouraging contributions from employees who work in diverse locations (Shex, 2011).

Case in Point: Department of Radiology at University of Maryland

As is to be expected, the Microsoft Corporation claims to have over 300,000 internal blogs and wikis. However, technology companies are not the only organizations who utilize this wikis. The Department of Radiology at the University of Maryland, School of Medicine, developed a knowledge base for creating and dispersing technical information to the support staff in a timely manner. This expert advice was distributed in the form of a wiki and was supported by the Radiology IT support team. Within a period of 18 months, the site had 248 pages of content and 5,138 pages edits for a total of 20,647 page views. This wealth of information was quickly adopted by other employees and provided a centralized knowledge management repository, establishing a mechanism for creating decision trees and accessing required policies and procedures. After prolonged use and exposure to the resource, the final outcome was an increased consistency of response by staff members (Gibson, 2006).

Challenges to Implementation

The drawbacks to wikis are the same as with social bookmarking and blogs. Personal opinion can easily distract an employee from his/her assigned task. Care must be taken when implementing a wiki so that employees remain focused on project goals, and resources present a sound view of issues contributing to the wellbeing of the organization.

Social Networking and Learning Management Systems

Social networking and Learning Management Systems (LMS) focus on the building and maintenance of online social networks and learning communities. These networks allow individuals to share common interests and collaborate on instructional activities. Both social networking and LMS can be used to communicate within an organization, utilize mechanisms such as RSS feeds to provide updated content, and establish structure for professional development trainings and webinars (Shex, 2011). Additionally, LMS provide a framework from which courses can be developed online and face-to-face, and provide employees with a central location with which to obtain course resources, documents and assignments (Shex, 2011).

Some popular examples of public social networking applications are Facebook (http://www.facebook.com), MySpace (http://www.myspace.com), and LinkedIn (http://www.linkedin.com). All of these resources can be easily integrated within organizational intranets. Other networks such as Socialtext (http://www.socialtext.com) and Yammer (http://www.yammer.com) are less public, and market their products to businesses and organizations. Corporate solutions such as Microsoft SharePoint (http://sharepoint.microsoft.com) and IBM Lotus (http://www-01.ibm.com/software/lotus) incorporate social networking functionality into their Enterprises 2.0 software packages. A common example of a LMS is Blackboard (http://www.blackboard.com).

Professional Development

Learning Management Systems allow for the creation of an online discussion board, the formation of discussion groups, a centralized location for course communications, and a predesigned structure for learning content. Additionally, some LMS also provide functionality for the creation of podcasts, blogs, wikis, journals, audio announcements and email (i.e., see http://www.blackboard.com for more information). An advantage to using a LMS is that it provides a centralized location where training professionals and administrators can easily disseminate information, thus, providing opportunities for both formal and informal learning experiences. Moreover, a LMS allows for the incorporation of various file types, such as Microsoft PowerPoint, Word, and Excel documents, into the network for easy file sharing end employee access.

Social networking, on the other hand, provides a different perspective to workplace collaboration. The primary purpose of social networking websites is to facilitate connections between individuals locally and in different regions and countries. Therefore, the advantages of utilizing social networking within professional development programs is that they are familiar, (i.e., many employees are active users of other social networks such as Facebook), easy to use, require low bandwidth (i.e., they exist in the cloud), and possess the ability to create separate groups for departmental, or individual, training opportunities. Additionally, websites such as Facebook have the added functionality of chat and email communications. This allows for conferencing between organizational personnel and provides individuals with the ability to connect with others who are active members of the organization's social network (Shex, 2011; Bullas, 2010).

Case in Point: BlueShirt Nation

Best Buy Inc. implemented a social media platform for their employees by integrating forums, wikis, videos, and a MySpace (i.e., social networking) like communication known as *BlueShirt Nation* (Thibodeau, 2009). *BlueShirt Nation* enables employees to remain connected with one another through email, SMS, and common online channels of communication (i.e., chat). Information can be created and accessed anywhere, anytime. This creates a wealth of knowledge, for both employees and senior management, arising from the combined experience of the company's nearly 170,000 employees (Bullas, 2010). It is within internal networks, such as *BlueShirt Nation* that employees increase company innovation, provide feedback to organizational initiatives, present suggestions to senior management, and respond to company policy changes.

Challenges to Implementation

The drawbacks to social networking are the same as with social bookmarking and blogs. Personal opinion and displays of individuality are rampant on public access social networking sites and some organizations may not approve of their use in the work environment. The main drawback to LMS lies within the cost of access to the network. Although there are free and low cost networks, these applications have a tendency to have a reduced functionality, and this may hinder implementation into the organization's virtual environment. Public networks have their place, but in order to protect corporate interests, it is essential that all employee networks reside behind a firewall (Allen & Naughton, 2011), and under the jurisdiction of organizational rules and guidelines of acceptable employee communication.

Social Media Sharing

Social media sharing is the simplicity of posting and sharing information on the Web. This information can be text, audio, images and/or video (Shex, 2011). Due to the wealth of resources available, it is easy to find some relevant content to reinforce organizational professional development and informal learning networks.

Some common examples of social media sharing applications are: YouTube (http://www.youtube.com), Flickr (http://www.flickr.com), Jing (http://www.jingproject.com), Podcast.com (http://www.podcast.com), and Slideshare (http://www.slideshare.net).

Professional Development

Social media sharing can be used to enrich professional development experiences by creating video and audio trainings, recording and viewing subject matter experts, presenting case studies, exchanging instructional resources (i.e., similar to using wikis and blogs), introducing a country or different culture to employees in different parts of the world (i.e., diversity training) and updating employees on organizational initiatives.

Case in Point: Enterprise 2.0 and Social Media Sharing

Many larger companies implement Enterprise 2.0 software solutions in order to provide secure social media sharing to their employees (IBM, 2011). For example, scientists at Astra Zeneca, use file sharing through IBM Documentum eRoom which provides a Web based workspace to distribute content to their local and geographically dispersed workforce (Warr, 2008). Another application, Microsoft SharePoint, is used by companies such as Microsoft, UNISYS, Eastman Chemical Company and the US Department of Agriculture for a combined social media solution (Sharepoint, 2011). Companies implement the SharePoint software solution behind a firewall, utilizing the internal company network to collaborate, share social media (i.e., text, audio, and video), create databases for employee use, communicate in real time and build professional relationships both within the network and with business partners.

Challenges to Implementation

The drawbacks to social media sharing are the same as with social bookmarking and blogs. Personal opinion and displays of individuality are rampant on social media sharing sites, and some organizations may not approve of their use. Care must be taken when implementing social media resources, and it is advisable to consider resources that can be placed behind firewalls in order to protect intellectual property and organizational interests. These precautions will also assist in assuring the authenticity of content; reducing the chances of misinformation being distributed to employees, or to the public at large.

Mashups

A mashup is a Web page and/or application that combine the functionality of two or more sources in order to create a new service (Podcastfaq, 2011). Mashups allow non-technical individuals to mix up data sources in order to find new meanings and represent it in interesting and different ways. Mapping mashups, for example, allow maps to be overlaid with various types of information. A music mashup, on the other hand, allows for the mixing of two different tracks in order to create a new musical formation (Shex, 2011). Many organizations have created their own individualized mashups for use by customers and employees.

Some collaborative examples of mashups are: mapping mashup-earthquakes (http://earthquakes.tafoni.net), IBM Many Eyes—visual data analysis (http://manyeyes.alphaworks.ibm.com/manyeyes/), GapMinder UN data visualization (http://www.gapminder.com), and heath map (http://healthmap.org/en).

Professional Development

Mashups can be used for the creation of maps, data visualization, examining organizational research, tracking of concepts over time (i.e., see GapMinder), creating semantic Web anthologies with the use of various media, creating knowledge maps (i.e., see IBM Many Eyes), tracking illnesses and creating a just-in-time learning location combining essential employee resources into one application (Shex, 2011).

Case in Point: Elsevier

Elsevier is a leading publisher of scientific, medical, and technical books and information products. The company employed the use of Socialtext, a wiki based social networking platform, to strengthen internal communications and unify the 7,000 employees worldwide under one network. Socialtext allows for easy communication, secure collaboration, and a user friendly interface that encourages employees to update and edit content quickly (Socialtext, 2011). What makes Socialtext a mashup is the mixture of wiki databases with social networking (i.e., similar to Facebook) capabilities and a microblogging interface (i.e., similar to Twitter). Users can create content, add images, video, and music, update profiles and easily identify others who have similar positions or who might be an information resource in the future. All of these features can be integrated into an organization's current content management system.

Challenges to Implementation

The drawbacks to mashups are the same as with social bookmarking and blogs. Mashups lend to personal interpretations that may not line up with organizational objectives. Although these collaborative applications allow for the presentation of a concept in multiple ways, administrators should be mindful that the clear establishment of goals will present employees with a strong framework with which to utilize mashups appropriately.

Synchronous Communication and Conferencing

Synchronous communication and conferencing is the ability to use text messaging, audio and video in real time in order to enhance collaborative and creative work projects (Shex, 2011). These applications are usually housed online, utilizing cloud-based computing technologies. Cloud-based computing technologies, or cloud computing, use the Internet in addition to centrally located servers to maintain applications and data (Siegle, 2010).

One of the most popular and common examples of synchronous communication and conferencing technologies is Google Apps for Business (http://www.google.com/apps/intl/en/business/index.html). This workspace allows for a centralized location for email, calendar, documents (i.e., including Google presentations, spreadsheets, and forms) and Google Sites. All of these apps are unified under one central login account. This allows for the instructor to facilitate collaboration and sharing between instructor-student and student-student (Google, 2010a, 2010b). Google has similar Apps for government, educational, and for nonprofit organizations.

Another example of synchronous communication is Adobe Connect (http://www.adobe.com/products/adobeconnect/features.html). Adobe Connect uses a simple interface in order to facilitate collaboration more effectively between groups of individuals. The interface is customizable and allows for the selective invitation, admission, and communication capabilities of all participants. The Adobe Connect interface allows for one main facilitator of each meeting. This facilitator can grant access, rights, and privileges to whomever he/she chooses. The facilitator can also upload documents to share with all of the participants, allowing attendees to review, edit, and make suggestions to any collaborative project under discussion. As a cloud computing application, Adobe Connect allows individuals to reduce the amount of technology needed to host collaborative meetings (Adobe, 2010).

Additional examples of synchronous communication and conferencing applications include Skype (http://www.skype.com), DimDim (http://www.DimDim.com), Wimba voice (http://www.wimba.com/products/wimba_voice), and Camtasia Relay (http://www.techsmith.com/camtasiarelay.asp).

Professional Development

Synchronous communication can be used for expert or guest presentations (i.e., without the added expense of travel), virtual team projects/collaborative team work, brainstorming and idea creation, online presentation review, developing learning resources (i.e., pre-recorded Web conferences), creating Web video clips, and broadcasting live trainings for viewing later.

Case in Point: Adobe Connect

Adobe Connect is used by various industry leaders to enhance their professional development and training programs. Both Toshiba and Xerox cite benefits for using Adobe Connect as reduced travel expenses, deliverable interactive training, increased problem resolution, improved knowledge transfer between divisions, increased training attendance, the consolidation of employees training records and the ability to increase training initiatives by instituting blended learning options (i.e., a mixture of face-to-face and online instruction). Other organizations who use Adobe Connect are, SAP, 3G Selling, Franklin Covey, and Constellation Wines. However, Adobe Connect is not just used by corporations, the US Defense In-

formation Services Agency, The Graduate School @ USDA, Utah Department of Transportation, and Arizona State University all use the software to facilitate training and provide diverse professional development opportunities (Adobe, 2011).

Challenges to Implementation

There are few drawbacks to synchronous communication and conferencing systems, especially since they can easily be implemented as closed networks with limited access. This fact may gain additional support from organizations who are concerned with protecting intellectual property. Additionally, much of this software is comprised of cloud-based technologies that allow for the utilization of informal learning and professional development opportunities from home. This also reduces hardware requirements, increasing the longevity of the equipment, and proliferation of the learning experiences to a diverse employee population.

Visual Worlds and Gaming

Visual worlds and gaming are synchronous interactions that occur within immersive 3-D worlds (Shex, 2011). Robinson (2009) the director of the Digital Media Center at the Illinois Institute of Technology defines immersive as "a synthetic world that makes the user feel a part of it by a number of means, including realistic video graphics, collaborative tasks, and luminal time." These worlds support collaboration and creativity, providing variety from common training lectures and text based resources to even audio-visual communications.

A few common visual world and applications are: Second Life (http://www.secondlife.com), Active Worlds (http://www.activeworlds.com), Muse (http://www.musecorp.com), The Palace (http://www.thepalace.com), and Moove (http://www.moove.com).

Professional Development

Virtual worlds and gaming can be used for creating avatars to make trainings more interactive, conducting simulations as a component of virtual research studies, facilitating virtual team projects, keeping in contact with a mentor or organizational expert, collaborating with employees in different countries, learning different languages and cultural customs. Virtual worlds can also be used for training employees through simulated workspaces, real estate appraisals, creating buildings to experiment with building materials, creating a role play or theater production, and exploring professional duties through the creation of virtual interactions (Shex, 2011).

Case in Point: Human Interface Technology Team

Robert Stone, the director of the Human Interface Technology Team at the University of Birmingham, UK, uses virtual worlds (i.e., game technology) to create training environments for military trainers. These "serious games" where military trainers use various scenarios for teaching and learning skills, allow military recruits to acclimate to the workplace environment, practice procedures and discuss situations with experienced personnel of how procedures unfold in the real world. Stone states that initial evaluations of soldiers who utilized virtual software programs indicate that trainees demonstrate improved real world performance (Cressey, 2011).

Challenges to Implementation

The drawbacks to visual worlds and gaming are the same as with social bookmarking and blogs. Displays of individuality are rampant on public networks, and offline identities do not always match online and/or gaming personas. Therefore, some organizations may not approve of their use. Although some larger corporations such as IBM

have an online presence in networks like Second Life (Gandhi, 2010), care must be taken when selecting and implementing virtual world applications for professional development. Therefore, it is advisable to consider working with virtual world developers (i.e., see http://www.musecorp.com) to create an individualized solution that fits organizational goals.

FUTURE OF COLLABORATIVE APPLICATIONS

Recently, a gaming technology entitled Kinect for Xbox 360 (see http://www.xbox.com/en-US/kinect) was released in the US. Kinect contains not only the ability to play games through the use of kinesthetic movement, but also possesses an interface that recognizes the skeleton of an individual, and allows him/her to interface with the technology to access additional social media applications.

The revolutionary nature of this interface is not its ability to use physical movement, because this was already established within the Nintendo Wii game system released approximately five years prior. However, it is the integration of social media, entertainment, and collaborative applications that provide a glimpse into the future of collaboration, virtual teamwork, and professional development. Kinect makes it possible to collaborate with the wave of a hand. The system also tracks an individual's movement across the room, possesses a voice recognition system, and has a seamless integration of social applications providing a wealth of information at the user's fingertips. Through this system, individuals have the opportunities to play games, watch movies, listen to music and share video chat conversations with love ones located many miles away (Microsoft, 2010).

These features, coupled with an ability to place a user within an immersive virtual reality game world, have culminated in a device that combines the characteristics of the collaborative applications discussed previously. From a professional development perspective, a user can easily be placed in a virtual environment that will allow for training and skill development. This technology is only a few steps away from possessing the capabilities to create unique employee training opportunities that can be completed from the comfort of a home, or office. Kinect is the future of collaborative applications, and although it may take time to be adopted within organizations, it demonstrates that online professional development has a bright outlook.

CONCLUSION

Within this chapter, we have attempted to present a fresh look at collaborative applications and their use in professional development and informal learning. In general, collaborative application technologies are transplanted from developed countries into regions of the world that are only beginning to understand their significance. Since the fundamental ontology, or generic meaning, of these tools varies, it is important to allow for cultural variation and differences in usage, contingent upon the individuals and/or organizations involved. Although these technologies possess great potential for both professional development and informal learning, it is imperative that external considerations, such as culture and community, be taken into account before, during, and after implementation.

In some ways, employee satisfaction can be one measure of success (Walters, 2009). However, in cross-cultural situations, cultural sensitivity must be employed in order to perceive when technology directly clashes with cultural norms and experiences (Williams, Warren, & Olaniran, 2009). Creating a professional development training program will take planning, insight, and understanding. Each individual (employee and/or student) is a unique learner who has the potential to contribute significantly to the organization as a whole and with the right structure, increased productivity can become a reality.

REFERENCES

Adobe Inc. (2010). *Adobe connect for web meetings.* Retrieved from http://www.adobe.com/products/adobeconnect/web-meetings.html.

Adobe Inc. (2011). *Showcase.* Retrieved from http://www.adobe.com/products/adobeconnect/showcase.html.

Allen, M., & Naughton, J. (2011). Social learning: A call to action for learning professionals. *T + D, 65*(8), 50-55.

Apegga. (2011). *Professional development.* Retrieved from http://www.apegga.org/members/ProfDev/toc_map.html.

Beckman, M. (1990). Collaborative learning: Preparation for the workplace and democracy. *College Teaching, 38*(4), 128–133.

Bullas, J. (2010). *How Best Buy energized 170,000 employees with social media.* Retrieved from http://www.jeffbullas.com/2010/05/26/how-best-buy-energized-170000-employees-with-social-media/.

Burnham, B. (2005). *The adult learner and implications for the craft of instructional design.* Paper presented at the 9th Annual Global Conference on Computers in Chinese Education. Laie, HI.

Campbell, A., McNamara, O., & Gilroy, P. (2004). *Practitioner research and professional development in education.* London, UK: Paul Chapman Publishing.

Caverly, D. C., & Ward, A. (2008). Techtalk: Wikis and collaborative knowledge construction. *Journal of Developmental Education, 32*(2), 36–37.

Chickering, A. W., & Gamson, Z. F. (1991). Applying the seven principles for good practice in undergraduate education. In Chickering, A. W., & Gamson, Z. F. (Eds.), *New Directions for Teaching and Learning.* San Francisco, CA: Jossey Bass.

Collier, K. G. (1980). Peer-group learning in higher education: The development of higher-order skills. *Studies in Higher Education, 5*(1), 55–62. doi:10.1080/03075078012331377306

Cooper, J. (1990). *Cooperative learning and college instruction.* Long Beach, CA: California State University.

Cox, E. J. (2009). The collaborative mind: Tools for 21st-century learning. *Multimedia & Internet@ Schools, 16*(5), 10-14.

Cressey, D. (2011). Q & A: The virtual trainer. *Nature, 477*(7365), 406. doi:10.1038/477406a

Daniel, D. (2007). Five tips for bringing Web 2.0 into the enterprise. *CIO Magazine.* Retrieved from http://www.cio.com/article/115300/Five_Tips_for_Bringing_Web_2.0_Into_the_Enterprise.

AccountingDegree.com. (2010). *25 CEO blogs every biz student should read.* Retrieved from http://www.accountingdegree.com/blog/2010/25-ceo-blogs-every-biz-student-should-read/.

Economides, A. A. (2008). Culture-aware collaborative learning. *Multicultural Education & Technology Journal, 2*(4), 243–267. doi:10.1108/17504970810911052

Educause Learning Initiative. (2005). *7 things you should know about social bookmarking.* Washington, DC: Educause.

Gandhi, S. (2010, January 19). *IBM dives into Second Life.* Retrieved from http://www.ibm.com/developerworks/opensource/library/os-social-secondlife/?ca=drs-.

GDRC. (2011). *What is collaborative learning.* Retrieved from http://www.gdrc.org/kmgmt/c-learn/what-is-cl.html.

Gibson, S. (2006, November 20). *Wikis are alive and kicking in the enterprise.* Retrieved from http://www.eweek.com/c/a/Messaging-and-Collaboration/Wikis-Are-Alive-and-Kicking-in-the-Enterprise/.

Glowacki-Dudka, M., & Brown, M. P. (2007). Professional development through faculty learning communities. *New Horizons in Adult Education & Human Resource Development, 21*, 29–39.

Goodsell, A. (1992). *Collaborative learning: A sourcebook for higher education.* University Park, PA: The Pennsylvania State University.

Google. (2010a). *For educators: Teach collaborative revision with Google Docs.* Retrieved from http://learn.googleapps.com/.

Google. (2010b). *Google Apps: Apps learning center for users.* Retrieved from http://www.google.com/a/help/intl/en/edu/customers.html.

Graham, J. (2004, December 14). Google's library plan a huge help. *USA Today.* Retrieved March, 13, 2011, from http://www.usatoday.com/money/industries/technology/2004-12-14-google-usat_x.htm.

Grebow, D. (2002). *At the water cooler of learning. Transforming Culture: An Executive Briefing on the Power of Learning.* Charlottesville, VA: The Darden School Foundation.

Hanley, M. (2009). Are you ready for informal learning? *Information Outlook, 13*(7), 13–18.

Hofstede, G. (1980). *Culture's consequences: International differences in work-related values.* Beverly Hills, CA: Sage Publications.

Hoover, J. N. (2007, June 20). *Motorola's IT department takes on Enterprise 2.0.* Retrieved from http://www.informationweek.com/news/199905701.

IBM. (2011). *Customers on social business.* Retrieved from http://www-01.ibm.com/software/lotus/socialbusiness/customers.

Johnson, D. W., & Johnson, R. T. (1989). *Cooperation and competition: Theory and research.* Edina, MN: Interaction Book Company.

Johnson, D. W., Johnson, R. T., & Smith, K. A. (1991). *Cooperative learning: Increasing college faculty instructional productivity. ASHE-FRIC Higher Education Report 4.* Washington, DC: George Washington University.

Johnson, L., Levine, A., Smith, R., & Stone, S. (2010). *The 2010 horizon report.* Austin, TX: The New Media Consortium.

Jones, S. (2011). Refresh for success: Moonee Valley libraries online database training wiki. *Aplis, 24*(2), 91–93.

Jue, A. L., Marr, J. A., & Kassotakis, M. E. (2009). *Social media at work: How networking tools propel organizational performance.* San Francisco, CA: Josey-Bass.

Kohn, A. (1986). *No contest: The case against competition.* Boston, MA: Houghton Mifflin.

Kojiri, T., Ogawa, Y., & Watanabe, T. (2001). Agent-oriented support environment in web-based collaborative learning. *Journal of Universal Computer Science, 7*(3), 226–239.

Konstantinidis, A., Tsiatsos, T., & Pomportsis, A. (2009). Collaborative virtual learning environments: Design and evaluation. *Multimedia Tools and Applications, 44,* 279–304. doi:10.1007/s11042-009-0289-5

Kukulska-Hulme, A., & Pettit, J. (2008). Semiformal learning communities for professional development in mobile learning. *Journal of Computing in Higher Education, 20,* 35–47. doi:10.1007/s12528-008-9006-z

Lenhart, A., Horrigan, J. B., & Fallows, D. (2004). Content creation online. *Pew Internet & American Life Project.* Retrieved March 13, 2011 from http://www.pewinternet.org/Reports/2004/Content-Creation-Online.aspx.

Liu, A. (2004). *Transcendental data: Toward a cultural history and aesthetics of the new encoded discourse.* Chicago, IL: University of Chicago.

Lund, N. (2010, April 25). *The use of Web 2.0 technology for professional development in Australia information associations.* Retrieved from http://networkconference.netstudies.org/2010/04/the-use-of-web-2-0-technology-for-professional-development-in-australian-information-associations/.

McKeachie, W. J., Pintrich, P. R., Lin, Y.-G., & Smith, D. A. F. (1986). *Teaching and learning in the college classroom: A review of the research literature.* Ann Arbor, MI: University of Michigan.

Meenan, C., King, A., Toland, C., Daly, M., & Nagy, P. (2010). Use of a wiki as a radiology department knowledge management system. *Journal of Digital Imaging, 23*(2), 142–151. doi:10.1007/s10278-009-9180-1

Michailidou, A., & Economides, A. A. (2003). Elearn: Towards a collaborative educational virtual environment. *Journal of Information Technology Education, 2,* 131–152.

Microsoft Inc. (2010). *Introducing Kinect for Xbox 360.* Retrieved from http://www.xbox.com/en-US/kinect.

Motorola. (2011). *Corporate responsibility: Training and development.* Retrieved from http://responsibility.motorola.com/index.php/employees/trainingdevelop/.

Olaniran, B. (2007a). Challenges to implementing e-learning in lesser-developed countries. In Edmundson, A. (Ed.), *Globalized e-Learning Cultural Challenges* (pp. 18–34). Hershey, PA: IGI Global. doi:10.4018/978-1-59904-301-2.ch002

Olaniran, B. A. (2007b). Culture and communication challenges in virtual workspaces. In St-Amant, K. (Ed.), *Linguistic and Cultural Online Communication Issues in the Global Age* (pp. 79–92). Hershey, PA: IGI Global. doi:10.4018/978-1-59904-213-8.ch006

Olaniran, B. A. (2010). Challenges facing the semantic web and social software as communication technology agents in e-learning environments. *International Journal of Virtual and Personal Learning Environments*, *1*(4), 18–30. doi:10.4018/jvple.2010100102

Olaniran, B. A., & Agnello, M. F. (2008). Globalization, educational hegemony, and higher education. *Journal of Multicultural Educational & Technology*, *2*(2), 68–86. doi:10.1108/17504970810883351

Olaniran, B. A., & Williams, I. M. (2009). Web 2.0 and learning: A closer look at transactional control model in e-learning. In Lambropoulos, N., & Rodriga, M. (Eds.), *Educational Social Software for Context-Aware Learning: Collaborative Methods and Human Interaction* (pp. 23–37). Hershey, PA: IGI Global. doi:10.4018/978-1-60566-826-0.ch002

Pew Internet and American Life Project. (2011). *Who's online: Internet user demographics.* Retrieved from http://pewinternet.org/Trend-Data/Whos-Online.aspx.

Podcastfaq. (2011). *Mashups.* Retrieved from http://www.podcastfaq.com/glossary/blogging-and-podcasting-terms/.

Ramburuth, P., & Tani, M. (2009). The impact of culture on learning: Exploring student perceptions. *Multicultural Education & Technology Journal*, *3*(3), 168–181. doi:10.1108/17504970910984862

Robinson, J. (2009, June 2). *The terminology of it all.* Retrieved from http://blog.joyrobinson.com/2009/06/the-terminology-of-it-all/.

Rogers, P., Graham, C., & Mayes, C. (2007). Cultural competence and instructional design: Exploration research into the delivery of online instruction cross-culturally. *Educational Technology Research and Development*, *55*(2), 197–217. doi:10.1007/s11423-007-9033-x

Samarawickrema, G., Benson, R., & Brack, C. (2010). Different spaces: Staff development for Web 2.0. *Australasian Journal of Educational Technology*, *26*(1), 44–49.

Sharepoint. (2011). *Customer success stories.* Retrieved from http://sharepoint.microsoft.com/en-us/customers/.

Shex. (2011). *Collaborative learning technologies.* Retrieved from http://shex.org/wiki/Collaborative_learning_technologies.

Siegle, D. (2010). Cloud computing: A free technology option to promote collaborative learning. *Gifted Child Today*, *33*(4), 41–45.

Slavin, R. E. (1983). When does cooperative learning increase student achievement? *Psychological Bulletin*, *94*(3), 429–445. doi:10.1037/0033-2909.94.3.429

Slavin, R. F. (1980). Cooperative learning. *Review of Educational Research, 50*(2), 315–342.

Smith, B. L., & MacGregor, J. T. (1992). *What is collaborative learning?* Retrieved from http://www.evergreen.edu/washcenter/natlc/pdf/collab.pdf.

Smith, K. A. (1986). Cooperative learning groups. In Schmoberg, S. F. (Ed.), *Strategies for Active Teaching and Learning in University Classrooms*. Minneapolis, MN: University of Minnesota.

Scovic, S. (2008). *Lost in transition?* London, UK: University of the Arts.

Sundar, M. (2006, July 9). *Top 10 CEO blogs*. Retrieved from http://mariosundar.com/2006/07/09/top-10-ceo-blogs/.

Socialtext (2011). *Customer case studies*. Retrieved from http://www.socialtext.com/customers.

Thibodeau, P. (2009, March 3). *Best Buy getting results from social network*. Retrieved from http://www.computerworld.com/s/article/9128877/Best_Buy_getting_results_from_social_network_.

Walters, G. (2009, March 1). Learning integration: Can informal learning be formalized?. *Training Journal,* 51-54.

Wang, X., Jiang, T., & Ma, F. (2010). Blog-supported scientific communication: An exploration analysis based on social hyperlinks in a Chinese blog community. *Journal of Information Science, 36*, 690–704. doi:10.1177/0165551510383189

Warr, W. A. (2008). Social software: Fun and games, or business tools? *Journal of Information Science, 34*, 591–604. doi:10.1177/0165551508092259

Whitman, N. A. (1988). *Peer teaching: To teach is to learn twice*. Washington, DC: Association for the Study of Higher Education.

Williams, I. M., Warren, H. N., & Olaniran, B. A. (2009). Achieving cultural acquiescence through foreign language e-learning. In Chang, M., & Kuo, C. (Eds.), *Handbook of Research on Learning Culture and Language via ICTs: Methods for Enhanced Instruction* (pp. 88–102). Hershey, PA: IGI Global. doi:10.4018/978-1-60566-166-7.ch006

ADDITIONAL READING

Alge, B. J., Wiethoff, C., & Klein, H. J. (2003). When does medium matter: Knowledge-building experiences and opportunities. e*Organizational Behavior and Human Decision Processes, 91,* 26–37.

Benford, S., Greenhalgh, C., Rodden, T., & Pycock, J. (2001). Collaborative virtual environments. *Communications of the ACM, 44*(7), 79–85. doi:10.1145/379300.379322

Brouse, P. L., Fields, N. A., & Palmer, J. D. (1992). A multimedia computer supported cooperative work environment for requirements engineering. In *Proceedings of the International Conference on Systems, Man and Cybernetics,* (pp. 954-959). Chicago, IL: IEEE.

Byrne, T. (2008). Enterprise social software technology. *KM World, 17*(8), 8–9.

Davis, A., Murphy, J., Owens, D., Khazanchi, D., & Zigurs, I. (2009). Avatars, people, and virtual worlds: Foundations for research in metaverses. *Journal of the Association for Information Systems, 10*(2), 90–117.

Ess, C. (2002). Cultures in collision philosophical lessons from computer-mediated communication. *Metaphilosophy, 33,* 229–253. doi:10.1111/1467-9973.00226

Gruman, G. (2006). Enterprise mashups. *Info-World, 28*(31), 19–23.

Hammond, T., Hannay, T., Lund, B., & Scott, J. (2005). Social bookmarking tools (I): A general review. *D-Lib Magazine, 11*(4). Retrieved from http://www.dlib.org/dlib/april05/hammond/04hammond.html doi:10.1045/april2005-hammond

Hansen, M. M. (2008). Versatile, immersive, creative and dynamic virtual 3-D healthcare learning environments: A review of the literature. *Journal of Medical Internet Research, 10*(3), e26. doi:10.2196/jmir.1051

Hofstede, G. (2001). *Culture's consequences: Comparing values, behaviors, institutions and organizations across nations* (2nd ed.). Thousand Oaks, CA: Sage.

Jones, W. (2008, June 16). *Wiki your office's technical knowledge and reduce support calls.* Retrieved from http://blogs.techrepublic.com.com/helpdesk/?p=106.

Lynch, P. K. (2010). New & noteworthy: Golden nuggets: Share your knowledge on the BMET Wiki. *Biomedical Instrumentation & Technology, 44*(6), 454–455. doi:10.2345/0899-8205-44.6.454

Mahmood, I., Hartley, R., & Rowley, J. (2011). Scientific communication in Libya in the digital age. *Journal of Information Science, 37*(4), 379–390. doi:10.1177/0165551511408846

Morse, K. (2003). Does one size fit all? Exploring asynchronous learning in a multicultural environment. *Journal of Asynchronous Learning Networks, 7*(1), 37–55.

Mullin, R. (2007). Seeing the forest at Pfizer. *Chemical and Engineering News, 85*(36), 29. doi:10.1021/cen-v085n036.p029

Mullin, R. (2007). The big picture: Drug firms forge an information management architecture to take on the research data glut. *Chemical and Engineering News, 85*(40), 13–17. doi:10.1021/cen-v085n040.p013

Nevo, S., Nevo, D., & Carmel, E. (2011). Unlocking the business potential of virtual worlds. *MIT Sloan Management Review, 52*(3), 14–17.

Newswire, P. R. (2011). *NAUTIS maritime simulators receive DNV certification.* Retrieved from http://www.prnewswire.com/news-releases/nautis-maritime-simulators-receive-dnv-certification-133870833.html.

O'Reilly, T. (2005, October 1). Compact definition. *O'Reilly Radar.* Retrieved from http://radar.oreilly.com/archives/2005/10/web_20_compact_definition.html.

O'Reilly, T. (2005, September 30). *What is Web 2.0? Design patterns and business models for the next generation of software.* Retrieved from http://www.oreillynet.com/lpt/a/6228.

Pascopella, A. (2011). Professional development 2.0. *District Administration, 47*(2), 14.

Perryer, G., Lambe, C. S., Attrill, D., & Walmsley, A. D. (2007). Podcasts, wikis, videos, and blogs: A case study in dental education. *MEDEV Bulletin, 22*, 6–7.

Redfern, S., & Naughton, N. (2002). Collaborative virtual environments to support communication and community in internet-based distance education. *Journal of Information Technology Education, 1*(3), 201–211.

Richardson, W. (2007). Teaching in a Web 2.0 world. *Kappa Delta Pi Record, 43*(4), 150–151.

Sorani, M. D., Ortmann, W. A., Beirwagen, E. P., & Behrens, T. W. (2010). Clinical and biological data integration for biomaker discovery. *Drug Discovery Today, 15*, 741–748. doi:10.1016/j.drudis.2010.06.005

KEY TERMS AND DEFINITIONS

Collaborative Applications: Online technologies used to create small group interactions and can be employed to implement active, collaborative, and real world instruction.

Cloud Computing: Applications and data housed on centrally located Internet servers.

Lifetime Learning: The continual re-education, renewal, and refinement of professional skills necessary to improve work performance.

Informal Learning: Learning that lacks structure and occurs during the course of daily life, work, or leisure time.

Formal Learning: Intentional learning associated with learning objectives that lead to a particular outcome such as a certificate or a degree and usually obtained from an institution.

Professional Development: A combination of formal learning provided by an educational or training institution and informal learning provided by mentorship, observations and discussions with more experienced employees.

Collaborative Learning: A method of instruction, where learners work together and share ideas to accomplish an educational goal.

Chapter 2
Web 2.0, the Individual, and the Organization:
Privacy, Confidentiality, and Compliance

Kerry J. Burner
Walden University, USA & Florida State University, USA

ABSTRACT

This chapter explores the issues that can arise when professionals employ Web 2.0 social networking technologies in service of their professional development by way of informal learning. Issues around privacy, confidentiality, and compliance are discussed and possible actions organizations and individuals can take are presented.

INTRODUCTION

Web 2.0 social networking tools are increasingly used by individuals to connect with each other while at work and on their own time about work. Frequently, these social networking tools support informal learning in service of professional development. Beers and Burrows (2007) use the term Web 2.0 to refer to "a cluster of new applications and related online cultures that possess a conceptual unity only to the extent that it is possible to decipher some significant socio-technical characteristics that they have in common" (para 1.3). Not only do Web 2.0 social networking tools

offer unprecedented access to employees by employees for informal learning goals, the role Web 2.0 social networking tools play in contemporary workplaces is redefining the relationship between the individual and the workplace.

What began with pagers and early mobile telephones—used to connect workers to their workplace in times of need—has evolved into a mutually ubiquitous presence: via the Internet, the worker and the workplace both can be accessible 24/7. The benefits of this constant access are many, especially in critical industries like medicine and emergency response fields. What of the emerging issues for both organizations and individuals?

DOI: 10.4018/978-1-4666-1815-2.ch002

This chapter will explore the issues around the Web 2.0-based relationship of the individual and the organization, particularly issues of privacy, confidentiality, and compliance in an effort to contribute to the ongoing conversation about working in the cloud. Specifically, this chapter will seek to give shape to these issues and attempt to identify what is working as well as focus on what work needs to be accomplished as the ever-expanding array of Web 2.0 social networking tools continues to become part of the daily practice of work and learning. Working in the cloud, or cloud computing, means that information and tools reside outside of the local, personal computing devices people use. Wang, von Laszewski, Younge, He, Kunze, Tao, and Fu (2008) provide an early definition of cloud computing: "A computing Cloud is a set of network enabled services, providing scalable, QoS guaranteed, normally personalized, inexpensive computing infrastructures on demand, which could be accessed in a simple and pervasive way" (p.3).

As we put this information out into the cloud, what are the near and far consequences of having it there for ourselves or even our social networks? This chapter explores the issues that can arise when professionals employ Web 2.0 social networking technologies in service of their professional development by way of informal learning. Issues around privacy, confidentiality, and compliance are discussed, and possible actions organizations and individuals can take are presented.

THE LANDSCAPE OF INFORMAL PROFESSIONAL DEVELOPMENT IN THE CLOUD

What is meant by informal professional development in the cloud? This section presents a brief overview of this concept as well as establishes definitions for privacy, confidentially, and compliance, as they will be used in this chapter.

Informal Learning and Professional Development

Informal learning is an essential part of how humans learn. Eraut (2004) defines informal learning as:

learning that comes closer to the informal end than the formal end of a continuum. Characteristics of the informal end of the continuum of formality include implicit, unintended, opportunistic, and unstructured learning and the absence of a teacher. In the middle come activities like mentoring, while coaching is rather more formal in most settings (p. 250).

Learning that happens by way of casual social interaction can be considered informal. Informal learning can be an unintended result of casual social interaction, or informal learning can be intentional on the part of the learner. For example, when we are cooking in the kitchen with our children, we are not just spending time together, they are learning—how to measure, that ovens should be pre-heated, that the mixer should be off when adding dry ingredients, and so forth. At work, we learn informally by seeking out information and knowledge, perhaps by looking over completed documents and comparing them to our own efforts.

Professional development is just that—developing the professional in terms of knowledge, skills, and attitudes. From schools to industry to the military, workers are often required to participate in continuing education in order to maintain their positions. In most work settings, formal professional development or staff development initiatives originate from the organization or an ancillary, approved provider, but these formal setting are not the only way in which professionals are developing themselves. Informal learning—learning without a teacher in an unexpected way—plays a role as well. At its most simple, workers who ask questions of more experienced colleagues and learn more than they anticipated are engaging in informal professional development. Web 2.0 technologies have expanded access—enlarging the pool of people with whom professionals can interact and engage in formal learning.

Traditionally, informal learning has not received a lot of organizational support. In 2008, ASTD and the Institute for Corporate Productivity (i4cp) reported that "while more than 70 percent of the knowledge that employees acquire comes from informal learning experiences, 78 percent of companies surveyed allocate less than 10 percent of their budgets to informal learning" (Pace, 2009, p. 20). This could be changing as Web 2.0 technologies change the landscape of informal learning. Organizations have long recognized the benefits of and have sought to maintain a well-developed workforce, and with the advent and proliferation of Web 2.0 technologies, more and more organizations are recognizing the roles both Web 2.0 and informal learning can play in that pursuit.

Web 1.0 vs. Web 2.0

Plainly described, Web 1.0 connects people with information using computers while Web 2.0 connects people with people using computers. Web 1.0 functionalities offer users the ability to do a wide range of activities—from shopping to learning—but the emphasis is not on an interpersonal connection. Web 2.0 technologies have at their center personal interaction. Blogs, discussion forums, wikis, social networking, social bookmarking, and podcasting are all examples of Web 2.0 technologies. Each offers people different ways to interact with other people; this interaction ranges from asynchronous conversations via posted messages to interacting in real time via social networking tools like Facebook or Twitter. Even podcasting has become interactive with the advent of podcasting technologies like Voicethread, which allows viewers to embed comments.

What does this mean for informal learning and professional development? It means that instead of searching static websites, professionals can participate in web-based, informal discussions with other professionals, becoming both consumers and producers of information. They can also create professional connections via social networking sites. boyd and Ellison (2007) define social networking:

as Web-based services that allow individuals to (1) construct a public or semi-public profile within a bounded system, (2) articulate a list of other users with whom they share a connection, and (3) view and traverse their list of connections and those made by others within the system. The nature and nomenclature of these connections may vary from site to site (p. 2).

Social networking sites target both professionals and the casual Internet user. Sites like LinkedIn offer a conduit for professionals to interact at a variety of price points, starting with a free account. Free social networking websites like Facebook, MySpace, and Google+ offer the casual Internet user places to interact with anyone else using the websites. Opportunities for professional and personal interaction are co-located on these sites, which can lead to overlaps—sometimes unfortunate ones that breach privacy, confidentiality, or compliance with regulations.

Privacy, Confidentiality, and Compliance

Conversations centering around the Internet and privacy, confidentiality, and compliance are not new, but Web 2.0 technologies have brought new features to the landscape and added to the conversation. What do these terms mean? For this discussion, they will be defined as follows. Privacy and confidentiality both involve limits on what is known and how information is distributed. At its most specific, privacy means to be in seclusion. Professionally, privacy typically refers to an individual's personnel information, the data an organization maintains about its members, and his personal life, a time when he is not functioning within the scope of work—off the radar. Personnel information is typically confidential, as is proprietary organizational information. Confidentiality, on the other hand, refers to the act of keeping information out of the professional or public arena. Compliance means to act in accordance with established rules, regulations, and laws either at the individual or organizational level. Informal interactions between professionals in the cloud can present privacy, confidentiality, and compliance issues for organizations. The next section explores those issues.

ISSUES WHEN INFORMAL PROFESSIONAL DEVELOPMENT HAPPENS IN THE CLOUD

Organizational Perspective

Privacy and Confidentiality

Since organizations do not have privacy in the same way individuals do, the focus becomes keeping confidential the private information of its workforce. In addition to ensuring confidentiality of private personnel information, organizations need to ensure that their own proprietary or classified information is kept confidential. Both are types of privileged information, known only to those who need to know it for the completion of their assigned duties. How does this relate to professional development, informal learning, and Web 2.0 technologies? It is important that all members of any organization understand both the legal restrictions and the organization's position about the use and distribution of privileged information and that they understand the manner in which they

should represent themselves and the organization in the cloud.

A US Government Accounting Office publication that addresses the challenges federal agencies face when using Web 2.0 technologies outlines the following privacy and security challenges:

- Determining how the Privacy Act of 1974 applies to government use of social media;
- Ensuring that agencies are taking appropriate steps to limit the collection and use of personal information through social media;
- Extending privacy protections to the collection and use of personal information by third party providers;
- Safeguarding personal information from security threats that target Web 2.0 technologies; and
- Training government participants on the proper use of social networking tools (GAO, 2010).

While this publication centers on government agencies, which might have more stringent policies, these issues are ones that every organization faces to some degree, depending on the industry.

Maintaining confidentiality, including controlling proprietary information, brings forth another set of issues for governmental agencies and governmentally regulated organizations that handle classified information. In the case of the military members who used a wiki to help with their battlefield mission, potentially classified information was shared via user-driven and user-controlled Web-based tools (Rid, 2007). Contrasted with the intentional distribution of classified information via the "Wikileaks" organization, this grassroots application of Web 2.0 social networking tools to assist in the troops' duties exemplifies the way in which the power and usefulness of Web 2.0 social networking tools is outpacing the norms and standard operating procedures of organizations. As Mergel (2009) points out:

The difference between this 'phase' of government IT and past phases such as the move from centralized mainframes to desktop PCs or the move from stovepiped organizations to ones connected via email and the uni-directional Web, is the ease at which organizations can interact and the ease at which these technologies can be deployed, often by people with very low technological abilities (p. 32).

As these "there's no rule for that" issues emerge, there are commonalities across all organizational settings, but there are also differences based on the setting.

Academic and accrediting institutions must contend not only with the issues around employees using Web 2.0 social networking tools—both faculty and staff—but also with the use of Web 2.0 by students in service of their learning both informally and formally. For example, students posting their coursework for the public to access opens the door for issues of plagiarism as well as fair use of course materials owned by Universities. Students like those who blog all of their coursework—from discussion board postings to formal submissions—not only share their unique learning processes and products, but also expose curricular requirements to non- and future students alike. The institution has no control over this type of student-generated content yet must contend with the impacts.

Compliance

Organizations are expected to be in compliance with local, state, and federal laws as well as government and industry regulations that govern everything from emissions to privacy. While this chapter is not a source of legal advice, organizations should seek the input of counsel; there are quite a few federal laws that directly impact the ways in which organizations handle private, confidential information:

- Administrative Procedure Act
- Cable Communications Policy Act of 1984
- Census Confidentiality Statute of 1954
- Computer Security Act of 1987
- E-government Act of 2002
- Fair and Accurate Credit Transactions Act (2003)
- Fair Credit Reporting Act (1970)
- Family Education Rights and Privacy Act (1974)
- Freedom of Information Act (1966)
- Gramm-Leach-Bliley Act (1999)
- Health Insurance Portability and Accountability Act of 1996 (HIPAA)
- Privacy Act of 1974
- Privacy Protection Act of 1980
- Right to Financial Privacy Act (1978)
- Taxpayer Browsing Protection Act (1997)
- Telephone Consumer Protection Act of 1991
- The Electronic Communications Privacy Act (1986)
- Video Privacy Protection Act of 1988

On the state level, laws are being passed to address specific acts of misconduct. For example, Missouri recently passed Missouri State Senate Bill 54, also known as the "Amy Hestir Student Protection Act" and informally as the "Facebook Law," in response to misconduct by a K12 teacher. While the primary focus of the law is the protection of children from sexual predators, it prohibits teachers and students from being friends on social network sites that are not also accessible to administrators and parents. As Web 2.0 technologies become more prevalent in the workplace, more laws will be written in response to problems and criminal acts.

Another aspect of compliance for organizations is documenting and archiving communication and collaborative processes in order to capture and manage proprietary information. "To approach records management from a siloed technology perspective complicates discovery and the ability to logically view information, regardless of where it came from, in its original business context" (HP, 2010, p. 2). Other aspects of compliance issues at universities in particular involve fair use/copyright issues, ownership of user-generated content, and putting educational activities in the public arena.

Individual Perspective

In as much as an individual's personal privacy can be under her control, she must seek to maintain a clear separation between personal and professional, particularly when working in the cloud.

Privacy

Privacy is likely the biggest issue facing individuals who have both personal and professional public identities—a Web presence. The always fine line between one's public and professional personas has been irrevocably blurred by Web 2.0 social networking tools; blogging and social networking tools like Blogspot and Facebook, for example, offer space for individuals to share their experiences with others. Recent news stories highlight the way in which social networking sites, specifically, have played a role in the professional lives of teachers—professors, PK12, and pre-service alike. Consider the recent case of an NYC schoolteacher who is slated to be fired because of a post on her personal Facebook account: Christine Rubino posted what can only be described as distasteful and inappropriate comments about wishing her students dead, and these comments were brought to the attention of her administration by a fellow teacher who had access to her page (Edelman, 2011). Similarly, Gloria Gadsden, a sociology professor at East Stroudsburg University in Pennsylvania, was dismissed for making comments on Facebook about wishing her students dead on two occasions (Stripling, 2010).

Words are not the only problem. Pictures of herself holding an alcoholic beverage during a vacation resulted in Ashley Payne's resignation; the photos on her Facebook wall were meant for only those with access, but a student's parent was able to view them and Ms. Payne was brought under disciplinary action (CBS, 2011). And pre-service teachers are also being impacted: Millersville University in Pennsylvania denied Stacy Snyder her degree in teaching over a photo the then student posted to MySpace. The photo was of the 25-year-old Synder consuming an unidentifiable beverage from a cup and was captioned "drunken pirate"; she was accused of promoting underage drinking (Michels, 2008). All of these cases bring to light questions about an individual's rights to both privacy and freedom of expression juxtaposed with an organization's responsibility to maintain and enforce professional standards.

Confidentiality and Compliance

For individuals, issues of confidentiality and compliance are more a matter of maintaining organizational policy to avoid any issues. If an individual's personnel information were to be made public, the individual would likely have grounds for legal action. Likewise, if an individual is responsible for a breach in confidentiality or compliance, there may be cause for legal action. The following section delves more deeply into the steps that both organizations and individuals can take to avoid problems with informal learning in the cloud.

RECOMMENDATIONS FOR INFORMAL PROFESSIONAL DEVELOPMENT IN THE CLOUD

What Organizations Can Do

Organizational leadership can take a wide array of approaches to informal learning in the cloud–from ignoring it to banning it to embracing it. The following section discusses three recommendations:

draft policy, create a code of ethics, and support these types of learning efforts by employees.

Policy

The first step for any organization is to draft policy that clearly spells out expectations. Virtually any member of an organization can access and use Web 2.0 social networking tools, and unless clear policy is both in place and enforced, the kinds of information shared via Web 2.0 social networking tools is boundless. Security approaches typically are top-down, monitoring and blocking of social networking (Clearswift, 2010). This can be too draconic an approach. Cisco Systems, the company largely responsible for the proliferation of the Internet, has a publically accessible policy about Internet posting that defines then discusses Internet activities of their employees.

Cisco's Internet Postings Policy

With the rise of new media and next generation communications tools, the way in which Cisco employees can communicate internally and externally continues to evolve. While this creates new opportunities for communication and collaboration, it also creates new responsibilities for Cisco employees. This Internet Postings Policy applies to employees who use the following:

- *Multi-media and social networking websites such as MySpace, Facebook, Yahoo! Groups and YouTube*
- *Blogs (Both Cisco Blogs and Blogs external to Cisco)*
- *Wikis such as Wikipedia and any other site where text can be posted*

All of these activities are referred to as "Internet postings" in this Policy. Please be aware that violation of this policy may result in disciplinary action up to and including termination. Com-

mon sense is the best guide if you decide to post information in any way relating to Cisco. If you are unsure about any particular posting, please contact the Cisco "Internet postings" email alias for guidance. For instance, if you are writing about Cisco business where you have responsibility, you may wish to make sure your manager is comfortable with your taking that action.

Your Internet postings should not disclose any information that is confidential or proprietary to the company or to any third party that has disclosed information to Cisco. If you comment on any aspect of the company's business or any policy issue in which the company is involved and in which you have responsibility, you must clearly identify yourself as a Cisco employee in your postings or blog site(s) and include a disclaimer that the views are your own and not those of Cisco. In addition, Cisco employees should not circulate postings they know are written by other Cisco employees without informing the recipient that the author of the posting is a Cisco employee. Your Internet posting should reflect your personal point of view, not necessarily the point of view of Cisco. Because you are legally responsible for your postings, you may be subject to liability if your posts are found defamatory, harassing, or in violation of any other applicable law. You may also be liable if you make postings which include confidential or copyrighted information (music, videos, text, etc.) belonging to third parties. All of the above mentioned postings are prohibited under this policy.

When posting your point of view, you should neither claim nor imply you are speaking on Cisco's behalf, unless you are authorized in writing by your manager to do so. If you identify yourself as a Cisco employee on any Internet posting, refer to the work done by Cisco or provide a link on a Cisco website, you are required to include the following disclaimer in a reasonably prominent place: "the views expressed on this post are mine and do not necessarily reflect the views of Cisco." Your Internet postings should not include Cisco's logos or trademarks, and should respect copyright, privacy, fair use, financial disclosure, and other applicable laws. Cisco Blogs (located on http:// blogs.cisco.com) are blogs requiring corporate approval in which employees may blog about Cisco and our industry. Only Cisco Blogs may include the company's logo. Cisco Blogs may also include links back to Cisco Web destinations. All Cisco Blogs must include a legal disclaimer stating that all posts by the author, guest author and visitors reflect personal thoughts and opinions which are not necessarily those of the company.

Cisco may request that you avoid certain subjects or withdraw certain posts from a Cisco Blog if it believes that doing so will help ensure compliance with applicable laws, including securities regulations. Cisco reserves the right to remove any posted comment on Cisco Blog site(s) that is not appropriate for the topic discussed or uses inappropriate language. Cisco also reserves the right to post particular communications on a Cisco Blog. If a member of the news media or blogger contacts you about an Internet posting that concerns the business of Cisco, please refer that person to Cisco public relations, see: http://tools.cisco.com/newsroom/contactSearch/jsp/prSearch.jsp Your Internet postings should not violate any other applicable policy of Cisco, including those set forth in the Employee Resource Guide and the Code of Business Conduct. You agree that Cisco shall not be liable, under any circumstances, for any errors, omissions, loss or damages claimed or incurred due to any of your Internet postings. Cisco reserves the right to suspend, modify, or withdraw this Internet Postings Policy, and you are responsible for regularly reviewing the terms of this Internet Postings Policy (Cisco Systems, 2008).

How to craft a policy statement? Organizations can use relevant, available examples like Cisco as a guide; additionally, the Department of Justice (2008) provides a development guide, the Privacy and Civil Liberties Policy Development Guide and Implementation Templates, to help justice practitioners craft privacy and civil liberties policy. Developing a policy statement and ensuring that the policy is known and understood by employees will help organizations hopefully avoid but certainly address issues should they arise.

Code of Ethics

The Association for Educational Communications and Technology (AECT), the International Society for Performance Improvement (ISPI), and the American Society for Training and Development (ASTD), three of the largest professional organizations for professionals engaged in the myriad ways of supporting performance improvement at the individual level in an organizational setting, all have a code of ethics to guide their members and, because they are freely accessible on each organization's website, non-members as well. These codes detail the ways in which professionals in these fields should—simply put—be when they are acting in a professional capacity.

From reading these three codes, it is plain to see that consideration of individual privacy is not a new notion for professionals responsible for designing learning and instruction. Among other issues and with differing degrees of granularity, each of these three codes addresses privacy, confidentiality, and compliance. Below are relevant excerpts from these three codes.

- Privacy
    ◦ 1.4. Shall conduct professional business so as to protect the privacy and maintain the personal integrity of the individual. (AECT)
    ◦ Be honest and truthful in representations to your client, colleagues, and

others with whom you may come in contact with while practicing performance technology. (ISPI)

- ◦ I strive to recognize the rights and dignities of each individual (ASTD)
- Confidentiality
  - ◦ 2.1. Shall honestly represent the institution or organization with which that person is affiliated, and shall take adequate precautions to distinguish between personal and institutional or organizational views. (AECT)
  - ◦ Maintain client confidentiality, not allowing for any conflict of interest that would benefit yourself or others. (ISPI)
  - ◦ I strive to maintain confidentiality and integrity in the practice of my profession (ASTD)
- Compliance
  - ◦ 3.8. Shall inform users of the stipulations and interpretations of the copyright law and other laws affecting the profession and encourage compliance. (AECT)
  - ◦ Do not use information for any personal gain or in any manner that would be contrary to the law or detrimental to the legitimate and ethical objectives of the client's organization. (ISPI)
  - ◦ I strive to comply with all copyright laws and the laws and regulations governing my position. (ASTD)

Whether the learning arm of an organization opts to adopt one of the extant codes from an organization or develop one of their own, a clearly articulated code of ethics helps define the expectants an organization can have of its members, which in turn can help to define the organizational culture.

Support It

Organizations can see the proliferation of Web 2.0 technologies as an opportunity to shape the kinds of informal learning their employees are engaging in. Web 2.0 technologies can be internal to the organization's intranet or be in the public domain. If an organization hosts Web 2.0 technologies on an intranet, for example, the organization has the opportunity to foster an environment of shared learning. Further, monitoring the information for accuracy is far less onerous than attempting to monitor all the information on the Internet. Hosting Web 2.0 technologies is not the only resource required, however. Rossett and Hoffman (2011) discuss the costs of moving organizationally sponsored informal learning into the wild world of Web 2.0 technologies, namely that someone internal to the organization needs to be responsible for updating, validating, and working with "attorneys to balance freedom and risk" (p. 172). Supporting it also allows organizations to intervene should issues of privacy, confidentiality, or compliance emerge.

Organizations that do decide to support Web 2.0 technologies in service of learning can draw on a number of theories to develop their particular learning plan. Siemens (2004) has proposed a learning theory—connectivism—that considers the medium and the activity. Connectivism could guide the development of Web 2.0 oriented learning, both formal and informal. The theory relies on an understanding of the fluidity of knowledge, knowledge building, and the media by which it can happen. The principles of connectivism are:

- Learning and knowledge rests in diversity of opinions.
- Learning is a process of connecting specialized nodes or information sources.
- Learning may reside in non-human appliances.
- Capacity to know more is more critical than what is currently known

- Nurturing and maintaining connections is needed to facilitate continual learning.
- Ability to see connections between fields, ideas, and concepts is a core skill.
- Currency (accurate, up-to-date knowledge) is the intent of all connectivist learning activities.
- Decision-making is itself a learning process. Choosing what to learn and the meaning of incoming information is seen through the lens of a shifting reality. While there is a right answer now, it may be wrong tomorrow due to alterations in the information climate affecting the decision (Siemens, 2004).

Further, Pettenati, and Cigognini (2010) outline four stages of a connectivist learning experience: (1) awareness and receptivity, (2) connection forming and selection filtering, (3) contribution and involvement, and (4) reflection and meta-cognition (pp. 13-14). These stages reflect the activities learners would engage in in a more structured environment and, hopefully, what the professionals engaged in informal learning in the cloud are experiencing.

Assuming that an organization is supporting it, one appealing aspect of Web 2.0 technologies is that they allow for intra-departmental interaction. Often, formal learning groups are unit or department based, and efforts to foster informal learning groups or communities of practice are also unit or department based. Web 2.0 technologies, like blogging or wikis, remove this boundary, and professionals are able to build networks independent of their particular job functions. In their study of communities of practices and informal learning, Boud and Middleton (2003) did not find that tightly defined communities of practice emerged in the variety units they studied, but they did find three areas of informal learning occurred across units, regardless of the type of work being performed: (1) mastery of organizational processes, (2) negotiating the political, and (3) dealing with

the atypical. These three areas are a great fit for Web 2.0 technologies as they all involve finding out more from other people who have had similar professional experiences.

What Individuals Can Do

Regardless of the organizational approach, it is at the individual level that issues or problems are created or avoided. The recommendations to be ethical, informed, and aware are ways the individual can work to ensure that problems with privacy, confidentiality, and compliance stay at bay.

Be Ethical

Ethics are standards of behavior that are generally agreed upon by members of a society. It should go without saying, but, for example, the fact that student-teacher relationships are being regulated at the level of state law means that it still needs to be said: people should act ethically. This means acting with integrity, honesty, and with authenticity. Acting ethically requires being fully informed about any given situation and the factors that influence it or result from it.

The effectiveness of Web 2.0 social networking tools depends greatly on the participants' willingness to be vulnerable and to disclose personal information (Luehmann, 2008; Luehmann & Tinelli, 2008). This can easily lead to disclosing too much information or disclosing information about other people. Smaldino, Donaldson, and Herring's (2011) discussion of AECT's code of ethics for instructional technology (IT) professionals includes some advice: "one related golden piece of advice to pass along to it professionals is to consider when in public that you act as if a colleague of the person you are discussing is sitting nearby" (p. 344). They were specifically addressing the code that calls for ethical behavior with regard to individual privacy, reminding it professionals that privacy is more a matter of taking the right measures than it is location.

Be Informed

Professionals should keep abreast of their organization's rules and regulations and any laws that might be applicable to their job. Do not rely on a passive approach—mandatory training or being told by a supervisor. A proactive approach means seeking out the information on policy, regulations, and laws that might apply to one's profession and being fully cognizant of the places where online activities intersect with professional responsibilities.

Be Aware

Few people do not have a Web-presence, and everyone should monitor it. Searching for your name using one or more of the available search engines is a fast way to find out what is on the Internet about you and what other people have access to. Not only is the location amorphous, because of the density of information and the power of search engines, it is nearly impossible to know how far one's Web-presence reaches. It is easy to extend Smaldino, Donaldson, and Herring's (2011) advice about acting ethically to all professionals engaged in professional development in the cloud—envision your professional peers right next to you when working.

What Both Organizations and Individuals Can Do

While the issues and approaches differ between an organizational perspective and an individual one, there are commonalities. Both should be patient and should cooperate.

Move Forward at a Moderate Pace

As Web 2.0 technologies become as ubiquitous as the Internet, the legalities will continue to be worked out. For example, the ultimate fate of the Facebook Law will set national precedent and will inform both policy and practice. Creating policy that is responsive to the current legal climate is appropriate, but so is creating a schedule for regular reviews and updates to keep it current.

Technology adoption should also be part of the overall approach to integrating Web 2.0 into organizational learning efforts. A new generation of software and hosted Web 2.0 social networking tools are coming to the market. For example, software company HP has recently developed TRIM, a program to assist companies who use Microsoft Sharepoint with archiving their user-generated content—to include Web 2.0 social networking tools. There are also sites specifically for educationally oriented social networking; Edmodo, for example:

Edmodo is a free and secure social learning network for teachers, students, and schools. Edmodo provides classrooms a safe and easy way to connect and collaborate, offering a real-time platform to exchange ideas, share content, and access homework, grades and school notices.

And Google+ has introduced a simple way to group social network associations by category with corresponding permissions, acknowledging the need for separation between levels of privacy and disclosure in a streamlined, single environment. The platform and software solutions will, much like the laws, move forward at the pace of demand and will be shaped by the users.

Co-Develop Data-Driven Solutions

As employees explore new technologies in service of their own professional development, organizations will need to develop policies and procedures appropriate to these explorations. Professionals who are harnessing these technologies should consider bringing the need for policy to the appropriate member of their organization. Organizations would be wise to employ proactive approaches to policy development that include tapping early adopters of technology for their insight and embracing those same technologies in support of organizational success.

CONCLUSION

Why do people engage in professional development via informal learning in the cloud? Researchers are seeking definitive answers to this question, but it is not hard to imagine an answer: it is a way of connecting with like-minded people who have similar experiences and interests. Humans are social beings, after all. We do know that learners using Web 2.0 technologies are more engaged than counterparts not using them (Chinn & Williams, 2009). Web 2.0 technologies are not going to disappear. Likely they will evolve, which brings emphasis to the position that shunning Web 2.0 technologies is not the best approach for organizations to take. Instead, they should focus on figuring out how to make their efforts to support and nurture this type of professional development pay off. Connectivism may be able to help shape that approach: connectivism presents a model of learning that acknowledges the tectonic shifts in society where learning is no longer an internal, individualistic activity (Siemens, 2004). Fostering professional development via internal Web 2.0 technologies could be a powerful way for companies to support their members, but, as with any solution, be it a performance or policy issue, analyzing the situation and basing the solution on an understanding of the circumstance and the data is key to that solution's viability. Both the organization and individual should have a clear understanding of the possibilities and features of Web 2.0 technologies in order to better integrate them into professional development efforts—informal or formal.

REFERENCES

AECT. (2011). *AECT Code of Ethics*. Retrieved June 9, 2011, from http://www.aect.org/About/Ethics.asp.

ASTD. (2011). *ASTD Code of Ethics*. Retrieved June 9, 2011, from http://www.astd.org/ASTD/aboutus/missionAndVision/.

Beer, D., & Burrows, R. (2007). Sociology and, of and in Web 2.0: Some initial considerations. *Sociological Research Online, 12*(5), 17. Retrieved March 4, 2011, from http://www.socresonline.org.uk/12/5/17.html.

boyd, d. m., & Ellison, N. B. (2007). Social network sites: Definition, history, and scholarship. *Journal of Computer-Mediated Communication, 13*, 210–230. doi:10.1111/j.1083-6101.2007.00393.x

CBS News. (2011, February 6). Did the Internet kill privacy? Facebook photos lead to a teacher losing her job: What expectations of privacy exist in the digital era? *CBS News*. Retrieved March 4, 2011, from http://www.cbsnews.com/stories/2011/02/06/sunday/main7323148.shtml.

Chinn, S. J., & Williams, J. (2009). Using Web 2.0 to support the active learning experience. *Journal of Information Systems Education, 20*(2), 165.

Cisco. (2011). *Cisco's Internet Postings Policy*. Retrieved June 9, 2011, from http://blogs.cisco.com/news/ciscos_Internet_postings_policy/.

Clearswift Limited. (2010). *Web 2.0 in the workplace today*. Whitepaper. Retrieved March 4, 2011, from https://info.clearswift.com/express/clients/clearhq/papers/Web2_0_InTheWorkplaceToday.pdf.

Department of Justice. (2008). *Privacy and civil liberties policy development guide and implementation templates*. Retrieved June 9, 2011, from http://it.ojp.gov/documents/Privacy_Guide_Final.pdf.

Edelman, S. (2011, March 13). Facebook vent burns teacher. *New York Post*. Retrieved March 14, 2011, from http://www.nypost.com/p/news/local/brooklyn/facebook_vent_burns_teacher_Ji HBB6wQwDljiYVfcUiIpN#ixzz1GhODXHPx.

GAO. (2010, November 28). *Information management: Challenges in federal agencies' use of Web 2.0 technologies – GAO testimony before the Subcommittee on Information Policy, Census, and National Archives, Committee on Oversight and Government Reform, US House of Representatives*. Retrieved June 9, 2011, from http://www.whitehouse.gov/omb/circulars_a130_a130appendix_iii.

HP. (2010). *HP TRIM software and Microsoft SharePoint HP*. Whitepaper. Retrieved March 4, 2011, from http://h20195.www2.hp.com/V2/GetPDF.aspx/4AA2-1196ENW.pdf.

ISPS. (2011). *ISPI code of ethics*. Retrieved June 9, 2011, from http://www.ispi.org/content.aspx?id=418.

Luehmann, A. L. (2008). Blogging as support for teacher learning and development: A case-study. *Journal of the Learning Sciences, 17*(3), 287–337. doi:10.1080/10508400802192706

Luehmann, A. L., & Tinelli, L. (2008). Teacher professional identity development with social networking technologies: Learning reform through blogging. *Educational Media International, 45*(4), 323–333. doi:10.1080/09523980802573263

Mergel, I. A., Schweik, C. M., & Fountain, J. E. (2009). *The transformational effect of Web 2.0 technologies on government*. Retrieved May 30, 2011, from http://ssrn.com/abstract=1412796.

Michels, S. (2008, May 6). Teachers' virtual lives conflict with classroom: Teacher in training says she was denied credential for online photos. *ABC News*. Retrieved March 4, 2011, from http://abcnews.go.com/TheLaw/story?id=4791295andpage=1.

Missouri State Senate. (2011). *Bill 54*. Retrieved June 9, 2011, from http://www.senate.mo.gov/11info/BTS_Web/Bill.aspx?BillID=4066479&SessionType=R.

NIST. (1987). *Computer Security Act of 1987*. Retrieved June 9, 2011, from http://www.nist.gov/cfo/legislation/Public%20Law%20100-235.pdf.

Pettenati, M. C., & Cigognini, E. (2007). Social networking theories and tools to support connectivist learning activities. *International Journal of Web-Based Learning and Teaching Technologies, 2*(3), 42–60. doi:10.4018/jwltt.2007070103

Rid, T. (2007). *War and media operations: The US military and the press from Vietnam to Iraq*. New York, NY: Routledge.

Rossett, A., & Hoffman, B. (2011). Informal learning. In Reiser, R. A., & Dempsey, J. V. (Eds.), *Trends and Issues in Instructional Design and Technology* (3rd ed., pp. 169–177). Upper Saddle River, NJ: Pearson Education.

Smaldino, S., Donalsdson, J. A., & Herring, M. (2011). Professional ethics: Rules applied to practice. In Reiser, R. A., & Dempsey, J. V. (Eds.), *Trends and Issues in Instructional Design and Technology* (3rd ed., pp. 342–347). Upper Saddle River, NJ: Pearson Education.

Stripling, J. (2010). Not so private professors. *Inside Higher Ed*. Retrieved March 4, 2011, from http://www.insidehighered.com/news/2010/03/02/facebook.

US Department of Justice. (2008). *Privacy and civil liberties development guide*. Retrieved June 9, 2011, from http://it.ojp.gov/documents/Privacy_Guide_Final.pdf.

Wang, L., von Laszewski, G., Younge, A., He, X., Kunze, M., Tao, J., & Fu, C. (2008). Cloud computing: A perspective study. *New Generation Computing, 28*(2), 137–146. doi:10.1007/s00354-008-0081-5

ADDITIONAL READING

Alexander, P., & Brown, S. (1998). *Attitudes toward information privacy: Differences among and between faculty and students.* Paper presented at the Americas' Conference on Information Systems. Baltimore, MD.

Barth, S. R. (2003). *Corporate ethics: The business code of conduct for ethical employees.* Boston, MA: Aspatore.

De George, R. T. (2003). *The ethics of information technology and business.* Malden, MA: Blackwell Publishing. doi:10.1002/9780470774144

Earp, J. B., & Payton, F. C. (2001). Data protection in the university setting: Employee perceptions of student privacy. In *Proceedings of the 34th Annual Hawaii International Conference.* Maui, HI: IEEE.

Hann, I.-H., Hui, K.-L., Lee, T., & Png, I. (2002). *Online information privacy: Measuring the cost-benefit trade-off.* Paper presented at the Twenty-Third International Conference on Information Systems. Barcelona, Spain.

Imperatore, C. (2009). What you need to know about Web 2.0. *Techniques: Connecting Education and Careers, 84*(1), 20–23.

Kaptein, M., & Johan, W. (2002). *The balanced company: A theory of corporate integrity.* Oxford, UK: Oxford University Press.

McNutt, K. (2006). Research note: Do virtual policy networks matter? Tracing network structure online. *Canadian Journal of Political Science, 39*(2), 391–405. doi:10.1017/S0008423906060161

Milberg, S. J., Smith, H. J., & Burke, S. J. (2000). Information privacy: Corporate management and national regulation. *Organization Science, 11*(1), 35–57. doi:10.1287/orsc.11.1.35.12567

Raab, J. (2003). Where do policy networks come from? *Journal of Public Administration: Research and Theory, 12*(4), 581–623. doi:10.1093/oxfordjournals.jpart.a003548

Solove, D. J. (2008). *Understanding privacy.* Boston, MA: Harvard University Press.

KEY TERMS AND DEFINITIONS

Privacy: Refers to the state of solitude and/or being free from public attention.

Confidentiality: The act of keeping personal or proprietary information from being public.

Compliance: Being in accordance with rules, regulations, and laws.

Web 2.0: A set of tools or technologies designed to connect people with each other.

Informal Learning: Incidental often unintentional learning.

Professional Development: Actions taken by professionals to improve their knowledge, skills, and attitudes.

Community of Practice: A group of individuals with common interests or goals who come together willingly in service of those interests or goals.

Chapter 3
Turn On Your Mobile Devices:
Potential and Considerations of Informal Mobile Learning

Shuang Hao
Florida State University, USA

ABSTRACT

The number of mobile devices and active users is growing. Mobile devices expand the reach of technology-mediated communication possibilities for many people. They have become a convenient, and in many instances preferred, way for people to communicate with each other as well as to access the Internet. In terms of learning, this means that people can increasingly access both content and resources from any number of locations. This chapter explores how mobile devices can be used to support informal learning practices, and it provides practical tips for researchers in conducting studies of informal mobile learning.

INTRODUCTION

Currently, mobile devices provide reliable and ubiquitous access to information (Wagner, 2008). Although mobile learning has been discussed for years, researchers are still examining ways to make the best use of this medium to promote meaningful learning. Various educational applications have been put into use within mobile devices, especially mobile phones on and out of curricula. Informal learning activities with mobile devices that support individual growth and professional development caught attention of more

and more researchers, yet there is still a lack of research with regards to an integrated learning mode (Kukulska-Hulme & Pettit, 2008). Unlike traditional learning activities, the impact of informal learning, especially informal mobile learning, is very hard to evaluate (Sharples, Arnedillo, & Vavoula, 2007). In addition, with all the research initiatives, no clear pedagogical agreement has been made about successful instructional strategies in the field of informal mobile learning that supports self and professional development. Thus, conducting a literature review on this topic seems necessary and essential to draw patterns and to guide future research.

DOI: 10.4018/978-1-4666-1815-2.ch003

In an effort to contribute to the existing knowledge of informal mobile learning that facilitates individual growth and professional development, this chapter is aimed to achieve two objectives. By going through current literature, the first part of this chapter will summarize the crux of good mobile learning practices on learner-initiated, informal learning activities through mobile devices, as well as provide notes for balancing informal mobile learning activities with daily professional practices. After drawing from theoretical background that support this type of learning activities, these features will then be linked to real context, when research is targeted to design, conduct, and evaluate research in this realm of informal mobile learning activities. As opposed to formal instruction design, informal mobile learning activities do not have clear stated goals and strict standards to evaluate the effectiveness of these activities and how they influence individual growth and professional development. The second part of this chapter will provide information about how to design and evaluate such learning activities and reveal opportunities in making informal mobile learning meaningful.

GENERAL BACKGROUND OF MOBILE LEARNING

In order to achieve the objectives of this chapter, it is important to first examine the current perspectives about mobile learning. The eLearning Guild defined mobile learning in their 2008 report as "any activity that allows individuals to be more productive when consuming, interacting with or creating information mediated through a compact digital portable device that the individual carries on a regular basis, has reliable connectivity and fits in a pocket or purse" (Wexler, Brown, Metcalf, Rogers, & Wagner, 2008, p. 7). With this definition, it becomes clear that mobile phones, PDAs,

touch pads and portable laptops fall in the mobile device category. Mobile phones are still considered as the major tool for mobile learning because of its ubiquitous feature. The number of mobile phone users is growing. Cochrane and Bateman (2010) noted that the total number of mobile phone users worldwide were over four billion in 2010, comparing to 800 million computer owners. Mobile phones give people freedom to interact with each other and to reach out for information (Ally, 2005). The proliferation and adoption of mobile phones makes most people choose them as a major communication gateway (Chapel, 2008), which provides the user with a foundation that makes the idea of learning through mobile phones possible. The Smartphone market is gaining in popularity, and users are beginning to have more integrated services from their daily-used phones. It is predicted that by 2014, the Smartphone market will reach 30% of the worldwide mobile phone market, and the users of Smartphones will exceed computer users by then (Hendery, 2009). Thus, mobile phones are generally considered as the default tool when researching mobile learning.

The use of portable computing technology was advocated ever since 1981 for the reason that learners are mobile (Kay & Goldberg, 1981). The mobility of mobile devices enables learners to use them in diverse settings, indoor or outdoor and on or off campus (Roger, Connelly, Hazlewood, & Tedesco, 2010). The versatility of mobile devices makes educators and researchers posit and conduct different instructional activities within them. Peters (2007) indicated that the delivery method of these devices enables the demand of "just enough, just in time, and just for time" (p. 3) of the twenty-first century learners. Through mobile-accessible platforms, learners have the freedom to study according to their own needs and preferences (Koole, McQuilkin, & Ally, 2010).

Various projects have been conducted over the past years in schools, workplaces, museums, cities and rural areas around the world (Sharples, Amedillo, & Vavoula, 2007). Holding the belief that mobile tools have the revolutionary potential to change learners' learning behaviors (Soloway, et al., 2001), researchers are working to find a unified educational framework and pedagogical meanings for mobile learning.

Previous research shows that the great potential of mobile learning was expressed by learners' favorable feedback. The small size and portability of a mobile device allow learners to easily take it into real-world environments (Koole, McQuilkin, & Ally, 2010). According to Cochrane and Bateman (2010), mobile devices engage collaborative learning through conversations between students and lecturers, between student peers, students and subject experts, and between students and authentic environments within any context. Through the immersive interaction, learning via mobile devices can lead to a sense of real time and continuous availability of the instructor and the peers (Koole, McQuilkin, & Ally, 2010).

On the other hand, however, as Sharples et al. (2007) noted, "Ten years of research into mobile learning has revealed no single 'killer application' for mobile technology in learning" (Sharples, Amedillo, & Vavoula, 2007, p. 246), and lot of problems were unfolded with this learning method. Most reported limitations include limited access to resources (Burge & Polec, 2008), small screen sizes for viewing information, limited input and output capabilities, weak processing powers, and limited memories (Kinshuk, 2003). All of the aforementioned limitations make information learned through mobile devices fragmented. Such interaction with a mobile device can detract learners from their ongoing learning experiences (Roger, Clnnelly, Hazlewood, & Tedesco, 2010). Learner's access to and use of advanced mobile technologies (e.g., Waycott, Jones, & Scanlon, 2005) and learner motivations (e.g., Goh, Chua, Lee, & Ang, 2009) also correlates to successful mobile learning activities.

DEFINING MOBILE LEARNING

Early definitions of mobile learning were anchored on technology usage: eLearning through mobile computational devices, e.g., Palms, Windows CE machines, and your digital cell phone (Quinn, 2000). Brown summarized several definitions and terms and identified mobile learning as "an extension of eLearning" (Brown, 2005, p. 299). Peters (2007) viewed mobile learning as a useful component of the flexible learning model and stated that it was a subset of eLearning, a step toward making the educational process "just in time, just enough and just for me" (Peters, 2007). Sharples et al. (2007) considered that mobile learning is a dimensional concept that should consider the technology aspect, conceptual space aspect, social space aspect, and the aspect of leaning dispersed over time (Sharples, Amedillo, & Vavoula, 2007). Wexler et al. (2008) defined mobile learning as "any activity that allows individuals to be more productive when consuming, interacting with, or creating information, mediating through a compact digital portable device that the individual carries on a regular basis, has reliable connectivity, and fits in a pocket or purse" (Wexler, et al., 2008, p. 7).

Nevertheless, there is still no agreement on a definition for mobile learning because each of the definitions has a different focal point. For example, the earlier definitions of mobile learning highlight the mobile technology and devices, rather than reflect much of the learning nature (e.g., Sharples, Amedillo, & Vavoula, 2007). These researchers use mobile devices as a media to deliver instruction and generate human-device interaction that would otherwise be hard to implement without the device. As observed by Steve Wexler (2008), for example, there are still a large number of eLearning practitioners that narrowly see mobile learning as taking training courses on a small screen. Some other practitioners in mobile learning hardly accept the categorization of mobile learning into eLearning and argue that the difference between mobile learning and eLearning should be at least as great as the difference between eLearning and traditional face-to-face learning (Feser, 2010). This is similar to when Web-based learning was first introduced and referred to by people as learning without an instructor, but now we know that the computer-mediated, Web-based learning means much more than just taking a face-to-face class on a computer. It changes learning behaviors in a way such that learners have vastly increased access to information and learning materials. Not only does the new technology fascinate people, but it also brings them new learning opportunities. Now people can participate in a class from in almost any setting and through different approaches instead of solely sitting in a classroom facing a teacher. This is the same situation for mobile learning. With mobile learning, people can carry a small device with them and get information in situ, rather than face a computer screen with no learning context.

Thus, what is so unique about mobile learning, beyond the 'wow' factor of the technology, is not just how it can put eLearning activities on smaller, portable devices (although that is definitely something people can do), but rather, how it changed the learning behavior, by augmenting the learning resources, the learning environment and as a result, the learner performances. In his book *mLearning* (2006), Metcalf mentioned that a fundamental way to think about mobile learning is about augmentation. Macdonald and Chiu (2011) found that Smart phones are used to augment rather than completely replace eLearning, especially considering that it can be hard to transfer all eLearning initiatives to a small mobile device. Quinn (2011) analyzed the function of human brains in relation to how mobile learning can best help people to achieve their learning goals. He then gives a broader definition of learning, which includes problem solving, creativity, information access, collaboration, innovation, experimentation and more. In this sense, Quinn argues that mobile learning is about augmenting our learning and performance, providing:

The answers we need, the people we need to communicate with, the just-in-time assistance, the special information relevant to where and when we are the capture of context to share, and more (Quinn, 2011, p. 18).

By adopting this notion, this chapter considers mobile learning as a learning activity that is mediated by mobile devices, giving the learners more flexibility and customized learning needs by negotiating meaning with place, time, and context in realizing the augmentation of knowledge and performance. Koole (2009) developed a Framework for the Rational Analysis of Mobile Education (FRAME) model for mobile learning (Figure 1). This model revealed mobile learning as the combination of the technology device, the social environment, and the learner's characteristics. As in the center of the vein diagram, mobile learning integrated the technology mediation (Device Usability), the social affordance (Social Technology) and collaborative context negotiation (Interaction Learning).

INFORMAL LEARNING AND MOBILE LEARNING

Learning activities can be dramatically diverse. A general categorization distinguishes between formal learning activities and informal learning activities. Informal learning itself is a very broad term. For example, informal learning might occur when person looks up a word from a pocket dictionary, begins to memorize the order of streets in her city, or even discusses a new term, such as 'coning,' with a friend. At the same time, it might also mean that an employee watched a YouTube video and learned how to say *thank you* in Spanish, or that a teacher had a conversation about daily experiences with a senior teacher and learned how to more effectively structure her teaching time. In the context of mobile learning, informal learning inherently shares two common characteristics:

Figure 1. The FRAME model (Adapted from Koole (2009))

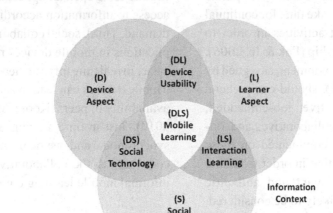

both tend to be impromptu and in situ. Learners can acquire previously known or unknown information and as a result can further develop knowledge base and support their performance in a particular domain.

Cross (2007) notes that according to a report from Inspire Innovation and Performance only 20 percent of what is learned on the job comes from formal learning, either in face-to-face or online settings. That means that the remaining 80 percent comes from informal learning, a topic about which various definitions abound. Tough (1979) referred to informal learning projects as a deliberate effort to gain or change performance skills and knowledge. Livingstone (1999) defined informal learning as any learning activity outside the institutional curricula. He then extended the definition in 2006 and included both intentional and tacit learning that might occur either individually or collaboratively. In distinguishing informal learning from social learning, Quinn (2011) noted that informal learning could include both individual learning and social learning. Informal social learning, however, is the basis of collaboration, which is becoming increasingly important. Either individually or collaboratively, informal learning

can happen anywhere, anytime. The motivation for these learning efforts generally and mainly comes from the individuals (Jones, Eileen, & Patrick, 2009). Finally, Tough (1979) noted that in the absence of a formal, externally imposed learning framework, the techniques, resources, tools, and technologies that informal learners will adopt are the ones conceived to best suit learning needs and personal preferences.

One important impetus for knowledge and performance augmentation comes from the demand for professional development, which is generally seen as one of the most readily available routes to both individual growth (Fullan, 1982) and career advances. Bell and Gilbert (1996) raised the idea that professional improvement is directly linked to new knowledge, skills and values and the development of beliefs and conceptions. Self-directed individuals normally relate their learning activities to their personal interests and goals (Woodill, 2011), which are aligned to social suggestions from the workplace, and/or other social regulatory practices (Billett & Pavlova, 2005). Thus, the growth of their knowledge base directly contributes to their professional improvement.

Many professional organizations stipulate that their members should take time for continual professional development activities in order to stay qualified for membership (Fok & Ip, 2006). Effective professional development, as argued by Lom and Sullenger (2011), should comprehend activities that are supportive, job-embedded, instructionally focused, collaborative, and ongoing. Hunzicker (2011) commented on these characteristics and stated that in order to enable these characteristics, relevant and authentic learning context is more likely to be considered. Researchers started to promote ongoing, self-directed, and collaborative informal learning activities (e.g., Cochran-Smith & Lytle, 1999; Darling-Hammond, 2005; Loucks-Horsley, et al., 2003). Lom and Sullenger (2011) considered that this type of informal, self-directed professional development has three key features: 1) learning is made easier; 2) learning is made contextual-related and practical; and 3) learning is collaborative and situated in networking with others.

Because workshops and conferences for professional development are not always available when people seek them, informal mobile leaning has created a convenient and powerful venue for individual improvement. First, thanks to its relatively low cost and portability, mobile technology is largely available, providing the technology base and easier access to information around the many other activities in which the users may involve themselves. Koole et al. (2010) reported that mobile access would also be helpful to those who do not have Internet connections, especially when traveling. Second, through informal mobile learning, learners have the freedom to study according to their own needs and preferences (Koole, McQuilkin, & Ally, 2010). The current 3G and 4G networks make the access to the Internet possible and fast. Whenever a learning need is identified, whether it is a discussion during coffee hour, 5 minutes before a presentation, or just a flash of a thought at leisure time, a mobile tool is available to help with these practical issues. In other words,

Mobile tools open an opportunity of just-in-time access to information according to the learner's demand. Third, social collaboration tools and applications in mobile devices made collaboration easier in real time informal learning environment. Mobile devices can lead to a sense of continuous availability of peers (Koole, McQuillkin, & Ally, 2010). Just-in-time sharing of information and synchronous and asynchronous feedback also contribute to the collaborative improvement in informal mobile learning environment.

EDUCATIONAL THEORIES BEHIND INFORMAL MOBILE LEARNING

As computers provide more opportunities of learning rather than completely replacing or changing traditional learning theories, mobile devices bring also an opportunity of learning augmentation. In their paper, Sharples et al. (2007) presented the dilemma of mobile learning: that the diversity of current mobile leaning projects makes it difficult to capture the essence of mobile learning and difficult to show their contributions to the theory and practice of education. In a recent paper, Keskin and Metcalf (2011) summarized and listed 15 educational theories that tie into the existing mobile learning research. Researchers are looking for a coherent theoretical frame for understanding the unique features of informal mobile learning. When tracing back to the basic learning theories, it is found that the traditional learning theories still perform the fundamental role to explain learning with modern tools. To be specific to the informal mobile learning topic, situated learning theory and constructivist learning theory most appropriately reflect the meaning of these learning activities.

Situated learning refers to knowledge acquisition through the process of social participation (Brown, et al., 1989). Informal mobile learning, by creating an immersive environment for learner, their peers and the learning context, makes these types of activities easier than it ever has been. The individual's perception of a specific situation can raise their understanding of the context and they integrate their competency in coping with practical problems. Mobile devices serve as venues for learners to create a rich interactive experience effortlessly both for themselves and their peers (Winters, 2007) when interacting with context. Such venues encourage learners to reflect and participate in collaborations that allow them to utilize a greater variety of situations in which to measure real time context and negotiate meaning (Koole, 2009). Cognitive apprenticeships also provide the affordance of situated learning because mentoring enables reflection (Field, 2011) and addresses contextual factors (e.g., just-in-time situation) and personal factors (e.g., personal sensibility protection, stress) at the same time.

Some informal learning applications that can help reach this goal include content management systems, context-aware notification applications, navigational and information retrieval applications, augmented realities, etc. Various generating and sharing applications are also developed and made available to the general public, including, to name a few, the information acquisition and sharing tools (e.g., screen capture tools, voice and notes sharing tools, QR code capture tools), and social networking and sharing tools (e.g., macro-blogging, macro-twitting, location exchange tools, and traditional Web 2.0 tools on mobile devices). These information publication and exchanging activities enabled by the mobile tools can be shown by the popularity of virtual teams and virtual communities of practice. In return, the mobile technology is continuously transforming to greater advance to meet people's interactive needs.

Constructivist learning refers to the learning activities in which learners construct new ideas or concepts based on their prior knowledge (Bruner, 1966). Brown et al. (1989) in their later research indicated the goal of the constructivist learning: Knowledge must develop and continue to change with the activity of the learner. Learning is a con-

tinuous life-long process resulting from acting in situations (Brown, et al., 1989, p. 33). Context is a central construct of mobile learning (Sharples, Taylor, & Vavoula, 2007). It is continuously created by people when they interact with other people, with their surroundings and with various everyday tools. People with mutual developing goals constantly build temporarily stable context with each other throughout the day and learning occurs by sharing their experiences and knowledge. Mobile learning enables simple activities as SMS text messaging and phone calls, mid-level activities as emailing and blogging, and sophisticated activities as interactive virtual worlds. These constructs disregard locations and create context and content-dependent learning activities as well as collaboration and interaction in mobile learning activities (Keskin & Metcalf, 2011).

Both individual constructivist learning and collaborativist constructive learning are made possible through informal mobile learning activities. Quinn (2011) believed that such characters cannot be wholly relied on individual learning, but are rather built up by conversations and teamwork, which are powerful parts of research, creativity, problem solving, and more (Quinn, 2011). Besides, Quinn (2011) also argued that collaborative social learning provides a powerful adjunct to individual learning. The knowledge construction can arise from personal experienced problems and concerns, or it can also come from scenarios that are shared by other people that do not necessarily reflect, but concerns, the correspondence of real world practices of this person. Especially through mobile learning, the learners are dispersed into different geographical locations around the world. This provides a greater scope of professional knowledge that the learners can have access to that could have been more difficult to access if they are learning by themselves.

With the fast rate of change of technology and the explosion of information, the ability to continually learn and be innovative will be critical, especially for individual growth and professional development purposes. While most informal mobile learning happens in leisure time, learners have their own control for the balance between work and life. Anderson (2002) found that people were willing to give their time to voluntarily contribute with their knowledge and experiences to collaborate with people, even colleagues with whom they would not normally work. By making contributions through mobile networking, the working place turns into a virtual place built by members' mutual knowledge. This type of mobile workplace is characterized by empowerment of each individual contributor to the ad-hoc temporary project team and network organizations, and by a high level of contextual awareness as well as membership responsibilities (Schaffers, Carver, Brodt, Fernando, & Slagter, 2006). More responsibilities then induce more demand for learning, and thus create a geographically flexible but structurally stable informal mobile learning environment for learning and performance augmentation.

EFFECTIVENESS AND CONSIDERATIONS OF INFORMAL MOBILE LEARNING ACTIVITIES

While researchers try to design and define the best instructional or informal practices, they must realize that the purpose for mobile learning is to meet learners' learning needs, rather than simply transform any existing learning content to mobile devices. As Maxl and Tarkus (2009) categorized, the important factors of learning activities through mobile phones include fun, excitement, respect, challenge, feedback, social experiences, allegiance and enhanced knowledge. Researchers need to understand both the medium and the targeted learners when designing and conducting such research. In the following sections, four key aspects of informal mobile learning research are presented: learner analysis, learning goals, learning activities, and data collection and evaluation

methods. Bringing up these issues will help better design and evaluate learning and performance augmentation.

LEARNER'S ANALYSIS

Learning though mobile technology cannot happen if the learners refuse to use, are reluctant to use, or do not know how to use the technology at hand. Before designing any informal mobile learning activities, the learner analysis is a key step. Van and Renaud (2008) summarized technology acceptance models in different disciplines at the 27th International Conference on Conceptual Modeling and found that the common factor across all models is the perceived ease of use of the mobile technology. Although mobile devices such as telephones are prevalent nowadays, it is hard to generalize user behaviors. For example, in the qualitative study of the applicability of technology acceptance models by senior mobile phone users, Van and Renaud (2008) considered that elderly mobile phone users are getting far less than the optimal value out of their devices due to their perception of the mobile phone usage and the unsupported user experience for this learning group. The small screen and relatively awkward inputting methods makes the mobile devices elude this group. In fact, this is not the problem reported only by this group of users. Tremblay (2010) also observed a negative correlation between the perceived benefits of an activity conducted with mobile phones and age and post-secondary experience. Nevertheless, in Macdonald and Chiu's research report (2011), they found no apparent correlation between age and degree of positive responses of mobile learning. In Quinn's observation (2011), once people get familiar with the mobile technology, it starts to bring benefits to people in return. A summary organized by Koszalka and Ntloedibe-kuswani (2010) from different papers shows that disadvantaged people (such as homeless, offenders, disabled, sick, and rural poor) could also benefit from mobile phone learning activities.

The characteristic of mobile learning may be multi-faceted. Now with new technologies, such as Siri—the personal intellectual assistant that debuted with iPhone 4S—more personalized and automatic learning environments that may guide the user through more efficient and effectively learning activities are becoming a reality. Three factors, learning patterns. styles, and motivation, continuously affect a learner's willingness to adopt mobile learning (Koole, McQuilkin, & Ally, 2010). Thus, a user profile is an important part of determining user requirements to establish an effective and well-designed application (Mayhew, 1999). The user profile may include (but not be limited to): familiarity with mobile technologies, frequency of mobile phone utilization, and use of social network platforms. These characteristics are not necessarily positive correlated with learning augmentation. Certain user attributes can be gleaned on through accessing their social networks' profiles, their frequently visited online locations or virtual check-ins, their usernames (or real names) and so on. Collecting data on other attributes may require interaction with the learners. The list below indicates some important considerations when analyzing the learners involved in informal mobile learning activities:

1. Access to technology. Accessing a mobile device is the basic step for conducting learning activities through mobile devices. To conduct research with users who are not equipped with such devices and/or tools, the first step may be to provide the devices and/ or tools to the users when they are at home or on the move (Naismith & Corlett, 2006).

2. Ownership (Naismith & Corlett, 2006). No matter if the devices are owned by the users originally or given to the users by the researchers, the user's sense of ownership over the mobile technology is another important factor as users may not venture

into more sophisticated functions of mobile technology to assist their learning if they have a sense of lack of ownership (Chan, Corlett, Sharples, Ting, & Westmancott, 2005; Kukulska-Hulme & Pettit, 2008).

3. Awareness of information channels and skills to access these channels. There are tools that can expand the scope of real-life information acquisition and communication venues and bring to the users much more informal learning opportunities. However, the users may or may not be aware of all the tools available for different learning purposes. Researchers need to consider the reliability and accessibility of these channels on the mobile devices and make sure the learners have the skills or potential skills to master them.

4. Motivation. The learning effect based on similar learning activities may vary based on the learner's motivations, especially for informal mobile learning, in which the learner has almost full control over the learning pace, learning style, and learning content. More prepared learners may find that their investment in learning yields greater results than those who are not prepared (Waycott & Scanlon, 2005). Since motivation comes from mainly intrinsic sources, within the learner, rather than from extrinsic, outside forces in informal settings (Jones, Eileen, & Patrick, 2009), the researcher might extend beyond passive observations. For example, learners might be presented with the links between their informal mobile learning activities and the practical applications of the knowledge. Further, motivation may be related not only to individual learning, but also collaborative learning. Goh, Chua, Lee, and Ang (2009) organized learner motivation into five categories in mobile sharing: (1) creation/maintenance of social relationships; (2) reminding of individual and collective experiences; (3) self-presentation; (4)

self-expression; and (5) task performance. All of these motivation categories reflect a user's social needs in informal learning environments.

LEARNING GOALS

Informal learning activities do not have explicit, specific goals in the same way that formal learning activities do. Incidental learning experiences occur all the time through mobile technology. For example, learning may occur during phone conversations, while watching YouTube videos, or when reading Facebook status updates. However, more in-depth learning is enabled if the person is motivated specifically to ask or search for more details regarding incidental information that she has encountered. In other words, this learning is driven by curiosity. In fact, this emergent learning desires can be considered a potential learning goal, and it may shape subsequent informal mobile learning activities. Thus, unintended learning becomes intentional learning.

Consider a simple life example. John planned a trip for the weekend with his family. He gathered information for the trip, such as directions, several days in advance. While driving to the destination, John and his family wanted Italian food. He could use GPS to find one near them, of course, and he could also use his Smartphone and find the most highly rated Italian restaurant within a certain geographic boundary. In this activity, John's purposefully looking up for information is guided by a goal: wanting Italian food.

There are more readily observed goals in the collaborative group learning activities in the informal mobile learning setting. Most informal learning groups give descriptions of what the group wants to achieve. Hertel et al. (2004) considered that by setting common goals, the dispersed team members will be more guided and motivated. On the other hand, in informal settings when collaborators may not know each other, there are fewer restrictions as to individual's obligations and contributions. The commitment level is positively correlated (Erez & Zidon, 1984) with the performance of the team and thus, the knowledge gain of the team members. When informal mobile learning intervenes in learner's personal life, the learner looks for the life-work balance, and less committed learners give up their learning goals earlier (Richter, Meyer, & Sommer, 2006). Thus, considering how to keep the balance to evade stress and other negative effects is an important issue to research on, especially when the demands of work are beginning penetrating the personal lives (Guest, 2002). Mobile technology helps leverage this problem. Its just-in-time availability enables learners to have more choices as to when and where to contribute their experience and expertise. Most importantly, learners can choose different ways to contribute with mobile technology to many possibilities for communicating and sharing.

The question that researchers need to think about is which goal should be aligned to the learning outcomes besides the general goal for self and professional development. If a mobile phone learning activity is to be conducted, a need analysis and deployment planning should be undertaken before executing the activity. A goal statement will also draw more attention from other professionals in informal learning activities. For example, if a teacher starts a new blog, he or she may want to describe what this blog is about to engage followers. As mentioned by Vavoula (2004), the difficulties inherited in researching informal learning occur not only because such learning activities occurs intentionally and unintentionally, but also because people may even be unaware of the learning that took place. Thus, this question can also help, when designing and evaluating informal mobile learning activities, to uncover more informal learning activities with the mobile technology that the learners may or may not recognize by themselves. For instance, if one is researching learner's informal learning activities to improve his or her time management skills, in addition to asking questions about setting up calendars in mobile devices she might also ask the learner about his daily tasks and how he progresses toward these tasks (e.g., mark completions, delete old tasks, and categorize tasks).

LEARNING ACTIVITIES

There are many documented mobile learning initiatives. People are excited about this new technology and consider the convenience when they are at remote locations from a classroom or a computer. Certain knowledge of a new technology can always serve as a motivator when used for educational purposes. However, this learning method presents a lot of drawbacks. Burnett and Meadmore (2002) noted that technology is often rushed into use before adequate assessments are conducted about its pedagogical merits. Researchers must realize that the aim for mobile learning is to meet learners' learning needs, rather than simply apply any learning content to mobile platforms. Maxl and Tarkus (2009) categorized the important factors of learning activities (i.e., games) through mobile phones, which include fun, excitement, respect, challenge, feedback, social experiences, allegiance, and enhanced knowledge. These factors can be applied to both formal and informal mobile learning activities. Jones, Eileen, and Patrick (2009) summarized seven categories of informal mobile learning activities:

- Collaborative applications that encourage knowledge sharing, making use of the learner's physical location and mobility.
- Location aware applications that contextualize information, allowing learners to interact directly with their environment; for example, collecting environmental data linked to geographical context or accessing contextually relevant reference material.
- Data collection applications that use the handheld device's ability to record data in the form of text, image, video, and audio.
- Referential applications that use dictionaries, translators, and e-books to deliver content when and where it is needed.
- Administrative applications that employ the typical scheduling, information storage, and other calendar functions available on mobile devices.
- Interactive applications that use both the input and output capabilities of mobile devices, allowing the learner to input information and obtain some form of feedback that aids the learning process.
- Virtual world applications model real world domains to enable learners to use practice in a constrained version of the learning scenario.

When designing and implementing these kinds of activities, researchers need to look into both 'big' and 'small.' Cochrane and Bateman (2010) noted that it takes significant time for a paradigm shift to pedagogically integrate mobile learning into formal learning settings, because it requires the lecturer's involvements and students' efforts in gaining the skills required to maximize the potential of this new learning method until the learners are prepared to benefit from this investment (Waycott, Jones, & Scanlon, 2005). At the same time, some informal, not strictly structured learning activities through mobile devices can be more promising, although they do not seem as 'exciting' as well-structured formal learning activities. The informal mobile learning researches can help people to better understand the nature of informal mobile learning and make better use of their mobile devices.

For example, Cornelius and Marston (2009) conducted a learning activity of disaster management among participants (the number and background of the participants were not mentioned).

They were required to make rapid decisions in order to affect the progress and outcome of situations. The participants used their imagination to picture the virtual context. The study adopted certain rules for the simulation based on the disaster context. For example, the responses were required in a certain format, or within a specific timeframe. As a result, all of the questionnaire respondents "strongly agreed" or "agreed" that they enjoyed the real time aspect of the simulation and were happy to receive messages which disrupted their lives outside normal "working" hours (Cornelius & Marston, 2009). This study focused on the advantages of using mobile phone features as a medium and adopted SMS text messages as the major communication tool to provide "anywhere, anytime" (Geddes, 2004) access to learners and a channel for communication with which they were generally familiar and comfortable (Koole, McQuilkin, & Ally, 2010). This type of mobile phone learning helped create contexts that would be hard to create with conventional learning devices such as books (Wali, Winters, & Oliver, 2008) or traditional learning methods (e.g., lecture, group discussion), and it appears successful.

In addition, researchers need to keep in mind that there is no good and bad, only appropriate application. Not all constraints of mobile devices are necessarily negative (Dron, 2007). Once we understand the best utilization of mobile devices is the augmentation of learning and performances, it is not hard to conceive the idea that even the most basic functions carried out by these devices can make a great use. It is the researchers' task to include the features of mobile phones and adopting the features to cater to learning needs. For example, the small size of the screen of mobile devices would go against long text reading (Ally, 2004). Thus, learning can happen in short time periods so that users can make use of small pieces of time, such as when they are waiting for a bus (Maxl & Tarkus, 2009). In this way, the learners can gain back hours of useful time each day

(Howard, 2007). Batpurev and Uyanga (2006) claimed that segmented messages, such as push in voice mail or instant messages, could promote higher-order thinking by forcing the learners to prioritize the message. Roger, Connelly, Hazlewood, and Tedesco (2010) also proposed the idea that comparing learning using mobile devices such as mobile phones tend to be useful for short bursts of time (e.g., looking up and reviewing information) to support learning activities, especially foregrounded physical activities in a particular environment. Koszalka, Tiffany, and Ntloedibe-Kuswani's (2010) summary also found that mobile phone learning could bring two perspectives: safe learning and disruptive learning. The concept of safe learning compares mobile phones as computers that can provide the learners broader range of information that they could not be able to access otherwise. Disruptive learning, on the other hand, suggests that mobile phone learning interrupts the traditional paradigms of teacher directedness and immerses learners in a personalized, self-regulated learning environment. In their argument (Koszalka, Tiffany, & Ntloedibe-Kuswani, 2010), both learning experiences can be beneficial with instructionally sound activities.

In Vavoula and Sharples (2002) research, they found that learning is mobile with respect to place, time, and different areas of life. They considered single learning experiences as episodes and collaborative and more purposeful learning experiences as activities, and found that learners used various kinds of mobile learning resources with dramatically different ways of organizing the learning behaviors that they feel most beneficial. Researchers also need to be familiar with the prevalent mobile applications and keep an open mind as to how these tools can be used to facilitate learning activities.

DATA COLLECTION AND EVALUATION METHODS

Because it often occurs within a short period of time and without a fixed schedule or location, informal mobile learning activities can be really tricky to evaluate. Traxler (2007) referred these attributes as personal, contextual, and situated. However, just because evaluation is difficult does not mean it is impossible. Learning surveys conducted nationally show that a large proportion of informal learning has historically pertained to the learner's personal and professional needs as well as life demands (Tough, 1971). With the mobile devices, informal mobile learning continues to grow into people's daily learning behavior at a fast pace. It will be valuable for researchers to develop assessment measures in order to encourage these personal-improvement learning activities by understanding and creating a supportive individual and social learning environment. By summarizing the literature, the most used and shown effective methods of evaluating informal mobile learning activities are survey and self-reported diary. Each of these two methods is applied in different situations.

A survey is easy for takers to answer questions and easy for researchers to aggregate the data (Quinn, 2011). Jones, McAndrew, and Scanlon (2008) considered that a direct observation method for informal mobile activities is not practical. Web-based surveys are the most appropriate methods to allow participants to provide information about their learning practices and experiences. Surveys, especially Web-based surveys, have a timely impact and can reach a wider range of people, whoever has an Internet access. However, using surveys for informal mobile learners can face difficulties. It seems, by filling in online surveys through mobile devices, that dispersed users are all in the participant pool. The reality is, however, that only network connected people are real participants. In other words, people who use unconnected PDAs and regular phones without regular internet

access are excluded. As mentioned earlier, even the simplest mobile technology such as phone calls and SMS text messages can be effectively used as informal mobile learning aids, and it will create bias if researchers do not consider these people as potential learners. In addition, surveys are pre-developed by researchers and cannot be inclusive of every aspect of informal mobile learning practices, especially because such practices are impromptu and different person by person. In this case, some important learning aspects may be missed. Partial or wrongly answered questions by misunderstanding survey questions are also possible.

A second favorable approach for evaluation informal mobile learning is self-reported diaries. Diaries can be reported in situ in a non-intrusive way as the activities occur (Goh, Chua, Lee, & Ang, 2009). Diary entries, thus, allow much more flexibility to the users and sometimes create some 'surprises' that the researchers would not be able to anticipate beforehand. On the other hand, an issue raised with this method is that sometimes people are not aware of their informal learning activities, and/or they do not want to share details about their every experience with the mobile devices. Interviews can serve as a correction step of such situation. A diary-interview method was brought up by Zimmerman and Wieder in 1977 for their ethnographic study. In their research, they argued that the diaries took a role as "an observational log maintained by subjects that can then be used as a basis for intensive interviewing" (Zimmerman & Wieder, 1977, p. 481). A drawback for diary method as a more qualitative way of gathering and evaluating data is that it takes much longer to organize the collected data and conduct content analysis.

In evaluating the effectiveness of informal mobile learning, Sharples et al. (2007) developed three-level results that should be examined for mobile learning. At the micro level, individual learning activities should be considered, such as mobile technology usability issue and satisfaction factor of user experience. Meso level examines the transferable knowledge to learners' practical activities as a whole and how well the learning experience integrates with other types of learning experiences. At the macro level, long-term impact of technology integration into learning should be examined and evaluated to see if they match the initial aspirations, intentions, and expectations (Sharples, Taylor, & Vavoula, 2007). Although these three levels mainly focus on mobile learning, as a subcategory, in informal mobile learning, these three levels still applies. As every technology is not perfect, researchers should not be intimidated by the possible drawbacks when designing evaluation and interview questions. In Waycott, Jones, and Scanlon's (2005) study that use PDAs as informal reading devices, for example, the users found that this tool caused eyestrain, headaches and blurred vision. Nevertheless, the result on the supportive effect of this learning tool was overwhelmingly positive when the reading activities were well adopted around their other life activities. In informal learning activities, thoughtfully designed evaluation items are helpful. Multiple measurement methods may also be needed for certain situations. Researchers are advised to continuously reflect on the contribution of information mobile learning and adapt to the topic of life-long learning.

CONCLUSION AND FUTURE RESEARCH DIRECTIONS

This chapter revisited the definition of mobile learning and informal learning, and then found meaning for informal mobile learning, which is for self-growth and performance development by the augmentation of learner behaviors. As new as informal mobile learning is considered, situated learning theory and constructivist learning theory provide strong theoretical background and support. Thus, it is rewarding to research learner behaviors and their knowledge gain through this new way. With its promises and drawbacks, educators and

researchers of informal mobile learning can learn lessons from prior research, as well as proactively adopt solid strategies in designing learning activities. A few more issues regarding this topic are discussed below, and worth contemplation in future informal mobile learning researches.

First, researchers should keep in mind both the cost and geographic locations regarding learner's access to a network through mobile phones (Koole, McQuilkin, & Ally, 2010). The cost is always a limitation for implementing mobile learning widely. It is the researcher's job to appropriately choose mobile devices and supported software and applications. These applications need to be reliable and accessible. Besides, the researchers may want his or her research group have equal access to the same resources under the same conditions.

In addition, Wagner (2008) emphasized the importance of establishing a mobility policy. She urged mobile device industries to provide more functional mobile devices, more powerful mobile phone networks, and better development tools to create learning content and applications for mobile platforms. At the same time, the researchers are responsible for distinguishing the good applications from the bad ones, enlightening users of the educational implications of these tools, and sometimes design engaging and rewarding instructional activities through these advanced features of mobile devices.

Researchers will benefit from the realization that mobile devices are just another technology tool that can be used to facilitate learning. Mobile learning can create a learning environment that differs from traditional classroom teaching and learning. Researchers need to dialectically think about the current issues involved in mobile learning in informal settings. If researchers and designers try to integrate all possible learning activities into mobile devices, they may impede learning at the end. In contrast, constrains of mobile phone learning are not necessarily negative elements (Dron, 2007). Informal mobile learning reveals huge potentials in education. However, it still takes time to reach a consensus about the most effective learning strategies. Only through researchers' continued effort can the critical benchmarks of mobile phone learning be reached in the future.

REFERENCES

Ally, M. (2005). Multimedia information design for mobile devices. In Pagani, M. (Ed.), *Encyclopedia of Multimedia Technology and Networking* (pp. 704–709). Hershey, PA: IGI Global. doi:10.4018/978-1-59140-561-0.ch099

Anderson, S. (2002). Working together to develop a professional learning community. In *Proceedings of the 2002 Annual International Conference of the Higher Education Research and Development Society of Australasia (HERDSA)*, (pp. 20-26). Perth, Australia: HERDSA.

Batpurev, B., & Uyanga, S. (2006). *Using open source software for open and distance learning*. Paper presented at the Information and Communications Technology for Social Development: An International Symposium. Jakarta, Indonesia.

Bell, B., & Gilbert, J. (1996). *Teacher development: A model from science education*. London, UK: Falmer Press.

Billett, S., & Pavlova, M. (2005). Learning through working life: Self and individuals' agentic action. *International Journal of Lifelong Education, 24*(3), 195–211. doi:10.1080/02601370500134891

Brown, J. S., Collins, A., & Duguid, P. (1989). Situated cognition and the culture of learning. *Educational Researcher, 28*(1), 32–42.

Brown, T. H. (2005). Towards a model for m-learning in Africa. *International Journal on E-Learning, 4*(3), 299–315.

Bruner, J. S. (1966). *Toward a theory of instruction*. Cambridge, MA: Belknap Press of Harvard University Press.

Burge, E. J., & Polec, J. (2008). Transforming learning and teaching in practice: Where change and consistency interact. In Haughey, M., Evans, T., & Murphy, D. (Eds.), *International Handbook of Distance Education* (pp. 237–258). Bingley, UK: Emerald Group Publishing Ltd.

Burnett, B., & Meadmore, P. (2002). Streaming lectures: Enhanced pedagogy or simply 'bells and whistles'? In *Proceedings of the International Education Research Conference*. Brisbane, Australia: Australian Association for Research in Education.

Chan, T., Corlett, D., Sharples, M., Ting, J., & Westmancott, O. (2005). Developing interactive logbook: A personal learning environment. In *Proceedings of the IEEE International Workshop on Wireless and Mobile Technologies in Education (WMTE 2005)*, (pp 73–75). IEEE Computer Society Press.

Chapel, E. (2008). Mobile technology: The foundation for an engaged and secure campus community. *Journal of Computing in Higher Education, 20*(2), 15–23. doi:10.1007/s12528-008-9002-3

Clough, G., Jones, A. C., McAndrew, P., & Scanlon, E. (2008). Informal learning with PDAs and smartphones. *Journal of Computer Assisted Learning, 24*(5), 359–371. doi:10.1111/j.1365-2729.2007.00268.x

Cochran-Smith, M., & Lytle, S. L. (1999). Relationships of knowledge and practice: Teacher learning in communities. *Review of Research in Education, 24*, 249–305.

Cochrane, T., & Bateman, R. (2010). Smartphones give you wings: Pedagogical affordances of mobile Web 2.0. *Australasian Journal of Educational Technology, 26*(1), 1–14.

Cornelius, S., & Marston, P. (2009). Towards an understanding of the virtual context in mobile learning. *ALT-J, 17*(3), 161–172. doi:10.1080/09687760903247617

Cross, J. (2007). *Informal learning: Rediscovering the natural pathways that inspire innovation and performance*. San Francisco, CA: Pfeiffer.

Darling-Hammond, L., & Bransford, J. (2005). *Preparing teachers for a changing world: What teachers should learn and be able to do*. San Francisco, CA: Jossey-Bass.

Dron, J. (2007). *Control and constraint in e-learning: Choosing when to choose* (1st ed.). Hershey, PA: IGI Global. doi:10.4018/978-1-59904-390-6

Erez, M., & Zidon, I. (1984). Effects of goal acceptance on the relationship of goal difficulty to performance. *The Journal of Applied Psychology, 69*, 69–78. doi:10.1037/0021-9010.69.1.69

Feser, J. (2010) *mLearning is not eLearning on a mobile device*. Retrieved from http://floatlearning. com/2010/04/mlearning-is-not-elearning-on-a-mobile-device/.

Field, K. (2011). Reflection at the heart of effective continuing professional development. *Professional Development in Education, 37*(2), 171–175. doi:10.1080/19415257.2011.559700

Fok, A. W. P., & Ip, H. H. S. (2006). An agent-based framework for personalized learning in continuing professional development. *International Journal of Distance Education Technologies, 4*(3), 48–61. doi:10.4018/jdet.2006070105

Fullan, M. (1982). *The meaning of educational change*. New York, NY: Teachers College Press.

Geddes, S. J. (2004). Mobile learning in the 21st century: Benefit for learners. *The Knowledge Tree e-Journal, 6*. Retrieved from http://knowledgetree.flexiblelearning.net.au/edition06/download/geddes.pdf.

Goh, D. H., Ang, R. P., Chua, A., & Lee, C. S. (2009). Why we share: A study of motivations for mobile media sharing. In *Proceedings of the Fifth International Conference on Active Media Technology (AMT 2009)*, (pp. 195-206). Beijing, China: IEEE.

Guest, D. E. (2002). Perspectives on the study of work-life balance. *Social Sciences Information. Information Sur les Sciences Sociales, 41*, 255–279. doi:10.1177/0539018402041002005

Hendery, S. (2009, July 9). Great gadget, stratospheric price. *New Zealand Herald*, p. B4. Retrieved 9 July 2009 from http://www. nzherald.co.nz/technology/news/article.cfm?c_ id=5&objectid=10583290&pnum=0.

Hertel, G., Konradt, U., & Orlikowski, B. (2004). Managing distance by interdependence: Goal setting, task interdependence and team-based rewards in virtual teams. *European Journal of Work and Organizational Psychology, 13*(1), 1–28. doi:10.1080/13594320344000228

Howard, C. (2007). *m-Learning: The latest trends, development and real-world applications*. Oakland, CA: Bersin Associates.

Hunzicker, J. (2011, April 01). Effective professional development for teachers: A checklist. *Professional Development in Education, 37*(2), 177–179. doi:10.1080/19415257.2010.523955

Jones, C. G., Eileen, A. S., & Patrick, M. (2009). Informal learning evidence in online communities of mobile device enthusiasts. In Ally, M. (Ed.), *Mobile Learning: Transforming the Delivery of Education and Training* (pp. 25–47). Edmonton, Canada: AU Press.

Kay, A., & Goldberg, A. (1981). Personal dynamic media. In Wasserman, A. I. (Ed.), *Software Development Environments*. New York, NY: IEEE Computer Society.

Keskin, N. O., & Metcalf, D. (2011). The current perspectives, theories and practices of mobile learning. *Turkish Online Journal of Educational Technology, 10*(2), 202–208.

Kinshuk. (2003). *Adaptive mobile learning technologies*. Retrieved from http://www.globaled. com/articles/Kinshuk2003.pdf.

Koole, M., McQuilkin, J., & Ally, M. (2010). Mobile learning in distance education: Utility or futility? *Journal of Distance Education, 24*(2), 59–82.

Koole, M. L. (2009). A model for framing mobile learning. In Ally, M. (Ed.), *Mobile Learning: Transforming the Delivery of Education and Training* (pp. 25–47). Edmonton, Canada: AU Press.

Koszalka, T. A., & Ntloedibe-Kuswani, G. S. (2010). Literature on the safe and disruptive learning potential of mobile technologies. *Distance Education, 31*(2), 139–157. doi:10.1080/015879 19.2010.498082

Kukulska-Hulme, A., & Pettit, J. (2008). Semi-formal learning communities for professional development in mobile learning. *Journal of Computing in Higher Education, 20*(2), 35–47. doi:10.1007/s12528-008-9006-z

Livingstone, D. W. (1999). Exploring the icebergs of adult learning: Findings of the first Canadian survey of informal learning practices. *Canadian Journal for the Study of Adult Education, 13*(2), 49–72.

Lom, E., & Sullenger, K. (2011). Informal spaces in collaborations: Exploring the edges/ boundaries of professional development. *Professional Development in Education, 37*(1), 55–74. doi:10 .1080/19415257.2010.489811

Loucks-Horsely, S., Love, N., Stiles, K., Mundry, S., & Hewson, P. W. (2003). *Designing professional development for teachers of science and mathematics* (2nd ed.). Thousand Oaks, CA: Corwin Press.

Macdonald, I., & Chiu, J. (2011). Evaluating the viability of mobile learning to enhance management training. *Canadian Journal of Learning and Technology, 37*(1). Retrieved from http://www.cjlt.ca/index.php/cjlt/article/view/535

Maxl, E., & Tarkus, A. (2009). Definition of user requirements concerning mobile learning games within the mGBL Project. *Serious Game on the Move, 1,* 91–104. doi:10.1007/978-3-211-09418-1_6

Mayhew, D. (1999). *The usability engineering life-cycle: A practitioner's handbook for user interface design*. San Francisco, CA: Morgan Kaufmann.

Metcalf, D. (2006). *mLearning: Mobile learning and performance in the palm of your hand*. Amherst, MA: HRD Press

Naismith, L., & Corlett, D. (2006). *Reflections on success: A retrospective of the mLearn conference series 2002-2005*. Paper presented at the Fifth World Conference on mLearn 2006: Across Generations and Cultures. Banff, Canada.

Peters, K. (2007). m-Learning: Positioning educators for a mobile, connected future. *International Journal of Research in Open and Distance Learning, 8*(2), 1–17.

Quinn, C. (2000). mLearning: Mobile, wireless, in-your-pocket learning. *LiNE Zine*. Retrieved from http://www.linezine.com/2.1/features/cqmmwiyp.htm.

Quinn, C. N. (2011). *Designing mLearning: Tapping into the mobile revolution for organizational performance*. San Francisco, CA: Pfeiffer.

Richter, P., Meyer, J., & Sommer, F. (2006). Well-being and stress in mobile and virtual work. In Andriessen, J. H. E., & Vartiainen, M. (Eds.), *Mobile Virtual Work: A New Paradigm?* (pp. 231–252). Berlin, Germany: Springer. doi:10.1007/3-540-28365-X_10

Roger, Y., Connelly, K., Hazlewood, W., & Tedesco, L. (2010). Enhancing learning: A study of how mobile devices can facilitate sensemaking. *Personal and Ubiquitous Computing, 14*(2), 111–124. doi:10.1007/s00779-009-0250-7

Schaffers, H., Carver, L., Brodt, T., Fernando, T., & Slagter, R. (2006). Mobile workplaces and innovative business practice. In Andriessen, J. H. E., & Vartiainen, M. (Eds.), *Mobile Virtual Work: A New Paradigm?* (pp. 343–368). Berlin, Germany: Springer. doi:10.1007/3-540-28365-X_15

Sharples, M., Milrad, M., Arnedillo, S. I., & Vavoula, G. (2007). *Mobile learning: Small devices, big issues.* Retrieved from http://www.lsri.nottingham.ac.uk/msh/Papers/Mobile%20learning%20-%20Small%20devices,%20Big%20Issues.pdf.

Soloway, E., Norris, C., Blumenfeld, P., Fishman, B., Krajcik, J., & Marx, R. (2001). Log on education: Handheld devices are ready-at-hand. *Communications of the ACM, 44*(6), 15–20. doi:10.1145/376134.376140

Tough, A. (1979). *The adult's learning projects: A fresh approach to theory and practice in adult learning.* Toronto, Canada: Ontario Institute for Studies in Education.

Traxler, J. (2007). Defining, discussing, and evaluating mobile learning: The moving finger writes and having writ. *International Review of Research in Open and Distance Learning, 8*(2), 1–12.

Tremblay, E. A. (2010). Educating the mobile generation: Using personal cell phones as audience response systems in post-secondary science teaching. *Journal of Computers in Mathematics and Science Teaching, 29*(2), 217–227.

Van, B. J., & Renaud, K. (2008). A qualitative study of the applicability of technology acceptance models to senior mobile phone users. In *Proceedings of the 27th International Conference on Conceptual Modeling,* (pp. 228-237). Springer.

Vavoula, G. (2004). *KLeOS: A knowledge and learning organisation system in support of lifelong learning.* Unpublished Doctoral Dissertation. Bringham, UK: University of Birmingham.

Vavoula, G., & Sharples, M. (2009). Lifelong learning organisers: Requirements for tools for supporting episodic and semantic learning. *Journal of Educational Technology & Society, 12*(3), 82–97.

Wagner, E. (2008). Realizing the promises of mobile learning. *Journal of Computing in Higher Education, 20*(2), 4–14. doi:10.1007/s12528-008-9008-x

Wali, E., Winters, N., & Oliver, M. (2008). Maintaining, changing and crossing contexts: An activity theoretic reinterpretation of mobile learning. *ALT-J, 16*(1), 41–57. doi:10.1080/09687760701850190

Waycott, J., Jones, A., & Scanlon, E. (2005). PDAs as lifelong learning tools: An activity theory based analysis. *Learning, Media and Technology, 30*(2), 107–130. doi:10.1080/17439880500093513

Wexler, S., Brown, J., Metcalf, D., Rogers, D., & Wagner, E. (2008). *eLearning guild research 360 report: Mobile learning.* Santa Rosa, CA: eLearning Guild.

Winters, N. (2007). periLEARN: Contextualised mobile learning in the era of Web 2.0. In *Proceedings of IADIS International Conference on Mobile Learning.* Lisbon, Portugal: IADIS.

Woodill, G. (2011). *The mobile learning edge: Tools and technologies for developing your teams.* New York, NY: McGraw-Hill.

Zimmerman, D. H., & Wieder, D. L. (1977). The diary: Diary-interview method. *Journal of Contemporary Ethnography, 5*(4), 479–498. doi:10.1177/089124167700500406

ADDITIONAL READING

Bereiter, C., & Scardamalia, M. (1993). *Surpassing ourselves: An inquiry into the nature and implications of expertise.* Chicago, IL: Open Court.

Bruce, B. (2008). *Ubiquitous learning, ubiquitous computing, and lived experience*. Paper presented at Symposium Making the Transition to Ubiquitous Learning. Athens, Greece.

Clough, G., Jones, A. C., McAndrew, P., & Scanlon, E. (2008). Informal learning with PDAs and smartphones. *Journal of Computer Assisted Learning, 24*(5), 359–371. doi:10.1111/j.1365-2729.2007.00268.x

Cornelius, S., Gemmell, A., & Marston, P. (2008). *Real-time simulation on the move: The learner context*. Paper presented at Online Educa 08, 14th International Conference on Technology Supported Leaning and Training. Berlin, Germany.

Fischer, G., & Konomi, S. (2007). Innovative socio-technical environments in support of distributed intelligence and lifelong learning. *Journal of Computer Assisted Learning, 23*(4), 338–350. doi:10.1111/j.1365-2729.2007.00238.x

Goh, D. H., Ang, R. P., Chua, A., & Lee, C. S. (2009). Why we share: A study of motivations for mobile media sharing. In *Proceedings of the fifth International Conference on Active Media Technology (AMT 2009)*, (pp. 195-206). Beijing, China: Springer.

Hager, P. J., & Halliday, J. (2006). *Recovering informal learning: Wisdom, judgement and community*. Dordrecht, The Netherlands: Springer.

Jacucci, G., Oulasvirta, A., & Salovaara, A. (2007). Active construction of experience through mobile media: A field study with implications for recording and sharing. *Personal and Ubiquitous Computing, 11*(4), 215–234. doi:10.1007/s00779-006-0084-5

Koole, M., McQuilkin, J., & Ally, M. (2010). Mobile learning in distance education: Utility or futility? *Journal of Distance Education, 24*(2), 59–82.

Koole, M. L. (2009). A model for framing mobile learning. In Ally, M. (Ed.), *Mobile Learning: Transforming the Delivery of Education and Training* (pp. 25–47). Edmonton, Canada: AU Press.

Koszalka, T., & Ntloedibe-Kuswani, G. S. (2010). Literature on the safe and disruptive learning potential of mobile technologies. *Distance Education, 31*(2), 139–157. doi:10.1080/01587919.2010.498082

Lom, E., & Sullenger, K. (2011). Informal spaces in collaborations: Exploring the edges/ boundaries of professional development. *Professional Development in Education, 37*(1), 55–74. doi:10.1080/19415257.2010.489811

Maxl, E., & Tarkus, A. (2009). Definition of user requirements concerning mobile learning games within the mGBL project. *Serious Games on the Move, 1*, 91–104. doi:10.1007/978-3-211-09418-1_6

Mckinney, D., Dyck, J. L., & Luber, E. S. (2009). iTunes university and the classroom: Can podcasts replace professors? *Computers & Education, 52*(3), 617–623. doi:10.1016/j.compedu.2008.11.004

Pachler, N., Bachmair, B., & Cook, J. (Eds.). (2010). *Mobile learning: Structures, agency, practices*. Berlin, Germany: Springer.

Pachler, N., Cook, J., & Bachmair, B. (2010). Appropriation of mobile cultural resources for learning. *International Journal of Mobile and Blended Learning, 2*(1), 1–21. doi:10.4018/jmbl.2010010101

Pachler, N., Pimmer, C., & Seipold, J. (Eds.). (2011). *Work-based mobile learning: Concepts and cases*. Oxford, UK: Peter Lang.

Patten, B., Sánchez, I. A., & Tangney, B. (2006). Designing collaborative, constructionist and contextual applications for handheld devices. *Computers & Education*, *46*(3), 294–308. doi:10.1016/j.compedu.2005.11.011

Quinn, C. N. (2011). *Designing mLearning: Tapping into the mobile revolution for organizational performance*. San Francisco, CA: Pfeiffer.

Richter, P., Meyer, J., & Sommer, F. (2006). Well-being and stress in mobile and virtual work. In Andriessen, J. H. E., & Vartiainen, M. (Eds.), *Mobile Virtual Work: A New Paradigm?* (pp. 231–252). Berlin, Germany: Springer. doi:10.1007/3-540-28365-X_10

Schaffers, H., Carver, L., Brodt, T., Fernando, T., & Slagter, R. (2006). Mobile workplaces and innovative business practice. In Andriessen, J. H. E., & Vartiainen, M. (Eds.), *Mobile Virtual Work: A New Paradigm?* (pp. 343–368). Berlin, Germany: Springer. doi:10.1007/3-540-28365-X_15

Stald, G. (2008). Mobile identity: Youth, identity, and mobile communication media. In Buckingham, D. (Ed.), *Youth, Identity, and Digital Media* (pp. 143–164). Cambridge, MA: MIT Press.

Wagner, E. D. (2008). Realizing the promises of mobile learning. *Journal of Computing in Higher Education*, *20*(2), 4–14. doi:10.1007/s12528-008-9008-x

Wali, E., Winters, N., & Oliver, M. (2008). Maintaining, changing and crossing contexts: An activity theoretic reinterpretation of mobile learning. *ALT-J*, *16*(1), 41–57. doi:10.1080/09687760701850190

Wexler, S., Brown, J., Metcalf, D., Rogers, D., & Wagner, E. (2008). *eLearning guild research 360 report: Mobile learning*. Santa Rosa, CA: eLearning Guild.

Woodill, G. (2011). *The mobile learning edge: Tools and technologies for developing your teams*. New York, NY: McGraw-Hill.

KEY TERMS AND DEFINITIONS

Augmentation: In this chapter, augmentation refers to the learner's individual improvement and professional knowledge growth through the on-demand and context-immersive informal mobile learning activities.

Constructivist Learning: Constructivist learning refers to the learning activities in which learners construct new ideas or concepts based on their prior knowledge (Bruner, 1966).

GPS: GPS is short for Global Positioning System. GPS is a satellite navigation system that can provide information on time, user location, and route maps.

Informal Learning: Impromptu and in situ learning activities, through which learners can acquire known or unknown information that can build up their knowledge base and support their performance. Sometimes the learning activity is not planned to happen.

Mobile Learning: Any learning activity that is mediated by mobile devices, giving the learners more flexibility and customized learning needs by negotiating meaning with place, time and context in realizing the augmentation of knowledge and performance.

Situated Learning: Situated learning refers to knowledge acquisition through the process of social participation (Brown, et al., 1989).

Siri: Siri is an intelligent voice-recognition personal assistant application integrated into Apple iPhone 4S Smartphones. Siri sends user voice commands through a remote server using Wi-Fi or 3G network, and complete the user task such as set up calendar and clock, prepare tasks and reminders, make phone calls and conduct Internet searching.

Virtual World: Any immersive online social environment that can engage participants to conduct learning and other social activities through self-representative avatars. Second Life is an example of a virtual world.

Section 2
Lenses and Approaches

Chapter 4

An Activity Theoretical Approach to Examining Virtual Professional Development and Informal Learning via Social Networks

Joseph M. Terantino
Kennesaw State University, USA

ABSTRACT

This chapter discusses the adoption of activity theory (Engeström, 1987, 2001; Leont'ev, 1978, 1981) as a conceptual framework for analyzing learning processes related to professional development and informal learning via social network environments. The discussion includes an overview of professional development and informal learning via social networks, which highlights the need for a related analytical framework. Activity theory is then described and applied to an example of professional development. This operationalization of activity theory demonstrates the ability of the framework to enable viewing and analyzing learning via social networks such as Facebook communities, wiki and blog spaces, listservs, and discussion forums. The chapter ends with several key points related to implementing activity theory as a solution to investigating behaviors in social networks and potential directions for future research.

INTRODUCTION

In today's society, earning a certificate or degree that accompanies the completion of various formal education programs is a fundamental prerequisite to being considered for many professional positions. For example, teaching certificates, nursing licenses, Ph.D.s, and similar products of formal education are often considered rites of passage. However, while completing these programs many pre-service professionals turn to the Web for additional professional development and informal learning to supplement their in-class experiences. In addition, others who have already entered the workforce have expanded the more traditional and

DOI: 10.4018/978-1-4666-1815-2.ch004

more formal methods of professional development via coursework and organized seminars and workshops to include social network environments. In many cases turning to online resources as a means to expanding professional development options has been a result of tough economic times (Gandel & Golden, 2004). Whether it be due to the changing needs of workplace professionals or financial concerns it has become increasingly more common for both pre-service and in-service professionals to pursue professional development and informal learning via social networking platforms such as Facebook, Twitter, and YouTube, and other Web 2.0 tools such as field-specific blogs, discussion forums, listservs, and wikis.

This relatively new pattern in professional development, creating less formal, virtual communities of practice, has evolved primarily as a byproduct of the social nature of humans and the inherent interactive qualities and widespread use of social media and Web 2.0 tools. Combined, these related forces are steadily changing the manner in which individuals and groups gather, create, and exchange information worldwide for personal and professional purposes. With these rapid changes in mind, a new challenge has also arisen for those of us who are interested in analyzing and understanding these unique practices. How should we attempt to organize and analyze the behaviors related to professional development, which are now situated in a virtual environment? The following chapter aims to answer this question.

Building on this general introduction to professional development and informal learning via social networks, the purpose of this chapter is to present activity theory (Engeström, 1987, 2001; Leont'ev, 1978, 1981) as a viable conceptual framework for viewing, analyzing, and better understanding these processes. To accomplish this feat, the following section of this chapter presents a historical overview of social networks and their impact on society. This is followed by a discussion of professional development and informal learning via social networks, which highlights the need for a related analytical framework. Then, activity theory

is explicated and operationalized with regards to professional development and informal learning. Last, the chapter ends by describing several key points related to implementing activity theory as a solution to investigating behaviors in social networks and potential directions for future research.

THE ROLE OF SOCIAL NETWORKS

The role of social networks in our society has evolved rapidly over the past several decades. This has been due in large part to the ever-increasing availability and capabilities of computer and internet-based technologies. Because the role of these technologies continues to evolve so rapidly, often researchers are unable to maintain up-to-date investigations. Thus, applying an appropriate theoretical framework to such innovative research, as presented by this chapter, is paramount. In addition to defining social networks and their role in our society, this section reviews social networks, professional development, and informal learning as a means to highlighting the need for implementing an analytical framework for future research related to social networking technologies.

An Overview of Social Networks

Social networks are online platforms, sites, services, and tools that individuals use to establish connections and relationships with other users. The modern version of social networks emerged in the 1990s when social networking sites began to further develop the ability to search for and connect with friends (boyd & Ellison, 2007). Often these "friends" are established based on offline relationships, familial ties, or similar interests. Currently, two of the most popular social networking platforms are Facebook and Twitter. Consider that Facebook now hosts more than 700 million active users (Social Bakers, 2011), and Twitter reports having more than 106 million active users (Online Marketing Trends, 2011).

This explosion in the availability and widespread use of social media sites has also provided users a more extensive means of communicating with others from across the globe. Many people use social networks for personal reasons related to connecting with friends and family members to share pictures and status updates; however, others also use social media for alternative reasons related to education, work, and professional development. Documenting how widespread this type of professional development is has been difficult due to its informal nature. Despite not having formal statistics to account for the use of social networks for professional development, one often hears of or personally participates in these social network exchanges. In this manner, users have been able to participate in a collaborative form of knowledge construction enabled by tools for creating and sharing information, which has revolutionized the way in which our society views learning. It is this use of social media, related to professional development and informal learning, which will be further explored here.

Professional Development and Informal Learning via Social Networks

Professional development is a process by which individuals attempt to gain knowledge for the purpose of improving their ability to perform job-related duties. Many people participate in professional development to refine, enhance, or broaden knowledge and skills related to their field. It is important to note that professional development can be formal or informal. For example, formal professional development opportunities are often offered via workshops or seminars, while informal professional development can occur in a variety of contexts. In particular, informal learning begins at the individual level in which a person seeks information via an array of semi-structured sources such as chatting with colleagues, watching a video, or joining an online community.

Grebow's (2002) description of learning to play golf demonstrates the difference between formal and informal learning and the overall importance of informal learning in developing specific skills sets and capabilities. Specifically Grebow states:

Real learning, then, is the state of being able to adopt and adapt what you know and can do—what you have acquired through formal learning—under a varying set of informal circumstances. It accounts for about 75 percent of the learning curve.

As Grebow explains, an individual may learn how to play golf formally through organized instruction; however, to play golf well one has to expand this formal learning to informal settings. In short, this means that an individual must have an outlet to practice and engage informally in the field. This brief conceptualization of professional development and informal learning also carries over to the use of social networks. Professionals from an assortment of fields, including medicine, academia, law, and technology, have joined online communities of practice as a form of continuing their professional development during and after completing formal training. Many online communities have been forged using tools such as Facebook, Twitter, and YouTube, and other Web 2.0 tools such as field-specific blogs, discussion forums, listservs, and wikis.

Current Issues and Problems with Research Related to Social Networks

Thus far, research conducted with social networks has focused extensively on the number of users (Mislove, Koppula, Gummadi, Druschel, & Bhattacharjee, 2008), patterns of use (Ellison, Lampe, & Steinfield, 2009; Huberman, Romero, & Wu, 2008; Madge, Meek, Wellens, & Hooley, 2009), privacy and security concerns (Bilge, Strufe, Balzarotti, & Kirda, 2009; Gross & Acquisti, 2005; Guha, Tang, & Francis, 2008), and the role of relationship building as it relates to formal education (Kane, Robinson-Combre, & Berge, 2010; Pempek, Yermolayeva, & Calvert, 2009). Research related to learning processes via social networks is still evolving. Some researchers have noted a perceived change in the manner in which individuals are learning via social networks. Specifically, McGuire and Gubbins (2010) describe how approaches to education and training via technology in general have recently become more informal, which has contributed to the "slow death of formal learning." On the contrary, others feel that adopting social networking tools may assist in bridging the gap between formal and informal learning (Helou, Li, & Gillet, 2010).

Based on these brief descriptions there is an obvious disparity in how scholars view the role of social networks in learning. This indicates that more research is needed to clarify the interplay between formal and informal learning based in social networks. For example, some scholars have called for redefining learning via social networks, "The potential for learning with social software tools compels us to reconsider how we conceptualize the dynamics of student learning" (McLoughlin & Lee, 2008). This implies that how individuals learn has changed, because the use of social networking tools has modified the external conditions that promote learning. If we assume learning processes have changed as a result of this modified social environment, what specific behaviors are individuals displaying? There is a need for research that examines individuals' actions and behavioral patterns via social networks, especially in relation to other social factors.

Similarly, there is a need to further define what professional development or informal learning via social networks means. There is often an overlap among terms associated with professional development and informal learning via social networks. For example, among other terms scholars refer to: professional development, informal learning, formal learning, lifelong learning, e-learning, and incidental learning. How do these terms relate to each other? Many of these terms have

overlapping characteristics, yet they are slightly different. Consider that lifelong "learning is not restricted to the classroom and to formal learning inside learning institutions; it is an activity which happens throughout life, at work, play, and home" (Klamma, Chatti, Duval, Hummel, Hvannberg, Kravcik, Law, Naeve, & Scott, 2007). Can we assume that lifelong learning is synonymous to informal learning? Probably not, the distinguishing characteristic of lifelong learning is that it takes place over a long period of time, not that it is informal. With this in mind, examining the specific behaviors that take place in social networks may aid in further redefining the type of learning that is occurring.

DEFINING ACTIVITY THEORY

The purpose of this section is to demonstrate how applying an activity theoretical framework to research with social networks allows scholars to address some of the aforementioned shortcomings in the field. "Broadly defined, activity theory is a philosophical and cross-disciplinary framework for studying different forms of human practices as development processes, with both individual and social levels interlinked at the same time" (Kuutti, 1996, p. 25). Activity theory is particularly useful because it provides a conceptual framework for describing human activity in relation to its social context. For example, activity theoretical analysis relates both the actions of the individual and the surrounding environment. Here, the discussion of activity theory will include an overview of the theoretical model, the three levels of the activity, and the role of contradictions and transformation.

Activity Theoretical Model

So, what is the "activity" in activity theory? "Any (activity) carried out by a subject includes goals, means, the process of molding the object, and the results. In fulfilling the activity, the subjects also

Figure 1. Model for an activity system (Adapted from Engeström (1987))

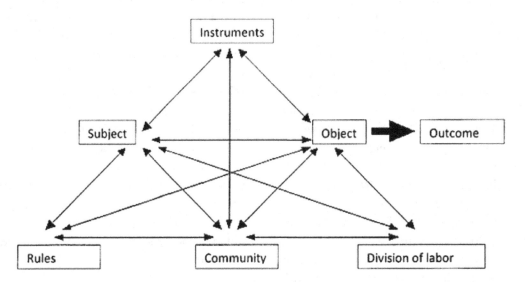

change and develop themselves" (Davydov, 1999, p. 39). More specifically, the activity is object-oriented and tool-mediated (Leont'ev, 1981, p. 59). This asserts that the activity is aimed at achieving a particular outcome and in doing so the activity is aided by the use of particular tools or instruments. To expand on this conceptualization of the activity, the following discussion addresses the activity theoretical model (See Figure 1).

Within this model the structure of an activity system includes the subject, the object and related outcomes, mediational tools and artifacts, the community or communities, the division of labor, and rules (Engeström, 1987, 1993, 2001; Engeström & Mittienen, 1999). This model is useful for understanding how a wide range of factors work together to impact an overall activity. In most research, the *subject* is the focus of the analysis within the context of the activity system, because it represents an individual or a group attempting to complete the particular activity. The arrows in the model represent the interaction between the elements. The *object* is the subject's motivation for an achieving an *outcome* or result for an activity. *Instruments* are the tools used that mediate the activity and aid the subject

in achieving the outcome. These tools can be cultural, mediational, or psychological. "The (reciprocal) relationship between the subject and the object of activity is mediated by a tool, into which the historical development of the relationship between subject and object thus far is condensed" (Kuuti, 1996, p. 27). A tool may be a physical object or a thinking tool. In this manner, a mediational tool may be a physical computer or other instrument, or a mental plan of action.

Furthermore, the subjects of an activity are grouped into communities, with rules mediating between *subject* and *community* and a *division of labor* mediating between *object* and *community*. The *community* consists of the participants in an activity that share the same object. Kuuti asserts that *rules* or regulational norms "cover both explicit and implicit norms, conventions, and social relations within a community (Kuutti, 1996, p. 28). These *rules* provide guidelines for what may and may not happen within an activity system. "Division of labor refers to the explicit and implicit organization of the community as related to the transformation process of the object into the outcome" (Kuuti, 1996, p. 28).

Figure 2. Model for interacting activity systems (Adapted from Engeström (2001))

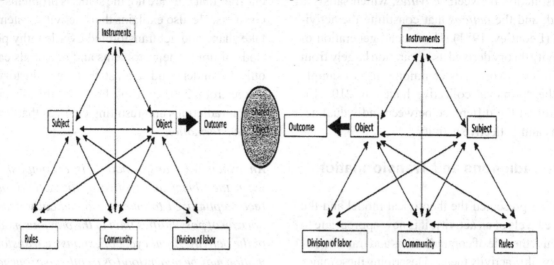

Engeström (2001) also explains that the basic model for an activity system may be expanded to include more than one interacting activity systems (See Figure 2). The two systems function in the same manner; however, it is possible that they interact with each other and potentially share an object, such as completing a collaborative task (i.e. a student and a teacher working together so that the student may learn). It is this structure of interacting concepts that makes activity theory a viable tool for complex analysis. Later in the chapter, this description of an activity system will be applied directly to the context of professional development and informal learning via social networks.

Three Levels of the Activity

The conceptual framework provided by the activity theoretical model can also be characterized as a hierarchical structure of activity with three unique levels. This hierarchy, as described by Leont'ev (1981, pp. 64-65), contains the *activity*, the *action*, and the *operation*. For example, an *activity* is a system of human behavior in which a subject attempts to work on an object to obtain a desired

outcome. This activity is considered the unit of analysis in activity theory. Also, these activities can be further divided into *actions* which are used to achieve a specific goal related to accomplishing the object of the broader activity (Leont'ev, 1981). As a result actions are performed consciously and they are implemented through *operations*. Leont'ev describes an operation as "the result of the transformation of an action" (Leont'ev, 1981, p. 64). This implies that as the *action* is internalized by the subject, it becomes an automatic procedure or *operation*. Kuutti (1996, p. 31) portrays operations related to driving a manual-shifting car. In short, the automatized operations of driving a car may include breaking and accelerating, because they have become natural functions of driving and although they are intended to fulfill a purpose, they do not directly achieve the outcome of the activity (reaching the destination).

Leont'ev expanded on the notion of mediation to develop activity theory by adopting *activity* as the unit of analysis. He argued that people perform *actions* that contribute towards the satisfaction of a particular need. In many cases, these actions must be viewed in their social context to be completely understood. In this manner Leont'ev made a distinction between *activities*, which satisfy a need, and the *actions* that constitute the activities (Leont'ev, 1981). The second generation of activity theory derived its inspiration largely from Leont'ev's work. His commonly used example of the "primeval collective hunt" (p. 210-213) solidified the difference between individual actions and collective activity.

Contradictions and Transformation

Having presented the theoretical model and the three levels of an activity, it is now appropriate to discuss the role of contradictions and transformation within activity theory. Describing these major components will offer a thorough explanation of how an activity system is formed and ultimately how it can be used to investigate learners' activities via social networks.

Contradictions, or internal tensions, are considered to be the motivating forces behind development (Engeström & Miettienen, 1999, p. 8). With the end goal of describing changes, transformations, or development, activity theory calls for investigating individuals within the context of their activity system. As such, development proceeds as the subject or subjects resolve *contradictions* in the activity. Nardi (1996) offers the following explanation of contradictions:

Activity theory uses the term contradiction to indicate a misfit within elements, between them, between different activities, or between different developmental phases of a single activity. Contradictions manifest themselves as problems, ruptures, breakdowns, clashes. Activity theory sees contradictions as sources of development; activities are virtually always in the process of working through contradictions (p. 34).

Thus, contradictions are tensions within or between activity systems. They are seen as sources of development; however, Engeström (2001)

clarifies that they are not the same as problems or conflicts. He also explains that "activity systems take shape and get transformed over lengthy periods of time. Their problems and potentials can only be understood against their own history" (Engeström, 2001, p. 136). Last, it is this history of contradictions and resulting changes that lead to *transformation*:

An expansive transformation is accomplished when the object and motive of the activity are reconceptualized to embrace a radically wider horizon of possibilities than in the previous mode of the activity. A full cycle of expansive transformation may be understood as a collective journey through the zone of proximal development of the activity" (Engeström, 2001, p. 137).

Transformation, coupled with the outcome, is the end product of the activity system. However, neither transformation nor the outcome should be viewed in isolation. They must be analyzed in the context of the activity system, highlighting the social factors involved. In the end, it is the transformation or outcome of an activity system or interacting activity systems, which serves as a major focal point of analysis.

APPLYING THE ACTIVITY THEORETICAL FRAMEWORK

Building on this general explanation of activity theory, now the theoretical framework will be applied more directly to the context of learning via social networks. Here, the activity theoretical framework will be operationalized with regards to a specific example of professional development and informal learning via social networks. This is followed by a discussion of solutions and recommendations, which address the issues and problems with social networks presented previously in this chapter.

Operationalizing the Theoretical Framework

The purpose of this section is to provide a better idea of how the conceptual framework of activity theory can be operationalized. In the context of this book the activity is related to virtual professional development and informal learning, and it is situated in the social network. Furthermore, the tools available in this type of social network afford individuals the opportunity to exert control over their environment and ultimately transform it and themselves. In this manner the online tools mediate the human activity of professional development and informal learning so that individuals may achieve a desired outcome.

For the purpose of further operationalizing the theoretical framework in relation to social networking tools, consider the following example:

Jan, a self-employed female business consultant, age 35, sought online professional development to increase her knowledge and skills related to technology implementation with larger corporations. Specifically, Jan was experiencing an inner tension because she felt unprepared and uncomfortable to work with larger corporations. Feeling that she would not further benefit from general workshops or coursework, she decided to join a Facebook community (11,000 members) related to business consulting for technology management. In addition, she joined a similar ListServ (8,450 members) and discussion board forum (440 members), which were dedicated specifically to technology implementation. Within each of these communities she has posted several questions, comments, and responses over a period of two years; however, for the most part she has not taken any leadership roles. In these communities she has been able to address her specific needs with other members related to the ongoing challenge, which she has encountered in her work. As a result of processing these challenges with others online, her initial anxieties began to disappear. She has modified her means of practicing business consulting to bring about an appropriate solution and to overcome her initial struggles and fears related to working with larger companies.

Using this example the focus now shifts to applying the activity theoretical model to demonstrate how it can be used to analyze and understand the social processes related to professional development and informal learning in social networks. The primary *subject* of this activity system is the female business consultant. The primary *communities* include the members of the Facebook, ListServ, and discussion board communities. The *mediating artifacts* or instruments include the specific technologies used and the other members of the communities. The *rules* and *division of labor* are established within each community, and they may include regulations for who can post, what can be posted, how to join the group, the responsibilities of leadership and the members, and other guiding principles for behavior while participating in the social network. The *object* of the activity is to obtain the overall learning outcomes associated with business consulting including knowledge and skills related to the primary concerns of the subject. The *outcome* is the acquired knowledge or skill gained. Figure 3 is a graphic representation of Jan's activity system as it relates to her professional development via social networks.

To further this discussion we should also consider the three levels of the activity, contradictions, and transformation as they apply to Jan's activity. First, Jan's activity is the act of seeking knowledge to overcome her anxiety related to working with larger companies. Second, some of the actions of her activity include searching for and joining online communities to get in contact with other technology professionals. Third, the operations are the commonplace steps required to participate in the online communities such as logging in and reading and posting comments.

Figure 3. Graphic representation of Jan's activity system via social networks

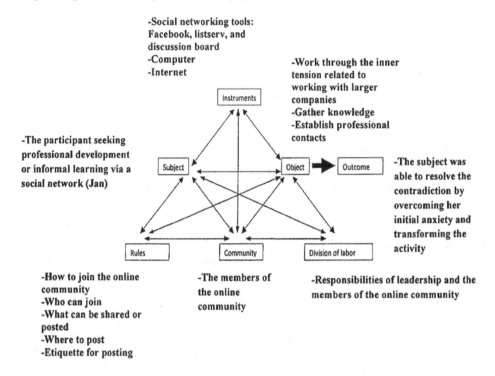

Last, as described previously, contradictions are seen as the motivating force behind the activity. In this example, Jan's primary contradiction was the inner tension experienced with relation to feeling unprepared and uncomfortable in dealing with larger companies. In essence, this was the root cause for seeking further information via social networks. If left unresolved the contradiction, the anxiety felt by Jan, would continue to stall the activity of technology consulting and adversely affect her business practice. In Jan's case, she was able to resolve the contradiction by seeking assistance from others via social networking tools. In this manner, the technology-based tools and the other participants of the online communities mediated her activity. By interacting with others, she was able to regain control over the activity. The resulting changes in her consulting practices represent the individual transformation, or professional development, experienced as a result of the activity described.

Solutions and Recommendations

Utilizing activity theory as an analytical model for investigating human behaviors and development, as operationalized in the previous section, enables a more thorough understanding of how and why individuals use social networking tools. It also offers several noteworthy solutions to remedy the shortcomings of current research related to learning processes via social networks. By focusing on the object-oriented, tool-mediated activity, activity theory accounts for individuals' use of social networking tools and the social factors involved. Implementing the activity theoretical framework for analysis of such factors enables researchers to answer the questions posed by Leont'ev (1981) in his description of the three analytical levels of activity theory: why, what, how (See Table 1).

Table 1. Description of three analytical levels for activity theory

Analytical level	Factor involved	Question answered
Activity	Object/motive	Why is the activity taking place?
Action	Specific goal	What is the subject doing to complete the activity?
Operation	Conditions: constraints and affordances	How is the subject completing the activity?

Adapted from Leont'ev (1981)

Answering these questions for any particular activity allows researchers to view the activity in its full context, examine individuals' specific behaviors, and track the outcome of the activity. This type of analysis has the potential to allow researchers to track and define the evolving learning processes of those who participate in social networks.

In addition to addressing the three levels of the activity, there are other recommendations for research related to professional development in social networks and utilizing Web 2.0 tools. Specifically, based on her work in the field of human-computer interaction Nardi (1996) describes the following four requirements for utilizing activity theoretical analysis:

A. A research time frame long enough to understand users' objects
B. Attention to broad patterns of activity
C. The use of a varied set of data collection techniques
D. A commitment to understanding things from users' points of view (pp. 94-95).

These suggestions demonstrate that utilizing activity theory as a conceptual framework to investigate learning via social networks requires distinguishing the research from more traditional and experimental studies. Within activity theory research it is important to understand "the interpenetration of the individual, other people and artifacts in everyday activity" (Nardi, 1996, p. 7), not simply cause and effect relationships. This type of research enables viewing and analyzing professional development via social networks as an activity embedded in its own social context including the online community and the social networking tools.

FUTURE RESEARCH DIRECTIONS

The future of professional development and informal learning via social networks will continue to evolve, especially as new and innovative technologies are created. As these new technologies are created, new variations of online communities will also appear. For this reason future research will have to account for *multi-voicedness* and *historicity* of the activities (Engeström, 2001). First, the community of an activity consists of the participants that share the same object. This refers in part to what Engeström (2001) calls *multi-voicedness*. It will be important for future research to gather data from multiple viewpoints to fully understand the online communities that are forged via social networking tools. Thus, we can compare and incorporate multiple views and stakeholders within the activity. Engeström explains "an activity system is always a community of multiple points of view, traditions, and interests" (p. 136). A subject may be part of several communities and a community, itself, may be part of other communities, but multiple points of view are always present. For example, one can observe a social network through the lens of the principal user and the other community members. Collecting this type of data in future research will offer the potential to further understand the inner workings of an online community from multiple perspectives.

Second, it is essential that future research investigates the cultural and historical context of each online community including the evolution of the specific technology, the formal and informal education of the members, and the history of the community itself. Historicity is relevant in this case because it helps in understanding problems as they develop. "Parts of older phases of activities stay often embedded in them as they develop" (Kuutti, 1996, p. 26), and thus, sources of tension may be revealed by examining these consecutive activity systems. As such, the foundation of an online community via social networking tools is based on the previous variations of the same community and the history of its members, which have led up to the current activity under examination. Often these previous forms of the same activity are unexamined. However, by examining these multiple layers of the same activity system (Engestrom, 2001, p. 136), future research may be able to identify key changes in regards to the interacting components of the online community. This will also enable a deeper understanding of the activity itself, learning via social networks.

CONCLUSION

This chapter has presented activity theory as a conceptual framework for analyzing professional development and informal learning via social networks. Through the operationalization of the framework, we can see how the focus of activity theory research is different from most previous research related to social networks. The descriptions of activity theory, provided in this chapter, demonstrate that activity theory is an appropriate analytical framework to use with learning via social networks because development is its main focus. By tracking the development of the subject or subjects within the online community, activity theory highlights the interplay between the individual(s), the social environment, and

the specific technology used. At the same time utilizing activity theory as an analytical tool demonstrates how using social networks and Web 2.0 tools mediates the individual's professional development and ultimately transforms the overall activity and future professional activities. In this manner, the technology itself becomes part of the activity and it contributes to the overall development within the activity.

REFERENCES

Bilge, L., Strufe, T., Balzarotti, D., & Kirda, E. (2009). All your contacts are belong to us: Automated identity theft attacks on social networks. In *Proceedings of the 18th International Conference on World Wide Web,* (pp. 551-560). New York, NY: IEEE.

boyd, D. M., & Ellison, N. B. (2007). Social network sites: Definition, history, and scholarship. *Journal of Computer-Mediated Communication, 13*(1). doi:10.1111/j.1083-6101.2007.00393.x

Davydov, V. (1999). The content and unsolved problems of activity theory. In Engstrom, R. M. Y., Miettinen, R., & Punamaki, R.-L. (Eds.), *Perspectives on Activity Theory* (pp. 39–52). Cambridge, UK: Cambridge University Press.

Ellison, N., Lampe, C., & Steinfield, C. (2009). Social network sites and society: Current trends and future possibilities. *Interactions Magazine, 16*(1).

Engeström, Y. (1987). *Learning by expanding: An activity-theoretical approach to developmental research*. Helsinki, Finland: Orieta-Konsultit.

Engeström, Y. (1993). Developmental studies of work as a testbench of activity theory: The case of primary care medical practice. In Chaiklin & Lave (Eds.), *Understanding Practice: Perspectives on Activity and Context,* (pp. 64-103). Cambridge, UK: Cambridge University Press.

Engeström, Y. (2001). Expansive learning at work: Toward an activity theoretical reconceptualization. *Journal of Education and Work, 14*(1), 133–156.

Engeström, Y., & Mittienen, R. (1999). Introduction. In Engeström, Y., Miettinen, R., & Punamaki, R. (Eds.), *Perspectives on Activity Theory* (pp. 1–16). Cambridge, UK: Cambridge University Press.

Gandel, P. B., & Golden, C. (2004). Professional development in tough financial times. *EDUCAUSE Quarterly Magazine, 27*(1).

Grebow, D. (2002). *At the water cooler of learning. Executive Briefing.* Arlington, VA: University of Virginia.

Gross, R., & Acquisti, A. (2005). *Information revelation and privacy in online social networks.* Paper presented at the Workshop on Privacy in the Electronic Society (WPES). Alexandria, VA.

Guha, S., Tang, K., & Francis, P. (2008). *NOYB: Privacy in online social networks.* Paper presented at the 1st ACM SIGCOMM Workshop on Online Social Networks (WOSN'08). Seattle, WA.

Helou, S. E., Li, N., & Gillet, D. (2010). *The 3A Interaction Model: Towards bridging the gap between formal and informal learning.* Paper presented at the Third International Conference on Advances in Computer-Human Interactions, Saint Maarten, Netherlands.

Huberman, B. A., Romero, D. M., & Wu, F. (2009). Social networks that matter: Twitter under the microscope. *First Monday, 14*(1).

Kane, K., Robinson-Combre, J., & Berge, Z. L. (2010). Tapping into social networking: Collaborating enhances both knowledge management and e-learning. *Vine, 40*(1), 62–70. doi:10.1108/03055721011024928

Klamma, R., Chatti, M. A., Duval, E., Hummel, H., Hvannberg, E. H., & Kravcik, M. (2007). Social software for life-long learning. *Journal of Educational Technology & Society, 10*(3), 72–83.

Kuuti, K. (1996). Activity theory as a potential framework for human-computer interaction research. In Nardi, B. A. (Ed.), *Context and Consciousness: Activity Theory and Human-Computer Interaction* (pp. 17–44). Cambridge, MA: MIT Press.

Leont'ev, A. N. (1978). *Activity, consciousness, and personality.* Englewood Cliffs, NJ: Prentice-Hall.

Leont'ev, A. N. (1981). *Problems of the development of the mind.* Moscow, Russia: Progress Publishers.

Madge, C., Meek, J., Wellens, J., & Hooley, T. (2009). Facebook, social integration and informal learning at university: It is more for socialising and talking to friends about work than for actually doing work. *Learning, Media and Technology, 34*(2), 141–155. doi:10.1080/17439880902923606

McGuire, D., & Gubbins, C. (2010). The slow death of formal learning: A polemic. *Human Resource Development Review, 9*(3), 249–265.

McLoughlin, C., & Lee, M. J. W. (2008). Future learning landscapes: Transforming pedagogy through social software. *Innovate, 4*(5).

Mislove, A., Koppula, H., Gummadi, K. P., Druschel, P., & Bhattacharjee, B. (2008), *Growth of the Flickr social network.* Paper presented at the 1st ACM SIGCOMM Workshop on Social Networks (WOSN 2008). Seattle, WA.

Nardi, B. A. (1996). *Context and consciousness: Activity theory and human-computer interaction.* Cambridge, MA: The MIT Press.

Online Marketing Trends. (2011). *The latest online media trends, analysis, news, research on online advertising, social media, search marketing and more*. Retrieved June 15, 2011 from http://www.onlinemarketing-trends.com/2011/03/twitter-statistics-on-its-5th.html.

Pempek, T., Yermolayeva, Y., & Calvert, S. (2009). College students' social networking experiences on Facebook. *Journal of Applied Developmental Psychology, 30*(3), 227–238. doi:10.1016/j.appdev.2008.12.010

Social Bakers. (2011). *Heart of social media statistics*. Retrieved July 15, 2011 from http://www.socialbakers.com/.

ADDITIONAL READING

Adamson, A. (2009). Companies should encourage social networking among employees. *Forbes.com*. Retrieved from http://www.forbes.com/2009/06/02/charles-schwab-spy-facebook-leadership-cmo-net.

Backstrom, L., Huttenlocher, D., Kleinberg, J., & Lan, X. (2006). *Group formation in large social networks: Membership, growth, and evolution*. Paper presented at the 12th ACM SIGKDD International Conference on Knowledge Discovery and Data Mining. Philadelphia, PA.

Bannon, L., & Bødker, S. (1991). Beyond the interface: Encountering artifacts in use. In Carroll, J. (Ed.), *Designing Interaction: Psychology at the Human-Computer Interface*. Cambridge, UK: Cambridge University Press.

Bennett, J., Owers, M., Pitt, M., & Tucker, M. (2010). Workplace impact of social networking. *Property Management, 28*(3), 138–148. doi:10.1108/02637471011051282

Bertelsen, O. W., & Bødker, S. (2003). Activity theory. In Carroll, J. M. (Ed.), *HCI Models Theories, and Frameworks: Toward a Multidisciplinary Science* (pp. 291–324). San Francisco, CA: Morgan Kaufmann. doi:10.1016/B978-155860808-5/50011-3

Bødker, S. (1991). *Through the interface: A human activity approach to user interface design*. Hillsdale, NJ: Lawrence Erlbaum Associates.

Ellison, N. B., Steinfield, C., & Lampe, C. (2007). The benefits of Facebook "friends": Social capital and college students' use of online social network sites. *Journal of Computer-Mediated Communication, 12*(4), 1143–1168. doi:10.1111/j.1083-6101.2007.00367.x

Engeström, Y. (2008). *From teams to knots: Activity-theoretical studies of collaboration and learning at work*. Cambridge, UK: Cambridge University Press.

Greenhow, C., & Robelia, B. (2009). Informal learning and identity formation in online social networks. *Learning, Media and Technology, 34*(2), 119–140. doi:10.1080/17439880902923580

Griffiths, M., Heinze, A., Light, B., & Kiveal, P. (2010). *FaceBook, YouTube, MySpace: Can Web 2.0 social networking sites nudge the boardroom – The evolution of CRN 2.0 research agenda?* Paper presented at UK Academy for Information Systems Conference. London, UK.

Jeffs, T., & Smith, M. K. (2005). *Informal education: Conversation, democracy and learning*. Retrieved from http://www.infed.org/i-intro.htm.

Kaptelinin, V. (1996). Activity theory: Implications for human-computer interaction. In Nardi, B. A. (Ed.), *Context and Consciousness: Activity Theory and Human-Computer Interaction* (pp. 103–116). Cambridge, MA: The MIT Press.

Kaptelinin, V., Kuutti, K., & Bannon, L. (1995). Activity theory: Basic concepts and applications. In Blumenthal, (Eds.), *Human-Computer Interaction*. Berlin, Germany: Springer. doi:10.1007/3-540-60614-9_14

Lenhart, A., & Madden, M. (2007). *Teens, privacy & online social networks: How teens manage their online identities and personal information in the age of MySpace*. Washington, DC: Pew Internet & American Life Project.

Murphy, E., & Rodriguez-Manzanares, M. A. (2008). Using activity theory and its principle of contradictions to guide research in educational technology. *Australian Journal of Educational Technology*, *24*(4), 442–457.

Roth, W. M., & Lee, Y. J. (2007). Vygotsky's neglected legacy: Cultural-historical activity theory. *Review of Educational Research*, *77*(2), 186–232. doi:10.3102/0034654306298273

Russell, D. L., & Schneiderheinze, A. (2005). Understanding innovation in education using activity theory. *Journal of Educational Technology & Society*, *8*(1), 38–53.

Smith, T. (2009). The social media revolution. *International Journal of Market Research*, *51*(4), 559–561. doi:10.2501/S1470785309200773

Subrahmanyam, K., Reich, S. M., Waechter, N., & Espinoza, G. (2008). Online and offline social networks: Use of social networking sites by emerging adults. *Journal of Applied Developmental Psychology*, *29*(6), 420–433. doi:10.1016/j.appdev.2008.07.003

Vygotsky, L. (1962). *Thought and language*. Cambridge, MA: MIT Press. doi:10.1037/11193-000

Vygotsky, L. (1978). *Mind in society: The development of higher psychological processes*. Boston, MA: Harvard University Press.

Warlick, D. (2006). A day in the life of web 2.0. *Technology & Learning*, *27*(3), 20–26.

Wertsch, J. (1981). The concept of activity in soviet psychology: An introduction. In Wertsch, J. (Ed.), *The Concept of Activity in Soviet Psychology* (pp. 3–36). Armonk, NY: ME Sharpe.

Wertsch, J. V. (1985). *Vygotsky and the social formation of mind*. Cambridge, MA: Harvard University Press.

Wertsch, J. V. (1998). *Mind as action*. Oxford, UK: Oxford University Press.

KEY TERMS AND DEFINITIONS

Action: An action is a specific behavior directed towards a goal. Actions are best understood in their full context, and they are subordinate to the larger activity.

Activity: An activity is a system of human behaviors aimed at obtaining a desired outcome. To accomplish this, the individual may use available tools to aid in the activity.

Contradictions: In Activity Theory contradictions are tensions that arise between elements of an activity system, between multiple activity systems, between different activities, or between phases of a single activity. These contradictions are viewed as problems, ruptures, breakdowns, or clashes. Contradictions are viewed as a source of development, and they are also referred to as disturbances, tensions, and conflicts.

Goal: This is the object of an individual action. It is the desired result of an action.

Mediation: This is the idea that all human activity is affected or controlled by artifacts, which are used as tools in the activity. Mediation serves to assist the individual in the completion of the proposed activity by enabling control over the world and the self.

Motive: This is the motivation for a specific action. Motive is what drives a particular action in the activity. This is different from the object, which is the motivation for the larger activity. It is an object that satisfies a need.

Object: This is the motivation for achieving a desired outcome for an activity. It drives the activity.

Operation: These are actions in an activity that have become automatic procedures. Operations are performed without conscious attention.

Transformation: This is the process of development as something changes throughout an activity. Typically, it refers to the process of moving from the object of an activity to the outcome.

Chapter 5
Applying Social Network Analysis and Social Capital in Personal Learning Environments of Informal Learning

Xiaojun Chen
Purdue University, USA

Jea H. Choi
Purdue University, USA

Ji Hyun Yu
Purdue University, USA

ABSTRACT

Recently, researchers in the instructional technology and learning sciences arenas have started to pay attention to the concept of Personal Learning Environments (PLE). With the aim to investigate how social network theory could indicate the desired indicators for successful Personal Learning Environments, the authors are addressing social capital theory as a conceptual framework to understand the network landscape within informal learning environments. Social capital is an inherent property of network and collaboration dynamics, along with key indicators related to personal network measurements. Personal network analysis as a means to evaluate the social capital is discussed later in this chapter. This chapter is not about learning what or learning as becoming, but about how people learn with whom, and with what degree of influence. It will be helpful to educators or researchers who are interested in measuring academic and psychosocial outcomes within the presence of social capital when applying personal social network analysis in personal learning networks.

DOI: 10.4018/978-1-4666-1815-2.ch005

INTRODUCTION

The Personal Learning Environment (PLE) concept has emerged as a label associated with the application of the technologies of Web 2.0; yet, there has been little agreement on which theory could guide the investigation on the ecology of networks that constitutes the Personal Learning Environments. No coherent model has been established or introduced to analyze the key indicators, relationships, or ties, and networks in a Personal Learning Environment. This chapter introduces a network-based social capital theory, which increases our understanding of how people learn with whom, or how people learn to be contributors to local and global society with some degree of influence in Personal Learning Environments. More importantly, we seek to address the following question: how could the frequent utilized or naturally occurring socio-technological features is best incorporated into the Personal Leaning Environments.

PERSONAL LEARNING ENVIRONMENTS

The concept of Personal Learning Environments has been advocated by computer scientists in the United Kingdom from the network perspective since the late 1990s (Johnson & Liber, 2008). It has recently become significant in learning and teaching research and in professional development research (Ross & Welsh, 2007). Especially in teachers' education, major researchers have devoted time to better understanding the phenomenon of the Personal Learning Environments in order to help teachers build their efficacy of using technology as well as to build their own developmental pace (Ross & Welsh, 2007).

Personal Learning Environments (PLEs) allow learners to control their own teaching and learning environments (Greehow, 2011). The Personal

Learning Environment supports both completely individualized, personal life-long learning efforts and trajectories, and learning within more structured learning contexts (for example, courses at an institution) where there is some organized or facilitated activity (Severance, Hardin, & Whyte, 2008). However, Personal Learning Environments differ from online course management systems. The online course management systems normally have very well structured platforms with specific tools or applications provided to the designated institutions (Wilson, Liber, Johnson, Beauvoir, Sharples, & Milligan, 2007). At the same time, learners in their own Personal Learning Environment can construct the tools of their choice by taking advantage of the growth of the Web 2.0 applications. Personal learning environments also differ from online communities of practice, which provides a virtual space where a group of people share an interest or a profession and localize new information based on their personal needs and living environment (Gray, 2004; Reverin, 2008). Wenger (2006) proclaims, "communities of practice enable practitioners to take collective responsibility for managing the knowledge they need, recognizing that, given the proper structure, they are in the best position to do this." Likewise, while both the Personal Learning Environments and the online communities of practice provide benefits for informal learning (Greenhow & Robelia, 2009a), learners are permitted to interact more loosely within Personal Learning Environments than within communities of practice.

In a Personal Learning Environment, learners would utilize a single set of tools, customized to their needs and preferences, inside a single learning environment. People, tools, communities, and resources interact very loosely within these personal learning environments. Learners are enabled to construct the environment for themselves, in part, by deciding upon: the tools they choose, the communities they start and join, the resources they assemble, and the things they write (Wilson, 2008). The chosen tools allow the learner to better interact with other people, for example, by better managing their relationships with their tutors and peers, as well as by permitting the formation of stronger links between contacts that are not generally part of their formal learning network. In this way, the Personal Learning Environment can enable learners to control their learning resources by enabling learners to structure, share, and annotate the resources that they have found or created by themselves or those, which they have received from their peers. The Personal Learning Environment also provides learners with the opportunity to set up and join varied activities, such as study groups, which bring together particular groups of people, along with the appropriate and available educational resources. Most importantly, a Personal Learning Environment helps the learners to integrate their learning processes. This environment provides learners with the opportunity to combine learning from different institutions and to continue successfully in their re-use of previously generated evidence of competency or in their establishment of links between formal and informal learning (Milligan, Johnson, Sharples, Wilson, & Liber, 2006).

Moreover, the Personal Learning Environment is designed as a "mash-up" of distributed services and offers a single window from which learners can track their activity and other people's activity, search and retrieve content, edit their own content, share digital resources, and collaborate with peers (Casquero, Portillo, Ovelar, Benito, & Romo, 2010). These characteristics of the Personal Learning Environment provide a promising platform for professional development and informal learning, where learners can take advantage of the self-control of the environment.

With the advent of Web 2.0, Personal Learning Environments constitute a new research strand that represents a new way of thinking about technology-enhanced learning (Johnson & Liber, 2008). The Personal Learning Environment is

considered as the educational manifestation of the Web's "small pieces loosely jointed," a "world of pure connection, free of the arbitrary constraints of matter, distance, and time" (Mott, 2010), when compared with the institution centered and monolithic model of traditional virtual learning environments (Casquero, et al., 2010).

Researchers have attempted to understand the patterns (Wilson, 2008) and applications used in Personal Learning Environments (Johnson & Liber, 2008). Though sample Personal Learning Environments have been found at the lesson plan or course level (Ross & Welsh, 2007; Casquero, et al., 2010), researchers are now working to better comprehend what is behind the wired connections between the learners and the technologies. As social network applications are having an increasingly important impact on society, a growing number of scholars and educators are arguing that the online network sites may serve as both supports for and sites of learning. For instance, students can use their online social networking skills to fulfill social learning functions within and across informal and formal learning spheres of activity—as in cases of informal sharing, peer validation and feedback, alumni support, and spontaneous help with school-related tasks (Greenhow & Robelia, 2009a, 2009b). However, it is not an easy task to examine the relationships or characteristics represented by the individualized learning networks. Therefore, educators should work to identify what learning resources are particularly exchanged throughout the network, the individuals involved in exchanges, and the impact of these as they occur over time (Christakis & Fowler, 2009; Greenhow, 2011) from a network-based approach. One of the network-based approaches is personal network analysis. In personal network analysis, the data will show trends in user's interaction with the learning content via Web 2.0 and social networking over the Internet. Adamic, Zhang, Bakshy, and Ackerman (2008) found that the analysis on ego-networks easily revealed Yahoo Answer categories where discussion threads tended to dominate. It is hypothesized that implementing personal network analysis over Personal Learning Environments will help researchers to evaluate successful factors to enhance informal learning from the social capital perspective.

Within this context, we will provide an overview of the personal network analysis (i.e. egocentric network analysis), with respect to the basic network measures of social capital and network ties. We propose to use social network analysis to examine the relationships within the Personal Learning Environments with the support of social capital theory. Social capital broadly refers to the resources accumulated through the relationships among people (Coleman, 1988). Prominent sociologists, such as Burt (1992, 1997), Coleman (1988), and Granovetter (1973) argue that variance or inequality in the success of individuals cannot be explained solely by their personal attributes, but is more significantly determined by the extension of social capital accumulated in their respective networks. In other words, social capital takes on an important role for the individual's success or organizational performance.

SOCIAL CAPITAL IN LEARNING NETWORKS

Social capital has received increased attention as a new perspective, as evidenced by its application to various disciplines and numerous subject areas (Griffith & Harvey, 2004). There is no commonly agreed upon definition of social capital across disciplines (Claridge, 2004; Robison, et al., 2002). However, scholars seem to agree that social capital is a term regarding the value of social networks, a bonding of similar people and bridging between diverse people, with norms of reciprocity (Bourdieu & Wacquant, 1992; Burt, 1992, 2000; Coleman, 1988); and social capital, as an inherent property of social relationships, is a key indicator of social networks based on shared

norms, values, and understandings that facilitate cooperation within or among groups (Jong, 2010). Putnam (2000) suggests two different concepts, such as *bridging social capital* and *bonding social capital*. Bridging social capital is related to 'weak ties,' which are loose connections between individuals who may provide useful information or new perspectives for one another but do not provide emotional support (Granovetter, 1982). Alternatively, bonding social capital is found between individuals in tightly knit, emotionally close relationships, such as with family and close friends.

For the development of a definition of social capital, there have been two main considerations within social capital theory. The first consideration regards social capital as a structural characteristic of social relations, whereas the second consideration regards social capital as a quality of social relations. From the structural consideration of social capital, social capital is defined as "the sum of the resources, actual or virtual that accrue to an individual or group by virtue of possessing a durable network of more or less institutionalized relationships of mutual acquaintance and recognition" (Bourdieu, 1986, p. 248). Following this definition, Burt (1997) defined that "social capital is a function of brokerage opportunities and draws on network concepts and also the structural autonomy created by complex networks" (p. 340). In this structural view, resources (e.g. information, ideas, and support) are social, in which they are only accessible in and through these specific relationships, unlike physical or human capital that are essentially the property of individuals (Jong, 2010). Therefore, if individuals occupy key strategic positions in the network, they can have more social capital than their peers, because their network position gives them heightened access to more and better resources (Burt, 2000).

In contrast, the relational consideration of social capital holds to the fact that social capital is rooted in the relationships, such as trust and trustworthiness. Putnam (2000) argued that the nature and extent of one's involvement in the social networks result in certain benefits for social actors, rather than just the structure itself (Kostova & Roth, 2003). From the relational perspective, social capital is expected to allow for potential benefits derived from the content of their social ties as indicated by the beliefs and attitudes among social actors who create a psychological environment designed to enhance collaboration and mutual support (Nahapiet & Ghoshal, 1998).

In this chapter, we take a mixed approach toward this distinction between the structural and relational consideration in terms of the definition of social capital, following Adler and Kwon (2002). They argued that learning is influenced by both structural aspects (e.g. structural composition) and relationship aspects (e.g. level of mutual trust and reciprocity) so that the learning processes leading to knowledge productivity can be understood by both considerations. The following paragraph describes two different types of social capital based on these two considerations.

From the two considerations of social capital, there continues to be a controversy over which type of network structure among 'closed' and 'open' network generates positive outcomes for social actors (Burt, 2000). To empirically investigate the concept of social capital in real-world settings, there are two perspectives regarding the mechanisms by which social capital is created and mobilized: *network closure* (strongly interconnected networks) and *structural holes* (loosely coupled networks). According to Coleman (1988), closed networks facilitate social actors to build up trust and cohesive ties so that they can bind themselves to each other through mutual obligations and expectations. In contrast, open networks provide brokerage opportunities, which include multiple disconnected clusters, termed as '*structural holes*' (Burt, 2000, 2004). In other words, within an open network, individuals can broker connections between otherwise disconnected segments. These two opposite views provide drastically different prescriptions for developing

and maintaining social capital. We shall illustrate how these two perspectives of social capital may have impact on both knowledge production and the sharing of individual learners.

Network Closure

Some pioneering researchers of social capital, such as Coleman (1988), assert that dense and closed networks in which nodes are highly connected to each other are the essential means of creating and maintaining social capital. We term this perspective 'network closure,' which is focused on the strength of relationships and the density of the social network based on the strong tie assumption that social capital is more effectively generated within rather than between network segments. The closed structures benefit productive outcomes, such as knowledge sharing, reduced opportunism, and well-coordinated conflict resolution (Gargiulo & Benassi, 2000). The network closure view holds that a closed network formation can enhance each individual's academic performance. Berg and his colleagues (1982) have revealed that a cohesive network with many direct and/or indirect ties leads to an extensive amount of knowledge sharing between members. Arora and Gambardella have also shown that members of a closed network were well acquainted with their partners' particular strengths and weaknesses, which efficiently facilitated complementary collaboration. Similarly, Gargiulo and Benassi (2000) found that individuals trusted each other to honor obligations, diminishing the uncertainty of their exchanges and enhancing their ability to cooperate in the pursuit of their interests. Additionally, opportunistic behavior is less likely to occur within a strongly connected network because of established trust and norms (Oh, et al., 2006). Previous studies have reported that the members of a closed network tend to find mutually satisfactory solutions through a resolution process (Ahuga, 2000; Gargiulo, et al., 2000; Gulati & Gargiulo, 1999; Oh, et al., 2006; Walker, et al., 1997).

Structural Holes

The relational consideration of social capital that the existence of ties between individuals defines both the structure of networks and the opportunity to build social capital has led directly to the current interest in a structural holes theory (Kilduff & Tsai, 2003). The concept of "structural holes" refers to "disconnections between nodes" or "a relationship of non-redundancy between two contacts as gaps in the social network across which there are no current connections, but that can be connected by 'brokers' who control the flow of information across gaps" (Burt, 1992). The structural holes theory addresses the potential drawbacks of network closure, for instance, the idea that strong bonds within a homogenous group of members are mostly productive through collaboration, but at the same time, there are inherent disadvantages, such as a lack of fresh knowledge due to *relational inactivity* and *cognitive lock-in* that prevent members from accepting new ideas by expanding social ties (Gargiulo & Benassi, 2000; Lin, et al., 2001). Therefore, this theory asserts that the position of the actor within the network is expected to be more critical than on the strength and density of the actor's relations. Several empirical studies have demonstrated that social capital produced by structural holes affects employee's job performance more positively than social capital generated within closed networks (Lin, et al., 2001); and structural holes were found to be significantly associated with a higher innovation rate (Stuart & Podolny, 1999), faster revenue growth (Baum, et al., 2000), and higher individual researcher's academic performance (Oh, et al., 2006). Specifically, loosely coupled networks rich in structural holes allow individual actors to gain fresh insights and diverse ideas that are critical features for knowledge production.

Both network closure and the structural holes theory consider reciprocity as the mechanism that turns relationships into assets. However, these two theories have differing assessments of the effects of amplified reciprocity on social action (Jong, 2010). According to the network closure views, the amplification of reciprocity necessitates the creation of a normative environment and trust among members, whereas the structural holes theory views the amplifying effect as 'structural arthritis' which makes it harder to coordinate complex collaboration and organizational tasks (Gargiulo & Benassi, 2000).

In order to clarify which characteristics of social capital in Personal Learning Environments impact learning and how those characteristics can be measured using network-based approaches, we aim to integrate the structural holes theory and network closure view. Because learning is a social process within social networks, it is important to understand the two key indicators of the network structure: the properties of networks and characteristics of social network members. In terms of the properties of networks, several research studies have suggested 'network size' and 'network density' as social capital indicators. For instance, Boase, and Wellman (2004) have shown that the larger the network, the greater the chance of finding at least one member able to provide resources. In addition, the larger the network, the more individuals who possess the same resources, as well as, the greater the chance they will exchange resources amongst themselves. For the characteristics of the members of a social network, we recommend 'network diversity' as a representative indicator. Three types of typology have been used to examine the degree of diversity among the members of a network and provide an idea of the types of resources that circulate within the network. That is, the more diversity between the members of a network, the greater likelihood that their resources will be diverse. The three types of typology are: bonding, bridging, and linking connections. Bonding connections refer to close ties between homogeneous individuals or groups; bridging connections refer to ties between fairly similar but more loosely knitted individuals, such as people with a shared interest; linking connections refer to ties between individuals or groups from dissimilar backgrounds.

Relational properties among the members of a network can also document the value of social capital. As noted earlier, a number of studies have revealed that strong ties—namely, frequent contact, emotional intensity, and mutual support—are transitive so that they create dense groups in which members share the same affinities and resources. In contrast, weak ties create bridges among groups and circulate 'fresh' information and resources, because weak ties are a connection with the outside world (Burt, 1992; Erickson, 2004). In addition, Wellman (1996) suggested a geographic perspective by revealing the impact of spatial proximity on social capital. These literature and theories have laid the ground for us to make recommendations for analyzing social capital in Personal Learning Environments.

Social Network Analysis

After introducing the concept and basics of the social capital theory, we recommend applying social network analysis to examine the ties or relationships of social capital in the Personal Learning Environment. The Social Network Analysis (SNA) is a study that views the relationship within the social situations. A Social Network Analysis focuses on the relationship between actors rather than on the attributes of individual actors (Mika, 2007). A Social Network Analysis can explain social change; presuppose ideas about the relational texture of society; and operationalize these ideas (Vera & Schupp, 2006). Another important function of the social network analysis is the modeling of ties between actors, so as to explain or predict the observed network (van Duijn & Vermunt, 2006). As interest on Social Network Analysis has grown, studies using Social Network Analysis in education and online learning to investigate the communication patterns, program evaluation, and lines of informational sharing have been introduced (Shen, Nuankhieo, Huang,

Amelung, & Laffey, 2008; Van Cleemput, 2010). Hogan (2008) has illustrated that online interaction is almost always social network-oriented. Social networks refer to a series of nodes such as people, organizations, or Web pages, and the specific links existent between two or more of these nodes. Much research on social capital in learning environments has been focused on the structural ecology of networks by social network analysis (Burt, 2001; Jong, 2010). There are several Social Network Analysis terms that are used a lot when talking about the network results. The key terms are centrality, closeness, betweeness, and degree.

Centrality is the main concept of Social Network Analysis. It measures a person's position in the network. A person with high centrality is well-connected to other people in the network and therefore has better access to information, resources, and influence than do people with lower centrality (Reid & Smith, 2009). Chan and Liebowitz (2006) noted that "centrality is important to understanding power, stratification, ranking, and inequality in social structures." There are several main approaches to measure centrality: degree, closeness, and betweenness.

Closeness is the term that denotes the distance between two given nodes. It is referred to as the number of 'steps' it takes for a node to reach all of the other nodes and means, thus, a generalization of what are popularly known as 'degrees of separation' between two given nodes (Vera & Schupp, 2006). This is the inverse of the average distance to others in the network (Valente, Gallaher, & Mouttapa, 2004). Closeness centrality of a node is equal to the total distance of the node from all other nodes. A high closeness for an actor means that he or she is related to all others through a small number of paths (Otte & Rousseau, 2002).

Betweenness refers to the extent to which a node serves to connect different sections of the network (Vera & Schupp, 2006). This may be defined loosely as the number of times a node needs a given node to reach another node. Betweenness gauges the extent to which a node facilitates the flow in the network. This measure is based on the number of shortest paths passing through an actor (Otte & Rousseau, 2002).

Degree is the number of direct ties an actor has. If the actor has higher degree, it is likely to be seen that the actor is more powerful in the network. With directed data, centrality can be categorized to in-degree and out-degree. An actor with a high in-degree is regarded to be prominent or to have higher prestige, as many other actors may seek to directly connect with them. An actor is often said to be influential if it has a high out-degree as it is able to make others aware of its views (Chan & Liebowitz, 2006). Density also has a similar meaning to degree as it represents the actual number of ties in a network as a ratio of the total maximum ties that are possible with all the nodes of the network (Shen, Nuankhieo, Huang, Amelung, & Laffey, 2008). It is also an indicator for the general level of connectedness in the graph (Otte & Rousseau, 2002). Durland et al. (2006) said that the density shows the proportion of total available ties. The higher the density, the more rapidly information will circulate between network members (Reid & Smith, 2009).

These terms are important since they show the strength and density of how people/artifacts are connected among the social network. Terms show to what degree the network was formed and what is the key personnel/artifact of the social network. With the knowledge of the social network analysis, we would like to recommend several methods to utilize personal network analysis in the Personal Learning Environment.

Personal Network Analysis

There are three network types that are covered in Social Network Analysis: whole networks, personal networks, and partial networks (Fielding, Lee, & Blank, 2008; Garton & Wellman, 1999; Haythornthwaite, 1996; Mika, 2007). The distinction between whole/complete networks and personal/egocentric networks is largely de-

pendent on how analysts have been able to gather data. Whole networks describe the relationships within a clearly demarcated population such as an e-mail list or social community. Personal network analysis examines the differences of the personal network, focusing on the size, shape, and quality of a number. Partial networks are used on snowball sampling to relational data (Fielding, et al., 2008).

In this section, we focus on the personal network analysis for the interpretation of effective factors in the Personal Learning Environment (PLE). A personal network is also called an egocentric network. Haythornthwaite (1996) said that a personal network focuses on a picture of a typical actor in a particular environment and shows how many ties individual actors have to others, what types of ties they maintain, and what kind of cocoon they give to and receive from others in their network. This approach is particularly useful when the population is large, or the boundaries of the population are hard to define. Each sampled case in the context is referred to as 'ego' and the nodes connected to ego are referred to as 'alters' (See Figure 1).

Boase (2008) said that "the personal network approach is ideally suited for understanding the personal communication system because it takes the individual's relationships as its primary focus of analysis." Personal networks are used quite often in the study of social support, i.e. the study of social relationships that aid the health or well-being of an individual (Wasserman & Faust, 1994). Haythornthwaite (1996) gave an example of egocentric networks as mentioning Wellman's case; Wellman et al. used egocentric networks to explore how a sense of community was maintained through ties, rather than through geographical proximity, among the residents of Toronto's East York neighborhood. As illustrated in the previous section, the Personal Learning Environment is "a concretization of operational spaces in the network where the subject is at the center of his network of learning resources" (Bonaiuti, 2006; as cited in Pettenati & Cigognini, 2007). Moreover, the

Figure 1. A sample diagram of egocentric network (Abraham, 2010)

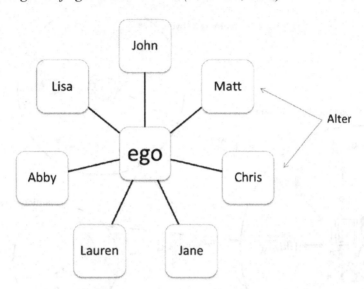

overall view of the Personal Learning Environment resembles the diagram of the personal network (See Figure 2).

Thus, personal network analysis is the most suitable method to show the network between the core member and other personnel, and also the most effective factor between the nodes.

For evaluating the Personal Learning Environment (PLE), social software sites, communication, and Web pages are the place to collect personal networks (Fielding, Lee, & Blank, 2008). Using personal network analysis, researchers are able to know the frequency of social network site usage and how much the members feel supported by the Web community. Referring to Boase's study, transferring a node from the 'people' to 'website or Web 2.0' (Hogan, 2008) would be a method to evaluate over Personal Learning Environment. Typically, the personal networks studied are often small ranging from 2-30 people with the strongest connection to the person at the center. Thus, analysts rarely use fancy network analytic techniques such as UNICET or Pajek. Instead, the researchers often use the more prosaic and less structural SPSS (Muller, et al., 1999; as cited in Wellman, 2007). For those readers who want to learn more about

social network analysis software, please refer to the additional reading section. The methods for data collection usually include surveys, interviews, and use of site databases (Boase, 2008; Fu, 2005; Hogan, 2008; Wellman, 2007).

Survey based collection is usually used for larger samples. They usually ask the participants to rate certain network members or other artifacts that seem to be close. Since surveys are generally large, the researchers usually do not analyze the whole personal network, but only the close network of the actor (Wellman, 2007). Boase (2008) used Pew Internet and American Life Project's Social Ties Survey (Boase, 2006) to investigate personal networks in use of communication technology. Social Ties Survey asked respondents to report the number of people with whom they "feel very close" to in a variety of relational roles, and then to report the number of people with whom they "feel somewhat close" in the same relational roles. In the case of the Personal Learning Environments, 'people' could be changed to the social capital, which would be artifacts from the other persons; Facebook, Twitter, Google document, etc.

Interviews can be given to gather additional details, which can be added to the survey. Oth-

Figure 2. Overview of an exemplar personal learning environment (Wilson, 2008)

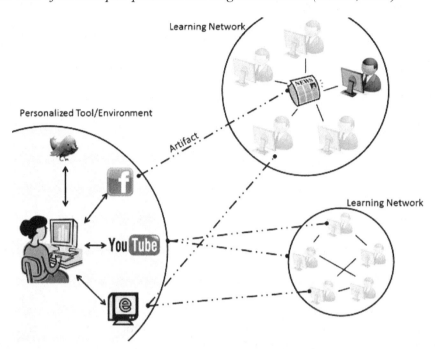

erwise, it could be used as a form of 'name generator' (Wellman, 2007). Examples of the name generator used in this view can be "Over the last six months, who are the people with whom you discussed matters important to you?"(Boase, 2008) That is, it does not give the list of the artifacts (or website), but asks the participant directly to think of the first thing that came up to their minds.

Database of the Site (Hogan (2008)) illustrated the way of collecting data from social software sites. One of the methods was to use the Application Program Interface (API), which can 'scrape' a page directly and extract the list of friends. With this method, the researcher was able to see the linking between the users in the site. Facebook also can provide some applications, which can illustrate the personal network of the site (see Figure 3).

Varied studies for developing the program that is collecting data from Web 2.0, personal blogs, and emails are also being introduced. These are still in the developmental phase; however, this could be another potential method by which to gather the data for personal network analysis. The program also features showing the egocentric network diagram for the users (Ching-Yung, Ehrlich, Griffiths-Fisher, & Desforges, 2008; Ehrlich, Lin, & Griffiths-Fisher, 2007).

Recommendations

The presence of social capital in personal social networks has been linked to a number of learning outcomes, including educational achievement, educational attainment, and other academic and psycho-social outcomes (Dika & Singh, 2002). Despite the burgeoning literature on network-based informal learning that spans numerous disciplines; few studies have utilized network measures of this construct within the field of education. The goal of this chapter is to define the key indicators for the maintenance and formation of social capital in social networks drawn from network-based approaches and to determine how these indicators may be used to measure social capital in Personal Learning Environments.

Figure 3. Example of the social network diagram generate by Facebook application

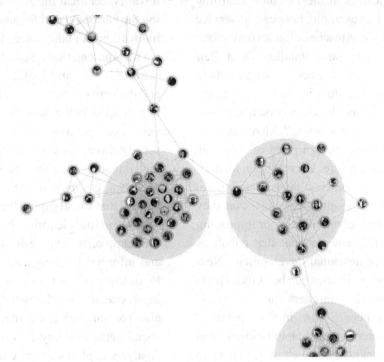

Based on our discussion on social capital theory and social network analysis approaches, we recommend to use the personalized network analysis via survey, interview, and database site to examine the relations, ties, and network structures in Personal Learning Environments. We also recommend examining the following social capital indicators in Personal Learning Environments from the perspective of the subcategories of the structural aspect and those of the relational aspect of the social capital theory.

Recommended indicators from structural dimensions:

- **Network Size**: The number of people with whom we maintain different types of relationships
- **Network Density**: The degree of interconnections among the members of a network
- **Network Diversity**: Heterogeneity of the backgrounds of members or, the type of organizations

Recommended indicators from relational dimensions:

- **Relationship Frequency**: The number and duration of contacts among the members of a network (e.g. collective social capital)
- **Relational Intensity**: The strength and nature of a relationship in terms of emotional investment
- **Spatial Proximity of Members**: Members with whom we maintain face-to-face relationships on a regular basis

FUTURE RESEARCH DIRECTIONS

The current literature suggests that to study the learning outcomes in the Personal Learning Environments requires the researchers to decide on the focus of the study; in the future, researcher are encouraged to investigate the structural dimension or relational dimension to address the key components of indicators in the Personal Learning Environments. For example, how can in-service professionals, such as teachers, nurses or doctors, work to gain a better understanding about their own learning from their practices with the help of social capital indicators in their learning, the leading resources, and the main person to whom they will go for their learning? Also, research from the instructional design point-of-view can be conducted in the future. For example, instructional design researchers can investigate how to apply instructional design theories so that they may meet the needs of maintaining or improving a personal learning environment that enhances an individual's professional development. New instructional design theories can be derived from empirical studies if researchers can understand thoroughly how people learn in their personal learning environments. Social capital and personal social network analysis can help researchers to start this kind of research.

CONCLUSION

This chapter explores social capital approach in order to more fully investigate the network that constitutes a Personal Learning Environment (PLE). More importantly, we seek to introduce possible indicators to measure the structural/relational aspects of the networks so that we might understand what role social capital plays in facilitating dynamics between personal learning networks.

We started this inquiry with the question "Why are some informal learning networks more successful in achieving innovation than others?" In an environment where knowledge is the main drive of the organization, it is very challenging to facilitate and support social dimension to enable knowledge productivity in the field of learning and development (Harrison & Kessels, 2004). While the current debate about innovations in terms of knowledge productivity is still strongly biased towards technical innovation, thereby overlooking the various social features of networks where innovation can take place. To explore this issue, we recommend that researchers and educators to start searching and looking at the social capital and the network theory to investigate the innovation process in the day-to-day personal learning networks. Social capital is a valuable indicator of social networks based on shared norms, values, and understanding that facilitate cooperation within or among groups (OECD, 2001). Therefore, we believe that social capital theory offers a new perspective to study learning that leads to innovation; for example, it can move professional development and informal learning away from an individual focus towards a network focus in studying learning processes and knowledge productivity. We also recommend some measures suggested by social network analysis theory. Social Network Analysis explains social changes by examining the social networks between people or artifacts (Hogan, 2008; Vera & Schupp, 2006). Specifically using personal network analysis, which focuses on the personal part of the social network, it helps evaluating the achievement of the social capital in Personal Learning Environment. For example, researchers or participants can see the frequency of social network site usage and how much the members feel supported by the Web community by using this type of analysis. This will eventually enable researchers to see what artifact and what type of Personal Learning Environment effects more on the informal learning (Wilson, 2008).

The indicators addressed in this chapter may contribute to further research in order to study the relationship between social networks, social capital, and knowledge productivity in practice from the student-centered learning perspective. In addition, this will provide an academic basis for practitioners within educational institutions who seek to both improve the quality of social networks and enhance social capital in order to stimulate knowledge productivity among personal learning networks; similarly, this will guide individual learners from various environments who are interested in their increasingly flexible and distributed lifelong learning experiences.

REFERENCES

Abraham, A. (2010). *Computational social network analysis: Trends, tools and research advances*. New York, NY: Springer.

Adamic, L. A., Zhang, J., Bakshy, E., & Ackerman, M. S. (2008). *Knowledge sharing and yahoo answers: Everyone knows something*. Paper presented at the Proceeding of the 17th international conference on World Wide Web. Beijing, China.

Adler, P. S., & Kwon, S. W. (2002). Social capital: Prospects for a new concept. *Academy of Management Review*, *27*(1), 17–40.

Ahuja, G. (2000). Collaboration networks, structural holes, and innovation: A longitudinal study. *Administrative Science Quarterly*, *45*(3), 425–455. doi:10.2307/2667105

Arora, A., & Gambardella, A. (1990). Complementarity and external linkages: The strategies of the large firms in biotechnology. *The Journal of Industrial Economics*, *38*(4), 361–379. doi:10.2307/2098345

Baum, J., Calabrese, T., & Silverman, B. (2000). Don't go it alone: Alliance network composition and startups' performance in Canadian bio-technology. *Strategic Management Journal*, *21*(3), 267–294. doi:10.1002/(SICI)1097-0266(200003)21:3<267::AID-SMJ89>3.0.CO;2-8

Berg, S., Duncan, J., & Friedman, P. (1982). *Joint venture and corporate innovation*. Cambridge, MA: Oelgeschlager, Gunn & Hain.

Boase, J. (2008). Personal networks and the personal communication system. *Information Communication and Society*, *11*(4), 490–508. doi:10.1080/13691180801999001

Boase, J., Horrigan, J., Wellman, B., & Rainie, L. (2006). The strength of internet ties. *Pew Internet & American Life Project*. Retrieved from http://www.pewinternet.org/Reports/2006/The-Strength-of-Internet-Ties.aspx.

Boase, J., & Wellman, B. (2004). *Suggested questions on social networks and social capital*. Paper presented to the Policy Research Initiative. Ottawa, Canada.

Bourdieu, P. (1986). The forms of capital. In Richardson, J. (Ed.), *Handbook of Theory and Research for the Sociology of Education* (pp. 241–258). New York, NY: Greenwood.

Bourdieu, P., & Wacquant, L. J. D. (1992). *An invitation to reflexive sociology*. Chicago, IL: University of Chicago Press.

Burt, R. (1992). *Structural holes: The social structure of competition*. Cambridge, MA: Harvard University Press.

Burt, R. (1997). The contingent value of social capital. *Administrative Science Quarterly*, *42*(2), 339–365. doi:10.2307/2393923

Burt, R. S. (2000). The network structure of social capital. *Research in Organizational Behavior*, *22*, 345–423. doi:10.1016/S0191-3085(00)22009-1

Burt, R. S. (2004). Structural holes and good ideas. *American Journal of Sociology*, *110*(2), 349–399. doi:10.1086/421787

Casquero, O., Portillo, J., Ovelar, R., Benito, M., & Romo, J. (2010). iPLE network: An integrated eLearning 2.0 strategy from university's perspective. *Interactive Learning Environments*, *18*(3), 293–308. doi:10.1080/10494820.2010.500553

Chan, K., & Liebowitz, J. (2006). The synergy of social network analysis and knowledge mapping: A case study. *International Journal of Management and Decision Making, 7*(1), 19–35. doi:10.1504/IJMDM.2006.008169

Ching-Yung, L., Ehrlich, K., Griffiths-Fisher, V., & Desforges, C. (2008). SmallBlue: People mining for expertise search. *IEEE MultiMedia, 15*(1), 78–84. doi:10.1109/MMUL.2008.17

Christakis, N., & Fowler, J. (2009). *Connected: The surprising power of our social networks and how they shape our lives.* New York, NY: Little, Brown & Co.

Claridge, T. (2004). *Social capital and natural resource management.* Unpublished Master Thesis. Brisbane, Australia: University of Queensland.

Coleman, J. S. (1988). Social capital in the creation of human capital. *American Journal of Sociology, 94*, 95–120. doi:10.1086/228943

de Jong, T. (2010). *Linking social capital to knowledge productivity.* Master's Thesis. Retrieved from http://josephkessels.com/sites/default/files/thesis_t_de_jong.pdf.

Dika, S. L., & Singh, K. (2002). Applications of social capital in educational literature: A critical synthesis. *Review of Educational Research, 72*(1), 31–60. doi:10.3102/00346543072001031

Durland, M. M., Fredericks, K. A., & American Evaluation Association. (2006). *Social network analysis in program evaluation.* San Francisco, CA: Jossey-Bass.

Ehrlich, K., Lin, C.-Y., & Griffiths-Fisher, V. (2007). Searching for experts in the enterprise: Combining text and social network analysis. In *Proceedings of the 2007 International ACM Conference on Supporting Group Work.* ACM Press.

Erickson, B. H. (2004). The distribution of gendered social capital in Canada. In Flap, H., & Volker, B. (Eds.), *Creation and Returns of Social Capital a New Research Program* (pp. 27–50). London, UK: Routledge.

Fielding, N., Lee, R. M., & Blank, G. (2008). *The Sage handbook of online research methods.* Thousand Oaks, CA: Sage.

Fu, Y. (2005). Measuring personal networks with daily contacts: A single-item survey question and the contact diary. *Social Networks, 27*(3), 169–186. doi:10.1016/j.socnet.2005.01.008

Gargiulo, M., & Benassi, M. (2000). Trapped in your own net? Network cohesion, structural holes, and the adaptation of social capital. *Organization Science, 11*(2), 183–196. doi:10.1287/orsc.11.2.183.12514

Garton, L., & Wellman, B. (1999). Studying online social networks. *Doing Internet Research: Critical Issues and Methods for Examining the Net, 75.*

Granovetter, M. (1973). The strength of weak ties. *American Journal of Sociology, 78*(6), 1360–1380. doi:10.1086/225469

Granovetter, M. S. (1982). The strength of weak ties: A network theory revisited. In Mardsen, P. V., & Lin, N. (Eds.), *Social Structure and Network Analysis* (pp. 105–130). Thousand Oaks, CA: Sage Publications. doi:10.2307/202051

Gray, B. (2004). Informal learning in an online community of practice. *Journal of Distance Education, 19*(1), 20–35.

Greenhow, C. (2011). Online social networks and learning. *Horizon, 19*(1), 4–12. doi:10.1108/10748121111107663

Greenhow, C., & Robelia, E. (2009). Old communication, new literacies: Social network sites as social learning resources. *Journal of Computer-Mediated Communication, 14*(4), 1130–1161. doi:10.1111/j.1083-6101.2009.01484.x

Greenhow, C., & Robelia, E. (2009b). Informal learning and identity formation in online social networks. *Learning, Media and Technology, 34*(2), 119–140. doi:10.1080/17439880902923580

Gulati, R., & Gargiulo, M. (1999). Where do interorganizational networks come from? *American Journal of Sociology, 104*(5), 1439–1493. doi:10.1086/210179

Harrison, R., & Kessels, J. W. M. (2004). *Human resource development in a knowledge economy: An organizational view*. New York, NY: Palgrave Macmillan.

Haythornthwaite, C. (1996). Social network analysis: An approach and technique for the study of information exchange. *Library & Information Science Research, 18*(4), 323–342. doi:10.1016/S0740-8188(96)90003-1

Hogan, B. (2008). Analyzing social networks via the Internet. In *The SAGE Handbook of Online Research Methods* (pp. 141–160). Thousand Oaks, CA: Sage.

Johnson, M., & Liber, O. (2008). The personal learning environment and the human condition: From theory to teaching practice. *Interactive Learning Environments, 16*, 3–15. doi:10.1080/10494820701772652

Kilduff, M., & Tsai, W. (2003). *Social networking in organizations*. London, UK: Sage.

Kostova, T., & Roth, K. (2002). Social capital in multinational corporations and a micro-macro model for its formation. *Academy of Management Review, 28*(2), 297–317.

Lin, N., Cook, K., & Burt, R. (2001). *Social capital: Theory and research*. New York, NY: Walter de Gruyter.

Mika, P. (2007). *Social networks and the semantic web*. Doctoral Dissertation. Retrieved from http://dare.ubvu.vu.nl/bitstream/1871/13263/5/7915.pdf.

Nahapiet, J., & Ghoshal, S. (1998). Social capital, intellectual capital and the organizational advantage. *Academy of Management Review, 23*(2), 242–266.

OECD. (2001). *The well-being of nation: The role of human and social capital*. Paris, France: OECD.

Oh, W., Choi, J. N., & Kim, K. (2006). Coauthorship dynamics and knowledge capital: The patterns of cross-disciplinary collaboration in information systems research. *Journal of Management Information Systems, 22*(3), 265–292. doi:10.2753/MIS0742-1222220309

Otte, E., & Rousseau, R. (2002). Social network analysis: A powerful strategy, also for the information sciences. *Journal of Information Science, 28*(6), 441–453. doi:10.1177/016555150202800601

Pettenati, M., & Cigognini, M. (2007). Social networking theories and tools to support connectivist learning activities. *International Journal of Web-Based Learning and Teaching Technologies, 2*(3), 42–60. doi:10.4018/jwltt.2007070103

Putnam, R. D. (2000). *Bowling alone*. New York, NY: Simon & Schuster.

Reagans, R., & Zuckerman, E. (2008). Why knowledge does not equal power: The network redundancy trade-off. *Industrial and Corporate Change, 17*(5), 903–944. doi:10.1093/icc/dtn036

Reid, N., & Smith, B. W. (2009). Social network analysis. *Economic Development Journal, 8*(3), 48–55.

Reverin, S. (2008). Sustaining an online community of practice: A case study. *Journal of Distance Education, 22*(2), 45–58.

Robison, L. J., Schmid, A. A., & Siles, M. E. (2002). Is social capital really capital? *Review of Social Economy, 60*, 1–24. doi:10.1080/00346760110127074

Ross, M. B., & Welsh, M. P. (2007). Formative feedback to improve learning on a teacher education degree using a personal learning environment. *International Journal of Emerging Technologies in Learning, 2*(3), 1–7.

Severance, C., Hardin, J., & Whyte, A. (2008). The coming functionality mash-up in personal learning environments. *Interactive Learning Environments, 16*(1), 9–14. doi:10.1080/10494820701772694

Shen, D., Nuankhieo, P., Huang, X., Amelung, C., & Laffey, J. (2008). Using social network analysis to understand sense of community in an online learning environment. *Journal of Educational Computing Research, 39*(1), 17–36. doi:10.2190/EC.39.1.b

Stuart, T., & Podolny, J. (1999). Positional consequences of strategic alliances in the semiconductor industry. In Knoke, D. (Ed.), *Research in the Sociology of Organizations* (pp. 161–182). Greenwich, CT: JAI Press.

Valente, T. W., Gallaher, P., & Mouttapa, M. (2004). Using social networks to understand and prevent substance use: A transdisciplinary perspective. *Substance Use & Misuse, 39*(10-12), 1685–1712. doi:10.1081/JA-200033210

Van Cleemput, K. (2010). I'll see you on IM, text, or call you: A social network approach of adolescents' use of communication media. *Bulletin of Science, Technology & Society, 30*(2), 75–85. doi:10.1177/0270467610363143

van Duijn, M. A. J., & Vermunt, J. K. (2006). What is special about social network analysis methodology. *European Journal of Research Methods for the Behavioral and Social Sciences, 2*(1), 2–6. doi:10.1027/1614-2241.2.1.2

Vera, E. R., & Schupp, T. (2006). Network analysis in comparative social sciences. *Comparative Education, 42*(3), 405–429. doi:10.1080/03050060600876723

Walker, G., Kogut, B., & Shan, W. (1997). Social capital, structural holes and the formation of an industry network. *Organization Science, 8*(2), 109–125. doi:10.1287/orsc.8.2.109

Wasserman, S., & Faust, K. (1994). *Social network analysis: Methods and applications.* Cambridge, UK: Cambridge University Press.

Wellman, B. (1996). Are personal communities local? A dumptarian reconsideration. *Social Networks, 18*(3), 347–354. doi:10.1016/0378-8733(95)00282-0

Wellman, B. (2007). The network is personal: Introduction to a special issue of social networks. *Social Networks, 29*(3), 349–356. doi:10.1016/j.socnet.2007.01.006

Wenger, E. (2006). *Communities of practice: A brief introduction.* Retrieved from http://www.ewenger.com/theory/.

Wilson, S. (2008). Patterns of personal learning environments. *Learning Environments, 16*(1), 17–34. doi:10.1080/10494820701772660

Wilson, S., Liber, O., Johnson, M., Beauvoir, P., Sharples, P., & Milligan, C. (2007). Personal learning environments: Challenging the dominant design of educational systems. *Journal of e-Learning and Knowledge Society, 2*(3), 27-38. Retreived from http://je-lks.maieutiche.economia.unitn.it/index.php/Je-LKS_EN/article/viewFile/247/229.

ADDITIONAL READING

Attwell, G. (2007). The personal learning environments - The future of eLearning? *eLearning Papers, 2*(1). Retrieved from http://citeseerx.ist.psu.edu/viewdoc/download?doi=10.1.1.97.3011&rep=rep1&type=pdf.

Batagelj, V., & Mrvar, A. (2003). Pajek-analysis and visualization of large networks. In Jünger, M., & Mutzel, P. (Eds.), *Graph Drawing Software* (pp. 77–103). Berlin, Germany: Springer.

Dawley, L. (2009). Social network knowledge construction: Emerging virtual world pedagogy. *Horizon*, *17*(2), 109–121. doi:10.1108/10748120910965494

Favell, A. (1993). James Coleman: Social theorist and moral philosopher. *American Journal of Sociology*, *99*(3), 590–613. doi:10.1086/230317

Freeman, L. C. (2004). *The development of social network analysis: A study in the sociology of science*. North Charleston, VA: Empirical Press.

Gillet, D., Law, E. L.-C., & Chatterjee, A. (2010). Personal learning environments in a global higher engineering education web 2.0 realm. In *Proceedings of Education Engineering 2010 IEEE*, (pp. 897-906). IEEE Press.

Huisman, M., & van Duijn, M. A. J. (2005). Software for social network analysis. In Carrington, P. J., Scott, J., & Wasserman, S. (Eds.), *Models and Methods in Social Network Analysis* (pp. 270–316). Cambridge, UK: Cambridge University Press.

Johnson, M., & Liber, O. (2008). The personal learning environment and the human condition: From theory to teaching practice. *Interactive Learning Environments*, *6*(1), 3–15. doi:10.1080/10494820701772652

Lin, N. (2001). *Social capital: A theory of social structure and action*. Cambridge, UK: Cambridge University Press.

Lin, N., Cook, K. S., & Burt, R. S. (2001). *Social capital: Theory and research*. New York, NY: Aldine de Gruyter.

Narayan, D., & Cassidy, M. F. (2001). A dimensional approach to measuring social capital: Development and validation of a social capital inventory. *Current Sociology*, *49*(2), 59–102. doi:10.1177/0011392101049002006

Pajek. (2009). *Networks/Pajek*. Retrieved from http://vlado.fmf.uni-lj.si/pub/networks/pajek/.

Portes, A. (1998). Social capital: Its origins and applications in modern sociology. *Annual Review of Sociology*, *24*(1), 1–25. doi:10.1146/annurev.soc.24.1.1

Portes, A. (2000). Social capital: Promise and pitfalls of its role in development. *Journal of Latin American Studies*, *32*(2), 529–548. doi:10.1017/S0022216X00005836

Portes, A., & Patricia, L. (1996). The downside of social capital. *The American Prospect*, *26*, 18–23.

Putnam, R. D. (1993). The prosperous community: Social capital and public life. *The American Prospect*, *13*(2), 35–42.

Putnam, R. D. (1995). Bowling alone: America's declining social capital. *Journal of Democracy*, *6*(1), 65–78. doi:10.1353/jod.1995.0002

Sclater, N. (2008). Web 2.0, personal learning environments, and the future of learning management systems. *EDUCAUSE Center for Applied Research Research*, *13*. Retrieved from http://pages.uoregon.edu/not/LMS/future%20of%20LMSs.pdf.

Scott, J. (1996). A toolkit for social network analysis. *Acta Sociologica*, *39*(2), 211–216. doi:10.1177/000169939603900205

Severance, C., Hardin, J., & Whyte, A. (2008). The coming functionality mash-up in personal learning environments. *Interactive Learning Environments*, *6*(1), 47–62. doi:10.1080/10494820701772694

UCINET. (2009). *UCINET*. Retrieved from http://www.analytictech.com/ucinet/.

Wasserman, S., & Faust, K. (1994). *Social network analysis: Methods and applications*. Cambridge, UK: Cambridge University Press.

KEY TERMS AND DEFINITIONS

Personal Learning Environment: An environment where individual learners can utilize any tools, person or resources available to create meaningful learning and to be engaged in social activities.

Social Network Analysis: An analysis that evaluates the relationship between the people or artifacts.

Personal Social Network Analysis: Evaluating the network having one person as a central of the relationship.

Degree: Number of relation between the people. (How many times did they collaborate?)

Centrality: Shows whether the person is in the center of the network.

Closeness: Shows whether the links are direct or whether it should go through several persons.

Betweenness: Similar to closeness, also shows the degree of each node's tie.

Social Capital: The sum of the actual and latent resources that actors derive from certain social structure as the web of cooperative relationship.

Network Closure: Social structures promoting a normative environment that enhance trust and cooperation among actors in the presence of cohesive ties.

Structural Holes: Gaps in which there are no current connections, but that can be possibly connected by 'brokers' who thereby control the flow of interaction across gaps.

Bonding: Connections, which closely tie among those who have a very similar background.

Bridging: Connections, which bring people with a shared interest from fairly similar backgrounds.

Linking: Connections, which bring people from dissimilar backgrounds.

Chapter 6
Linguistic Aspects of Informal Learning in Corporate Online Social Networks

Magdalena Bielenia-Grajewska

University of Gdansk, Poland & Scuola Internazionale Superiore di Studi Avanzati, Italy

ABSTRACT

This chapter discusses the role of corporate online social networks in the process of informal learning. The first part of these studies offers some introduction to the issue of online social networks used in the corporate setting. The second component of the investigation is dedicated to discussing the notion of informal learning in online social networks. To limit the scope of the research, in the subsequent sections the author concentrates on the linguistic aspect of spontaneous and unofficial education acquired online by corporate members. To discuss these issues in greater detail, the concepts of homophilous and heterophilous networks in corporate online learning will be presented and discussed.

INTRODUCTION

Modern times are very dynamic, with changes and flows (i.e., circulations of material and non-material entities) determining one's life course (Papastergiadis, 2000). The latter can be divided into capital flows, information flows, technology flows, and know-how flows (Coskun Samli,

2002) or, similarly, into flows of capital, flows of information, flows of technology, flows of organizational interaction, flows of images, sounds, and symbols (Castells, 2010). Another term used to describe the mobility of entities in the twenty first century is *the object in motion*, a concept that encompasses the portability of ideas, ideologies, people, goods, images, and messages as well as technologies and techniques (Appadurai, 2001).

DOI: 10.4018/978-1-4666-1815-2.ch006

This chapter focuses specifically on technology, which is not only one of the flows, but also the factor responsible for creating, maintaining, and catalyzing other flows. Moreover, technology is responsible for limiting or lowering the weight of entities since it has enabled a virtual rather than physical transport of ideas, people, and goods (Ritzer, 2010a).

Narrowing this discussion to the role of Information Technology (IT) in the corporate environment, it is IT that influences the flows of workers, money, ideas, services and goods in terms of both quality and quantity. The Internet is "an electronic Klondike, a new gold rush for all sorts of companies" (Rosenoer, Amstrong, & Gates, 1999, p. 15), which offers many business opportunities for all types of corporations and firms. Among these opportunities is the possibility of engaging more workers in the process of product design and organizational change as well as providing effective information input into the company (DiMaggio, 2001). New information technologies offer this possibility of attracting and involving more employees in organizational processes, regardless of their geographical location. Moreover, the Web is an important space where identity, both professional and social, is created and maintained (e.g. Holt, 2004). Simultaneously, technology is one of the most important factors shaping organizational identity (Carr, 2004; Fernandez, 2004). Thus, the modern tools of online communication influence the way the organizational personae is shaped, sustained, and perceived.

It should be noted that the relationship between technology and organizations is symbiotic. Because the attitude toward technology reflects organizational culture (Jex, 2002), the choice of online communication tools available to those participating in corporate communication is a commentary on the values, opinions and artifacts that create the organization's corporate identity. The selection of online communication methods also depends on the level of online communication: virtual social networks, online communities,

virtual teams and organization as well as computer-mediated communication (Panteli, 2009). Since the increasing popularity of social media is visible in private and professional spheres, the author aims to discuss the role of social networking in organizational life by showing how the companies operating in the Facebook Era (Shih, 2010) benefit from social networking in various corporate activities, including knowledge creation and distribution.

ONLINE SOCIAL NETWORKS

In the past, the Internet was mainly used for one way communication (i.e., presentation of information), whereas nowadays it is a place of dialogue and interaction, with the user acting not only as the reader, but also as the author (Jung, 2010), and not only as the receiver, but also as the co-creator, or even the *prosumer* (Ritzer, 2010b), who produces and consumes simultaneously. This change in the position of individuals acting online is related to the possibility of many people interacting at the same time (Servon, 2002), simultaneously as passive recipients and active creators of online content. The possibility of active participation in the information superhighway has shifted many formerly face-to-face social activities into cyberspace and has catalyzed the proliferation of new social networks.

ONLINE SOCIAL NETWORKS: HISTORY AND BASIC CHARACTERISTICS

The first Online Social Networks (OSNs) appeared in 1979 (Bhulyan, Josang, & Xu, 2010) and since that time such networks have been an important part of modern life. Online social networks have been defined as "a Web site that encourages members in its online community to share their interest, ideas, stories, photos, music, and videos with other registered users" (Shelly & Vermaat, 2011, p. 202). Considering the relationship between personal and public dimensions, OSNs differ from other technological innovations since in the past new technologies were the result of work-related activities, whereas nowadays online social networks first influence the private life and later shape the professional sphere (Shih, 2010).

Online social networks developed and grew in popularity for several reasons. First, social networks allow the user to concentrate more on the personal sphere, whereas other tools of online communication are more content-directed. Second, the motivation for creating communities has changed. In the past geographical proximity was of primary importance, whereas nowadays common interests and goals constitute the main determinants of people choosing groups (e.g. Doktorowicz, 2003; McPherson, Lovin, & Cook, 2001). As far as the reasons for joining networks are concerned, people engage in such groupings to get support, to express oneself, to gain popularity, to share knowledge (Ala-Mutka, Punie, & Ferrari, 2009), and to realize the need of belonging (Ma & Yuen, 2011; Preece, 2000). Moreover, online networks in most cases offer unlimited access to their sources (Powazek, 2002). Health-related online networks for patients, their families and friends are one example of online networking; their popularity is connected with a multitude of simultaneous functions (e.g. offering sympathy, advice and information) and a vast array of users simultaneously benefiting from them (e.g. patients, doctors, and medicine producers). The mentioned diversity of grouping as well as the proliferation of group functions cannot be found in traditional communities (Greene, et al., 2010).

Another important feature of social networks is the ability to track the information flow since all members have the potential to see participants' online interactions as they unfold (Bambina, 2007). At the same time, the asynchronous character of social media makes it possible for each person to decide when to visit the online network and engage in on-going discussions (Pitta & Fowler, 2005). The user is not restricted by any timetables or time limits as far as entering the network is concerned.

Additionally, the lack of technological barriers reduces geographical, political, and cultural distance (Gannon, 2008), and, consequently, the access to useful resources is provided regardless of geographical location or time (Bambina, 2007). Taking into account the characteristics of social networking, traditional networks are often substituted with the online ones (Monge & Contractor, 2003). In addition to these already discussed features of online networks that differentiate them from face-to-face groups, the dynamism of the twenty-first century also influences the popularity of virtual communities.

Individuals exist in fluid times (Bauman, 2003) and the change from *solids* to *liquids* (Ritzer, 2011), visible in the increased mobility of people and things, leads to the intensified performance of people, in both the private and the social sphere. Modern liquid individuals not only change their physical location very often, but they are also more eager to adapt to changes and accept novelties. Moreover, this liquidity determines modern identity that is not given once and forever, is not fixed and stable (e.g. Papacharissi, 2011; Tosoni, 2008), and can be chosen according to one's needs and preferences (Magala, 2003). Moreover, postmodern identity is rather contradictory. Taking into account the amount of data to which individuals are exposed, people are hyper-socialized because they are confronted with more messages than they can readily understand or utilize. At the same time, they are hypo-socialized since they do not have the access to normative social environments (Mantovani, 1995), the ones that will help them to navigate in the jungle of everyday issues. Thus, modern sources, although rich in messages, do not provide the user with the answers to the questions regarding e.g. morality and proper behavior.

Additionally, there are certain features of online identities that influence social networking. For example, taking into account the fact that face-to-face communication is absent in virtual contacts, it allows the user to mask or change his or her identity (Brey & Søraker, 2009; Burnett, Consalvo, & Ess, 2010; Wallace, 2001). Thus, this type of personae requires more effort on the recipient side to discover the real characteristics and the true intentions of the identity "owner." Consequently, social networks that enable the active participation in information exchanges are not only the efficient tool of identity creation and maintenance, but also the powerful instrument of personae control and correction.

Online social networking has been a popular research topic in the social sciences as well as professional fields; this phenomenon has been investigated in politics (e.g. Di Bari, 2010; Gargiulo, 2010; Vergeer, Hermans, & Sams, 2011), marketing (e.g. Foglio, 2010; Prunesti, 2010a), advertising (Di Bari, 2010), as well as professional and business contacts (e.g. Cutillo, Manulis, & Strufe, 2010; Prunesti, 2010b). Since individuals deal with companies on everyday basis as customers, workers or stakeholders, in the next parts of this chapter attention will be focused on the role of social networking in organizational environments.

ONLINE SOCIAL NETWORKS IN ORGANIZATIONS

Online social networks are popular in corporate settings for a number of reasons. First, corporate social networking speeds up the communication process. Online social networks allow companies to communicate quickly with workers as well as with stakeholders (Guffey, 2010), especially when more traditional forms of contact would be difficult, expensive or impossible. Second, due to the low cost of adding and changing information in online environments (Cantoni & Tardini, 2010; Lipsey, Fischer, & Poirier, 2007) and the ability to interact with others and share information having minimal technological expertise (De

Choudhury, et al., 2010), social networks are an attractive form of communication for a great number of stakeholders (Blanchard, 2011; Kerpen, 2011; Lagioni, 2004) and can readily help companies to reach niche markets (Bosman & Zagenczyk, 2011). Moreover, they are used in e.g. viral marketing to strengthen the brand awareness by people disseminating information among the network members (Pastore & Vernuccio, 2008). Third, since they offer their users the possibility to meet various needs, such as sharing interests and exchanging opinions as well as having entertainment and fun (Buzzo, 2007), they manage to attract various stakeholders for a considerably extensive amount of time and in various moments of their daily activities.

Additionally, online social media offer people and corporations lacking standard media coverage the possibilities of attracting public attention (Vergeer, Hermans, & Sams, 2011). Thus, the companies that cannot afford media campaigns due to financial reasons or that are not in the centre of attention of regular mass media can run online networks to inform the customers and potential stakeholders about their activities. Moreover, social networking proves to be very useful in crisis situation, e.g. when telephone lines are overloaded or when the access to other modes of communication such as television or radio is limited or unavailable due to e.g. language barrier. They are used for example in aviation industry to inform passengers about delays caused by bad weather, strikes or natural disasters (Bielenia-Grajewska, 2011).

Apart from the organizational dimension of networking, the economic sphere of social contacts is also visible at the individual level since it helps in personal branding, which is especially useful when one is looking for a job (Salpeter, 2011; Schepp & Schepp, 2010). For example, there are various online networks that gather professionals and provide information about their expertise. Moreover, the ones active in various discussion groups or other online networks may post a job add themselves in their profile. However, it should be stated that wrong behavior in online networks can blight chances for professional success. For example, vulgar statements or morally dubious pictures that accompany one's profile may destroy the chance of employment or promotion. The role of social media in the economic reality can be summarized in the following words:

relationships are the ultimate source of advantage, the new heavy-weight champion of the marketing ring. Social media, however, is the champ's head trainer (Meyerson, 2010, p. 4).

Thus, social networking is responsible for different relations in corporate settings since it determines various aspects of organizational life, including corporate learning. One aspect of organizational education, namely, informal learning, will be discussed in the next section.

INFORMAL LEARNING: BASIC CHARACTERISTICS

Learning is an indispensable part of social life, connected with being part of a community; by acquiring new information one learns also how to function in a given grouping (Brown & Duguid, 1991). Additionally, learning is a transactional type of activity, with learners and environment evolving together (Hager & Halliday, 2009), and, consequently, it is continuously responding to the changes in the background as well as the changing needs and characteristics of the participants. Additionally, it appears when one exploits other experiences, attitudes as well as their interpretations, in both formal as well as informal learning (Nelkner, Magenheim, & Reinhard, 2009). In other words, it is informal learning that occurs outside the bounds of structured or classroom experiences. A general definition of informal learning would describe it as the type of skill acquisition, which results from the experience related to having contacts with other people and things (Wain, 2004). Informal learning has also been categorized as "just-in-time and just the amount necessary to put to immediate use" (Mason & Rennie, 2007, p. 197) and as "a style of learning that allows the student to learn at his or her own pace" (Tomei, 2010, p. 120). According to other scholars, informal learning is experiential and non-institutional (Marsick & Volpe, 1999; Marsick & Watkins, 1990), initiated by the learner (Carliner, 2004) who is responsible for the learning process (Ala-Mutka, Punie, & Ferrari, 2009; Attwell, 2009). This learning process often happens subconsciously, without the learner knowing that he or she is acquiring new skills (Marsick & Watkins, 1990).

It should be noted that the success of unofficial training depends on several determinants, with the type of community being one of them. Closed communities have the advantage of trust and effectiveness, whereas open networks have the primacy of diversity and innovativeness (Ala-Mutka, Punie, & Ferrari, 2009). These characteristics determine the process of informal learning; people belonging to communities with restricted access are more likely to believe in the knowledge disseminated by group members than trust the data provided by those outside the group. Since an individual's attitude toward recommendations and opinions received via the Internet is connected to the network level of trust (Bhulyan, Josang, & Xu, 2010), virtual environments (e.g., those with no face-to-face feedback), especially value a high degree of reliability in terms of both knowledge acquisition and dissemination. In contrast, people participating in open communities have the access to diversified and innovative information.

INFORMAL LEARNING IN CORPORATE SETTINGS

Taking into account the learning sphere in corporations, many companies would rather focus on how workers perform their duties and routines in the short term rather than concentrate on the long-lasting impact of learning, such as the infusion of innovations and ideas (Moore, 2010). Thus, social networking offers the workers, in this case corporate learners, some opportunities to share knowledge independently of the main corporate communication channel. An important feature of organizational learning is the instance of *experience traps* since companies rely on previous observations and skills, even if in the past false decisions were made (Lomi & Larsen, 1999). Thus, workers are likely to repeat known behaviors and strategies, without trying to find novel and better solutions. In this case, informal social networks offer the employees the possibility to discuss past mistakes in an informal setting, provide constructive criticism, and implement corrective procedures to mistakes. Moreover, taking into account the fact that knowledge communication requires reciprocal interaction between interlocutors often possessing fragmentary understanding of the matter (Lurati & Eppler, 2006), the informality of social networking diminishes social barriers and accelerates the eagerness of participants to exchange information, regardless of their corporate position.

The other aspect of corporate learning is related to personal features of workers and stakeholders. For example, shyness, which may be a challenge for some people in face-to-face communication (Cantoni & Piccini, 2004), is not the same kind of obstacle in online discourse; even people who are not socially skilled can create and maintain relationships in the virtual sphere (McKenna, Green, & Gleason, 2002). One of the reasons for this openness on the Web is the lack of social inhibitors that are frequently present in face-to-face evaluative interaction (Stritzke, Nguyen, & Durkin, 2004). Consequently, taking into account the online perspective, online social networks speed up the learning process of shy people (Baker & Oswald, 2010).

Another important feature of informal learning is that sharing knowledge online relies to a large

extent upon the kindness of strangers (Constant, Sproull, & Kiesler, 1996). Thus, knowledge transfer depends on whether or not unknown people will disclose information. In the case of corporate online networking, it is the task of managers to create such a corporate online identity that will make workers and stakeholders eager to participate in knowledge creation and diffusion. Additionally, it should be stressed that informal learning is also related to treating coworkers with dignity and respecting social ethics at work (Garrick, 1998). Thus, the relation between learners (individuals and groups) and the learning environment is reciprocal (Ellström, 2011) since both workers as well as the broadly understood corporate environment determine the success or failure of corporate informal learning. Learning does not exist without shared contacts since it involves the give and take process in creating and disseminating information. Those participating in learning must bear in mind that the success of knowledge creation and acquisition depends on their willingness to ask questions as well as provide answers. Since it is communication that determines new knowledge creation and dissemination (Pfeffermann & Hülsmann, 2011) as well as proper corporate climate, in the following section the attention will be focused on the linguistic side of corporate social networking.

LINGUISTIC ASPECTS OF INFORMAL LEARNING IN CORPORATE SETTINGS

Since "a modern *homo loquens* is also a *homo technologicus* who relies on technology in the process of communication" (Bielenia-Grajewska, 2012, p. 41), online media play an important role in human interactions. Some of the most popular online technologies are social media, including blogs, social networking sites, virtual social worlds, collaborative projects, content communities and virtual game worlds (Kaplan & Haenlein,

2010). As far as measuring their performance is concerned, the most often utilized social media metrics include volume, sentiment, topics, and sources. Although language as such belongs, together with demographics, outbound links and location, to the less common metrics used in measuring and monitoring social media (Barlow & Thomas, 2011), there are certain reasons why the linguistic aspect of online social networking should not be omitted in the studies on social networking. The role of language in shaping and maintaining corporate online social networks is at least threefold. Taking into account the product of learning into account, it is through language that knowledge is developed (Kimmerle, Moskaliuk, Cress, & Thiel, 2011; Wasko & Faraj, 2005) since linguistic activities accompany all actions and stages of handling information. As far as the processes of knowledge acquisition are concerned, language is an indispensable element of learning, be it formal or informal schooling, training or any other form of knowledge distribution and comprehension. Moreover, language serves as an identity marker (Scollon & Wong, 2001; Cabre Castellvi, 1997). The way in which one speaks and writes discloses information about one's personal and social personae, and about one's individual and group identity. For example, the linguistic repertoire used by the individual provides some data about his or her profession or the place occupied in the organizational hierarchy. Looking at the corporate sphere, language can be the factor determining social exclusion in workgroups, and consequently, the access or lack of access to organizational informal learning (Rainbird, et al., 2004).

Focusing the discussion solely on unofficial learning, language is not only the determinant of informal learning as such, but also constitutes the output of it. An example can be the specialized language, genre, unique corporate lingo or just new words and terms that result from informal interaction. Furthermore, informal learning may lead to some new communicative strategies at both

the organizational level and the personal stratum. As a result, organizations may benefit from both novel corporate rhetoric and individual speaker innovation (Milroy & Milroy, 1985). Taking into account the online communication, abbreviations and acronyms serve not only as a tool for condensing information, but also as an identity marker because their meaning can be often perceived only the group members (Posteguillo, 2003). An example can be FYI (For Your Information), which is only understood by those using online communication in their daily activities.

Since the peripheral positions in any community resulting from physical or social isolation determine the learning process (Brown & Duguid, 1991), it should be also remembered that language can be the decisive factor for ones occupying the central or the secondary position. For example, the workers with limited linguistic skills in the company official language have fewer possibilities to benefit from colleagues' knowledge. The same applies to the ones who find communication as such very difficult. Even if occupying central positions in the company, with an easy access to the sources of formal and informal learning, the employees with low interaction skills find it burdensome to engage in network knowledge exchange and diffusion. At the same time, even the ones in the tangential positions, but with high Willingness To Communicate (WTC), are more likely to engage in new network linkages (Cho, et al., 2007).

It should be noted that the type of language used in social networking tends to reflect the social position of the speaker. For example, people communicating in an academic or business environment rely on the conventionalized linguistic forms to mask personal language preferences (Hudson, 2010), including some elements of regional jargons, gender characteristic forms of communication and age-related expressions. Thus, companies count on standard linguistic strategies to reach a possibly vast spectrum of stakeholders. Moreover, language skills determine the selection of social media. For example, online synchronous discussions are not popular among those with low linguistic skills. The rapid nature of such discussions and their dependence on immediate response hinder their use (Fontaine & Chun, 2010). Thus, corporate online networks are very useful for the stakeholders not proficient in the official language of the company. For example, workers have time to prepare their comments or translate the ones they find difficult to understand. In result, online social networks are often the only possibility to engage in interactions for the ones avoiding corporate face-to-face communication. Since these messages can be thought over carefully and checked linguistically, the opinions or pieces of information in asynchronous interactions are often less spontaneous but tend to be more comprehensive from the language perspective. Moreover, online tools themselves often suggest some dialogue or interaction, e.g. by such comments as download, share, etc. (Tan, 2010). Consequently, the customer is not only the passive receiver of corporate news, but is also the author of information on companies since he or she can add comments, opinions, or ask questions. Taking into account the fact that asynchronous communication is less fragmentary and more focused on one topic (Kern, Ware, & Warschauer, 2008) than synchronous tools, it is very efficient in corporate exchanges with workers and stakeholders.

HOMOPHILY VS. HETEROPHILY IN ONLINE SOCIAL NETWORKS

The communicative patterns within online social networks can be discussed by the use of the concepts called *homophily* and *heterophily*. Both terms have already been employed in the discussion on communication (e.g. Rogers & Bhowmik, 1970); however, the issues of homophily and heterophily in online social networking and their implication for corporate online learning have not been covered extensively in scientific writing.

Homophily is used to describe the similarity of interlocutors, in terms of things like education, gender and social status. On the other hand, heterophily denotes the opposite, namely, the issue of dissimilarity among participants of communicative exchanges. The phenomenon of homophily is very common in human interactions since people who share similar beliefs or interests are more eager to interact with the ones who are not much different (Rogers, 1995). Thus, individuals often select homophilous partners for interaction. The reasons for choosing similar interlocutors are as follows. First of all, it is easier to start relations with the ones who share something in common since the choice of topic for conversation comes easier, the flow of exchange is often quite predictable and the goals are often easier achieved. Secondly, these collaborations offer rewards at limited emotional costs (Schaefer, Kornienko, & Fox, 2011) since due to the similarities in personalities or interests the interlocutors do not have to adapt themselves psychologically and do not suffer from the high level of stress related to communicating with strangers. Taking into account the mentioned features, the homophilous ties tend to be stronger (Brown, Broderick, & Lee, 2007), are likely to last longer and repeat when a new opportunity for collaboration appears. Homophily is related to both positive and negative conditions since it entails individuals who are successful as well as the ones who suffer from poverty. This is also in line with Schachter's statement (1959): "Misery doesn't love just any kind of company, it loves only miserable company" (p. 24). When in trouble, people favor the ability to talk to the ones in a similar situation. For example, this phenomenon can be observed among those suffering from depression (Tanis, 2007).

Schaefer, Kornienko, and Fox (2011) discuss two types of homophily, namely, *homophily through avoidance* and *homophily through withdrawal*. Homophily through avoidance occurs when individuals are excluded due to some features and that is why they stay within the group of rejected ones. The second type is related to homophily that results from not participating in social contacts due to some conditions (Schaefer, Kornienko, & Fox, 2011).

As stated earlier, homophily has different dimensions including race and ethnicity, sex and gender, age, religion, education, occupation and social class, network positions, behavior, attitudes, abilities, and beliefs and aspirations (McPherson, Lovin, & Cook, 2001). Taking into consideration the importance of technologies in modern life another dimension can be added, namely, the ability to use the Internet for both private and professional use. In this case, the Web serves as the factor for forming homophilous networks. It does not only accelerate the formation of these networks, but also can hinder relationships among similar interlocutors. For example, in the corporate sphere, access to social networking offers new possibilities of forming homophilous networks with workers and stakeholders. At the same time, these relationships do not develop when access to the Internet is not unavailable or unreliable or when the individual is not familiar with such communication tools.

It should be stated that social networking shares both the homophilous and heterophilous features. To start with homophily, it is present in online social networks since people, as in traditional communities, often prefer to connect with the ones of the same age, gender and geographical location (Mazur & Richards, 2011), although the geographical proximity is of little importance (Bisgin, Agarwal, & Xu, 2010). In the case of corporate settings, workers engage in contacts with the ones doing similar jobs, having similar skills or occupying the same level of an organizational ladder. Moreover, homophily in online social networks is more related to having common interests (Brown, Broderick, & Lee, 2007). Taking into account the categorization of Lazarsfeld and Merton (1954) who divided homophily into *status homophily* and *value homophily*, online setting gives primacy to value homophily since online

users prefer interactions with people thinking in a similar way, with their social status being of secondary importance (Bisgin, Agarwal, & Xu, 2012). Homophily is also related to multiplexity, which represents the different flows between a pair of persons. It can be categorized as *activity multiplexity* that encompasses shared actions and *content multiplexity* that involves common issues (Mesch & Talmud, 2007). In the case of online homophilous networks present in organizational settings, both forms of multiplexity can be found since workers and stakeholders do not only share similar activities, but also perform similar tasks, both in online and offline sphere of their corporate life. Taking the heterophily into account, at the same time, people search for corporate online networks to find information they do not possess or to exchange knowledge with the ones who are often not informed in exactly the same way, being more or less competent in the subject than the other interlocutor. Since in the case of homophily innovations spread only within a closed group (Rogers, 1995), heterophilous networks allow for effective knowledge diffusion. They are very important in the communication between the specialists from different departments as well with diversified stakeholders trying to find relevant information. To add, heterophilous networks should be also an element of vicarious learning when an individual acquires new skills by observing the behaviors of others, together with their consequences, and later makes use of new knowledge not only for his or her own benefit, but also for the benefit of the organization he or she works for. This feature makes it possible for workers to acquire new skills without having to learn these abilities first by trial and error actions (Hellriegel & Slocum, 2007). Individuals should not only imitate the behaviors of similar nature, but also benefit from diverse experience. Consequently, although homophily encompasses people of similar features or expectations, it also divides the group (Yuan & Gay, 2006) since people have no access to new knowledge. As Rogers (1995) states, individuals can be homophilous as far as education or socioeconomic status is concerned, but they are heterophilous as far as their level of innovation is taken into account. Thus, individuals should simultaneously benefit from homophilous and heterophilous networks. One of the factors determining one's place in both homophilous and heterophilous networks is the language itself, being for the sake of this chapter understood mainly as the communication style by the individual and his or her social environment.

LINGUISTIC HOMOPHILY AND HETEROPHILY IN ONLINE SOCIAL NETWORKS

Language is an instrument of creating heterophilous or homophilous networks in online settings that is not fixed and stable, but is continuously responding to the changes in organizations. For example, people adjust their conversational styles mainly to assimilate or to deviate from others, thus their communication interactions can be described through the prism of divergence, maintenance, and convergence. Divergence happens when one does not want to be associated with somebody. The other option is maintenance, which happens when one does not change his or her communicative behavior when speaking to a different person (Aritz & Walker, 2010). When one wants to be perceived as a part of the group, he or she will adjust their way of speaking to match that of their interaction partner. The degree of convergence is related to the desire for social approval. When the need to gain social acceptance is high, the tendency to "synchronize" with the interlocutor is more important for the individual (Giles, Coupland, & Coupland, 1991). Additionally, using a similar language or discourse style helps in reaching agreements (Huffaker, Swaab, & Diermeier, 2011).

It should be stressed that all of these communicative adaptation styles are connected with both losses and gains. For example, converging

to the interlocutor's conversational style increases understanding and effectiveness of the discourse. At the same time, it may lead to some loss of personal identity (Giles & Ogay, 2009). It should be remembered that both ways could happen during the interaction among the same group of people. For example, divergence takes place to discipline the speaker, which can occur between people of not equal status (Dainton & Zelley, 2010), e.g. in the corporate settings. However, patronizing speech makes the recipient feel less comfortable, passive, and dependant (Dennen, 2011; Giles & Ogay, 2009), and consequently, this technique may hinder informal learning since a worker may feel insecure and may not want to share knowledge or opinions. As has already been stated, in the case of divergence in communication, the interlocutor uses linguistic tools to differentiate himself or herself from the other speaker. It can be stated that he or she creates heterophilous networks that in the case do not offer much possibility of learning new skills.

The use of unknown phrases and comments, together with patronizing communicative behavior, may hinder informal learning. This assertion is aligned with one of the features of communication between dissimilar interlocutors: the greater the heterophily, the more difficult it is to influence others (Hargie, 2003). People are not likely to listen to those who they do not understand and whose beliefs and opinions they do not follow. One idea for dealing with the heterogeneous elements in corporate communication is to opt for what Dwyer calls *consultative power* (Vine, 2004). The mentioned linguistic strategy, also called *social poetics*, is connected with managers negotiating meaning with their subordinates, asking questions and discussing issues with their workers (Shotter & Cunliffe, 2002). The difficulties in communication are connected with both linguistic and cultural difficulties. As far as the language level is concerned, the knowledge of corporate official language is crucial in comprehending organizational messages. Thus, the language used in online social networks should be the standard variation of the language, deprived of archaic or lesser-used phrases. The same applies to branch or department specific names that may be incomprehensible for workers from other sectors of the same company, not to mention external audience, not familiar with the professional jargon. Taking the cultural level into account, heterophilous communication may result in problems with cognition since people have to deal with messages that may be in conflict with their beliefs (Rogers, 1995). The mentioned resistance may result from cultural differences as well as different aims and interests of the interlocutors. The example can be a worker of a factory being at the same time an inhabitant of the village the industrial plant is situated in. Taking care about his or her place of living, the individual may not favor e.g. the negative influence of the factory on the local environment.

The mentioned issues are of huge importance to the ones in charge of facilitating corporate social networking who should remember about the balance between homophilous and heterophilous features in informal learning. Although heterophilous communicative networks accelerate innovation flow in the organization, homophilous communicative style should be employed to discuss unknown methods and solutions.

FUTURE RESEARCH DIRECTIONS

There are a number of directions for future research that can enrich the discussion on the role of online corporate informal learning, looking at the issue from the linguistic perspective. Taking into account the increasing role of technology in the life of modern companies, it can be predicted that online informal learning will be more and more crucial in the organizational activities since workers and stakeholders rely on social networking in both private and professional life. Consequently, the importance of these communicative tools should be noticed by those responsible for corporate communication. It should be remembered, however, that not all employees, customers and potential users of company's products and services are familiar with social networking tools. Thus, standard forms of communication should be maintained to enable the effective distribution of corporate information. Consequently, in the future the author would like to conduct a study showing the synergy effect of using the social networking tools together with various standard forms of communication.

CONCLUSION

The aim of this chapter was to discuss the role of corporate online social networks in the process of informal learning taking place within the organizational setting. Thus, the issue of corporate informal learning has been studied, focusing on the linguistic perspective. The concepts of homophily and heterophily have been employed to present the complexities related to the communicative side of corporate informal online learning. The aim of the author was to show that corporate informal online learning has both homophilous as well as heterophilous features, which determine the shape of unofficial training in organizational settings. Additionally, both types of network are important and, when handled properly, they can facilitate and accelerate the corporate learning process.

REFERENCES

Ala-Mutka, K., Punie, Y., & Ferrari, A. (2009). Review of learning in online networks and communities. *Lecture Notes in Computer Science, 5794,* 350–364. doi:10.1007/978-3-642-04636-0_34

Appadurai, A. (2001). Grassroots globalization and the research imagination. In Appadurai, A. (Ed.), *Globalization* (pp. 1–21). Durham, NC: Duke University Press.

Aritz, J., & Walker, R. C. (2010). Cognitive organization and identity maintenance in multicultural teams: A discourse analysis of decision-making meeting. *Journal of Business Communication*, *47*(1), 20–41. doi:10.1177/0021943609340669

Attwell, G. (2009). The social impact of personal learning environments. In Wheeler, S. (Ed.), *Connected Minds, Emerging Cultures: Cybercultures in Online Learning* (pp. 119–136). Charlotte, NC: Information Age Publishing.

Baker, L. R., & Oswald, D. L. (2010). Shyness and online social networking services. *Journal of Social and Personal Relationships*, *27*(7), 873–889. doi:10.1177/0265407510375261

Bambina, A. (2007). *Online social support: The interplay of social networks and computer-mediated communication*. Youngstown, NY: Cambria Press.

Barlow, M., & Thomas, D. B. (2011). *The executive's guide to enterprise social media strategy: How social networks are radically transforming your business*. Hoboken, NJ: John Wiley & Sons.

Bauman, Z. (2003). *Liquid modernity*. Cambridge, UK: Polity Press.

Bhulyan, T., Josang, A., & Xu, Y. (2010). Managing trust in online social networks. In Furht, B. (Ed.), *Handbook of Social Network Technologies and Applications* (pp. 471–496). New York, NY: Springer.

Bielenia-Grajewska, M. (2011). Rola Internetu w komunikacji prowadzonej przez polskie lotniska: Na przykładzie sytuacji kryzysowych spowodowanych trudnymi warunkami atmosferycznymi. *Pieniądze i Więź*, *51*, 156–162.

Bielenia-Grajewska, M. (2012). Linguistics. In Bainbridge, W. S. (Ed.), *Leadership in Science and Technology. A Reference Handbook* (pp. 41–48). Thousand Oaks, CA: SAGE.

Bisgin, H., Agarwal, N., & Xu, X. (2010). Investigating homophily in online social networks. In *Proceedings of the 2010 IEEE/WIC/ACM International Conference on Web Intelligence and Intelligent Agent Technology*, (pp. 533-536). IEEE Press.

Bisgin, H., Agarwal, N., & Xu, X. (2012). A study of homophily on social media. In Ting, I.-H., Hong, T.-P., & Wang, L. (Eds.), *Social Network Mining, Analysis and Research Trends* (pp. 17–34). Hershey, PA: IGI Global. doi:10.4018/978-1-61350-513-7.ch002

Blanchard, R. (2011). *Creating wealth with a small business: Strategies and models for entrepreneurs in the 2010s*. Bloomington, IN: iUniverse.

Bosman, L., & Zagenczyk, T. (2011). Revitalize your teaching: Creative approaches to applying social media in the classroom. In White, B., King, I., & Tsang, P. (Eds.), *Social Media Tools and Platforms in Learning Environments* (pp. 3–15). Berlin, Germany: Springer-Verlag. doi:10.1007/978-3-642-20392-3_1

Brey, P., & Søraker, J. H. (2009). Philosophy of computing and information technology. In Gabbay, D. M., Meijers, A., Thagard, P., & Woods, J. (Eds.), *Philosophy of Technology and Engineering Sciences* (pp. 1341–1408). Amsterdam, The Netherlands: North Holland. doi:10.1016/B978-0-444-51667-1.50051-3

Brown, J. S., Broderick, A. J., & Lee, N. (2007). Word of mouth communication within online communities: Conceptualizing the online social network. *Journal of Interactive Marketing*, *21*(3), 2–20. doi:10.1002/dir.20082

Brown, J. S., & Duguid, P. (1991). Organizational learning and communities-of-practice: Toward a unified view of working, learning, and innovation. *Organization Science*, 2(1), 40–57. doi:10.1287/orsc.2.1.40

Burnett, R., Consalvo, M., & Ess, C. (2010). *The handbook of internet studies*. Malden, MA: John Wiley & Sons.

Buzzo, B. (2007). *Governare la comunicazione d'impresa: Modelli, attori, tecniche, strumenti e strategie*. Milan, Italy: Franco Angeli.

Cabre Castellvi, M. T. (1997). Standardization and interference in terminology. In Labrum, M. B. (Ed.), *The Changing Scene in World Languages: Issues and Challenges* (pp. 49–64). Philadelphia, PA: John Benjamins Publishing Company.

Cantoni, L., & Piccini, C. (2004). *Il sito del vicino è sempre più verde: La comunicazione fra committenti e progettisti di siti Internet*. Milan, Italy: Franco Angeli.

Cantoni, L., & Tardini, S. (2010). The internet and the web. In Albertazzi, D., & Cobley, P. (Eds.), *Media: An Introduction* (pp. 220–232). Harlow, UK: Pearson Education Limited.

Carliner, S. (2004). *An overview of online learning*. Amherst, MA: HRD Press.

Carr, N. G. (2004). *Does IT matter? Information technology and the corrosion of competitive advantage*. Boston, MA: Harvard Business School Publishing Corporation.

Castells, M. (2010). *The rise of the network society*. Chichester, UK: Blackwell Publishing.

Cho, H., Gay, G., Davidson, B., & Ingraffe, A. (2007). Social networks, communication styles, and learning performance in a CSCL community. *Computers & Education*, *49*, 309–329. doi:10.1016/j.compedu.2005.07.003

Constant, D., Sproull, L., & Kiesler, S. (1996). The kindness of strangers: The usefulness of electronic weak ties for technical advice. *Organization Science*, *7*(2), 119–135. doi:10.1287/orsc.7.2.119

Coskun Samli, A. (2002). *In search of an equitable, sustainable globalization: The bittersweet dilemma*. Westport, CT: Quorum Books.

Cutillo, L. A., Manulis, M., & Strufe, T. (2010). Security and privacy in online social networks. In Furht, B. (Ed.), *Handbook of Social Network Technologies and Applications*. New York, NY: Springer. doi:10.1007/978-1-4419-7142-5_23

Dainton, M., & Zelley, E. D. (2010). *Applying communication theory for professional life: A practical introduction*. Thousand Oaks, CA: SAGE Publications, Ltd.

De Choudhury, M., Sundaram, H., John, A., & Seligmann, D. D. (2010). Analyzing the dynamics of communication in online social networks. In Furht, B. (Ed.), *Handbook of Social Network Technologies and Applications* (pp. 59–94). New York, NY: Springer Science and Business Media, LLC. doi:10.1007/978-1-4419-7142-5_4

Dennen, V. P. (2011). Facilitator presence and identity in online discourse: Use of positioning theory as an analytic framework. *Instructional Science*, *39*(4), 527–541. doi:10.1007/s11251-010-9139-0

Di Bari, R. (2010). *L'era della web communication: Il futuro è adesso*. Trento, Italy: Tangram Edizioni Scientifiche.

DiMaggio, P. (2001). Introduction: Making sense of the contemporary firm and prefiguring its future. In DiMaggio, P. (Ed.), *The Twenty-First-Century Firm: Changing Economic Organization in International Perspective* (pp. 3–30). Princeton, NJ: Princeton University Press.

Doktorowicz, K. (2003). Społeczności wirtualne-cyberprzestrzeń w poszukiwaniu utraconych więzi. In Haber, L. W. (Ed.), *Społeczeństwo Informacyjne - Wizja Czy Rzeczywistość?* (pp. 59–66). Kraków, Poland: Uczelniane Wydawnictwa Naukowo Dydaktyczne.

Ellström, P. E. (2011). Informal learning at work: Conditions, processes and logics. In Malloch, M., Cairns, L., Evans, K., & O'Connor, B. N. (Eds.), *The SAGE Handbook of Workplace Learning* (pp. 105–119). London, UK: Sage Publications, Ltd.

Fernandez, J. (2004). *Corporate communications: A 21st century primer*. New Delhi, India: Response Books.

Flynn, N. (2006). *Blog rules: A business guide to managing policy, public relations, and legal issues*. New York, NY: AMACON.

Foglio, A. (2010). *E-commerce e web marketing: Strategie di web markeing e tecniche di vendita in internet*. Milan, Italy: Franco Angeli.

Fontaine, G., & Chun, G. (2010). Presence in teleland. In Rudestam, K. E., & Schoenholtz-Read, J. (Eds.), *Handbook of Online Learning* (pp. 30–56). Thousand Oaks, CA: Sage Publications, Ltd.

Gannon, M. J. (2008). *Paradoxes of culture and globalization*. Thousand Oaks, CA: SAGE.

Gargiulo, M. (2010). Lingua e Identitá. La politica nella rete di Facebook. In Cresti, E., & Korzen, I. (Eds.), *Language, Cognition and Identity. Extensions of the endocentric/exocentric language typology* (pp. 155–166). Florence: Firenze University Press.

Garrick, J. (1998). *Informal learning in the workplace: Unmasking human resource development*. New York, NY: Routledge.

Giles, H., Coupland, N., & Coupland, J. (1991). Accommodation theory: Communication, context and consequence. In Giles, H., Coupland, J., & Coupland, N. (Eds.), *Contexts of Accommodation: Developments in Applied Sociolinguistics* (pp. 1–68). New York, NY: The Press Syndicate of the University of Cambridge. doi:10.1017/CBO9780511663673.001

Giles, H., & Ogay, T. (2009). Communication accommodation theory. In Whaley, B. B., & Samter, W. (Eds.), *Explaining Communication: Contemporary Theories and Exemplars* (pp. 325–344). Mahwah, NJ: Lawrence Erlbaum Associates, Inc.

Greene, J. A., Choudhry, N. K., Kilabuk, E., & Shrank, W. H. (2010). Online social networking by patients with diabetes: A qualitative evaluation of communication with Facebook. *Journal of General Internal Medicine, 26*(3), 287–292. doi:10.1007/s11606-010-1526-3

Guffey, M. E. (2010). *Essentials of business communication*. Mason, OH: Cengage Learning.

Hager, P., & Halliday, J. (2009). *Recovering informal learning: Wisdom, judgment and community*. Dordrecht, The Netherlands: Springer Science + Business Media.

Hargie, O. (2003). *Skilled interpersonal communication: Research, theory and practice*. Hove, UK: Routledge.

Hellriegel, D., & Slocum, J. W. (2007). *Organizational behavior*. Mason, OH: Thompson Higher Education.

Holt, R. (2004). *Dialogue on the internet: Language, civic identity, and computer-mediated communication*. Westport, CT: Greenwood Publishing Group.

Hudson, B. (2010). Candlepower: The intimate flow of online collaborative learning. In Rudestam, K. E., & Schoenholtz-Read, J. (Eds.), *Handbook of Online Learning* (pp. 267–300). Thousand Oaks, CA: SAGE.

Huffaker, D. A., Swaab, R., & Diermeier, D. (2011). The language of coalition formation in online multiparty negotiations. *Journal of Language and Social Psychology, 30*(1), 66–81. doi:10.1177/0261927X10387102

Jex, S. M. (2002). *Organizational psychology: A scientist-practitioner approach*. New York, NY: John Wiley & Sons.

Jung, B. (2010). *Wokół świata mediów ery Web 2.0*. Warsaw, Poland: WAIP.

Kaplan, A. M., & Haenlein, M. (2010). Users of the world, unite! The challenges and opportunities of social media. *Business Horizons, 53*, 59–60. doi:10.1016/j.bushor.2009.09.003

Kern, R., Ware, P., & Warschauer, M. (2008). Network-based language teaching. In N. Van Deusen-Scholl & N. H. Hornberger (Eds.), *Encyclopedia of Language and Education*, (pp. 281-292). New York, NY: Springer Science+ Business Media LLC.

Kerpen, D. (2011). *Likeable social media: How to delight your customers, create an irresistible brand, and be generally amazing on Facebook (and other social networks)*. Columbus, OH: McGraw-Hill.

Kimmerle, J., Moskaliuk, J., Cress, U., & Thiel, A. (2011). A systems theoretical approach to online knowledge building. *AI & Society, 26*(1), 49–60. doi:10.1007/s00146-010-0281-7

Lagioni, I. (2004). *CMI: Comunicazione di marketing integrate: Una nuova cultura della comunicazione d'impresa*. Milan, IT: Tecniche Nuove.

Lipsey, M. J., Fischer, R. R., & Poirier, K. L. (2007). *Systems for success: The complete guide to selling, leasing, presenting, negotiating & serving in commercial real estate*. Gretna, LA: Pelican Publishing Company.

Lomi, A., & Larsen, E. (1999). Learning without experience: Strategic implications of deregulation and competition in the electricity industry. *European Management Journal, 17*(2), 151–163. doi:10.1016/S0263-2373(98)00074-7

Lurati, F., & Eppler, M. J. (2006). Communication and management: Researching corporate communication and knowledge communication in organizational settings. *Studies in Communication Sciences, 6*(2), 75–98.

Ma, W. W. K., & Yuen, A. H. K. (2011). Understanding online knowledge sharing: An interpersonal relationship perspective. *Computers & Education, 56*, 210–221. doi:10.1016/j.compedu.2010.08.004

Magala, S. (2003). Elective identities: Culture, identification and integration. In Zdanowski, J. (Ed.), *Globalizacja a Tożsamość* (pp. 135–151). Warsaw, Poland: Wydawnictwo Naukowe ASKON.

Mantovani, G. (1995). Virtual reality as a communication environment: Consensual hallucination, fiction, and possible selves. *Human Relations, 48*(6), 669–683. doi:10.1177/001872679504800604

Marsick, V. J., & Volpe, M. (1999). The nature and need for informal learning. *Advances in Developing Human Resources, 1*, 1–9. doi:10.1177/152342239900100302

Marsick, V. J., & Watkins, K. E. (1990). *Informal and incidental learning in the workplace*. London, UK: Routledge.

Mason, R., & Rennie, F. (2007). Using web 2.0 for learning in the community. *The Internet and Higher Education, 10,* 196–203. doi:10.1016/j.iheduc.2007.06.003

Mazur, M., & Richards, L. (2011). Adolescents' and emerging adults' social networking online: Homophily or diversity? *Journal of Applied Developmental Psychology, 32,* 180–188. doi:10.1016/j.appdev.2011.03.001

McKenna, K. Y. A., Green, A. M., & Gleason, M. E. J. (2002). Relationship formation on the Internet: What's the big attraction? *The Journal of Social Issues, 58*(1), 9–31. doi:10.1111/1540-4560.00246

McPherson, M., Lovin, L. S., & Cook, J. M. (2001). Birds of a feather: Homophily in social networks. *Annual Review of Sociology, 27,* 415–444. doi:10.1146/annurev.soc.27.1.415

Mesch, G., & Talmud, I. (2007). The quality of online and offline relationships: The role of multiplexity and duration of social relationships. *The Information Society, 22*(3), 137–148. doi:10.1080/01972240600677805

Meyerson, M. (2010). *Success secrets of social media marketing superstars.* Irvine, CA: Entrepreneur Media.

Milroy, J., & Milroy, L. (1985). Linguistic change, social network and speaker innovation. *Journal of Linguistics, 21*(2), 339–384. doi:10.1017/S0022226700010306

Mislove, A., Marcon, M., Gummadi, K. P., Druschel, P., & Bhattacharjee, B. (2007). Measurement and analysis of online social networks. In *Proceedings of the 5th ACM/USENIX Internet Measurement Conference (IMC 2007).* ACM Press. Retrieved October 3, 2011 from http://www.mpi-sws.org/~amislove/publications/SocialNetworks-IMC.pdf.

Monge, P. R., & Contractor, N. (2003). *Theories of communication networks.* New York, NY: Oxford University Press.

Moore, S. (2010). *Strategic project portfolio management: Enabling a productive organization.* Hoboken, NJ: John Wiley & Sons.

Nelkner, T., Magenheim, J., & Reinhard, W. (2009). PLME as a cognitive tool for knowledge achievement and informal learning. In Tatnall, A., & Jones, A. (Eds.), *WCCE 2009, IFIP AICT 302* (pp. 378–387). International Federation for Information Processing. doi:10.1007/978-3-642-03115-1_40

Newman, B. M., & Newman, P. R. (2009). *Development through life: A psychosocial approach.* Belmont, CA: Wadsworth Cengage Learning.

Panteli, N. (2009). *Virtual social networks: Mediated, massive and multiplayer sites.* Basingstoke, UK: Palgrave Macmillan.

Papacharissi, Z. (2011). Conclusion: A networked self. In Papacharissi, Z. (Ed.), *A Networked Self: Identity, Community, and Culture on Social Network Sites* (pp. 304–318). Abingdon, UK: Routledge.

Papastergiadis, N. (2000). *The turbulence of migration: Globalization, deterritorialization, and hybridity.* Cambridge, UK: Polity Press.

Pastore, A., & Vernuccio, M. (2008). *Impresa e comunicazione: Principi e strumenti per il management.* Milan, Italy: Apogeo Editore.

Pfeffermann, N., & Hülsmann, M. (2011). Communication of innovation: Marketing, diffusion and frameworks. In Hülsmann, M., & Pfeffermann, N. (Eds.), *Strategies and Communications for Innovations: An Integrative Management View for Companies and Networks* (pp. 97–104). Berlin, Germany: Springer Verlag. doi:10.1007/978-3-642-17223-6_7

Pitta, D. A., & Fowler, D. (2005). Internet community forums: An untapped resource for consumer marketers. *Journal of Consumer Marketing, 22*(5), 265–274. doi:10.1108/07363760510611699

Posteguillo, S. (2003). *Netlinguistics: An analytical framework to study language, discourse and ideology in internet.* Castelló de la Plana, Italy: Publicacions de la Universitat Jaume I.

Powazek, D. M. (2002). *Design for community: The art of connecting real people in virtual places.* Indianapolis, IN: New Riders Publishing.

Preece, J. (2000). *Online communities: Designing usability and supporting sociability.* New York, NY: John Wiley & Son.

Prunesti, A. (2010a). *Social media e comunicazione di marketing.* Milan, Italy: Franco Angeli.

Prunesti, A. (2010b). *Enterprise 2.0: Modelli organizzativi e gestione dei social media in azienda.* Milan, Italy: Franco Angeli.

Rainbird, H., Munro, A., & Holly, L. (2004). The employment relationship and workplace learning. In Rainbird, H., Munro, A., & Holly, L. (Eds.), *Workplace Learning in Context* (pp. 38–53). London, UK: Routledge.

Ritzer, G. (2010a). *Globalization: A basic text.* Chichester, UK: Blackwell Publishing.

Ritzer, G. (2010b). *Enchanting a disenchanted world: Continuity and change in the cathedrals of consumption.* Thousand Oaks, CA: Pine Forge Press.

Ritzer, G. (2011). *Globalization: The essentials.* Malden, MA: John Wiley & Sons.

Rogers, E. M. (1995). *Diffusion of innovations.* New York, NY: The Free Press.

Rogers, E. M., & Bhowmik, D. K. (1970). Homophily- heterophily: Relational concepts for communication research. *Public Opinion Quarterly, 34*(4), 523–538. doi:10.1086/267838

Rosenoer, J., Amstrong, D., & Gates, J. R. (1999). *The clickable corporation: Successful strategies for capturing the Internet advantage.* New York, NY: The Free Press.

Salpeter, M. (2011). *Social networking for career success.* New York, NY: Learning Express.

Schachter, S. (1959). *The psychology of affiliation: Experimental studies of the sources of gregariousness.* Stanford, CA: Stanford University Press.

Schaefer, D. R., Kornienko, O., & Fox, A. M. (2011). Misery does not love company: Network selection mechanisms and depression homophily. *American Sociological Review, 76*, 764–785. doi:10.1177/0003122411420813

Schepp, B., & Schepp, D. (2010). *How to find a job on LinkedIn, Facebook, Twitter, MySpace, and other social networks.* New York, NY: McGraw-Hill.

Scollon, R., & Wong Scollon, S. (2001). *Intercultural communication-A discourse approach.* Oxford, UK: Blackwell Publishers Ltd.

Servon, L. J. (2002). *Bridging the digital divide: Technology, community, and public policy.* Oxford, UK: Blackwell Publishers Ltd. doi:10.1002/9780470773529

Shelly, G. B., & Vermaat, M. E. (2011). *Discovering computers 2011.* Boston, MA: Course Technology.

Shih, C. (2010). *The Facebook era: Tapping online social networks to market, sell, and innovate.* Boston, MA: Prentice Hall.

Shotter, J., & Cunliffe, A. L. (2002). Managers as practical authors: Everyday conversations for action. In Holman, D., & Thorpe, R. (Eds.), *Management and Language: The Manager as Practical Author* (pp. 15–37). London, UK: SAGE.

Stritzke, W. G. K., Nguyen, A., & Durkin, K. (2004). Shyness and computer-mediated communication: A self-presentational theory perspective. *Media Psychology*, 6, 1–22. doi:10.1207/s1532785xmep0601_1

Tan, S. (2010). Modeling engagement in a web-based advertising campaign. *Visual Communication*, 9(1), 91–115. doi:10.1177/1470357209352949

Tanis, M. (2007). Online social support group. In Joinson, A., McKenna, K., Postmes, T., & Reips, U. D. (Eds.), *The Oxford Handbook of Internet Psychology* (pp. 139–154). Oxford, UK: Oxford University Press.

Tomei, L. A. (2010). *Lexicon of online and distance learning*. Plymouth, MA: Rowman and Littlefield Education.

Tosoni, S. (2008). *Identitá virtuali: Comunicazione mediata da computer e procesi di constuzione dell'identitápersonale*. Milan, Italy: Franco Angeli.

Vergeer, M., Hermans, L., & Sams, S. (2011). Online social networks and micro-blogging in political campaigning: The exploration of a new campaign tool and a new campaign style. *Party Politics*, (n.d), 1–25.

Vine, B. (2004). *Getting things done at work: The discourse of power in workplace interaction*. Philadelphia, PA: John Benjamins.

Wain, K. (2004). *The learning society in a postmodern world: The education crisis*. New York, NY: Peter Lang Publishing, Inc.

Wallace, P. (2001). *The psychology of the internet*. Cambridge, UK: Cambridge University Press.

Wasko, M. M., & Faraj, S. (2005). Why should I share? Examining social capital and knowledge contribution in electronic networks of practice. *Management Information Systems Quarterly*, 29(1), 35–57.

Williams, J. B., & Jacobs, J. (2004). Exploring the use of blogs as learning spaces in the higher education sector. *Australasian Journal of Educational Technology*, 20(2), 232–247.

Yuan, Y. C., & Gay, G. (2006). Homophily of network ties and bonding and bridging social capital in computer-mediated distributed teams. *Journal of Computer-Mediated Communication*, 11, 1062–1084. doi:10.1111/j.1083-6101.2006.00308.x

ADDITIONAL READING

Anderson, T. (2008). *The theory and practice of online learning*. Edmonton, Canada: AU Press.

Bielenia-Grajewska, M. (2011). Actor-network theory in medical e-communication: The role of websites in creating and maintaining healthcare corporate online identity. *International Journal of Actor-Network Theory and Technological Innovation*, 3(1), 39–53. doi:10.4018/jantti.2011010104

Bielenia-Grajewska, M. (2011). The influence of technology on business expatriate performance in host countries. In German, M., & Banerjee, P. (Eds.), *Migration, Technology and Transculturation: A Global Perspective* (pp. 222–233). St Charles, MO: Lindenwood Press.

Boud, D., & Middleton, H. (2003). Learning from others at work: Communities of practice and informal learning. *Journal of Workplace Learning*, 15(5), 194–202. doi:10.1108/13665620310483895

Cantoni, L., Botturi, L., & Succi, C. (2007). *E-learning: Capire, progettare, comunicare*. Milan, Italy: Franco Angeli.

Carliner, S. (2004). *An overview of online learning*. Amherst, MA: HRD Press, Inc.

Cheetham, G., & Chifers, G. (2005). *Professions, competence and informal learning*. Cheltenham, UK: Edward Edgar Publishing Limited.

Coffield, F. (2000). *The necessity of informal learning*. Bristol, UK: The Policy Press.

Conlon, T. J. (2004). A review of informal learning literature, theory and implications for practice in developing global professional competence. *Journal of European Industrial Training, 28*(2/3/4), 283-295.

Cross, J. (2007). *Informal learning: Rediscovering the natural pathways that inspire innovation and performance*. San Francisco, CA: John Wiley & Sons.

Dennen, V. P. (2005). From message posting to learning dialogues: Factors affecting learner participation in asynchronous discussion. *Distance Education, 26*(1), 127–148. doi:10.1080/01587910500081376

Dennen, V. P., & Wieland, K. (2007). From interaction to intersubjectivity: Facilitating online group discourse processes. *Distance Education, 28*(3), 281–297. doi:10.1080/01587910701611328

Enos, M. D., Thamm Kehrhahn, M., & Bell, A. (2003). Informal learning and the transfer of learning: How managers develop proficiency. *Human Resource Development Quarterly, 14*(4), 369–387. doi:10.1002/hrdq.1074

Eraut, M. (2004). Informal learning in the workplace. *Studies in Continuing Education, 26*(2), 247–273. doi:10.1080/158037042000225245

Folkestad, G. (2006). Formal and informal learning situations or practices vs formal and informal ways of learning. *British Journal of Music Education, 23*, 135–145. doi:10.1017/S0265051706006887

Garrison, R., & Cleveland-Innes, M. (2005). Facilitating cognitive presence in online learning: Interaction is not enough. *American Journal of Distance Education, 19*(3), 133–148. doi:10.1207/s15389286ajde1903_2

Gray, B. (2004). Informal learning in an online community of practice. *Journal of Distance Education, 19*(1), 20–35.

Greenhow, C., & Robelia, B. (2009). Informal learning and identity formation in online social networks. *Learning, Media and Technology, 34*(2), 119–140. doi:10.1080/17439880902923580

Hiltz, S. R., & Goldman, R. (2009). *Learning together online: Research on asynchronous learning networks*. Mahwah, NJ: Lawrence Erlbaum Associates, Inc.

Macneil, C. (2001). The supervisor as a facilitator of informal learning in work teams. *Journal of Workplace Learning, 13*(6), 246–253. doi:10.1108/EUM0000000005724

Malcolm, J., Hodkinson, P., & Colley, H. (1989). The interrelationships between informal and formal learning. *Journal of Workplace Learning, 15*(7/8), 313–318. doi:10.1108/13665620310504783

Northcote, M., & Kendle, A. (2001). Informal online networks for learning: Making use of incidental learning through recreation. In P. L. Jeffery (Ed.), *Proceedings of the International Education Research Conference*. Melbourne, Austalia: Australian Association for Research in Education. Retrieved 3 October, 2011 from http://www.aare.edu.au/01pap/nor01596.htm.

Salmon, G. (2002). *E-tivities: The key to active online learning*. London, UK: Kogan Page Limited.

Svensson, L., Ellström, P. E., & Åberg, C. (2004). Integrating formal and informal learning at work. *Journal of Workplace Learning, 16*(8), 479–491. doi:10.1108/13665620410566441

Wilson, B., & Lowry, M. (2000). Constructivist learning on the Web. *New Directions for Adult and Continuing Education, 88*, 79–88. doi:10.1002/ace.8808

KEY TERMS AND DEFINITIONS

Informal Learning: Learning in informal environment or by using non-standard methods of knowledge acquisition.

Online Social Networks: Networks taking place in online settings, by using social media instruments.

Linguistic Networks: Networks determined by linguistic factors, such as language preferences and skills of their users.

Heterophilous Networks: Networks constituting of dissimilar material and nonmaterial entities.

Homophilous Networks: Networks constituting of similar material and nonmaterial entities.

Section 3
Cases and Research in Higher Education

Chapter 7
Creating Ongoing Online Support Communities through Social Networks to Promote Professional Learning

Maria Elena Corbeil
The University of Texas at Brownsville, USA

Joseph Rene Corbeil
The University of Texas at Brownsville, USA

ABSTRACT

Professionals who want to remain competitive in their fields are turning to Web 2.0 to learn the knowledge and skills they need in order to do their work more efficiently and effectively. Through a detailed description of how one instructor transformed his online graduate courses into dynamic, interactive, ongoing online learning communities that extended beyond the classroom, this chapter provides academics and practitioners a model for establishing a professional network that learners can participate in, and replicate in their workplaces for their professional development and informal learning. An overview of the role of social networking in creating professional development and informal learning opportunities for cognitive apprenticeship, knowledge brokering, and ongoing online support communities, as well as the results of a survey conducted on students' perceptions of the impact of the social networking strategies and tools on their professional development and informal learning in and out of class will also be discussed.

DOI: 10.4018/978-1-4666-1815-2.ch007

INTRODUCTION

More than ever before, professionals are being required to keep up with fast-paced changes in technology, information, and ways of doing their jobs. While formal training and higher education programs have traditionally been the primary source of formal learning and professional development, research (Halx, 2010; Nair & Webster, 2010; McKinsey Global Institute, 2011) revealed that many of these programs, even those delivered online, employ traditional instructor-led content-centered strategies, such as lectures, isolated hands-on activities, and reading of texts, while in the workplace, professionals are required to learn in new ways and direct their own learning. To address this disparity, one professor turned to social media to create a virtual learning network, where his students could connect with a group of like-minded professionals. Over the past two years, this virtual learning network has grown to include over 120 students and alumni. Through tools like social networking sites, blogs and wikis, faculty, students, and alumni share their knowledge and experiences, successes and challenges, and views on events impacting their profession. When students need program advice, assistance with a technical issue or a course-related assignment, or help in addressing an issue at work, they turn to this cohort for assistance. An informal, professional learning network has naturally developed from the active and sustained participation of current students, faculty, and alumni, who are professionals in their fields.

This chapter presents a model for academics and practitioners through a case study that describes how one instructor transformed his online graduate courses into dynamic, interactive, ongoing online support communities that extended beyond the limitations of the courseware-managed classroom. Using tools like social networking sites, blogs, and wikis, current and former students interact with each other to build professional relationships, share ideas, and seek answers to challenges they faced at school and at work. A survey of the students' perceptions of the impact of social networking, revealed that having discovered the value of the social networks, they applied the knowledge and skills they acquired in these online graduate courses by setting up social networking sites to promote professional and informal learning opportunities in their own workplaces. An overview of the role of social networking in creating ongoing online support communities that support cognitive apprenticeship and knowledge brokering for sustained professional development and informal learning, as well as the results of a survey conducted on students' perceptions of the use of social media and its impact on their professional development and informal learning on-the-job are also discussed.

BACKGROUND

Until recently, the term professional development typically described formal learning and training activities, usually provided by experts to train professionals in the knowledge and skills they required to carry out their jobs. Fast-paced changes in Internet and mobile technologies have changed professional development by putting the tools for the creation, selection, and sharing of learning into the hands of the end users. Stevens (2006) noted that in addition to basic learning resources available online, Web 2.0 has changed the landscape for professional development by providing tools not available in previous versions of the Web. For example, accompanying Web 2.0 is a host of communication services, commonly known as social networking tools or social media. "Web 2.0 is where anyone can not only take information down from it but also create content and upload to it. In this respect the Web is not simply a one-way means of obtaining knowledge, but also a place where you interact with the material and annotate and contribute to the content" (p. 3). Through the use of social media such as Facebook®, Twitter®,

LinkedIn®, MySpace®, and others, users stay connected, oftentimes in real-time, and become active creators, not just recipients of content and information.

The changes in the technological landscape have prompted changes in learning for professionals.

As a result, researchers such as Bitter-Rijpkema and Verjans (2010), differentiate between *professional development*- information that is presented to employees by those with expertise in the area, and *professional learning*- "learning activities initiated and performed by the learner" (p. 2). The main difference lies in the level of learner control and direction of the learning. Professional learning, for example, "... is not limited to a specific time or place, i.e. it can happen in preparation of, during, or after professional activities, and it is not limited to a single location..." (Bitter-Rijpkema & Verjans, 2010, p. 2). It is in these aspects that professional learning takes on many of the characteristics of informal learning. As its name implies, in informal learning, learning usually take place in an unstructured, informal environment that does not require an instructor or trainer because learners direct the goals, content, time, location, and resources of their learning.

Given the availability and ease of use of social media, "there is growing evidence that many people are engaged in a wide range of technology-based informal learning at home and the community" (Selwyn, 2007, p. 2). Sewlyn (2007) recognized that while some critics deem social networking as unofficial and unqualified sources of learning, their ever-increasing value cannot be denied, as current-day professionals require authentic applications of learning and Web 2.0 additionally offers "communities of users adding value to Web applications in collaborative and creative ways which would not be possible on an individual basis" (Selwyn, 2007, p. 2). Therefore, today, as social media become more accessible and mobile technologies give individuals anytime, anywhere access to Web-based resources, profes-

sionals are able to harness the power of ongoing online support communities to achieve cognitive apprenticeship and knowledge brokering, for their professional development and informal learning.

Cognitive Apprenticeship

Collins, Brown, and Holum (1991) observed that before formal schooling, knowledge and skills were learned through apprenticeships—that is, learning how to do something, such as carpentry or speaking a language, by working alongside and modeling those who had mastered the art. They added that formal schooling changed the way people were taught and apprenticeships were relegated to limited uses such as on the job training. However, noting the value of this form of learning, in 1989, Collins, Brown, and Newman (Collins, Brown, & Holum, 1991) developed a model of *cognitive apprenticeship*, that integrates apprenticeship strategies into current academic practices. The authors recognized that although traditional teaching methods employed in schools have effectively helped learners acquire large amounts of content, "too little attention is paid to the reasoning and strategies that experts employ when they acquire knowledge or put it to work to solve complex or real-life tasks" (p. 1). The development of thinking skills is usually addressed in isolation using classroom-based examples, and when students are faced with different challenges in the workplace, they may not possess the problem-solving skills or knowledge of the use of resources needed to tackle the situations effectively (Collins, Brown, & Holum, 1991).

Incorporating cognitive apprenticeship in classroom learning provides a model for students, as well as opportunities for them to develop expertise and increase their motivation. In the cognitive apprenticeship model, students not only learn by modeling the instructor, but developing and applying the problem-solving strategies, thereby becoming experts themselves. According to Collins, Brown, and Holum (1991), "teachers need to encourage students to explore questions teachers cannot answer, to challenge solutions the 'experts' have found- in short, to allow the role of 'expert' and 'student' to be transformed" (p. 17). In addition, Lombardi and Oblinger (2007) noted that although students reported increased motivation when learning by doing, incorporating authentic learning, that is, solving real-life problems in an educational setting has been challenging up to now. However, with advancements in social networking technologies, "we can offer students a more authentic learning experience based on experimentation and action" (p. 2), replicating the contexts, technologies, and tasks required in their workplaces, while helping them "make valuable connections with mentors around the world" (p. 2), "just as it is in the actual workplace" (p. 2). Since social media tools allow the users to not only participate in, but also create and build content, they provide ample opportunities for incorporating cognitive apprenticeship strategies into formal and informal learning environments. Rosencheck (2010) summarized, "using Web 2.0 and social media technologies, cognitive apprenticeship offers a map to help chart a course toward faster proficiency, innovation and results" (p. 1). There is no question then, why learners of all ages and in a myriad of professions are engaging in social networking for their personal and professional development.

Knowledge Brokering

Advancements in social networking technologies have also helped in knowledge transfer, "the process of bridging the gap between knowledge and action" (Ward, et al., 2010, p. 6). According to Ward et al. (2010), the challenge faced in many professions today is the slow or virtually non-existent transfer of knowledge from research to practice. The authors noted that lack of communication of relevant research to the end-users who need the findings for improved processes and procedures are oftentimes due to differences

in the language of researchers and practitioners, the time required for a study, as well as the way each views and applies research. For example, researchers take years to complete a study and work with theories that may be too abstract for practitioners' needs. On the other hand, as Ward et al. observed, practitioners need to make quick decisions based on clear, understandable data presented in easy-to-understand language.

Given the fast-paced changes in technology and the global economy, there is a need for employees who have the skills to: know where to find relevant research and information; sift through thousands of pieces of information; analyze the reliability and validity of sources; extract the relevant information; figure out how it applies to their needs; and synthesize and communicate the results. Therefore, the students in higher education programs need more than ever, to graduate with skills that help them become highly analytical consumers of information, as well as the change agents that promote the transfer of knowledge process to facilitate decisions and processes in their workplaces.

In order to facilitate the transfer of knowledge, graduates also need to become adept at knowing how to consume and communicate information using social media. Social media puts the tools of knowledge transfer into the hands of the creators and end-users of information, so for the first time, they can inhabit the same space. However, knowing how to effectively use social media, in and of itself, is not a quick fix and graduates need additional skills to be effective. Although on the surface it would seem that the solution to the challenge of knowledge transfer can be solved through the one way transmittal of information from researchers to practitioners and that the challenge is greatly alleviated today with the explosion of communication tools afforded by social media, the effective transfer of knowledge is more complicated and requires the development of the more complex skills of knowledge brokering. "Brokering focuses on identifying and bringing together people interested in an issue, people who can help each other develop evidence-based solutions. It helps build relationships and networks for sharing existing research and ideas and stimulating new work" (Canadian Health Services Research Foundation, 2003, p. ii). By building social media networks, users, who can now more readily access, apply, and share their professional experiences with the research to facilitate the transfer of knowledge at their workplaces, become knowledge brokers. "By definition, they are go-betweens; their core function is connecting people to share and exchange knowledge" (Canadian Health Services Research Foundation, 2003, p. ii). As the knowledge brokers of their organizations, professionals are being called upon to learn new skills, more quickly, and on their own.

Ongoing Online Support Communities and Social Learning

As professionals increasingly leverage the benefits of knowledge brokering for transfer of learning and professional development using social networking tools, the workplace learning process shifts from being developed and led by an instructor to being co-created in ongoing online support communities. Web 2.0 allows learners to individualize their learning by balancing the level of individuality and interactivity they are comfortable engaging in. Sewlyn (2007) noted that the professional online learning communities developed through social networking "are potentially fertile sites for informal learning" (p. 3). Consequently, professionals are engaging in social networks outside of formal educational and professional settings. "At its most basic level, new social learning can result in people becoming more informed, gaining a wider perspective, and being able to make better decisions by engaging with others. It acknowledges that learning happens with and through other people, as a matter of participating in a community, not just by acquiring knowledge" (Bingham & Conner, 2010, p. 7). Web 2.0 tools

are not only changing the technologies available for communication and collaboration, but are actually changing the landscape of learning and the culture of the workplace.

Bingham and Conner (2010) observed, "social tools are powerful building blocks that can transform the way we enable learning and development in organizations. They foster a new culture of sharing, one in which content is contributed and distributed with few restrictions or costs" (p. 8). Yet, to facilitate social learning and professional development in the new landscape created by social media, specialized skills are required to navigate and identify the appropriate tools and resources for the specific learning task. As Bitter and Verjans (2010) noted, "new opportunities for learning present themselves, but these opportunities require new strategies to ensure effective and productive learning" (p. 4). Consequently, higher education is often looked upon to prepare graduates to pursue their own professional development and informal learning. However, oftentimes, the instructors do not possess these skills themselves and courses, even online ones, are far more content-centered, instead of student-centered, and replicate face-to-face strategies, such as lectures. "Many higher education institutions have been utilizing learning management systems in their teaching. These systems and the ways they are used, however, usually implement a traditional instructivist approach to teaching" (Salavuo, 2008). The intrepid faculty who do promote cognitive apprenticeship, knowledge brokering, and ongoing online support communities through Web 2.0 and social media, oftentimes had to acquire the skills through their own informal learning pursuits because there were no formal training opportunities available at their own institutions. In addition, there are numerous research studies regarding the potential uses of social networking in medical (Kamel Boulos & Wheeler, 2007), educational (edWeb.net, et al., 2009; Vogel, 2009), and business environments (Eyrich, et al., 2008) for professional collaboration, networking, informal learning, and professional development, but insufficient research regarding actual applications and results.

In order to help fill the abovementioned gap between research and application, one instructor, who had no formal, institution-based professional development resources to turn to, engaged in informal learning himself to figure out what Web 2.0 social networking tools were available and how to apply them in his online graduate classes. The resulting online class, described in the following sections, provides a model for building opportunities for cognitive apprenticeships, knowledge brokering, ongoing online support communities, and social learning that academics and professionals can implement in their own learning environments, whether it is in an academic or professional setting.

TRANSFORMING AN ONLINE COURSE THROUGH SOCIAL MEDIA

In order to prepare his Educational Technology graduate students to meet the rigors and challenges of learning in the 21st century workforce, one university professor used social media to transform his online graduate courses into dynamic, interactive learning environments that modeled strategies for cognitive apprenticeship and knowledge brokering. To extend the professional collegiality he fostered beyond his courses, social networking tools were employed to keep learners engaged in professional discourse throughout their graduate studies and beyond, as well as to provide them with examples of how the social media tools could be used to establish ongoing learning communities in their workplaces.

The courses are facilitated through the latest version of one of the most popular Learning Management Systems (LMS) on the market. Although the LMS claims to integrate Web 2.0 tools such as blogs, wikis, and discussion forums, in actuality,

all three asynchronous communication tools are delivered using the same discussion forum tool. In order to give students an authentic social learning experience, it became necessary to replace the courseware managed forum tools with actual social networking tools. The challenge became to integrate social media into every aspect of the course without losing continuity. The revamped courses provide multiple avenues and opportunities for learning through student-to-student, student-to-instructor and student-to-content interactions.

Setting up a New Course Communications Hub

To facilitate the transfer of knowledge and ongoing learner communication and collaboration, the Home/Announcements pages of each course were replaced with a blog. The enhanced Home page, now serves as a telecommunications hub for the entire course. Students have immediate access to all course and program-related communication, news, and information when they log in. To further enhance knowledge transfer, students can subscribe to the live RSS blog feed to receive the up-to-the-minute information on their laptop computers and mobile devices without having to log in to the course. Figure 1 shows a screenshot of the enhanced course Home page.

The Home page informs students of the week's reading assignments, daily work activities, and upcoming project due dates. Links to a weekly podcast, discussion forum, Ed Tech Blog, and other resources needed for the week are also posted. On the side bar, an online status indicator and live chat app notifies students when the instructor is online and available to answer questions. Also located in the sidebar is a Twitter® feed for the Educational Technology program, as well as a feed for the course microblog. These feeds provide up-to-the-minute program and course related news and information.

Figure 1. Screenshot of the course home page, managed by a blog

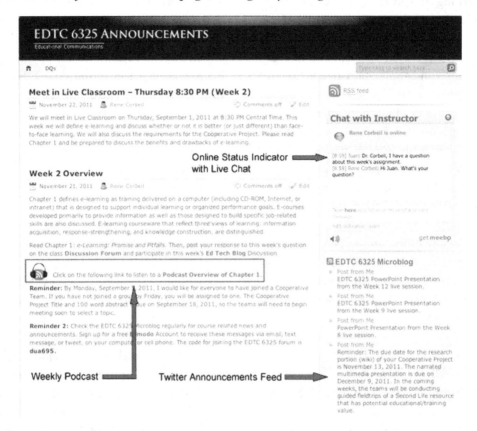

Enhancing the Class Discussions

In order to model social media technologies that students could employ in their workplaces to promote online communities of learning, and engage students in professional dialogues that promoted their transfer of learning, as well their building of cognitive apprenticeships, the LMS discussion board was also replaced with a blog (Figure 2). While the featureless courseware-managed discussion forums are static and frustratingly non-user friendly, the class blogs, in contrast, are attractive, customizable, and much more personal. By allowing participants to create a personal profile with a picture, students and the instructor are able to "see" each other every time they post a comment to the blog.

Each week, students are asked to submit their viewpoints to issue questions pertaining to the class reading assignments, thus becoming the experts in a cognitive apprenticeship model.

The questions are intended to get students to synthesize, evaluate, and extend their knowledge and understanding of the materials they have read. To promote interactivity with their peers, in order to receive full participation credit, they must read, reflect upon, and respond to at least 2 of their classmate's responses to the discussion questions.

In addition to the class discussion forum, a separate blog (Figure 3) was created to generate discussion and debate of field-related topics and issues, helping students become consumers, as well as creators of learning content. The weekly posts to the EdTech Blog expose current (and former) Educational Technology students to the opportunities and issues facing the professional practitioner. Each week students from multiple classes address a new topic, taken straight from the headlines.

Figure 2. Screenshot of the class discussion forum facilitated by a blog

Figure 3. Screenshot of the EdTech blog

Working Collaboratively In and Out of the Class

The Cooperative Project is a group effort that includes a report and a group presentation. Working in groups of 4-5, students conduct research on a 3D virtual environment to analyze its potential for instructional and/or training applications. Working in Second Life®, the teams establish a virtual community and use the virtual environment and its collaborative tools to meet, plan, prepare, and present their reports and multimedia presentations to the class. They also organize and conduct instructional field trips for other members of the class. Students document their work through a team wiki, a website that enables groups to collaborate and share their work. A screen shot of a class session is provided in Figure 4.

The social networking tools described above were seamlessly integrated into the course to provide learner support through built in and just-in-time access to ongoing online support communities and social learning opportunities. These tools also provide a dynamic and participatory e-learning environment that engage students to be active creators and consumers of learning materials; and promote critical reflection strengthened by consistent, reciprocal communication between the learners, the instructor, and the content that they can model for their own virtual professional development outside of the classroom.

Using Social Media for Professional Development and Informal Learning

In addition to the social networking tools used within the instructor's courses, several additional social networking tools are being employed to engage students in dialog and debate outside of the classroom. While the majority of users of these social networking tools are current students (i.e., students currently enrolled in the program), a significant percentage of students are graduates, who have chosen to remain active. Several social media tools, including Facebook®, Twitter®, YouTube®, and LinkedIn®, are used to engage the Educational Technology students and alumni.

One of the most active social networking tools is The EdTech Facebook® Fan Page (http://www.facebook.com/EDTConline), which was created to bring current and former Educational Technology students together as a community of educational technology practitioners. This forum, which exists outside of the formal classroom setting, is used to post job openings, program and industry-related news, and announcements celebrating former and current students' achievements. Since its inception, the Educational Technology program has produced over 300 graduates. More than one third of those graduates are "fans" of the site and contribute regularly.

In order to promote the Educational Technology program, and encourage student participation outside of the class environment, an EdTech@ UTB Twitter® page (https://twitter.com/#!/EDTECH_UTB) was also established. It, too, serves as a forum for current, former, and future educational technology students to interact with one another in a professional environment. Less than a year old, EdTech@UTB already has hundreds of followers, most of whom are current and former students.

Summary of Social Media Tools and Their Purpose

The following section provides a summary of the social media tools and their purposes for enhancing communication, interaction, and learning, both formal and informal.

Wordpress®. The LMS discussion forum was replaced with a blog to make the class discussions more interactive and easier to follow. The class blog improves social presence and teacher immediacy by allowing participants to create personal profiles with pictures, enabling students and instructors to "see" each other every time they posted a new comment to the blog.

Figure 4. Screenshot of the class meeting in Second Life®. The team on the stage is preparing to take the members of the class on a virtual fieldtrip.

Blogger®. The EdTech Blog is a program-related blog facilitated through *Google Blogger®*. Students enrolled in multiple courses (as well as former students who continue to visit the blog) interact with one another on topics and issues related to the profession. Each week a new topic, taken straight from the headlines, is addressed. The weekly posts to the EdTech Blog are in addition to the weekly class discussion questions.

PBWorks®. Working in groups of 4-5, students conduct research on a selected topic and document their work in a wiki. One of the benefits of wikis is that all drafts are saved and archived, making them ideal for group work.

YouTube®. Individual and cooperative multimedia projects are developed and uploaded to the EdTech YouTube® Channel to share with fellow classmates and the general public. Many of the student-generated products are publically viewable video tutorials for a host of software applications. This venue makes it easy for students to integrate their multimedia projects into their E-Portfolios for private and public viewing, as well to share them with their co-workers, thereby

creating a repository for informal learning and professional development.

Edmodo®. A Twitter®-like service designed specifically for education is used to post short course and program-related news, announcements, and reminders on the course home page. The messages appear on the course Home page through an RSS feed. Students can opt to receive the messages via email, SMS text message, or Twitter®. Students in cooperative groups also use Edmodo® to stay in continuous communication with team members throughout the day, enabling them to discuss team activities without having to log in to the course. Through a smartphone app, students are also able send and receive messages while on the go.

Podcasts. Weekly 5-minute podcasts are produced to engage students in critical reflection and to provide examples of authentic applications of the weekly topics and the underlying concepts addressed in class. Podcasts are a convenient method of knowledge transfer since they can be easily shared and accessed by professionals while on the go.

Second Life®. Working in groups, students explore and conduct research on the instructional and/or training potential of this 3D virtual environment. The cooperative teams plan and facilitate virtual fieldtrips for other members of the class. This is an ideal platform for facilitating cognitive apprenticeships for informal learning and professional development opportunities.

Facebook®. A Facebook® Fan Page brings current and former Educational Technology students together as a community. This forum is used to post job openings, program and industry-related news, and announcements celebrating former and current students' achievements.

Twitter®. The Educational Technology Twitter® account serves as a forum for current, former, and future educational technology students to interact with one another in a professional, yet informal environment.

SURVEY: USING SOCIAL MEDIA FOR PROFESSIONAL DEVELOPMENT AND INFORMAL LEARNING

In order to assess the impact of social networking on professional development and informal learning practices, current and former students from the Master of Education in Educational Technology were invited to participate in an informal survey of their social networking behaviors. Over the past 10 years, this fully online program has produced over 300 graduates. A significant majority of current and former students are adult learners who must balance work and family responsibilities. Approximately 53% are male and 47% are female. The largest group of students are K-12 teachers (56%), with 13% of the student population coming from a higher education background, and 31% coming from the public sector.

What distinguishes this program from other educational technology programs is that the students learn the theories behind educational technology through the application of educational

technology, and social media, and content-sharing tools are heavily integrated into all of the core courses through peer-to-peer and group collaborations. Students learn by doing and are encouraged to integrate the newly acquired knowledge and skills to their work and personal lives in meaningful ways.

The instructor-generated survey consisted of four questions designed to elicit information on current and former students' specific social networking and content-sharing tool preferences and how their use contributed to their professional development and informal learning, both in and out of the classroom. The survey asked the following questions:

1. What social networking and content-sharing tools do you regularly use and for what purposes?
2. How do you use these social networking and content-sharing tools?
3. Do you use these social networking for your professional development and/or informal learning?
4. How do you use social networking for professional development and/or informal learning?

The online survey was posted on the *Educational Technology Facebook® Page*, which has 120 active members. Of the 120 total active members, 35 current and former students volunteered to participate anonymously in the survey for a response rate of 29 percent. The results of the survey are presented below and in Tables 1, 2, and 3.

Table 1 presents a summary of students' social networking and content-sharing tool preferences and uses. The survey question listed the 12 most popular social networking and content-sharing tools and asked students to indicate if they used these tools for educational, personal, and/or professional use. Not surprising, since all of these tools were used extensively in their online class-

Table 1. Summary of social networking tool uses and purposes (N=35)

What social networking and content-sharing tools do you use?	Educational Use	Personal Use	Professional Use	Response Count
Facebook®	36.7% (11)	90.0% (27)	43.3% (13)	30
MySpace®	0.0% (0)	80.0% (4)	20.0% (1)	5
Wikipedia®	90.3% (28)	87.1% (27)	67.7% (21)	31
YouTube®	78.8% (26)	100.0% (33)	72.7% (24)	33
Google Docs®	90.5% (19)	57.1% (12)	71.4% (15)	21
Twitter®	78.6% (11)	78.6% (11)	64.3% (9)	14
Photo Sharing	63.2% (12)	94.7% (18)	31.6% (6)	19
LinkedIn®	29.4% (5)	41.2% (7)	82.4% (14)	17
Edmodo®	92.3% (12)	7.7% (1)	30.8% (4)	13
Wikis®	100.0% (29)	51.7% (15)	48.3% (14)	29
Blogs®	96.2% (25)	46.2% (12)	53.8% (14)	26
Podcasts	91.3% (21)	26.1% (6)	43.5% (10)	23
Answered question				35
Skipped question				0

Table 2. Summary of social networking and content-sharing tool use (N=33)

I regularly use social networking and content-sharing tools to...	Response Percent	Response Count
Share information and resources with other professionals	63.6%	21
Network with peers and colleagues	90.9%	30
Create professional learning communities	39.4%	13
Improve communication between peers and colleagues	69.7%	23
Create groups to collaborate on projects	39.4%	13
Receive online professional development support	30.3%	10
Get support from peers to cope with job/educational challenges	51.5%	17
Learn how Social Networking and Web 2.0 can be incorporated into my work	42.4%	14
Find job and career opportunities	36.4%	12
Find information on products and services	42.4%	14
Learn about topics that interest me	69.7%	23
Answered questions		33
Skipped questions		2

es, the most popular social media platforms for educational use, were wikis (100%), blogs (96.2%), Edmodo® (92.3%), podcasts (91.3%), Google Docs® (90.5%), and Wikipedia® (90.3%). Under the category of personal use, YouTube® (100%), photo sharing sites (94.7%, and Facebook (90%) were listed among students' favorite social media and content-sharing tools. Lastly, students listed LinkedIn® (82.4%), YouTube® (72.7%),

Table 3. Summary of use of social networking for professional development and/or informal learning (N=35)

Do you use social networking for your professional development and/or informal learning?	Response Percent	Response Count
Yes	80.0%	28
No	20.0%	7
Answered question		35
Skipped question		0

and Google Docs® (71.4%) as their social media tools of choice for professional use.

Table 2 provides a summary of the types of activities and interactions current and former students engaged in through social media and content-sharing tools. A clear majority, (90.9%) indicated that they regularly used social media and content-sharing tools to network with peers and colleagues. A significant majority also indicated that they used social media and content-sharing tools to learn about topics that interested them (69.7%), improve communication between peers and colleagues (69.7%), and share information and resources with other professionals (63.6%). Interestingly, over half of survey respondents (51.5%) indicated that they used social media and content-sharing tools to get support from peers to cope with job/educational challenges.

Table 3 presents the outcome of current and former student responses to the question of whether or not they use social networking for professional development and/or informal learning. Not surprising, a significant majority (80.0%) indicated that they did currently use social networking to enhance their professional development and/or informal learning practices.

Student Comments

In order to gain a deeper insight into current and former students' practices regarding their use of social networking and content-sharing tools for professional development and informal learning,

the following open-ended question was asked: "How do you use social networking tools for professional development and/or informal learning?"

- *Little current use as most of my peers are educational luddites. I have discovered and use the social networking aspects of virtual worlds, Diigo®, Google®, Twitter®, discussion groups, etc. for expanding my resource horizons and awareness about what others are doing.*

- *Social media is a valuable resource for staying connected with other professionals both in my current field and in the areas that I am targeting for future career development. I am able to learn from other professionals and ask questions to inform me of trends and directions.*

- *For me, LinkedIn® is the most valuable resource as I can select groups with similar interests, network with those individuals and learn about options. I can look at career paths that I would like to pursue and see how others got to similar positions. I can follow companies of interest. I can increase my visibility in my field. But most importantly, stay connected.*

- *I probably use wikis more than any other tool. I have my court reporting audio recordings on several WIKIs. I personally purchased the campus version. Have had great success in the past two years that I have used it. My students don't seem to like it when teachers are their friends on Facebook®, so I have avoided that.*

- *I offer in-district and out of district staff development opportunities for educators on social networking tools and how these can be utilized to enhance instruction.*
- *I hope to continue the informal, yet professional dialogue that has begun in the blog discussion forums and wikis.*
- *I rely on Facebook® to get updates from personal/professional groups that interest me. For example, the UTB Educational Technology program has a Facebook® page that I keep up with.*
- *I currently use social networking tools as a part of my personal educational endeavors and for professional development. Since I am a part of an online educational masters program, social networking tools are often used for collaboration, sharing, communication, and research.*
- *Now that I am in the master's program, I am finding out that these social networking sites that I previously used for personal use, would be of great use in the educational setting and I am planning to incorporate this type of instruction when I teach.*
- *My past work experience as a minister has positioned me to be an ed-tech evangelist in my current circles of influence. I am passionate about educational technology and love connecting others to it.*
- *I currently use social networking for classes I am attending and personal use. After completion of my degree, I plan to have more time to dedicate towards managing and implementing more social networking tools I have learned about to use in a professional and educational manner.*
- *Through social networking, it is easy to find individuals who share my professional interests, who can guide me to the resources I need. This kind of networking sometimes*

works faster and better than doing my own Web searches.

As the results of this informal survey suggest, student exposure to social media through their online courses reinforces their continued use both in and out of the classroom. The fact that current and former students are choosing to interact voluntarily with one another through a host of social media resources is further evidence that students find value in networking with like-minded individuals. Furthermore, in monitoring the Educational Technology program social media sites, continued student activity is increasingly observed between semesters and long holiday breaks, suggesting that students are using the tools without being required to as part of a course activity. As social media resources become more easily accessible through the penetration of increasingly user-friendly and affordable smart phones and tablets, individuals will be able to take advantage of anytime, anywhere online support communities to sustain their personal cognitive apprenticeship and knowledge brokering, for professional development and informal learning. These preliminary findings provide sufficient justification for continued investigation into the use of social networking and content-sharing resources for formal and informal learning, as well as ongoing professional development.

FUTURE DIRECTIONS

What does the future hold for online professional development and informal learning? Our imagination is the limit. Recent advancements in augmented reality and virtual reality are adding new dimensions to social media, making formal and informal learning possible anywhere, through mobile devices and smart phones.

One new technology being explored and used for informal learning and professional development are 3D virtual worlds. Virtual worlds simulate real-world work environments that permit individuals to communicate, interact, and collaborate with others to acquire and practice skills in safe, non-threatening surroundings. Since these virtual environments are on the Internet, they can be accessed at any time, from anywhere, fostering apprenticeships between professionals that are no longer bound by location.

Different from virtual reality, augmented reality involves the combining or overlapping of computer-generated data and imagery with reality to enhance the user's perception of the world around him. The benefit of the marriage between social media and augmented reality is that through smart phones and other portable computing devices, individuals can instantaneously access just-in-time information about everyday objects and places in their immediate surroundings. A digital image is projected using a phone or other mobile device, onto a photo, object, or structure to create a type of three-dimensional display. For example, people taking a tour in a historic part of a city, can use their smart phones to scan a code imprinted on the building's descriptive plaque. As users move their phones over the building, they are able to see the original blueprints superimposed over the structure. According to Ira and Berge (2009), one of the biggest benefits of augmented reality is that it "immerses participants in workplace contexts that closely match the actual contexts of their jobs" (p. 638). As professionals discover the uses of augmented reality, a host of applications can be developed for professional development and informal learning in a wide range of fields.

As educators, trainers, and practitioners experiment with these new social media tools, researchers will need to evaluate their effectiveness and usefulness for providing high-quality education and professional development to workforce professionals. Hart (2010) noted, "organisations need agile and flexible systems as the world is changing under their feet" (para. 7). While social media provides such a system, Paus-Hasebrink et al. (2010) cautioned that there is also a need

for further research on the "effects of Internet-based learning environments on actual learning outcomes" (p. 46), and "the advantages as well as the challenges related to new ways of teaching and learning based on the social Web" (p. 46). Coupled with effective research, new technologies, such as virtual and augmented realities, can afford professionals unlimited opportunities to direct their own learning, build ongoing online learning communities, as well as to create and contribute to the learning of other professionals world-wide.

CONCLUSION

The demands of the ever-changing, increasingly competitive workplace are forcing workers to adopt new methods of learning and acquiring information. This need has helped to fuel the growth of the social media phenomenon, and is exerting pressure on higher education and professional development providers to make learning more relevant. As educators and trainers, it is important to recognize and adapt to this emerging paradigm shift or risk becoming irrelevant. Already, a profusion of information is available at the worker's fingertips, diminishing the need for colleges, universities, and even, libraries to exist. Instead of waiting for the impending shift to happen, institutions of higher education should prepare themselves and their graduates to capitalize on opportunities these seismic movements will create.

In order to add value to their college degrees in this era of free information, institutions need to reemphasize the intellectual skills and competencies graduates will need to capitalize on the accessibility and availability of information. Information without understanding is worthless, but information with understanding is priceless.

Through a detailed description of how one instructor transformed his online graduate courses into dynamic, interactive, ongoing online learning communities that extended beyond the classroom, this chapter provides academics and practitioners a model for establishing a professional learning network that learners can participate in, and replicate in their workplaces to promote their professional development and informal learning. As corroborated by the students' responses to the social media survey, learners are beginning to recognize the value of social media and content-sharing tools for broadening their professional development and informal learning.

As the Millenial learners enter and professional workers return to higher education, they will select programs that are relevant to their interests and needs. As Ketter (2010) observed, "change is happening quickly, whether organizations are ready for it or not. So it is now time for learning professionals to adapt to these changes; create new strategies for learning, employee development, and engagement; and find their place in this new workplace structure" (p. 40). This is an exciting time for higher education and professional development providers, during which partnerships can be forged between the learners and the learned to create and share knowledge and develop new ways for improving workplace performance.

REFERENCES

Bingham, T., & Conner, M. (2010). *The new social learning*. Alexandria, VA: ASTD Press & Berett-Koehler.

Bitter-Rijpkema, M., & Verjans, S. (2010). Hybrid professional learning networks for knowledge workers: Educational theory inspiring new practices. In L. Creanor, D. Hawkridge, K. Ng, & F. Rennie (Eds.), *ALT-C 2010 Conference Proceedings: Into Something Rich and Strange: Making Sense of the Sea-Change,* (pp. 166-174). Nottingham, UK: ALT-C. Retrieved from http://dspace.ou.nl/bitstream/1820/2575/6/bitter_verjans%20ALTC_2010_HybridprofessionalLN.pdf.

Canadian Health Services Research Foundation. (2003). *The theory and practice of knowledge brokering in Canada's health system.* Retrieved from http://www.sandy-campbell.com/sc/Knowledge_Translation_files/Theory_and_Practice_e.pdf.

Collins, A., Brown, J. S., & Holum, A. (1991). Cognitive apprenticeship: Making thinking visible. *American Educator*. Retrieved from http://elc.fhda.edu/transform/resources/collins_brown_holum_1991.pdf.

edWeb.net. MCH, Inc., & MMS Education. (2009). *Preliminary findings: A survey of D-12 educators on social networking and content-sharing tools*. Retrieved from http://www.edweek.org/media/k-12socialnetworking.pdf.

Eyrich, N., Padman, M. L., & Sweetser, K. D. (2008). PR practitioners' use of social media tools and communication technology. *Public Relations Review, 34*, 412–414. Retrieved from http://uga.academia.edu/sweetser/Papers/121858/PR_practitioners_use_of_social_media_tools_and_communication_technology doi:10.1016/j.pubrev.2008.09.010

Halx, M. D. (2010). Re-conceptualizing college and university teaching through the lens of adult education: Regarding undergraduates as adults. *Teaching in Higher Education, 15*(5), 519–530. doi:10.1080/13562517.2010.491909

Hart, J. (2010, August 1). *The future of social media in the enterprise*. Retrieved from http://janeknight.typepad.com/socialmedia/2010/08/futureenterprise.html.

Ira, K., & Berge, Z. (2009). Online learning's future in the workplace with augmented reality. In Cartelli, A., & Palma, M. (Eds.), *Encyclopedia of Information Communication Technology*. Hershey, PA: IGI Global.

Kamel Boulos, M. N., & Wheeler, S. (2007). The emerging Web 2.0 social software: An enabling suite of sociable technologies in health and health care education. *Health Information and Libraries Journal*, 24(1), 2–23. doi:10.1111/j.1471-1842.2007.00701.x

Ketter, P. (2010). Six trends that will change workplace learning forever. *ASTD Training and Development*. Retrieved from http://www.astd.org/TD/Archives/2010/Dec/Free/December+2010+2010+Trends.htm.

Lombardi, M. M., & Oblinger, D. G. (2007). Authentic learning for the 21st century: An overview. *EDUCAUSE Learning Initiative*. Retrieved from http://alicechristie.org/classes/530/EduCause.pdf.

McKinsey Global Institute. (2011). An economy that works: Job creation and America's future. *McKinsey Global Institute Report*. Retrieved from http://www.mckinsey.com/~/media/McKinsey/dotcom/Insights%20and%20pubs/MGI/Research/Labor%20Markets/An%20economy%20that%20works%20Job%20creation%20and%20Americas%20future/MGI_US_job_creation_full_report.ashx.

Nair, M., & Webster, P. (2010). Education for health professionals in the emerging market economies: A literature review. *Medical Education*, 44(9), 856–863. doi:10.1111/j.1365-2923.2010.03747.x

Paus-Hasebrink, I., Wijnen, C. W., & Jadin, T. (2010). Opportunities of web 2.0: Potentials of learning. *International Journal of Media and Cultural Politics*, 6(1), 45–62. doi:10.1386/macp.6.1.45/1

Rosencheck, M. M. (2010). Navigating the interactive workplace. *Chief Learning Officer*. Retrieved from http://www.cedma-europe.org/newsletter%20articles/Clomedia/Navigating%20the%20Interactive%20Workplace%20(May%2010).pdf.

Salavuo, M. (2008). Social media as an opportunity for pedagogical change in music education. *Journal of Music, Technology and Education, 1*(2), 121-136. Retrieved from http://miikkasalavuo.fi/SalavuoSocialMedia.pdf.

Selwyn, N. (2007). Web 2.0 applications as alternative environments for informal learning - A critical review. In *Proceedings of the OECD-KERIS Expert Meeting*. OECD-KERIS. Retrieved from http://www.oecd.org/dataoecd/32/3/39458556.pdf.

Stevens, V. (2006). Revisiting multiliteracies in collaborative learning environments: Impact on teacher professional development. *TESL-EJ, 10*(2), 1-12. Retrieved from http://tesl-ej.org/pdf/ej38/int.pdf.

Vogel, M. P. (2009). Exploring the conditions for academic teachers' informal collegial learning about teaching: A social network approach. *Educate, 9*(2), 18-36. Retrieved from http://www.educatejournal.org/index.php?journal=educate&page=article&op=viewFile&path%5B%5D=200&path%5B%5D=209.

Ward, V., Smith, S., Carruthers, S., Hamer, S., & House, A. (2010). *Knowledge brokering: Exploring the process of transferring knowledge into action*. Retrieved from http://www.leeds.ac.uk/lihs/psychiatry/research/TransferringKnowledgeIntoAction/documents/Knowledge%20Brokering%20Final%20report.pdf.

ADDITIONAL READING

Anderson, T., & Kanuka, H. (1997). On-line forums: New platforms for professional development and group collaboration. *Journal of Computer-Mediated Communication, 3*(3), 1–15. Retrieved from http://www.eric.ed.gov:80/PDFS/ED418693.pdf

Bingham, T., & Conner, M. (2010). *The new social learning*. Alexandria, VA: ASTD Press & Berett-Koehler.

Canadian Health Services Research Foundation. (2003). *The theory and practice of knowledge brokering in Canada's health system*. Retrieved from http://www.chsrf.ca/migrated/pdf/Theory_and_Practice_e.pdf.

Cheong, C., Tandon, R., & Cheong, F. (2010). A project-based learning internship for it undergraduates with social support from a social networking site. In *Proceedings of the Information Systems Educators 2010 Conference*. Information Systems Educators. Retrieved from http://proc.isecon.org/2010/pdf/1389.pdf.

Chung Wei, R., Darling-Hammond, L., & Adamson, F. (2010). *Professional development in the United States: Trends and challenges*. National Staff Development Council Technical Report. Retrieved from http://www.nsdc.org/news/NSDCstudytechnicalreport2010.pdf.

Conole, G., Galley, R., & Culver, J. (2011). Frameworks for understanding the nature of interactions, networking, and community in a social networking site for academic practice. *International Review of Research in Open and Distance Learning, 12*(3), 119–138. Retrieved from http://www.irrodl.org/index.php/irrodl/article/view/914

Cranefield, J., & Yoong, P. (2010). Knowledge brokers in overlapping online communities of practice: The role of the connector-leader. In Yoong, P. (Ed.), *Leadership in the Digital Enterprise: Issues and Challenges*. Hershey, PA: IGI Global.

Cross, J. (2007). *Informal learning: Rediscovering the natural pathways that inspire innovation and performance*. San Francisco, CA: Pfeiffer.

Downes, S. (2010). New technology supporting informal learning. *Journal of Emerging Technologies in Web Intelligence, 2*(1), 27–33. Retrieved from http://nparc.cisti-icist.nrc-cnrc.gc.ca/npsi/ctrl?action=rtdoc&an=15336784&article=0 doi:10.4304/jetwi.2.1.27-33

Ebner, M., Lienhardt, C., Rohs, M., & Meyer, I. (2010). Microblogs in higher education – A chance to facilitate informal and process-oriented learning? *Computers & Education, 55*(1), 92–100. doi:10.1016/j.compedu.2009.12.006

Jarche, H. (2010, February 24). *A framework for social learning in the enterprise*. Retrieved from http://www.jarche.com/2010/02/a-framework-for-social-learning-in-the-enterprise/.

Kane, K., Robinson-Combre, J., & Berge, Z. (2010). Tapping into social networking: Collaborating enhances both knowledge management and e-learning. *The Journal of Information and Knowledge Management Systems, 40*(1), 62–70.

LeNoue, M., Hall, T., & Eighmy, M. A. (2011). Adult education and the social media revolution. *Adult Learning, 22*(2), 4–12.

Lightle, K. (2010). Using social media to build an online professional network of middle level educators. *Knowledge Quest*. Retrieved from http://pathfinder.utb.edu:2081/pdf25_26/pdf/2010/5F8/01Nov10/57458491.pdf?T=P&P=AN&K=57458491&S=R&D=a9h&EbscoContent=dGJyMNXb4kSeprE4v%2BvlOLCmr0mep7VSsqi4SbKWxWXS&ContentCustomer=dGJyMPGptlGxq7ZLuePfgeyx44Dt6fIA.

Lombardi, M. M., & Oblinger, D. G. (2007). Authentic learning for the 21st century: An overview. *EDUCAUSE Learning Initiative*. Retrieved from http://alicechristie.org/classes/530/EduCause.pdf.

Luehmann, A. L., & Tinelli, L. (2008). Teacher professional identity development with social networking technologies: Learning reform through blogging. *Educational Media International, 45*(4), 323–333. doi:10.1080/09523980802573263

Nafukho, F. M., Graham, C. M., & Muyia, H. M. A. (2010). Harnessing and optimal utilization of human capital in virtual workplace environments. *Advances in Developing Human Resources, 12*(6), 648–664. doi:10.1177/1523422310394791

Park, Y., Heo, G. M., & Lee, R. (2011). Blogging for informal learning: Analyzing bloggers' perceptions using learning perspective. *Journal of Educational Technology & Society, 14*(2), 149–160.

Paus-Hasebrink, I., Wijnen, C. W., & Jadin, T. (2010). Opportunities of web 2.0: Potentials of learning. *International Journal of Media and Cultural Politics, 6*(1). doi:10.1386/macp.6.1.45/1

Polin, L. (2010). Graduate professional education from a community of practice perspective: The role of social and technical networking. In Blackmore, C. (Ed.), *Social Learning Systems and Communities of Practice*. London, UK: Springer London. doi:10.1007/978-1-84996-133-2_10

Redecker, C., Ala-Metka, K., & Punie, Y. (2010). Learning 2.0 - The impact of social media on learning in Europe. *IPTS Learning 2.0 Policy Brief*. Retrieved from http://ftp.jrc.es/EURdoc/JRC56958.pdf.

Rosencheck, M. M. (2010). Navigating the interactive workplace. *Chief Learning Officer*. Retrieved from http://www.cedma-europe.org/newsletter%20articles/Clomedia/Navigating%20the%20Interactive%20Workplace%20(May%2010).pdf.

Shepherd, C. (2011). Does social media have a place in workplace learning? *Strategic Direction, 27*(2), 3–4. doi:10.1108/02580541111103882

Thompson, T. L. (2011). Work-learning in informal online communities: Evolving spaces. *Information Technology & People, 24*(2), 184–196. doi:10.1108/09593841111137359

Vogel, M. P. (2009). Exploring the conditions for academic teachers informal collegial learning about teaching: A social network approach. *Educate, 9*(2), 18–36.

Wang, M. (2011). Integrating organizational, social, and individual perspectives in web 2.0-based workplace e-learning. *Information Systems Frontiers, 13*(2), 191–205. doi:10.1007/s10796-009-9191-y

Wenger, E., McDermott, R., & Snyder, W. (2002). *Cultivating communities of practice*. Boston, MA: Harvard Business School Press.

Westera, W. (2011). On the changing nature of learning context: Anticipating the virtual extensions of the world. *Journal of Educational Technology & Society, 14*(2), 201–212.

KEY TERMS AND DEFINITIONS

Authentic Learning: In authentic learning activities, real-life problems or situations are identified, which are relevant to the learners' personal or professional lives. As a strategy of cognitive apprenticeship, learners will oftentimes first see an expert carry out the task, then, do the task themselves.

Cognitive Apprenticeship: Cognitive apprenticeship is a social constructivist approach to learning, where novice learners (apprentices) observe an expert carry out an action and then practice doing it themselves under the guidance of the mentor/expert.

Informal Learning: Informal learning refers to ongoing learning activities that are determined by the learner and occur outside of structured academic or professional environments.

Knowledge Brokering: Knowledge brokering refers to the activities designed to aid in the exchange of knowledge between researchers and practitioners.

Professional Development: Professional development refers to the learning activities that help professionals acquire the knowledge and skills they need for career advancement or to carry out their job responsibilities.

Social Networking/Social Media: Social media refers to Web 2.0 services and tools that facilitate communication and collaboration.

Social Learning: Social learning is a term that has emerged in recent years to describe the type of learning facilitated through social media. The term describes the learning that occurs when individuals use social media to exchange information, collaborate on and improve their work, as well as develop knowledge and skills.

Web 2.0: Web 2.0 refers to a new generation of Internet services and tools that facilitate communication and collaboration. A characteristic feature of Web 2.0 is the explosion of social networking tools that allow users to not only download content from the Internet but to also create and share information.

Chapter 8
Developing Professional Competencies through International Peer Learning Communities

Hanna Yakavenka
University of Greenwich, UK

ABSTRACT

This chapter utilizes a peer learning community as an example to explore whether and how information exchange, learning, and knowledge creation occur when students undertake professional internships. Observation and analysis of the learners' views on their interaction are conducted by studying peer-generated blogs to determine if learners working in companies worldwide, but connected via an informal virtual community, can communicate effectively and produce a useful pool of information, thus creating meaningful knowledge and expertise to assist in future career development. The objective is to utilize the lessons learned to incorporate effective elements of the peer learning experience into formal programs of study and so increase the employability focus of business education.

INTRODUCTION

This chapter presents the findings of investigative research conducted on a group of learners with the intention of exploring how effective use of online social networking tools can assist participants within an informal international professional peer community to learn from each other. A number of research areas including communication across cultures, professional development, and com-

munities of learning were used as a background to the study. The prime data was derived from the informal, learner initiated online reflective blogs, where postgraduate, culturally diverse students utilize their peers' knowledge and expertise when undertaking work placements abroad and completing their internship reports. Whilst adopting a social constructivist approach, the intention was to find out whether learners can effectively learn from each other by exchanging internship experiences and exploring how knowledge is

DOI: 10.4018/978-1-4666-1815-2.ch008

generated within an informal peer initiated learning community, thus enhancing the professional development and employment opportunities of the participants.

BACKGROUND

There is sufficient evidence to indicate that knowledge can be shared in a community of learning given that reflective communication enables the enculturation of professional activities (e.g. Steinbring, 2005). A primary focus of learning within the community is *social participation* i.e. an individual as an active participant in the interactions of the community and in the construction of the knowledge base through the community. Many have suggested that knowledge is socially constructed (Berger & Luckmann, 1966); often tacit (Polanyi, 1966; Hedlund, 1994); a function of the play of meanings, material, as well as mental and social (Latour, 1987); acquired through participation within communities of practice (Wenger, et al., 2002). In contrast to the objectivist epistemology view, Polanyi (1966) argued that there is an inescapable and essential personal element that is a structural component of all knowledge which he called "personal," saying that when we know anything at all, we "dwell in" its particulars in order to understand the "comprehensive entity" which is the meaning of these particulars, which includes them as their sense. Davenport and Prusak (1998) claimed, "knowledge is a fluid mix of framed experience, values, contextual information and expert insight... it originates and is applied in the minds of knowers" (p. 5). Nonaka (in von Krogh, et al., 2000) concluded that in any way knowledge is context-specific, as it depends on a particular time and space. While the sender of the knowledge is giving it meaning in according with its home context, the receiver is decoding it in accordance with the host framework in order to apply it. Overall this chapter argues that knowledge is constructed on the bases of social

circumstances, the characteristics and personal history of individual learners (Billet, 1996), the level of trust generated among the members (Bekmeier-Feuerhahn & Eichenlaub, 2010) and specific work-based settings.

It is essential to understand the fundamentals of the communication process in order to fully comprehend the many and varied enablers and barriers that are an integral part of knowledge sharing which occurs in the process of learning. While "communication is *already* a complex process of information exchange, that involves the perception and judgment of all involved" (Nance quoted in Buckley, et al., 1999, p. 79), effective communication incorporates how that information is conveyed and received. Some explanations of human communication behavior derive directly from an examination of how individuals acquire and modify ideas through communication with others. The learning, diffusion, and change processes, all involve the communication route. Schramm (1965) found that the transfer of ideas occurs most receptively between those who are alike and similar in certain attributes, such as beliefs, values, and education. When the parties involved share common understandings, have a mutual language, and are alike in personal characteristics, the communication of ideas is likely to have a greater effect in terms of knowledge gained, attitude formation, and change. As a whole, the interactions are more rewarding to both the sender and receiver of the information the more they have in common. When encoding information to communicate to others, the degree of common ground varies with the particular relationship, complicating the process of information perception. Schramm (1965, p. 17) suggested that it is the area formed by the overlapping field of experience of communicators—a desirable area of "common interest/ground"—that enhances the possibility of knowledge creation as a result of the communication process. This has been further developed by social constructivists, who believed knowledge to be socially and culturally constructed by individuals through interaction (Kukla, 2000) and that shared understanding or inter-subjectivity not only forms the necessary ground for human communication, but also supports people in their willingness to extend their learning and understanding of new ideas (Rogoff, 1990; Vygotsky, 1987).

Learning something new can be exciting, particularly when it is stimulating and motivational, especially if one feels it is really worthwhile and ultimately useful. How one learns however differs greatly depending on the person. Each individual brings different approaches that are grounded in his/her past learning experiences and value systems (Laurillard, 1993). Therefore it is only natural to have different perspectives and expectations on what is considered to be effective learning. In accordance with behavioral perspectives, learning is not self-initiated but rather a reactive behavior. Learners gain knowledge by mainly responding to external stimuli (Skinner, 1968; in Fang, 2001). Supporters of cognitive perspectives believe that learning is natural and hierarchical, and learners come with a certain background of experience and value systems (Ausubel, 2000). As a result, knowledge and skills can be easily transferred from the short-term memory (surface learning) to the long-term memory (deep learning) which can be retrieved later for a specific application. The responsibility for learning in such scenarios is mainly on the learners themselves. At the same time constructivists view learning as a natural and self-initiated process, taking place by transforming new information into personal knowledge with learners critically identifying its relevance and usefulness, especially if it assists in solving immediate work related challenges (Cobb, 1995; Gredler, 1997). This would indicate that learning success does not necessarily depend on the content as such, but rather on the system of information management that allows individuals to effectively learn, therefore what to know may potentially be less important than where to know and above all, how to know.

Online Communities of Learning (CoL)

Learning is influenced by participation in a community (Rafaeli, et al., 2004) where learners construct their knowledge through social interaction with peers, through applying ideas in practice, and through reflection and modification of ideas (Bruner, 1990; Tobin, 1990). Communities of Practice / Learning (CoL) trace their roots to constructivism (Oliver & Herrington, 2000; Palloff & Pratt, 1999; Persichitte, 2000; Squire & Johnson, 2000). Lave and Wenger (1991) discussed the notion of legitimate peripheral participation, implying a significant shift of control among members of the community. Today CoL are described as groups of people informally bound together by shared expertise and passion for a joint enterprise, which promises to radically stimulate knowledge sharing, learning and change (Wenger, et al., 2002).

A well-designed CoL encourages a wide diversity of actions: one-to-one conversations, group discussions, learning, and development of new ideas and communication with experts on specific issues. In the learning environment, central direct leadership and guidance is replaced by self-management and work ownership by the learners themselves. Among some of the major factors needed for the best results are trust, voluntary activeness, non-hierarchical status, duration, and intensity of the partnership (Eisen, 2001). The learning that evolves from a community of learners is collaborative, and hence greater than would be generated by an individual. In addition to the end knowledge itself, the process of its development is an important factor to recognize (Gherardi & Nicolini, 2000). People in CoL share their experiences and knowledge in free-flowing creative ways fostering new approaches to knowledge creation, learning and decision-making. In addition to generating new knowledge, effective CoP solves problems, promotes the spread of best practice, and enhances professional skills.

Those requiring new knowledge and skills today are faced with additional opportunities provided by the e-learning environment. Flourishing online communities coupled with the increasing need for efficient knowledge sharing, has created a need for a better understanding on how online communications promote learning, facilitating and the diffusion of knowledge within a group of learners.

A social environment undergoing profound change through a tsunami-like flood of innovative tools and services that foster new modes of collaboration and social organization. The rapid evolution of blogs, wikis, social networking... and related applications offer rich user experiences where the process of knowing is a community-based, collaborative endeavor (Alexander, 2006, p. 32).

It has been taken for granted that social interaction will automatically occur just because technology allows it (Häkkinen, et al., 2004). When considering *learning through technology*, one should consider *technology* to be broadly defined as the application of learning science (by whatever means). Learning through technologies enables people from radically different locations to readily communicate, creates new possibilities that support a range of learning types, including information retrieval, transfer of knowledge to application, as well as new ways of working collaboratively with knowledge. However, along with the extra opportunities generated by technological advancements, they also present communicational challenges preventing the generation of new ideas, knowledge and the 'building' of expertise. It is only within communities built on systemic and interpersonal trust where participants go beyond superficial exchanges and enjoy sharing and benefiting from each other's knowledge and expertise, while being jointly committed to developing better practices (Bekmeier-Feuerhahn & Eichenlaub, 2010; Antonijevic & Gurak, 2009; Gilroy, 2001).

Professional World Expectations: Cross-Cultural Awareness

In today's global knowledge-based economy, companies require a whole spectrum of new higher-order metacognitive skills and dynamic competencies from their employees to manage innovation and organizational changes. Metacognitive skills related to purposeful use, planning, monitoring, and regulating the learning processes are central in order to take full advantage of the benefits of computer-supported learning environments (Pifarre & Cobos, 2010; Abel, 2007). The same significance is given to the characteristics of learners, their tasks, and learning preferences as these characteristics also affect skills development within a computer-supported learning environment (Winter, et al., 2008). According to Kirch and Tucker (2001), 20% of success in any career is based on the ability to learn, understand, and reason. The other 80% depends on the ability to understand the value and apply soft skills. Within professional practice communities, specialists are also required to continuously develop their subject specific knowledge and skills by engaging in Work-Based Learning (WBL) which involves conscious reflection on *learning by action* in workplace interaction (Raelin, 2008).

There are several dimensions of cultural and prior learning experiences, which shape how a learner reacts to the challenges experienced within a new learning environment (Akande, 1998; Black, 1999). People from different cultures can have difficulty in communicating with and understanding one another to the extent that their respective communication 'codes' differ (Fox, 1997; Triandis, 1995; Buckley, et al., 1999), this can be further exacerbated by cultural and language differences. Hence, learning (knowledge sharing) efficiency within multicultural groups can be significantly reduced if cultural diversity is not taken into account, particularly if communication occurs online. As an example, in the case of Asian learners, knowledge acquisition consists of teaching and asking; making the educator the central figure in the learning process, whereas in Western education, learners are strongly encouraged and are expected to do further investigation themselves to enhance their understanding of the subject (Durkin, 2008; Currie, 2007). According to market research by the British Council in 2007, 69% of learners worldwide said they learned most effectively when socializing informally, suggesting that people learn most from friends or those who have something in common. When learning occurs outside the formal learning environment (particularly in a real business setting) it creates an entirely different experience, atmosphere and dynamic for learning and self-development, which can assist one to achieve own learning goals even more efficiently.

There is a strategic need for people of different cultures to better understand each other to be able to perform complex tasks and take decisions. The argument over whether cultural differences impact upon the process of knowledge sharing and creation in cross-cultural communities prevails. Some researchers disagree, not finding empirical support (e.g. Frost & Zhou, 2005) while others confirmed the supposition (Day, et al., 1995). There are also those who consider that on the one hand cultural differences cause misunderstandings and complicate the process while, on the other, new knowledge is likely to originate in unfamiliar contexts (Chini, 2004; Subramaniam & Venkatraman, 2001). Nonetheless, even if difficult to define in practice, culture is widely accepted as an important element, able to affect the transfer of knowledge and expertise internationally. As expressed by Chini (2004) "human capability to capture and understand complex facts is rooted in a cultural setting and thus tends to differ across cultural areas" (p. 2). In international settings, critical cross-cultural awareness becomes another essential employee quality, which enables individuals to conduct cross-cultural interaction by reducing misunderstandings and inappropriate behavior. It is essential to recognize that it is not always

easy to make people comprehend the concept of culture, as everyone is accustomed to seeing the world from their own perspective. The subtlety and depth of culture's influence often surprises even those people who consider themselves as being aware and tolerant of other ways of being. Cross-cultural awareness increases the ability of individuals to communicate better and adapt their behavior when interacting within the international community (Brislin & Yoshida, 1994; Triandis, 1995). "Thinking outside the box" entails the appropriation of cultural tools to transform not only the relation of individuals to situations, but also their relation to other members of a 'community' by participating in their practices.

By adopting a social constructivist approach this chapter observes an online community of practice, presuming it is individuals who build reality around them and create meanings through their interactions with each other. It investigates:

- Whether cultural differences of the participants create significant barriers to effective learning;
- The key factors which motivated and enabled the participants to learn from their peers and develop competencies sought after by global employers;
- If any useful knowledge was generated by the participants.

METHODOLOGICAL APPROACH AND THE SETTING FOR THE STUDY

The objectives outlined in this chapter and complexity of the phenomena under investigation necessitated a mixed method approach, which enables taking into account the context and outcome of the learning process. Data about individuals and their cultural background was collected via a concise purpose designed questionnaire. For analysis purposes, the reflective blogs were followed closely throughout the year to identify how the learning community was created and how the messages were being communicated. Towards the end of the observation, participants were also asked a number of simple reflective questions to identify their general feelings about the whole experience. Blogs were further content-analyzed with the help of NViVo software.

The example used in this chapter is based on the analysis of online blog conversations within the informal peer learning community formed by fifty-eight MBA International Business students undertaking their internships. The group was predominantly male (75%), with the majority of Asian origin (87%), including students from India, Bangladesh, Pakistan, China, Thailand, and Vietnam, the remainder being of European origin.

After spending a year in the classroom, the students secured employment with companies situated in Dubai, Nigeria, Kuwait, Ghana, Bangladesh, India, Nepal, Malaysia, Iran, France, and the UK, where they had to face real business reality. They were employed in a range of managerial posts—e.g. Marketing/HR/Customer Relationships Managers; Business/Product/Project Development Managers; International Trade/Operations Managers. In each role, they had to rapidly engage in the company context, culture and day-to-day activities in order to acquire, understand, develop, and implement their knowledge in authentic work scenarios to develop their professional competences. Students were employed in diverse industries—e.g. Manufacturing/Chemical/Home/Office Appliances and Accessories; Information Technologies, Hard/Software Design; Hospitality and Resorts; Textile, Fashion, and Clothing; Health Care/Energy Providers; Education, all of which presented different work practices and expectations.

Within a university, experiential learning can take place in various forms, from formal educational programs to informal learner-initiated activities. In the current example of a Professional Practice (internship) course, academics adopted the role of facilitators while students were expected to control and direct their own learning experiences. The goal was to increase motivation and improve learning by encouraging the formation of a rich source of knowledge, which could be used to improve skill levels in actual work situations. In order to promote social interaction and enhance knowledge sharing as well as smoothing the transition, students were offered an open Web space where they could connect with study colleagues who were going through a similar process (via reflective blogs), and if necessary receive feedback from academics (via learning logs). Within this space, learners were engaged into a social practice intrinsic to organizational networks to enable exchange of information and learning. In learning logs (open only between a learner and an academic), students were asked to map steps in their learning throughout the placement, particularly the development of practice locally, nationally or internationally and the learners' own continuing professional development. Unlike learning logs, reflective interaction blogs are open for all learners to read and comment, providing an opportunity to both reflect and interact by sharing experiences.

The introduction of the Professional Practice course into the study curricula was stimulated by the recent debate on the effectiveness of management education, which highlighted the importance of collective, multidisciplinary, reflective practice on management development and autonomous integrity. Rogers (1969) compared education to therapy in respect of sharing similar goals for personal change, self-knowing, personal growth, and development. Students who engage in authentic business related learning tasks acquire associated facts and skills much better because they must understand the whole complex of things to accomplish their job related task. Critical reflection on practice, including different technical, social, and economic influences drawn from local, national and/or international perspectives, is a valuable resource that can be used to enhance a learners' judgment, increase their professional autonomy and to promote change. Together with problem based learning during in-class activities WBL could be conceived as a system where learning is developed and applied by relating academic and workplace practices enhancing learners' transferrable skills for Lifelong Career Development. Consequently, this course has been designed to focus on reflective practice within the experiential learning context of the professional role (the business situation).

The course aims to:

- Consolidate, in a practical context, advanced understanding of organizations, their management and the changing external context in which they operate;

- Enhance the application of knowledge and understanding of complex international business and management issues, both systematically and creatively, to improve business and management practice.

- Increase students' capacity to reflect on and learn from events and thus integrate new knowledge with past experience and apply it to new situations

The learning outcomes of the course centre on individual's reflections on a year of managerial work experience related to the previous pathway of studies. The use of computer-moderated communications as a distance-learning medium provides a flexible means to facilitate the individual's learning experiences, enrich the collaborative nature of practice, and broaden the dialogue between learners and academics. Learners are expected to master reflective skills to critically assess the nature, efficiency, and effectiveness of their current knowledge and to practice and apply an action inquiry approach to develop strategies for effecting change.

LEARNING COMMUNITIES: HOW DO THEY WORK IN PRACTICE

An online learning environment works most effectively among those wishing to look at and study issues from a number of perspectives. Dependant on their chosen or adopted role within the community, participants can choose to just read and reflect on the contributions from others or respond within a secure environment, enabling them to express their true thoughts. This combination of certain anonymity together with a sense of connectedness allows participants to open up and take risks to express their thoughts, going through the process of thinking rather than adopting a fixed position, especially in uncertain areas of knowledge. As expressed by one of the participants in the community under investigation:

The best channel of peer networking is online, as not everyone feels comfortable putting their views forward in front of others in a face-to-face environment. Using blogs has been an excellent way of testing my ideas with peers and learn from them.

Since most of the participants come from different cultural backgrounds and undertook their professional practice placements in different parts of the world, there was a fear that there would be a significant level of tension and misunderstanding in the community. Social behavior and interaction does differ from country to country, being under the strong influence of the internal cultural forces that makes the transfer of tacit knowledge in particular more complicated. With communication being the foundation for knowledge sharing, these problems will be exacerbated if the source and receiver do not share a common culture.

It became apparent that the community under investigation fits well with a similarity-attraction hypothesis (by Byrne, 1969; in Bochner, 1996), stating that individuals are more likely to seek out, enjoy, understand, want to work with, trust, believe and generally prefer people with whom they share salient characteristics, including interests, values, religion, skills, language and all other aspects on which human beings differ as shown by the following blogs.

... cross-cultural management is considered important in every organization today. My networking with peers provides me with an invaluable chance to share our differences, work ethics and attitudes to work at different levels of organization. This creates an awareness of the multicultural working environment with its challenges and opportunities.

...as I work in an international business department, I daily come across people who belong to different cultures. By talking to my peers, who also come from different backgrounds and who I can trust to share my fears, I learn from them how to address potential challenges in cross-cultural behavior.

...by reading my peers' blogs and by interacting with them, I have gained a lot of experience, exposure, awareness about culture, working styles, diverse work ethics and codes of professional practice in different countries.

...my interactive blog experience has helped to eliminate the barriers between peers, their industries, their work cultures irrespective of the different geographical locations.

Most of the participants (82%) noted that working and interacting with peers belonging to different cultural backgrounds, helped them to better understand and work easier with people who belong to other cultures in their work places. When a topic was generated which everybody could relate to (e.g. work/study problems; useful general practices etc.) discussion was readily taken up and exchanges could easily involve up to six people irrespective of their cultural background.

If someone brought up culture specific experiences (e.g. festivals, negotiation behavior) there would be at least two with three others interested who may later engage into further conversation. It helped significantly that most of the participants had studied together before; this provided greater directional stability and some common ground while newer members brought fresh ideas initiating new topics for discussion. Despite the diversity of backgrounds of members, there were no major disagreements and dysfunctional communication exchanges.

The vibrancy of the community very much depends on the participants and their willingness to get involved, share their experiences, and reflect on the experiences of others. Some students appreciated the freedom in choosing the topics for their blog discussions and were curious about the blogs of others, as "it brings wealth of learning and breadth of information." Others were more self-oriented and focused on their own personal learning and development and were not keen to share, but might have read what others were saying. The third group of participants were those who liked to be directed in learning 'what,' 'where' and 'how' and had a marked unwillingness to explore new things and interact with others in the community. However, overall general flexibility, openness to new ideas and adaptability to change allowed the community to share experiences and generate a great deal of new knowledge and practices.

Yamazaki and Kayes (2004) who also studied occurrences of knowledge absorption as a result of cross-cultural interpersonal interaction concluded that in fact, they provide additional opportunities for accumulating new knowledge. They stressed that an individual's competences are learned rather being inherited which helps with the understanding, managing, and development in the knowledge absorption process. In spite of language and cultural differences, learners in the community studied did establish the necessary level of trust enabling knowledge sharing and creation, feeling that they belonged to a professional community and were happy to share in the "spirit of professionalism." Informality within the community was a vital tool in the success of cross-cultural interactions and experience exchange, with the participants more willing to share information on a casual basis. The degree to which knowledge was shared was strongly related to the cognitive, motivational, and emotional capacity of the participants of the community. Communication challenges were also minimized if people were eager to communicate and had previously participated in similar activities.

Developing Professional Competencies

Rather than setting performance goals (which had been already done within the formal setting of the course in parallel to learners' internships) the informal learning community aimed to aid the sharing of knowledge; the increase of understanding (Wenger, et al., 2002) and professional development by effective collaborative discussion (Bielaczyc & Collins, 1999). While in the traditional educational situation, learners are required to absorb the same thing at the same time, in their informal learning community, newly adopted roles of idea generators, discussion motivators and humble listeners played an important part by developing and using skills requiring collaboration and different types of expertise, necessitating trust development among members (Grisham, Bergeron, & Brink, 1999; Palloff & Pratt, 1999). Below is a selection of statements from the participants about their blogging interaction:

...informal peer learning is more effective than any other way as it is just like talking to your own buddies who willingly sharing their knowledge and ideas. In this forum I am not afraid to speak and share my doubts as all of us are going through similar experiences.

...as my peers work in different industries (e.g. textiles, automobile, IT) the knowledge they share from their experiences helps me significantly to relate theoretical knowledge gained in the classroom to practical settings.

...unlike a traditional classroom this learning community is open 24/7... it gives me a great morale boost to know that my work is being appreciated by an authentic audience of my peers.

...talking to my peers I understood how valuable it is to be in possession of such skills as self-awareness, networking, negotiation skills, team working ability, the decision-making skills and the ability to cope with uncertainty.

...after reading other people's experiences I started putting myself forward at work when I had some good ideas. Talking to my peers helped me to boost my confidence levels.

...peer networking and information sharing helped me to gain knowledge and exchange diverse ideas, as well as getting exposure to different organizational practices, roles and responsibilities in different cultural settings. When I came across something interesting and relevant to my organization in my peers' blogs I always tended to try it out, often helping my organization to find alternative solutions to the problems. This experience has motivated me a lot during my professional practice.

...our peer discussions were not merely confined to workplace experiences, they also stimulated collaborative knowledge building approach between peers and hence it gradually became a weaving community which accelerated open and transparent information sharing.

As most of the participants did not work in similar jobs or industries it was not always easy to directly apply other peoples' experiences to their own situation, unless they had the necessary level of critical thinking skills to reflect on the blog of another participant and utilize it in their own work place. In these cases individuals stimulated further interaction and discussion with more regular exchanges on other social networking sites, e.g. Facebook (15%), LinkedIn (27%).

The students noted that relating to others in similar circumstances made their own experiences more valid and enabled useful comparisons. Some said that blog experience reduced their levels of anxiety (8%), helped to build up confidence (42%), as well as exploring and understanding their individual strengths and weaknesses (19%). A significant number of participants stressed that communicating with others motivated them to express more initiative at work (34%) and encouraged them take on more responsibility (17%).

Busy work schedules meant that some took longer to get involved with blogging, but once participating, they became quite active. Students with a high aptitude for learning were more willing to ask questions, comment on the work of others, and hence were probably perceived as sources of reliable information by other peers. Three or four students intently followed certain blogs that mirrored specific incidents/practices at their own place of work. They did not appear to say much about their own experiences, but were keen to ask further questions or request clarification, resulting in more in depth conversations. Occasionally they would also do additional research and propose alternative solutions to the issues raised. This type of communication often generated further communication on other social network web sites.

Evidence from the study suggests that students with stronger social networks (study; friendship; advice) also contributed more to the community by bringing new ideas and stimulated learning. The effective combination of studying and socializing with peers allowed learners to create their own *Personal Professional Learning Environments*, helping them to achieve targets by setting their own learning goals, managing their own learning,

sharing, and gaining knowledge by communicating with others in the learning process. From the students' blogs, it was evident that most learners felt included in the learning process and joined the 'conversation' when they felt ready to do so:

...the online interactive blog became a discussion board, where all of us could comment, share and discuss our roles, professional activities and most of all, our fears.

...one quite noticeable point is that my peers' professional practice updates provide me with a chance to directly learn and virtually experience the challenges and joys associated with their professional roles and responsibilities. I have deep appreciation for all the bloggers in the community who are contributing to this vast expanding pool of knowledge and making this a great learning experience for me.

In accordance with the science of learning, people develop better learning skills when given feedback. This feedback does not necessarily have to be from the academics and/or professionals. There is strong evidence that students in the studied community learned a lot from their peers:

...in our interactive blog which everyone is sharing, I could analyze, reflect, and improve my working style with others.

... it helped to boost my skills and confidence not only during the internship but also contributed to a better focus in my future professional career.

... I have learned and further developed my knowledge on various topics with the help of informal peer networking as well as shared ideas, expertise, and suggestions with others.

...when I read something interesting in the blogs of my peers it generated my curiosity and stimulated further reading on a particular subject. Updating

blogs also helped me to keep track of things that I have learned over a period of time. Sharing ideas with others made me reflect on my strengths and weaknesses in the professional settings.

Most indicated that the online support they received from their peers was very important to them and boosted their confidence, stating the openness of discussions made them feel comfortable about sharing their own concerns and challenges. Common online space was characterized as a "pool of knowledge" which could be tapped into when specific advice was needed, stimulating their creativity, boosting initiative, and exposing them to broad-based experiences across multiple business settings worldwide.

Knowledge Generation within an Informal Learning Community

Among the crucial questions in the investigation was whether any *specialist* knowledge had being created through the interaction processes. Although most of the participants agreed that a process of knowledge transfer initially begins with identification of the source (internal or external), followed by identification of whether that knowledge might be of value to the acquiring side, it is not always acknowledged that is essential for the receiver to really understand the transferred 'message' and be comfortable with it. This can only be achieved by 'translating' the meaning of the intended message in accordance with the existing knowledge of the recipient and enriching it with relevant new knowledge (Major & Cordey-Hayes, 2000). Hence only when the recipients were finally comfortable with the new knowledge could they assimilate it into wisdom leading to commitment and its further application.

It was evident that the content of the interactions between the participants of the community of learning under investigation went much further than pure exchange of practices and ideas.

...my peers work in different sectors and countries and I have learned much about the business practices of companies outside my normal sphere and have implemented some of the practices in my own work placement.

...I value my relationships with my peers as I learned a lot from them and saw potential for future business ventures in a number of countries, where I could expand my business.

...a number of my peers are working in companies dealing with a shortage of resources and how those are being addressed. As companies are spread around the world I was able to compare efficient and less so solutions to the problem.

...with my peers working in different companies all over the world, it is interesting to know how these companies employ cultural and social policies.

...from my peers' blogs I have learnt various things about software marketing, event management, retail management and distribution channels.

...a while back I read the blog of XXX where he shared his experience working in a UK based company. Two months later I was asked to meet one of UK based clients. The preparation for and the actual meeting went well as I was well aware of behavioral issues which could have come up during the negotiations. Now I am regularly chatting with another peer of mine, who works in Australia, as I am working on the project with the Australian partners of my company.

...I read and studied a lot in class on the Corporate Social Responsibility of companies, but when I read the blogs of one of my peers who actually works on a CSR project I saw how theoretical knowledge has been applied on practice.

...the interactive blogs of my colleagues have become my knowledge bank of information, which I have used when I came across similar problems at work.

These reflections suggest that students feel that when issues discussed by others related directly to them, it validated their contributions to the general discussion as well contributing to their existing pool of knowledge. It also indicates that when someone communicates to another learner in an online community, they developed a stronger motivation towards understanding their own situation and benefited by learning and investing themselves in it. Reading through the learning experience of other peers and reflecting on their own, helped students to understand the relevance of the theoretical material learned in class. Participants also seemed to have appreciated that knowledge sharing is a common essential business practice that should be encouraged, as it contributes greatly to the sustainable competitive advantage of organizations. Hence, the sharing of ideas with and learning from peers gained a totally new meaning.

Value of the Professional Practice Learning Community

When CoL is formed, it is not always apparent what its value is; moreover, the value often changes over the life of the community as the development of an easily accessed systematic body of knowledge becomes more important. Studying the level and quality of exchanges within the community investigated, participants enjoyed having the Web space to connect with their peers and showed a keenness to share specific work practices and ethics from their respective companies (24%); discuss problems they had to deal with and mistakes they made (32%); propose solutions to problems (11%); and debate resources and accessible training opportunities (21%). Much discussion centered on

individual roles, responsibilities, and management expectations in different organization (57%) with direct feedback to each other (14%).

As there were no set topics, the majority of participants often reported day-to-day practices and how they 'felt' in a specific situation. Each participant tended to share what was important for them personally in a given moment of time and work situation, making it difficult at times for others to follow, as it could be very specific to that individual. This generated an element of frustration among the participants. In spite of the general desire to have a more focused discussion on critical work occurrences and their solutions, only few were willing to take the initiative and lead such discussions. There was, however, some evidence that individuals working in similar sectors, job positions or countries, communicated more and shared their contact network establishing stronger relationships, even meeting occasionally to discuss specific situations (9%).

It was evident that each participant treated the experience differently. There was a strong feeling that pressure of work limited some peoples' involvement unless they had a specific interest in something or had a problem that needed solving. While some were eager to start communicating and sharing with others from the very first day by initiating dialogue and proposing topics for discussion, others, being cautious, preferred to observe, and only later, once confidence was gained, learned to appreciate the experience and began contributing more to the ongoing discussions.

...when I first joined the learning community, I did not know much about social networking and was not sure about the rules....the more I read what others shared, the more I felt confident that I wanted to express my own opinions and let people in the community know about my experiences. Now it is more like a routine for me to spend half an hour here and there to see what my peers are doing and whether I can comment on or add something.

Communities of Learning are rarely created from scratch, with members probably belonging to other pre-existing networks, therefore any new development needs to be shaped rather than newly created, this being the case for the community under investigation. To combine familiarity and enthusiasm for new initiatives, an open dialogue between inside and outside perspectives was useful, allied to an in-depth understanding of community issues, which were developed by utilizing an outsider, interchange with the core members. By inviting different levels of participation, each learner was allowed to satisfy their individual desire to belong to the community. Members participated in the community for varying reasons, some because the community directly provided value, some for personal connection and others for the opportunity to improve their professional development skills. After the community was given some time to establish itself, a number of academics performed the roles of facilitators to motivate the development of critical learning skills rather than a simple exchange of ideas and experiences.

Egege and Kutieleh (2004) when reviewing some definitions of critical thinking pointed out that what counts as evidence of critical thinking is not usually shared with the student, even though many academics "can reliably ascertain the presence or lack of critical thinking skills" (p. 75). All humans may well have a reasoning capacity, possibly in a generic cognitive way, but the way that it is valued (if at all) can vary tremendously between cultures. Evidence of good reasoning by Western standards, the tools used to reason with, the language and structure of the argument actually is a cultural representation and perception rather than a universal approach. By adopting the facilitators' role, academics in the current case only stepped into discussions when especially interesting and valuable ideas or experiences were being exchanged among learners. This promoted a deeper investigation of the issue, connecting it with material learned in the classroom, and hence enabling the critical thinking/learning process

in an explicit way. The idea was to promote the development of critical thinking skills in a culturally sensitive way and encourage cross-cultural awareness across diverse cultural backgrounds and business sectors.

Recommendations

Communities of Learning can be difficult to build and sustain with their organic, spontaneous, and informal nature making them resistant to supervision and interference, the members themselves deciding if they wish to belong to the group and build and share knowledge. It is the passion and commitment of the participants that hold the community together. In the community examined, maintaining the 'learning vibe' by means of focused facilitation increased the viability of the collaboration within the group as well as enhancing the learning outcomes. The diverse cultural backgrounds of the members being used as an additional facilitator to master the critical culture-aware competencies required in modern business.

Facilitators and group members themselves encouraged fellow learners to master their critical thinking and writing skills, which was a very steep learning curve for some. Although chatting and blogging is on an informal basis, thinking and reflecting on their professional practices and sharing their experiences did prove a complex and challenging task. Some preferred having an explicit theme or topic to motivate them to get involved, more so if they did not consider themselves a social blogger by nature. It was evident that well organized and supported collaboration helped reduce the effort and pressure associated with a specific task, while simultaneously helping individuals to learn to accommodate different personality types. Even so, it still required dynamic participants with shared fundamental values and visions, who were truly committed to achieving a goal, whether in general learning or professional development.

The location of some members in different time zones meant that asynchronous communication could be a problem, with posts appearing at different times and often in random sequence, resulting in someone responding to one query while another addressing a totally unrelated point. In a face to face situation both parties can quickly get back on track, but online this proved more problematical. Posts that were out of context or irrelevant still remained part of the online conversation, whereas in a face-to-face context they would be quickly discarded. Conversely, most of the participants noted that by having more time to create a blog entry they could think more and do more research, particularly in response to existing postings. Overall, it was evident that correcting participants or refocusing the discussion was essential to encourage the creation of further knowledge; this requires a sensitive facilitator using tactful strategies (Collison, et al., 2000). It was also suggested that as the community expanded it would have been more effective to introduce smaller topical or industry focused sub-groups to reinforce the focus and increase the levels of trust and motivation.

When engaging with people from different cultural backgrounds, it is important to acknowledge that the concept of culture is not always easy to grasp; many people are accustomed to seeing the world in their own certain way. The subtlety and depth of culture's influence often surprises even those who already recognize these differences. By enabling learners to understand that cultural differences can affect communications within a multi-cultural group and how that impacts on the learning process of others, facilitators can help to progress learners' sensitivities and competences. Effective support of work and problem based learning with facilitated peer learning in cross-cultural communities enables the development of viable transferrable skills and critical culture competencies.

FUTURE RESEARCH DIRECTIONS

There are a number of directions that future research on this topic can develop. Although previously acknowledged (e.g. Chen, Gully, Whiteman, & Kilcullen, 2000; Mooradian, et al., 2006) that the personal characteristics of the participants in the online communities are important factors influencing the process of information sharing, more in-depth research into the personal aspirations and attitudes towards learning would be beneficial to see how it affects the creation of collective knowledge within the community. It would be also interesting (the author having launched a pilot study already) to study whether the willingness to share individual knowledge/expertise and an openness to learning, positively correlate to the performance of individuals whether in study or work settings and how it contributes to future professional development. This would further develop the research of Matzler and Mueller (2011, p. 325) who found, that there is a relationship between learning orientation and the knowledge sharing behavior of individuals.

CONCLUSION

Increasingly in higher education, practice situated experiential learning, supported via an online environment is becoming a key method of learning for students with international placements. Given this growth in online learning involving learner-to-learner interaction, it is important to consider how situational learning and interaction is related to the actual intended learning outcomes of the work placement experience. A deeper understanding of the interaction patterns and linkages between the theory of learning and practical situations is necessary in order to provide the required support to the process: this would make it more learner oriented and empower students to achieve potentially higher learning outcomes. As found by Reychav and Te'eni (2009, p. 1276) and further confirmed by this study, there is a strong connection between knowledge sharing in formal and informal settings. While formal settings motivate more the actual subject related knowledge exchange, informal communications contribute significantly to the creation of social relationships between participants of the community.

An observed level of trust and developed professionalism among members did allow the sustainable development of the community. Members appreciated that to become successful in business they needed to learn how to communicate effectively, recognizing that interpersonal skills and the ability to work with others was essential in the real world (Cottrell, 2003). Mature students and/or ones with some prior experience were more willing to share with and learn from the experience of others. In turn, younger learners and particularly those with minimal practical experience needed more guidance, structure, and facilitation from the academic facilitators to critically evaluate the value of experience and knowledge being shared within the community.

Benefits cited by online participants were increased understanding of specialist subject areas, access to specialist data/information, support for new ideas and problem solving, increased confidence in their own abilities, collaboration and support for new ideas allied to valued membership of a community of like-minded individuals in an atmosphere of trust and openness. Participants identified benefits that relate to the social context of learning as the most valuable—"sharing information and experience" was cited as the most useful aspect of the online community.

Even a highly stimulating learning experience is not sufficient to guarantee actual learning and knowledge creation. Desire and willingness of learners, specific learning skills are also required such as information utilization, past remembrances/future imaginations, the understanding and

looking for, organizing and seeing relationships, patterns, regularities. Hence, a person with very high learning skills would learn significantly more to one without. The whole information sharing process moves onto to another level when members of the community start critically engaging in the knowledge creation process. This is best described by Holden's (Glisby & Holden, 2011) 'participative competence,' which states that the characteristics, experiences and traits held by the participants may affect the willingness and ability to exchange and value knowledge. If members of the community are willing to learn new things and have the capacity to do so, there is a higher probability that they will value and use this knowledge. Successful facilitation and support of e-learning activities could substantially solve the problem of meeting the varying needs of each particular learner, providing stronger focus and control while maintaining wider access and flexibility over their learning process.

REFERENCES

Abel, R. (2007). Innovation, adoption, and learning impact: Creating the future of IT. *EDUCAUSE Review*, *42*(2), 12–30.

Akande, A. (1998). Towards the multicultural validation of a western model of student approaches to learning. *Education*, *119*(1), 37–47.

Alexander, B. (2006). Web 2.0: A new wave of innovation for teaching and learning? *EDUCAUSE Review*, *42*(2), 32–44.

Antonijevic, S., & Gurak, L. J. (2009). Trust in online interaction: An analysis of the socio-psychological features of online communities and user engagement. In *Proceedings on Cultural Heritage Online: Empowering Users: An Active Role for User Communities,* (pp. 1-7). Fondazione Rinascimento Digitale.

Ausubel, D. P. (2000). *The acquisition and retention of knowledge*. Dordrecht, The Netherlands: Kluwer Academic Publishers.

Bastiaens, T. J., & Martens, R. L. (2000). Conditions for web-based learning with real events. In Abbey, B. (Ed.), *Instructional and Cognitive Impacts of Web-Based Education* (pp. 1–31). Hershey, PA: IGI Global. doi:10.4018/978-1-878289-59-9.ch001

Bekmeier-Feuerhahn, S., & Eichenlaub, A. (2010). What makes for trusting relationships in online communication? *Journal of Communication Management, 14*(4), 337–355. doi:10.1108/13632541011090446

Berger, P., & Luckmann, T. (1966). *The social construction of reality: The sociology of knowledge*. New York, NY: Penguin Books.

Bielaczyc, K., & Collins, A. (1999). Learning communities in classrooms: A reconceptualization of educational practice. In Reigeluth, C. (Ed.), *Instructional-Design Theories and Models. A New Paradigm of Instructional Theory* (pp. 269–292). Mahwah, NJ: Lawrence Erlbaum Associates.

Billet, S. (1996). Situated learning: Bridging socio-cultural and cognitive theorizing. *Learning and Instruction, 6*(3), 263–280. doi:10.1016/0959-4752(96)00006-0

Black, B. (1999). National culture and high commitment management. *Employee Relations, 21*(4), 389–404. doi:10.1108/01425459910285519

Bochner, S. (1999). Cultural diversity within and between societies: Implications for multicultural social systems. In Pedersen, P. B. (Ed.), *Multiculturalism as a Fourth Force* (pp. 19–60). Washington, DC: Taylor and Francis.

Brislin, R. W., & Yoshida, T. (1994). *Intercultural communication training: An introduction*. London, UK: Sage.

Bruner, J. S. (1990). *Acts of meaning*. Boston, MA: Harvard University Press.

Buckley, P. J., & Carter, M. J. (1999). Managing cross-border complementary knowledge: Conceptual developments in the business process approach to knowledge management in multinational firms. *International Studies of Management and Organisation, 29*(1), 80–92.

Burch, R. (2001). Effective web design and core communication issues: The missing components in web-based distance education. *Journal of Educational Multimedia and Hypermedia, 10*(4), 357–367.

Chen, G., Gully, S. M., Whiteman, J.-A., & Kilcullen, R. N. (2000). Examination of relationships among trait-like individual differences, state-like individual difference, and learning performance. *The Journal of Applied Psychology, 85*(6), 835–847. doi:10.1037/0021-9010.85.6.835

Chini, T. C. (2004). *Effective knowledge transfer in multinational corporations*. Basingstoke, UK: Palgrave Macmillan. doi:10.1057/9780230005877

Cobb, P. (1995). Continuing the conversation: A response to Smith. *Educational Researcher, 24*(6), 25–27.

Collier, J., & Esteban, R. (1999). Governance in the participative organisation: Freedom, creativity and ethics. *Journal of Business Ethics, 21*(2/3), 173–188. doi:10.1023/A:1006250627410

Collison, G., Elbaum, B., Haavind, S., & Tinker, R. (2000). *Facilitating online learning: Effective strategies for moderators*. Madison, WI: Atwood Publishing.

Cottrell, S. (2003). *Skills for success*. New York, NY: Palgrave.

Currie, G. (2007). Beyond our imagination: The voice of international students on the MBA. *Management Learning, 38*(5), 539–556. doi:10.1177/1350507607083206

Davenport, T., & Prusak, L. (1998). *Working knowledge: How organisations manage what they know*. Boston, MA: Harvard Business School Press.

Day, D., Dosa, M., & Jorgensen, C. (1995). The transfer of research information within and by multicultural teams. *Information Processing & Management, 31*(1), 89–100.

Durkin, K. (2008). The middle way: East Asian master's students' perceptions of critical argumentation in UK universities. *Journal of Studies in International Education, 12*(1), 38–55. doi:10.1177/1028315307302839

Eastmond, D. V. (1995). *Alone but together: Adult distance study through computer conferencing*. Cresskill, NJ: Hampton Press.

Egbert, J., & Thomas, M. (2001). The new frontier: A case study in applying instructional design for distance teacher education. *Journal of Technology and Teacher Education, 9*(3), 391–405.

Egege, S., & Kutieleh, S. (2004). Critical thinking: Teaching foreign notions to foreign students. *International Education Journal, 4*(4), 75-85. Retrieved from http://ehlt.flinders.edu.au/education/iej/articles/v4n4/Egege/paper.pdf.

Eisen, M. J. (2001). Peer-based learning: A new-old alternative to professional development. *Adult Learning, 12*. Retrieved from http://www.questia.com/googleScholar.qst?docId=5000657294

Fang, Y. W. (2001). *Does technology hinder or enhance learning and teaching technology in language education: Meeting the challenges of research and practice*. Retrieved from http://www.sjsu.edu/people/waimei.fang/articles/hinder-enhance.pdf.

Fox, S. (1997). From management education and development to the study of management learning. In Burgoyne, J., & Reynolds, M. (Eds.), *Management Learning: Integrating Perspectives in Theory and Practice* (pp. 21–37). Thousand Oaks, CA: Sage.

Frost, T. S., & Zhou, C. (2005). R&D co-practice and 'reverse' knowledge integration in multinational firms. *Journal of International Business Studies, 36*(6), 676–687. doi:10.1057/palgrave.jibs.8400168

Gherardi, S., & Nicolini, D. (2000). The organizational learning of safety in communities of practice. *Journal of Management Inquiry, 9*(1), 7–18. doi:10.1177/105649260091002

Gilroy, K. (2001). Collaborative e-learning: The right approach. *ArsDigita Systems Journal*. Retrieved from http://www.eveandersson.com/arsdigita/asj/elearning/.

Glisby, M., & Holden, N. (2011). Mastering tacit corridors for competitive advantage: Cross-cultural knowledge creation and sharing at four international firms. *Global Business and Organisational Excellence, 30*(5), 64–77. doi:10.1002/joe.20396

Gredler, M. E. (1997). *Learning and instruction: Theory into practice* (3rd ed.). Upper Saddle River, NJ: Prentice-Hall.

Grisham, D., Bergeron, B., & Brink, B. (1999). Connecting communities of practice through professional development school activities. *Journal of Teacher Education, 50*(3), 182–191. doi:10.1177/002248719905000304

Häkkinen, P., Arvaja, M., & Mäkitalo, K. (2004). Prerequisites for CSCL: Research approaches, methodological challenges and pedagogical development. In Littleton, K., Faulkner, D., & Miell, D. (Eds.), *Learning to Collaborate, Collaborating to Learn* (pp. 161–175). New York, NY: Nova Science Publishers, Inc.

Hedlund, G. (1994). A model of knowledge management and the N-form corporation. *Strategic Management Journal, 15*, 73–90. doi:10.1002/smj.4250151006

Hennemann, S., & Liefner, I. (2010). Employability of German geography graduates: The mismatch between knowledge acquired and competences required. *Journal of Geography in Higher Education, 34*(2), 215–230. doi:10.1080/03098260903227400

Kirch, D. P., Tucker, M. L., & Kirch, C. E. (2001). The benefits of emotional intelligence in accounting firms. *The CPA Journal, 70*(8), 60–61.

Kukla, A. (2000). *Social constructivism and the philosophy of science.* New York, NY: Routledge.

Latour, B. (1987). *Science in action.* Milton Keynes, UK: Open University Press.

Laurillard, D. (1993). *Rethinking university teaching: A framework for the effective use of educational technology.* London, UK: Routledge.

Lave, J., & Wenger, E. (1991). *Situated learning: Legitimate peripheral participation.* Cambridge, UK: Cambridge University Press.

Major, E., & Cordey-Hayes, M. (2000). Knowledge translation: A new perspective on knowledge transfer and foresight. *The Journal of Future Studies, Strategic Thinking and Policy, 2*(4), 411–423. doi:10.1108/14636680010802762

Matzler, K., & Mueller, J. (2011). Antecedents of knowledge sharing – Examining the influence of learning and performance orientation. *Journal of Economic Psychology, 32*(3), 317–329. doi:10.1016/j.joep.2010.12.006

Metaxiotis, K., Psarras, J., & Papastefanatos, S. (2002). Knowledge and information management in e-learning environments: The user agent architecture. *Information Management & Computer Security, 10*(4), 165–170. doi:10.1108/09685220210436958

Moller, L. (1998). Designing communities of learners for synchronous distance education. *Educational Technology Research and Development, 46*(4), 115–122. doi:10.1007/BF02299678

Mooradian, T. A., Renzl, B., & Matzler, K. (2006). Who trusts? Personality, trust and knowledge sharing. *Management Learning, 37*(4), 523–540. doi:10.1177/1350507606073424

Oliver, R., & Herrington, J. (2000). Using situated learning as a design strategy for web-based learning. In Abbey, B. (Ed.), *Instructional and Cognitive Impacts of Web-Based Education* (pp. 178–191). Hershey, PA: IGI Global. doi:10.4018/978-1-878289-59-9.ch011

Palloff, R., & Pratt, K. (1999). *Building learning communities in cyberspace: Effective strategies for the online classroom.* San Francisco, CA: Jossey-Bass.

Persichitte, K. (2000). A case study of lessons learned for the web-based educator. In Abbey, B. (Ed.), *Instructional and Cognitive Impacts of Web-Based Education* (pp. 192–199). Hershey, PA: IGI Global. doi:10.4018/978-1-878289-59-9.ch012

Pifarre, M., & Cobos, R. (2010). Promoting metacognitive skills through peer scaffolding in a CSCL environment. *Computer-Supported Collaborative Learning, 5*(2), 237–253. doi:10.1007/s11412-010-9084-6

Polanyi, M. (1966). *The tacit dimension.* New York, NY: Anchor Day Books.

Raelin, J. (2008). *Work-based learning: Bridging knowledge and action in the work place.* New York, NY: Wiley Publishers.

Raelin, J. (2008). *Work-based learning: Bridging knowledge and action in the work place.* New York, NY: Wiley Publishers.

Rafaeli, S., Barak, M., Dan-Cur, Y., & Toch, E. (2004). QSIA – A web-based environment for learning, assessing and knowledge sharing in communities. *Computers & Education, 43*(3), 273–289. doi:10.1016/j.compedu.2003.10.008

Reychav, I., & Te'eni, D. (2009). Knowledge exchange in the shrines of knowledge: The "how's" and "where's" of knowledge sharing processes. *Computers & Education, 53*(4), 1266–1277. doi:10.1016/j.compedu.2009.06.009

Rogoff, B. (1990). *Apprenticeship in thinking: Cognitive development in social context.* Oxford, UK: Oxford University Press.

Schramm, W. (1965). How communication works. In Schramm, W. (Ed.), *The Process and Effects of Mass Communication* (6th ed., pp. 3–26). Urbana, IL: University of Illinois Press.

Squire, K., & Johnson, C. (2000). Supporting distributed communities of practice with interactive television. *Educational Technology Research and Development, 48*(1), 23–43. doi:10.1007/BF02313484

Steinbring, H. (2005). *The construction of new mathematical knowledge in classroom interaction: An epistemological perspective.* New York, NY: Springer.

Subramaniam, M., & Venkatraman, N. (2001). Determinants of transnational new product development capability: Testing the influence of transferring and deploying tacit overseas knowledge. *Strategic Management Journal, 22*(4), 359–378. doi:10.1002/smj.163

Tobin, K. G. (1990). Social constructivist perspectives on the reform of science education. *The Australian Science Teachers Journal, 36*(4), 29–35.

Tosey, P. (1999). The peer learning community: A contextual design for learning? *Management Decision, 37*(5), 403–410. doi:10.1108/00251749910274171

Triandis, H. C. (1995). *Individualism and collectivism.* Boulder, CO: Westview Press.

von Krogh, G., Ichijo, K., & Nonaka, I. (2000). *Enabling knowledge creation: How to unlock the mystery of tacit knowledge and release the power of innovation.* Oxford, UK: Oxford University Press.

Vygotsky, L. (1987). *Mind and society.* Cambridge, MA: Harvard University Press.

Wenger, E., McDermott, R., & Snyder, W. (2002). *Cultivating communities of practice: A guide to managing knowledge.* Boston, MA: Harvard Business School Press.

Wenger, E., & Snyder, W. (2000). Communities of practice: The organizational frontier. *Harvard Business Review, 78*(6), 139–146.

Winter, F. I., Greene, J. A., & Costich, C. M. (2008). Self-regulation of learning within computer-based learning environments: A critical analysis. *Educational Psychology Review, 20*(4), 369–372.

Yamazaki, Y., & Kayes, D. C. (2004). An experiential approach to cross-cultural learning: A review and integration of success factors in expatriate adaptation. *Academy of Management Learning & Education, 3*(1), 4–16.

ADDITIONAL READING

Baldwin, T. T., Bedell, M., & Johnson, J. J. (1997). Social networks in a team-based MBA program: Effects on student satisfaction and performance. *Academy of Management Journal, 40*, 1369–1397. doi:10.2307/257037

Boden, R., & Nedeva, M. (2010). Employing discourse: Universities and graduate 'employability'. *Journal of Education Policy, 25*(1), 37–54. doi:10.1080/02680930903349489

Byrne, R. (2001). Employees: Capital or commodity. *Career Development International, 6*(6), 324–330. doi:10.1108/EUM0000000005988

Campbell, J. A. (2000). Using internet technology to support flexible learning in business education. *Information Technology Management, 1*(4), 351–362. doi:10.1023/A:1019193513024

Capon, N., & Kuhn, D. (2004). What is so good about problem-based learning? *Cognition and Instruction, 22*(1), 61–79. doi:10.1207/s1532690Xci2201_3

Chory, R. M., & McCroskey, J. C. (1999). The relationship between teacher management communication style and affective learning. *Communication Quarterly, 47*, 1–11. doi:10.1080/01463379909370120

Combs, A. W. (1982). Affective education or none at all. *Educational Leadership, 39*(7), 494–497.

Drucker, P. F. (2002). *Managing in the next society*. New York, NY: St. Martin's Press.

Goos, M., Galbraith, P., & Renshaw, P. (1999). Establishing a community of practice in a secondary mathematics classroom. In Burton, L. (Ed.), *Learning Mathematics: From Hierarchies to Networks* (pp. 36–61). London, UK: Routledge.

Guest, R. (2005). Will flexible learning raise student achievement? *Education Economics, 13*(3), 287–297. doi:10.1080/09645290500073761

Hann, D., Glowacki-Dudka, M., & Conceicao-Runlee, S. (2000). *147 practical tips for teaching online groups: Essentials of web-based education*. Madison, WI: Atwood Publishing.

Ivanitskaya, L., Clark, D., Montgomery, G., & Primeau, R. (2002). Interdisciplinary learning: Process and outcomes. *Innovative Higher Education, 27*(2), 95–111. doi:10.1023/A:1021105309984

Knowles, M., Holton, E., & Swanson, R. (1998). *The adult learner: The definitive classic in adult education and human resource development* (5th ed.). Houston, TX: Gulf Publishing.

Ludwig-Hardman, S., & Woolley, S. (2000). Online learning communities: Vehicles for collaboration and learning in online learning environments. In *Proceedings of World Conference on Educational Multimedia, Hypermedia and Telecommunication*, (pp. 1556–1558). Chesapeake, VA: AACE.

McLoughlin, C. (2000). Cultural maintenance, ownership, and multiple perspectives: Features of web-based delivery to promote equity. *Journal of Educational Media, 25*(3), 229–241.

Milliken, R. J., & Martins, L. L. (1996). Searching for common threads: Understanding the multiple effects of diversity in organisational groups. *Academy of Management Review, 21*(2), 402–433.

Nystrom, S., & Dahlgren, M. (2008). A winding road - Professional trajectories from higher education to working life: A case study of political science and psychology graduates. *Studies in Continuing Education, 30*(3), 215–229. doi:10.1080/01580370802439896

Rothwell, A., & Herbert, I. (2008). Self-perceived employability: Construction and initial validation of a scale for university students. *Journal of Vocational Behavior, 73*(1), 1–12. doi:10.1016/j.jvb.2007.12.001

Silius, K., & Tervakari, A.-M. (2003). The usefulness of web-based learning environments: The evaluation tool into the portal of Finnish Virtual University. In *Proceedings of International Conference on Network Universities and e-Learning*. Retrieved from http://matriisi.ee.tut.fi/arvo/liitteet/usefulness_of_web.pdf.

Simonin, B. (1999). Transfer of marketing know-how in international strategic alliances: An empirical investigation of the role and antecedents of knowledge ambiguity. *Journal of International Business Studies, 30*(3), 463–490. doi:10.1057/palgrave.jibs.8490079

Taylor, J. A., & McDonald, C. (2007). Writing in groups as a tool for non-routine problem solving in first year university mathematics. *International Journal of Mathematical Education in Science and Technology, 38*(5), 635–655. doi:10.1080/00207390701359396

Tomlinson, M. (2008). The degree is not enough: Students' perceptions of the role of higher education credentials for graduate work and employability. *British Journal of Sociology of Education, 29*(1), 49–61. doi:10.1080/01425690701737457

Wenger, E. (1998). *Communities of practice: Learning, meaning, and identity.* Oxford, UK: Oxford University Press.

Wilton, N. (2011). Do employability skills really matter in the UK graduate labour market? The case of business and management graduates. *Work, Employment and Society, 25*(1), 85–100. doi:10.1177/0950017010389244

Yakavenka, H. (2009). *Transfer of international knowledge: The role of host educators.* Berlin, Germany: VDM Verlag.

Yeh, Y.-C. (2009). Integrating e-learning into the direct-instruction model to enhance the effectiveness of critical-thinking instruction. *Instructional Science, 37*, 185–203. doi:10.1007/s11251-007-9048-z

Zibit, M. (2004). The peaks and valleys of online professional development. *eLearn Magazine.* Retrieved from http://elearnmag.acm.org/featured.cfm?aid=975815.

KEY TERMS AND DEFINITIONS

Informal online Communities of Learning: A group of individuals amalgamating via an online medium to share thoughts, experiences and practices outside of formal educational settings

Knowledge Sharing: The exchange of information, ideas, and practices resulting in their application in new settings

Learning: The willingness to be open-minded about the experiences of others and practice new ideas

Metacognitive / Higher Level Critical Skills: The ability to understand and critically reflect on the level of one's knowledge and executive processes

Professional Competencies: The ability to apply theoretical knowledge in practical situations

Chapter 9
Use of Social Network Analysis to Create and Foster Interdisciplinary Research, Projects, and Grants among Faculty

Kyle Christensen
Columbus State University, USA

Iris M. Saltiel
Columbus State University, USA

ABSTRACT

This chapter describes one university-based social network created for peer mentoring, knowledge brokering, and resource sharing for faculty and students to collaborate to increase research and scholarship. First, the case study describes the process utilized to survey interests of faculty as the basis for an affiliation network of faculty research interests. The benefits of social network analysis and its applications are discussed and utilized. Next, a conversation is presented about the use of social network analysis to foster faculty collaboration through targeted programming. Finally, recommendations for practice are presented.

INTRODUCTION

In the United States, expectations for increased scholarship as well as grants have grown for faculty at regional teaching universities, as well as at research universities in order to generate necessary operating funds. ABC University (a pseudonym) is a regional, medium sized university with 250

full-time faculty members. At ABC University, the task of developing faculty members to be more productive and skillful in scholarly endeavors as well as grant writing is essential to remaining viable during times of increasing costs and decreasing availability of funds from traditional sources. Given this challenge, we wanted to create opportunities for faculty to interact with one another, create fluid informal networks crossing

DOI: 10.4018/978-1-4666-1815-2.ch009

disciplines, colleges, campuses and eventually, other universities. Coordinated programming from three one-person offices (Faculty Development, Social Research, and Sponsored Programs) allowed us to pool resources, skills, and areas of expertise to do more than we probably would have attempted individually. We decided to use professional development as the vehicle to facilitate collaboration among faculty and to develop both scholar endeavors and grant writing skills of faculty members.

Promotion of an intra-university affiliation network that emphasizes the building of relationships is an important area for faculty collaboration and activities. Traditional methods of collaboration and social networking focus on interuniversity relations within a particular field. Examples of these mechanisms include websites such as academia. edu, citation indices, or academic conferences that reinforce these linkages. However, our focus on intra-university collaboration is based on the need to provide meaningful service to the institution, the faculty, and the broader community of stakeholders. This method of coordination also compliments current existing forms of inter-university collaboration by developing new avenues for research that allow faculty members to include existing research networks.

We knew that in order to be effective we had to serve as the catalyst to facilitate individual professional development and initiate collaborative efforts. The challenge for us was how to best provide the structures and climate to promote scholarly productivity, as well as increase efforts in competing externally for grants. We wanted to create an environment where professional and personal expectations could be expressed in an atmosphere of trust so that individual and organizational needs could be met. By sponsoring and facilitating opportunities for faculty networking and collaboration, we developed a climate in which we hoped success would precipitate as naturally as rain falling from clouds.

Following a survey used to measure faculty research interests, skill sets, and needs (described in greater detail later in the chapter), we developed and conducted a series of collaborative programs as "Lunch N' Learns" to increase the collegiality, scholarship, and grants among the faculty. Food was served and time was allotted for brief overviews of the services offered by the three offices and a discussion about how and why to collaborate. Attendees were encouraged to share interests and needs. Networking analysis tools were used to capture personal interactions in order to enhance and expand scholarly activities and grantsmanship.

In this case study, we explain how social networking analyses were used towards the creation of interdisciplinary research, projects, and grants among faculty. The objective of this chapter is to depict the processes utilized in this endeavor. Specifically, the chapter describes how the professional development needs of faculty were assessed using Web 2.0 technology; how the professional development networks across disciplines were designed and developed; and, how the strategies aligning institutional and personal needs and goals were developed. Faculty development practices employing informal and formal learning strategies in social networks were utilized, and the program was assessed through a variety of evaluation metrics.

This case study also allows us to present the visual representation of the research interests of our faculty, which helped to further faculty collaboration. The ability to illustrate and effectively portray research affiliations greatly improves the ability of institutional offices to develop programming to support faculty development. These techniques also make identifying groups for collaboration much simpler because self-reported research area interests are a reliable source of information. We bypassed the existing constraints of academia, namely departmental and disciplinary boundaries, and opened up multiple options for collaboration.

These points of interest served as the impetus for the development of intra-university mechanisms to foster and facilitate activities among faculty, students, and staff.

USING SOCIAL NETWORKS AMONG FACULTY

The Academy

Teaching, scholarship, and service are the foundation on which colleges were founded. Within the academy, we often refer to ourselves as a "teaching" or "research" university, referencing the Carnegie Foundation for the Advancement of Teaching classification system (McCormick & Zhao, 2005). What these designations mean to faculty is how much scholarship one needs for promotion and if they must bring in grant money. One's primary responsibility at a teaching institution is to teach. At a research university, faculty members expect to spend most of their time on research and generating grants. That does not mean a faculty member is not expected to publish or bring in external dollars at a teaching institution. The difference is in the percentage of time one spends on these pursuits (Fox, 1992).

In the last decade (Youn & Price, 2009; Prince, Felder, & Brent, 2007), there has been an increase of scholarly expectations at teaching universities in response to the economic changes higher education has faced. This increase manifests itself through innocuous statements like, "You are expected to publish," during hiring protocols. Specific and finite expectations (such as "You are expected to publish one article per year") for scholarship at any university or in any particular field are rarely found. Instead, promotion and tenure requirements often stress quality, peer review, excellence, and impact in the field (Lamont, 2009). Lamont describes how this is because standards and expectations of scholarship differ by field.

Those outside the academy consider universities to be the ultimate professional learning community, with faculty members learning alongside both each other and students, with all engaged in the pursuit of knowledge acquisition. Inside the ivory tower, it is a different picture. Collaborative activities relating to teaching and research are fraught with problems of collective action, namely uncertain outcomes and a substantial investment of time and energy (Olson, 1971). Any scholarly endeavor attempted takes time and energy. Faculty members who collaborate on scholarly projects seem to be more productive (Baldwin & Austin, 1995). However, if a collaboration goes bad, "the co-taught class may be canceled, or a book advance may have to be returned to the publisher" (Chaddock & Saltiel, 2004, p. 3). In a time of economic contraction, the competition for resources, position, and status increases can contribute further problems to the process of collaboration. As Fox (1992, p. 302) says, "Faculty may be hired to do one thing (teach) and be rewarded for doing another (research)." The professoriate must produce scholarship in order to receive promotion and/or tenure. The interest of the individual faculty person is naturally focused on their own needs for recognition of their contributions and achievements. Multiple authored works can present problems for faculty from author order to roles and responsibilities in each scholarly work (Chaddock & Saltiel, 2004).

However, the nature of academic collaboration has a number of inherent benefits. First, research collaborations tend to occur among relatively small groupings of scholars, thus allowing for high levels of appreciable gains from successful endeavors. Second, the linkages formed in these endeavors assist in building an individual's professional network, thus providing new and continued opportunities for increased productivity. This is similar to Putnam's (2000) idea of two elements of Social Capital, bridging and bonding linkages. Putnam's ideas regarding social capital illustrates mechanisms to reinforce existing ties within a field, thus building traditional notions of bonding capital, or deepening relations, associated with networking for a traditional scholarly agenda. Applications of bridging capital occur across academic disciplines when faculty contacts facilitate interdisciplinary research. Thus, we believe individuals working on interdisciplinary projects are able to develop a wider array of connections across fields from which they can draw support and potential collaborators.

Another benefit of the academic collaboration, which facilitates its establishment and continuance, is the economic benefit achieved by securing grants. When the source of the funding is external to the institution, the competition associated with pursuing dollars in the zero sum game of the university budget is overcome. However, many of the benefits of increased research productivity are non-excludable such as institutional overhead from grants and increased prestige associated with major academic achievements. In essence, faculty benefit from working together and their success does not diminish anyone within the university's community from achieving similar success in different areas.

CREATION OF A SOCIAL NETWORK

To create the affiliation network at ABC University, three primary tasks were undertaken: (1) faculty were surveyed electronically to determine research interests and capacities, (2) network analysis and visualization tools were used to generate linkages between researchers and interests, and (3) university resources and training to foster and sustain collaboration was established. In this section, we describe how the social network was created among ABC faculty. Clearly, in order to implement any new programming a baseline measure of research interests and capacity was needed, which is what this study offers.

We chose to use an electronic survey because it provided an efficient and cost effective method for reaching out to the faculty (Dillman, 2000). A survey of full and part-time faculty was conducted in the fall semester of 2010 to gauge interest in faculty members' collaborative research and grantsmanship, as well as interest areas. Additionally, this survey was designed to explore the research interests of faculty. The instrument also allowed faculty members to indicate willingness to collaborate based on research interests, student research, grants, or other faculty development activities. Data from the survey was used to classify faculty research interests into dichotomous affiliations with particular topics. The collective linkages of the responding faculty served as the basis for an affiliation network of research interests.

In creating a collaborative online and face-to-face network at ABC University, our goal in part was to facilitate casual on-the-job exchanges of information to encourage the sharing of informal as well as incidental learning (Marsick & Watkins, 1990) among faculty. Understanding that university research networks (Newell & Swan, 2000) encourage faculty from different disciplines to work together collaboratively and even across institutions, we wanted to encourage interdisciplinary dialogues. Meanwhile, the use of an affiliation network provided a powerful mechanism to explore relations between faculty and their research interests. The use of network analysis allowed for creative analysis and visualization of the complex data in order to uncover attributes of the network (Scott, 2000; Wasserman & Faust, 1994). This application utilized network analysis to develop clusters for specific programming applications designed to promote intra-university linkages for interdisciplinary research opportunities. Training programs designed and conducted as part of the Lunch N' Learn sessions to foster collaboration were designed to promote reciprocity and trust in collaborations, thus supporting more effective collaboration across the affiliation network (Gould, 1993). This programming also focused on building sustained collaborations using a range of institutional offices and resources.

METHOD

In order to implement this project, a baseline measure of faculty research interests and skill sets was needed. During the fall semester of 2010, we conducted a three wave electronic survey of the entire faculty at a medium sized, southern university. The survey waves were conducted in one-week intervals to provide the panel of faculty sufficient time to respond prior to being invited to participate again. This survey mode was selected because of the low cost and relative ease of implementation. The survey consisted of a twenty-two question instrument designed to measure faculty research interests, skill sets, and needs for support. This survey was pre-tested by individuals in departments across campus prior to implementation. This survey was conducted as a part of the establishment of a research center to provide research support within the university while meeting potential external needs of clients in the broader community. This initial survey of faculty was an outgrowth of our ongoing administrative efforts, but it could easily be replicated or implemented at other universities or research institutions.

The survey also measured the needs that faculty possessed in order to determine what resources could be targeted to departments to increase the research productivity. These measures were part of a broader institutional shift toward increasing scholarly productivity as a part of a changing institutional mission.

The response rate from the faculty was modest among full time faculty, but lower among part-time faculty. All full time and part time faculty were included in the three survey waves. We included all part time faculty members in the study because of a desire to be inclusive of all possible collaborative endeavors. Table 1 presents the response rates for full time and part time faculty members. Full time faculty members responded at a rate of 20% while part time faculty members responded

Table 1. Faculty survey of research interests

	Total Faculty	Number Responding	Response Rate
Part Time Faculty	806	27	0.03
Full Time Faculty	366	75	0.20
Total Faculty	1172	102	0.09

at only 3%. Part time faculty members consisted of any instructor or adjunct who taught at the University within the last two academic years. The large number of these individuals lowers the overall response rate among total faculty, but the full time rate gives a better indication of actual response. The survey also saw higher levels of response from faculty in the sciences, social sciences, education, and public health fields with lower rates of response from business faculty.

The data in Table 1 indicate relatively low levels of participation in the study. However, we advertised future training or research endeavors to allow faculty to opt-in, even if they did not respond. This allowed any faculty member who might have missed responding to one of the three survey waves an opportunity to join the programmatic options that were formatted based on the results of the surveys.

Data from the survey was analyzed and disseminated to various university offices to provide services to faculty members who indicated an interest in receiving assistance on the survey. The self-reported faculty research interests and skill sets questions were coded to produce relational data between individual faculty members, their research interests, and their research skill sets. Coding was conducted by the Director of Social Research in conjunction with discipline specific experts to ensure the accuracy of the classifications. These groupings are summarized in Table 2, with coding separated by broad categories and in nuanced topical area. These data provided a quick and simple method to coordinate across disciplinary boundaries to promote targeted programming for faculty with similar interests.

These data were then entered into UCINET, a social network analysis software package, to produce a visual representation of faculty research interests across the university. Social network analysis allows for visual representation of relational data.

Relational data are represented by nodes, the actors, and ties, their relations with other actors, institutions, or ideas (Wasserman & Faust, 1994; Scott, 2000). Data for this project consist of directed ties between faculty and their research topics. The ties or linkages between faculty and their research concept are present only if a faculty member indicated a relationship with a particular research concept. The data in this project is unweighted, but other forms of analysis can use weighted data. This allows for a host of different analytical and visualization options related to faculty collaboration.

The results from the affiliation networks were surprising. First, the data reflected the self-reported research interests from faculty, which frequently did not correspond with discipline specific titles. This presented an image of research across campus that transcends disciplinary boundaries that could have deterred or limited interactions between faculty members. The networks also had relatively low levels of overall centralization, meaning that each individual faculty person was frequently connected only to a limited number of topics or affiliations. This made identifying clusters of faculty with similar interests fairly straightforward, as these groupings were easily apparent. This allowed for clearly discernible groupings of faculty to be observed across categories

Second, the wealth of data about faculty research interests and skills could easily be converted based on related attribute data to reflect or represent multiple levels of information in a single diagram. This is done simply by modifying

Table 2. Faculty research topics

Cluster Categories and Attributes	Counts
Education	23
Educational Technology	6
Education/Science	4
Service Learning	1
General Education Cluster	28
Admin/Organizational Theory	17
Public Health	7
Criminal Justice	7
Computer Science	7
Environmental Science & Policy	3
Geography	2
Psychology	4
Law	3
Government	4
Applied Social Science Cluster	44
Race	4
Gender Studies	5
French	2
Spanish	2
Cultural Studies	14
Cultural Studies Cluster	18
Biology	6
Chemistry	1
Geology	2
Math	4
Physics	2
Science Cluster	14
Political Theory/Philosophy	1
Religion	2
History	9
English	4
Creative Writing	4
Arts	2
Music	8
Humanities Cluster	23
Quantitative Methodology	9
Mixed Methodology	4
General Research Methods Cluster	12
Entrepreneurship	2
Economic Development	2
Accounting	1
General Business	6
Business Cluster	8

colors, or displaying different shapes to reflect the attribute data of various faculty or their relations in question, thus allowing a much richer presentation of information. This provides a powerful visual tool for exploring vast quantities of information related to research interests (Tufte, 2001). This tool also makes the results of these surveys understandable for non-expert audiences as well.

Third, data from the survey and the research interests present served to start several standing conversations about methods to improve and enhance mechanisms for intra-university collaboration. The following figures provide a visual display of faculty research interests in an affiliation network. Figure 1 presents the social network of faculty research interests grouped by general themes and Figure 2 provides a diagram of our University social network of faculty research interests based on specific research topics. These models are only examples of the usefulness of social networks to clearly and concisely present visual information. Data collected from the surveys can be used to change multiple properties in these images to convey several aspects of the individual members or their linkages in one visual image. The data provided below consist of faculty, anonymized using the letter F and a number linked to their self-defined research topics.

With the rise of online communities and social networking tools, such as Web 2.0 opportunities for virtual "learning Webs" (Illich, 1970) can be used to encourage informal (Marsick & Watkins, 1990) as well as formal learning to occur through professional development. These networks were also bolstered by the institutional use of Google technologies for chat, collaborative editing of documents, formation of online groups, and use of email lists. The use of these technologies provides an excellent slate of tools for advancing collaboration based on the social networks.

FINDINGS AND RECOMMENDATIONS

These results indicate a potential wealth of knowledge for universities of all sizes. First, we provided a relatively quick, but low cost method for measuring and visualizing the research capacity within an organization. The ability to accurately measure faculty interests based on self-reported indices provides numerous outlets for institutional collaboration across multiple offices in a modern university to assist faculty with research activities related to the institutional mission.

Second, faculty members that are able to collaborate with colleagues are consistently seen as being more productive (Newell & Swan, 2000). This was one of the strongest benefits of the research, but also led to a crucial limitation. The initial survey of faculty research interests included protections for anonymity for participants. This meant that unless faculty self-selected into certain types of collaboration, they were not invited or included in those activities. This limited our ability to fully connect with the entire faculty as we might have liked, but did allow individual faculty members the freedom to engage in the process, as they were comfortable.

Third, our use of social networking techniques coupled with the use of Web-based technologies presented key problems due to differentiated rates of adoption amongst the faculty. Our campus utilizes the Google's suite of technologies for chat, website hosting, and shared collaboration of documents. These technologies are integrated into university email system seamlessly, though faculty members have different rates of adoption for other applications. Some faculty members are completely comfortable using a variety of different technologies such as user groups, online editing software, discussion groups, and listservs to promote collaboration. However, there are significant numbers of faculty that find some or all of these technologies daunting due to a lack of familiarity. This limitation presents a non-trivial

Figure 1. Social network of faculty research interests grouped by general themes

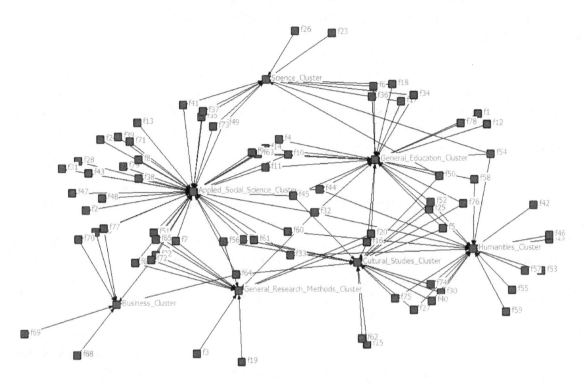

Figure 2. Social network of faculty research interests

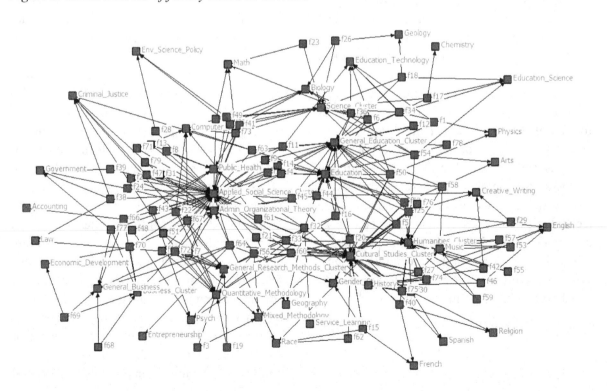

barrier to participation, which needs to be carefully monitored to promote the highest levels of collaboration in other contexts.

Fourth, this case study provides an example that had strong institutional support. Multiple universities offices participated across a range of programming in order to make this initiative a successful endeavor. In addition, administrators at the highest levels of the institution saw the need for this type of collaboration. Failure to have buy-in from appropriate administrators or other "gatekeeper" types in the process could dramatically limit the effectiveness of this type of endeavor at another institution.

Fifth, the ongoing effects of this case study are difficult to empirically evaluate, particularly in the short term. Rarely, will new partnerships or collaborations immediately result in visible productivity. This makes this type of programming suited for long term strategic endeavors on behalf of colleges and universities seeking to increase interdisciplinary scholarship and grants productivity that are willing to experiment with ways to work with faculty.

INITIAL PERFORMANCE EVALUATION

Given all of the issues identified, the question is, "Where are we and how do we know if this strategy is effective or worth pursuing for a second year?" For example, several individual faculty members moved to different institutions and they were working on grants with faculty from other departments. Those efforts stopped when the individuals left for other positions. The remaining faculty were surprised by the sudden departure of their colleagues, and expressed sentiments of demoralization and not knowing how to proceed without their colleagues. The loss of trust was felt personally as well as professionally. Their trust in others for university research collaboration was broken. Newell and Swan (2000) discuss this

necessary aspect of relationships in their work on trust and inter-organizational networking for university research productivity. Often the professional loss of scholarship outweighs the personal relationship for all involved. Hopefully, the work may continue as an inter-institutional collaboration at a future date.

A significant challenge is not only cultivating faculty collaborative efforts in scholarship and grantsmanship, but also tracking the results in ways that are not offensively intrusive. Faculty enjoy informing us when a conference presentation or publication is accepted. They do not often share when their attempts do not produce a positive outcome. For us to know if this initiative is successful we need to document the processes and efforts, not just the results. Early analysis indicates that this way of working is blossoming at our university. In 2010, 10 of 37 external grants submitted in a 5-month period were from faculty who had been connected to each other through our social networking efforts. Faculty participation rates were also consistent and recurring in face-to-face sessions focused on promoting collaboration in faculty research clusters. Thirty-eight faculty members participated in faculty collaboration events, with eight faculty members participating in multiple training events. These preliminary results show that a nucleus of faculty developed over the course of this programming. The challenge remains building on the initiatives started last year, monitoring their progress and opening the door for new partnerships.

FUTURE RESEARCH DIRECTIONS

This chapter presented a preliminary examination of a low cost method to increase research productivity at one university by developing purposeful social networks. This case study presents an idea for innovation brought about by a changing institutional mission, coupled with a fascination by the use of social networking as a tool for collaboration.

Applications of this technique at larger institutions with more clearly defined research missions could provide an even more fertile case for collaboration and adoption. Similarly, the use of this technique to explore research dynamics found in liberal arts colleges would also be interesting. These models might have an emphasis on a range of scholarship, civic engagement, or service components to reflect the special missions of these institutions.

Studying and finding ways to use this type of approach became extremely popular with the 2010 release of the movie, "The Social Network," about the creation of Facebook, a social networking website. Examples of networking in the academic sphere include websites such as Academia.edu, citation indices, and conferences. Colleges and universities as well as corporations and nonprofits are all using social networking tools to further their goals. The challenge of monitoring progress towards goals is complicated by the increasing ways in which we can track interactions; reminding ourselves that data in and of itself is not always meaningful.

Faculty conducting collaborative research and writing with each other and possibly even students, might in fact be paving the way to improving aspects of higher education. This fad of more scholarship among faculty is not going away (Prince, Felder, & Brent, 2007). The interaction among peers in different disciplines encourages seeking linkages where they previously did not exist.

Another potential area ripe for more research is interestingly enough, that of the use of collaborative writing in academe (Lowry, Curtis, & Lowry, 2004). The dynamics present in collaborative writing for publication are fraught with complexities and challenges. Yet, when it works... it works! In addition, the benefits far outweigh the disadvantages. Foster (2004) suggests we consider a nonlinear model of information-seeking behavior in how we conduct the analysis of informal learning. The intersection of collaborative writing and how we seek information might provide for the development of social networks.

In this way, using virtual social networking for professional development and informal learning creates unique opportunities for interdisciplinary research, projects, and grants among faculty where previously we were limited in the ways in which we met each other and interacted with each other. In earlier times, faculty only met each other through campus committees, social gatherings, or professional meetings. Asking about mutual interests may be the impetus for new ways of examining phenomena. After all, it might not only be politics that creates strange bedfellows.

CONCLUSION

We believe we are developing a new use of network analysis as we attempt to measure the impact of social networks on a professional developers' ability to create interdisciplinary research, projects, and grants among faculty. This is an exciting venture for the academy. Longitudinal reporting on the development of social networks created specifically for these pursuits should yield the impact of such methods on professional development efforts.

As expectations for increased scholarship and grantsmanship continue to increase in higher education, we will continue to seek strategies to assist faculty to meet the demands placed upon them in creative and informal ways.

REFERENCES

Baldwin, R. G., & Austin, A. E. (1995). Toward a greater understanding of faculty research collaboration. *Review of Higher Education, 19*(1), 45–70.

Chaddock, K. R., & Saltiel, I. M. (2004). *When faculty collaborations crumble: How to know if the benefits outweigh the costs.* Paper presented at the 29th Annual Conference of the Association for the Study of Higher Education. Kansas City, MO

Dillman, D. A. (2000). *Mail and internet surveys: The tailored method* (2nd ed.). New York, NY: Wiley & Sons.

Foster, A. (2004). A nonlinear model of information-seeking behavior. *Journal of the American Society for Information Science and Technology, 55*(3), 228–237. doi:10.1002/asi.10359

Fox, F. F. (1992). Research, teaching, and publication productivity: Mutuality versus competition in academia. *Sociology of Education, 65*(4), 293–305. doi:10.2307/2112772

Illich, I. D. (1970). *Deschooling society.* New York, NY: Harper & Row.

Lamont, M. (2009). *How professors think: Inside the curious world of academic judgment.* Boston, MA: Harvard University Press.

Lowry, P. B., Curtis, A., & Lowry, M. R. (2004). Building a taxonomy and nomenclature of collaborative writing to improve interdisciplinary research and practice. *Journal of Business Communication, 41*(1), 66–99. doi:10.1177/0021943603259363

Marsick, V. J., & Watkins, K. (1990). *Informal and incidental learning in the workplace.* New York, NY: Routledge.

McCormick, A. C., & Zhao, C. M. (2005). Rethinking and reframing the Carnegie classification. *Change, 9*(10), 51–57. doi:10.3200/CHNG.37.5.51-57

Newell, S., & Swan, J. (2000). Trust and inter-organizational networking. *Human Relations, 53*(10), 1287–1328.

Olson, M. (1971). *The logic of collective action: Public goods and the theory of groups.* Boston, MA: Harvard University Press.

Prince, M. J., Felder, R. M., & Brent, R. (2007). Does faculty research improve undergraduate teaching? An analysis of existing and potential synergies. *Journal of Engineering Education, 96*(4), 283–294.

Putnam, R. (2000). *Bowling alone: The collapse and revival of American community.* New York, NY: Simon and Schuster.

Scott, S. (2000). *Social network analysis: A handbook* (2nd ed.). Los Angeles, CA: Sage.

Tufte, E. (2001). *The visual display of quantitative information* (2nd ed.). Cheshire, CT: Graphics Press.

Wasserman, S., & Faust, K. (1994). *Social network analysis: Methods and applications.* New York, NY: Cambridge University Press.

Youn, T., & Price, T. (2009). Learning from the experience of others: The evolution of faculty tenure and promotion rules in comprehensive institutions. *The Journal of Higher of Higher Education, 80*(2), 204–237. doi:10.1353/jhe.0.0041

ADDITIONAL READING

Austin, A. E., & Baldwin, R. G. (1992). *Faculty collaboration: Enhancing the quality of scholarship and teaching.* San Francisco, CA: Jossey Bass.

Bayer, A. E., & Smart, J. C. (1988). *Author collaborative styles in academic scholarship.* Paper presented at the Annual Meeting of the American Educational Research Association. New Orleans, LA.

Bohen, S. J., & Stiles, J. (1988). Experimenting with models of faculty collaboration: Factors that promote success. *New Directions for Institutional Research, 100*, 39–55.

Calkins, S., & Drane, D. (2010). Engaging faculty in conversations about teaching through a research proposal workshop. In Nilson, L. B., & Miller, J. E. (Eds.), *To Improve the Academic Academy: Resources for Faulty, Instructional, and Organizational Development* (*Vol. 28*, pp. 265–277). San Francisco, CA: Jossey-Bass.

Czaja, R., & Blair, J. (2005). *Designing surveys: A guide to decisions and procedures*. Thousand Oaks, CA: Sage Publications, Inc.

Daley, J. M., Zanna, M. P., & Roediger, H. L. (2004). *The complete academic: A career guide*. Washington, DC: American Psychological Association.

Deneef, A. L., & Goodwin, C. D. (1995). *The academic handbook*. Durham, NC: Duke University Press.

Dillman, D. A. (2000). *Mail and internet surveys: The tailored design model*. New York, NY: John Wiley & Sons.

Gilbert, G. (2010). Making faculty count in higher education assessments. *Academe, 96*(5), 25–27.

Gillespie, K. J. (2010). Organization development. In Gillespie, K. J. (Eds.), *A Guide to Faculty Development* (2nd ed., pp. 379–396). San Francisco, CA: Jossey-Bass.

Hurd, S. N., & Stein, R. F. (2004). *Building and sustaining learning communities: The Syracuse University experience*. Bolton, MA: Anker Publishing.

Kennedy, E. L. (1995). In pursuit of connection: Reflections on collaborative work. *American Anthropologist, 97*(1), 26–33. doi:10.1525/aa.1995.97.1.02a00060

Lamont, M. (2009). *How professors think: Inside the curious world of academic judgment*. Boston, MA: Harvard University Press.

Middaugh, M. F. (2001). *Understanding faculty productivity: Standards and benchmarks for colleges and universities*. San Francisco, CA: Jossey-Bass.

Oakes, G., & Vidich, A. (1999). *Collaboration, reputation, and ethics in American academic life*. Urbana, IL: University of Illinois Press.

Olson, M. (1965). *The logic of collective action: Public goods and the theory of groups*. Boston, MA: Harvard University Press.

Pye, K. A. (2007). University governance and autonomy: Who decides what in the university. In Deneef, A. L., & Goodwin, C. D. (Eds.), *The Academic's Handbook* (3rd ed., pp. 349–366). Durham, NC: Duke University Press.

Salant, P., & Dillman, D. A. (1994). *How to conduct your own survey*. New York, NY: John Wiley & Sons.

Schroeder, C. M. (2011). Knowing and facilitating organizational change processes. In Schroeder, C. M. (Eds.), *Coming in from the Margins: Faculty Development's Emerging Organizational Development Role in Institutional Change* (pp. 199–217). Sterling, VA: Stylus Publishing.

Sgroi, A., & Saltiel, I. M. (1998). Human connections. In Saltiel, I. M., Sgroi, A., & Brockett, R. G. (Eds.), *The Power and Potential of Collaborative Learning Partnerships: New Directions of Adult and Continuing Education* (*Vol. 79*, pp. 87–92). San Francisco, CA: Jossey-Bass.

Stephenson, F. (2001). *Extraordinary teachers: The essence of excellent teaching*. Kansas City, MO: Andrews McMell Publishing.

Stewart, P. (2007). The academic community. In Deneef, A. L., & Goodwin, C. D. (Eds.), *The Academic's Handbook* (3rd ed., pp. 387–394). Durham, NC: Duke University Press.

Tufte, E. R. (2001). *The visual display of quantitative information*. Cheshire, CT: Graphic Press.

Walker, G. E., Golde, C. M., Jones, L., Bueschel, A. C., & Hutchings, P. (2008). *The formation of scholars: Rethinking doctoral education for the twenty-first century*. San Francisco, CA: Jossey-Bass.

Wasserman, S., & Faust, K. (1994). *Social network analysis: Methods and applications*. Cambridge, UK: Cambridge University Press.

KEY TERMS AND DEFINITIONS

Faculty Collaboration: Collaborative arrangement that involves a coordinated effort and product for which collaborators (which may include students) share responsibility and credit.

Faculty Research Interests: Subjects, topics or areas of interest to faculty for research, scholarly endeavors, and/or creative works.

Interdisciplinary Research: Interdisciplinary research brings together perspectives, research and interest from different disciplines to address a particular purpose, issue or study.

Intra-University Collaboration: Collaboration from different departments within the same university.

Network Analysis: Analysis of social network and the linkages among and between them.

Social Network: Social structure comprised of individuals who are connected by a friendship, relationship, or common interest.

Chapter 10
Social Media as a Learning Tool in Medical Education:
A Situation Analysis

Mariliis Vahe
Florida State University, USA

Khawaja Zain-Ul-Abdin
Florida State University, USA

Yalın Kılıç Türel
Firat University, Turkey

ABSTRACT

Social media has become one of the most dominant information phenomena of our time. As its commercial, social, activist, and informational uses multiply, questions are raised as to its efficiency as a learning tool. The authors focus this chapter on social media use in higher education, specifically in the field of medical education, and provide a modern definition of social media and its tools while elaborating on its educational uses and efficiency. Furthermore, they present a situation analysis through a review of original research published on the topic in the last five years, culminating in an identification of the gaps in literature and recommendations for future research endeavors.

INTRODUCTION

Social media is very much *en vogue*, with many academic database search engines showing hundreds and sometimes thousands of academic documents published in only the last year (2010) referring to the term "social media" (Google Scholar: 13100; EBSCO Host: 282; ProQuest

ABI/INFORM GLOBAL: 1038). The excitement may be ascribed to the recently realized financial potential of the social media networks (Foreman, 2011), or equally to the smorgasbord of opportunities it allows students, businessmen, and researchers in the form of collaborative learning, distributed intelligence, online communities of practice, diverse respondent populations, and many others (Kaplan & Haenlein, 2009). In

DOI: 10.4018/978-1-4666-1815-2.ch010

this chapter, we present an overview of recent research studies into the use of social media as a tool for enhancing learning in higher education, specifically in the field of medical education. We aim to provide an accounting of recent research (2007-2011) published in the field and present a situation analysis as a guide to further forays for researchers and academics.

BACKGROUND

Defining Social Media

The power, impact, and importance of social media is evident through its usage statistics, as shown in Table 1, provided by the Nielsen Company (2010), showing average usage times and the number of monthly unique visitors to social networking sites.

However, even though social media is such a widespread and active phenomenon, it does not have any one commonly accepted definition. We found numerous authors using a variety of semantics to define social media. Studies have taken the construct to be everything from "user generated content" (Castillo, Donato, Gionis, & Mishne, 2008, p. 1) to "media with possibilities of relationships" (Gilbert & Karahalios, 2009, p. 1) with no real semantic consensus or exact agreement upon what is and what is not considered social media. One major reason behind this definitional uncertainty is the arrival of new technologies almost every year. These new technologies not only introduce new forums and avenues of usage, but also serve to update and evolve existing traditional technologies and applications into having social media components. As an example, computer games, online news articles, online company and product sites and many other applications that were originally considered to be *traditional*, i.e. non-social online media, have in recent years been taken under the wing of social media with

Table 1. Unique visitors to social networking sites in December 2009 (in millions)

Country	Unique Audience (000)	Time per Person (hh:mm:ss)
United States	142,052	6:09:13
Japan	46,558	2:50:21
Brazil	31,345	4:33:10
United Kingdom	29,129	6:07:54
Germany	28,057	4:11:45
France	26,786	4:04:39
Spain	19,456	5:30:55
Italy	18,256	6:00:07
Australia	9,895	6:52:28
Switzer-land	2,451	3:54:34
Source: The Nielsen Company, 2010		

the addition of comment boards, online gaming communities, fan blogs and other tools opening the way for social interaction. Social scientists and researchers have reacted to this evolving technology by continuously widening their definitions of it (Social Media Defined, 2007), more recently including tools by name like wikis, blogs, social networking platforms, and others (Xiang & Gretzel, 2009). The element of connectivity is the recurring theme within most definitions, the social aspect of the communication, however, is open for interpretation.

In this chapter, we define social media as any private or public network based application that allows the exchange of information and social interaction between two or more individuals. The information may be *live* or synchronous (e.g. instant messaging), or linear time gapped or asynchronous (such as bulletin boards and wikis). The tools that qualify as social media must allow two-way communication between the initiator of the conversation and intended partners, or the author of the information and his audience. Whether the

Table 2. Social media tools

Tools	Explanation
Bulletin Boards (BBS)	A computer simulation of a real world bulletin board where different people post messages and are responded to by other members or passers-by.
Wikis	Webpages or forums where users can contribute, edit, and delete information, leading to communally edited works.
Blogs (Weblogs)	Blogs are akin to personal journal entries posted on publically accessible websites that allow readers to place comments and responses to the posted material.
User generated audio/video – Podcasts	Made famous by Apple's iPod media players, this tool alludes to serialized personal broadcasts that are available for download via the Internet. They may include audio or video and are produced both professionally and in amateur capacities. This term has recently come to encompass most user generated video and audio media. As per our definition of social media, podcasts or user generated audio/video qualify as social media only when they are interactive and allow for audience feedback e.g. through a comments section.
Instant Messaging (IM)	A synchronous communication tool that allows for two or more users to converse via text based exchanges through the tool's platform. It is also possible to exchange files and play basic games collaboratively.
Video chat	Although initially a component feature of IM because of its high bandwidth needs, with the proliferation of high speed Internet in homes today, video chat has become a social media tool itself. People converse in pairs or in groups face to face from diverse locations and are able to transfer files and engage in professional and casual social exchanges.
Social networking platforms	A collection of social networking tools that include personal information pages, instant messaging, blogs, and wikis all provided under singular platforms. They are the premiere social networking application and are widely thought to best embody the term social media.
Online social simulations	These simulations of the real world allow for people to be represented through avatars which they can customize to represent themselves. The virtual worlds allow for enhanced synchronous social interaction as they model real world social exchanges and relationships.
Games	In today's world, online, computer based and console games have all evolved to include a network playing element, allowing users to play against each other or in collaboration. The exchanges are not limited to gameplay and may include chat, video, and exchange of game based items and points.

audience/partners choose to reply or comment in turn does not have a bearing on the qualification of the exchange as a social media message.

Social Media Tools

There exists an extensive body of literature that explains what social media tools are and how they work. However, because of the aforementioned dynamic and constantly evolving nature of the definition, we are including a summary list of the most commonly used tools (Table 2) considered to embody social media at the present time, allowing our future readers to assess the shape of social media at the time of writing this chapter.

SOCIAL MEDIA, HIGHER EDUCATION, AND LEARNING THEORIES

The advent of social media in higher education was met with what can at best be called careful optimism, many established institutions feared competition as they expected online resources to replace rather than reinforce their business models (Katz, 2008). Over the last couple of years, however, academia seems to have warmed up to the idea of using social media as a learning tool. With several maiden implementations across various fields and areas of expertise, the use of this tool in higher education seems to be constantly growing. The increased accessibility of information and ease of collaboration making the world one large classroom, unhindered by the brick and mortar boundaries of traditional schools (Harris & Rea, 2009). One of the reasons for this increased acceptability of social media in academia and in particular higher education, seems to be related to the current generation of students who have grown up and have been living with Internet and social tools most of their lives. These digital natives, millennium or next generation students (Prensky, 2001) experience the Internet in a much more organic way than their predecessors, considering the online social tools to be an ongoing part of their lives (Katz, 2008).

As expected, there is more to the science of using social media in higher education than just making it available to the students. Groups of researchers have examined the need for the use of social media tools in terms of current instructional theories, models, and approaches (Ferdig, 2007; Ajjan & Hartshorne, 2008). Coming to the conclusion that any technology cannot offer instructional success alone unless it is founded upon appropriate instructional strategies and approaches for the learning context (Ferdig, 2007).

However, the question remains as to what theories within the fields of instructional systems or education psychology can be best used as frameworks for building social media uses in higher education. As with most social science, depending on the situation there might be several answers that satisfy the needs at hand. Judging from recent studies, however, the researchers seem to gravitate towards the constructivist learning theory as the foundation for learning through social media. Based on the constructivist learning theory, knowledge is constructed through different ways including participation, reflection, collaboration, and interaction (Brooks & Brooks, 1999; Jonassen, 1994) and learning is taken to be a social process through which students construct meaning and understanding by means of interaction with each other and the environment (Bruner, 1996;

Vygotsky, 1978). In the same vein, Rovai (2001) asserts that a student's sense of community, which can be provided by interaction and collaboration, is a key element for the student's satisfaction and retention. It is therefore inductively posited that when used appropriately, social media tools can provide constructivist learning environments and community in which students participate in learning experiences actively and collaboratively resulting in satisfactory learning and increased retention.

Formal Use of Social Media in Medical Education

Although a growing number of medical professionals and educators use Web applications like e-mail or the websites of professional journals in their day to day practice and instruction, a far lesser number are cognizant of the opportunities that social media provides to them, especially in the field of medical education. As a result, over the past decade, several Web-based technologies have become integral to health communication but the use of social media for health education is still in infancy. There are only a few studies that focus on applying social media technologies in the health education sector and most of them focus on the growing spectrum of social media applications targeted to health care provider-patient interaction (e.g. Hawn, 2009; Bonilla-Warford, 2010) and patient-patient communication (e.g. Brennan & Fink, 1997; Demiris, 2006; Wright, 2009; Wright & Bell, 2003).

A far more limited number of publications have discussed some examples of how social media tools have been applied in higher education environments in the medical and nursing fields. Since social media software allows for new and innovative ways of creating, exchanging, repurposing, and categorizing information, it could have great potential in medical education and professional development in health care. Social media could potentially help overcome the challenges in medical education caused by shortage of faculty, aging workforce and limited teaching knowledge and experience that expert clinicians may have (Bassell, 2010).

Informal Use of Social Media Use among Medical Students

The assumption that social media based student-centered learning tools for medical students are an important need is supported by the finding that medical students need to acquire skills for maintaining life-long learning, not only focus on core knowledge of their chosen field (General Medical Council, 2009), a need that can be well served by social media forums because of their ability to reinforce knowledge already learned and introduce knowledge as yet unknown (to the learner). Furthermore, medical students already seem to have great interest in using social media. Research data indicate that medical students are regularly engaged in using social media, especially instant messaging and social networking. Confirming this trend, studies have shown that medical students' use of instant messaging ranges from 80 to 90% of their population (Sandars, Homer, Pell, & Crocker, 2010; Kennedy, Krause, Judd, Churchward, & Gray, 2006; White, 2007) and social networking sites as MySpace and Facebook are used by 60% to 70% of students (Sandars, et al., 2010; White, 2007). Blogs are read by about a fifth of medical students and a small number (8%) write their own blogs (Sandars, et al., 2010).

However, even though social media seems to be such a global phenomenon, the use of social media by students in aforementioned medical education settings may depend on the structure of the education system as well. As studies conducted in the UK show, besides instant messaging, social networking, and blogs, other social media applications are barely used by medical students (Sandars & Schroter, 2007). Since both the US and the UK have very high Internet penetration

among population (InternetWorldStats.com, 2010) and the popularity of social media tools is constantly growing in all developed countries around the world, it may be assumed that differences in educational systems possibly account for the minimal use of social media by medical students in the U.K.

Focusing on the U.S., however, the suggestion that social media tools may work well for medical students is reinforced by Sandars and Schroter (2007), who found that in spite of low knowledge and skills for educational uses of social media applications, medical students are interested in using these technologies in their studies. Thus, with proper training of how to integrate social media in undergraduate and graduate medical studies, social media technologies could have the popularity and the potential to overcome most awareness based shortcomings currently hindering such progress.

Social Media in Medical Curricula

It is fair to say that even though there is currently little research to measure the effectiveness of social media applications in medical education, there is realization of their potential. Some innovative and open-minded medical and nursing programs have already added social media tools in their curricula. Lemley and Burnham (2009) found that 53% of nursing schools and 45% of medical schools in the U.S. use social media in their curricula and blogs, wikis, videocasts, and podcasts being the most commonly used tools in campus-based courses, as well as mixed online and campus-based courses. The same study indicated that whereas nursing students used social media mainly in non-nursing courses, medical schools use social media tools in both preclinical and clinical courses. In addition, according to Lemley and Burnham (2009), half of medical schools and 58% of nursing schools planned to integrate social media applications in their curricula during 2010, so far no report on the actual realization of these goals exists.

METHODOLOGY

Since the topic at hand required analysis of software products in terms of online applications, we chose to use a guide for systematic review of software applications developed by Kitchenham (2004). This guide itself is based on the Cochrane Reviewer, Australian National Health and Medical Research Council and Center for Reviews and Dissemination (CRD) guides, which are more commonly used in medical systematic reviews. This guide matched our intended goals for this chapter since it was geared towards producing reviews that look to summarize research, identify gaps and provide a background for further research.

Review Questions

This current review was structured as per the summary outline of the Kitchenham guide presented above. Consistent with this guide the following *review questions* provided focus for this review:

RQ 1: What are the prevalent formal (official) and informal (student /privately initiated) uses of social media reported in available literature on medical education?

RQ 2: Is there adequate original research testing the effectiveness of social media based learning applications in formal (official) medical education?

Data Sources

These questions are exploratory in nature and were adopted to guide the research with a singular composite discussion serving as their answer. In order to formulate that discussion, articles published over the last five years (2007 to 2011) were searched through the following databases: EBSCOHost (ERIC), Academic Search Premier, ScienceDirect, PubMed, Informa Healthcare, and MedLib.

Search Terms

The search terms referred to general use of social media in medical, professional health and nursing education as well as specific applications' (podcast, wiki, blog, instant messaging, RSS, social bookmarking, social networking, and simulations) implementation in these educational programs. A list of basic search terms was used as a base dictionary to create Boolean logic statements in the search categories. The basic search terms used were: Social+Media, "Social Media," Medical+Education, "Medical Education," Blogs, Wikis, Collaborative+Learning, "Collaborative Learning," Social+Simulations, "Social Simulations," Podcasts, Social+Network, "Social Network," Nursing, nursing+education, and "Nursing Education." Boolean permutations of these terms were used to create complex search queries.

Pre-Selection Results

The search was limited to articles published between 2007 and 2011 as most of the widely used social media technologies of today were developed in the last 5 years (facebook.com opened to public at the end of 2006, twitter.com opened to public in 2006), academic research on their use (relevant to our topic) is therefore a fairly new development. The initial search resulted in 601 articles (Table 3).

Table 3. Initial search results

Database	Number of articles
EBSCOHost (ERIC)	36
Academic Search Premier	58
ScienceDirect	283
PubMed	117
Informa Healthcare	44
Medlib	63

Selection Criteria

Using the review questions as guides, selection criteria were developed to enable review of relevant studies. The selection criteria mandated the article contribute towards answering the review questions, thereby, articles that contained any of the following were deemed to have met the selection criteria and were considered for further review:

- Original studies that measured the effectiveness of social media in medical education;
- Refer to other original studies that examine social media in medical education; or
- List uses of social media applications in medical education or by medical students.

Research Design Assessment

Using a research design categorization from Merisotis and Phipps (1999), we selected the articles and categorized and tagged them accordingly (Table 4).

Since this chapter presents an academic situation analysis of the prevalence of social media in medical education, only studies that qualified within these research design categories were deemed to have enough information to perform analysis and were included for reporting in the results section of this chapter. In order to undertake the situation analysis, which is a term ascribed to the thorough examination of a situation (Roy, 2001), we first read through the abstracts of each article within the search results, if they met aforementioned selection criteria; if they did, we proceeded to review the methodology and results sections to determine which Merisotis and Phipps (1999) best suited the work.

Table 4. Categorization of articles

Abbreviation	Category	Description
Des	Descriptive	Collection of data to answer a specific question
Cas	Case Study	In-depth investigation and narrative of a single unit
Cor	Correlational	Collection of data to investigate relationship between two or more variables
Exp	Experimental Research	Testing of hypothesis concerning cause and effect relationships

Note. Adapted from Merisotis and Phipps (1999)

RESULTS

Post Selection Results

Out of the 601 total search returns (initial results), 408 were excluded after review of abstracts for either redundancy or the absence of a focus on the use of social media in medical education, leading to the exclusion of those articles that only contained brief mentions of the keywords without any proper analysis or review dedicated to them. The remaining 193 articles were then reviewed (abstract, methodology, and results sections) and subjected to the selection criteria leaving 18 for extraction of data for this review.

By categorizing the articles per search criteria, a majority of articles (11) referred to other studies that examined social media in medical education. Five studies listed uses of social media applications in medical education or by medical students; and two articles measured the effectiveness of social media tools in medical education.

The selected studies were divided into the research design categories (Table 5). The results of the analysis indicated that the number of original research studies scientifically analyzing the effectiveness of social media applications in medical or nursing education is still very limited (5 studies). Furthermore, even though there are several officially used applications that facilitate online

Table 5. Results per research design category

Category	Results	Article Reference
Des (Descriptive)	6	Kamel Boulos, Hetherington, & Wheeler, 2007; Gorini, Gaggioli, Vigna, & Riva, 2008; Jain, 2009; Chretien, Goldman, & Faselis, 2008; Black, Thompson, Duff, Dawson, Saliba, & Black, 2010; Poonawalla & Wagner, 2006
Cas (Case Study)	10	Chu, Young, Zamora, Kurup, & Macario, 2010a; Srinivasan, 2009; Bratsas, Kapsas, Konstantinidis, Koutsouridis, & Bamidis, 2009; Cain & Fox, 1999; Abdo, Pashnyak, & Dennen, 2011; McGee & Begg, 2008; Paton, Bamidis, Eysenbach, Hansen, & Cabrer, 2011; George & Dellasega, 2011; Chatterjee & Biswas, 2011; George, 2011
Cor (Correlational)	0	
Exp (Experimental Research)	2	Youngblood, Harter, Srivasrtava, Moffett, Heinrichs, & Dev, 2008; Fischer, Haley, Saarinen, & Chretien, 2011

learning, 29 as per the results, near 20 (70%) of them do not allow two-way communication (e.g. Simulation Atlas of Physiology and Pathophysiology developed by Charles University in Prague, http://www.physiome.cz/atlas/index_en.html).

We found that almost 91% (175/193) of the published articles in the last five years that met our search criteria (pre-selection) focused on needs or potency analysis rather than providing case studies of social media use in medical education or original research on the topic. This may be ascribed to the infancy of the medium in medical education settings. We noted however, that this gap in original research does not mean that social media in medical education has remained just an idea; it has in fact found several avenues of use in the field. For instance, our review showed that there are higher education facilities and enthusiastic professors who have included social media applications in their medical or nursing programs in the form of blogs, wikis, social simulations, or podcasts. This ready acceptance of the new technology into the learning spectrum is a testament to the usability of social media and indeed an indication of its possible effectiveness.

However, as alluded to before, since there is a significant gap in research measuring the effectiveness of these tools among medical and nursing students, we found little concrete basis to validate social media's potential for this field. Furthermore,

since the technology has been mostly inducted on small scale experimental basis, often by singular professors and/or students themselves, it is often unclear which (if any) theoretical frameworks were used when designing these social media learning tools or if they were designed at all and not simply adopted from general use. Indeed, we found the most widely reported uses of social media use in medical education came from private student endeavors, which used template based Web technologies that are designed to enable general communication rather than an explicit facilitation of learning. In addition, most (12/18) of the selected articles did not specify whether the mentioned applications were targeted to undergraduate, graduate or post-graduate students, a possible effect of the absence of formal design structure on behalf of the application creator.

The following is a summary of research in the last five years (as per our results) that reported social media applications in medical education. As an answer to Review Question 1 (RQ1), this summary of research is categorized according to the social media tool that was used in each implementation.

Social Simulations

As medical science requires real world practical training, a wide variety of simulations in virtual environments were broadly discussed in the articles as a viable alternative. As per the operationalization of social media in our study, only articles focusing on simulations that facilitate two-way communication were analyzed.

We found an innovative study by Youngblood et al. (2008) that provided an analysis of virtualization and social media communication as it measured the effectiveness of Online Virtual Emergency Departments (OVED). An online environment was used by teams of four to communicate with each other synchronously over Internet protocol to manage computer-controlled patients who exhibited signs and symptoms of physical trauma. The study indicated that OVED proved to be as effective for learning team skills as the patient simulators, which are the predominant and costly method for training healthcare teams in situations that require trainees be present in the same place at the same time (Youngblood, et al., 2008).

Additionally, a well-known virtual reality environment Second Life has been recently used for medical training through innovative simulations. The Heart Murmur Sim for Second Life developed by Dr. Kemp from San José State University, allows medical students to practice and test their skills on cardiac auscultation (Kamel Boulos, Hetherington, & Wheeler, 2007). Similarly, Ann Myers Medical Center in Second Life allows medical students to practice skills such as listening skills during initial exam history and physicals (Chu, et al., 2010a). Another implementation is the Gene Pool's interactive genetics lab in Second Life, which involves experiments, tutorials, quizzes, and animations. Whereas, the Virtual Neurological Education Centre (VNEC) in Second Life facilitates training and provides a virtual experience of a neurological disorder (Gorini, Gaggioli, Vigna, & Riva, 2008).

Blogs

The social media tools applied in medical education involved mostly blogs and social networking tools. According to Poonawalla and Wagner's (2006) study conducted among blog users, the blog and most of its features were evaluated to be useful and therefore are likely to have had a positive impact on medical education. According to a content analysis of 30 blogs initiated by medical students from various countries, Abdo, Pashnyak, and Dennen (2011) suggested that blogging is foremost a channel that provides informal support for medical students and creates a sense of community. Blogging may help medical students share their ideas and experiences, find and offer solutions to professional problems, socialize with other students and provide real life experiences for prospective medical students as well as the current ones (Abdo, Pashnyak, & Dennen, 2011).

In addition, there are blogs initiated by educational institutions that serve as a platform for professional information change and interaction. For example, a blog called DIG@UTMB (http://digutmb.blogspot.com/) developed by the University of Texas Medical Branch Dermatology Interest Group is a resource for medical students interested in dermatology as well as for dermatologists and residents but is not directly used as part of coursework.

Finally, there are a few blogs that have been integrated in medical schools' curriculum and provide an official learning tool for their students. Fischer et al. (2011) conducted a comparative study among students at two medical schools in the U.S., asking them to either use online blogging or a traditional format for writing their essays. As the study showed that there was no statistically significant difference in topics addressed or in depth of reflection between students in two study arms, the authors suggested that blogs could be a suitable substitution for traditional essay writing among medical students and helps to address students' different learning styles.

In addition, a study conducted by Chretien, Goldman, and Faselis (2008) suggested that blogs are a suitable medium for promoting medical students' reflection, collaboration, and provide opportunities to promote their professional development. In the program, the students were asked to post two reflective posting to a class blog during their four-week basic medicine clerkship. The students could also read fellow students posts, leave feedback and get feedback from the instructor. In the end of the task, 177 posts were submitted by 91 students and one third of them commented fellow students' threads. Overall, the students found the task to be enjoyable and found instructor's feedback helpful.

In addition, Stanford University School of Medicine has several initiatives where social blogs are used as a learning tool. For example, EtherBlog (http://med.stanford.edu/anesthesia/etherblog/) features videos, lecture capture, questions and answers section, as well as educational quizzes for anesthesia residents (Chu, et al., 2010a).

Wikis

Medicine and medical education wikis are increasing in popularity (Chu, Zamora, Young, Kurup, & Macario, 2010b) and could have potential to become a source of information and platform of collaboration for medical students and professionals. For instance, a wiki Ganfyd is born as a collaboration of nearly 500 medical professionals, students, and non-medical experts who have contributed as authors and editors (http://www.ganfyd.org).

As Kamel Boulos, Maramba, and Wheeler (2006) concluded in their article, there is very little reliable original pedagogic research and evaluation evidence about Web 2.0 tools. This is especially the case for wikis in medical education. In spite of their increasing popularity and potential, the search results indicated that there is very limited information about the wikis that have been initiated by universities or used as medical education tools

within schools' curricula. One of the prominent users is the University of Edinburgh, which has used wikis as a teaching tool for undergraduate student group projects facilitating collaborative group work and peer reviewing; as well as for collaborative research base for staff members (McGee & Begg, 2008). Another innovative example is University of Florida's wiki Virtual Anesthesia Machine (http://vam.anest.ufl.edu/) that involves information about different anesthesia simulations.

Podcasts

Although a number of universities have used podcasts in medical education, there is limited information about them from an instructional design perspective. University of Pittsburgh has captured and digitalized all core curriculum lectures (Laboratory for Educational Technology, 2011) and Vanderbilt University and St. Louis University have developed a podcast collection of Anesthesia and Critical Care lectures (Chu, et al., 2010b); however, it is not known what learning design factors were followed when creating these podcasts. More importantly, it is not known as to what extent the podcasts allowed for interactivity or two-way communication, making it difficult to even classify them as social media tools under the definition used in this article.

Social Networking Platforms

Some universities have been involved in medical education applications that allow social networking among students and professors. For example, students at University of Pittsburgh are asked to create their own collaborative websites where they develop their own course-related content when developing school projects. These sites facilitate students' group discussions, and allows them both to help create and critique each other's presentations, and to review journal articles (McGee & Begg, 2008). According to McGee and Begg

(2008), over 2000 unique collaborative websites have been maintained by the 600 undergraduate medical students.

CONCLUSION

As can be seen from the results section, social media tools have almost all found a place within medical education, be it formal or informal. The on-demand nature of online information, coupled with the cost and time effective nature of online communication, come together to form a very lucrative package in the form of social media. The tools, which allow information exchanges to be stored either latently or actively, eventually allow for an encyclopedic storage of curricula-alternate information, enabling users to asynchronously benefit from these exchanges. An example would be blog posts that often survive as long as the server will host them, allowing past, current and future students' access to the information and unlimited avenues of update.

The collaborative nature of the social media tools also open up considerable opportunities for application of collective knowledge to problem solving in the field, a boon for diagnostic medicine and for further innovations in established practices. For example, we found several concept papers that discuss extensions of aforementioned Second Life implementations in medical education, the extensions ranged from robotic surgical assistants plugged in as avatars performing real time surgery based on directions from other users, to intelligent know-it-all avatar agents that can be approached or called in during a virtual diagnosis, surgery or medical procedure. We must add, however, that such collaboration is susceptible to producing false, biased or misleading information, mainly because of the lack of consequence and lack of vetting for the author of such information, especially in open forums. This issue however

can be addressed through an active monitoring and moderation of content to allow for only sound medical advice to filter through. This can be achieved either through community appointed moderators, as done in the Wikipedia project and several other forums, or through a certification process that allows the forum's administrators to vet the qualifications of the moderator to be, for the purpose of medical education, the latter seems much more practical.

Furthermore, as a direct answer to our second question, we found a gap in the available literature: there is very little original research focusing on the effectiveness of social media in medical education. In fact we found only two relevant studies (Youngblood, et al., 2008; Fischer, et al., 2011) with small sample sizes that included measures of effectiveness on learning performance when social media are used. In terms of a recommendation in light of this situation analysis, given the possible benefits of social media, its ready acceptability and adoption, we would point to an immediate need for original research experiments measuring the efficiency of social media tools in medical education. Knowing the efficiency of this medium, as well as a scientific assessment of its limitations, would allow instructional designers to formally incorporate social media into medical curricula, while allowing the instructors and students better accuracy in utilizing this new medium within their study plans. We end this chapter by adding that social media is not infallible, with many platforms rising to fame and falling fast (e.g., Orkut.com and MySpace), however it is the longevity of the concept as a whole rather than any single implementation that gives most promise to this new technology. The fact that it is not just a fleeting trend that makes social media in medical education a worthwhile subject for academic research, as we expect researchers to add to the body of literature for years to come.

REFERENCES

Abdo, S. N., Pashnyak, T. G., & Dennen, V. P. (2011). Medical students' international blogging community: A coping mechanism to survive the difficult years of medical school. *International Journal of Web Based Communities*, *7*(3), 342–356. doi:10.1504/IJWBC.2011.041203

Ajjan, H., & Hartshorne, R. (2008). Investigating faculty decisions to adopt Web 2.0 technologies: Theory and empirical tests. *The Internet and Higher Education*, *11*(2), 71–80. doi:10.1016/j.iheduc.2008.05.002

Bassell, K. (2010). Social media and the implications for nursing faculty mentoring: A review of the literature. *Teaching and Learning in Nursing*, *5*, 143–148. doi:10.1016/j.teln.2010.07.007

Black, E. W., Thompson, L. A., Duff, W. P., Dawson, K., Saliba, H., & Black, N. M. P. (2010). Re-visiting social network utilization by physicians-in-training. *Journal of Graduate Medical Education*, *2*(2), 289–293.

Bonilla-Warford, N. (2010). Many social media options exist for optometrists. *Optometry - Journal of the American Optometric Association*, *81*(11), 613–614. doi:10.1016/j.optm.2010.09.006

Bratsas, C., Kapsas, G., Konstantinidis, S., Koutsouridis, G., & Bamidis, P. D. (2009). A semantic wiki within Moodle for Greek medical education. In *Proceedings of CBMS 2009: The 22nd IEEE International Symposium on Computer-Based Medical Systems*, (pp. 1-6). IEEE Press. Retrieved from http://ieeexplore.ieee.org/xpl/freeabs_all.jsp?arnumber=5255417.

Brennan, P. F., & Fink, S. V. (1997). Health promotion, social support, and computer networks. In Street, R. L., Gold, W. R., & Manning, T. (Eds.), *Health Promotion and Interactive Technology: Theoretical Applications and Future Directions* (pp. 157–169). Mahwah, NJ: Lawrence Erlbaum Associates.

Brooks, J. G., & Brooks, M. G. (1999). *In search of understanding: The case for constructivist classrooms*. Alexandria, VA: American Society for Curriculum Development.

Bruner, J. (1996). *Culture of education*. Boston, MA: Harvard University Press.

Cain, J., & Fox, B. I. (1999). Web 2.0 and pharmacy education. *American Journal of Pharmaceutical Education*, *73*(7), 120. Retrieved from http://www.ncbi.nlm.nih.gov/pmc/articles/PMC2779632/ doi:10.5688/aj7307120

Castillo, C., Donato, D., Gionis, A., & Mishne, G. (2008). Finding high-quality content in social media. In E. Agichtein (Ed.), *Proceedings of the 2008 International Conference on Web Search & Data Mining*. Palo Alto, CA: ACM Press.

Chatterjee, P., & Biswas, T. (2011). Blogs and twitter in medical publications - Too unreliable to quote, or a change waiting to happen? *South African Medical Journal*, *101*(10), 712–714. Retrieved from http://samj.org.za/index.php/samj/article/view/5213

Chretien, K., Goldman, E., & Faselis, C. (2008). The reflective writing class blog: Using technology to promote reflection and professional development. *Journal of General Internal Medicine*, *23*(12), 2066–2070. doi:10.1007/s11606-008-0796-5

Chu, L., Young, C., Zamora, A., Kurup, V., & Macario, A. (2010a). Anesthesia 2.0: Internet-based information resources and web 2.0 applications in anesthesia education. *Current Opinion in Anaesthesiology*, *23*(2), 218–227. doi:10.1097/ACO.0b013e328337339c

Chu, L., Zamora, A. K., Young, C., Kurup, V., & Macario, A. (2010b). The role of social networking applications in the medical academic environment. *International Anesthesiology Clinics*, *48*(3), 61–82. doi:10.1097/AIA.0b013e3181e6e7d8

Demiris, G. (2006). The diffusion of virtual communities in health care: Concepts and challenges. *Patient Education and Counseling, 62*(2), 178–188. doi:10.1016/j.pec.2005.10.003

Ferdig, R. (2007). Examining social software in teacher education. *Journal of Technology and Teacher Education, 15*(1), 5–10.

Fischer, M. A., Haley, H.-L., Saarinen, C. L., & Chretien, K. C. (2011). Comparison of blogged and written reflections in two medicine clerkships. *Medical Education, 45*(2), 166–175. doi:10.1111/j.1365-2923.2010.03814.x

Foreman, T. (2011, March 8). How much is Facebook really worth? *CNN*. Retrieved from http://edition.cnn.com/2011/TECH/social.media/03/08/facebook.overvalued/.

General Medical Council. (2009). *Tomorrow's doctors: Recommendations on undergraduate medical education.* Retrieved from http://www.gmc-uk.org/education/undergraduate/tomorrows_doctors_2009.asp.

George, D., & Dellasega, C. (2011). Social media in medical education: Two innovative pilot studies. *Medical Education, 45*(11), 1158–1159. doi:10.1111/j.1365-2923.2011.04124.x

George, D. R. (2011). Friending facebook? A minicourse on the use of social media by health professionals. *The Journal of Continuing Education in the Health Professions, 31*(3), 215–219. doi:10.1002/chp.20129

Gilbert, E., & Karahalios, K. (2009). Predicting tie strength with social media. In *Proceedings of the 27th International Conference on Human Factors in Computing Systems.* Boston, MA: ACM Press.

Gorini, A., Gaggioli, A., Vigna, C., & Riva, G. (2008). A Second Life for eHealth: Prospects for the use of 3-D virtual worlds in clinical psychology. *Journal of Medical Internet Research, 10*(3). doi:10.2196/jmir.1029

Harris, A. L., & Rea, A. (2009). Web 2.0 and virtual world technologies: A growing impact on IS education. *Journal of Information Systems Education, 20*(2), 137–144. Retrieved from http://learningtechworld.com/Documents/Virtual%20World%20Technologies.pdf

Hawn, C. (2009). Take two aspirin and tweet me in the morning: How Twitter, Facebook, and other social media are reshaping health care. *Health Affairs, 28*(2), 361–368. doi:10.1377/hlthaff.28.2.361

InternetWorldStats.com. (2010). *Internet usage statistics.* Retrieved from http://internetworldstats.com/stats.htm.

Jain, S. H. (2009). Practicing medicine in the age of Facebook. *The New England Journal of Medicine, 361*, 649–651. doi:10.1056/NEJMp0901277

Jonassen, D. H. (1994). Thinking technology: Toward a constructivist design model. *Educational Technology, 34*(4), 34–37.

Kamel Boulos, M., Hetherington, L., & Wheeler, S. (2007). Second Life: An overview of the potential of 3-D virtual worlds in medical and health education. *Health Information and Libraries Journal, 24*(4), 233–245. doi:10.1111/j.1471-1842.2007.00733.x

Kamel Boulos, M., Maramba, I., & Wheeler, S. (2006). Wikis, blogs and podcasts: A new generation of web-based tools for virtual collaborative clinical practice and education. *BMC Medical Education, 6*(41).

Kaplan, A. M., & Haenlein, M. (2009). Users of the world, unite! The challenges and opportunities of social media. *Business Horizons, 52*(1), 59–68.

Katz, R. N. (2008). The gathering cloud: Is this the end of the middle. In R. N. Katz (Ed.), *The Tower and the Cloud: Higher Education in the Age of Cloud Computing,* (pp. 2-42). Washington, DC: Educause. Retrieved from http://net.educause.edu/ir/library/pdf/PUB7202.pdf.

Kennedy, G., Krause, K.-L., Judd, T., Churchward, A., & Gray, K. (2006). *First year students' experiences with technology: Are they really digital natives?* Melbourne, Australia: University of Melbourne. Retrieved from http://www.ascilite. org.au/ajet/ajet24/kennedy.pdf.

Kitchenham, B. (2004). *Procedures for performing systematic reviews*. Technical Report TR/SE0401. Newcastle-under-Lyme, UK: Keele University.

Laboratory for Educational Technology. (2011). *Lecture recording and podcasting*. Retrieved from http://let.pitt.edu/ProjectsAndPrograms/ podcast.html.

Lemley, T., & Burnham, J. F. (2009). Web 2.0 tools in medical and nursing school curricula. *Journal of the Medical Library Association, 97*(1), 50–52. doi:10.3163/1536-5050.97.1.010

McGee, B., & Begg, M. (2008). What medical educators need to know about Web 2.0. *Medical Teacher, 30*(2), 164–169. doi:10.1080/01421590701881673

Merisotis, J., & Phipps, R. (1999). *What's the difference? A review of contemporary research on the effectiveness of distance learning in higher education*. Retrieved from http://www.ihep.org/ Publications/publications-detail.cfm?id=88.

Nielsen Company. (2010, January 22). *Led by Facebook, Twitter, global time spent on social media sites up 82% year over year*. Retrieved from http://blog.nielsen.com/nielsenwire/global/ led-by-facebook-twitter-global-time-spent-on-social-media-sites-up-82-year-over-year/.

Paton, C., Bamidis, P., Eysenbach, G., Hansen, M. M., & Cabrer, M. (2011). Experience in the use of social media in medical and health education. *Yearbook of Medical Informatics, 6*(1), 21–29. Retrieved from http://www.schattauer. de/en/magazine/subject-areas/journals-a-z/imia-yearbook/imia-yearbook-2011/issue/special/ manuscript/16534.html

Poonawalla, T., & Wagner, R. F. (2006). Assessment of a blog as a medium for dermatology education. *Dermatology Online Journal, 12*(1). Retrieved from http://dermatology.cdlib.org/121/ commentary/blog/wagner.html

Prensky, M. (2001). Digital natives, digital immigrants. *Horizon, 9*(5), 1–6. doi:10.1108/10748120110424816

Rovai, A. P. (2001). Building classroom community at a distance: A case study. *Educational Technology Research and Development Journal, 49*(4), 33–48. doi:10.1007/BF02504946

Roy, J. (2001). From data fusion to situation analysis. In *Proceedings of the Fourth International Conference on Information*. Montreal, Canada.

Sandars, J., Homer, M., Pell, G., & Crocker, T. (2010). Web 2.0 and social software: The medical student way of e-learning. *Medical Teacher*. Retrieved from http://www.scribd.com/ doc/47545552/Medical-Teacher-Web-2-0-and-Social-Software.

Sandars, J., & Schroter, S. (2007). Web 2.0 technologies for undergraduate and postgraduate medical education: An online survey. *Postgraduate Medical Journal, 83*, 759–762. doi:10.1136/ pgmj.2007.063123

Social Media Defined. (2007). *What is social media?* Retrieved from http://www.socialmedi-adefined.com/what-is-social-media/.

Srinivasan, M. (2009). Visualizing the future: Technology competency development in clinical medicine, and implications for medical education. *Academic Psychiatry, 30*(6), 480–490. doi:10.1176/appi.ap.30.6.480

Vygotsky, L. S. (1978). *Mind in society: The development of higher psychological processes*. Boston, MA: Harvard University Press.

White, D. (2007). *Results of the "online tool use survey" undertaken by the JISC funded SPIRE project*. Retrieved from http://www.scribd.com/doc/464744/Online-Tool-Use-Survey.

Wright, K. B. (2009). Increasing computer-mediated social support. In Parker, J. C., & Thorson, E. (Eds.), *Health Communication in the New Media Landscape* (pp. 243–265). New York, NY: Springer Pub.

Wright, K. B., & Bell, S. B. (2003). Health-related support groups on the internet: Linking empirical findings to social support and computer-mediated communication theory. *Journal of Health Psychology*, *8*(1), 39–54. doi:10.1177/1359105303008001429

Xiang, Z., & Gretzel, U. (2009). Role of social media in online travel information search. *Tourism Management*, *31*(2), 179–188. doi:10.1016/j.tourman.2009.02.016

Youngblood, P., Harter, P. M., Srivastava, S., Moffett, S., Heinrichs, W. L., & Dev, P. (2008). Design, development, and evaluation of an online virtual emergency department for training trauma team. *Society for Simulation in Healthcare*, *3*(3), 146–153. doi:10.1097/SIH.0b013e31817bedf7

ADDITIONAL READING

Al-Deen, H. S. N., & Hendricks, J. A. (2011). *Social media: Usage and impact*. Lexington, KY: Lexington Books.

Boateng, B. A., & Black, E. W. (2012). *Social media in medicine: The impact of online social networks on contemporary medicine*. Stillwater, OK: New Forums Press.

Fraser, R. (2011). *The nurse's social media advantage*. Indianapolis, IN: Sigma Theta Tau Intl.

Hobbs, R. (2011). *Digital and media literacy: Connecting culture and classroom*. Thousand Oaks, CA: Corwin Press.

Newson, A., Houghton, D., & Patten, J. (2008). *Blogging and other social media: Exploiting the technology and protecting the enterprise*. Farnham, UK: Gower Publishing, Ltd.

Thielst, C. B. (2010). *Social media in healthcare: Connect, communicate, collaborate*. Chicago, IL: College of Healthcare Executives.

KEY TERMS AND DEFINITIONS

Social Media: Any private or public network based application that allows the exchange of information and social interaction between two or more individuals.

Health Education: The field of educating people about health.

Medical Education: Education associated with the practice of being a medical practitioner such as doctors and nurses.

Wiki: Webpages or forums where users can contribute, edit, and delete information, leading to communally edited works.

Blog (Weblog): Blogs are akin to personal journal entries posted on publically accessible websites that allow readers to place comments and responses to the posted material.

Podcast: Made famous by Apple's iPod media players, this tool alludes to serialized personal broadcasts that are available for download via the Internet. They may include audio or video and are produced both professionally and in amateur capacities. This term has recently come to encompass most user generated video and audio media. As per our definition of social media, podcasts or user generated audio/video qualify as social media only when they are interactive and allow for audience feedback e.g. through a comments section.

Online Social Simulation: These simulations of the real world allow for people to be represented through avatars which they can customize to represent themselves. The virtual worlds allow for enhanced synchronous social interaction as they model real world social exchanges and relationships.

Social Networking: A collection of social networking tools that include personal information pages, instant messaging, blogs, and wikis all provided under singular platforms. They are the premiere social networking application and are widely thought to best embody the term social media.

Virtual Worlds: Online community in which users can interact and collaborate with each other, create new things and share them with each other.

Health Communication: The field of informing and influencing people about essential health issues.

Section 4
Cases and Research Regarding Pre- and In-Service Teachers

Chapter 11
It's All about Personal Connections:
Pre-Service English Teachers' Experiences Engaging in Networked Learning

Luke Rodesiler
University of Florida, USA

Lauren Tripp
University of Florida, USA

ABSTRACT

Given the potential of informal online learning via social networks for supporting the career-long professional growth of in-service teachers, research must be conducted to better understand the ways in which today's future teachers are being prepared for and experiencing such practice. This chapter presents the authors' efforts to move in that direction, a qualitative study describing six pre-service secondary English language arts teachers' perceptions of self-directed networked learning during a teaching internship. Findings suggest that participants perceived networked learning as a viable and valuable approach to supplementing professional growth despite also perceiving challenges in the form of context, identity, and time.

INTRODUCTION

During the summer of 2009, we had the pleasure of working with pre-service secondary English Language Arts (ELA) teachers as they explored the potential of Web 2.0 applications for supporting

literacy instruction in the ELA classroom. After spending the final semester investigating the role technology plays in supporting literacy learning, one pre-service teacher expressed his dismay about leaving the program and, seemingly, being cut off from a pipeline of valuable information and resources:

DOI: 10.4018/978-1-4666-1815-2.ch011

I have some vague idea that there are a lot of really good resources out there, but I just have no idea of, like, how to connect with them. And even after this class, you know, I don't know how I'm going to be able to connect...to find other resources.... I just don't know. It'd be nice to get a newsletter or something, you know, that says, like, 'You should check this out,' or something like that.

Those words—a pre-service teacher bemoaning his uncertainty about how he will connect with others and continue his professional learning post-graduation—have fueled our interests in preparing pre-service teachers to engage in their own self-directed professional learning. This chapter presents research investigating pre-service secondary English teachers' perceptions regarding their experiences engaging in networked learning during a teaching internship.

BACKGROUND

Integrating online technologies in the ELA classroom to support student learning has received extensive coverage (e.g., Hicks, 2009; Kajder, 2003; Rozema & Webb, 2008). Accordingly, much attention has also been paid to how teacher educators prepare pre-service English teachers to incorporate the latest technologies into their practice (e.g., Grabill & Hicks, 2005; Pope & Golub, 2000; Swenson, Rozema, Young, McGrail, & Whitin, 2005; Young & Bush, 2004). However, it seems that secondary students are not the only ones whose learning can benefit from the active use of online technologies. Given recent endorsements for the potential of social media—defined for our purposes as interactive online technologies used to make connections with others for the purposes of sharing and receiving ideas and other information—to extend teachers' professional learning (e.g., Boss, 2008; Couros, 2008; Demski, 2010; Jakes, 2007; Trinkle, 2009), it seems that

attention must also be paid to how pre-service English teachers are taught to harness the latest online technologies in order to connect with professionals in the field, to engage in discourse about ideas and theories that are shaping their practice, and to locate and share resources of value in the ELA classroom. In other words, attention must be paid to how pre-service teachers are prepared to partake in "networked learning" (Steeples & Jones, 2002, p. 2).

The powerful learning that takes place for individuals plugged into a social network of teachers who collaborate, share inquiries into their own and others' practice, and engage in thoughtful professional discourse face-to-face as described by Cercone (2009) may be enhanced with the use of social media. Such technologies allow learners to extend the reach of their networks beyond the local geographic area to include professionals with shared interests and practices from across the globe. Networked learning empowers learners to diversify their influences and gain perspectives that would likely be unattainable otherwise. Steeples and Jones (2002) describe networked learning as "learning in which information and communication technology is used to promote connections: between one learner and other learners, between learners and tutors; between a learning community and its learning resources" (p. 2). Utilizing social media tools to support networked learning affords teachers opportunities to engage with others in collaborative spaces where they can reflect on their practice, share knowledge, and develop fresh understandings about teaching and learning (Riel & Fulton, 2001). Such technologies are characterized by the ability to bring individuals together to share insights, to make connections where there were none before, and to enhance the learning experience for all parties, making them viable options for teachers, both in-service and pre-service, to carry out self-directed professional learning.

RESEARCH METHODS

Given the potential of online social media technologies for connecting teachers, facilitating discourse, and ultimately supporting teachers' professional learning as their needs dictate, we believe English teacher educators must consider introducing pre-service English teachers to and engaging them in networked learning before they embark on what may be an isolated start to a career as a classroom teacher (McCann, Johannessen, & Ricca, 2005). However, if teacher educators are to effectively prepare pre-service teachers to engage in self-directed professional learning that is timely and efficient throughout their careers, research must be conducted to illuminate pre-service teachers' experiences engaging in networked learning to supplement their education and developing practice. In this chapter, we share our efforts to introduce six pre-service secondary English teachers to the concept of networked learning and to online social media technologies that may help them extend their learning during a teaching internship and beyond. Qualitative research methods, which focus on research participants' "experiences, perspectives, and histories" (Ritchie & Lewis, 2003, p. 3), were used throughout this study. Our investigation was guided by the following question: *What perceptions do pre-service secondary English language arts teachers hold with regard to engaging in networked learning during a teaching internship?*

Epistemology and Theoretical Perspective

This study is rooted in constructionism, an epistemology that suggests that knowledge is constructed, not discovered. In contrast with an objectivist epistemology, which posits that objects hold meaning independent of consciousness and experience, constructionism presumes multiple realities (Grbich, 2007) and suggests that different people may construct knowledge in different ways (Crotty, 1998). Researchers who position their work within constructionism focus on investigating the ways in which people make sense of their experiences as they engage with the worlds they inhabit (Crotty, 1998; Grbich, 2007), positioning participants as knowledge producers (Koro-Ljungberg, Yendol-Hoppey, Smith, & Hayes, 2009). Moreover, constructionism as an epistemological stance informs constructivism, the theoretical perspective guiding our methods. Constructivism suggests that each individual's sense of the world is a valid one (Crotty, 1998). Accordingly, this study explored pre-service secondary English teachers' individual perceptions regarding their engagement in networked learning during a teaching internship.

Participants

The pre-service teachers participating in this study consisted of four women and two men, with little ethnic diversity among them; all participants appeared to be predominantly Caucasian. Ranging in age from the early-twenties to mid-thirties, each participant possessed a bachelor's degree in English or a related field. Enrolled in the second semester of a three-semester graduate-level teacher certification program at a large, public university in the southeast United States, each participant was assigned to complete a 10-week teaching internship in an ELA classroom at a local public high school or middle school. Three participants were placed in middle school classrooms, and three were placed in high school classrooms. Participants reported being generally comfortable navigating the Web and having familiarity with Facebook and other popular social networking sites prior to the beginning of the study.

Context of the Study

For additional support during their teaching internships, participants met weekly in a seminar required for all pre-service English teachers. The content of the course was driven by the pre-service teachers' classroom experiences during the internship and addressed topics such as responding to student work, culturally responsive teaching, and teaching with technology.

Early in the course, and prior to starting their internships, the pre-service teachers were introduced to the notion of networked learning and the concept of a Personal Learning Network (PLN). A PLN, as Warlick (2009) describes it, is the network of colleagues, instructors, associates, friends, family, books, and other resources that supplement our knowledge and understanding. Pre-service teachers discussed the resources that comprised their respective networks and began thinking about how they might expand those networks using social media. The pre-service teachers completed online modules introducing them to social media tools that have the potential to connect them with teachers in the field and to promote discourse and the sharing of ideas, inquiries, and resources. The modules featured blogs, microblogs, Really Simple Syndication (RSS), and professional social networking sites such as those created through Ning.

Each module took on the same basic structure. The pre-service teachers viewed a brief video overview of each technology via Common Craft's "In Plain English" series and followed that by reading a more detailed introduction to the technologies featuring the "7 Things You Should Know About…" series from Educause Learning Initiative. The modules continued by prompting the pre-service teachers to explore examples of professionals in the field using social media before finally charging them to begin using each technology to enhance their PLNs. For example, participants were prompted to create a Twitter account, to join professional social networking sites and groups within those sites that spoke to their interests, to set up an RSS aggregator (used to check subscribed feeds of blogs or websites regularly for new work and download it to one location for ease of access and reading), and to

subscribe to blogs relevant to the teaching of English. After reflecting on how the use of each technology might benefit teachers, the pre-service teachers were invited to participate in this study. It should be noted that participants were not required to use any of the social media technologies introduced in the course or to maintain the digital components of their personal learning networks beyond what was required to complete each introductory module.

Data Collection and Analysis

Data collection began with the introduction of the modules at the start of the semester and continued until a focus group interview was conducted at the end of the semester. Though individual interviews would have been preferred, participant availability dictated the use of a focus group. Sources of data for this study included artifacts such as the participants' written reflections, observations of participants' communication with other educators within professional social networking sites and through Twitter, written notes from informal conversations with participants, and the transcript of the focus group interview conducted at the end of the semester. Participants wrote four reflections during the course of data collection. Because online communication was self-directed, the review of participants' communication with others varied per participant.

Data analysis was ongoing and recursive, beginning during data collection. Borrowing from ethnographic methods, data were analyzed using Spradley's (1980) guidelines for domain analysis, an approach intended to help researchers explore "categories of meaning" (p. 88). We used domain analysis as the primary method in order to systematically categorize patterns in participants' perceptions about engaging in networked learning to supplement and extend their professional growth. We followed Spradley's recommended steps independently, first selecting a semantic relationship—a "rationale" relationship (X is a reason for doing Y), in this case—to begin. From there, we prepared domain analysis worksheets independently to organize included terms and cover terms, selected a sample of the data with which to begin working, and then searched for possible cover terms and included terms that fit the semantic relationships. This process continued until all sources of data were considered.

Once all data sources were exhausted and domain analysis worksheets were complete, we met to compare domain analysis worksheets, including semantic relationships, cover terms, and included terms. We also reviewed and compared the data sources and grouped domains that were related. We continued this process until we were both satisfied with the final domains, which are presented in the findings.

Trustworthiness

Multiple measures were taken to ensure the trustworthiness of this study, including accounting for triangulation, maintaining an audit trail, and providing a thick description.

Denzin (1970) contends that by "combining multiple observers, theories, methods and data sources [researchers can] overcome the intrinsic bias that comes from single-method, single-observer and single-theory studies" (p. 313). This study utilizes two types of triangulation: data triangulation and researcher triangulation. Triangulating data requires researchers to use a variety of data sources in a study, comparing and cross-checking the consistency of data collected at various points in time and by different means (Patton, 2002). As noted previously, data sources included participant-generated artifacts, notes from informal conversations with participants, and a focus group interview. Researcher triangulation requires that two or more researchers engage in analyzing data so as to compensate for single-researcher bias (Denzin, 1989), which we did.

Maintaining an audit trail, a systematic form of documenting all aspects of a research project,

including data collection and analysis, is another technique researchers use to establish trustworthiness (Lincoln & Guba, 1985). While conducting this research, we systematically recorded decisions made along each step of the research process. Additionally, we attempted to provide a thick description (Geertz, 1973), including details related to the context and circumstances of the study, to afford readers the opportunity to develop a nuanced understanding of our work, enhancing their capacity to evaluate the trustworthiness of our observations and interpretations.

SUMMARY OF FINDINGS

The perceptions of networked learning shared by the participants in this study provide insight for teacher educators in similar contexts who are considering introducing networked learning as a means of fostering informal and self-directed career-long learning. The domains that emerged through data analysis provide insight into participants' thoughts on the viability and value of engaging informally in networked learning as a means of extending professional growth, as well as the roles that context, professional experience, and time play in pre-service teachers' networked learning experiences.

Authentic Support and Expert Advice

In sharing their perceptions of networked learning as a means of extending professional growth during a teaching internship and into their careers as English teachers, participants resoundingly described positive experiences that enhanced their learning. Many, like Suzy (all participant names are pseudonyms), recognized the value of networked learning, noting the potential to connect with and engage others in the field: "It's all about personal connections. It's a chance to 'talk shop' and get real ideas and advice from real educators. I love it!" Her sentiments were echoed by her peers. Kyle, for example, also saw the potential for connecting with his teaching colleagues to explore inquiries and discuss relevant content: "[A professional social networking site] is an easy way for me to stay in touch with my peers and discuss relevant information and pose questions." Tara shared her enthusiasm for networked learning that puts her in touch with teachers from across the globe and described the important role such learning plays in her professional development: "I am excited to connect with professional colleagues and associations through social networking and blogs. Most of my learning occurs through connecting with professional and academic colleagues." Kristy expressed a similar view as she described how the use of RSS and blogs, in particular, are significant to her engagement in networked learning:

RSS can constantly keep me updated with the latest teacher resources and techniques, as well as critical shifts in education. RSS can help me quickly find tools that will not only benefit me as a teacher, but my class. Blogs help me interact with the teaching community. Through blogs, I will be able to comment on topics of interest. Having already set up two blogs, I can see myself creating teacher-related blogs to help address critical issues and provide useful feedback to educators.

The enthusiasm with which participants described their perceptions of networked learning for supporting their professional growth is evident. Consistently, participants described an appreciation for the ease with which they can build connections with professionals in the field in order to overcome problems in their own classrooms or to keep up with the latest resources, trends, and shifts related to the teaching of English.

In addition to the connections that can be made with others, we found that participants recognized networked learning as a way of diversifying their sources of information and, thus, potentially broadening their own perspectives on teaching and learning. Darla, for example, described as

much when addressing the ways participating in professional social networking sites may enhance her professional learning:

These professional social networks add to my [professional learning] because they will help broaden my views on teaching as well as get me in contact with teachers who face the same struggles and successes I may have while teaching. This will help get me in contact with others who can possibly help with any teaching questions I have, as well as provide me with good resources to use for lesson planning in my classes.

Like Darla, Kyle also described the potential for networked learning to help him branch out and extend his reach: "Social networks on the Internet allow my questions to reach thousands of teachers rather than just the handful I come in contact with everyday—a valuable asset to any teacher's toolbox." Such responses are characteristic of the potential and viability of networked learning as a form of professional development perceived by participants throughout the study.

Discovering Like-Minded Others

This domain, which captures participants' perceptions of the importance of context, was reflected in data collected from each participant in this study. Participants claimed that engaging in networked learning was most helpful when they discovered a community of educators working in situations similar to their own. For example, Suzy stated, "Sometimes I just want to know that there is someone else out there grappling with the same problems and questions I have." In a similar vein, Kyle shared that his routine reading of the Digital Writing, Digital Teaching blog was most powerful because the contributors (both the blogger and readers providing comments) shared their struggles with and solutions for their students' lack of technology access, which was also a problem at his high school. Likewise, those participants who were teaching English for Speakers of Other Languages (ESOL) found ESOL networks to be particularly helpful in offering suggestions and strategies for differentiating instruction.

However, these same participants noted that the contextual nature of teaching also prevented them from fully engaging in networked learning. Rather than relying heavily on networked learning to support them during the internship, some participants opted instead to rely on connections they had made face-to-face. Kyle, for example, described frequently turning to previously established connections he had made with practicing teachers: "I would say I tapped into former teachers more than I tapped into anything else. People that knew me and people that I'd seen in action before because when I was in their class that kind of thing worked for me." This "apprenticeship of observation," in which pre-service teachers tend to assume the teaching practices of teachers they witnessed as students, rather than attempting those, which they learn in their teacher education programs, is a daunting hurdle to overcome, especially in situations where the pre-service teacher feels uncertain or uncomfortable (Lortie, 1975). Those "tried and true" practices, despite being seen from an angle which ignores any planning, adaptation, or reflection on the teacher's part, tend to be utilized because they are familiar and they provide teachers with default options.

In a similar fashion, Douglas described his preference for turning to the veteran teachers in his building with whom he could sit down: "In my planning time, I would spend it speaking with my cooperating teacher or I would go to the 11th grade teacher's classroom and get ideas from him....I was just so satisfied with the resources around me that I didn't feel the need to [reach out to others in an online setting]." Still others, like Darla, recognized the opportunities for learning that were presented to her each week when she met with fellow pre-service teachers in her weekly seminar: "We had the additional resources from being in this class. We posed questions to each other and answered them in class. I know Kyle

would email me and ask me what I was doing, and, you know, if I had any ideas for him, I'd respond. It was all relatable because we were all doing similar things." Recognition of the "personally maintained synchronous connections" (Warlick, 2009, p. 13), those traditional sources of information we have long turned to in order to supplement our understandings and achieve our goals, was evident as participants described their perceptions of engaging in networked learning.

Intimidation and Inexperience

Among the ten "Opportunities Essential in Effective Teacher Preparation Programs" recognized by the National Council of Teachers of English (2006) is "Develop[ing] a sense of belonging to a professional community and a desire for professional growth that will help them, as ELA teacher candidates, sustain their commitment to the profession over time" (p. 11). As teacher educators, we believe that engaging pre-service teachers in networked learning can go a long way toward developing the sense of professional belonging that NCTE advocates. We believe that by helping pre-service teachers build connections with professionals in the field and with other pre-service teachers from across the nation who, like them, are trying to find their way in the field, teacher educators are providing opportunities for pre-service teachers to develop a taste for professional growth and to carve out a place for themselves within the professional community. However, our participants spoke at length about the role their identities as pre-service teachers played in limiting their willingness to engage in-service teachers in substantive discourse about pressing issues they faced, or even responding to the inquiries posed by others. This domain reflects participants' perceptions and concerns about where they, with their limited classroom experience, fit into the professional online conversations with more experienced teachers that are characteristic of networked learning.

Kyle described the trouble he had posing alternative perspectives when engaged in discourse with an experienced in-service teacher, given the fact that his experience is so limited:

And it's like, how do you respond to someone when you completely, whole-heartedly disagree? You know? I mean, when they have experience and that's how they run their classroom. I don't disagree—I mean I do disagree—but...um, I think etiquette was a big deal. How do you, as a preservice teacher, how do you form your own ideas and talk to people who have different ideas when I feel so strongly one way, but she's been running her classroom for twelve years a different way, and she has a job? For me, it's like I don't have job, so, at this point, arguing with someone who does doesn't seem like a good idea.

In the excerpt above, Kyle describes how his perceived lack of experience compromises his ethos, or his credibility as a knowledgeable source on matters pertaining to teaching English in a secondary classroom. For him, it seems, a true sense of belonging to the professional community is lacking, for he lacks experience, the proverbial ticket into the conversation. Kyle was not alone in expressing this sentiment. Kyle's perception that because he lacks experience his contributions to professional conversations are less valid than those offered by a more-experienced teacher are echoed by his peers in the following exchange about responding to other professionals while engaged in networked learning:

1. **Author**: Something else that's been pretty steady in our conversation is the idea of us searching for resources, finding resources, asking questions, and these sorts of activities that bring information to us. How much responding to others did we do with these tools? Did we share ideas of our own? And if not, why not?

2. **Suzy**: I think there's still that part that a lot of us feel where we're not—yeah, we might [be working toward] a master's degree, but we don't have the same experience as veteran teachers, so I almost feel as though, even if I know the answer, I don't feel like it's my place yet—

3. **Tara**: Or that there's something you're missing—you don't even know that you don't know.

4. **Author**: Okay, again, so perception.

5. **Tara**: You don't want to come across as this uppity, know-it-all graduate student who hasn't been in the trenches for the past 20 years.

6. **Darla**: Also, time. Internship, school, time.

7. **Author**: You've got enough things to worry about?

8. **Kyle**: I'd respond to my friends, like Douglas, because we have that type of relationship that if I saw Douglas post a question, I'd answer him because he knows me and he knows whatever I respond to it, I don't mean it maliciously if I disagree with him or anything like that. So the personal relationship that we already have allows us to answer those sorts of questions. Also, I still don't have a job, like I said earlier. For me, I have a hard time being an authority on anything if I'm unemployed.

In this exchange, other participants, like Kyle, describe their reticence to respond to more experienced professionals—even when they think they might have something valuable to offer—when engaging in networked learning. Whether due to concerns about how they may be perceived, due to fears that they may be overlooking an important element in their response and not even know it because they lack experience, or due to the belief that it is simply "not [their] place" to speak up and join the conversation, participants clearly expressed a hesitance to fully engage in the discourse of the professional community online.

In line with concerns about their inexperience, participants described their status as pre-service teachers preparing to hit the job market as a factor influencing their engagement in networked learning. According to the participants, their identities as job-seeking pre-service teachers made them cautious about what they shared online. Even when they could acknowledge, as Kyle did, that reading about other teachers' successes and failures through their blogs acted as a form of personal motivation for them, they did not extend that motivation to posting their own successes or failures. Tiffany elaborated on her hesitance: "I think it's just because I'm—we're all looking for jobs and I just don't want to inadvertently put something out there that's negative. I'm very much aware of the public profile I'm putting out on the Web, so I don't think that I [would use it] for personal support issues." Participants perceived concerns about how others (i.e., future employers and colleagues) might view them based on the content they posted online as inhibiting their networked learning experiences.

On paper, networked learning seems to have great potential for fostering "a sense of belonging to a professional community and a desire for professional growth" (NCTE, 2006, p. 11) as pre-service teachers work side-by-side in digital environments with professionals from across the globe and experience the rewarding feeling that comes with getting your professional learning "at the point of need" (Swenson, 2003, p. 263). However, as the experiences described by these participants suggest, this potential may be quickly derailed if lacking that sense of belonging prevents pre-service teachers from fully engaging in networked learning in the first place.

A Shortage of Time

Undoubtedly, when serving an internship as a pre-service secondary English teacher, time is difficult to come by. Consider the many ways in which teacher interns must divide their time during any given week: Time must be split between attending a full load of classes in the evening at the local university; reading and writing to complete the accompanying coursework; conferring with an internship supervisor; conferring with a cooperating teacher; locating, designing, and organizing resources for classroom use; developing lesson plans; reading, evaluating, and responding to student work; contacting parents; and, yes, also actually teaching five days a week. That is to say nothing about the time teacher interns may spend trying to find their footing as novice teachers and reflecting upon their practice. Despite these many responsibilities, some teacher interns also make time to engage in networked learning to support their growth during the course of the internship, and a perceived lack of time was recognized as a prominent domain within the data analyzed. We found that participants frequently and consistently referred to limited available time when describing their experiences with and perceptions of networked learning. This domain captures participants' perceptions related to the importance of accounting for time when engaging in networked learning during the completion of a teaching internship.

Each participant detailed spending the limited time he or she did have to devote to networked learning by searching through archived discussion forums within professional social networking sites to locate classroom resources and ideas from other English teachers. Participants' experiences typically mirrored Darla's: "I would say for an assignment that I had a lot of time on I could search for hours and would really get lost in the search just looking up information…in between classes or when I had my off periods or my prep periods and when I had more time to look things up, that's when I used those resources the most." We found that descriptions of such immersion within the incredible amount of information shared and housed in professional social networking sites suggest a need for understanding how to most effectively navigate such sites in order to locate the content one seeks. Tara notes as much in describing her own experience losing valuable time while searching asynchronous discussion forums within professional social networking sites: "These technologies could be really helpful but you really have to know what it is you're looking for and where to look…I mean, I definitely wasted many hours just searching. And searching. At some point the search has to stop." Elaborating further, Tara described her typical experience seeking resources while engaged in networked learning:

I would start going down one path and, you know, I'd read someone's lesson plan and think, 'That's really great.' So I'd start heading off in that direction just to hit a brick wall. So, I think I ended up—I mean those searches and those paths would influence my lessons in the long run, but I spent a lot of time in the process, which I probably—I don't know if it was the best use of my time or not.

In addition to time-consuming searches, participants described posing queries in the discussion forums of professional social networking sites as an effective method of "just in time" professional learning. However, some participants, like Kyle, described a lack of control over the direction a unit might take, which was commonly guided by the cooperating teacher, as prominently limiting the time he spent engaging in networked learning:

I didn't know what I was teaching very far in advance… if I had more time and if I knew what I was teaching, say I planned out my own curriculum calendar for the entire year, then I would be able to look in advance, say plan two weeks in advance, three weeks in advance, and then have that time to look for activities and the things I needed to do. As far as the internship was concerned, I didn't have the time, I wasn't afforded the time because I didn't know what I was teaching day-to-day.

Darla echoed Kyle's description of having limited time to engage in networked learning due to the reliance on a cooperating teacher to provide the direction a unit might take: "We were dependent on what our teachers wanted and whether it was a day-to-day, three days in advance, or a week-to-week kind of thing, it wasn't us, you know, doing the whole year and knowing in three weeks this is what I want to do so I can start now." Elaborating further, Darla described how such short-notice limited her networked learning experience:

You know, I posted a question [via a group discussion forum within a professional social networking site] and I didn't get any responses until almost the next day… and it's not a long wait—a day—but if you have something that needs to be done that day or early the next morning, waiting sometimes isn't an option. Whereas when I email [my internship supervisor] writes back right away. A teacher [known through personal connections] might write back right away. My [cooperating teacher] wrote back right away.

In describing such experiences, these participants illuminate the importance of allotting adequate time in order for any professional learning endeavor to be effective, a sentiment shared by scholars who study effective professional development (e.g., Garet, Porter, Desimone, Birman, & Yoon, 2001).

IMPLICATIONS AND DISCUSSION

The findings of this study present points regarding the fostering of informal professional development practices and activities over the long-term and practical implications for English teacher education programs that are worthy of discussion.

Fostering a Welcoming Environment

Developing a traditional learning community of teachers who are comfortable engaging in the challenging and substantive conversations that promote teacher learning is both difficult and time-consuming (Borko, 2004; Grossman, Wineburg, & Woolworth, 2001; Stein, Smith, & Silver, 1999). Findings indicate that the individuals participating in this study perceived similar challenges as they worked independently to extend their personal learning networks. Whereas online discussion forums with limited access have proven to be safe ground for novice teachers in a cohort or class to connect with one another and seek support during trying times (Paulus & Scherff, 2008; Scherff & Paulus, 2006; Singer & Zeni, 2004), the findings of this study indicate that online spaces open to the public, such as the discussion forums of professional social networking sites, open Twitter accounts, and comment forums for individual blogs, did not prove to be inviting spaces in the eyes of participating pre-service teachers. This is problematic, particularly when attempting to foster informal professional learning practices and activity for the long-term.

Whether student or teacher, sharing one's practice with the world and turning to another to express inquiry are potentially vulnerable tasks that are not easily done (Buehler, 2005; Dillon, 1981). However, as Lieberman and Mace (2010) suggest, "When teachers go public with their work, they open themselves up to learning, not only from their own practice, but also from research and others who help expand their knowledge" (p. 86). While professional conversations that foster critical analysis of teaching practices may take place between and among teachers via social media, for this study's participants, they are unlikely to occur without establishing trust and developing a sense of worth to others online. In order for these pre-service English teachers to reap the potential benefits of making their work public in online spaces for the world to see, teacher educators and practicing teachers experienced in professional learning online must foster a safe, inviting environment, an environment that values the unique experiences and ideas pre-service and early-career teachers have gained during their

brief yet valid stints teaching English. Given the reported scarcity of professional conversations that foster the critical analysis of teaching practices (Borko, 2004; McLaughlin & Talbert, 2001; Putnam & Borko, 1997), working to foster such environments is surely a worthwhile endeavor.

Expanding Learning Networks

The findings of this study highlight participants' reluctance to engage practitioners outside of their particular contexts or pre-existing learning networks, as participants opted instead to turn to those with whom they were already familiar. In the realm of social networking, such moves seem commonplace. Ellison, Steinfield, and Lampe (2007) note that, for college students, social networking typically entails communicating online with others they are already familiar with from interactions in face-to-face settings. However, if pre-service English teachers are to make the most of networked learning, both while preparing for and living the life of an in-service English teacher, teacher educators must consider the ways they might nudge their students into expanding their networks and looking beyond the local to invite and entertain diverse perspectives on teaching and learning.

What might such nudging look like? How might English teacher educators promote an expansion of online networks and active engagement in informal professional learning? Providing opportunities to connect face-to-face might be a start. Teacher educators could, for example, capitalize on the networking opportunities that often arise at their respective state and local conferences. English teacher preparation programs have been known to require students to attend professional conferences such as local NCTE affiliate conferences (Smagorinsky & Whiting, 1995), where pre-service teachers can meet and connect with practicing English teachers and expand their learning networks. Moreover, face-to-face conferences increasingly feature "tweet-ups," where contributors to online networks have the opportunity to meet in-person, providing additional opportunities for those looking to expand their networks to find willing and available parties. Beyond promoting conference attendance, establishing partnerships among universities may be another way to help pre-service teachers diversify and expand their networks. English teacher educators from universities in different regions of the country might, for example, use hash tags to organize synchronous chats, invite students to connect with one another, and engage in the exchange of lesson plans or other materials via their networked connections. In this way, teacher educators may promote diversity in the expansion of networks and begin to negotiate the challenge of effectively incorporating networked learning in an English education program.

Negotiating the Demands of English Teacher Preparation

The findings of this study indicate that participants struggled to find a place in their schedules for networked learning among the many responsibilities placed upon them as English teacher interns. This challenge appears to reflect the many demands that are placed on English teachers and, accordingly, English teacher educators. While the features and provisions of English education programs may vary (Smagorinsky & Whiting, 1995), the demands are universally high and wide-ranging, as teacher educators are charged with supporting pre-service teachers as they work to develop pedagogical content knowledge (Shulman, 1987) and, as appropriate, technological pedagogical content knowledge (Mishra & Koehler, 2006) related to language, literature, media literacy, reading, writing, speaking, and listening (NCTE, 2006).

Despite the great demands already placed on English educators, consideration must be given to how and where networked learning fits into an English teacher preparation program if the potential for networked learning to promote career-long

professional growth is valued by English teacher educators. Given the findings of this study, synthesizing opportunities for networked learning into the threadwork of a program seems ideal. After providing a brief introduction to networked learning, the supporting technologies, and the ways practicing teachers employ them to supplement their learning and their practice, teacher educators could prompt students to draw upon their networks throughout the program. For example, students might be tasked to crowdsource perspectives on issues raised in the course readings as they prepare for class discussion, to follow-up class discussions by reporting their own perspectives to their networks, or to make their practice public by sharing lesson plans, mini-lessons, or syllabi with their networks and soliciting feedback from seasoned professionals. In this way, English teacher educators may enrich their students' learning and prepare them to direct their own career-long development in the future without sacrificing time that might be devoted to the countless pedagogical issues of importance. Through extensive experience, pre-service teachers may find a reduction in the burden that often accompanies turning to another for support. Likewise, in an ideal situation, by the time pre-service teachers reach the internship—often one of the final requirements of a teacher education program—they may find that networked learning is an integral part of their work, not something they try to fit into their schedules as time allows.

LIMITATIONS

This study is not without its limitations. With a duration of 10 weeks, the brief nature of the teaching internship limits this study to capturing only a short glimpse into the experiences the participating pre-service teachers have engaging in networked learning. Additionally, participant availability dictated the use of focus groups rather than individual interviews. Given our constructivist theoretical perspective and intention to explore the individual perceptions and experiences of our participants, individual interviews would have been a preferred method of data collection. However, given participants' limited availability and Morgan's (2002) contention that focus group interviews have the potential to generate data that share a similar degree of depth and detail as data generated through individual interviews, we proceeded with a focus group. It should also be noted that the qualitative nature of this study does not afford generalizing the findings beyond the unique participants involved in this study. Rather, readers must rely upon the provision of our description in order to draw their own conclusions regarding the applicability of the findings to their unique contexts.

FUTURE RESEARCH DIRECTIONS

The findings of this study also point us in the direction of future research and the methods that may support it. With an understanding of how these unique participants perceived their experiences engaging in networked learning, we can take a closer look at the specific issues uncovered. For example, exploring the role that status plays in networked learning experiences (e.g., identifying as a pre-service teacher within a community of practicing teachers) through a critical discourse analysis may shed light on the challenges pre-service teachers face and the ways they are welcomed into the Discourse or denied entrance. Moreover, a closer look at the stories and specific experiences of pre-service teachers who actively engage in networked learning—say, through a narrative analysis approach—may provide insight into how pre-service teachers experience networked learning, balance professional learning among their many other responsibilities, and apply what they learn by connecting with professionals online. Additionally, while the findings of this study indicate that participants perceive

networked learning as a valuable enterprise, future research may take a closer look at how individuals interact and converse while engaged in online professional activities via the various digital mediums that foster networked learning, such as microblogs and discussion forums within professional social networking sites. Through conversation analysis, for example, researchers may help us better understand the rules for social behavior when interacting via particular social media technologies.

Future research regarding pre-service teachers' engagement in networked learning may also look beyond professional sites for learning, a key element of this study. In much the same way that teachers who use technology in their personal lives are not necessarily using it in their classrooms (National Council of Teachers of English, 2007), the findings of this study seem to suggest that—at least for these participants—using social media in their personal lives, particularly mainstream social networking sites, does not ensure carry over to their professional lives. While participants expressed hesitance to engage others in professional online forums, this study did not consider the role and use of more personal, mainstream social networking sites, such as Facebook, for example. Teacher educators may benefit from future research that explores the ways pre-service teachers use more personal, mainstream social networking sites for connecting with others and for sharing and exchanging ideas and resources that inform their developing practice.

CONCLUSION

Networked learning, in which learners utilize interactive online technologies that foster the sharing of professional resources and the exchange of ideas while facilitating cooperation and collaboration, has great potential for supporting the continued professional growth of teachers, both in-service and pre-service. While the social media tools that make networked learning possible provide the pipeline that connects individuals with one another and allows for the quick and efficient sharing of ideas, inquiries, and classroom resources, it is not the technologies themselves that matter most. Rather, the connections made with one another serve as the linchpin of networked learning. If those connections are perceived to be absent, learning will suffer, as evident in this study when participants felt that they lacked the expertise to be part of the conversation or that their experiences were too different from those in their networks. While the technologies will undoubtedly change, the power of turning to another and the human connection that often results will sustain the continued growth of professional networks and communities and, ultimately, the growth of all learners.

REFERENCES

Borko, H. (2004). Professional development and teacher learning: Mapping the terrain. *Educational Researcher*, *33*(8), 3–15. doi:10.3102/0013189X033008003

Boss, S. (2008). Twittering, not frittering: Professional development in 140 characters. *Edutopia*. Retrieved from http://www.edutopia.org/twitter-professional-development-technology-microblogging.

Buehler, J. (2005). The power of questions and the possibilities of inquiry in English education. *English Education*, *37*(4), 280–287.

Cercone, J. (2009). We're smarter together: Building professional social networks in English education. *English Education*, *41*(3), 199–206.

Couros, A. (2008, February 25). *What does the network mean to you?* Retrieved from http://educationaltechnology.ca/couros/799.

Crotty, M. (1998). *Foundations of social research: Meaning and perspective in the research process.* Thousand Oaks, CA: Sage.

Demski, J. (2010). Tweets for teachers. *Technological Horizons in Education Journal*, *37*(2), 16–18.

Denzin, N. (1970). *The research act in sociology.* London, UK: Butterworth.

Denzin, N. (1989). *Interpretive biography.* Thousand Oaks, CA: Sage.

Dillon, J. T. (1981). A norm against student questions. *Clearing House (Menasha, Wis.)*, *55*(3), 136–139.

Ellison, N. B., Steinfield, C., & Lampe, C. (2007). The benefits of Facebook "friends": Social capital and college students' use of online social networking sites. *Journal of Computer-Mediated Communication*, *12*(4). Retrieved from http://jcmc.indiana.edu/vol12/issue4/ellison.html doi:10.1111/j.1083-6101.2007.00367.x

Garet, M. S., Porter, A. C., Desimone, L., Birman, B. F., & Yoon, K. S. (2001). What makes professional development effective? Results from a national sample of teachers. *American Educational Research Journal*, *38*(4), 915–945. doi:10.3102/00028312038004915

Geertz, C. (1973). Thick description: Towards an interpretive theory of culture. In Lincoln, Y., & Denzin, N. (Eds.), *Turning Points in Qualitative Research: Tying Knots in a Handkerchief* (pp. 143–168). Walnut Creek, CA: Altamira Press.

Grabill, J. T., & Hicks, T. (2005). Multiliteracies meet methods: The case for digital writing in English education. *English Education*, *37*(4), 301–311.

Grbich, C. (2007). *Qualitative data analysis: An introduction.* Thousand Oaks, CA: Sage.

Grossman, P., Wineburg, S., & Woolworth, S. (2001). Toward a theory of community. *Teachers College Record, 103*(6), 942–1012. doi:10.1111/0161-4681.00140

Hicks, T. (2009). *The digital writing workshop.* Portsmouth, NH: Heinemann.

Jakes, D. (2007). Professional development and web 2.0. *Technology and Learning, 27*(9), 20.

Kajder, S. (2003). *The tech-savvy English classroom.* Portland, ME: Stenhouse.

Koro-Ljungberg, M., Yendol-Hoppey, D., Smith, J. J., & Hayes, S. B. (2009). Epistemological awareness, instantiation of methods, and uninformed methodological ambiguity in qualitative research projects. *Educational Researcher, 38*(9), 687–699. doi:10.3102/0013189X09351980

Lieberman, A., & Mace, D. P. (2010). Making practice public: Teacher learning in the 21st century. *Journal of Teacher Education, 61*(1-2), 77–88. doi:10.1177/0022487109347319

Lincoln, Y. S., & Guba, E. G. (1985). *Naturalistic inquiry.* Beverly Hills, CA: Sage.

Lortie, D. (1975). *Schoolteacher: A sociological study.* Chicago, IL: University of Chicago Press.

McCann, T. M., Johannessen, L. R., & Ricca, B. P. (2005). *Supporting beginning English teachers: Research and implications for teacher induction.* Urbana, IL: National Council of Teachers of English.

McLaughlin, M., & Talbert, J. (2001). *Professional communities and the work of high school teaching.* Chicago, IL: University of Chicago Press.

Mishra, P., & Koehler, M. J. (2006). Technological pedagogical content knowledge: A framework for teacher knowledge. *Teachers College Record, 108*(6), 1017–1054. doi:10.1111/j.1467-9620.2006.00684.x

Morgan, D. L. (2002). Focus group interviewing. In Gubrium, J., & Holstein, J. (Eds.), *Handbook of Interview Research: Context & Method* (pp. 141–159). Thousand Oaks, CA: Sage.

National Council of Teachers of English. (2006). *Guidelines for the preparation of teachers of English language arts.* Urbana, IL: NCTE. Retrieved from http://www1.ncte.org/library/files/Store/Books/Sample/Guidelines2006Chap1-6.pdf.

National Council of Teachers of English. (2007). *21st century literacies: A policy research brief.* Urbana, IL: NCTE. Retrieved from http://www.ncte.org/library/NCTEFiles/Resources/PolicyResearch/21stCenturyResearchBrief.pdf.

Patton, M. (2002). *Qualitative evaluation and research methods* (3rd ed.). Newbury Park, CA: Sage Publications.

Paulus, T., & Scherff, L. (2008). Can anyone offer any words of encouragement? Online dialogue as a support mechanism for preservice teachers. *Journal of Technology and Teacher Education, 16*(1), 113–136.

Pope, C., & Golub, J. (2000). Preparing tomorrow's English language arts teachers today: Principles and practices for infusing technology. *Contemporary Issues in Technology & Teacher Education, 1*(1), 89–97. Retrieved from http://www.citejournal.org/vol1/iss1/currentissues/english/article1.htm

Putnam, R. T., & Borko, H. (1997). Teacher learning: Implications of new views of cognition. In Biddle, B. J., Good, T. L., & Goodson, I. F. (Eds.), *The International Handbook of Teachers and Teaching* (pp. 1223–1296). Dordrecht, The Netherlands: Kluwer.

Riel, M., & Fulton, K. (2001). The role of technology in supporting learning communities. *Phi Delta Kappan, 82*(7), 518–523.

Ritchie, J., & Lewis, J. (Eds.). (2003). *Qualitative research practice: A guide for social science students and researchers*. Thousand Oaks, CA: Sage.

Rozema, R., & Webb, A. (2008). *Literature and the web: Reading and responding with new technologies*. Portsmouth, NH: Heinemann.

Scherff, L., & Paulus, T. (2006). Encouraging ownership of online spaces: Support for preservice English teachers through computer-mediated communication. *Contemporary Issues in Technology & Teacher Education, 6*(4), 354–373. Retrieved from http://www.citejournal.org/vol6/iss4/languagearts/article1.cfm

Shulman, L. S. (1987). Knowledge and teaching: Foundations of the new reform. *Harvard Educational Review, 57*(1), 1–22.

Singer, N. R., & Zeni, J. (2004). Building bridges: Creating an online conversation community for preservice teachers. *English Education, 37*(1), 30–49.

Smagorinsky, P., & Whiting, M. E. (1995). *How English teachers get taught*. Urbana, IL: National Council of Teachers of English.

Spradley, J. P. (1980). *Participant observation*. New York, NY: Holt, Rinehart and Winston.

Steeples, C., & Jones, C. (2002). Perspectives and issues in networked learning. In Steeples, C., & Jones, C. (Eds.), *Networked Learning: Perspectives and Issues* (pp. 1–14). New York, NY: Springer.

Stein, M. K., Smith, M. S., & Silver, E. A. (1999). The development of professional developers: Learning to assist teachers in new settings in new ways. *Harvard Educational Review, 69*(3), 237–269.

Swenson, J. (2003). Transformative teacher networks, on-line professional development, and the write for your life project. *English Education, 35*(4), 262–321.

Swenson, J., Rozema, R., Young, C. A., McGrail, E., & Whitin, P. (2005). Beliefs about technology and the preparation of English teachers: Beginning the conversation. *Contemporary Issues in Technology & Teacher Education, 5*(3/4), 210–236. Retrieved from http://www.citejournal.org/vol5/iss3/languagearts/article1.cfm

Trinkle, C. (2009). Twitter as a professional learning community. *School Library Monthly, 26*(4), 22–23.

Warlick, D. (2009). Grow your own personal learning network: New technologies can keep you connected and help you manage information overload. *Learning and Leading with Technology, 36*(6), 12–16.

Young, C. A., & Bush, J. (2004). Teaching the English language arts with technology: A critical approach and pedagogical framework. *Contemporary Issues in Technology & Teacher Education, 4*(1), 1–22. Retrieved from http://www.citejournal.org/vol4/iss1/languagearts/article1.cfm

ADDITIONAL READING

Beauchamp, C., & Thomas, L. (2009). Understanding teacher identity: An overview of issues in the literature and implications for teacher education. *Cambridge Journal of Education, 39*(2), 175–189. doi:10.1080/03057640902902252

Boekaerts, M. (1997). Self-regulated learning: A new concept embraced by researchers, policy makers, educators, teachers, and students. *Learning and Instruction, 7*(2), 161–186. doi:10.1016/S0959-4752(96)00015-1

DeWert, M. H., Babinski, L. M., & Jones, B. D. (2003). Safe passages: Providing online support to beginning teachers. *Journal of Teacher Education, 54*(4), 311–320. doi:10.1177/0022487103255008

Duncan-Howell, J. (2010). Teachers making connections: Online communities as a source of professional learning. *British Journal of Educational Technology, 41*(2), 324–340. doi:10.1111/j.1467-8535.2009.00953.x

Educause Learning Initiative. (2007a). *7 things you should know about... blogs*. Retrieved from http://net.educause.edu/ir/library/pdf/ELI7006.pdf.

Educause Learning Initiative. (2007b). *7 things you should know about... RSS*. Retrieved from http://net.educause.edu/ir/library/pdf/ELI7024.pdf.

Educause Learning Initiative. (2007c). *7 things you should know about... Twitter*. Retrieved from http://net.educause.edu/ir/library/pdf/ELI7027.pdf.

Educause Learning Initiative. (2008). *7 things you should know about... Ning*. Retrieved from http://net.educause.edu/ir/library/pdf/ELI7036.pdf.

Ellison, N. B., Lampe, C., & Steinfield, C. (2009). Social network sites and society: Current trends and future possibilities. *Interaction, 16*(1), 6–9. doi:10.1145/1456202.1456204

Faulkner, G. (2009). English teachers find an online friend: The English companion Ning. *National Writing Project*. Retrieved from http://www.nwp.org/cs/public/print/resource/2848.

Ferguson, H. (2010). Join the flock! *Learning and Leading with Technology, 37*(8), 12–15.

Ferriter, W. M. (2010). Why teachers should try Twitter. *Educational Leadership, 67*(5), 73–74.

Fletcher, J. D., Tobias, S., & Wisher, R. (2007). Learning anytime, anywhere: Advanced distributed learning and the changing face of education. *Educational Researcher, 36*(2), 96–102. doi:10.3102/0013189X07300034

Galland, P. (2002). Techie teachers — Web-based staff development at your leisure. *TechTrends, 46*(3), 11–16.

Huber, C. (2010). Professional learning 2.0. *Educational Leadership, 61*(8), 41–46.

Kist, W. (2010). *The socially networked classroom: Teaching in the new media age*. Thousand Oaks, CA: Corwin.

Laferrière, T., Lamon, M., & Chan, C. K. K. (2006). Emerging e-trends and models in teacher education and professional development. *Teaching Education, 17*(1), 75–90. doi:10.1080/10476210500528087

Luehmann, A. L. (2008). Using blogging in support of teacher professional identity development: A case study. *Journal of the Learning Sciences, 17*(3), 287–337. doi:10.1080/10508400802192706

Luna, C., Botelho, M., & Fontaine, D. (2004). Making the road by walking and talking: Critical literacy and/as professional development in a teacher inquiry group. *Teacher Education Quarterly, 31*(1), 67–80.

Rich, E. (2009). The world's largest English department. *Teacher Magazine, 3*(1), 26-29. Retrieved from http://www.teachermagazine.org/tsb/articles/2009/10/01/01ning.h03.html.

Richardson, W., & Mancabelli, R. (2011). *Personal learning networks: Using the power of connections to transform education*. Bloomington, IN: Solution Tree.

Seglem, R. (2009). Creating a circle of learning: Teachers taking ownership through professional communities. *Voices from the Middle, 16*(4), 32–37.

Shanklin, N. (2009). Being proactive about your professional learning: Where's the payoff? *Voices from the Middle, 16*(4), 45–47.

Webster-Wright, A. (2009). Reframing professional development through understanding authentic professional learning. *Review of Educational Research, 79*(2), 702–739. doi:10.3102/0034654308330970

Wenger, E. (1998). *Communities of practice: Learning, meaning, and identity.* Cambridge, UK: Cambridge University Press.

KEY TERMS AND DEFINITIONS

Blog: An online collection of commentaries, reflections, and resources that typically revolve around a particular topic. Organized chronologically, blogs are commonly embedded with graphics or video, and they typically offer interactive comment features, which openly invite readers to join the conversation. Blogging circles are often recognized for their sense of community, a byproduct of meaningful interaction between bloggers and their readers.

Hashtag: The combination of a hash symbol or pound sign preceding a tag (e.g., #ncte) in a tweet in order to mark keywords or topics, allowing Twitter users to categorize messages.

Microblog: An online collection of brief comments, observations, and reflections that are organized chronologically yet distinguished from blogs by the limited number of characters available for each post. As is the case with blogs, a sense of community among microbloggers may form as users follow each other's posts and routinely respond to one another. Links to images, videos, documents, and websites are often shared within individual posts.

Pre-Service Teacher: A student enrolled in a teacher education program preparing him or her to work as a teacher in K-12 classrooms.

Professional Social Networking Site: A site in which users are connected through a shared interest in and passion for a particular profession. Professional social networking sites differ from mainstream social networking sites such as Facebook in that they are primarily driven by professional purposes. Through the site's features, users can share images, videos, and other files, contribute to discussion forums, and form groups within the greater online community. English Companion Ning and Making Curriculum Pop are examples of professional social networking sites of which many English language arts teachers are members.

Really Simple Syndication (RSS): A Web feed protocol used to publish works that are updated routinely, such as blogs or news websites. An RSS aggregator, such as Google Reader, is used to check subscribed feeds regularly for new work and download it to one location for ease of access and reading. This allows users to avoid checking multiple websites in order to stay up-to-date on new publications.

Chapter 12

Online Mentoring as a Tool for Professional Development and Change of Novice and Experienced Teachers:
A Brazilian Experience

Aline Maria de Medeiros Rodrigues Reali
Federal University of São Carlos, Brazil

Regina Maria Simões Puccinelli Tancredi
Presbyterian University Mackenzie, Brazil & Federal University of São Carlos, Brazil

Maria da Graça Nicoletti Mizukami
Presbyterian University Mackenzie, Brazil & Federal University of São Carlos, Brazil

ABSTRACT

This chapter examines the results of an investigation carried out by the researchers from a Brazilian public institution and experienced teachers (mentors) that aimed to produce knowledge on teacher professional development and learning, investigate educational processes of mentors interacting with novice teachers by e-mail, evaluate the continued education methodology adopted, and contribute to existing knowledge on online continued teacher education. The main sources of data were email communications between mentors and novice teachers, the mentors' and novice teachers' reflective journals, and the researchers' observations from weekly meetings between the mentors and the teachers. The development of the online Mentorship Program has been a much more complex enterprise than a face-to-face equivalent program would have been because it demands entirely new logistics, but it promoted the establishment of professional and affective bonds among the participants, the broadening of professional knowledge, the mastery of online adult education technologies, and the participants' professional growth.

DOI: 10.4018/978-1-4666-1815-2.ch012

INTRODUCTION

Despite much investment in basic education in the past years, it is clear that the quality of education imparted to Brazilian children, even in developed urban centers, has been rather dismal. According to Libâneo (2011), there have been contradictions between the number of students who are having access to school and the quality of education received, as well as "among pedagogical and socio-cultural aspects, and between a vision of schools based on knowledge and other in their social missions." It is evident the "duality of aggravation of the current Brazilian public schools, characterized as a school of knowledge for the rich and the school of social care for the poor. Such dualism... is perverse because it reproduces social inequalities and maintains social inequalities" (p. 3).

In spite of the fact that there is no consensus with respect to how and how much teacher education influences student performance, this work presupposes that there is a strong relation between professional education and proficiency. In Brazil, most of the teacher education programs usually are conceived according to a technical rationality paradigm, and we do not have public policies directed to novice teachers. We observe a lack of integration between theoretical and practical-pedagogic content courses, which compromises the connection between theory and practice.

Bearing in mind that learning to teach and being a teacher are ongoing and lifelong processes, it is important to remark that teaching proficiency is not just derived from pre-service education. On the contrary, proficient teaching is associated with the capacity to understand the other, students, curricular content, pedagogy, curriculum development, and strategies and techniques related to facilitating students' learning (Mizukami, et al., 2010; Mizukami, Reali, & Tancredi, 2010).

Being a teacher does not encompass characteristics inherent to teaching alone; it goes beyond them. It involves participating in the school, the locus of the professional community par excellence (Knowles, Cole, & Presswood, 2008; Pérez Gomes, 2010; Mizukami, Reali, & Tancredi, 2010). Hence, taking into consideration the characteristics of teaching and being a teacher as well as those of today's world, it is vital that teachers be supported in order to be able to evolve professionally during their careers.

Notwithstanding, continuing education programs have traditionally treated teacher education—even when held at the workplace—as an undifferentiated process, thus failing to place proper emphasis on the peculiarities of different career phases. These phases display unique characteristics and problems; future, novice, and experienced teachers show distinct professional competencies and different educational necessities.

To Garcia (2011) it is necessary to pay attention to a critical period in teachers' professional development: the first years of teaching. This is a phase in which professionals seem to become myopic since they primarily focus on their teaching competencies and the management of immediate classroom demands (Grossman, Hammerness, & MacDonald, 2009). Their thoughts temporarily concentrate on the most pressing practical aspects, and they struggle to develop a repertoire of professional behaviors related to teaching and being a teacher, to their specific teaching contents and adequate representations about the way their students learn.

Brazilian literature on the initial phases of the teaching career and on mentorship programs is rather limited, and it seems that public policies (regarding any educational systems or teaching levels) that take into consideration these aspects are also lacking. Moreover, there are no studies on expert teachers teaching novice teachers how to teach.

Brazilian professional teaching contexts seldom allocate resources to mitigate the difficulties inherent to this or subsequent career phases because, traditionally, schools in this country are not loci for systematized professional development or induction of novice teachers. Although novice teachers have been the object of many studies, there have been few investigations on how their particular difficulties could be identified, faced, and overcome by means of support programs involving more experienced professionals through mentoring programs.

This chapter concerns an investigation of teachers' educational specificities at different career phases by means of an online mentoring program designed to help novice teachers to explain, understand, face, and overcome their everyday professional difficulties. It aimed to contribute to their professional development processes.

Experienced teachers (mentors) offer this online support to novices asynchronously. Researchers of a public university and experienced teachers (mentors) conducted this investigation. It aimed to produce knowledge on teacher professional development and learning, investigate educational processes of mentors interacting with novice teachers by e-mail, evaluate the continued education methodology adopted, and contribute to existing knowledge on online continued teacher education.

MENTORSHIP AS A TOOL FOR PROFESSIONAL DEVELOPMENT AND CHANGE

To Gatti, Barreto, and André (2011), in spite of the spaces where teaching and learning processes take place, good teachers—those concerned about teaching and their students' learning, committed to their professional development, and capable of providing their students with proper frameworks—will always be in great demand. In addition, today's teachers are not only required to merely transmit knowledge so that their students may perform well at exams, but also to teach them to solve problems and integrate knowledge and understanding into new different situations.

According to Marcelo, Garcia, and Vaillant (2009), it is necessary that teachers learn from their students, by studying, doing, and reflecting in collaboration with colleagues, and by carefully observing their students and their work and sharing what they learn. It is also necessary that teachers as well as students actively construct their modes of knowing.

In view of these demands, it is important to reexamine the role of teacher education programs and its aspects that concern teachers' professional development and learning. It seems that such programs can only offer a weak antidote to the overwhelming, and often defective, socialization process that teachers experience as students. Many times these experiences differ desirable and adequate to today's school scenarios. Thus, it is essential that teacher education should help these professionals to transcend what they experienced as elementary and secondary students as well as in teacher education.

Every year a great number of novice teachers enter the job market, experiencing a period often referred to as induction or professional initiation. During this period, the teachers face the complex school reality as well as contradictions that they will not always be able to overcome. Their professional knowledge is put to the test. Their attitudes may be range from an adaptation and reproduction—often with little criticism—of the school context and practice, to an innovative and autonomous approach, aware of the possibilities, challenges, and professional knowledge that support the classroom. Talking about the length of professional initiation is to consider an approximation of personal and professional factors as well as structural and organizational aspects, which the teachers face (Papi & Martins, 2010).

The first years of teaching constitute a period of conflict and intensive learning in unknown contexts, when teachers stop being students to become professionals with specific competencies and knowledge. Novice teachers face a multiplicity of challenges and demands, which influence the development of their practices and their convictions about their role. As professionals, they must display skills, competencies, and knowledge, which have not yet been fully developed. During the first years, they have to perform numerous tasks, such as socializing in the school system, building up the teacher role, and constructing their professional identity, which involve bi-directional processes. Moreover, novice teachers' works receive influence of multiple variables. These variables are related to their personal and schooling histories, classes taught (students, contents, teacher-student relationships, etc.), schools (peers, administration, curriculum, etc.), and broader social context (educational policies, economic and social environment, etc.). In order to survive in this complex setting, they often conceive routes that are not necessarily conducive to good teaching and/or permanence in the career.

In Brazil, there is evidence that the first years of teaching constitute a particularly complex period, because novice teachers usually receive the most difficult classes in the most troublesome schools. Notwithstanding these complications, novices are hardly ever provided with institutional support. When this support is ever given, it is more likely to come from caring colleagues. Though there are some in-service teacher education programs, they are of short duration. We still do not have educational polices towards effective teaching induction, and little attention has been given, in terms of professional development, to the specific needs of each stage of the career.

The deficiencies found in different Brazilian basic and continued teacher education initiatives reinforce the need for support to teachers, especially novices. The importance of this support becomes more apparent when one considers that teachers act in a complex, uncertain and changing world, whose problems cannot be solved by mere application of available theoretical-technical knowledge. Taking effective action demands constant decision-making and construction of solutions, which, in turn, involve prioritizing, organizing and evaluating often-contradictory issues, and proposing reasonable actions.

We assume that teacher education and online education can promote changes in elementary education, and consequently help to alter the present picture of student underachievement in Brazil. We assume also that teacher education should encourage teachers, individually and collectively, to reflect upon their conceptions, beliefs, ideas and practices, and be responsible for their own professional development in environments that promote self-directed learning and sharing of knowledge. Continued teacher education programs should provide teachers with time, space and support from experienced professionals—those who have already gone through the initial phases of teaching, and have overcome obstacles towards proficiency (Mizukami, Reali, & Tancredi, 2010; Reali, Tancredi, & Mizukami, 2008).

Ingerson and Strong (2011), analyzing several initiatives to support novice teachers, such as mentorship or induction programs, show positive impact of such initiatives on three sets of outcomes: teacher commitment and retention, teacher instructional practices and student achievement. Although mentoring may apply to all phases of the teaching career, it is possible to define a mentorship or induction program as a set of formative activities following pre-service education that aim at assisting teachers throughout their first professional years (induction period). According to Marcelo Garcia (2011), a mentorship program contains three components: a teaching and formative concept; a set of knowledge deemed as important to novice teachers; and a concept of teacher learning and how it may be accomplished. Additional components may be: classroom situations and dilemmas likely to be encountered by novice teachers; tasks and goals of mentorship; professional profile; mentors' role; and professional education as well as limitations.

Selecting mentors is central to the successful development and implementation of mentorship programs. Mentors should be expert teachers, experienced in daily classroom situations and school matters; those who are capable of helping novices to learn the school philosophy and cultural values as well as of demonstrating a repertoire of professional behaviors expected by the school community. They can counsel and orientate novice teachers, provide general information, look for/ suggest teaching materials, supervise practices, propose solutions to problems, and share experiences by establishing and maintaining significant interactions. However, despite the fact that good mentorship programs depend heavily on their mentors' qualifications, there is scarce literature on how to prepare them.

Although experienced, mentors also need to be prepared to exercise its tasks of mentoring. Such preparation implies to consider specificities related to the nature of their mediation work with the novice teachers, as teacher educators. It is necessary that the mentors learn to teach other teachers how to teach.

We believe that both experienced teachers, especially mentors, and novice teachers should be motivated to examine their beliefs about teaching and learning to teach, to construct teaching practices consistent with research findings, and in the case of mentors, to develop the disposition to learn how to teach. We assume that mentoring goes beyond helping novices to learn how to teach. It constitutes also an excellent opportunity for mentors to grow professionally.

Considering the professional learning potential of teacher mentoring programs, the shortcomings in initial teacher education and in the first professional teacher experiences and the fact that there are no educational policies in Brazil towards effective teaching induction, we assume that teacher education and online education can promote help to novice teachers.

THE ONLINE MENTORSHIP PROGRAM OF THE "PORTAL DOS PROFESSORES" (UFSCAR)

Distance education may be a valid response to the increasing demand for quality continued professional education. It has the advantage of being capable of reaching many more students than face-to-face instruction can. By means of distance education, it is possible to broaden the knowledge spectrum, and reach people who may not be able to attend school.

The Internet allows fast access to available information in a global world, and facilitates individualized learning, learning at the learners' pace/available time and meeting their knowledge needs. Despite the fact that information is not equivalent to knowledge, acquiring information does not make anyone knowledgeable; the Internet can promote learning because previous acquisition of information is a *sine qua non* in knowledge construction. Users are not mere consumers of information. They are eminently social beings; they participate in collectivities and affirm their political, cultural, and professional ideas. Distance education expands opportunities for individuals and social groups 'confined' by the space or the social agenda, that is, by its rhythms of life and work" (Moraes, 2010).

The Mentoring Program of the Portal dos Professores (www.portaldosprofessores.ufscar.br) from Federal University of São Carlos, Brazil, may be characterized as an online distance program that implies frequent communication between mentors and novice teachers on its own platform. Its goal was to assist novice K-4 teachers.

In this study, a mentor is a more experienced professional who guides and assists a novice teacher in solving practical problems, mitigating dilemmas and doubts related to teaching. Although experienced in relation to elementary education, the mentors had little experience as teacher educators. They participated of the elaboration of the mentorship program foundations, defining with the researchers its curriculum and characteristics.

The mentors were teachers with more than 15 years of teaching experience. Despite their different majors and professional backgrounds, these 10 teachers had two characteristics in common: they had firmly invested in their professional development throughout their careers, and generally evaluated as good professionals by their peers.

The development of a mentorship program implied the adoption of a methodology that promotes the mentors' decision-making processes and subsequent actions. This methodology should also provide the means for the apprehension, interpretation, and description of difficulties indicated by the novice teachers and their professional development processes when constructing viable solutions to problems.

Additionally, the methodology promoted the apprehension of educational processes of all participants (novice teachers, mentors, and researchers). To this end, we adopted a constructive-collaborative approach to research because it makes it possible to apprehend knowledge and monitor the process. Such an approach can be broadly described as:

[...] the 'constructivist' camp in which teaching is understood to be a complex and personal phenomenon continually influenced and made meaningful by factors and conditions both inside and outside classrooms and schools. Also implicit is our belief that each teacher's practice is idiosyncratic, an expression of a personal and professional way of knowing that is shaped by events and experiences, both past and present, that take place at home, school, and in the broader societal and political spheres. Personal and professional backgrounds, experiences and perceptions, attitudes, beliefs, and goals underlie and inform the manner in which teachers carry out their lives and work in classroom communities and within the larger communities of schools and society (Cole & Knowles, 1993, pp. 474-475).

As constructive-collaborative research, it can be characterized by the development of intervention strategies that allowed the construction and implementation a professional development process emphasizing: problems of practice; specificities of pedagogical action and organization of teachers' work; specificities of school contexts and classrooms; mutual understanding and consensus, democratic decision-making; collective responsibility in mapping, understanding, and solving problems identified by the participants, and mutual support. By assuming a constructive-collaborative approach, we were at the same time aiming to investigate the professional development process of novice and experienced teachers and to promote said process.

The option for a constructive-collaborative work among researchers, mentors, and novice teachers implied conceiving and adopting procedures/activities that favors partnership and mutual learning processes (Cole & Knowles, 1993). It entails the systematic investigation of the collaborative work to change the social relations existing in the context/community under consideration. In addition, when studying teachers' professional development processes, it is relevant that researchers observe, participate, and discuss teaching, learning, and other educational aspects with the main actors.

The Mentorship Program had three phases. In the *first phase*, the ten experienced teachers, selected by their competence as well as their social recognition by the community have participated in a Mentor Education Program, carried out by the researchers. At weekly meetings, they have developed a set of formative activities, such as elaboration and analysis of cases, reading of theoretical texts, discussions, written reports, and so forth. During this phase, the researchers elaborated educational strategies to foster the mentors' professional development as regards mentoring activities, and the mentors defined what they deemed as necessary to play the role of mentor, the presuppositions, the "curriculum," the possible actions and the duration of the Mentorship Program.

The initial foundations of the Mentorship Program were collaboratively constructed with the mentors-to-be. Consistent with the research-intervention model adopted it was necessary to get to know the future mentors' ideas and what and why they did when teaching, collaboratively reflect upon situations they have experienced during their professional trajectories, and design/construct ways to deal with possible demands that would be posed by novice teachers. As a result, the experienced teachers defined what they deemed as necessary to play the role of mentor, the presuppositions, the "curriculum," the possible actions and the duration of the Mentorship Program.

In the *second phase* mentors participated in training programs considering the use of Internet and the specificities of the Web platform adopted by the Mentorship Program. This platform was developed by professionals from the Federal University of São Carlos, in order to dispense any type of training face-to-face for the novice teachers, considering enormous distances between different cities/states. The environment provided easy access to e-mails, posting multiple documents, return of corrected documents, as well as the entire record of the interaction process. Researchers and mentors could at any time assess the files stored.

The *third phase* constituted the implementation of the Mentorship Program involving mentors and their mentees. When the mentoring activities began, the researchers monitored the mentors' work closely through discussions and studies at weekly meetings and by means written accounts of activities carried out by them and the e-mails between each mentor and their novice teacher partner. In addition to monitoring their work, the researchers met with the mentors on a weekly basis to discuss how the Mentoring Program was evolving, and to assist in their professional development.

Each one of the mentors assisted two or three mentees. The mentors' work was primarily monitored on a person-to-person basis. This phase was depth in two modules. We planned the Program to last 120 hours, spread over one year. This was considered the first module of its development. During the course, some novice teachers requested to continue working with the mentor dealing with additional issues. A second module was conceived for who chose to remain in the Program.

The data sources for this study were: emails exchanged between the mentors and their novice teachers, between the mentors themselves and between the mentors and the researchers; the mentors' and novices' reflective journals; and the transcriptions of weekly meetings between the mentors and researchers.

Fifty-two novices were involved in the mentorship program, out of which thirteen gave up in the beginning of the process. A total of 39 novices completed first module 1, and ten of them concluded second module. It should be remembered that the mentorship program assisted teachers with less than five years of teaching experience, selected according to their answers to a questionnaire about their difficulties and their familiarity with the Internet.

The novices' age ranged between 22 to 52 years; their classroom experience varied from one to five years but some of them had more years of practice in another educational level. These teachers conduct their teaching activities in public schools, in the Social Service for Industry (SESI) and some of them also work in private schools and five in rural schools. Forty-seven (90%) were residents in the state of São Paulo (three in São Carlos and the others in other cities in the region) and five in the state of Santa Catarina.

Since the beginning of the Mentorship Program, the researchers have closely followed the mentors' work, holding weekly meetings to discuss the implementation of the program and carry on the mentors' professional development process. These meetings have been audio-recorded and later transcribed. Some of them were videotaped. After transcription, the meetings underwent an analytical process and some categories were defined. The mentors' work has been monitored by means of journals, in which they report the activities they do with the novice teachers, and studies carried out at the weekly meetings.

The purpose of the researchers' constant meetings with mentors and specialists at the university were to study and analyze the educational process carried out by the mentors and their partner novice teachers, propose solutions to the problems encountered in mentoring, and contribute knowledge and experiences to individual mentor's work. Therefore, the group became stronger and committed to reciprocal learning.

Regarding the data collected by observation, one of the challenges faced by the researchers has been how to systematize conversations so that knowledge and processes involved could be identified and understood, especially the knowledge and processes associated with the construction of teachers' learning communities. In order to meet this challenge, the researchers have relied on Carrol's (2005) model to analyze dialogs and collective construction of ideas, Little's (2002) model to analyze modes of practice and participation throughout time, keeping in mind the dilemmas inherent to the internal analysis of teacher communities, and Grossman, Wineburg and Woolworth's (2001) indicators of professional community building.

With respect to the documents, this work considers the teachers' (novices and mentors) texts as narratives, a type of knowledge that enables the characterization, understanding and representation of human experience. We consider the experiences as lived stories and reflection triggers, whereas narratives are considered to be told stories.

The option for e-mails and reflective journals to identify and comprehend the teachers' personal views was based on the assumption that these artifacts can effectively elicit the knowledge and beliefs that underpin their pedagogical practices. By doing so, we presuppose that teachers know what they say they know. That is to say that we assume that words are the thinking medium par

excellence and can isomorphically represent what exists in people's minds; that people's thoughts, beliefs and feelings are rooted in their words. Therefore, we consider that the novices' and mentors' texts and accounts verily represent their actual experiences.

Consistent with the methodology adopted, data analysis was done simultaneously with the mentors in an on-going fashion: an on-going cycle of reflection on conceived and implemented actions.

Written communication distance education is different from face-to-face communication: the absence of tone/impact markers of words—usually provided by gesture or by visually examining students' work in face-to-face interactions—has raised much anxiety and doubt on the part of the mentors. In order to curb this limitation some mentors have requested that the novices send them their students' written work or have arranged visits with their partner novices. Written communication, on the other hand, has the advantage of being asynchronous; it presents fewer opportunities for the mentors to act on impulse, consequently higher chances of proper construction of messages/answers. Indeed, the mentors have devoted a lot of time to preparing answers to their novice teachers' questions.

The mentors have participated in processes of collective reflection and have put their new understandings into practice: interdependence of group members; testing individual understandings and making the passage from the personal level to the public one.

The mentor-researcher, mentor-mentor, and mentor-novice dyads have systematically produced interactive conversations via weekly meetings and e-mail messages. On these occasions, they often establish relations with the ideas discussed at researchers-mentors meetings or through mentor-mentor and mentor-novice teacher contacts. These relations have also been observed at other times during the mentoring process, when the mentors implicitly or explicitly count on other mentors to agree with their explanations or offer alternative explanations.

The participants were often invited/induced to go beyond the mere description of a particular circumstance, relate it to other examples, and view it from another standpoint—in light of more comprehensive ideas, principles or assumptions.

RESULTS

The most significant difficulties faced by the participating novices elicited in the beginning of the Mentorship Program were: interaction with their colleagues and school administration; specific classroom aspects, such as use of didactic material; teaching at rural schools; and precarious teaching facilities. We identified other difficulties as the program progressed, such as troublesome induction into teaching, especially in reference to choosing grades/school and contacting the school.

In spite of the fact that most Brazilian schools are required to allocate time and space for collective planning and pedagogical learning, many novice teachers express a strong feeling of isolation together with dilemmas about what and how to teach children with different academic repertoires, how to evaluate their performance, and how to relate to colleagues.

One thing has drawn the researchers' attention: the novice teachers' high functional mobility within short periods. For instance, two teachers that used to teach regular classes were relocated to remedial classes, where they were made responsible for almost 120 students with multiple learning deficiencies. This aspect also shows that anxiety, dilemmas, and tensions may not be inherent to the period of induction into teaching alone, they may also happen every time teachers face major changes throughout their careers.

E-mail was the chosen tool of communication between the mentors and their partner novices: almost 30,000 messages were exchanged. A longitudinal investigation of this process indicates the existence of phases relative to the rhythm the e-mail messages were exchanged and the manner they are structured, which, in turn, displays a close relation to the mentoring process development. The analysis reveals that written accounts of practices—reflective journals and emails—have allowed the mentors to examine, discuss, and improve the strategies they adopted in their work with the novice teachers. The same was observed with the novice teachers.

The content of the first messages is characterized by the mentors probing, approaching, eliciting the novices' needs, creating a common language with them, individually and collectively. Some mentor-novice dyads produced up to 80 e-mail exchanges in the first month, and have even made an effort to exchange messages synchronously, i.e., in "chat rooms." The content of the first messages also shows that some mentors were uneasy about the development of the Program activities.

In this initial phase the mentors displayed patterns of professional behavior similar to those of their partner novice teachers. Their reflective journals and oral accounts at the meetings with the researchers showed that they were going through a process of anxiety, uncertainty, and expectation and were experiencing grief, conflict, and dilemmas without pre-established solutions, feelings inherent to the induction period. However, unlike most novice professionals, they expressed that they felt they could count on the researchers for support.

From the initial contacts, which varied in duration for each dyad, the mentors moved on to a phase of mapping out the novices' professional routes and conceptions and understanding the causes of their difficulties. The content of their e-mail messages in this phase shows that they wanted to meet the needs indicated by their partner novice teachers, though sometimes they were the ones to define the focus. These e-mail exchanges revealed the complexity and vicissitudes of the first teaching years and the novices' lack of stability with respect to their work conditions.

The subsequent monitoring work comprised the development of teaching and learning experiences, structured situations planned by the mentors with their partner novices, and implemented by the latter from themes that they deemed relevant. These situations derived from practical difficulties encountered by the novice teachers, and their development may be depicted as a circumscriptive process involving actions of diverse natures on the part of the mentors and novices. They also involved, depending on the case, the novice teachers' students. Data made clear the difficulties, dilemmas, perceptions, fears, beliefs, successes experienced by teachers at the beginning of their careers.

Every mentor displayed an idiosyncratic and individual pattern of relationship and communication with their novice teachers. Each one performed a personal translation of the objectives, ends, contents, and educational strategies of the Mentorship Program, despite having participated in the consensual establishment of its theoretical and methodological basis. Their expertise was embedded in their mentoring practices.

All mentor-novice dyads constructed unique routes as regards the development of the Program. They display distinctive rhythms and patterns when performing the Program activities. A dyad's rhythm and patterns also modified during the process.

The obtained data suggest that the Online Program showed positive impact on teacher communication with different members of school community (principals and students' parents), teacher commitment, and teacher classroom instructional practices, especially in keeping students on task, adjusting classroom activities to meet student's interests, maintaining a positive classroom atmosphere, and demonstrating successful classroom management.

The mentors' processes of professional development and learning are not similar to the novice teachers' processes. Both the mentors and novice teachers experience individual processes of meaning attribution, in dyads and collectively, deriving from their interactions and actions related to Program.

Establishing precise goals and clear interaction strategies—which were translated as teaching and learning experiences—seems to have promoted the professional development and learning processes of the mentors' and novice teachers' alike.

Mentorship seems to be best performed by practicing professionals: the fact that the mentors in question are in touch with practical classroom situations themselves seems to favor their mentoring performance. The mentors' knowledge base is modeled by: (a) the context to which it is exposed (the context of virtual interaction with the novice teacher or that of face-to-face interaction with the researchers and other mentors); (b) the context in which it is used and practiced (the context of novice teachers' practice or that of their own practice, including herein the correspondence with the novice teachers); and (c) the processes of construction/reconstruction of new/old knowledge. Interactive conversations and written narratives should be highlighted in this modeling process as rich spaces for the construction of new knowledge.

Some mentors have carried out the mentoring process around the themes and contents they have more mastery of and/or more experience with. As teacher educators, they have, in addition to online teaching-related knowledge, a multidisciplinary knowledge base at least on two levels: (1) related to the novice teachers they mentored; and (2) associated with the students of these novice teachers. There was also indication that they hold a *multifocal vision* about what they need to know to teach novice teachers how to teach, since they simultaneously and permanently articulated and took into consideration their novice teachers' formative needs and those of their novice teachers' students, the teaching learning processes they (mentors and novices) were subject to, intervening factors, and contexts of teaching practice.

The mentors' work emphasized the difficulties faced by the novice teachers concerning the teaching of specific contents (pedagogical content knowledge), which involves teaching content knowledge on a new basis. They expect that the novice teachers will put their recommendations into use, and encourage them to develop reflective processes about their own practices.

It appears that no mentor can satisfactorily develop their educational activities without the other mentors' knowledge and assistance. All of them have habitually requested their peers' advice to solve problems encountered in the mentoring activities under their responsibility.

Both mentors and novice teachers have revealed systematic, rigorous and disciplined reflective processes in their accounts and journals. These processes imply experiencing situations, interpreting experiences, indicating problems/ issues, attempting to explain problems/issues, turning explanations into hypotheses, and experimenting with or testing these hypotheses. This process is most likely to occur in a culture—that accepts and invests in multiplicity of knowledge and conceptions, encourages expression of professional discourse and sharing of ideas by mapping out constructed professional knowledge and existing gaps, as happens in the research group under consideration—is of extreme importance.

Interactive conversation seems to insert an element of inquiry in the group's discourse. Paradigm clashes have taken place between some mentor-novice dyads as well as mentor-mentor dyads, which have led some mentors to express feelings of inconformity, discomfort, and inadequacy to work with dissimilar beliefs.

Little by little, the participants' frameworks (novice, mentors, and researchers) have been delineated; ideas have been examined and sometimes replaced; and a basis for collaborative conversation was created by them.

It was noticed that the development of dialog-based and practice-orientated educational programs for mentors provided opportunities for the abandonment of models experienced or received in other educational contexts as also the collec-tive construction of reflective practices leading to change especially when their teaching and learning conceptions and routines were questioned.

The group—mentors, specialists and researchers—was gradually bringing forth a learning community: there is evidence of a movement toward defining the group's identity, with the establishment of interaction rules. Although personal differences have been honored, there is a tendency to share responsibility for the learning of peers and novices as a group. The mentors and novice teachers have shown attitudes indicative of valorization of individual and collective intellectual growth.

CONCLUSION

The development of the Online Mentoring Program has been a rather challenging process, but enriching as well. It has promoted the establishment of professional and affective bonds among the participants, the broadening of professional knowledge, the mastery of online adult education technologies and the participants' professional growth. These kind or intervention/research offered a way to maintain a close look into the process of dialogue considering novice teachers-experienced teachers (mentors) researchers. Using the collaborative-constructive model of research, it was possible to create a dialog process involving different partners.

It emphasize that it has been a much more complex enterprise than a face-to-face equivalent program would have been because it demands entirely new logistics. As pointed by Schlager et al. (2009) it is necessary to explore new frameworks, tools, and techniques to understand and maximize the benefits of teacher professional online networks. We point some challenges or questions that remain without answer considering our data and have to be further understood and better managed.

1. What is the adequate time, a key variable in successful development and implementation of formative actions, to support the mentors and novice teachers and simultaneously to do a research? What is the necessary time between the novices posing a problem or dilemma and the mentors' subsequent work? What is the adequate time to promote the process of knowledge construction, involving thinking up hypotheses, testing alternatives, and evaluating courses of action?

2. What criteria adopt to prioritize the novice demands? Which demands should/could get prompt answers or be answered later during the process?

3. How to equilibrate the novices' demands with the individual mentors teaching knowledge base?

4. How to meet all the needs of a novice teacher since no mentor knowledge base is comprehensive and diversified enough?

5. How to develop adequate distance education actions without face-to-face contact? How to apprehend the novices' pedagogical practices only by their narrative accounts? How accurate are the words and ideas expressed by the novice teachers?

In conclusion, these results were very significant because they expanded the vision about the potentially of mentoring programs considering the Brazilian teacher education characteristics and the use of the Internet as a professional educational context and narrative account as formative and investigative tools. The study also indicated how much there is to learn and investigate in experienced teachers' and novice teachers' educational processes and the importance of public policies that foster assisted teacher induction, while respecting the characteristics of this professional phase and not demanding from novice teachers the responsibilities usually expected of more experienced teachers as well the use of the Internet as formative tool.

REFERENCES

Carroll, D. (2005). Learning through interactive talk: A school-based mentor teacher study group as a context for professional learning. *Teaching and Teacher Education, 21*(5), 457–473. doi:10.1016/j.tate.2005.03.005

Cole, A. L., & Knowles, J. G. (1993). Teacher development partnership research: A focus on methods and issues. *American Educational Research Journal, 30*(3), 473–495.

de Moraes, R. C. C. (2010). Educação a distância e efeitos em cadeia. *Cadernos de Pesquisa, 40*(140), 547–559. Retrieved from http://www.scielo.br/scielo.php?script=sci_arttext&pid=S0100-15742010000200012&lng=pt&nrm=iso doi:10.1590/S0100-15742010000200012

Gatti, B. A., Barreto, E. S. S., & André, M. D. A. (2011). *Políticas docentes no Brasil: Um estado da arte*. Rio de Janeiro, Brasília: UNESCO.

Grossman, P., Hammerness, K., & MacDonald, M. (2009). Redefining teaching, re-imaging teacher education. *Teachers and Teaching: Theory and Practice, 15*(2), 273–289. doi:10.1080/13540600902875340

Grossman, P., Wineburg, S., & Woolworth, S. (2001). *What makes teacher community different from a gathering of teachers*. Retrieved from http://depts.washington.edu/ctpmail/PDFs/Community-GWW-01-2001.pdf.

Ingersoll, R. M., & Strong, M. (2011). The impact of induction and mentoring programs for beginning teachers: A critical review of the research. *Review of Educational Research, 81*(2), 201–233. doi:10.3102/0034654311403323

Knowles, J. G., Cole, A. L., & Pressword, C. S. (2008). *Through preservice teachers' eyes: Exploring field experiences through narrative and inquiry*. Halifax, Canada: Backalong Books.

Libâneo, J. C. (2011). *O dualismo perverso da escola pública brasileira: Escola do conhecimento para os ricos, escola do acolhimento social para os pobres.* Educação e Pesquisa.

Little, J. W. (2002). Locating learning in teachers communities of practice: Opening up problems of analysis in records of everyday work. *Teaching and Teacher Education, 18*(8), 917–946. doi:10.1016/S0742-051X(02)00052-5

Marcelo Garcia, C. (2011). *Políticas de inserción en la docência: De eslabón perdido a puente para el desaroollo professional docente.* Retrieved from http://www.inet.edu.ar/programas/formacion_docente/biblioteca/formacion_docente/marcelo_garcia_politicas_insercion_docente.pdf.

Marcelo Garcia, C., & Vaillant, D. (2009). *Desarrollo professional docente: Cómo se aprende a esneñar?* Madrid, Spain: Narcea.

Mizukami, M. G. N., et al. (2010). *Escola e aprendizagem da docência: Processos de investigação e formação.* São Carlos, Spain: EDUFSCar.

Mizukami, M. G. N., Reali, A. M. M. R., & Tancredi, R. M. S. P. (2010). Elementary public school and university partnership: Promoting and analyzing development processes of school teachers. In Slater, J. J., & Ravid, R. (Eds.), *Collaboration in Education* (pp. 54–60). New York, NY: Routledge.

Papi, S. O. G., & Martins, P. L. O. L. (2010). As pesquisas sobre professores iniciantes: Algumas aproximações. *Educational Review, 26*(3), 39–56. doi:10.1590/S0102-46982010000300003

Pérez Gómez, A. (2010). Nuevas exigências y escenarios para la profesión docente em la era de la información y de la incertidumbre. *Revista Interuniversitaria de Formación del Professorado, 68*(24), 17–36.

Reali, A. M. M. R., Tancredi, R. M. S. P., & Mizukami, M. G. (2008). Programa de mentoria on-line: Espaço para o desenvolvimento profissional de professoras iniciantes e experientes. *Educação e Pesquisa, 34*(1), 77–96.

Schlager, M. S., Fusco, J., Schank, P., & Dwyer, N. (2009). Analyzing online teacher's networks. *Journal of Teacher Education, 60*(1), 86–100. doi:10.1177/0022487108328487

Tancredi, R. M. S. P., & Reali, A. M. M. R. (2011). O que um mentor precisa saber: Ou: Sobre a necessidade de um mentor construir uma visão multifocal. *Exitus, 1*(1), 33–44.

ADDITIONAL READING

Achinstein, B., & Athanases, S. Z. (2006). *Mentors in the making: Developing new leaders for new teachers.* New York, NY: Columbia University.

Alen, B., & Allegroni, A. (2009). *Acompañar los primeros pasos en la docencia, explorar una nueva práctica de formación.* Buenos Aires, Brazil: Ministerio de Educación, Série: Acompañar los primeros pasos en la docencia.

Ariav, T., & Imanuel, D. (2007). *How mentor teachers in professional development schools (PDS) perceive their professional growth: Barriers and opportunities.* Chicago, IL: AERA.

Ball, A. S., & Tyson, C. A. (2011). *Studying diversity in teacher education.* London, UK: Rowman & Littlefield.

Cochran-Smith, M., & Lytle, S. (2009). *Inquiry as stance: Practitioner research in the next generation.* New York, NY: Teachers College Press.

Dal-Forno, J., & Reali, A. M. M. R. (2009). Formação de formadores: Delineando um programa de desenvolvimento profissional da docência via internet. *Revista Profissão Docente, 9*, 1–20.

Darling-Hammond, L. (2010). *The flat world and education: How America's commitment to equity will determine our future*. New York, NY: Teachers College Press.

Gatti, B. A. (2008). Análise das políticas públicas para formação continuada o Brasil, na última década. *Revista Brasileira de Educação, 13*(37), 58–70.

Gatti, B. A., & Barreto, E. S. S. (2009). *Professores do Brasil: Impasses e desafios*. Rio de Janeiro, Brasília: UNESCO.

Giolo, J. (2008). A educação a distância e a formação de professores. *Education et Sociétés, 29*(105), 1211–1234.

Lieberman, A., Hanson, S., & Gless, J. (2012). *Mentoring teachers: Navigating the real-world tensions*. San Francisco, CA: Jossey-Bass.

Marcelo, C. (1999). *Formação de professores – Para uma mudança educativa*. Porto-Portugal, Portugal: Porto Editora.

Marcelo, C. (2007). Empezar con buen pie: Inserción a la enseñanza para profesores picipiantes. *Política Educativa: Docência, 33*, 27–38.

Marcelo García, C. (2011). *Políticas de inserción en la docencia: De eslabón perdido a puente para el desarrollo profesional docente*. Serie documentos de PREAL (No. 52). Retrieved from http://prometeo.us.es/idea/miembros/01-carlos-marcelo-garcia/archivos/preal.pdf.

Marcolino, T. Q., & Reali, A. M. M. R. (2010). El trabajo del mentor: Análisis de los feedbacks de diarios reflexivos a lo largo de un proceso de mentoría en grupo. *Revista Iberoamericana de Educación, 52*, 1–12.

Migliorança, F., & Tancredi, R. M. S. P. (2010). *Programa de mentoria online: A experiência de uma professora iniciante*. Paper presented at the II Congreso Internacional sobre profesorado iniciante y inserción profesional en la docência. Buenos Aires, Brazil.

Moon, B. (2008). O papel das novas tecnologias da comunicação e da educação a distância para responder à crise global na oferta e formação de professores: Uma análise da experiência de pesquisa e desenvolvimento. *Education et Sociétés, 29*(104), 791–814. doi:10.1590/S0101-73302008000300008

Nóvoa, A. (2009). Educación 2021: Para un historia del futuro. *Revista IberoAmericana de Educación, 49*, 181–199.

Olebe, M. (2005). Helping new teachers enter and stay in the profession. *Clearing House (Menasha, Wis.), 78*(4), 158–166. doi:10.3200/TCHS.78.4.158-163

Papi, S. O. G., & Martins, P. L. O. (2010). As pesquisas sobre professores iniciantes: Algumas aproximações. *Educational Review, 26*(3), 39–56. doi:10.1590/S0102-46982010000300003

Reali, A. M. M. R., Tancredi, R. M. S. P., & Mizukami, M. G. N. (2010). *Desenvolvimento profissional de professoras iniciantes e experientes: O programa de mentoria on-line do portal dos professores da UFSCar*. Paper presented at the II Congreso Internacional sobre profesorado iniciante y inserción profesional en la docencia. Buenos Aires, Argentina.

Reali, A. M. M. R., Tancredi, R. M. S. P., & Mizukami, M. G. N. (2010). Programa de mentoria on-line para professores iniciantes: Fases de um processo. *Cadernos de Pesquisa, 40*, 479–506. doi:10.1590/S0100-15742010000200009

Shulman, L. (2005). Conocimiento y enseñanza: Fundamentos de la nueva reforma. *Profesorado. Revista de Currículum y Formación del Profesorado, 9*(2), 1–30.

Strong, M. (2009). *Effective teacher induction and mentoring: Assessing the evidence*. New York, NY: Teachers College Press.

Tancredi, R. M. S. P. T., & Reali, A. M. M. R. (2010). Desenvolvimento profissional de professores no programa de mentoria do portal dos professores da UFSCar. *Caminhos Educacionais, 1*, 60–70.

Tartuce, G. L. B. P., Nunes, M. M. R., & Almeida, P. C. A. (2009). *Atratividade da carreira docente no Brasil. São Paulo, Brazil*. Fundação Carlos Chagas, São Paulo: Relatório Preliminar.

Terigi, F. (2010). *Desarrollo professional continuo y carrera docente em América Latina. Serie documentos de PREAL (No. 50). Washington, DC: Inter-American Dialogue. Salinas, S., et al. (2009). Los procesos de gestión en el acompañamiento a los docentes noveles. Buenos Aiores, Argentina: Ministerio de Educación, Série: Acompañar los primeror pasos en la docencia. Sherman, S., et al. (2007). Enhancing traditional mentoring with e-mentoring: Implications for state policy for the e-mentoring study.* Rio de Janeiro, Brazil: AERA.

UNESCO. (2006). *Teachers and educational quality: Monitoring global needs for 2015*. Montreal, Canada: UNESCO.

Vaillant, D. (2009). Políticas de inserción a la docencia en America Latina: La deuda pendiente. *Profesorado: Revista del Curriculum y Formación del Profesorado, 13*(1), 27–41.

Vaillant, D., & Rossel, C. (Eds.). (2006). *Maestros de la escuela basica en America Latina: Hacia una radiografia de la profesión.* Equadrao, Portugal: PREAL.

Valente, J. A., & Bustamante, S. B. V. (2009). *Educação a distância: Prática e formação do profissional reflexive.* São Paulo, Brazil: Avercamp.

Wang, J., Odell, S. J., & Schwille, S. A. (2008). Effects of teacher induction on beginning teachers' teaching: A critical review of the literature. *Journal of Teacher Education, 59*(2), 132–152. doi:10.1177/0022487107314002

Zeichner, K. M. (2008). Uma análise crítica sobre a "reflexão" como conceito estruturante na formação docente. *Education et Sociétés, 29*(103), 535–554. doi:10.1590/S0101-73302008000200012

KEY TERMS AND DEFINITIONS

Mentoring: Support and assistance that novice teachers can receive from more experienced teachers in a regular basis as induction programs

Teacher Professional Development and Learning: Learning to teach and be a teacher implies processes that are guided by different experiences and ways of knowing. These processes occur before the initial training, during the period of initial teacher education programs and throughout the professional experience. According to Marcelo (1999) professional development is a set of processes and strategies that facilitate teachers' reflection on their practice, which helps teachers, generate knowledge, strategies and learn from their experience. Such development must be closely related to the improvement of the school, curriculum development and innovation with the education progress and the growth of the teaching profession.

Mentors: Experienced teachers that act as teacher educators of novice teachers educating, supporting, coaching, and guiding them.

Teacher Reflection: Reflection can be considered as a professional development tool. By means of such process, we can promote a critical analysis about teaching and learning approaches/experiences especially when it is conducted among peers.

Novice Teachers: Teachers with less than five years of teaching experience.

Online Mentoring: Online support and assistance that novice teachers can receive from more experienced teachers.

Narratives: Considered here as mode of action research and formative strategy aiming to understand / reconstruct of knowledge and pedagogical practices of teachers as well as the interpretation and meanings they give to their actions, and knowledge.

Reflective Inquiry: Type of investigative reflection that teachers engage themselves (individually or in groups, with peers or researchers) from questions about their knowledge and practices. Raising questions about their work, they can turn it to better teach their students. It is also an investigative strategy and training for teachers and researchers.

Chapter 13
An Analysis of Teacher Knowledge and Emotional Sharing in a Teacher Blog Community

Jung Won Hur
Auburn University, USA

Thomas Brush
Indiana University, USA

Curt Bonk
Indiana University, USA

ABSTRACT

The purpose of this chapter is to discuss the findings of a research study analyzing knowledge and emotional sharing in a self-generated online teacher community. Although active informal learning occurs in online communities of teachers, scant information is available about the knowledge and emotions teachers share in these communities. The authors conducted a content analysis of 1,709 entries in a self-generated blog community and examined the types of activities teachers were engaged in. The data revealed that over 29% of entries were related to lesson plans or teaching resources. In addition, over 17% of the postings addressed teachers' positive or negative emotions. The authors argue that teacher participation in online communities should be promoted and encouraged since online communities help teachers with informal learning and emotional sharing.

DOI: 10.4018/978-1-4666-1815-2.ch013

INTRODUCTION

Diverse student demographics and expectations of high test scores require teachers to continue to develop their knowledge and skills through Teacher Professional Development (TPD). Hill (2007) reports that most US teachers are required to complete an average 120 hours of training every five years. At the same time, No Child Left Behind mandates a minimum of 25% of educational technology grants to be allocated for high quality teacher professional development. However, despite this emphasis, researchers report that many TPD programs have little impact on teacher knowledge and skill development (Duncan-Howell, 2010; Guskey, 1986; Wilson & Berne, 1999). Programs are largely developed based on knowledge transmission from experts (Richter, Kunter, Klusmann, Lüdtke, & Baumert, 2011). In such a model, teachers are asked to be passive listeners, consuming knowledge created by outside experts who often have little knowledge about local conditions (Richter, Kunter, Klusmann, Lüdtke, & Baumert, 2011; Wilson & Berne, 1999). The learning focus is mainly on mastering teaching skills and basic rules (Boyle, While, & Boyle, 2004; Darling-Hammond & McLaughlin, 1995). More importantly, teacher training is often provided separately from actual classes, such as during summer workshops. Unfortunately, in such situations, teachers have minimal, if any, opportunity to get feedback on the ideas learned and possible applications for the classroom with the experts who ran the workshop or institute when they attempt to place the skills learned into practice. Worse still, they often lack time to discuss their ideas even with fellow teachers in their own building or district (Fiszer, 2004; Hew & Hara, 2007).

Internet technology, however, has provided teachers with a new learning opportunity; teachers have created online communities to share ideas and concerns with peers (Duncan-Howell, 2010; Hew & Hara, 2007; Hur & Brush, 2009).

For example, Trinnifer, a middle school language arts teacher, asked members in a self-generated online community of teachers for practical ideas: "How do you differentiate for a class of widely varying abilities without drawing attention to any one student or set of students?" (Retrieved from Teaching community in LiveJournal on 2008, February 10). Increasing diversity in a classroom requires adept teaching abilities. Many teachers, like Trinnifer, search for such new skills and knowledge in online communities.

Online communities are "a collaborative means of achieving 'shared creation' and 'shared understanding,' in which mutual exchange between community members are encouraged to support individual and collective learning" (Yeh, 2010, p. 140). They are self-organizing and self-sustaining entities that entail a common practice and a joint enterprise (Ardichvili, Page, & Wentling, 2002; Schlager & Fusco, 2003). Social network technologies, such as Internet forums or blogs, are used for community development, and many teachers actively participate in these communities, sharing ideas, advice, and concerns (Hew & Hara, 2007; Hur & Brush, 2009). For example, Hur and Hara (2007) report that, since 2000, over 87,000 elementary school teachers in Korea have shared knowledge and resources through a teacher-generated Web-based community called Indischool.

Studies indicate that knowledge sharing is one of key reasons why teachers want to participate in online communities. For example, Hur and Brush (2009) found that teachers voluntarily took part in online communities because sharing online allowed teachers to explore a variety of new ideas and reflect on their own teaching practice. Similarly, Hew and Hara (2007) found that teachers wanted to share knowledge in online communities to improve their own skills while discussing with others. A teacher in Hew and Hara's study discussed, "When I share my knowledge, I usually get comments from other people, and we go back and forth in our discussions. It makes me think, stimulates my intellect and helps me gain a better understanding of the issue" (p. 585).

Although participation in an online teacher community is an important way for teachers to gain new knowledge and share concerns (Chalmers & Keown, 2006; Putnam & Borko, 2000), scant information is available about what is occurring in these communities (Hew & Hara, 2007; Hur & Brush, 2009). Examining the different types of activities and the knowledge shared in such communities is critical to understanding how teachers informally learn in virtual places. Consequently, this chapter discusses the findings of a research study analyzing teacher knowledge and emotional sharing in a self-generated online teacher community using a blog site, LiveJournal.

THEORETICAL FRAMEWORK

Teacher Knowledge

Darling-Hammond (2003) claims, "Well prepared capable teachers have the largest impact on student learning and they need to be treasured and supported" (p. 7). Given the direct connection to student learning, supporting teacher knowledge development has grown in importance among teacher educators and policy makers (Goldhaber & Anthony, 2007; Goldhaber & Brewer, 2001; Wilson, Floden, & Ferrini-Mundy, 2001). However, defining the types of knowledge that teachers need to understand is difficult because of the varied responsibilities that teachers need to perform. Shulman (1987) claims that if teacher knowledge were organized in a handbook or encyclopedia, the content would include the following items, among others:

- Content knowledge;
- General pedagogical knowledge in relation to classroom management and delivery of subject matter;

- Curriculum knowledge of materials and program;
- Knowledge of learners and their characteristics;
- Knowledge of educational contexts, including classroom, school, and community;
- Knowledge of educational goals, values, and philosophy and historical grounds.

These types of knowledge are also called formal knowledge or knowledge-for-practice (Cochran-Smith & Lytle, 1999a). Such types of knowledge is fundamental to improving teaching practices because of the scientifically-based approach which has accumulated the past few decades (Hiebert, Gallimore, & Stigler, 2002). This approach assumes that there is an explicitly defined knowledge base that teachers should master. From such a perspective, teachers are not those who generate knowledge; rather, they are the consumers of knowledge developed by university-based researchers. By this definition, an expert teacher is one who knows existing formal knowledge and continually updates his or her individual knowledge base.

Another view of teacher knowledge is called practical knowledge or knowledge-in-practice (Cochran-Smith & Lytle, 1999a). A basic assumption of this perspective is that teaching is situational and uncertain and is constructed in response to everyday practice in classrooms. Teachers gain knowledge through experience and reflection. From this perspective, expert teachers are defined as those who are able to articulate implicit knowledge explicitly for novices or less confident teachers. In this sense, novice teachers are expected to learn by observing and imitating the strategies of expert teachers.

Researchers argue that viewing knowledge dualistically poses problems, whether formal or practical. First, some knowledge, such as pedagogical content knowledge (Shulman, 1987), does not belong to either category (Carter, 1990; Fenstermacher, 1994). According to Shulman, pedagogical content knowledge is defined as "the blending of content and pedagogy into an understanding of how particular topics, problems, or issues are organized, represented, and adapted to the diverse interests and abilities of learners and presented for instruction" (p. 8). In other words, pedagogical content knowledge includes both formal and practical knowledge. When all knowledge is divided into two parts, an attempt to link two components, such as pedagogical content knowledge, proves troublesome (Cochran-Smith & Lytle, 1999a).

Another problem of looking at knowledge dualistically is that both approaches assume that there is knowledge that is already known. Formal knowledge emphasizes learning knowledge that is already known by someone else who constructed or discovered the knowledge, such as a researcher. Practical knowledge focuses on learning knowledge that is known by someone who gained that knowledge by experience, such as an expert teacher or practitioner.

Cochran-Smith and Lytle (1999a) propose a new conception of teacher knowledge called knowledge-of-practice. This view stands in contrast to the dualistic view of knowledge. Instead of being a synthesis of formal and practical knowledge, it is based on a fundamentally different assumption that understanding teacher knowledge goes beyond the idea of formal-practical distinction. It does not distinguish expert teachers from novice teachers. Instead, both types of teachers work together to construct the knowledge necessary for teaching. From this view, knowledge cannot be separated from the knower; rather, knowledge is constructed in the contexts in which it is utilized and connected to the knower. Such a perspective views a teacher as a researcher or knower who does not need more "findings" from university-based researchers but needs dialogue with other teachers in order to generate theories grounded in practice (Cochran-Smith & Lytle, 1999b). This view emphasizes teacher learning

across the professional life through participation in teacher communities. Cochran-Smith and Lytle (1999a) claim:

Working together in communities, both new and more experienced teachers pose problems, identify discrepancies between theories and practices, challenge common routines, draw on the work of others for generative frameworks, and attempt to make visible much of that which is taken for granted about teaching and learning (p. 293).

Garet, Porter, Desimone, Birman, and Yoon (2001) explain that teachers who work in a collaborative working environment experience several advantages within their peer community. Such advantages include having more opportunities to discuss concepts and problems that arise in school as well as greater chances to share common curriculum materials or assessment requirements.

The above discussion primarily targeted the cognitive side of teacher knowledge development. Although assisting teachers in acquiring content or pedagogical knowledge is critical to success in the classroom, an increasing number of scholars claim that teacher emotions should also be taken into consideration. Given that personal development involves the mind, body, and emotions, the role of emotions in the learning process cannot be discounted (Hoekstra & Korthagen, 2011). Thus, factoring in emotions will offer educators a more comprehensive understanding of teachers' learning and professional growth (Demetrious, Wilson, & Winterbottom, 2009).

Teachers' Emotional Sharing

Emotions teachers experience are typically divided into two categories: (a) positive and (b) negative. Positive emotions include the love, joy, and pleasure associated with teaching (Sutton & Wheatley, 2003). Teachers experience positive emotions when struggling students make progress, when former students come back to visit, when students cooperate without disruption, when they work with supportive colleagues, and when parents respect teachers' judgment (Hargreaves, 1998; Lasky, 2000; Lortie, 1975). On the other hand, negative emotions, such as anger or frustration, arise when teachers do not make adequate progress toward a goal (Sutton & Wheatley, 2003). Teachers also experience negative emotions when students misbehave or violate rules. Such emotions also emerge when colleagues or parents are disrespectful and when students lack motivation or have lazy study attitudes (Golby, 1996; Hur & Brush, 2009; Lasky, 2000).

There are serious repercussions to riding a negative emotional plane. Experiencing continuous negative emotions can result in emotional exhaustion, cynicism, lack of professional efficacy, and health problems such as a depressed mood or cardiovascular disorders (Kahn, Schneider, Jenkins-Henkelman, & Moyle, 2006). Teachers may even leave the teaching profession due to job burnout. In fact, the National Center for Educational Statistics (2001) reports that approximately 20-25% of new teachers leave the profession within two years and only 50% remain after five years. Sutton and Wheatley (2003) discuss that beginning teachers often experience anxiety when faced with the complexity of providing differentiated instructions, uncertainty about job performance, and difficulties interacting with parents.

Some studies (e.g., Zembylas, 2002) have demonstrated that teachers' emotions affect how they organize curriculum and interact with students. Demetrious, Wilson, and Winterbottom (2009) reported a study of two science teachers and discussed that one teacher, who was upset and discouraged by a lack of progress in the classroom, had communications issues with students, resulting in a lack of student motivation. By contrast, in a similar situation in which students misbehaved and did not put enough effort into learning, the other teacher studied maintained a positive, professional attitude. He was able to create a supportive

learning environment by incorporating various teaching methods and by repeating instruction several times, establishing a strong rapport with students. Hargreaves (2000) claims that teaching is an emotional practice, as teachers constantly interact with a number of students, colleagues, and parents. He argues, "Teaching, learning and leading may not be solely emotional practices, but they are always irretrievably emotional in character, in a good way or a bad way, by design or default" (Hargreaves, 2000, p. 812).

METHOD

Research Case

In order to understand how teachers share knowledge and emotions in online communities, the authors collected data from a Teaching community located in LiveJournal. Livejournal is a community publishing platform that combines blogging and social networking. As with many blogging tools, membership is free. One unique feature of LiveJournal is that any member can create communities. A community is a journal or blog where many people can post entries concerning a topic of interest, unlike a personal journal where only the owner posts. All users can create new communities or join communities created by others.

The teaching community on LiveJournal (T-LJ) is the most popular education-related community today, with over 2,500 members. As of March 2011, a total of 13,470 journal entries had been made to T-LJ since its inception. During the year 2008 alone, 1,709 new entries were posted. Only members can create a new post on T-LJ, but anyone can read the entries. Members are quite active within T-LJ. In fact, each new entry received 11.53 comments on average in 2008. Because membership information is not readily available, identifying and classifying members' teaching experience is difficult. However, based on the blog entries and comments, the authors noted that the experience of the members is quite diverse. For example, the community includes teachers who just started their first teaching jobs as well as who have over 25 years of experience. In addition, some members are pre-service teachers looking for practicing teachers' advice and ideas. The analysis of the community was guided by the following research questions:

1. In what types of topics were teachers engaged when participating in T-LJ?
2. What are the monthly patterns of topic postings?
3. Is there any relationship between types of topics and the number of comments?
4. What types of topics received relatively high numbers of comments?
5. How did members share knowledge in T-LJ?
6. How did members share emotions in T-LJ?

Data Analysis

To answer these research questions, a content analysis (Neuendorf, 2002) of T-LJ entries from 2008 was conducted. The year 2008 was selected because it offered the highest number of postings in T-LJ from 2001 to 2010. Due to the fact that no existing framework was deemed applicable to the types of activities that teachers tended to share in self-generated online communities, the authors designed a coding framework to analyze these postings based on the constant-comparative approach (Lincoln & Guba, 1985).

The unit of analysis was each new post. While the researchers read each blog entry, they documented emerging codes and compared and combined codes into several categories until no additional information emerged (Lincoln & Guba, 1985). To ensure the validity of the coding scheme, the researchers cross checked each other's categorization and revised the framework until they reached 100 percent agreement. Below are two examples demonstrating how each post was coded.

On March 10, a teacher wrote, "I'm in need of recommendations for songs that are upbeat and popular for my year 7 class (11-13 years old). The lyrics need to be appropriate and preferably uplifting or have some sort of positive message. Help anybody?" Given that this message sought specific materials for the classroom, it was coded as "Teaching Resources." A second example was posted on July 25. A teacher shared a link to a YouTube video of Dr. Randy Pausch's last lecture and said, "If you haven't seen his speech, you should. What an educator." This post was coded as "Sharing Education" because the author wanted to share Dr. Pausch's inspiring passion for teaching and life with other teachers.

The initial coding framework included nine codes. The two coders independently coded all the posts in January (a total of 147), obtaining 0.75 inter-coder reliability. To improve the reliability, they engaged in an extended long discussion of the coding process until they reached the same coding results. The initial coding framework was slightly modified (i.e., deleting and adding codes, redefining the definition of each category, etc.) after the discussion. The finalized framework included eight codes: Lesson Plan, Teaching Resources, Management, Job Search, College Training, Feelings about Education, Tips for Teachers, Sharing Education, and Others (see Table 1). All the codes in January were re-categorized based on the new framework together, reaching 100 percent agreement, and one coder analyzed the rest of the postings.

Different methods were utilized to categorize each blog entry. First, the coders examined the title of the post: members often specified what they wanted in the title (e.g., "Please help me with my lesson!"). Next, they carefully read the post, paying close attention to the words (e.g., advice, resources). When the main topic was unclear, the coders read the comments of the post to see how others interpreted it. If the message was related to Feelings about Education, they examined the mood sign[1] to identify the poster's specific emo-

Table 1. T-LJ activity coding framework

Topic	Explanation	Example
Lesson Plan	Asking for teaching strategies or ideas related to a specific lesson or school event	I want to teach a two day mini-unit on *Pyramus and Thisbe*. How would you suggest I sequence these two days?
Teaching Resources	Searching for information about books, websites, worksheets, or assignments related to classroom teaching or specific student populations (e.g., ELLs)	I'm looking for the biggest and most current world map. I teach English so I'm completely ignorant where all the best deals are for social studies gear.
Job Search	Seeking information about becoming a teacher (e.g., interview tips, certification) or job relocation; asking for advice on advanced degrees	I have a very basic interview on Thursday. I was wondering if someone here could take a look at my resume?
College Training	Pre-service teachers asking for advice about teaching in general	Does anyone have any tips for student teachers?
Management	Asking for information or advice on a specific school policy, use of software, classroom management, or evaluation strategies	Any tips on what a SMART Board is capable of or interesting ways to use one?
Feelings about Education	Sharing feelings related to classroom teaching or daily teaching experiences	The second year is a little bit less stressful than the first. I'm still working way too much, but I don't stress about things as frequently.
Tips for Teachers	Sharing tips, ideas, or resources that might be useful to other teachers	A colleague showed me that rubber cement thinner can remove almost any type of marker from whiteboards, laminated paper, etc.
Sharing Education	Sharing education-related policy, structures, social phenomena (e.g., survey, articles)	Has anyone's district/school moved to an online grade system that parents can access at any time? What is your take?
Others	Not directly related to classroom teaching	With the long weekend coming up and a lengthy train ride booked, I'm looking for some good light reading.

tional status. Assigning one code that represented the main idea of each post was the analysis rule, but they noted that some teachers asked specific questions related to two categories (e.g., Lesson Plan and Teaching Resources); additional codes were created for those postings.

To answer the first research question, types of topics, all 1,709 blog entries were coded and the frequency of each code was calculated. Only 79 postings (4.6%) required the additional codes; thus, the researchers removed these codes from further analysis. Chi-square test for goodness of fit and analysis of graphs on the types of postings by month were conducted to address the second research question, monthly patterns of topic postings. The researchers investigated whether the number of postings each month was the same and then carefully analyzed the trends of each code's occurrence by month. The third research question, the relationship between topics and comments,

was answered by conducting a one-way ANOVA. The authors analyzed the number of comments grouped by codes and compared differences in number. To address the fourth research question, types of topics received relatively high numbers of comments, the authors sorted the blog entries, pulling the top 10% of posts based on the number of comments (a total of 181 posts). Then, the researchers examined the frequency of code occurrences by types of topics.

To answer question five, examining how members shared knowledge in T-LJ, the researchers sorted the top 30 comment-earning entries from Lesson Plan and Teaching Resources (a total of 60 postings). They selected postings related to these two codes because the content of these messages was directly related to classroom teaching, critical knowledge for effective teaching. Although some postings from Management dealt with classroom issues, many were related to teacher administrative work; thus, entries from Management were not included. The researchers read all the comments (a total of 1,461) associated with the 60 postings and counted the number of lesson ideas and teaching resources that teachers shared. Finally, in order to answer the sixth research question, to assess how members share emotions in T-LJ, the researchers created three sub-categories for all messages related to Feelings about Education: positive, neutral, and negative. If the posters used terms or choose modes such as happy, excited, or amused, the entries were categorized as positive. Postings including words such as frustrated, depressed, or angry were coded as negative. When the directions of emotions were unclear, they were coded as neutral. The frequency of the sub-categories was calculated and a one-way ANOVA was conducted to examine differences in the number of comments received depending on each sub-category. Finally, the authors sorted the top 10 comment earning postings (a total of 519) and examined different kinds of advice or information that teachers shared.

RESULTS

Types of Topics in T-LJ

The results presented eight different types of topics: Lesson Plan, Teaching Resources, Management, Job Search, College Training, Feelings about Education, Tips for Teachers, Sharing Education, and Others. The postings asking for lesson plan development or ideas for classroom or school activities were coded as "Lesson Plan." A total of 217 postings (12.7%) were related to this topic (see Figure 1). For example, a high school English teacher wanted to develop a class project that put literary characters and historical figures on trial. She had broad ideas about the lesson but had several specific questions about ways to improve the quality of class activities. The teacher asked,

"How did you make certain that everyone had an equal share in the work? What products did you ask your students to create? Was it the same thing for each one? Or did certain roles require different projects?" (Posted on August 11).

If teachers searched for specific resources for a lesson, the entry was categorized as "Teaching Resources." There were a total of 282 postings (16.5%) in this category. In one instance, a teacher asked for book recommendations for 5th and 6th grade gifted students. She wrote:

Last year, I loved reading aloud to my class and I've got a couple of ideas about what to start with this year but a couple of problems too. First, I'm keeping some of my kids so I can't re-read anything. Second, the gifties are tricky: anything recent but not recent enough at least some of them have read... Any suggestions for me? Books that really worked? (Posted on August 27).

Postings related to classroom management, evaluation strategies, or technology systems were categorized as "Management." These postings were either indirectly related to classroom teaching or teacher responsibility in schools. A total of 113 postings (6.6%) belonged to this category, which included strategies on dealing with students who disrupted class on purpose, appropriate ways to report suspected student drug use, and the pros and cons of online grading systems. The "Job Search" code referred to postings related to job-hunting. Nearly 14 percent (n=235) of postings belonged to this category. Members asked about interview strategies, portfolio development methods, and the differences between private and public school systems. Some teachers asked about teacher certification issues because they wanted or needed to move to other states. Teachers also asked for advice regarding "should/should not" situations arising during the job seeking process. For example, one teacher asked how she should address her pregnancy while interviewing:

Figure 1. Frequency of types of topics in T-LJ

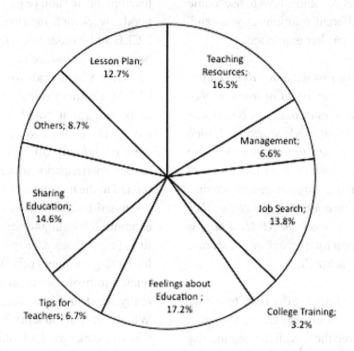

I have an interview tomorrow for a part time (3 days a week) position at a private school. I recently found out that I am about 10 weeks pregnant! ... What should I do? Should I offer the information if I get the job? Or should I mention it during the interview and risk not getting the job based on being pregnant? (Posted on August 3).

Some members of the community were pre-service teachers who asked questions about internships, practicums, and student teaching experiences. For example, one student teacher asked, "Does anyone have any tips for student teachers? If you have been a cooperating teacher, what are some traits in student teachers that you really admire?" (Posted on May 15). This type of posting by pre-service teachers was categorized as "College Training." There were 55 postings (3.3%) in this category. Teachers also shared amusement, excitement, frustration, and disappointment that emerged while they were teaching. Such postings

were coded as "Feelings about Education." This code included the largest number of postings: n=294 (17.2%). One teacher shared the following frustration with demanding job responsibilities:

I feel lost inside my job. I feel consumed by this ideal of being a "good teacher." I work very hard to craft a set of ideas and experiences for the kids to have a fair chance of learning how to think better, to reason, but in doing so, I'm losing myself.... It's hard to pump out so much energy to keep up the spirits and enthusiasm and confidence of 150 teenagers. It is literally and figuratively draining (Posted on March 5).

In contrast to the negative emotions described above, many teachers also shared positive emotions experienced during teaching. For instance, one 6th grade teacher noted that her students loved writing on the big whiteboard in the back of the room. To use the tool for a teaching purpose, she created a math competition: "Using 5 fives and any of the operations you know how to use, come up with as many different solutions as you can." After the event, the teacher expressed:

My class today really just made my day today... The most impressive part of all of this was that this group of 6th graders at the back board was nearly completely silent while working. Which allowed their classmates to continue working on their tests almost oblivious to the flurry of mathematical activity going on behind them... Seeing that many 6th graders doing math that they weren't required to do...made me REALLY happy. Especially nice after a tough week at school and home (posted on October 7).

When teachers found effective teaching methods, resources, or classroom management strategies, they shared them with the community members. These postings were categorized as "Tips for Teaching," and a total of 115 postings (6.7%) belonged to this category. For instance, a teacher shared useful website information: "I've just been introduced to the very cool concept mapping tool at http://bubbl.us—it would be great for kids of any age and adults, too" (Posted on April 5). "Sharing Education" referred to the postings where teachers discussed educational policy, school systems, or teaching in general. When teachers found news articles or videos related to teachers or educational policy, they linked them and asked members to share their perspectives on the issues. A total of 250 postings (14.6%) belonged to this category. Among them, 27 postings were polling questions[2] asking about teachers' experiences (e.g., "Does your school do the pledge every morning?") or school systems (e.g., "How many field trips do you take?"). Another 40 postings asked members to read news articles (e.g., teacher who taught Creationism instead of the science curriculum for 11 years) or videos (e.g., a reality show featuring school principals)

and comment on them. Teachers also discussed the teaching profession (e.g.," What makes a district good to work for?") and teaching methods (e.g., "If NCLB and standardized testing were eliminated, how would your teaching change?").

"Others" was a category that included postings (8.7%) not quite related to classroom teaching or postings that could not be categorized into any of the codes above. Although a few posts were completely off topic (e.g., advertisement, research participation solicitation), many were still related to the members of the community, as they discussed teachers' lives outside of school. For example, 39 postings discussed teachers' personal lives (e.g., "Does your spouse get angry with you for having summers off?") and 11 postings were related to professional appearances (e.g., "I am really short and look really young for my age. Where can I purchase professional, petite clothing that will make me look older?")

Monthly Patterns

The chi-square test for goodness of fit analysis results showed that the number of postings each month was significantly different, $\chi^2(11, n=1709) = 125.891$, $p<.001$. The total number of postings in each month ranged from 109 to 169, excluding the month of August (see Figure 2). However, the number in August increased significantly to 251. Further analysis of the results showed that the number of postings related to Feelings about Education, Teaching Resources, and Teaching Tips doubled in August, yielding a high total number of postings in August. For example, the overall average number of postings related to Feelings about Education was 23.25 but was 46 in this month.

The analysis of the number of postings each month signaled that the occurrence of codes differed each month. In addition, there was a relationship between changes in the number of postings and academic seasons (see Figure 3). For example, the number of postings related to Teach-

Figure 2. Patterns of number of postings and comments by month

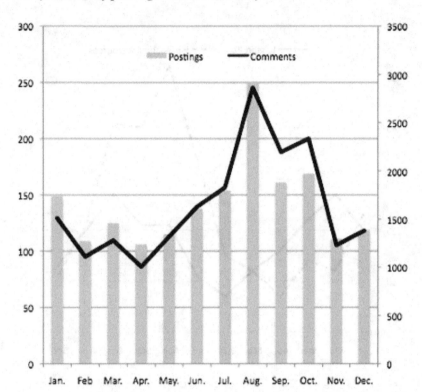

ing Resources was highest in August, as teachers prepared for the new academic semester. Not unexpectedly, the number of postings decreased gradually during the fall semester. Then, the number increased in January when the spring semester started. Similar patterns appeared for Management, Teaching Tips, and Sharing Education: the number of postings increased at the beginning of the new semester and decreased over time. However, a different pattern was noted for Lesson Plan postings. The total number of postings was steady throughout the semester but dropped during summer break. No noticeable pattern was found for entries related to Feelings about Education. The average number of postings (m= 23.25) was constant throughout the year except July and August. The number dropped to 13 in July but soared to 48 in August.

Relationship between the Types of Topics and the Number of Comments

The average number of postings each month was 142, while the average number of comments was 1,639; on average, 4.68 new postings were made daily, and each post received 11.53 comments. A one-way ANOVA was conducted to investigate whether the number of comments differed depending on the topic category. The results indicated a statistically significant difference in the number of comments among the categories, $F(8, 1697)= 16.458$, $p<.001$ with a moderate effect size ($\eta^2=0.72$). The analysis of LSD post hoc test revealed that the number of comments for Feelings of Education was significantly larger than Job Search, Lesson Plan, Teaching Resources,

Figure 3. Changes in number of postings of teaching resources and lesson plan

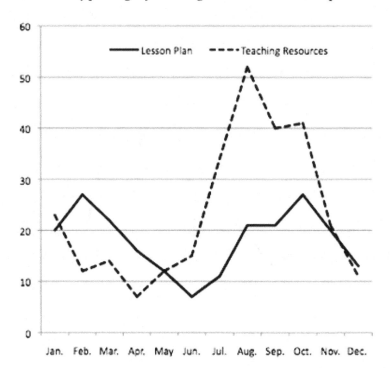

Table 2. Summary of number of postings and comments by types of topics

Topic	Postings		Comments		
	N	%	N	Mean	S.D.
Lesson Plan	217	12.7	1960	9.03	6.90
Teaching Resources	282	16.5	2724	9.66	8.57
Job Search	235	13.8	2090	8.89	7.61
College Training	55	3.3	517	9.57	7.32
Management	113	6.6	1941	17.18	15.95
Feelings about Education	294	17.2	3772	12.83	12.48
Tips for Teachers	115	6.7	861	7.49	8.19
Sharing Education	250	14.6	4197	16.92	16.90
Others	148	8.7	1615	10.91	13.01

and Tips for Teachers, while smaller than Sharing Education and Management, *p*<.001 (see Table 2 for the number comparison). The number of comments for Lesson Plan and Teaching Resources was significantly smaller than Sharing Education, Feelings about Education, and Management, *p*<.001.

Types of Topics with High Numbers of Comments

A total of 181 postings were ranked in the top 10% for comments; each one had over 26 comments. Entries related to Sharing Education had the largest portion: a total of 62 postings (34.3%).

For example, one teacher asked, "What do you do when a cell phone rings or you catch a student using one during class?" (Posted on April 2), and 57 comments were made on this issue, ranging from a zero tolerance policy to allowing students to use one if there was a family issue. Other topics related to Sharing Education and their respective number of comments included:

- How would your teaching change if NCLB was gone? (51 comments);
- If anybody puts their handouts/notes on their websites, and if you do, do the students regularly come to class with the material printed out? (48 comments);
- Does anyone still have Recess? My school doesn't. My students go to PE during specials, maybe two times every 6 days or so. Then, we have a 30 min exercise tape the kids do at the end of the day. Does anyone else do something like this? (42 comments).

Feelings about Education ranked second: 39 postings (21.5%). For example, one teacher shared the frustration with his new principal's policies on November 7, and the entry received 48 comments. The title of post said, "please let me vent" and the author wrote:

We just got a new principal midyear. He has instituted new policies, including "No grade lower than a 50. If a child doesn't turn in an assignment, lunch detention is assigned until the assignment is turned in. 75% of all tests and quizzes must be on scantron to let the kid get used to using scantrons for the TAKS test." I hate the new rules. If a kid earns a 30, he should get a 30.

A total of 48 comments were made on this topic, and teachers discussed similar policies recently instituted in their own schools and their opinions. One commenter wrote, "I've had a lot of these same frustrations lately, and I have to say I'm glad to see our school is not the only one going down this road" (Posted on November 10). Other topics related to Feelings about Education and the number of comments included:

- Frustrated that there is no time during the day to use the restroom (45 comments);
- Frustrated with standardized testing (41 comments);
- Amused by student's nice comment (34 comments).

Management ranked third (n=21, 11.6%) and Others ranked fourth (n=19. 10.5%). Both Lesson Plan and Teaching Resources had nine entries that received over 26 comments, while only two entries belonged to College Training.

Sharing Knowledge in T-LJ

In order to examine how teachers share knowledge in T-LJ, the researchers analyzed the top 30 comment-earning entries from Lesson Plan and Teaching Resources each. The analysis results of 30 entries from Lesson Plan showed that teachers from different subject areas shared knowledge together. Among the 30 postings, fifteen were related to language arts, five were from social studies, five were from math, and one was related to art; four postings did not specify a subject. Grade level was diverse too, including postings made by two kindergarten teachers, two second grade teachers, four eighth grade teachers, and five high school teachers. The analysis results of the 646 comments from the 30 entries indicated that when a teacher asked about specific lesson plan ideas, people shared an average of 8.1 ideas (ranging from 1 to 21). Many times, they included practical teaching resources for a particular topic. For example, one teacher asked, "Does anyone have any good methods for pre teaching vocabulary (the activities you do to familiarize kids with words before they read a piece of text)?" (Posted on March 29). For this question, eight teachers shared 14 different ideas, including open word sorts, closed word sorts, looking up definitions and making predictions, and listing the words on chart paper. Teachers often explained how they implemented the shared idea in their own classrooms:

We just fold a piece of paper into thirds. The kids will label each section with one of three things—I KNOW I know, I THINK I know, I KNOW I DON'T know. We then talk about what each category means....When we are finished writing the words and which category, the students do some talking and we see if we can come up with what the word means, etc. (posted March 30)

Additionally, two teachers shared one magazine article and two website links that explained direct vocabulary instruction.

The researchers analyzed 30 entries from Teaching Resources and found that an average of 20.7 resources per blog entry (ranging from 1 to 147) were shared over 815 related comments. For example, one social studies teacher asked, "Anybody know any good Civil War films that are appropriate for middle school? Maybe something that deals more with the social complexities of the war rather than just the fighting?" (Posted on May 18). Over ten possible movie names were shared, including *April 1865: The Month that Saved America, Glory,* and *North and South.*

Sharing Emotions in T-LJ

Among the total of 295 postings related to Feelings of Education, 113 postings were categorized as negative, while 80 postings contained positive message. The remaining 102 postings were coded as neutral. On average, negative postings received 16.86 comments, whereas positive and neutral postings received 8.27 and 12.01 comments, respectively. A one-way ANOVA was conducted to examine whether the number of comments differed depending on the three sub-categories.

The results indicated a statistically significant difference in the number of comments among the sub-categories, $F(2, 292) = 12.28$, $p < .001$ with a moderate effect size ($\eta^2 = 0.78$). The analysis of LSD post hoc test revealed that the number of comments for negative postings was significantly higher than neutral ($p < .05$) and positive postings ($p < .001$). The analysis of 10 postings that received the highest comments presented four common comment activities: giving advice, sharing similar emotions, encouragement, and appreciation. For example, on October 2, a teacher shared her negative emotions on teaching:

This is my fifth year of teaching and I honestly feel awful at the end of every day...I feel like a failure so much every single day and I came home crying today because I just felt I didn't do things well enough. I think I am a good teacher and all, but I feel so horrible every day that I just want to quit and give up. How I feel about myself truly makes me hate my job.

This posting received a total of 42 comments and many teachers provided advice and encouragement. For example, one teacher said, "You need a mentor—someone at your school who has had years and years of experience and still seems enthusiastic. You can bounce ideas and feelings off of her and perhaps she can help you see how great you are." Teachers often shared similar feelings. One teacher wrote, "Were you reading my mind when you wrote this? I've been struggling with this very thing (and this is my 10th year). I've been slowly learning to let some things go; and it is hard! Hang in there, and keep seeking out encouragement and support." The original poster commented on other members' comments many times. In fact, 10 comments out of 42 were made by the original poster. For instance, the original poster commented on the teacher who had the same experience to express her appreciation: "Thanks. Honestly, it's been really nice to hear that I'm not the only one that feels this way. I've been very close to quitting teaching because of it. Knowing I'm not the only one at least helps me to gain some perspective."

DISCUSSION AND IMPLICATIONS

The purpose of this study was to examine knowledge and emotional sharing in a self-generated online community of teachers. The results indicated that teachers actively sought out new knowledge and information in T-LJ. Over 29% of entries (Lesson Plan and Teaching Resources) were related to seeking knowledge-for-practice or knowledge-in-practice (Cochran-Smith & Lytle, 1999a). Teachers wanted to learn about appropriate teaching methods or resources that could assist their specific classroom lessons. Knowledge-of-practice (Cochran-Smith & Lytle, 1999a) was generated while teachers were engaged in discussions.

The wide range of knowledge and information posted and opportunities to share ideas with other educators promoted active informal learning occurrences in T-LJ. Hoekstra and Korthagen (2011) define informal learning as "learning in the workplace where systematical support of learning, such as professional development trajectories, is absent." (p. 663). Teachers gain new understanding while they are teaching, observing colleagues' classrooms, or talking with co-workers (Hoekstra, Beijaard, Brekelmans, & Korthagen, 2007). Teacher collaboration is an important indicator of informal learning in teacher communities (Richter, Kunter, Klusmann, Lüdtke, & Baumert, 2011). While teachers share and discuss, they learn from each other and gain new insights into teaching and learning (Putnam & Borko, 2000). However, such learning opportunities are limited in school environments as teachers rarely observe other classrooms or discuss their ideas with colleagues. T-LJ assisted teachers' active knowledge development by providing flexible learning environments in which teachers shared

a variety of ideas and experiences with educators without time and location limitations. Other studies (e.g., Duncan-Howell, 2010; Hur & Hara, 2007) also demonstrated that encouraging teachers to communicate through online communication technologies was useful for reducing teacher isolation, fostering teacher reflection, and supporting the formation of communities of learners.

Teachers' emotional sharing in the community must receive significant attention. The results presented that highest portion of postings were related to Feeling about Education (a total of 294 postings, 17.4%), and this category received significantly more comments than other categories including Lesson Plan and Teaching Resources. A number of scholars (e.g., Hargreaves, 1998; Sutton & Wheatley, 2003; Zembylas, 2002) emphasize the importance of emotions in teaching. Emotions affect not only the individual's mind but also human interactions and relationships; teachers' emotions affect overall classroom environments that influence student learning (Hargreaves, 1998). Despite its importance, teacher education has continued to focus squarely on cognitive aspects of teacher learning; the emotional aspects of teaching are typically ignored, forgotten, or disregarded (Hargreaves, 1998; Sutton & Wheatley, 2003). Hoekstra et al. (2007) claim:

The interrelatedness of cognitive, affective, motivational, and behavioural aspects in classroom teaching suggests that real change can only occur when all of these four aspects are addressed. The consequence for teacher professional development is that beside a focus on changing teachers' cognition, there should be ample attention for teachers' affect and motivation (p. 204).

Teachers in T-LJ shared both negative and positive emotions actively. Teachers' negative emotions were mostly related to job responsibilities or misbehaviors of students, whereas positive emotions occurred when they observed students' learning progress. Previous studies indicate that sharing both positive and negative emotions is important to cope with the stresses associated with teaching. For example, Kahn, Schneider, Jenkins-Henkelman, and Moyle (2006) reported, "the more teachers engaged in supportive communications in which they discussed pleasant aspects of the job, the less likely they were to experience burnout." (p. 803). They noted that opportunities to talk about pleasant aspects of teaching help reframe teachers' experience in a positive way, and sharing problems with colleagues effectively helped dissipate the feelings of stress. Similarly, Hur and Brush (2009) found that when teachers shared negative emotions in online communities, other teachers provided emotional support such as "you are not alone." This type of encouragements helped them understand other teachers struggle with similar problems and search for a variety of solutions to the challenges.

Based on the findings of the present study, the authors conclude that fostering participation in online communities of teachers is beneficial for teachers' continuous professional growth. While engaging in discussion with other educators, teachers gain new knowledge and broaden perspectives on teaching. Online communities also function as an emotional outlet: sharing emotions in communities help teachers cope with teaching related stresses. Consequently, teacher participation in online communities should be supported and encouraged.

Although the present study demonstrated teachers' active knowledge and emotional sharing in T-LJ, the results should be viewed cautiously due to potential limitations of content analysis. Because the researchers did not interview original posters, it is possible that final coding results did not accurately reflect on the underlying intentions of community members. However, to ensure reliable data analysis, researchers went through iterative development processes within the coding framework, and multiple coders analyzed the blog entries. The findings of this study suggest several important design considerations for future online communities of teachers:

- The online communities should provide spaces in which teachers can share both knowledge and emotions. If they focus solely on either knowledge or emotions, meeting teachers' diverse needs will likely prove difficult.
- The online community should allow everyone to share ideas, regardless of levels of teaching experience. This condition implies that educators should not lead teachers' learning processes; rather, teachers themselves must take control of their own learning processes.
- The online community should be designed to invite a wide variety of participants to share ideas and experiences. Diverse participants of an online community might include teachers with different experiences in terms of subject and grade level taught. It might also include teachers from rural, urban, and suburban communities.
- The online community should be developed based on teachers' needs, not educators' interests. Teachers should be given many opportunities to choose topics that they want to share and discuss. Teachers' new needs should be continually examined and reflected on in order to improve the community.

FUTURE RESEARCH DIRECTIONS AND CONCLUSION

What is clear is that teachers long for support and collegiality for the cognitive as well as emotional issues that they face on a daily, if not minute-to-minute, basis. Today that support can be found in online communities specifically designed for a diverse level of needs. These online communities can be emergent and based on the assorted participants flocking to them and their respective backgrounds and situations. They might also predesigned for specific occupational needs, levels of teaching experience, or familiarity with and acceptance of online environments. As a vital component of society that is too often lacking in sufficient funding, teaching stands to benefit more directly from the proliferation of online communities than many other fields and professions. Such environments are inexpensive, replicable, extendable, and reusable. As they quickly gain in acceptance and use, the Web offers a growing repository of knowledge, ideas, examples, and support structures; some of which practicing teachers never fathomed when studying to become a teacher. Equally important, like-minded individuals found in these communities can offer empathy, insights and sage advice.

It is conceivable that during the coming decades tens of millions of teachers around the planet will reach out to each other using similar types of forums and approaches. As their questions, advice, discussion threads, and overall support are better understood and utilized, we will need to plan for their economies of scale and ponder ingenious ways of reusing and recycling the ideas that arise there so that more teachers can benefit from them. We will also need to establish and maintain online sharing and mentoring tools and systems. Gigantic possibilities for impacting new as well as more established classroom teachers experiencing frustration and lack of confidence with timely support and cognitive apprenticeship are now possible.

There is definitely much at stake here. The teaching profession stands to gain enormous dividends from online support systems that we design, test, scale to large numbers, and continually refine. As this happens, teacher effectiveness in the classroom should improve while burn-out should drop significantly. All the while, students should learn more content. The actual learning communities that will be designed and learning gains that will be enjoyed are still to be determined. This study is but singular example of such a community

and one glimpse into how this technology-driven movement can make an impact. As such, there is a growing need for continued attention and investigation of online communities for educators.

REFERENCES

Ardichvili, A., Page, V., & Wentling, T. (2002). Virtual knowledge-sharing communities of practice at caterpillar: Success factors and barriers. *Performance Improvement Quarterly, 15*(3), 99–113.

Boyle, B., While, D., & Boyle, T. (2004). A longitudinal study of teacher change: What makes professional development effective? *Curriculum Journal, 15*(1), 45–68. doi:10.1080/1026716032000189471

Carter, K. (1990). Teachers' knowledge and learning to teach. In Houston, W. R. (Ed.), *Handbook of Research on Teacher Education: A Project of the Association of Teacher Educators* (pp. 291–310). London, UK: Collier Macmillan.

Chalmers, L., & Keown, P. (2006). Communities of practice and professional development. *International Journal of Lifelong Education, 25*(2), 139–156. doi:10.1080/02601370500510793

Cochran-Smith, M., & Lytle, S. L. (1999a). Relationships of knowledge and practice: Teacher learning in communities. *Review of Research in Education, 24*, 249–305.

Cochran-Smith, M., & Lytle, S. L. (1999b). The teacher researcher movement: A decade later. *Educational Researcher, 28*(7), 15–25.

Darling-Hammond, L. (2003). Keeping good teachers: Why it matters, what leaders can do. *Educational Leadership, 60*(8), 6–13.

Darling-Hammond, L., & McLaughlin, M. W. (1995). Policies that support professional development in an era of reform. *Phi Delta Kappan, 76*(8), 597–604.

Demetriou, H., Wilson, E., & Winterbottom, M. (2009). The role of emotion in teaching: Are there differences between male and female newly qualified teachers' approaches to teaching? *Educational Studies, 35*(4), 449–473. doi:10.1080/03055690902876552

Duncan-Howell, J. (2010). Teachers making connections: Online communities as a source of professional learning. *British Journal of Educational Technology, 41*(2), 324–340. doi:10.1111/j.1467-8535.2009.00953.x

Fenstermacher, G. D. (1994). The knower and the known: The nature of knowledge in research on teaching. In Darling-Hammond, L. (Ed.), *Review of Research in Education* (pp. 3–56). Washington, DC: American Educational Research Association. doi:10.2307/1167381

Fiszer, E. P. (2004). *How teachers learn best: An ongoing professional development model.* Lanham, MD: Scarecrow Education.

Garet, M. S., Porter, A. C., Desimone, L., Birman, B. F., & Yoon, K. S. (2001). What makes professional development effective? Results from a national sample of teachers. *American Educational Research Journal, 38*(4), 915–945. doi:10.3102/00028312038004915

Golby, M. (1996). Teachers' emotions: An illustrated discussion. *Cambridge Journal of Education, 26*(3), 423–434. doi:10.1080/0305764960260310

Goldhaber, D., & Anthony, E. (2007). Can teacher quality be effectively assessed? National board certification as a signal of effective teaching. *The Review of Economics and Statistics, 89*(1), 134–150. doi:10.1162/rest.89.1.134

Goldhaber, D., & Brewer, D. (2001). Evaluating the evidence on teacher certification: A rejoinder. *Educational Evaluation and Policy Analysis, 23*(1), 79–86. doi:10.3102/01623737023001079

Guskey, T. R. (1986). Staff development and the process of teacher change. *Educational Researcher, 15*(5), 5–12.

Hargreaves, A. (1998). The emotional practice of teaching. *Teaching and Teacher Education, 14*(8), 835–854. doi:10.1016/S0742-051X(98)00025-0

Hargreaves, A. (2000). Mixed emotions: Teachers' perceptions of their interactions with students. *Teaching and Teacher Education, 16*(8), 811–826. doi:10.1016/S0742-051X(00)00028-7

Hew, K. F., & Hara, N. (2007). Empirical study of motivators and barriers of teacher online knowledge sharing. *Educational Technology Research and Development, 55*(6), 573–595. doi:10.1007/s11423-007-9049-2

Hiebert, J., Gallimore, R., & Stigler, J. W. (2002). A knowledge base for the teaching profession: What would it look like and how can we get one? *Educational Researcher, 31*(5), 3–15. doi:10.3102/0013189X031005003

Hill, H. C. (2007). Learning in the teaching workforce. *The Future of Children, 17*(1), 111–127. doi:10.1353/foc.2007.0004

Hoekstra, A., Beijaard, D., Brekelmans, M., & Korthagen, F. (2007). Experienced teachers' informal learning from classroom teaching. *Teachers and Teaching: Theory and Practice, 13*(2), 189–206.

Hoekstra, A., & Korthagen, F. (2011). Teacher learning in a context of educational change: Informal learning versus systematically supported learning. *Journal of Teacher Education, 62*(1), 76–92. doi:10.1177/0022487110382917

Hur, J., & Brush, T. (2009). Teacher participation in online communities: Why do teachers want to participate in self-generated online communities of K-12 teachers? *Journal of Research on Technology in Education, 41*(3), 279–303.

Hur, J., & Hara, N. (2007). Factors cultivating sustainable online communities for K-12 teacher professional development. *Journal of Educational Computing Research, 36*(3), 245–268. doi:10.2190/37H8-7GU7-5704-K470

Kahn, J. H., Schneider, K. T., Jenkins-Henkelman, T. M., & Moyle, L. L. (2006). Emotional social support and job burnout among high school teachers: Is it all due to dispositional affectivity? *Journal of Organizational Behavior, 27*(6), 793–807. doi:10.1002/job.397

Lasky, S. (2000). The cultural and emotional politics of teacher-parent interactions. *Teaching and Teacher Education, 16*(8), 843–860. doi:10.1016/S0742-051X(00)00030-5

Lincoln, Y. S., & Guba, E. G. (1985). *Naturalistic inquiry*. London, UK: SAGE Publications.

Lortie, D. (1975). *Schoolteacher: A sociological study*. Chicago, IL: University of Chicago Press.

National Center for Education Statistics. (2001). *Attrition of new teachers among recent college graduates: Comparing occupational stablity among 1992-93 graduates*. Washington, DC: NCES.

Neuendorf, K. A. (2002). *The content analysis guidebook*. Thousand Oaks, CA: SAGE Publications.

Putnam, R., & Borko, H. (2000). What do new views of knowledge and thinking have to say about research on teacher learning? *Educational Researcher, 29*(1), 4–15.

Richter, D., Kunter, M., Klusmann, U., Lüdtke, O., & Baumert, J. (2011). Professional development across the teaching career: Teachers' uptake of formal and informal learning opportunities. *Teaching and Teacher Education, 27*(1), 116–126. doi:10.1016/j.tate.2010.07.008

Schlager, M., & Fusco, J. (2003). Teacher professional development, technology, and communities of practice: Are we putting the cart before the horse? *The Information Society, 19*(3), 203–220. doi:10.1080/01972240309464

Shulman, L. S. (1987). Knowledge and teaching: Foundation of the new reform. *Harvard Educational Review, 57*(1), 1–22.

Sutton, R. E., & Wheatley, K. F. (2003). Teachers' emotions and teaching: A review of the literature and directions for future research. *Educational Psychology Review, 15*(4), 327–358. doi:10.1023/A:1026131715856

Wilson, S., Floden, R., & Ferrini-Mundy, J. (2001). *Teacher preparation research: Current knowledge gaps and recommendations*. Seattle, WA: University of Washington.

Wilson, S. M., & Berne, J. (1999). Teacher learning and the acquisition of professional knowledge: An examination of research on contemporary professional development. *Review of Research in Education, 24*(6), 173–209.

Yeh, Y.-C. (2010). Analyzing online behaviors, roles, and learning communities via online discussions. *Journal of Educational Technology & Society, 13*(1), 140–151.

Zembylas, M. (2002). Constructing genealogies of teachers' emotions in science teaching. *Journal of Research in Science Teaching, 39*(1), 79–103. doi:10.1002/tea.10010

ADDITIONAL READING

Alavi, M., & Leidner, D. E. (2001). Knowledge management and knowledge management systems: Conceptual foundations and research issues. *Management Information Systems Quarterly, 25*(1), 107–136. doi:10.2307/3250961

Barab, S. A., MaKinster, J. G., Moore, J. A., & Cunningham, D. J. (2001). Designing and building an online community: The struggle to support sociability in the inquiry learning forum. *Educational Technology Research and Development*, *49*(4), 71–96. doi:10.1007/BF02504948

Barab, S. A., MaKinster, J. G., & Scheckler, R. (2003). Designing system dualities: Characterizing a web-supported professional development community. *The Information Society*, *19*(3), 237–256. doi:10.1080/01972240309466

Beatty, W. H. (1969). Emotions: The missing link in education. *Theory into Practice*, *8*(20), 86–92. doi:10.1080/00405846909542179

Borko, H. (2004). Professional development and teacher learning: Mapping the terrain. *Educational Researcher*, *33*(8), 3–15. doi:10.3102/0013189X033008003

Brown, J. S., Collins, A., & Duguid, P. (1989). Situated cognition and the culture of learning. *Educational Researcher*, *18*(1), 32–42.

Brown, J. S., & Duguid, P. (1991). Organizational learning and communities of practice: Toward a unified view of working, learning, and innovation. *Organization Science*, *2*(1), 40–57. doi:10.1287/orsc.2.1.40

de Souza, C. S., & Preece, J. (2003). A framework for analyzing and understanding online communities. *Interacting with Computers*, *16*, 579–610. doi:10.1016/j.intcom.2003.12.006

Ellis, D., Oldridge, R., & Vasconcelos, A. (2004). Community and virtual community. *Annual Review of Information Science & Technology*, *38*, 145–186. doi:10.1002/aris.1440380104

Gray, B. (2004). Informal learning in an online community of practice. *Journal of Distance Education*, *19*(1), 20–35.

Gray, J., & Tata, D. (2004). Sociocultural analysis of online professional development: A case study of personal, interpersonal, community, and technical aspects. In Barab, S., Kling, R., & Gray, J. H. (Eds.), *Designing for Virtual Communities in the Service of Learning* (pp. 404–435). Cambridge, UK: Cambridge University Press.

Grossman, P., Wineburg, S., & Woolworth, S. (2001). Toward a theory of teacher community. *Teachers College Record*, *103*(6), 942–1012. doi:10.1111/0161-4681.00140

Gunawardena, C. (1995). Social presence theory and implications for interaction and collaborative learning in computer conferences. *International Journal of Educational Telecommunications*, *1*(2/3), 147–166.

Guskey, T. R. (2002). Professional development and teacher change. *Teachers and Teaching*, *8*(3/4), 381–391. doi:10.1080/135406002100000512

Hargreaves, A., & Fullan, M. G. (2000). Mentoring in the new millennium. *Theory into Practice*, *39*(1), 50–56. doi:10.1207/s15430421tip3901_8

Hildreth, P. M., & Kimble, C. (2004). *Knowledge networks: Innovation through communities of practice*. Hershey, PA: IGI Global.

Hou, H., Chang, K., & Sung, Y. (2009). Using blogs as a professional development tool for teachers: Analysis of interaction behavioral patterns. *Interactive Learning Environments*, *17*(4), 325–340. doi:10.1080/10494820903195215

Jackson, P. W. (1992). Helping teachers develop. In Hargreaves, A., & Fullan, M. G. (Eds.), *Understanding Teacher Development* (pp. 62–74). New York, NY: Teachers College Press.

Jones, A., & Preece, J. (2006). Online communities for teachers and lifelong learners: A framework for comparing similarities and identifying differences in communities of practice and communities of interest. *International Journal of Learning Technology, 2*(2/3), 112–137. doi:10.1504/IJLT.2006.010615

Kling, R., & Courtright, C. (2003). Group behavior and learning in electronic forums: A sociotechnical approach. *The Information Society, 19*(3), 221–235. doi:10.1080/01972240309465

Lave, J., & Wenger, E. (1991). *Situated learning: Legitimate peripheral participation*. Cambridge, UK: Cambridge University Press.

Lieberman, A. (2000). Networks as learning communities: Shaping the future of teacher development. *Journal of Teacher Education, 51*(3), 221–227. doi:10.1177/0022487100051003010

Nicholson, S. A., & Bond, N. (2003). Collaborative reflection and professional community building: An analysis of preservice teachers' use of an electronic discussion board. *Journal of Technology and Teacher Education, 11*(2), 259–279.

Preece, J. (2002). Supporting community and building social capital. *Communications of the ACM, 45*(4), 37–39. doi:10.1145/505248.505269

Scribner, P. (1999). Professional development: Untangling the influence of work context on teacher learning. *Educational Administration Quarterly, 35*(2), 238–266.

Wenger, E. (1998). *Communities of practice: Learning, meaning and identity*. Cambridge, UK: Cambridge University Press.

Wenger, E., McDermott, R., & Snyder, W. M. (2002). *Cultivating communities of practice*. Boston, MA: Harvard University Press.

KEY TERMS AND DEFINITIONS

Online Communities: Social aggregations that emerge from the Internet technology; people in such groups share information, emotions, and advice.

Teacher Knowledge: Knowledge that teachers need to understand in order to provide appropriate guidance to students in classrooms.

Emotions: Feelings or physiological changes deriving from interactions with people or environments.

Informal Learning: Knowledge acquisition outside of formal education environments, including home or work place.

Teacher Professional Development: Formal teacher trainings designed to help teachers update knowledge and reflect on classroom teaching.

Blog (Weblog): A website that individual or group of people share opinions, information, and/or multimedia data.

Content Analysis: A research method that examines the content of communications or words (phrases) within texts.

ENDNOTES

[1] LiveJournal provides a mood function in which a user can select his or her current mood, such as angry, crazy, excited, and frustrated.

[2] LiveJournal provides a posting function called Create a Poll in which members can conduct a one-question survey with multiple choice and/or open-ended answers.

Section 5
Cases and Research in the Workplace

Chapter 14
Twitter–Based Knowledge Sharing in Professional Networks:
The Organization Perspective

Vanessa P. Dennen
Florida State University, USA

Wenting Jiang
Florida State University, USA

ABSTRACT

Social media provides professional organizations with a new means of distributing information and perhaps even facilitating learning among their members. This study compares Twitter use in two populations, academics and corporate professionals, and in two interaction contexts, conference and non-conference, looking at how knowledge is shared by organizations. Organizations in three fields—nursing, information technology, and educational technology—were included in the study. A content analysis showed that both types of organizations focused more on supplying original content than providing links or retweets. Conferences generated the greatest activity levels and industry organizations were more savvy with Twitter use, although on the whole hashtags were underutilized and much room remains to maximize use of social media. Nonetheless, a wealth of knowledge sharing that can support information learning and professional development is taking place in these online networks.

DOI: 10.4018/978-1-4666-1815-2.ch014

INTRODUCTION

Learning how to succeed in a career requires more than just earning a degree from an institution of higher education. Post-degree learning experiences may include employer-based training; discipline-based workshops, seminars, and continuing education courses; and a wide range of less formal experiences including mentoring, networking, and attending conferences. These ongoing learning experiences range from those that are highly regulated and organized to those that are more likely to be user-driven, just-in-time, and individualized.

Professional organizations are one source of support for career-based learning. Professional organizations often face the challenge of meeting the diverse needs of a dispersed membership. Although annual meetings and local chapters long have been used to bring together members in a face-to-face setting for professional interactions, increasingly new communication technologies such as Twitter are being used to help support interactions and communication, both between the organization and its members and among its members. In this chapter, we compare the cases of six different professional organizations and how they used Twitter to support professional communication with their membership over a six-month period, inclusive of their annual conference.

BACKGROUND

Traditional professional development has been didactic in nature, focused on disseminating knowledge to individuals. However, a paradigm shift may be in order, including increased efforts to provide professional learning opportunities that can be blended with authentic practice (Webster-Wright, 2009). In some ways, this trending toward embedded and embodied learning is not new, but rather represents a new respect and support for types of informal professional learning that have long occurred to meet the on-the-job needs of individuals.

Professional networks support a great deal of workplace and professional-oriented learning. On the local and more informal end, these networks may be as simple as a group of peers—either within one institution or representing different ones—with similar jobs who can contact each other as needed for learning, sharing, and support. However, larger professional networks may be formed either by individuals who mine their professional connections with an explicit intent to grow a network or by formal professional organizations whose purpose is to support continued learning and networking.

The impact of professional networks on the success of their members is a well-studied area. For example, successful university faculty are likely to interact regularly with and seek counsel from their colleagues (Hitchcock, Bland, Hekelman, & Blumenthal, 1995). Physicians, who often avoid the Internet in a professional capacity due to risks of lawsuits, can benefit from professional interactions and networking with colleagues in closed online communities (Hyman, Luks, & Sechrest). Online networks have the potential of connecting medical professionals with similar specialties across geographical boundaries which may ultimately result in better professional development for them as well as better care for their patients (Prasanna, Seagull, & Nagy, 2011).

Part of the reason why professional networks can have such an impact on member success is because they serve as informal knowledge hubs. Lam (2000) notes that professional knowledge may be individual or collective, and explicit or tacit. Each of these types of knowledge may be learned and transmitted in different ways within an organization—embrained, embodied, encoded, and embedded—with the tacit forms being most effectively transmitted via community or networks. With this in mind, participating in a combination of internal (within institution or company) and external (within field at large) networks may be desirable, with each enhancing the other and allowing the influx and outflow of new ideas with internal encouragement and support to try these new ideas (Morris, 2003).

However, professional networks are not a panacea for individuals who need knowledge and support, and studies of their impact in members' lives have yielded conflicting results. In one study, nurse managers indicated that their professional networks did not help them in dealing with management-related issues (Lindholm, Dejin-Karlsson, Östergren, & Udén, 2003). In another, nurse managers cited a professional network as critical to helping them adjust to their position and gain support from peers (Lindholm, 1999). To reconcile these conflicting results, it is worth noting that the two purposes cited for the networks—to deal with management issues and to adjust to a new position—may not have much in common. Further, individuals may have very different expectations and experiences within a network and networks can be as unique as the individuals who participate in them.

Learning within Professional Organizations

Professional organizations provide the core for a structured type of professional network. They combine formal professional development opportunities and official organization communications with the ability to network with other members. Table 1 compares three main types of networks that support professional learning and development.

Whereas informal networks tend to be user-driven and use a bottom-up approach to support network activities, professional organizations must find top-down ways of meeting their membership's needs. Bowes (2002) indicated the value of having structured activities for a professional network to thrive. She further notes how important the choice of communication technology is, in particular considering ease of use for the network's members and the value of having push technologies.

Ozgen and Baron (2007) studied mentors, informal networks, and participation in professional development opportunities (e.g., seminars) to see if there were differences in information

Table 1. Networks types that support professional learning and development

Type of Network	Individual Social/Professional Network	Informal Social/Professional Network	Professional Organization
Example	A person and their connections on LinkedIn	An open interest group on LinkedIn	A group with clear leadership structure and formal membership process
How it Works	Use one's own personal contacts to find individuals who might help or provide support or connections	Join a group of people with a self-identified interest on a topic and lurk or seek interactions as needed	Join a formal group and partake in their formal (conference, seminars, journals, etc.) and informal (membership networking) opportunities
Key Strengths	Ability to use personal connections to facilitate sharing	Ability to reach out to people not in an immediate social network; potential to add new people to individual social network	Ability to more passively benefit from organized activities and communications in addition to the ability to engage with other members; potential to add new people to individual social network

Table 2. Twitter features and terminology

Twitter Feature	Brief Description	Example
Tweet	A twitter message constructed of 140 characters or less, inclusive of all features described below.	This message could be a brief tweet
@mention	A tweet that includes a twitter username preceded by the @ symbol, which makes the tweet show up in that user's feed.	This message could be a brief tweet from @vanessadennen
@reply	A tweet that begins with a twitter username preceded by the @ symbol indicating that the tweet is directed at that person.	@wentingjiang this tweet is to you
Hashtag (#)	A marker that can be inserted into a tweet to allow it to be searched/aggregated along with other tweets containing the same mark. Users may self-designate a tag by putting any desired characters after the pound (#) sign.	This message could be a brief tweet #random
Retweet (RT)	Resending someone else's tweet, much like forwarding an email. The tweet then begins with RT and a reference to the person who previously tweeted it.	RT @vanessadennen This message could be a brief tweet

flow and thus an impact on opportunities found by individuals. All three were found to be useful, but interestingly degree of participation in informal social networks was found to be related to degree of self-efficacy, essentially suggesting that people who are active in forming social networks also believe highly in their own ability to achieve their goals. In this finding there is perhaps a bit of a self-fulfilling prophecy; as social networks increase, so do the chances of finding opportunities. Thus, professional organizations may wish to foster informal online networking opportunities for their members.

Twitter and Professional Development Networks

Twitter (twitter.com) is an online microblogging service that enables users to send messages of up to 140 characters. It provides an easy way for people to communicate with each other by broadcasting their status and opinions as well as to share text-based content and links. Table 2 provides an overview of Twitter terminology

and communication features. Even photos can be shared easily with facilitation through a third-party application such as twitpic (twitpic.com) or yfrog (yfrog.com).

Twitter users build and support individual networks as they post and read messages. Each user can select other users she wishes to "follow" and the messages written by those users will show up aggregated in her feed. Then those users may choose to reciprocate and follow her as well. Reciprocal following via Twitter is not automatic, and some Twitter users may maintain a private profile that requires approval for following.

Twitter use has become widespread. Per surveys done by the Pew Internet & American Life Project, between November 2010 and May 2011 Twitter use by adults who are online increased from 8% to 13% (Smith, 2011). These numbers can be somewhat deceiving, however, because not all people who have Twitter accounts are regular users. Another survey by the same project found that although approximately one-third of all users check in with Twitter daily, a larger percentage

(41%) checks in sporadically at best (Smith & Rainie, 2010). That same survey showed a potential connection between Twitter and work: 62% of their respondents indicated tweeting about work.

It is now commonplace for professional organizations and conferences to promote tweeting both at the organizational level (messages from organization to members via organization account) as well as at the membership level (messages among members via organization hashtags). The latter form of tweeting requires a means of aggregation, which for Twitter would be a hashtag (see Table 2 for a definition and example). Hashtags may be initiated and promoted by the organization, or may be elected by members who simply start using them and encouraging those in their Twitter network to do likewise. They have been found to effectively enable people within a profession to find relevant information (Letierce, Passant, Decker, & Breslin, 2010).

However, Twitter can be a very inward-looking technology. The brief nature of tweets has been criticized as useless for sharing meaningful information, and Twitter is far better known as a platform for celebrities, citizen journalists, and random navel-gazing than it is as a professional development platform. As noted by Dann (2010), Twitter communication can be lexically diverse, with tweets containing conversation, status updates, new, endorsements, and phatic elements.

Research on Twitter use in professional networks has shown that relatively little that is posted may be of use to others (Ebner, et al., 2010; Suh, Hong, Convertino, & Chi, 2010), reflecting both a tendency for individuals to use it for personal note-taking rather than for knowledge sharing with others (Naaman, Boase, & Lai, 2010) as well as the cryptic nature of some messages due to the character limit. Combating these issues, a study of conference hashtag use showed that contributors both included non-attendees who wished to engage in information exchange and made heavy use of URLs, linking to information resources (Dennen, 2011). Additionally, proponents of Twitter like

Boss (2008) claim that people can learn and gain ideas related to professional practice by observing the Twitter feeds of other—particularly more experienced—people in their field.

Purpose and Context of the Study

The purpose of this study is to examine how Twitter is being used by professional organizations in two contexts. The first context is during an annual conference, which has been shown to have potential benefits for both organizations and attendees and which constitutes three phases: pre, during, and post-conference (Dennen, 2011; Reinhardt, Ebner, Beham, & Costa, 2009). Previous studies have examined how Twitter can form a backchannel at conferences, networking users in a discussion of a wide variety of issues related to the conference while the official events are taking place (Ross, Terras, Warwick, & Welsh, 2011). However, the role of the organization in conference tweeting has not been explored.

The second context is everyday, non-conference use. In other words, this second context represents how an organization tweets as part of their regular activities. Social media provides an outlet for organizations to not only promote themselves, but also to share information and connect with their membership. An organization could potentially serve as a knowledge broker or hub for its members throughout the year.

Additionally, we chose to look at two different types of professional organizations: academic and industry. The reasons for making this distinction were based on our own informal observations while attending conferences and observing conference twitter feeds. It seemed to us that industry organizations were more savvy users of the technology than academic ones, perhaps because mobile devices are more likely to be employer-supplied and actively used in the service of work for those employees. By comparing both types of organizations, we are able to see if those initial perceptions are accurate.

This research is important because noting ways in which organizations are both successful and unsuccessful at using the medium can help the organizational learning process. Through this research, we strive to identify ways in which organizations might optimize their use of Twitter within both contexts.

The research questions that guided this study are:

1. Do academic professional organizations use Twitter differently from industry ones? In what ways?
2. Do professional organizations use Twitter differently during conferences? In what ways?
3. In what ways are professional organizations using Twitter to promote knowledge sharing?
4. How might the signal-to-noise ratio on a particular feed impact potential followers and contributors?

These questions were explored via structural and content analysis of professional organization Twitter feeds.

METHOD

Sample

For this study, we selected Twitter feeds from six professional organizations, three representing academe and three representing industry. We also sampled from three different fields of practice: educational technology, information technology, and nursing. These fields were selected because it was possible to find both academic and industry organizations that engaged in tweeting.

For each organization, we sampled six months worth of tweets. All tweets were from 2010 and 2011. We anchored each sample around the organization's annual conference, so each sample chronologically represented three months of regu-

lar tweeting, followed by the meeting, and then an additional three months of regular tweeting.

Data Analysis

Data analysis was a multi-stage process. First, we separated out the tweets by time, resulting in about three months of pre-conference tweets, three months of post-conference tweets, and the conference tweets. Then, we coded all tweets for evidence of structural features (retweets, @replies, hashtags, and URLs) and noted the frequency of these features by organization and time period. These structural features provide evidence of the different types of content the organization was providing as well as the ways in which the organization was potentially reaching individual users. Finally, we coded all of the tweets for content using the categories shown in Table 3. These categories were based on an initial review of tweet content. Frequencies were calculated for all codes.

FINDINGS

Activity Level

Overall Twitter activity levels ranged from a low of 48 tweets to a high of 678 tweets. In both educational technology and information technology, the industry organizations were more active on Twitter than the academic ones (see Table 4). For nursing, that trend was reversed, but the difference in rate of posting was not as great. Further, all three industry organizations and the nursing-academic one were posting at an average rate of 2-3 tweets per day, whereas the other two were posting far less frequently than daily.

Overall Structural Elements

Retweets were not a commonly used feature among the different organizations (see Table 5). Only the educational technology-industry group

Table 3. Content coding categories

Content element	Description
Announcement	Announcement of an event or service
Information Sharing	Providing non-announcement information either within the body of a tweet or via a URL
Phatic	A message that lacks real content but may convey a general greeting or sentiment
Conversation	Directed at a particular person, part of a discursive exchange of messages

Table 4. Total tweets per organization

Field	Academic	Industry
Educational Technology	48	433
Information Technology	63	581
Nursing	708	587

Table 5. Summary of structural feature use by organization

Element	Ed Tech - Academic	Ed Tech - Industry	Info Tech– Academic	Info Tech – Industry	Nursing – Academic	Nursing - Industry
Retweet	0 (0%)	120 (28%)	0 (0%)	21 (4%)	14 (2%)	36 (6%)
@reply	0 (0%)	152 (35%)	0 (0%)	311 (54%)	234 (35%)	242 (41%)
URL	39 (81%)	226 (52%)	20 (32%)	329 (57%)	529 (78%)	270 (46%)
Hashtag	12 (25%)	233 (54%)	50 (80%)	252 (43%)	328 (48%)	94 (16%)
Overall Tweets	48	433	63	581	678	587

sent them with any regularity, constituting around one-quarter of their messages, and two organizations did not use this feature at all. @replies were present in one-third to one-half of the tweets sent by the four more active organizations, whereas once again the educational technology and information technology academic organizations did not use these features at all.

URLs were quite popular among all organizations, included in 38-81% of all tweets across the organizations (See Table 5). Hashtag use was less consistent, with frequencies ranging from 16-86%. It is, however, worth noting that the organization with the lowest percentage of tweets with hashtags (nursing-industry) was also the second most active

organization, and 16% of their tweets are still more than the overall number of tweets for two of the organizations.

Structural Trends by Time Period

Looking at the trends over time, in three-month blocks with the annual conference in the middle, it becomes apparent that Twitter activity tends to be greater in the months immediately preceding a conference than in the months immediately following it (see Table 6). This finding makes sense upon reviewing the content of the Twitter feeds since conference-related announcements are sent out during the weeks leading up to the event.

Table 6. Summary of structural feature use by time period and type of organization

	Academic			Industry		
	Pre-Conf	**Conference**	**Post-Conf**	**Pre-Conf**	**Conference**	**Post-Conf**
Tweets	402 (49%)	56 (7%)	361 (44%)	843 (54%)	144 (9%)	564 (36%)
Ed Tech	20	6	22	225	37	171
Info Tech	8	46	9	281	101	149
Nursing	374	4	330	337	6	244
Retweet aggregate	5 (1%)	0 (0%)	9 (2%)	74 (9%)	29 (20%)	46 (8%)
Ed Tech	0 (0%)	0 (0%)	0 (0%)	37 (16%)	23 (62%)	30 (18%)
Info Tech	0 (0%)	0 (0%)	0 (0%)	12 (4%)	5 (5%)	4 (3%)
Nursing	5 (13%)	0 (0%)	9 (3%)	25 (7%)	1 (17%)	12 (5%)
@reply aggregate	118 (29%)	2 (5%)	114 (32%)	364 (43%)	91 (63%)	450 (80%)
Ed Tech	0 (0%)	0 (0%)	0 (0%)	70 (31%)	28 (76%)	54 (32%)
Info Tech	0 (0%)	0 (0%)	0 (0%)	189 (67%)	59 (58%)	63 (42%)
Nursing	118 (32%)	2 (50%)	114 (35%)	105 (31%)	4 (67%)	133 (55%)
URL aggregate	320 (80%)	10 (18%)	262 (73%)	462 (55%)	66 (46%)	405 (76%)
Ed Tech	20 (100%)	0 (0%)	19 (86%)	178 (79%)	13 (35%)	143 (84%)
Info Tech	8 (100%)	6 (13%)	6 (67%)	155 (55%)	50 (50%)	124 (83%)
Nursing	288 (77%)	4 (100%)	237 (72%)	129 (38%)	3 (50%)	138 (57%)
Hashtag aggregate	168 (42%)	46 (82%)	180 (50%)	350 (42%)	109 (76%)	120 (21%)
Ed Tech	2 (10%)	6 (100%)	4 (18%)	165 (73%)	33 (89%)	35 (20%)
Info Tech	8 (100%)	37 (80%)	5 (56%)	122 (43%)	74 (73%)	56 (38%)
Nursing	154 (41%)	3 (75%)	171 (52%)	63 (19%)	2 (33%)	29 (12%)

Noting that the pre and post conference periods each account for about 49% of the overall time, with the conferences (averaging 4 days in length) accounting for 2% of the time, it also becomes apparent that Twitter activity (in terms of tweets/day) tends to be greater during a conference. However, this finding did not hold true across all organizations. Whereas the information technology-academic organization did most of their tweeting during the annual conference, both nursing organizations had lower than typical rates of tweeting during their conference period.

Hashtag use typically increased during the conference period, with the highest percentage of use occurring during the conference in five of the organizations; in the remaining organization,

hashtag use was still high. The hashtags that were used during the conference period were either the standard hashtag for the organization or the one that was being used specifically to aggregate conference-related tweets.

Message Content

The findings related to message content are summarized in Table 7. The only commonalities shared among all of the organizations were low rates of sharing information directly within the body of a tweet and phatic messages, usually in the form of social greetings, via Twitter. Phatic messages represented only 13 tweets across the organizations, which is not surprising. Such tweets may

Table 7. Summary of message content

Content	Ed Tech – Academic	Ed Tech – Industry	Info Tech– Academic	Info Tech – Industry	Nursing – Academic	Nursing – Industry
Announce event	10 (21%)	58 (13%)	54 (86%)	47 (8%)	133 (20%)	137 (23%)
Share info in tweet	3 (6%)	51 (12%)	0 (0%)	7 (1%)	24 (4%)	4 (.7%)
Share info via URL	35 (73%)	306 (71%)	9 (14%)	282 (49%)	396 (58%)	133 (23%)
Phatic	1 (2%)	4 (1%)	0 (0%)	3 (.5%)	0 (0%)	5 (.9%)
Conversation	0 (0%)	14 (3%)	0 (0%)	242 (42%)	201 (30%)	307 (52%)

express a nice sentiment (e.g., Have a great conference!) but are neither substantive nor responsive to an information need. However, conversational use of Twitter was strikingly different across the organizations, with three organizations regularly engaging discussion-like tweets with other Twitter users and two not using Twitter in this manner at all.

Twitter use to announce events ranged between 8-23% in all but one organization, and that organization (information technology-academic) used their Twitter feed almost exclusively to announce events. In terms of meeting information needs, tweets with self-contained information were far less common than tweets that shared basic information and a URL leading to additional information.

When examining the content trends over the different time periods, organizations proved themselves to be rather consistent. In other words, if the person controlling the organization account was conversational during the pre-conference months, he was also conversational during the conference and post-conference.

Overall Organization Characterizations

In addition to being coded for structural and content elements, which allow for simple comparison across organizations, each organization's Twitter feed was examined more holistically to generate a synthesized description of the organization's approach to using Twitter.

Educational Technology: Academic

This organization trended toward posting announcements about accomplishments of the organization and its members. Links were used liberally, leading to longer news stories about these accomplishments. To a lesser degree, this organization shared and linked to information about special events and opportunities that were potentially of interest to the membership. There was no evidence of actual engagement with the membership; instead, Twitter was being used as a unidirectional means of transmitting information.

Educational Technology: Industry

This organization made common practice of sharing stories published online elsewhere as well as brief sayings and quotes. Often these stories and quotes were retweeted content. Many tweets contained the conference and/or organization name as a hashtag, providing an additional way of reaching their audience. The person running this account truly engaged with members who tweeted. For example, one post was a reply to someone who tweeted about a safe arrival at the conference.

Information Technology: Academic

This organization used Twitter in a manner that was entirely different from all of the others. Their primary use was to make announcements about and during their conference, and they included hashtags on these announcements, ensuring that the tweets would show up in the larger conference feed. Additionally, although far less frequently, this organization used Twitter to provide links to organization-related information.

Information Technology: Industry

This organization used Twitter to respond to personal queries from individuals, greeting them by name as well as using the @reply function. These response messages ranged in content from providing information about deadlines to comments about the weather and hotel rooms. They were interspersed among links to news stories and, to a lesser degree, announcements about the organization's events. This feed in particular had the feel that it was being authored by a person rather than by an organization.

Nursing: Academic

This organization was heavily self-promotional in their tweets. The feed also was used to respond to questions, such as what might be suitable for a proposal. All conversation-like transactions were very businesslike, with little personality shining through. That said, all of the information shared via this tweet had a decidedly upbeat feel to it.

Nursing: Industry

This organization frequently shared factoids and news stories on their feed. Additionally, the person running the feed was very personable when engaged in conversation with followers, complimenting them and thanking them for their suggestions. Giveaways were also promoted with winners announced via Twitter.

DISCUSSION

Although the industry organizations were consistently active on Twitter and the academic ones were not nearly as active, with a sample of six organizations it would be inappropriate to generalize that industry makes greater use of Twitter than higher education. However, there are some points worth noting about the overall trends. The two academic organizations that were not making heavy use of Twitter were both in technology disciplines, and it would seem logical for their memberships to be active on Twitter, if not the organization as well. However, this finding confirms our initial impressions prior to undertaking this study: We had noted that while industry organizations in our field had an active Twitter presence during their conferences our academic conferences had a comparably paltry level of activity.

Similarly, two of the academic organizations did not use two Twitter features, retweets and @replies, at all. Both of these features provide indicators that the Twitter user is aware of and following other users. In fact, this area represents a major difference in how the organizations used Twitter to serve and engage with their membership. They ranged on a continuum from uni-directional communication (posting information but never engaging with individuals) to multi-directional, conversational communication (engaging in both professional and social discourse with other Twitter users). These differences in engagement may have an impact on how the membership perceives and values the organization's electronic offerings.

Overall, the organizations were more focused on sending out unique messages than sharing messages from other sources. A variety of factors may have contributed to this trend. First, it is possible that the organizations believed that original content was more important and would better convey their value to their membership. In other words, the person controlling the organization's social media presence may have feared to some degree that acting as a conduit of information from various external sources would give the perception that the organization was not offering unique information and services. However, the heavy use of URLs seems to somewhat contradict this assertion, since many URLs do lead to non-organization Web sites (e.g., news, member, and government sites).

There is an alternate explanation for this phenomenon. Some of the organizations may have been treating Twitter primarily as a one-way form of communication rather than a network form of communication. In such a scenario, the person responsible for sending out tweets may not have been following other Twitter feeds and thus would have been unaware of relevant items that could be retweeted.

Returning to the topic of URLs, they clearly play a very important role in organizational Twitter use. In some ways, it appears that much of the information that people expect to be sent out to members via a listserv or posted to a web site is now also being tweeted. However, the character limitations of Twitter means that it is not used to supply the full information, but rather to give a pointer to the information. This type of Twitter use is what Dann (2010) calls pass along, and it is part of being both a content provider and, when the URL is from another source or the message is retweeted, an endorser. Thus, organizations should keep in mind that the value of Twitter is not just in the power of what can be stated in 140 characters or less, but in what can be shared or pointed at in 140 characters or less.

The organizations that did not use retweets or @replies had fairly streamlined and focused feeds, whereas the others had feeds that interspersed multiple message types and Twitter features. In the latter case, some messages were directed at the membership at large and others were directed at individuals. Taking the perspective of a member-follower, in terms of signal-to-noise ratio the more streamlined feeds may seem to have some distinct advantages. However, if one can look past the odd tweet that seems irrelevant or directed at someone else, the robust, multi-function feeds probably have more to offer in terms of informal learning and professional development.

Implications for Practice

These findings, and the contrast between the cases, shows how social media use often just evolves in a natural manner within an organization. Across the cases, there are various examples of how Twitter might be used, but ultimately each organization needs to determine what type of Twitter presence they desire. For example, will the organization control their Twitter network, or will they encourage members to help build the network? And does the organization wish to have uni- or multi-directional communication with its members? With myriad options for engaging with other people and sharing knowledge online, individual users may find their information and interaction needs met outside the organization. If an organization wants to maximize their value to their membership and knows that the membership is on Twitter, then using Twitter in a multi-directional manner and trying to foster community interaction may be a good idea.

An organization could potentially serve as a knowledge broker or hub for its members throughout the year. The flow of information need not be one way, from organization to members, but rather could be user-driven with a common hashtag. Alternately, if the organization were enterprising enough to mine the Web and other Twitter feeds (including member Twitter feeds) for items of interest to its membership, it could serve as an information conduit.

If we consider Twitter to be primarily an information medium and secondarily a social one, at least from the organizational perspective, then hashtag use might be more important than these organizations currently realize. Aside from when retweeting, none of the organizations studied used hashtags that were not directly related to the organization. That choice may be a limiting one. Hashtags not only serve the purpose of bringing together people who belong to an organization, but also can bring together messages on a common topic. By participating in other relevant hashtag networks, the organization might be able to bring both new ideas to the membership and new members to the organization.

In summary, to maintain both an active feed and an active network, organizations should consider setting Twitter guidelines for themselves regarding:

- Frequency of messages;
- Types of messages, and perhaps aspirational frequency for each type;
- Level of formality and conversation;
- Who to follow (users and hashtags) and perhaps retweet; and
- Use of organization-oriented and other hashtags.

CONCLUSION

The six organizations examined in this study each paint a different picture of Twitter use. None is inherently better or worse, but rather they represent different approaches and yield different results. The more active and conversational networks seem more likely to foster informal learning and professional development via their Twitter feeds than the strictly information-oriented feeds. However, those information-oriented feeds may nonetheless play a role in their member's professional development by alerting them to opportunities and important updates related to the field.

In response to our first research question, we cannot make any conclusive statement about differences in how academic and industry organizations use Twitter. We can, however, say with certainty that there is great variance in how organizations in general use Twitter to communicate with their membership. There are a number of factors that likely contribute to these differences, including the organization's reason for using Twitter (to communicate *with* or *to* their members) and the degree to which their members are using Twitter.

The answer to our second question confirmed that Twitter use does look different during a conference period, if for no reason other than a change (typically an increase) in level of activity. Conferences typically also represent a time when individual members are more likely to come together via a hashtag and engage in collective discourse. For an organization with a conversational Twitter presence, the conference period should be considered a prime time for not only face-to-face networking but also for building the organization's online network. If members see during the conference how useful the organization's Twitter-based network (both their controlled feed as well as the network of users they can bring together with a common hashtag), they may be more likely to continue to participate in the network on an ongoing basis.

Our third question was about how knowledge sharing was manifested via an organization's Twitter network. Across the six cases, many different types of knowledge sharing were observed. Explicit knowledge was shared in a pass along or information dissemination capacity, but some organizations engaged in open discourse with members about profession-related (and particularly organization-related) topics. This latter type of knowledge sharing is one that should be further explored, along with its capacity to be fostered more broadly and frequently via hashtag use. Of course, that supposes that the membership of a given organization has both the will and the means to be active contributors to such a network.

Finally, we asked about the signal-to-noise ratio on Twitter. As Honeycutt and Herring (2009) note, when a Twitter feed contains a lot of irrelevant (to an individual user) messages among the relevant ones, the feed becomes difficult to follow. Thus, this question brings to bear two sub-questions, neither of which could be directly addressed in this content analysis: First, what is relevant to a typical member? And second, how many extraneous messages will people be willing to pass over to read the relevant ones? Indirectly addressing these questions, we note that during our analysis, we did not find it overly difficult to follow the overall feed even when we lacked the context for understanding personal replies to individual users. Organization messages remained on relevant topics, and even seemingly social or off-topic messages such as those about weather or travel were nonetheless relevant in context (e.g., talking about conference conditions). Further, as noted by Chen (2011), Twitter fulfills a general need that people have for human connection. It is possible that these 'noisy' personal exchanges that may not be relevant to all followers still serve a purpose in that they indicate the promise of personal interaction fulfilled if it is sought.

In closing, we believe that Twitter use by professional organizations will continue to grow in both contexts, at conferences and in support of general organizational communication. Many organizations are just scratching the surface in terms of how they might serve members via Twitter, particularly in support of informal learning and ongoing professional development. With careful attention and planning, organizational leadership might foster an ongoing Twitter presence for its membership. However, the development of a robust organization-based Twitter network is not dependent solely on the organization's actions alone; the membership must be ready and interested in using Twitter to support informal learning and professional development as well.

REFERENCES

Boss, S. (2008). *Twittering, not frittering: Professional development in 140 characters*. Retrieved from http://www.edutopia.org/twitter-professional-development-technology-microblogging.

Bowes, J. (2002). Buliding online communities for professional networks. *Global Summit 2002*. Retrieved from http://www.educationau.edu.au/globalsummit/papers/jbowes.htm.

Chen, G. M. (2011). Tweet this: A uses and gratifications perspective on how active Twitter use gratifies a need to connect with others. *Computers in Human Behavior, 27*(2), 755–762. doi:10.1016/j.chb.2010.10.023

Dann, S. (2010). Twitter content classification. *First Monday, 15*(12). Retrieved from http://frodo.lib.uic.edu/ojsjournals/index.php/fm/article/view/2745/2681

Dennen, V. P. (2011). *Conversations on the hashtag: Does conference Twitter use promote professional discourse?* Paper presented at the International Conference on the e-Society. Avila, Spain.

Ebner, M., Mühlburger, H., Schaffert, S., Schiefner, M., Reinhardt, W., & Wheeler, S. (2010). Getting granular on Twitter: Tweets from a conference and their limited usefulness for non-participants. In Reynolds, N., & Turcsányi-Szabó, M. (Eds.), *Key Competencies in the Knowledge Society* (*Vol. 324*, pp. 102–113). Boston, MA: Springer. doi:10.1007/978-3-642-15378-5_10

Hitchcock, M. A., Bland, C. J., Hekelman, F. P., & Blumenthal, M. G. (1995). Professional networks: The influence of colleagues on the academic success of faculty. *Academic Medicine: Journal of the Association of American Medical Colleges, 70*(12), 1108–1116. doi:10.1097/00001888-199512000-00014

Honey, C., & Herring, S. C. (2009). *Beyond microblogging: Conversation and collaboration via Twitter.* Paper presented at the 42nd Hawaii International Conference on System Sciences. Hawaii, HI.

Hyman, J., Luks, H., & Sechrest, R. (2011). Online professional networks for physicians: Risk management. *Clinical Orthopaedics and Related Research.* Retrieved from http://www.springerlink.com/content/q353mj5425106452/fulltext.pdf.

Lam, A. (2000). Tacit knowledge, organizational learning and societal institutions: An integrated framework. *Organization Studies*, *21*(3), 487–513. doi:10.1177/0170840600213001

Letierce, J., Passant, A., Decker, S., & Breslin, J. G. (2010). *Understanding how Twitter is used to spread scientific messages.* Paper presented at the Web Science Conference 2010. Raleigh, NC.

Lindholm, M. (1999). Influence of nursing management education in changing organizations. *The Journal of Nursing Administration*, *29*, 49–56. doi:10.1097/00005110-199910000-00010

Lindholm, M., Dejin-Karlsson, E., Östergren, P. O., & Udén, G. (2003). Nurse managers' professional networks, psychosocial resources and self-rated health. *Journal of Advanced Nursing*, *42*(5), 506–515. doi:10.1046/j.1365-2648.2003.02650.x

Morris, M. (2003). Professional development that works: The power of two: Linking external with internal teachers' professional development. *Phi Delta Kappan*, *84*(10), 764.

Naaman, M., Boase, J., & Lai, C.-H. (2010). *Is it really about me? Message content in social awareness streams.* Paper presented at the 2010 ACM Conference on Computer Supported Cooperative Work. Savannah, GA.

Ozgen, E., & Baron, R. A. (2007). Social sources of information in opportunity recognition: Effects of mentors, industry networks, and professional forums. *Journal of Business Venturing*, *22*(2), 174–192. doi:10.1016/j.jbusvent.2005.12.001

Prasanna, P.M., Seagull, F., & Nagy, P. (2011). Online social networking: A primer for radiology. *Journal of Digital Imaging*, *24*(5), 908–912. doi:10.1007/s10278-011-9371-4

Reinhardt, W., Ebner, M., Beham, G., & Costa, C. (2009). How people are using Twitter during conferences. In Hornung-Prähauser, V., & Luckmann, M. (Eds.), *Creativity and Innovation Competencies on the Web* (pp. 145–156). Salzburg, Austria: EduMedia/Salzburg Research.

Ross, C., Terras, M., Warwick, C., & Welsh, A. (2011). Enabled backchannel: Conference Twitter use by digital humanists. *The Journal of Documentation*, *67*(2), 214–237. doi:10.1108/00220411111109449

Smith, A. (2011). *13% of online adults use Twitter*. Retrieved from http://pewinternet.org/Reports/2011/Twitter-Update-2011.aspx.

Smith, A., & Rainie, L. (2010). *8% of online Americans use Twitter*. Retrieved from http://pewinternet.org/Reports/2010/Twitter-update-2010.aspx.

Suh, B., Hong, L., Convertino, G., & Chi, E. H. (2010). *Sensemaking with Tweeting: Exploiting microblogging for knowledge workers.* Paper presented at the ACM Conference on Human Factors in Computing Systems. Atlanta, GA.

Webster-Wright, A. (2009). Reframing professional development through understanding authentic professional learning. *Review of Educational Research*, *79*(2), 702–739. doi:10.3102/0034654308330970

ADDITIONAL READING

boyd, d., Golder, S., & Lotan, G. (2010). Tweet, tweet, retweet: Conversational aspects of retweeting on Twitter. In *Proceedings of the 43rd Hawaii International Conference on System Sciences*. Kauai, HI: IEEE Press. Retrieved from http://ieeexplore.ieee.org/stamp/stamp.jsp?tp=&arnumber=5428313.

Diaz Ortiz, C. (2011). *Twitter for good: Change the world one tweet at a time*. San Francisco, CA: Jossey-Bass.

Dunlap, J. C., & Lowenthal, P. R. (2009). Tweeting the night away: Using Twitter to enhance social presence. *Journal of Information Systems Education, 20*(2), 129–136.

Huang, J., Thornton, K. M., & Efthimiadis, E. N. (2010). *Conversational tagging in Twitter*. Paper presented at the 21st ACM Conference on Hypertext and Hypermedia. Toronto, Canada.

Jacobs, N., & McFarlane, A. (2005). Conferences as learning communities: Some early lessons in using 'back-channel' technologies at an academic conference – Distributed intelligence or divided attention? *Journal of Computer Assisted Learning, 21*(5), 317–329. doi:10.1111/j.1365-2729.2005.00142.x

Kwak, H., Lee, C., Park, H., & Moon, S. (2010). *What is Twitter? A social network or a news media?* Paper presented at the 19th International Conference on World Wide Web. Raleigh, NC.

Lenhart, A., & Fox, S. (2009). Twitter and status updating. *Pew Internet & American Life Projects*. Retrieved July 10, 2010, from http://www.pewinternet.org/~/media//Files/Reports/2009/PIP%20Twitter%20Memo%20FINAL.pdf.

McCarthy, J. F., & boyd, d. m. (2005). *Digital backchannels in shared physical spaces: Experiences at an academic conference*. Paper presented at CHI 2005 Conference on Human Factors in Computing Systems. Portland, OR.

Sullivan, L. E. (2009). *Twitter*. Newbury Park, CA: Sage Publications.

Wagner, C. (2010). Exploring the wisdom of the tweets: Towards knowledge acquisition from social awareness streams. In Aroyo, L., Antoniou, G., Hyvönen, E., ten Teije, A., Stuckenschmidt, H., Cabral, L., & Tudorache, T. (Eds.), *The Semantic Web: Research and Applications* (*Vol. 6089*, pp. 493–497). Berlin, Germany: Springer. doi:10.1007/978-3-642-13489-0_50

KEY TERMS AND DEFINITIONS

@mention: A tweet that includes a twitter username preceded by the @ symbol, which makes the tweet show up in that user's feed.

@reply: A tweet that begins with a twitter username preceded by the @ symbol indicating that the tweet is directed at that person.

Aggregate: To collect a group of tweets that is related in some way.

Hashtag (#): A marker that can be inserted into a tweet to allow it to be searched/aggregated along with other tweets containing the same mark. Users may self-designate a tag by putting any desired characters after the pound (#) sign.

Retweet (RT): Resending someone else's tweet, much like forwarding an email. The tweet then begins with RT and a reference to the person who previously tweeted it.

Tweet: A twitter message constructed of 140 characters or less, inclusive of all features described below.

Twitter: A microblogging tool that permits users to send messages of 144 characters or less.

Chapter 15
Story–Based Professional Development:
Using a Conflict Management Wiki

Wayne A. Slabon
Columbus State University, USA

Randy L. Richards
St. Ambrose University, USA

ABSTRACT

In this chapter, the authors describe an initiative to create a cross-organization, knowledge building communal network built from the personal workplace stories voluntarily contributed by conflict management practitioners. They identify various wiki adoption and usage issues and provide recommendations and strategies for addressing these issues based on survey data from the wiki target member population. Moreover, the authors compare and contrast their wiki design with recommended practices from the wiki literature and provide some suggestions for future research.

INTRODUCTION

For nearly ten years, adult learners in a master's level conflict management course offered by a small private university in the Midwest have been introduced to a unique method of instruction. This instructional method was designed by Dr. Richards, the second author of this article, and has been researched by Dr. Slabon, the first author of this article. This instructional method is referred to in the literature as "learning by restorying" (Slabon, 2009).

Restorying uniquely engages learners in the rewriting and retelling of a personal, domain-relevant story based on the application of concepts, principles, strategies and techniques covered during each unit of instruction and again summarily at the end of the course. Through a five-week series of content application assignments, in-class story sharing and discussion, and a final integration paper, adult learners in the aforementioned conflict management course engaged in the restorying of a personally meaningful workplace story selected from their own, professionally relevant experience base (Slabon, 2009).

DOI: 10.4018/978-1-4666-1815-2.ch015

In March 2011, the authors of this chapter conceived of the idea to invite 250 former students who engaged in learning by restorying to co-construct a personal story-based wiki for professional development. The intent was to create a cross-organization, cross-industry knowledge-building communal network (Scardamalia & Bereiter, 2003, 2006) built from the personally meaningful, professionally relevant stories voluntarily contributed by conflict management practitioners. By providing an informal elearning space which enabled practitioners to share their real world conflict management stories along with critical insights and any unresolved issues or challenges for fellow practitioners to reflect and comment on, we believed that this wiki would have strong potential to serve its members as an ongoing professional development resource with an ever-growing inventory of professionally useful stories, insightful commentaries, and context-rich dialogue to inform member practice (Jonassen & Hernandez-Serrano, 2002; Lave & Wenger, 1991; Wenger 1998, 2000).

We noted from the instructional design and professional development literature that Schank (1990, 1999), Lave and Wegner (1991), and Schön (1993) have strongly advocated for the use of real world stories to promote problem solving skills and contextual reflection on difficult cases for all professions. Jonassen and Hernandez-Serrano (2002) have similarly asserted that "stories elicited from skilled problem solvers, indexed for the lessons they have to teach, and made available to learners in the form of case libraries can support a broader range of problem solving than any other strategy or tactic" (p. 66).

With respect to the use of wikis to promote professional growth through practitioner knowledge sharing, we looked at how wikis have been utilized in such domains as law, medicine, business, and education. Google searches produced a wealth of examples in each of these domains. For example, a list of 69 wikis devoted to the medical domain was provided on David Rothman's blog site at

http://davidrothman.net/list-of-medical-wikis/. Robert Ambrogi's (2007) "Legal Wikis Are Bound to Wow You" offered useful descriptions of how wikis are being employed to promote lawyer-to-lawyer collaboration. A business case study of wiki usage involving Dresdner Kleinwort Wasserstein, an investment bank with 6,000 employees across the world, was accessed at http://learningwith-wikis.wikispaces.com/Empirisk+grundlag. In education, the Educause web site offered wikis on a variety of topics in addition to over 130 wiki-related resources at http://www.educause.edu/Resources/Browse/Wiki/18426.

While we thought that a real world story-based wiki might have strong potential to serve its members as an ongoing professional development resource, questions immediately arose as to the extent to which practitioners would in fact adopt and actively utilize this resource to inform their practice. Even with privacy settings and story contributor instructions to change the names of actual parties and departments and to not disclose specific information that would reveal a company's identity, it was unclear whether these working adults would readily construe an online wiki as a *safe* environment for frank and open discussion about personal workplace conflicts.

Slabon's (2009) research involved face-to-face classroom story sharing and even in that environment, a number of learners expressed some initial concerns about openly sharing and discussing a personal workplace conflict with others. These initial concerns were however promptly allayed by the instructor and other class members who effectively modeled candid disclosure, which fostered a collective perception of a safe learning environment in the classroom for story sharing and discussion. We wondered if similar, or perhaps even greater, levels of concern would arise in an online wiki environment.

In the sections that follow, we describe our wiki design, survey design, implementation method, and the results of our efforts to create a cross-organization, knowledge building communal network built from the personal workplace stories voluntarily contributed by conflict management practitioners. We identify various wiki adoption and usage issues and provide recommendations and strategies for addressing these issues based on survey data from the wiki target member population. Moreover, we compare and contrast our wiki design with recommended practices from the wiki literature and provide some suggestions for future research.

WIKI DESIGN, SURVEY DESIGN, AND WIKI IMPLEMENTATION

Wiki Design

The wiki site design consisted of a Home welcome page, a Resources page, a Search tags page, and Share your story pages. The site was created using Wikispaces. As displayed in Appendix A, the Home welcome page included an audio greeting message and photo of Dr. Richards as site host along with text that described the purpose of the wiki. It also encouraged wiki members to select and edit a Share your story page to tell wiki members about a former or current workplace conflict and to solicit creative input from others if there were unresolved issues as each conflict story page provided the opportunity for exchanging comments.

The Resources page provided a series of .mp4 audio-video screen recordings to help acclimate new wiki members to using the site and various tools. For example, one recording focused on "How to Post and Reply to Comments on Story Pages" while another demonstrated "How to Add Search Tags to Your Story Page." A third recording was entitled "How to Receive Notifications of Wiki Activity (Specific Pages or Site-Wide)." A fourth recording demonstrated "How to Create an .mp3 file using Audacity and Embed it into a Wiki page." Contact information for Dr. Slabon was provided for those who may have questions with respect to site and tool usage.

The Search tags page provided a table of story tag search terms currently being employed on the site. It was pointed out that one could enter a term in the left margin search box and click on the arrow to locate related stories on the wiki site. As displayed in Appendix B, the Share your story pages consisted of a series of partially constructed template-based wiki pages with story prompts. The prompts were provided so that contributing members would not need to create pages from scratch but could simply add content through editing to produce page content that was consistent in look and feel as other contributors.

The first prompt directed the wiki member to click on the edit button to tell about a personal workplace conflict in a couple of paragraphs. If they wanted to include an audio file along with text, the story contributing member was advised that they could upload an .mp3 file as demonstrated in Story 001 and explained under Resources. To contextualize their story, the member was encouraged to include some general organizational details such as relative size (e.g., less than or more than 500 employees) and type of organization (e.g., non-profit, educational) but not to include any specific information that would reveal the organization. The member was also advised to change the names of the conflict parties and any specific references to actual departments.

The second prompt on the Share your story pages asked the wiki member as story contributor to describe how they defined the problem space for this conflict based on what they had learned through the restorying process. The third prompt asked the wiki member as story contributor how they defined the solution space for this conflict based on what they had learned through the restorying process. It also asked the member to describe what was the main 'takeaway' from this conflict.

The fourth prompt asked the wiki member as story contributor to describe any unresolved issues or questions regarding the conflict that they would like others to consider and comment on. Each Share your story page had an embedded discussion area at page bottom to provide opportunities for wiki members to offer comments and encourage dialogue among members about any issues or challenges stemming from the personal workplace conflict story described on that wiki page.

Survey Design

To obtain data that might shed light on issues related to wiki adoption and usage, a brief survey was created by the authors. A copy of the survey has been provided in Appendix C. The survey focused on such areas as practitioner resource consultation, the likelihood of non-members joining the wiki in the future, the identification of factors contributing to their not previously accepting an invitation to join the wiki, and the identification of factors that would likely encourage them to reconsider a membership invitation. The survey also asked how the wiki membership invitation process might be improved, how the conflict management wiki site might be improved, and if there was anything else they might like to add regarding the conflict management wiki.

Wiki Implementation

Dr. Richards recorded a welcome message and contributed an initial conflict story. Dr. Slabon added a conflict story from his prior research on the restorying method. Based on what others have suggested with respect to the merits of pre-loading site content, we thought it would be useful to add a few more conflict stories to the wiki space before we invited the former students to join the wiki space. Dr. Richards contacted three former students that he knew had interesting conflict stories they would be willing to submit. The students agreed and added their own stories using the Share your story page template prompts described above.

In April 2011, approximately 250 former students who engaged in learning by restorying were invited via mass email to join the professional development wiki. This email was sent using the wikispace email application and included a welcoming message and description of the intent of the wiki from the site host, Dr. Richards. While the authors were concerned about this email being filtered out as spam by their organizations, a greater concern was not to offend the target member population through aggressive marketing and multiple email solicitations. In June 2011, a second invitation was sent to the same group. A link to the online survey was sent in July using a personal email rather than wiki site originating point.

RESULTS

Wiki Adoption

Nineteen practitioners responded to the mass mailing invitations to join the conflict management wiki.

Wiki Usage

Wiki site usage statistics indicated that wiki members initially viewed wiki site content within the first thirty days of their membership. These wiki members were not "frequent flyers." They viewed the site content posted by others only once or twice and did not post any comments in relation to the stories provided by others. Ninety days into their membership acceptance, no one had as yet contributed a personal workplace story to the conflict management wiki site beyond the five previously supplied stories.

Wiki Survey

To obtain data that might shed light on issues related to wiki adoption and usage, a brief survey was sent to the 250 individuals who were originally

Table 1. Resource consultation for unfamiliar conflict management issue

Resource	Response % and Count
Colleagues within my organization	96% (23)
Professional acquaintances outside my organization that I contact frequently and know personally	71% (17)
Materials and resources provided by professional organizations (e.g., SHRM, ASTD)	33% (8)
Materials and resources freely accessible online through Web blogs, content communities, or wikis	29% (7)
Practitioner journals, texts, and guides	25% (6)
Materials and resources provided by my organization	17% (4)
Professional acquaintances outside my organization that I infrequently contact through a networking site	17% (4)

Table 2. Reaction statements

Statement	Strongly Disagree	Disagree	Agree	Strongly Agree	N/A
I am not currently a wiki site member but am likely to join the Conflict Management wiki in the future	0%	28% (7)	36% (9)	8% (2)	28% (7)
I think the personal story-based wiki approach has potential to help me address conflict management issues and inform practice	0%	16% (4)	56% (14)	16% (4)	12% (3)
I am likely to contribute a personal workplace conflict story to the Conflict Management wiki in the future	4% (1)	56% (14)	28% (7)	8% (2)	4% (1)
I am likely to comment on a wiki member's workplace conflict story and/or related discussion in the future	4% (1)	32% (8)	44% (11)	12% (3)	8% (2)

invited to join the wiki. The survey yielded a 10% response rate with 25 of 250 invitees completing the survey.

When asked which of the following resources they typically consult to resolve a conflict management issue they are unfamiliar it, the respondents gave the following responses as detailed in Table 1.

When asked to indicate the extent to which they agree or disagree with the following statements, respondents gave the following responses as detailed in Table 2.

When non-members were asked to identify which of the following factors contributed to their not previously accepting an invitation to join the conflict management wiki, they provided the following responses as detailed in Table 3.

With respect to the nine respondents who indicated "Other," seven stated that they did not

recall receiving any information about joining this wiki; that this survey was actually the first time that they heard about the conflict management wiki. One respondent indicated that uncertainties concerning the validity of the email source that was offering the membership played a factor in their not accepting an invitation.

When non-members were asked to identify which of the following factors would likely encourage them to reconsider an invitation to join the conflict management wiki, they provided the following responses as detailed in Table 4.

When asked how the wiki membership invitation process might be improved, respondents offered such recommendations as providing online reminder prompts, providing more regular communication, sending the invitation from a source known to be reliable, sending the invitation as a

Table 3. Contributing factors to not accepting wiki invitation

Factors	Response % and Count
Uncertainty regarding the utility of this wiki as a professional development resource	75% (9)
Other	75% (9)
Uncertainty regarding what wiki membership might entail	67% (8)
Lack of time to explore this matter	50% (6)
Uncertainty of this wiki as a safe environment for posting workplace stories and comments	33%(4)
Lack of interest in exploring this matter	8% (1)
Abundance of other resources to inform practice and address issues	8% (1)

Table 4. Reconsideration factors for wiki invitation acceptance

Factors	Response % and Count
Ability to preview the wiki without first having to join it to view its contents	71% (12)
Clarity re: what wiki membership entails	71% (12)
Recommendation from a colleague or professional acquaintance	59% (10)
Assurances re: the safety of the wiki environment for posting stories and comments	41% (7)
Assurances that wiki members choose their own levels of site engagement	35% (6)
Receiving an invitation to join at a later date	29% (5)

personal rather than a mass e-mail, providing membership information along with the invitation, and providing more detailed instructions and explanations regarding wiki access, usage, and expectations.

With respect to how the conflict management wiki site might be improved and if there was anything else they might like to add regarding the conflict management wiki, survey takers typically skipped these questions and did not provide a response. Two individuals who did respond mentioned the need to be prompted to check what is on the wiki. One individual felt that due to time constraints, unfamiliarity with the wiki platform, and extensive participation in a professional networking site that offers discussion groups, they most likely would not be inclined to use the conflict management site.

DISCUSSION

In April 2011, 250 graduates of a master's-level business program were invited to join a story-based professional development wiki. The intent was to create a knowledge-building communal network that was built from the personally meaningful, professionally relevant stories voluntarily contributed by conflict management practitioners. While we believed that this type of wiki could have strong potential to serve its members as an ongoing professional development resource, we recognized that the target membership population consisted of busy working professionals predisposed to using other information sources for professional development and assistance in addressing conflict management issues that may arise on the job.

While these working professionals were predisposed to using other information sources, we thought it not unreasonable to expect that at least some percentage of the target member popular would express interest and take the time to join and contribute to the wiki. Assumptions driving our expectations were largely based on the familiarity of the target membership population with: a) the wiki-site organizer as a respected and popular former instructor of this population, and b) the restorying method involving the sharing of personal workplace conflict stories with colleagues in their conflict management class as an effective and engaging method for promoting their learning (Slabon, 2009).

Wiki adoption results indicated that 19 of 250, about 8% of those invited, responded to the mass-mailed invitation and joined the conflict management wiki site. Those who joined primarily did so within a week of receipt of their invitation. Thereafter, wiki membership essentially flat-lined and wiki members typically viewed site content only once or twice. Moreover, over 90 days into their initial membership, members had not as yet contributed a personal workplace conflict story nor posted a comment in response to a story contributed by others.

While short-term adoption and usage results of this wiki initiative were disappointing, they were not altogether surprising given that site marketing strategies such as site reminder prompting techniques were not employed in this case. A low-key, organic approach to site adoption and usage was taken as the authors did not want to risk offending the target population through aggressive marketing tactics. However, weekly or bimonthly email announcements to point out new context-rich, story-based site additions on various conflict management issues and strategies may precisely have been needed to spur interest and encourage involvement. To mitigate the potential for annoying members of the target population, an "opt-out" notification feature could have been incorporated to remove designated individuals from the mailing list.

The survey results provided useful insights that shed light on various factors that appear to have played a role in the results obtained. The salient factors that appear to have inhibited wiki membership and usage in this case may well have implications for other cases. What we learned in this case will guide our future initiatives and we hope that others can similarly benefit from the information we have provided and the recommendations we have outlined below.

To increase the likelihood of wiki invitation acceptance:

- Employ site marketing strategies, especially site reminder prompts, that highlight the site's uniqueness, relevance and utility for the target member population
- Use a personal and recognized as trustworthy email origination source rather than a site-based mass emailing approach
- Include an "opt-out" email notification feature that enables mailing list removal to mitigate annoying the target member population through ongoing email solicitation efforts
- Encourage individuals to recommend wiki membership to their colleagues
- Offer preview access so that potential members can view the wiki without first having to join it to view its contents
- Include a clear description of wiki member expectations with the membership invitation
- Provide assurances that wiki members can choose their own site engagement levels
- Provide assurances regarding the safety of the wiki environment for posting stories and comments by describing the privacy measures that have been employed
- Consider expanding the target member population

To increase the likelihood of wiki usage:

- Employ site marketing strategies, especially site reminder prompts, that highlight the site's uniqueness, relevance and utility for the target member population
- Periodically encourage members to contribute their own workplace conflict stories and send out an announcement to members when a new story has been added to the site
- Stimulate dialogue among members by active hosting techniques such as site organizer posing domain-rich questions that encourage multiple perspectives
- Provide partially constructed wiki pages with prompts so that contributing members do not need to create pages from scratch but can simply add content through editing to produce page content that is consistent in look and feel as other contributors
- Provide "how to" screen capture video resources to facilitate new member site and tool acclimation.
- Consider expanding the target member population

Comparison to the Literature

In this section, we compare and contrast our wiki design with recommended practices from the literature. To identify and explore those characteristics that affected participation and promoted engagement in a wiki environment, Wagner and Majchrzak (2007) examined three cases of organizations that used wikis to enhance constructive customer engagement. They compared and contrasted wikis developed by the "Boomtown Times" (a pseudonym), Novell's Cool Solutions, and Wikimedia Foundations Wikipedia.

The "Boomtown Times" sought to engage customers in collaborative preparation of editorials but contrasting opinions dominated postings and no site blocking features were employed whereby the site was promptly discontinued after several site attacks. Novell's Cool Solutions was described

as moderately successful but member contributions were rather limited in scope and narrowly focused on FAQs rather than content co-creation. Wikipedia, the most successful example, exhibited a wide readership and authorship coupled with significant content co-creation, community monitoring and management.

Based on their analysis of these three cases, Wagner and Majchrzak (2007) proposed six enabling characteristics to explain how constructive customer engagement is effectively promoted in a wiki environment. As their results were based on an exploratory case study research design limited to these three cases, the authors acknowledged that these enabling characteristics should be construed as propositions, not conclusions. Further research on each characteristic or combination of characteristics is needed and other potential factors not considered in their study that may be contributing to successful engagement—e.g., market conditions, nature of the organization, population characteristics, type of content--should also be investigated.

Community custodianship with different forms of responsible self-help. Greater constructive customer engagement was promoted when customers were allowed to exert more rather than less custodianship within a wiki site. The cases that achieved higher levels of customer engagement had their customers take responsibility for content development and monitoring with varying governance and leadership roles; i.e., some create new content, some edit or reorganize existing content, and others manage process.

Goal alignment encompassing multiple purposes among participants. The motivations that drive individuals to engage in a wiki site are going to differ. Some may be altruistic, some may be seeking personal notoriety, and some may merely be looking for advice. Given this mixed-motive situation, wikis will not thrive unless all participants realize that helping others in one instance can result in helping oneself in another instance;

that mutual benefits are afforded through collaborative participation.

Value-added processes with methods and norms that make contribution processes explicit. In the case that evidenced the highest levels of constructive customer engagement, communal rules and processes for member contributions were explicitly stated and enforced. The least successful wiki case did not provide such rules for member contributions. Explicit rules and processes for contributions help to ensure that member artifacts that appear on the site are those that offer the most value to communal members.

Allowing and enabling the emergence of layers of participation. In all three cases, varying levels of participation were exhibited. Participation levels were not predefined for any group but were allowed to emerge. Constructive customer engagement appears to be promoted when various levels of participation are allowed to emerge.

Critical management and monitoring effort levels. Customer-centric wiki sites require performance monitoring and management mechanisms. A "lightweight" management system is needed to allow management functions to be handled by communal volunteers. On the other hand, the management system needs to be sufficiently robust to protect the system from destruction while driving growth and the ongoing success of the site.

Collaboration and engagement enabling technologies. All three cases employed the same wiki technology (Mediawiki) but each selectively incorporated technology features that were seemingly predicated on their assumptions about collaboration and the co-creation process. The range of available technology features included site usage statistics; registration; access rights; version history; IP address identification; auto-blocking of unacceptable language; auto-blocking of site policy violators based on IP address; auto-blocking of content by size and type; interaction frequency notification; and so forth.

According to Wagner and Majchrzak (2007), the least successful wiki case site assumed that contributions would be motivated by collaborative goodwill to achieve common understandings and shared knowledge. Consequently, the "Boomtown Times" employed a bare-bones registration process with no content or contributor blocking capabilities. As previously noted, this resulted in the site being discontinued after several site attacks. By contrast, the most successful wiki case site from Wikipedia appears to have construed collaboration as a complex, evolving process with communal members well informed about site processes and with behaviors monitored and managed via detailed metrics to promote high quality contributions.

The fit between "task" and "technology" in these cases suggested that customer-centric wiki sites will work best when they seek to obtain the collective wisdom from multi-user contributions rather than relying on a singular expert contributor. Task-technology fit is further enhanced when a wiki is employed to aggregate knowledge and information instead of opinions. As evidenced in the "Boomtown Times" case, opinion seeking can be detrimental to goal alignment and the promotion of collaborative participation. Task-technology fit is also enhanced when a wiki site has been seeded with a sufficient number of "starter pages" to engage and encourage site participants to create their own pages. It is recommended that a wiki avert an imbalance between a large number of authors and a small number of pages and consider a ratio of one page per author.

With respect to the story-based conflict management wiki site, it is interesting to note that most if not all of these enabling characteristics were evidenced in the site design and functionality. For example, wiki members were enabled to self-determine their level of participatory engagement. Members could determine whether they wanted to contribute to the site by posting a new domain-relevant story or by providing an informative response to someone else's story. They could consider posing questions in regards to issues raised by their own or someone else's story. They could also consider contributing to the site by responding to questions or issues raised by other site members in relation to their own story or someone else's conflict management story.

Explicit rules and clearly defined processes for posting site contributions to help ensure quality postings of value to communal members were evidenced in the *Share your story* page design. As previously described, and displayed in Appendix B, these pages consisted of a series of partially constructed template-based wiki pages with story prompts. The prompts provided value-added features by standardizing contribution processes so that contributing members could easily add new story content through page editing rather than new page creation to produce page content with consistency in look and feel to other communal member story contributors.

With respect to collaboration enabling, community custodianship, performance monitoring, and critical management, the conflict management wiki site was largely shielded from the threat of site attacks by operating as a members-only private site with membership obtained through site organizer invitation, reply and approval processes. Membership invitations were specifically sent to former students who previously engaged in learning by restorying in their master's level conflict management course. Collaboration enabling technologies were evidenced in such site features as posting and replying to comments on story pages, adding search tags to a story page, and receiving email notifications of wiki activity on specific pages or site wide. A series of .mp4 audio-video tutorials were provided to help acclimate and encourage wiki members to use these collaboration enabling site tools.

With respect to task-technology fit, the story-based conflict management wiki was designed to obtain the collective wisdom from multi-user contributions. The wiki design promoted a mutually beneficial, cross-organization, cross-industry knowledge building communal network based on professionally relevant stories contributed by conflict management practitioners previously educated in applying conflict management concepts, principles and strategies to their real world workplace stories. Moreover, the wiki site was seeded with a number of "starter pages" to both engage members with relevant examples and to encourage them to follow suit with contributing their own workplace conflict story, one page per authored story, to the wiki site.

In his analysis of online, multi-user communities and social networks, Jakob Nielsen (2006) has written about a phenomenon associated with such communities called "participation inequality." "Participation inequality" refers to the behavioral dynamic that a very small minority of communal members will usually account for a disproportionately large amount of content and activity. In most online communities that rely on users to contribute content, user participation tends to follow a 90-9-1 rule. Ninety percent of users are merely lurkers who read or observe but do not contribute. Nine percent of users are intermittent contributors who will contribute from time to time but are most often focused on other priorities. One percent of users of an online community are the heavy contributors who participate very often and account for most of the contributions.

Since member contribution is critical to a wiki's success, what steps can be taken to address participation inequality? Nielsen (2006) suggests that while this phenomenon is impossible to overcome, one may be able to reshape the participation distribution angle to a more equitable distribution; e.g., 80-16-4, with 80% lurkers, 16% contributing some, and 4% contributing the most. Recommended strategies for reshaping the distribution angle to better equalize participation with particular relevance for wikis include: make it easy for members to contribute by providing orientation tutorials and help resources; provide templates that users can readily modify and edit rather than having to create a site contribution from scratch; and promote quality contributions by calling attention to good contributions and rewarding good contributors with some form of public acknowledgement.

The story-based, conflict management wiki that we developed did incorporate Nielsen's recommendation to provide help resources and orientation tutorials. The wiki also provided a template-approach to content contribution whereby users did not have to create a site contribution story page from scratch but could easily edit a previously created page with text-based prompts to guide their content addition with consistency in look and feel across story contributors. Given the low levels of wiki adoption and usage, public acknowledgement of good contributions was not employed but it certainly strikes us as a plausible strategy worth incorporating to promote quality contributions.

As we reflected on the extent to which our story-based conflict management wiki site largely incorporated Wagner and Majchrzak's enabling characteristics as well as Nielsen's recommendations yet still resulted in low adoption and participation to date, it seemed reasonable to conclude that other factors and dynamics were in play here. As previously noted, the target member population was comprised of busy working professionals predisposed to using other information sources for job-related assistance and professional development. In order for a new resource to wedge its way into the pragmatic consciousness of its target member population as a "go to" source, it is likely going to require some convincing that the site is indeed worthy of their time and attention; that it offers useful information that busy practitioners can readily access and apply that is in some way unique and relevant for those it seeks to serve.

To underscore the importance of heightening awareness of a new wiki as a "go to" source among the target member population, our lists of recommendations to increase wiki invitation acceptance and wiki usage began with the notion of employing site marketing strategies, especially site reminder prompts. Based on our site and survey data, it appeared to us that the lack of

site reminder prompts to periodically highlight and remind the target member population of the site's uniqueness, relevance and utility may well have played a role in the results obtained. Future research in the respective effectiveness of various types of site marketing strategies, especially reminder prompts, to promote wiki membership and usage is clearly needed.

The lists of recommendations we proposed with respect to increasing wiki invitation acceptance and wiki usage concluded with a consideration to expand the wiki target member population. While the 250 former students who engaged in learning by restorying were initially considered the ideal population to join and contribute to a personal story-based conflict management wiki, they are by no means the only population who may be interested in and benefit from this type of wiki. We could, for example, repurpose this type of wiki site for large-scale adoption.

Consider, for example, that a national or international "Call for Storytellers" regarding workplace conflicts could be marketed to professional organizations and social networks as well as to relevant programs that offer conflict management courses in higher education. A weekly series of featured stories, topics and discussion facilitators could be developed and publicized along with ongoing notification of new stories and topical additions to the wiki site. In his book *Wikipatterns*, Stewart Mader (2008) identified and described useful strategies to promote large-scale adoption. Strategies, patterns and ideas to promote wiki collaboration can also be accessed at Wikipatterns.com, a community-built wiki resource site that Mader began in 2007.

Despite the low initial adoption rate and limited usage to date, our survey results suggest that the conflict management wiki site may yet evolve into a unique, relevant, "go to" source for conflict management practitioners. Interestingly, only one survey respondent indicated that the abundance of other resources to inform practice and address issues was a contributing factor for not accepting the invitation to join the conflict management wiki. Moreover, about 30% of survey respondents indicated that materials and resources freely accessible online through Web blogs, content communities, or wikis were among the resources they typically consult to resolve a conflict management issue they are unfamiliar it.

An identified obstacle to becoming a "go to" source for practitioners that surfaced in both the site results and the survey is adequately motivating members to overcome any story sharing insecurities and taking the time to contribute a personal workplace conflict story to the wiki site in the future. While about 60% of respondents indicated that they were likely to post comments regarding a wiki member's workplace conflict story, the same percentage of respondents also expressed reticence to contribute a personal workplace conflict story to the wiki in the future. Recall also that a sizable amount, about 40%, of non-members pointed to assurances regarding the safety of the wiki environment for posting stories and comments as a factor impacting their decision to join the conflict management wiki.

Instilling the notion that the online wiki environment is indeed a safe environment for sharing and discussing personal workplace conflict stories may pose special challenges. Candid disclosure modeling by their instructor and other classmates sufficiently allayed information sharing concerns when orally sharing personal workplace conflict stories in the classroom setting (Slabon, 2009), but this may not be sufficient in an online text-based wiki environment where users are typically engaged in written communications. The transitory nature of oral communication in a classroom setting may well be more likely to lessen personal hesitancies and promote confidence in sharing personal workplace stories among colleagues than the stored and retrievable postings and contributions members can repeatedly access within the wiki environment. The interpersonal communication dynamic that there are some things that I

would tell you in person that I would be hesitant to put in writing may play a role in these matters.

The above discussion would suggest that additional measures may need to be taken to foster member perceptions that the online wiki environment is indeed a safe environment for sharing and discussing personal workplace conflict stories. One such measure would be to have members provide consent to a site content privacy agreement as part of their membership expectations. On the other hand, it is relatively unclear and remains to be investigated whether any specific measures or combination of measures may adequately address information sharing safety concerns for a given segment of the target member population.

It should not go unnoticed that over 80% of respondents, 18 of 22 after factoring out the three N/A responses, indicated that they agreed or strongly agreed with the statement that the personal story-based wiki approach has potential to help them address conflict management issues and inform practice. In addition, we thought it was noteworthy that when asked about the likelihood of joining the wiki in the future, about 60% of non-members, 11 of 18, agreed or strongly agreed that they were likely to join in the future. Recall also that seven respondents who indicated "Other" as a contributing factor to their not previously accepting a wiki invitation stated that the survey was the first time they heard about the wiki; that they did not recall receiving any prior information about it.

The fact that several individuals indicated they did not recall receiving any information about the wiki prior to the survey underscores the importance of sending out periodic site reminder notifications to mitigate the chances of the site being overlooked by the target member population. It also serves to support the recommendation of using a personal and recognized-as-trustworthy email origination source to lessen the chance of email announcements being auto-filtered as unimportant communication.

As we reflected on this case, it also occurred to us that perhaps preloading the site with five stories was unnecessary and in some ways counterproductive. A better strategy and one that would have simultaneously addressed site adoption and site usage issues would have been to preload the site with a couple of stories and then employ a progressive roll-out marketing strategy with announcements sent to the target member population when a "new" story has been added to the wiki site. A progressive rollout strategy could also be employed to promote wiki adoption and usage by showcasing a specific story and related topics during a designated time period.

While a strategy such as this would bring additional formality into the mix of what is largely intended to be an informal, user-generated resource for professional development, it may provide requisite kindling to fuel member interest in the nascent phases of its existence before this type of wiki site can become self-sustaining. Additional research is needed to discern what kind of transitory phases this type of wiki site may need or likely go through before it can fulfill its potential as a professional development resource with an ever-growing inventory of practitioner-compiled stories, insightful commentaries, and context-rich reflections and dialogue to inform member practice.

CONCLUSION

In this chapter, we described the design and implementation of a wiki, which sought to serve conflict management practitioners as an ongoing professional development resource. The wiki aimed to create a cross-organization, knowledge building communal network built from the personal workplace stories voluntarily contributed by its members. We identified various adoption and usage issues and provided recommendations and strategies for addressing these issues. Moreover, we compared and contrasted our wiki design with recommended practices from the wiki literature and identified some areas for future research. While by no means conclusive given our exploratory approach, type of content, specific population and context in which our data and results were obtained, we hope that the strategies and recommendations provided herein may nevertheless be informative for others who may be interested in practitioner-built, story-based professional development using a wiki.

REFERENCES

Ambrogi, R. J. (2007, May 4). Legal wikis are bound to wow you. *Law Technology News*. Retrieved from http://www.law.com/jsp/lawtechnologynews/PubArticleLTN.jsp?id=900005480497&slreturn=1.

Jonassen, D. H., & Hernandez-Serrano, J. (2002). Case-based reasoning and instructional design: Using stories to support problem solving. *Educational Technology Research and Development*, *50*(2), 65–77. doi:10.1007/BF02504994doi:10.1007/BF02504994

Lave, J., & Wenger, E. (1991). *Situated learning: Legitimate peripheral participation*. Cambridge, UK: Cambridge University Press.

Mader, S. (2008). *Wikipatterns: A practical guide to improving productivity and collaboration in your organization*. Indianapolis, IN: Wiley Publishing, Inc.

Nielsen, J. (2006). *Participation inequality: Encouraging more users to contribute*. Retrieved September 2, 2011, from http://www.useit.com/alertbox/participation_inequality.html.

Rothman, D. (2011). *List of medical wikis*. Retrieved July 23, 2011 from http://davidrothman.net/list-of-medical-wikis/.

Scardamalia, M., & Bereiter, C. (2003). Knowledge building. In J. Guthrie (Ed.), *Encyclopedia of Education* (2nd ed.). New York, NY: Macmillan.

Scardamalia, M., & Bereiter, C. (2006). Knowledge building: Theory, pedagogy, and technology. In K. Sawyer (Ed.), *Cambridge Handbook of the Learning Sciences* (pp. 97–118). Cambridge, UK: Cambridge University Press.

Schank, R. C. (1990). *Tell me a story: Narrative and intelligence*. Evanston, IL: Northwestern University Press.

Schank, R. C. (1999). *Dynamic memory revisited*. Cambridge, UK: Cambridge University Press. doi:10.1017/CBO9780511527920doi:10.1017/CBO9780511527920

Schön, D. A. (1993). *The reflective practitioner: How professionals think in action*. New York, NY: Basic Books.

Slabon, W. A. (2009). *Learning by restorying: A naturalistic case study of an instructional strategy in a master's level conflict management course*. Unpublished Doctoral Dissertation. Tallahassee, FL: Florida State University.

Wagner, C., & Majchrzak, A. (2007). Enabling customer-centricity using wikis and the wiki way. *Journal of Management Information Systems*, *23*(3), 17–43. doi:10.2753/MIS0742-1222230302doi:10.2753/MIS0742-1222230302

Wenger, E. (1998). *Communities of practice: Learning, meaning and identity*. Cambridge, UK: Cambridge University Press.

Wenger, E. (2000). Communities of practice and social learning systems. *Organization*, *7*(2), 225–246. doi:10.1177/135050840072002doi:10.1177/135050840072002

ADDITIONAL READING

Aamodt, A., & Plaza, E. (1994). Case-based reasoning: Foundational issues, methodological variations, and system approaches. *AI Communications*, *7*(1), 39–59.

Ardichvili, A., Page, V., & Wentling, T. (2003). Motivation and barriers to participation in virtual knowledge-sharing communities of practice. *Journal of Knowledge Management*, *7*(1), 64–77. doi:10.1108/13673270310463626doi:10.1108/13673270310463626

Barry, D. (1997). Telling changes: From narrative family therapy to organizational change and development. *Journal of Organizational Change Management*, *10*(1), 30–46. doi:10.1108/09534819710159288doi:10.1108/09534819710159288

Barry, D., & Elmes, M. (1997). Strategy retold: Toward a narrative view of strategic discourse. *Academy of Management Review*, *22*(2), 439–452.

Bransford, J., Brown, A., & Cocking, R. (2000). *How people learn: Brain, mind, and experience & school*. Washington, DC: National Academy Press.

Brown, J. S., Collins, A., & Dugid, P. (1989). Situated cognition and the culture of learning. *Educational Researcher*, *18*, 32–42.

Bruner, J. (1991). The narrative construction of reality. *Critical Inquiry*, *18*(1), 1–21. doi:10.1086/448619doi:10.1086/448619

Callanan, G. A., & Perri, D. F. (2006). Teaching conflict management using a scenario-based approach. *Journal of Education for Business*, *81*(3), 131–139. doi:10.3200/JOEB.81.3.131-139doi:10.3200/JOEB.81.3.131-139

Carter, K. (1993). The place of story in the study of teaching and teacher education. *Educational Researcher*, *22*(1), 5–12, 18.

Carter, K. (1999). What is a case? What is not a case? In M. A. Lundeberg, B. B. Levin, & H. L. Harrington (Eds.), *Who Learns What from Cases and How? The Research Base for Teaching and Learning with Cases*. Mahwah, NJ: Lawrence Erlbaum. doi:10.1016/j.jss.2010.11.258doi:10.1016/j.jss.2010.11.258

Christensen, C. R., & Hansen, A. J. (1987). *Teaching and the case method*. Boston, MA: Harvard Business School Press.

Cobb, S. (1994). A narrative perspective on mediation. In J. Folger & R. Baruch Bush (Eds.), *New Directions in Mediation: Communication Research and Perspectives*. Thousand Oaks, CA: Sage.

Cohen, S. (2002). *Negotiating skills for managers*. New York, NY: McGraw-Hill.

Connelly, F. M., & Clandinin, D. J. (1990). Stories of experience and narrative inquiry. *Educational Researcher*, *19*(5), 2–14.

Denning, S. (2004, May 1). Telling tales. *Harvard Business Review*, (n.d), 1–7.

Denning, S. (2006). Effective storytelling: Strategic business narrative techniques. *Strategy and Leadership*, *34*(1), 42–48. doi:10.1108/1087857 0610637885doi:10.1108/10878570610637885

Doyle, W., & Carter, K. (2003). Narrative and learning to teach: Implications for teacher-education curriculum. *Journal of Curriculum Studies*, *35*(2), 129–137. doi:10.1080/002202702200002 3053doi:10.1080/0022027022000023053

Fisher, R., & Ury, W. (1981). *Getting to yes: Negotiating agreement without giving in*. Boston, MA: Houghton Mifflin.

Freedman, J., & Combs, G. (1996). *Narrative therapy: The social construction of preferred reality*. New York, NY: Norton.

Friedman, R. A., Tidd, S. T., Currall, S. C., & Tsai, J. C. (2000). What goes around comes around: The impact of personal conflict style on work conflict and job stress. *The International Journal of Conflict Management*, *11*, 32–55. doi:10.1108/ eb022834doi:10.1108/eb022834

Gabriel, Y. (2000). *Storytelling in organizations: Facts, fictions, and fantasies*. Oxford, UK: Oxford University Press.

Herman, D. (2002). *Story logic*. Lincoln, NE: University of Nebraska Press.

Herman, D. (2003). Stories as a tool for thinking. In D. Herman (Ed.), *Narrative Theory and the Cognitive Sciences*. Palo Alto, CA: CSLI Publications.

Hmelo-Silver, C. E. (2004). Problem-based learning: What and how do students learn? *Educational Psychology Review*, *16*(3), 235–266. doi:10.1023/B:EDPR.0000034022.16470. f3doi:10.1023/B:EDPR.0000034022.16470.f3

Hmelo-Silver, C. E., & Barrows, H. S. (2006). Goals and strategies of a problem-based learning facilitator. *The Interdisciplinary Journal of Problem-based Learning*, *1*(1), 21–39.

Jonassen, D. (1999). Designing constructivist learning environments. In C. M. Reigeluth (Ed.), *Instructional Design Theories and Models*. Mahwah, NJ: Erlbaum.

Jonassen, D. H. (2000). Toward a design theory of problem solving. *Educational Technology Research and Development*, *48*(4), 63–85. doi:10.1007/BF02300500doi:10.1007/ BF02300500

Knowles, M. S., Holton, E. F., III, & Swanson, R. A. (1998). *The adult learner*. Houston, TX: Gulf Publishing Co.

Kolodner, J. (1993). *Case-based reasoning*. New York, NY: Morgan Kaufman.

Perry, A., & Doan, R. E. (1994). *Story re-visions: Narrative therapy in the postmodern world*. New York, NY: Guilford Press.

Rahim, M. A. (2001). *Managing conflict in organizations* (3rd ed.). Westport, CT: Praeger.

Rahim, M. A. (2002). Toward a theory of managing organizational conflict. *The International Journal of Conflict Management, 13*(3), 206–235. doi:10.1108/eb022874doi:10.1108/eb022874

Riesbeck, C. K. (1996). Case-based teaching and constructivism: Carpenters and tools. In B. G. Wilson (Ed.), *Constructivist Learning Environments: Case Studies in Instructional Design*. Englewood Cliffs, NJ: Educational Technology Publications.

Savery, J. R., & Duffy, T. M. (1995). Problem-based learning: An instructional model and its constructivist framework. In B. G. Wilson (Ed.), *Constructivist Learning Environments: Case Studies in Instructional Design*. Englewood Cliffs, NJ: Educational Technology Publications.

Schank, R. C., Berman, T. R., & Macpherson, K. A. (1999). Learning by doing. In C. M. Reigeluth (Ed.), *Instructional Design Theories and Models: A New Paradigm of Instructional Theory* (pp. 161–181). Mahwah, NJ: Lawrence Erlbaum Associates.

Thomas, K. W. (1992). Conflict and negotiation processes in organizations. In M. D. Dunnette & L. M. Hough (Eds.), *Handbook of Industrial and Organizational Psychology* (2nd ed.). Palo Alto, CA: Consulting Psychologists Press, Inc.

Thompson, M. (2007). *Telling the story: Narrative techniques in conflict management*. Paper presented at the Meeting of the Texas Association of Mediators Conference. San Antonio, TX.

Watson, K., & Harper, C. (2008). Supporting knowledge creation: Using wikis for group collaboration. *Research Bulletin (Sun Chiwawitthaya Thang Thale Phuket), 3*. Washington, DC: EDUCAUSE Center for Applied Research. Retrieved from http://www.educause.edu/ecar

West, J. A., & West, M. L. (2009). *Using wikis for online collaboration: The power of the read-write web*. San Francisco, CA: Jossey-Bass.

White, M., & Epston, D. (1990). *Narrative means to therapeutic ends*. New York, NY: Norton.

Winslade, J., & Monk, G. (2000). *Narrative mediation: A new approach to conflict resolution*. San Francisco: Jossey Bass.

KEY TERMS AND DEFINITIONS

Conflict Management: The implementation of strategies and tactics to delimit the negative, dysfunctional aspects of conflict and promote the positive, constructive aspects of conflict to enhance learning and performance.

Professional Development: The expansion of knowledge and/or improvement of skills for personal and career growth which occurs through informal as well as formal learning opportunities.

Prompt: A cue that is intended to help elicit desired information from a contributor.

Restorying: The rewriting or retelling of a personal, domain-relevant story based on the application of concepts, principles, strategies and techniques covered during a unit or course of instruction (Slabon, 2009).

Search Tags: The assignment of a label to an artifact such as a wiki page to categorize and facilitate locating that artifact and similarly labeled artifacts through search and retrieval processes.

Story-Based: The strategic use of stories as the foundational basis for promoting learning and enhancing performance.

Wiki: A website that enables multiple users to contribute and edit content on site pages.

Appendix A: Conflict Management Wiki Home Page

Figure 1. Conflict management wiki home page

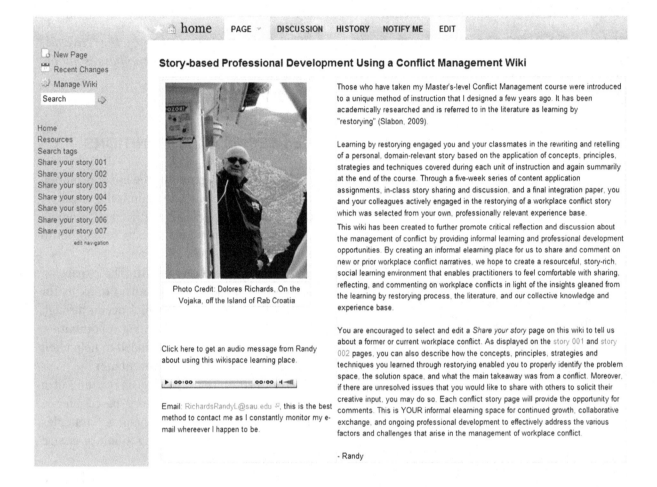

Appendix B: Conflict Management Wiki Share Your Story Page

Figure 2. Conflict management wiki share your story page

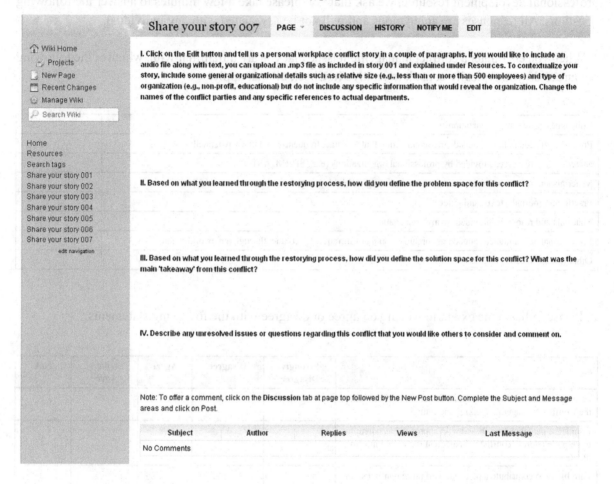

Appendix C: Survey

To help us discern whether the Conflict Management Wiki has any real potential to serve as an ongoing professional development resource, we ask that you please take a few minutes to answer the following questions. All responses are anonymous and will not be associated with any individual.

1. When you encounter a conflict management issue that you are unfamiliar with, which of the following resources do you typically consult to resolve it. Check all that apply.

Colleagues within my organization	
Professional acquaintances outside my organization that I contact frequently and know personally	
Materials and resources provided by professional organizations (e.g., SHRM, ASTD)	
Materials and resources freely accessible online through Web blogs, content communities, or wikis	
Practitioner journals, texts, and guides	
Materials and resources provided by my organization	
Professional acquaintances outside my organization that I infrequently contact through a networking site	
Other (please specify)	

2. Please indicate the extent to which you agree or disagree with the following statements.

	Strongly Disagree	Disagree	Agree	Strongly Agree	N/A
I am not currently a wiki site member but am likely to join the Conflict Management wiki in the future					
I think the personal story-based wiki approach has potential to help me address conflict management issues and inform practice					
I am likely to contribute a personal workplace conflict story to the Conflict Management wiki in the future					
I am likely to comment on a wiki member's workplace conflict story and/or related discussion in the future					

3. If you have NOT as yet joined the Conflict Management Wiki, please indicate which of the following factors contributed to your not previously accepting an invitation to join this wiki. Check all that apply. (If you have joined the wiki, skip this question).

Ability to preview the wiki without first having to join it to view its contents	
Clarity re: what wiki membership entails	
Recommendation from a colleague or professional acquaintance	
Assurances re: the safety of the wiki environment for posting stories and comments	
Assurances that wiki members choose their own levels of site engagement	
Receiving an invitation to join at a later date	
Other (please specify)	

4. If you have NOT as yet joined the Conflict Management Wiki, please indicate which of the following factors would likely encourage you to reconsider an invitation to join this wiki. Check all that apply. (If you have joined the wiki, skip this question).

Uncertainty regarding the utility of this wiki as a professional development resource	
Uncertainty regarding what wiki membership might entail	
Lack of time to explore this matter	
Uncertainty of this wiki as a safe environment for posting workplace stories and comments	
Lack of interest in exploring this matter	
Abundance of other resources to inform practice and address issues	
Other (please specify)	

5. How might the wiki membership invitation process be improved?

6. If you HAVE JOINED the Conflict Management wiki, please indicate how might the Conflict Management Wiki sight be improved (such as navigation, resources, search terms, content prompts)? (If you have NOT yet joined the wiki, skip this question).

7. We thank you for taking the time to complete this brief survey. Is there anything else you would like to add re: the Conflict Management wiki?

Chapter 16
Dermatological Telemedicine Diagnoses and Andragogical Training Using Web 2.0 Mobile Medicine Video Conferencing

Richard Brandt
Metroplex Dermatology, USA

Rich Rice
Texas Tech University, USA

ABSTRACT

Polymorphic innovations of Web 2.0 have both inspired and facilitated a near ubiquitous learning architecture centered on mobility, customization, and collective intelligence in a variety of fields. These reconfigurable pedagogical learning platforms have empowered participants by removing passive, standardized methods of unilateral knowledge delivery established by its Web 1.0 predecessor, and included a multitude of divergent, informal, and participant-driven social networks. These new technological devices and opportunities for self-guided, multidirectional knowledge exchange within newly established informal learning networks are affordable and flexible. Thus, McLoughin and Lee's (2007) moniker of "Pedagogy 2.0" is apropos (p. 672). The teaching and training of professional medical personnel, aligned with the flexibility and the capability of Web 2.0 platforms in the exchange of collaborative social learning, can be an authentic and productive knowledge-making andragogical approach to healthcare training. Such training must consider, study, and embrace social-constructivism, problem-based learning, andragogy, universal design for learning, media naturalness theory, divergent thinking, and the expanded rhetorical triangle in order to maximize the potential of mobile medicine through expanding the practice of telemedicine.

DOI: 10.4018/978-1-4666-1815-2.ch016

INTRODUCTION

The medical healthcare industry, in particular, is among the many industries embracing Web 2.0 technologies and protocols in an effort to enhance productivity and quality of service. Clinically based healthcare communication is often referred to as "telemedicine" (Mair & Whitten, 2000) or "e-health" (Karkalis, 2006), and it has been employed for decades to enhance patient care. Time, space, and modality have often limited these efforts; one antiquated example of such treatment protocols includes the use of ship-to-shore radios by land-based physicians to offer treatment and medical advice to deployed sea captains (Wootton, 2001, p. 557). Web 2.0 methodologies not only utilize more advanced tools than a ship radio, but more importantly, they symbolize a new learning paradigm for divergent knowledge creation, user-guided problem-based learning, and untethered mobility. We call this mobile medicine.

The term "medical education" may include public awareness efforts, standardized student instruction, postgraduate review, and professional Peer-to-Peer (P2P) collaborative or divergent learning praxis. Mobile medicine focuses its attention on the latter. Ongoing postgraduate learning and continual training within the medical profession have made significant use of Web 2.0's P2P social learning platforms, and has further engendered new dimensions of electronic medical communication and consultation among healthcare professionals, including professional physicians, postgraduate residents, physician assistants, and nurse practitioners. It is within this subset of medical education that the advances of Web 2.0 and social networking make profound contributions.

Adult learners in the professional workplace, long removed from academia, especially those in the medical professions, feel more comfortable with certain learning styles than others, based partially on the learning models introduced during their formal medical training and in part due

to how adults learn in general. For one example, adult learners need to utilize prior knowledge and experience as both an ongoing guide and a starting reference point for new learning experiences (Nelson, 2010, p. 101). Learning theorists Knowles, Holton, and Swanson (2005), in fact, go on to suggest that adult learners have a need to know as well as a need for a foundation of knowledge, a need for ready content as well as immediately relevant orientation, and a need for personal motivation. Further, they point out that adult learners need to play a direct role in planning and evaluating their own instruction. As such, the subject matter in patient-centric medical learning often elicits more knowledge transfer if the content is problem-centered rather than content-oriented (Knowles, Holton, & Swanson, 2005).

Andragogy, which is the study of how adult learners learn, is often in contrast to the pedagogical analogy of a "blank canvas" that didactic learners, and many medical students, are thought to utilize. As healthcare professionals transition from one paradigm, or from one discourse community to another, more familiar learning practices seem less intrusive. This is also the case for allied health professionals, such as physician assistants, nurse practitioners, physical therapists, and registered nurses. Medical school education is initially structured on a generalized, science-based learning architecture (e.g. anatomy, physiology, genetics) that is meant to fortify each student's knowledge foundation. This framework later evolves into an individualized, constructivist-like, problem-based learning model (e.g. why is Mrs. Smith having symptoms A, B, and C?), wherein each participant actively develops an individual learning framework. The social and rhetorical context—such as the hospital-based training setting—encourages collaborative and collective knowledge accumulation. These small group discussions do not require unilateral agreement. They have been found to have a "larger positive effect on prior knowledge activation than individual analysis" (Dolmans & Schmidt, 2006, p. 324), leading to customized, self-directed, knowledge management protocols tailored by each student to better fulfill personalized learning needs. Thus, the learning choices of these same individuals later in their careers would likely incorporate some similar social-constructivist and problem-based learning methodology.

Thus, while telephone and fax modalities may meet basic collaborative communication needs, uses of Web 2.0 technologies or more rhetorically or contextually driven training approaches, especially the capability to implement P2P social networking, significantly improves preparation for clinical patient care. Mobile devices, which can tap into reliable and valid yet immediately flexible and fluid content, are quite valuable. Newer generation mobile devices, such as smartphones and tablets, are becoming more powerful as they are being produced in smaller size, with increasing affordability, and with expanded flexibility and connectivity. Clinicians can more easily utilize collaborative Web 2.0 applications for professional learning activities. More importantly, using Web 2.0 tools, these same pedagogical protocols may be activated in real-time for peer consultation at the point of patient care, despite where the consulted physician is located.

WEB 2.0 AND MOBILE MEDICINE SOCIAL NETWORKING

We define Web 2.0 as a personalized, customizable second generation of the World Wide Web that affords active participatory learning, P2P collaboration, flexible retooling of information, and mobile accessibility. This enhanced framework "lies [in] an ensemble of standards, protocols, technologies, and software development architectures and approaches that enable the seamless communication of third party programs thus creating the communities and networks of services that bring people together" (Kaldoudi, 2010, p. 130).

Although the growth and popularity of Web 2.0 is relatively new, the origins are not. According to Rollett et al. (2007), Licklider and Taylor first identified the computer as a communication device in 1968, the original World Wide Web (Web 1.0) was released from CERN in 1993, and Ward Cunningham first devised a collaborative wiki platform in 1995 (p. 6). Wikipedia introduced wikis in a significant way to the public in 2001, Flicker utilized Application Programming Interface (API) to publically enable photo sharing in 2002, and Del.icio.us brand social bookmarking tools went public in 2003 (Rollett, et al., 2007, p. 6). Today, just a few years later, Web 2.0 is not only engrained into our social fabric, but the tools of Web 2.0 are easier to use and more ubiquitous.

Tim O'Reilly, founder of O'Reilly Publishing, with Dale Dougherty and MediaLive International, are often credited with developing the term "Web 2.0" along with some best practice design principles (O'Reilly, 2005; Rollett, et al., 2007). Characteristics and principles typically understood to be byproducts of Web 2.0 use:

1. Small, specialized communities increase focus on specific topics, allowing for easier information exchange.
2. Data is more valuable than the interface features.
3. Peers who co-create products add value because collective intelligence is developed.
4. Because there are more users there is more value.
5. Content is not, for the most part, guarded or restricted, but should be retooled and reused in different ways.
6. Upgrades can be constantly performed to ensure ongoing improvement.
7. Trusted cooperation from many rather than proprietary control by a few.
8. Cross function software is more important than any one device (Rollet, et al., 2007).

Table 1. Common web 2.0 applications and services

Application	Description of Application
Wiki	Social writing software and template-driven web space that allows invited users to read, post, edit, or delete collaborative content (e.g. PBWiki or Wikipedia).
Blog	Simple, turnkey content management tools, similar to a web-based digital diary, which lists the owner's chronologically sequenced entries and any associated reader commentary (e.g. Blogger[SM]).
Podcasting	Independently published audio/video contributions called feeds are distributed to subscribers automatically through RSS feeds or are individually transferred in MP3/MP4 format for use on portable devices (e.g. Apple iPod®).
Streaming Video	Short, user-generated videos are uploaded to a public database or repository for public viewing and utilization (e.g. YouTube[SM]).
Social Bookmarking	Participants bookmark and catalogue their preferred social sites and services, after which they may publically share their lists (e.g. Del.icio.us).
Video Conferencing	Web-based telephone conference calling that incorporates a real-time video connection link between users (e.g. Skype®).
FaceTime®	Mobile one-on-one video calls broadcast over a secure Wi-Fi connection using Apple's newer devices (e.g. iPad2®, iPhone4®, iPodTouch4®).

Some Web 2.0 application platforms and services are summarized in Table 1.

TELEMEDICINE

How do common Web 2.0 applications and services relate to telemedicine? Similar to applications and platforms mentioned in Table 1, "telemedicine" today is the use of electronic communication devices and protocols utilized in a cost effective manner by healthcare professionals to assist individuals at disparate locations. Electronic medical assistance can be enabled or applied in one of several ways: for instance, real-time video conferencing protocols; "store-and-forward" methods (Eedy, 2001, p. 696) wherein a digital photograph is electronically forwarded to others for consultation; and professionally mediated, asynchronous group collaboration in wikis. Web 2.0 affordances have expanded telemedicine's traditional focus now to incorporate interoffice professional collaboration, post-graduate medical learning (i.e. continuing medical education), resident training, and student development. Such protocols have also been embraced in medical spe-

cialties in addition to general medicine, including endocrinology (Martinez-Sarriegui, et al., 2008), emergency trauma medicine (Archambault, 2010), laboratory sciences (Dragoni, 2009), radiology (Rubin, 2008), psychiatry, cardiology, pathology, obstetrics, surgery (Eedy & Wooton, 2001), and dermatology (Tran, et al., 2011).

The flexible retooling of Web 2.0 platforms, the general learning theories of professional medical education, and the imminently affordable ubiquity of emerging mobile media devices have facilitated new opportunities for electronic medical education initiatives. In 2008 in Spain, for instance, Primary Care Physicians (PCPs) and endocrinology-trained diabetes specialists started using an information technology tool called Computer Supported Collaborative Work (CSCW), which provided an asynchronous, physician-mediated, multi-user workspace. Within this mobile "shared care" suite, registered patients were able to 1) access multi-channel messaging services that allowed electronic message exchange in any application format, 2) share information with disseminated group distribution, and 3) coordinate individual office visits and small group meetings (Martinez-Sarriegui, et al., 2008). Patients were able to take more ownership of their care through this semi-autonomous, yet supervised, patient care portal by uploading their daily blood sugar readings and receiving adjustment advice from the physician-lead healthcare support team.

For another example, in 2010 several Canadian Emergency Department physicians and trauma care professionals implemented an asynchronous wiki-based discussion board that served as a collaborative repository for updating medical education materials and as a reminder protocol for promoting policy improvements and healthcare delivery best practices (Archambault, 2010, p. 1). Benefits of such a system are not yet fully realized, as they may include updating new knowledge, softening information overload, homogenizing departmental standards, training students, disseminating ideas across rotating work schedules, and improving cost effectiveness.

More visually oriented medical specialties, such as Radiology departments, have developed applications for high-resolution mobile tablets. As early as 2008, a small group of radiologists in California developed a tablet-based, open-source application that could enable clinicians to author, embed, and extract "semantic information," such as text reports and biomedical data, within each image which ultimately allowed for the semi-automatic retrieval of non-image data during viewing and analysis (Rubin, 2008, p. 626).

Further, dermatology is another visually oriented specialty that has—and will continue to utilize—Web 2.0 architecture to enhance patient care outcomes, educate newer practitioners, and solidify the continuing education efforts of clinicians long removed from the university setting. The shortage of dermatologists and the remote location of some patients in Norway in 2010, for instance, inspired Schopf et al. to study how the follow-up care of children with atopic eczema could be administered through a Web-based counseling system that allowed physician feedback on patient-generated updates and photos (p. 1). Their conclusion: home-based follow-ups are "feasible" (Schopf, et al., 2010, p. 3). Given these examples,

it is not difficult to imagine the significance and impact that such strides in Web 2.0 enhanced telemedicine can bring to patient care and medical practice; however, to fully appreciate the educational implications that such protocols afford, the active andragogical apparatus of medicine's bifurcating instructional model must be more fully understood and implemented in praxis.

HEALTHCARE EDUCATION PROTOCOLS

Throughout the world's most medically advanced societies, a concerted effort to incorporate electronic devices and Internet utilities with the transfer of healthcare knowledge has played an important role. Once top-heavy and unilateral in its delivery, industry "experts" passed down various levels of translated medical information to students and laypersons alike. These efforts served to enhance medical school curricula, public healthcare awareness, and the lifelong, ongoing Continuing Medical Education (CME) needs of practicing clinicians. Stanford University's School of Medicine, for instance, was recently highlighted in the press for distributing an Apple iPad® to each of their incoming medical students because some popular medical school textbooks have been rewritten and retooled into interactive, multimedia editions (White, 2010). This learning has been applied to many hospitals in California.

However, personal clinical experience suggests that the less-structured and self-mediated nature of postgraduate continuing medical learning, whether individually driven or mandated by regulation, presents distinctively different teaching and learning challenges. Such obstacles can be, and have been, successfully and proficiently overcome using Web 2.0 social networking affordances, and mobile medicine in particular has specific ramifications for medical and healthcare training, public health information, and continuing medical education.

Medical and Healthcare Training

The study of medicine and allied health professions is typically a lengthy endeavor that requires years of schooling divided into a long biphasic framework of large-group, didactic book instruction in the early years; followed later by small group, problem-based, supervised clinical practice, which is extended further for physician residency training. Although allied health professionals (i.e. non-physicians) experience less rigorous and less lengthy training protocols, they too are trained using this two-fold approach.

In U.S. university hospital settings, as well as equivalent U.K. tertiary care center models, care delivery interactions involve a number of different individuals, some seemingly more knowledgeable and more highly ranked than others. The practice of what medical professionals call "rounding"—where a hierarchical small group of medical personnel gather "around" patients in order to talk "about" them—is especially important. Metaphorically, this time-honored medical tradition reminds one of a badelynge of ducks led by the most senior member with student ducks in tow. After leaving the patient's room, this flock of clinicians proceeds to the hallway or a conference room to discuss the intricacies of symptoms, physical findings, plausible diagnosis, and treatment options. Then, patients are informed of the flock's conclusions and, this time with patient inclusion, the group's recommended care is discussed again. These are two of medicine's most popular learning models in action: social-constructivist and problem-based health information learning.

Public Health Information

The term "health information" may also include the dissemination of new or updated medically based knowledge to the general public in the form of websites (e.g. Centers for Disease Control and Prevention), blogs (e.g. KevinMD), and asynchronous wikis (e.g. Shared Care Systems).

Once restricted to the limitations of unilateral Web 1.0 knowledge transfer, Web 2.0 tools enable lay-persons to more actively participate in their care, to research individual questions when they arise, and even to serve as mentors to newly diagnosed patients with similar conditions. Web 2.0 and informal social networking have redefined the traditional role of "patient" as "active participant." Patients can be prosumers rather than consumers of public health information.

Continuing Medical Education

Continuing Medical Education (CME) previously designated to describe standardized and regulated formal training often required yearly for practicing clinicians, has now become an all-encompassing term for lifelong, postgraduate training, regardless of the learning format or the clinician's motivation for participation. Self-guided training is important for practicing healthcare providers because it 1) can keep clinicians up-to-date with new medical information, 2) may teach, or enhance, new procedural skill sets, 3) might facilitate distribution and acquisition of inter-specialty knowledge (e.g. specialists to general practitioners), and 4) could improve patient care outcomes by reducing errors or omissions during the delivery of care. If we as a society wish to encourage our medical providers to incorporate such learning activities—exercises that will likely affect each one of us some day and plays an important role in general public health information—then we must study, understand, and continue to develop easy and applicable learning protocols.

THE ANDRAGOGY OF MEDICAL LEARNING THROUGH SOCIAL NETWORKING

In order to apply expertise as educators, as technical communicators, and as rhetoricians in an effort to assist healthcare professionals in their ongoing learning pursuits, we must first deconstruct the utilitarian needs of these adult learners. The concept of medical personnel making patient rounds or "rounding" in teaching hospitals illustrates two popular learning model theories that have been ingrained in medical training: social-constructivist and problem-based learning. These instructional paradigms can be enhanced by making use of subtler learning principles and learning designs, including social construction theory, principles of universal design for learning, media naturalness theory, divergent thinking, and the expanded rhetorical triangle. Dissecting, examining, and understanding how these theories of learning and communication can use Web 2.0's social networking can enhance knowledge accumulation models for medical professional and mobile medicine video conferencing.

Social-Constructivism

According to Dr. Ruey Shieh (2008), an information management specialist, the social-constructivist model relies on the approach that "knowledge is socially situated and is constructed through reflection on one's own thoughts and experiences, as well as other learner's ideas" (p. 707). The "social" side of this dichotomy emphasizes benefits that learners may extract from authentic interaction with their environmental and cultural surroundings. Advocates value diverse interests, goals, lessons, and experiences that various, ever-changing social circles readily engage in.

We equate social-constructivist learning models to the "buffet style of learning," a participatory learning theory approach which allows each participant to select his or her contextual lesson for a given time. The "constructivist" bifurcation encourages active, participatory learning whereby the learner must take ownership of educational curriculum and effectively construct an individual learning framework from pieces within a buffet of social learning opportunities. What matters more than which foods, or lessons, one

chooses to invest time in is that one, at the end of the project, is healthy and full and achieves the goals and objectives of the lesson. Selection and ownership of content is fundamental to the success of the adult learning platform, and enhances motivation, self-regulation, critical thinking, and collaboration (Zhu, 2009, p. 167).

Within the context of medical education, this theory offers clear practicality: environments change often, and lessons learned must adapt to change. This is precisely the reason medical professional routinely rotate through specialties, departments, clinics, and faculty knowledge-building groups during their formalized educational years. As medical professionals become more "academically sedentary learners," confined to one field of study or one brick-and-mortar clinic, they must work to maintain a cognitive, self-guided approach to their learning. P2P social networking via real-time, Face-to-Face (F2F) tablet communication can facilitate such needs, rooting every lesson in a specific and real yet variable context.

Problem-Based Learning (PBL)

PBL is a student-centered instructional model that was initially implemented with medical students to enhance diagnostic skills, problem-solving abilities, and critical thinking (Nelson, 2010, p. 99). PBL is loosely structured, entails environmental specificity, and requires both group collaboration and self-guided exploration. Similar to constructivist approaches, student outcomes of PBL may be more quantifiably measured when accessing overall patient outcomes through facilitator evaluation by supervising physicians. Savery and Duffy (2001) describe core tenets of PBL practice:

1. Environmental interaction facilitates understanding; as such, an individual's total cognition is a learned sum of the involved contextual parts: content, context, activity, and goals.

2. Cognitive puzzlement stimulates learning and determines the knowledge acquired, the pragmatic tools to be utilized, and the general purpose of being present at all.
3. Collaborative conflict and the social negotiation of that (mis)understanding serves to (in)validate our initial view and may result in new puzzlement and learning (p. 1).

Further, according to Erik Nelson (2010), an internationally recognized PBL researcher, PBL was originally designed for F2F instruction and knowledge delivery, but that "courses are being re-designed for delivery online" (p. 100). As a recent clinical study by one of the authors of this chapter illustrates, collaborative F2F peer interaction via video conferencing tablet technology adheres to well documented and accepted constructivist PBL principles (see Bowdish, 2003; Nelson, 2010; Savery & Duffy, 2001; Zhu, et al., 2009).

Universal Design for Learning (UDL)

Similar to principles of andragogy and PBL, UDL makes use of learners' interests in solving problems. In 1998, R. Orkwis and K. Maclane published an educational brief calling for a generalized improved awareness of universal design principles during curriculum development. They cite the non-profit Center for Applied Special Technology (CAST) because of CAST's advocacy to expand technological opportunities for everyone, particularly those with disabilities. The work of CAST was seminal in the development of UDL; their methodology planned and developed learning curriculum that promotes "access, participation, and progress in the general educational curriculum for all learners" (McGuire, 2006, p. 169). CAST guidelines include curricular efforts with multiple presentation media, a variety of means for expression, and multiple avenues of possible engagement (Orkwis & Maclane, 1998). UDL works to identify and remove barriers from learning by offering flexible curriculum, and new media provides new opportunity to design multimodal

artifacts, including representing information in multiple formats and types of media, providing multiple pathways for students, and providing multiple ways for students to engage content.

Media Naturalness Theory

Not to be confused with media richness theory, the "media naturalness hypothesis" postulates that an increase in the degree of naturalness of a communication effort or protocol will lead to: 1) decreased cognitive effort, 2) decreased ambiguity, and 3) increased physiological stimulation. Ned Kock (2005) writes that our human propensity is to prefer communications in a "co-located and synchronous manner" (p. 119), which enhances that interaction because of the allowance for non-verbal clues (i.e. facial expressions and body language) to augment the spoken word. He argues a Darwinian theory that evolutionary natural selection accounts for genetic enhancements, which ultimately, have come to improve the survival and mating abilities of the human species by allowing over "6,000 communicative expressions" (Kock, 2005, p. 120). Justine Cassell, et al. (1994), while at the University of Pennsylvania, found similar value in the benefits of gesture-based communication and concluded that facial expressions are not merely translated speech, but that "gesture and speech are so intimately connected that one cannot say which one is dependent on the other" (p. 3).

The benefits of using media types that are as close to being as "natural" as possible is clear, especially in medical training or exchanges between doctor and patient. Media naturalness theory, thus, relies on five basic components:

1. Co-location.
2. A synchronous exchange of ideas in (i.e. real-time).
3. Clear observation of the participant's facial expressions.
4. Ability to appreciate body language.
5. Understandable speech interaction and exchange (Kock, 2005).

Simulated, or virtual, communication through video conferencing tablet technology is not an exact substitute for co-located, F2F communication; however, this virtual alternative is vastly superior in telemedicine activities to traditional, fax, or email media to bridge time and distance.

Media naturalness in the context of telemedical communication is currently understudied. In theory, cognitive benefits of decreased effort and ambiguity, coupled with an increased psychological and intellectual stimulation, supports principles of andragogical learning theory. We have found increased communication efficiency while introducing video conferencing tablets and protocols into one of the author's clinical medical practice. These new protocols have enabled the collaborating providers to add real-time video imagery to what was once a simple verbal telephone discussion, giving both doctor and patient more opportunity to present information directly and divergently, which can lead to a better diagnosis and more immediate and effective treatment.

Divergent Thinking

Ken Robinson (2010), a leader in educational theory, describes divergent thinking as an essential capacity for creativity that leads to the "ability to see different answers and interpretations to a question" ("Changing Educational Paradigms" Video). Ramifications for physicians who can master such paradigms cannot be overstated as such ability lends itself to narrowing possible etiologies for a given patient ailment. Robinson advocates the removal of current learning paradigms—rigid book learning with standardized testing—developed during the Age of Enlightenment, and feels that "most great learning happens in groups" (Robinson, 2010, Video "Changing Educational Paradigms"). He advocates for lateral and collective group learning, instead of production-line-like linear or convergent methodologies. Similarly, Maudsley and Strivens (2000) equate such thinking and problem-solving skills to a session of brainstorming in which many possible answers

and ideas are generated in a "freewheel" approach and then later analyzed (p. 540). Robinson reminds us that school-based learning has a single correct answer, and that looking for that answer in the back of the book or asking a friend is "cheating"; while in the real world, it is called "collaboration." Robinson (2010) uses the practicality of the doctor Bones in *Star Trek* to illuminate (see Figure 1):

The Expanded Rhetorical Triangle

Aristotle introduced the rhetorical triangle of proofs as *logos* (reason/text), *ethos* (credibility/writer), and *pathos* (values, beliefs/audience) in the *Rhetoric* in the 4th century B.C.E., envisioning three types of rhetoric: political discourse, forensic or legal persuasion, and epideictic or ceremonial speaking. Archetypal situations and meaning, however, demand more complex representations. Developed as a taxonomic metaphor by I. A. Richards and Charles Kay Ogden in 1923, the "semantic triangle" describes the importance of divergence through paying close attention to situational elements of language, communicative experiences, and events. The three interdependent, and equally important, components, according to Richards and Ogden, are words (symbols), things (referents), and the thought of reference (Johnson, 1998, p. 34). The semantic triangle is often referred to as the communication triangle, and if any element in the triangle changes, so too must the angles and connections and other elements of the communication change. In *The Rhetoric of Motives,* published in 1950, the rhetorician and literary critic Kenneth Burke expanded the triangle to the shape of pentad, suggesting that all human activities are modes of symbolizing. The rhetorical elements of his dramatistic pentad include act, scene, agent, agency, and purpose (Burke, 2006). Dissatisfied with the scope of the semantic triangle, in 1969, rhetorician and teacher James Kinneavy created the rhetorical triangle to include all manifestations of text created through the relationships between reader, writer, and reality (see Figure 2).

Figure 1. Animated representation of Ken Robinson's talk (permission granted by RSA Animate)

Figure 2. Richards/Ogden's semantic triangle and Kinneavy's rhetorical triangle

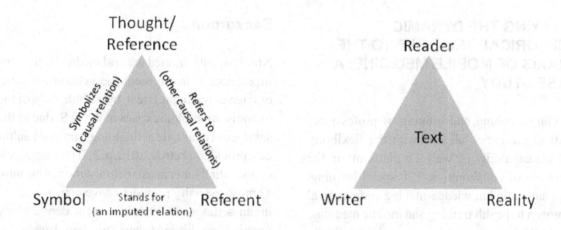

This extended lesson in rhetoric is significant because the notion of the rhetorical triangle in recent years has changed dramatically. In 1998 rhetorical theorist Robert Johnson wrote *User-Centered Technology* to further reconfigure the triangle's nomenclature into a user-centric model. He argued, "No technology is developed, disseminated, or used in a vacuum, and a user-centered theory would be remiss [...] if it bypassed this crucial concern" (p. 37), suggesting that users and technologies in addition to Aristotelian pur-pose, semantic relationships, and "dramatistic" (re)presentation of reality should become part of the metaphor. Finally, the use of Web 2.0 technologies today requires a new approach to the communication triangle in order to explain epistemological changes in communication, especially with mobile media devices.

Our interpretation of an expanded, user-centric, "expanded rhetorical triangle" mimics Johnson's user-centered principles, but accounts for dimensions of location and modality to appropriately represent communication media and protocols. The Dynamic Rhetorical Triangle (see Figure 3), thus, includes listener/speaker/speech as well as reader/writer/text, while embracing location and media type because the nature of meaning and purpose changes with the situationalized reception (i.e. home or hospital) and application (i.e. diagnosis or instruction to different stakeholders) of content. This representation includes InterActor (an active prosumer of variable content), a more dynamically-enabled communicator, content that is often database-driven and can be visual and immediate, various Web 2.0 enabled media devices, and personal and public and mobile environments which carry much more complex underpinnings of agency and authority. The connection to Burke's pentad, here, is clear.

APPLYING THE DYNAMIC RHETORICAL TRIANGLE TO THE PRAXIS OF MOBILE MEDICINE: A CASE STUDY

Ongoing teaching and training of professional medical personnel, aligned with the flexibility and the capability of Web 2.0 platforms in the exchange of collaborative, P2P social learning, is an authentic knowledge-making andragogical approach to health training and mobile medicine praxis. We have studied the approach specifically while developing teledermatology protocols for facilitating P2P medical consultations and information exchange between metropolitan dermatologists (i.e. specialists) and rural-based primary care providers (i.e. generalists). Of course, even before Web 2.0 tablet technology and hardware, scholars envisioned a network where clinicians, "especially those in isolated, rural areas," could connect to peers, tutors, conferences, and knowledge building interactions (Kamel Boulos, et al., 2007, p. 15). Still, participants in our study used mobile devices to communicate dynamically, and the principles of divergent thinking, problem-

Figure 3. The dynamic rhetorical triangle

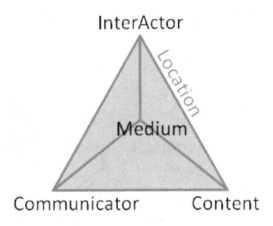

based learning, andragogy, universal design for learning, media naturalness, and social construction were each in effect.

Background

Non-specialty-trained general medical clinicians in practice (i.e. family medicine, general medicine, or internal medicine) treat, by default, 70% of the overall dermatologic cases in the U.S. due to the shortage of available dermatology-trained healthcare providers (Petrou, 2010, p. 2). This disparity is exponentially increased in rural America because 1) most specialty providers have congregated in urban settings, 2) 10% of current dermatology practices are shifting to cosmetic-based medicine, and 3) economically advanced patient populations (i.e. metropolitan cities) largely determine the distribution of resources (Cooper, 2002, p. 763).

Our research has been predicated on the use of Internet-based, personalized social networks, and the potential benefits such protocols may bring to this underserved patient population. Simple, affordable, and ubiquitous technological tools have been used to produce a coalescence of small P2P micro-networks. These professional networks can easily facilitate a responsive, real-time, and user-driven learning platform to improve the medical knowledge of general rural clinicians, as well as various types of other healthcare professionals, and could ultimately produce more accurate diagnoses and improved patient outcomes because of this collaborative effort.

Method

One of the authors of this chapter performed a clinical study in his dermatologic group. Regularly scheduled patients with a variety of dermatologic conditions, representative of all age groups and all Fitzpatrick skin types (i.e. an industry specific scale ranging from 1-6 that uniformly describes skin color), were evaluated and treated in accordance with customary office standards and policies; some of these patients were asked at the conclusion of their visit if they would like to participate in a study. Twenty patients were selected for the study based on their willingness to participate. A full explanation and consultation was performed, and informed consent was obtained and documented. The "presenting provider" then initiated a secure Wi-Fi videoconference call to the "consulting specialty physician" using the latest generation Apple® devices available at the time (e.g. iPad2® and iPod Touch4®) equipped with Apple FaceTime® video conferencing. The dermatologist (consultant) was not privy to the presenter's documented preliminary diagnosis and the dermatologist had not previously treated any of the participants. The patients' areas of concern were presented to and viewed by the consulting physician for analysis; he was able to interact with the patient, ask direct questions, and direct camera angles on the mobile devices (see Figure 4 for a simulation). After the consulting dermatologist formulated an independent diagnosis, the connection was closed. All parties verbally reported high levels of comfort, and the researchers noted a high quality of patient care and apparent personal agency through the approach.

The scientific significance and the statistical concordance of the corresponding diagnoses have been submitted for review and scientific publication, but some important theoretical, instructional, and rhetorical insights and theories can be constructed here.

Discussion of Findings

First, the value on this emerging teledermatology consultation technique must be considered in connection with time-honored medical teaching practices, such as social-constructivist and problem-based learning methodologies. New approaches expand capabilities of andragogical learning and patient care consultation by using real-time diagnosis and collaborative sharing of findings at the exact moment of a patient's visit. The previous store-and-forward method of emailing digital photos and waiting for a response (see Dragoni, 2009; Eedy & Wootton, 2001; Mair & Whittten, 2000; Tran, et al., 2011) can be effectively replaced with on-demand feedback and discussion, which may translate into a quicker diagnosis, the perception of attacking the problem more readily, and a more comfortable treatment selection process. The presenting clinician, while interacting with a real-world patient, can now incorporate a live transmission and implement a three-dimensional and more interactive learning scenario into their knowledge acquisition activities, instead of sending and receiving an email minutes, hours, or even days after the actual patient interaction. In this case study, observations and self-reporting of patients and clinicians indicated that incorporation of such technology, which includes paying attention to the medium and the location in the examination-training-diagnosis process, seemed intriguing and more effective to both patients and clinicians.

CONCLUSION

With Web 2.0 social networking and tablet technology, *mobile medicine* is a new, less-tethered approach for divergent knowledge creation through

Figure 4. Simulated tablet video conferencing between rural (Stratford, Texas) and urban (Houston, Texas) locations

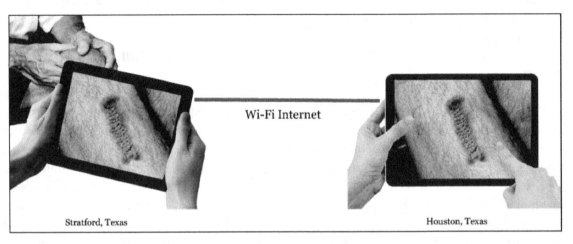

well-supported, user-driven, problem-based learning praxis. If lateral divergent thinking, as opposed to linear conceptualization, requires the ability to brainstorm and compile many possible answers, similar to a physician laboring to solve the case of a mysterious ailment, then collaborative problem-based learning and the resulting clinical decision-making is a positive step in increasing the quality of patient care.

We have researched and constructed our tablet-based, *mobile medicine* approach to engender affordable, mobile, and customizable learning opportunities with new technology familiar to the postgraduate, adult, clinical learner. Our Web 2.0 mobile medicine video conferencing approach 1) reinforces comfortable and well-rehearsed learning models, such as social-constructivist and PBL; 2) adheres to theories and principles of andragogy, universal design for learners, and social construction; 3) promotes collaborative divergent thinking to any clinical learner through recognizing dynamic complexities of the expanded rhetorical triangle; and 4) allows for real-time medical consultation, enabling the sharing of resources and expertise between rural and urban facilities, at the exact point of patient care. With the right tools, once a secure communication environment is activated, this exchange requires just three or four finger taps or swipes across the tablet's face (e.g. On > FaceTime > Select Contact).

Mobile medicine approaches to initiating on-demand, real-time consultation and collaboration will benefit clinicians and patients, and may facilitate universal access to healthcare resources in disparate locations as mobile technologies become increasingly flexible, affordable, and ubiquitous. The aforementioned clinical study and this manuscript were constructed within five months of the public release of the featured device, which underscores both the timeliness and the readiness of these technologies and this work. Additional time for further research, analysis, and industry acceptance will likely yield a greater breadth and depth of the andragogical and clinical learning opportunities afforded to practicing healthcare professionals by such technologies.

REFERENCES

Abarbanell, L. (2006). Universal design for learning in postsecondary education: Reflections on principles and their application. *Journal of Postsecondary Education and Disability*, *19*(2), 135–151.

American Academy of Dermatology. (2010). Find a dermatologist webpage. *American Academy of Dermatology*. Retrieved from http://aad.org/find-a-derm.

American Academy of Physician Assistants. (2008). AAPA physician assistant census report. *American Academy of Physician Assistants*. Retrieved from http://www.aapa.org/uploadedFiles/content/Common/Files/ob_gyn08c.pdf.

Archambault, P. M., Légaré, F., Lavoie, A., Gagnon, M. P., Lapointe, J., & St-Jaques, S. (2010). Healthcare professionals' intentions to use wiki-based reminders to promote best practices in trauma care: A survey protocol. *Implementation Science; IS, 5*, 45. doi:10.1186/1748-5908-5-45

Aristotle. (2011). *The rhetoric and the poetics of Aristotle*. Scotts Valley, CA: CreateSpace.

Benefield, H., Ashkanazi, G., & Rozensky, R. H. (2006). Communication and records: Hippa issues when working in health care settings. *Professional Psychology, Research and Practice, 37*(3), 273–277. doi:10.1037/0735-7028.37.3.273

Bowdish, B. E., Chauvin, S. W., Kreisman, N., & Britt, M. (2003). Travels towards problem based learning in medical education (VPBL). *Instructional Science, 31*(4-5), 231–253. doi:10.1023/A:1024625707592

Burke, K. (1978). Questions and answers about the pentad. *College Composition and Communication, 29*(4), 330–335. doi:10.2307/357013

Burke, K. (2006). *A grammar of motives*. Berkeley, CA: University of California Press.

Cassell, J., Steedman, M., Douville, B., Pelachaud, C., Achorn, B., & Prevost, S. … Stone, M. (1994). *Animated conversation: Rule-based generation of facial expression, gesture & spoken intonation for multiple conversational agents*. Philadelphia, PA: University of Pennsylvania. Retrieved from http://repository.upenn.edu/cgi/viewcontent.cgi?article=1342&context=cis_reports.

Cheng, C. E., Kimball, A. B., & Van Cott, A. (2010). A survey of dermatology nurse practitioners: Work setting, training, and job satisfaction. *Journal of the Dermatology Nurses Association, 2*(1), 19–23.

Clincy, V. A., & Ozturk, C. (2009). *Technological advances to distance learning*. Retrieved from http://ww1.ucmss.com/books/LFS/CSREA2006/FEC5134.pdf.

Cooper, R. A. (2002). There's a shortage of specialists: Is anyone listening? *Academic Medicine, 77*(8), 761–766. doi:10.1097/00001888-200208000-00002

Dolan, P. L. (2011). *Health care embraces the iPad: Doctors jump on new technology*. Retrieved from http://www.ama-assn.org/amednews/2011/02/07/bisa0207.htm.

Dolmans, D. H. J. M., & Schmidt, H. G. (2006). What do we know about cognitive and motivational effects of small group tutorials in problem-based learning? *Advances in Health Sciences Education: Theory and Practice, 11*(4), 321–336. doi:10.1007/s10459-006-9012-8

Dragoni, A. F. (2009). Stable communications and social networking for the netmedicine of tomorrow (or today). *AIM-Abridged Index Medicus, 17*(3), 161–164.

Eedy, D. J., & Wootton, R. (2001). Teledermatology: A review. *The British Journal of Dermatology, 144*(4), 696–707. doi:10.1046/j.1365-2133.2001.04124.x

Francis-Baldesari, C., & Pope, C. (2008). Syllabus selection: Innovative learning activity. *The Journal of Nursing Education, 47*(3), 143–144.

Howard, J. B. (2003). Universal design for learning: An essential concept for teacher education. *Journal of Computing in Teacher Education Summer, 19*(4), 113–118.

Johnson, R. (1998). *User-centered technology: A rhetorical theory for computers and other mundane artifacts*. Albany, NY: State University of New York.

Kaldoudi, E., Konstantinidis, S., & Bamidis, P. D. (2010). Web 2.0 approaches for active, collaborative learning in medicine and health. In Mohammed, S., & Fiaidhi, J. (Eds.), *Ubiquitous Health and Medical Informatics: Advancements in Web 2.0, Health 2.0, and Medicine 2.0* (pp. 127–149). Hershey, PA: IGI Global. doi:10.4018/978-1-61520-777-0.ch007

Kamel Boulos, M. N., & Wheelert, S. (2007). The emerging web 2.0 social software: An enabling suite of social technologies in health and health care education. *Health Information and Libraries Journal, 24*(1), 2–23. doi:10.1111/j.1471-1842.2007.00701.x

Karkalis, G. I., & Koutsouris, D. D. (2006). *E-health and the web 2.0*. Retrieved from http://medlab.cs.uoi.gr/itab2006/proceedings/eHealth/124.pdf.

Kinneavy, J. E. (1969). The basic aims of discourse. *College Composition and Communication, 20*(5), 297–304. doi:10.2307/355033

Knowles, M., Holton, E. F., & Swanson, R. A. (2005). *The adult learner: The definitive classic in adult education and human resource development* (6th ed.). Burlington, MA: Elsevier.

Kock, N. (2005). Media richness or media naturalness? The evolution of our biological communication apparatus and its influence on our behavior toward e-communication tools. *IEEE Transactions on Professional Communication, 48*(2), 117–130. doi:10.1109/TPC.2005.849649

Kock, N. (2007). Media naturalness and compensatory encoding: The burden of electronic media obstacles is on senders. *Decision Support Systems, 44*(1), 175–187. doi:10.1016/j.dss.2007.03.011

Mair, F., & Whitten, P. (2000). Systemic review of studies of patient satisfaction with telemedicine. *British Medical Journal, 320*(7248), 1517–1520. doi:10.1136/bmj.320.7248.1517

Martinez-Sarriegui, I., Garcia Saez, G., Hernando, M. E., Rigla, M., Brugues, E., de Leiva, A., & Gomez, E. J. (2008). Mobile telemedicine for diabetes care. In Xiao, Y., & Chen, H. (Eds.), *Mobile Telemedicine* (pp. 143–160). Boca Raton, FL: Auerbach Publications.

Maudsley, G., & Strivens, J. (2000). Promoting professional knowledge, experimental learning and critical thinking for medical students. *Medical Education, 34*(7), 535–544. doi:10.1046/j.1365-2923.2000.00632.x

McGuire, J. M., Scott, S. S., & Shaw, S. F. (2006). Universal design and its applications in educational environments. *Remedial and Special Education, 27*(3), 166–175. doi:10.1177/07419325060270030501

McLoughlin, C., & Lee, M. J. W. (2007). Social software and participatory learning: Pedagogical choices with technology affordances in the web 2.0 era. In *Proceedings Ascilite Singapore 2007* (pp. 664–675). Singapore: Ascilite Singapore.

Nelson, E. (2010). Elements of problem-based learning: Suggestions for implementation in the asynchronous environment. *International Journal on E-Learning, 9*(1), 99–114.

Orkwis, R., & McLane, K. (1998). *A curriculum every student can use: Design principles for student access*. Retrieved from http://eric.ed.gov/PDFS/ED423654.pdf.

Petrou, I. (2010, April 5). Feeling the impact: Shortage of dermatologists getting worse. *Modern Medicine: Dermatology Times*.

Quinn, C. N. (2011). *Designing mLearning: Tapping into the mobile revolution for organizational performance*. San Francisco, CA: Pfeiffer.

Richards, I. A., & Ogden, C. K. (1923). The meaning of meaning. In Bizzell, P., & Herzberg, B. (Eds.), *The Rhetorical Tradition: Readings From Classical Times to the Present* (pp. 1273–1280). New York, NY: St. Martin's Press.

Robinson, K. (Producer). (2010, October 14). *RSA animate: Changing educational paradigms*. Retrieved from http://www.youtube.com/watch?v=zDZFcDGpL4U&feature=player_embedded.

Roine, R., Ohinmaa, A., & Hailey, D. (2001). Assessing telemedicine: A systemic review of the literature. *Canadian Medical Association Journal, 165*(6), 765–771.

Rollett, H., Lux, M., Strohmaier, M., Dosinger, G., & Tochtermann, K. (2007). The web 2.0 way of learning with technologies. *International Journal of Learning Technology, 3*(1), 87–108. doi:10.1504/IJLT.2007.012368

Rose, D. H., Harbour, W. S., Johnson, C. S., Daley, S. G., & Abarbanell, L. (2006). Universal design for learning in postsecondary education: Reflections on principles and their application. *Journal of Postsecondary Education and Disability, 19*(2), 135–151.

Rubin, D. L., Rodriguez, C., Shah, P., & Beaulieu, C. (2008). Ipad: Semantic annotation and markup of radiological images. In *Proceedings of AMIA 2008 Symposium,* (pp. 626-630). Washington, DC: AMIA.

Savery, J. R., & Duffy, T. M. (2001). *Problem based learning: An instructional model and its constructivist framework*. Bloomington, IN: Center for Research on Learning and Technology.

Schopf, T., Bolle, R., & Solvoll, T. (2010). The workload of web-based consultations with atopic eczema at home. *BMC Research Notes, 3,* 71. doi:10.1186/1756-0500-3-71

Shieh, R. (2008). A case study of constructivist instructional strategies for adult online learning. *British Journal of Educational Technology, 41*(5), 706–720.

Topol, E. (2010, February 2). *Eric Topol: The wireless future of medicine*. Retrieved from http://www.ted.com/talks/eric_topol_the_wireless_future_of_medicine.html.

Tran, K., Ayad, M., Weinberg, J., Cherng, A., Chowdbury, M., & Monir, S. (2011). Mobile teledermatology in the developing world: Implications of feasibility study on 30 Egyptian patients with common skin diseases. *Journal of the American Academy of Dermatology, 64*(2), 302–309. doi:10.1016/j.jaad.2010.01.010

Walker, R., & Monin, N. (2001). The purpose of the picnic: Using Burke's dramatistic pentad to analyse a company event. *Journal of Organizational Change Management, 14*(3), 266–279. doi:10.1108/09534810110394886

White, T. (2010). iPads to be distributed in incoming class by Stanford medical students. *Stanford School of Medicine*. Retrieved from http://med.stanford.edu/ism/2010/august/ipad.html.

Whitten, P. S., Mair, F. S., Haycox, A., May, C. R., Williams, T. L., & Hellmich, S. (2002). Systemic review of cost effectiveness studies of telemedicine interventions. *British Medical Journal, 324,* 1434–1437. doi:10.1136/bmj.324.7351.1434

Wootton, R. (2001). Recent advances: Telemedicine. *British Medical Journal, 323*(8), 557–560. doi:10.1136/bmj.323.7312.557

Zhu, C., Valcke, M., & Schellens, T. (2009). Cultural differences in the perception of a social-constructivist e-learning environment. *British Journal of Educational Technology, 40*(1), 164–168. doi:10.1111/j.1467-8535.2008.00879.x

ADDITIONAL READING

Cook, J., Pachler, N., & Bachmair, B. (2011). Ubiquitous mobility with mobile phones: A cultural ecology for mobile learning. *e-Learning and Digital Media, 8*(3) 181-194.

Ebner, C., Wurm, E. M. T., Binder, B., Kittler, H., Lozzi, G. P., & Massone, C. (2007). Mobile teledermatology: A feasibility study of 58 subjects using mobile phones. *Journal of Telemedicine and Telecare, 14*(1), 2–7. doi:10.1258/jtt.2007.070302

Granlund, H., Thoden, C.-J., Carlson, C., & Harno, K. (2003). Realtime teleconsultations versus face-to-face consultations in dermatology: Immediate and six-month outcome. *Journal of Telemedicine and Telecare, 9*(1), 204–209. doi:10.1258/135763303322225526

Guy, R. (Ed.). (2010). *Mobile learning: Pilot projects and initiatives*. Santa Rosa, CA: Informing Science Press.

Kidd, T. T., & Chen, I. (Eds.). (2011). *Ubiquitous learning: Strategies for pedagogy, course design, and technology*. Charlotte, NC: Information Age Publishing.

Nordal, E. J., Moseng, D., Kvammen, B., & Lochen, M.-L. (2001). A comparative study of teleconsultations versus face-to-face consultations. *Journal of Telemedicine and Telecare, 7*(1), 257–265. doi:10.1258/1357633011936507

Pachler, N., Bachmair, B., & Cook, J. (2010). *Mobile learning: Structures, agency, and practices*. London, UK: Springer.

Thind, C. K., Brooker, I., & Ormerod, A. D. (2011). Teledermatology: A tool for remote supervision of a general practitioner with special interest in dermatology. *Clinical and Experimental Dermatology, 36*(1), 489–494. doi:10.1111/j.1365-2230.2011.04073.x

Warshaw, E. M., Hillman, Y. J., Greer, N. L., Hagel, E. M., MacDonald, R., Rutks, I. R., & Wilt, T. J. (2010). Teledermatology for diagnosis and management of skin conditions: A systematic review. *Journal of the American Academy of Dermatology, 64*(4), 759–772. doi:10.1016/j.jaad.2010.08.026

Weinstok, M. A., Nguyen, F. Q., & Risica, P. M. (2002). Patient and referring provider satisfaction with teledermatology. *Journal of the American Academy of Dermatology, 47*(1), 68–72. doi:10.1067/mjd.2002.119666

Wurm, E. M. T., Hofmann-Wellenhof, R., Wurm, R., & Soyer, H. P. (2008). Telemedicine and teledermatology: Past, present and future. *Journal der Deutschen Dermatologischen Gesellschaft, 6*(2), 106–112. doi:10.1111/j.1610-0387.2007.06440.x

KEY TERMS AND DEFINITIONS

Andragogy: The study of teaching adult learners. Adult learners have specific needs, such as the need to know, the need to a foundation of knowledge, the need to privilege a self-concept, the need for ready content, the need for immediately relevant orientation, and the need for personal motivation.

Divergent Thinking: A capacity for creativity that can lead to seeing different answers and interpretations to questions.

Dynamic Rhetorical Triangle: An expanded rhetorical or communication triangle that embraces Web 2.0 technologies and divergent thinking to include location and media type in addition to reader, writer, and text or listener, speaker, and speech.

Fitzpatrick's Skin Type: A skin classification system first developed by Dr. Thomas Fitzpatrick of Harvard Medical School in 1975. This system, and its recent revisions, is a uniformly accepted nomenclature among dermatologists and other healthcare professionals.

Media Naturalness Theory: A theory by Ned Kock that suggests the greater the "realness" or naturalness of any communication the less cognitive effort and ambiguity there is, and the more potential for increased physiological stimulation.

Mobile Medicine: The use of mobile technologies and Web 2.0 networking tools by healthcare practitioners, professionals, and/or patients to provide divergent knowledge creation, user-guided problem-based learning, and untethered mobility.

Pedagogy: The study of teaching and educational instruction.

Problem-Based Learning: A student-centered instructional model that includes environmental specificity, and requires both group collaboration and self-guided exploration in order to select, develop, and use various skills to solve specific problems.

Rhetoric: The art of persuasion, including attention to the reader, the writer, the text, the modality, and the location of the communicative moment and situation.

Social-Constructivism: Because knowledge is socially situated, it is always already constructed through reflection on one's own thoughts and experiences as well as through embracing others' ideas.

Telemedicine: The use of electronic communication devices and protocols utilized in a cost effective manner by healthcare professionals to assist individuals at disparate locations. Often referred to as e-health.

Universal Design for Learning: An approach to designing curriculum which promotes ready access, active participation, and steady individual progress.

Web 2.0: A personalized, customizable second generation of the World Wide Web that affords active participatory learning, peer-to-peer collaboration, flexible retooling of information, and mobile accessibility.

Compilation of References

Abarbanell, L. (2006). Universal design for learning in postsecondary education: Reflections on principles and their application. *Journal of Postsecondary Education and Disability, 19*(2), 135–151.

Abdo, S. N., Pashnyak, T. G., & Dennen, V. P. (2011). Medical students' international blogging community: A coping mechanism to survive the difficult years of medical school. *International Journal of Web Based Communities, 7*(3), 342–356. doi:10.1504/IJWBC.2011.041203

Abel, R. (2007). Innovation, adoption, and learning impact: Creating the future of IT. *EDUCAUSE Review, 42*(2), 12–30.

Abraham, A. (2010). *Computational social network analysis: Trends, tools and research advances.* New York, NY: Springer.

Adamic, L. A., Zhang, J., Bakshy, E., & Ackerman, M. S. (2008). *Knowledge sharing and yahoo answers: Everyone knows something.* Paper presented at the Proceeding of the 17th international conference on World Wide Web. Beijing, China.

Adler, P. S., & Kwon, S. W. (2002). Social capital: Prospects for a new concept. *Academy of Management Review, 27*(1), 17–40.

Adobe Inc. (2010). *Adobe connect for web meetings.* Retrieved from http://www.adobe.com/products/adobe-connect/web-meetings.html.

Adobe Inc. (2011). *Showcase.* Retrieved from http://www.adobe.com/products/adobeconnect/showcase.html.

AECT. (2011). *AECT code of ethics.* Retrieved June 9, 2011, from http://www.aect.org/About/Ethics.asp.

Ahuja, G. (2000). Collaboration networks, structural holes, and innovation: A longitudinal study. *Administrative Science Quarterly, 45*(3), 425–455. doi:10.2307/2667105

Ajjan, H., & Hartshorne, R. (2008). Investigating faculty decisions to adopt Web 2.0 technologies: Theory and empirical tests. *The Internet and Higher Education, 11*(2), 71–80. doi:10.1016/j.iheduc.2008.05.002

Akande, A. (1998). Towards the multicultural validation of a western model of student approaches to learning. *Education, 119*(1), 37–47.

Ala-Mutka, K., Punie, Y., & Ferrari, A. (2009). Review of learning in online networks and communities. *Lecture Notes in Computer Science, 5794,* 350–364. doi:10.1007/978-3-642-04636-0_34

Alexander, B. (2006). Web 2.0: A new wave of innovation for teaching and learning? *EDUCAUSE Review, 42*(2), 32–44.

Allen, M., & Naughton, J. (2011). Social learning: A call to action for learning professionals. *T + D, 65*(8), 50-55.

Ally, M. (2005). Multimedia information design for mobile devices. In Pagani, M. (Ed.), *Encyclopedia of Multimedia Technology and Networking* (pp. 704–709). Hershey, PA: IGI Global. doi:10.4018/978-1-59140-561-0.ch099

Ambrogi, R. J. (2007, May 4). Legal wikis are bound to wow you. *Law Technology News.* Retrieved from http://www.law.com/jsp/lawtechnologynews/PubArticleLTN.jsp?id=900005480497&slreturn=1.

American Academy of Dermatology. (2010). Find a dermatologist webpage. *American Academy of Dermatology.* Retrieved from http://aad.org/find-a-derm.

American Academy of Physician Assistants. (2008). AAPA physician assistant census report. *American Academy of Physician Assistants.* Retrieved from http://www.aapa.org/uploadedFiles/content/Common/Files/ob_gyn08c.pdf.

Anderson, S. (2002). Working together to develop a professional learning community. In *Proceedings of the 2002 Annual International Conference of the Higher Education Research and Development Society of Australasia (HERDSA)*, (pp. 20-26). Perth, Australia: HERDSA.

Antonijevic, S., & Gurak, L. J. (2009). Trust in on-line interaction: An analysis of the socio-psychological features of online communities and user engagement. In *Proceedings on Cultural Heritage Online: Empowering Users: An Active Role for User Communities*, (pp. 1-7). Fondazione Rinascimento Digitale.

Apegga. (2011). *Professional development.* Retrieved from http://www.apegga.org/members/ProfDev/toc_map.html.

Appadurai, A. (2001). Grassroots globalization and the research imagination. In Appadurai, A. (Ed.), *Globalization* (pp. 1–21). Durham, NC: Duke University Press.

Archambault, P. M., Légaré, F., Lavoie, A., Gagnon, M. P., Lapointe, J., & St-Jaques, S. (2010). Healthcare professionals' intentions to use wiki-based reminders to promote best practices in trauma care: A survey protocol. *Implementation Science; IS, 5,* 45. doi:10.1186/1748-5908-5-45

Ardichvili, A., Page, V., & Wentling, T. (2002). Virtual knowledge-sharing communities of practice at caterpillar: Success factors and barriers. *Performance Improvement Quarterly, 15*(3), 99–113.

Aristotle,. (2011). *The rhetoric and the poetics of Aristotle.* Scotts Valley, CA: CreateSpace.

Aritz, J., & Walker, R. C. (2010). Cognitive organization and identity maintenance in multicultural teams: A discourse analysis of decision-making meeting. *Journal of Business Communication, 47*(1), 20–41. doi:10.1177/0021943609340669

Arora, A., & Gambardella, A. (1990). Complementarity and external linkages: The strategies of the large firms in biotechnology. *The Journal of Industrial Economics, 38*(4), 361–379. doi:10.2307/2098345

ASTD. (2011). *ASTD code of ethics.* Retrieved June 9, 2011, from http://www.astd.org/ASTD/aboutus/missionAndVision/.

Attwell, G. (2009). The social impact of personal learning environments. In Wheeler, S. (Ed.), *Connected Minds, Emerging Cultures: Cybercultures in Online Learning* (pp. 119–136). Charlotte, NC: Information Age Publishing.

Ausubel, D. P. (2000). *The acquisition and retention of knowledge.* Dordrecht, The Netherlands: Kluwer Academic Publishers.

Baker, L. R., & Oswald, D. L. (2010). Shyness and online social networking services. *Journal of Social and Personal Relationships, 27*(7), 873–889. doi:10.1177/0265407510375261

Baldwin, R. G., & Austin, A. E. (1995). Toward a greater understanding of faculty research collaboration. *Review of Higher Education, 19*(1), 45–70.

Bambina, A. (2007). *Online social support: The interplay of social networks and computer-mediated communication.* Youngstown, NY: Cambria Press.

Barlow, M., & Thomas, D. B. (2011). *The executive's guide to enterprise social media strategy: How social networks are radically transforming your business.* Hoboken, NJ: John Wiley & Sons.

Bassell, K. (2010). Social media and the implications for nursing faculty mentoring: A review of the literature. *Teaching and Learning in Nursing, 5,* 143–148. doi:10.1016/j.teln.2010.07.007

Bastiaens, T. J., & Martens, R. L. (2000). Conditions for web-based learning with real events. In Abbey, B. (Ed.), *Instructional and Cognitive Impacts of Web-Based Education* (pp. 1–31). Hershey, PA: IGI Global. doi:10.4018/978-1-878289-59-9.ch001

Batpurev, B., & Uyanga, S. (2006). *Using open source software for open and distance learning.* Paper presented at the Information and Communications Technology for Social Development: An International Symposium. Jakarta, Indonesia.

Bauman, Z. (2003). *Liquid modernity*. Cambridge, UK: Polity Press.

Baum, J., Calabrese, T., & Silverman, B. (2000). Don't go it alone: Alliance network composition and startups' performance in Canadian bio-technology. *Strategic Management Journal, 21*(3), 267–294. doi:10.1002/(SICI)1097-0266(200003)21:3<267::AID-SMJ89>3.0.CO;2-8

Beckman, M. (1990). Collaborative learning: Preparation for the workplace and democracy. *College Teaching, 38*(4), 128–133.

Beer, D., & Burrows, R. (2007). Sociology and, of and in Web 2.0: Some initial considerations. *Sociological Research Online, 12*(5), 17. Retrieved March 4, 2011, from http://www.socresonline.org.uk/12/5/17.html.

Bekmeier-Feuerhahn, S., & Eichenlaub, A. (2010). What makes for trusting relationships in on-line communication? *Journal of Communication Management, 14*(4), 337–355. doi:10.1108/13632541011090446

Bell, B., & Gilbert, J. (1996). *Teacher development: A model from science education*. London, UK: Falmer Press.

Benefield, H., Ashkanazi, G., & Rozensky, R. H. (2006). Communication and records: Hippa issues when working in health care settings. *Professional Psychology, Research and Practice, 37*(3), 273–277. doi:10.1037/0735-7028.37.3.273

Berger, P., & Luckmann, T. (1966). *The social construction of reality: The sociology of knowledge*. New York, NY: Penguin Books.

Berg, S., Duncan, J., & Friedman, P. (1982). *Joint venture and corporate innovation*. Cambridge, MA: Oelgeschlager, Gunn & Hain.

Bhulyan, T., Josang, A., & Xu, Y. (2010). Managing trust in online social networks. In Furht, B. (Ed.), *Handbook of Social Network Technologies and Applications* (pp. 471–496). New York, NY: Springer.

Bielaczyc, K., & Collins, A. (1999). Learning communities in classrooms: A reconceptualization of educational practice. In Reigeluth, C. (Ed.), *Instructional-Design Theories and Models. A New Paradigm of Instructional Theory* (pp. 269–292). Mahwah, NJ: Lawrence Erlbaum Associates.

Bielenia-Grajewska, M. (2011). Rola Internetu w komunikacji prowadzonej przez polskie lotniska: Na przykładzie sytuacji kryzysowych spowodowanych trudnymi warunkami atmosferycznymi. *Pieniądze i Więź, 51*, 156–162.

Bielenia-Grajewska, M. (2012). Linguistics. In Bainbridge, W. S. (Ed.), *Leadership in Science and Technology. A Reference Handbook* (pp. 41–48). Thousand Oaks, CA: SAGE.

Bilge, L., Strufe, T., Balzarotti, D., & Kirda, E. (2009). All your contacts are belong to us: Automated identity theft attacks on social networks. In *Proceedings of the 18th International Conference on World Wide Web,* (pp. 551-560). New York, NY: IEEE.

Billet, S. (1996). Situated learning: Bridging socio-cultural and cognitive theorizing. *Learning and Instruction, 6*(3), 263–280. doi:10.1016/0959-4752(96)00006-0

Billett, S., & Pavlova, M. (2005). Learning through working life: Self and individuals' agentic action. *International Journal of Lifelong Education, 24*(3), 195–211. doi:10.1080/02601370500134891

Bingham, T., & Conner, M. (2010). *The new social learning*. Alexandria, VA: ASTD Press & Berett-Koehler.

Bisgin, H., Agarwal, N., & Xu, X. (2010). Investigating homophily in online social networks. In *Proceedings of the 2010 IEEE/WIC/ACM International Conference on Web Intelligence and Intelligent Agent Technology,* (pp. 533-536). IEEE Press.

Bisgin, H., Agarwal, N., & Xu, X. (2012). A study of homophily on social media. In Ting, I.-H., Hong, T.-P., & Wang, L. (Eds.), *Social Network Mining, Analysis and Research Trends* (pp. 17–34). Hershey, PA: IGI Global. doi:10.4018/978-1-61350-513-7.ch002

Bitter-Rijpkema, M., & Verjans, S. (2010). Hybrid professional learning networks for knowledge workers: Educational theory inspiring new practices. In L. Creanor, D. Hawkridge, K. Ng, & F. Rennie (Eds.), *ALT-C 2010 Conference Proceedings: Into Something Rich and Strange: Making Sense of the Sea-Change,* (pp. 166-174). Nottingham, UK: ALT-C. Retrieved from http://dspace.ou.nl/bitstream/1820/2575/6/bitter_verjans%20ALTC_2010_HybridprofessionalLN.pdf.

Black, B. (1999). National culture and high commitment management. *Employee Relations*, *21*(4), 389–404. doi:10.1108/01425459910285519

Black, E. W., Thompson, L. A., Duff, W. P., Dawson, K., Saliba, H., & Black, N. M. P. (2010). Re-visiting social network utilization by physicians-in-training. *Journal of Graduate Medical Education*, *2*(2), 289–293.

Blanchard, R. (2011). *Creating wealth with a small business: Strategies and models for entrepreneurs in the 2010s*. Bloomington, IN: iUniverse.

Boase, J., & Wellman, B. (2004). *Suggested questions on social networks and social capital*. Paper presented to the Policy Research Initiative. Ottawa, Canada.

Boase, J., Horrigan, J., Wellman, B., & Rainie, L. (2006). The strength of internet ties. *Pew Internet & American Life Project*. Retrieved from http://www.pewinternet.org/Reports/2006/The-Strength-of-Internet-Ties.aspx.

Boase, J. (2008). Personal networks and the personal communication system. *Information Communication and Society*, *11*(4), 490–508. doi:10.1080/13691180801999001

Bochner, S. (1999). Cultural diversity within and between societies: Implications for multicultural social systems. In Pedersen, P. B. (Ed.), *Multiculturalism as a Fourth Force* (pp. 19–60). Washington, DC: Taylor and Francis.

Bonilla-Warford, N. (2010). Many social media options exist for optometrists. *Optometry -. Journal of the American Optometric Association*, *81*(11), 613–614. doi:10.1016/j.optm.2010.09.006

Borko, H. (2004). Professional development and teacher learning: Mapping the terrain. *Educational Researcher*, *33*(8), 3–15. doi:10.3102/0013189X033008003

Bosman, L., & Zagenczyk, T. (2011). Revitalize your teaching: Creative approaches to applying social media in the classroom. In White, B., King, I., & Tsang, P. (Eds.), *Social Media Tools and Platforms in Learning Environments* (pp. 3–15). Berlin, Germany: Springer-Verlag. doi:10.1007/978-3-642-20392-3_1

Boss, S. (2008). Twittering, not frittering: Professional development in 140 characters. *Edutopia*. Retrieved from http://www.edutopia.org/twitter-professional-development-technology-microblogging.

Bourdieu, P. (1986). The forms of capital. In Richardson, J. (Ed.), *Handbook of Theory and Research for the Sociology of Education* (pp. 241–258). New York, NY: Greenwood.

Bourdieu, P., & Wacquant, L. J. D. (1992). *An invitation to reflexive sociology*. Chicago, IL: University of Chicago Press.

Bowdish, B. E., Chauvin, S. W., Kreisman, N., & Britt, M. (2003). Travels towards problem based learning in medical education (VPBL). *Instructional Science*, *31*(4-5), 231–253. doi:10.1023/A:1024625707592

Bowes, J. (2002). Buliding online communities for professional networks. *Global Summit 2002*. Retrieved from http://www.educationau.edu.au/globalsummit/papers/jbowes.htm.

boyd, D. M., & Ellison, N. B. (2007). Social network sites: Definition, history, and scholarship. *Journal of Computer-Mediated Communication*, *13*(1). doi:10.1111/j.1083-6101.2007.00393.x

Boyle, B., While, D., & Boyle, T. (2004). A longitudinal study of teacher change: What makes professional development effective? *Curriculum Journal*, *15*(1), 45–68. doi:10.1080/1026716032000189471

Bratsas, C., Kapsas, G., Konstantinidis, S., Koutsouridis, G., & Bamidis, P. D. (2009). A semantic wiki within Moodle for Greek medical education. In *Proceedings of CBMS 2009: The 22nd IEEE International Symposium on Computer-Based Medical Systems*, (pp. 1-6). IEEE Press. Retrieved from http://ieeexplore.ieee.org/xpl/freeabs_all.jsp?arnumber=5255417.

Brennan, P. F., & Fink, S. V. (1997). Health promotion, social support, and computer networks. In Street, R. L., Gold, W. R., & Manning, T. (Eds.), *Health Promotion and Interactive Technology: Theoretical Applications and Future Directions* (pp. 157–169). Mahwah, NJ: Lawrence Erlbaum Associates.

Brey, P., & Søraker, J. H. (2009). Philosophy of computing and information technology. In Gabbay, D. M., Meijers, A., Thagard, P., & Woods, J. (Eds.), *Philosophy of Technology and Engineering Sciences* (pp. 1341–1408). Amsterdam, The Netherlands: North Holland. doi:10.1016/B978-0-444-51667-1.50051-3

Brislin, R. W., & Yoshida, T. (1994). *Intercultural communication training: An introduction.* London, UK: Sage.

Brooks, J. G., & Brooks, M. G. (1999). *In search of understanding: The case for constructivist classrooms.* Alexandria, VA: American Society for Curriculum Development.

Brown, J. S., Broderick, A. J., & Lee, N. (2007). Word of mouth communication within online communities: Conceptualizing the online social network. *Journal of Interactive Marketing*, *21*(3), 2–20. doi:10.1002/dir.20082

Brown, J. S., Collins, A., & Duguid, P. (1989). Situated cognition and the culture of learning. *Educational Researcher*, *28*(1), 32–42.

Brown, J. S., & Duguid, P. (1991). Organizational learning and communities-of-practice: Toward a unified view of working, learning, and innovation. *Organization Science*, *2*(1), 40–57. doi:10.1287/orsc.2.1.40

Brown, T. H. (2005). Towards a model for m-learning in Africa. *International Journal on E-Learning*, *4*(3), 299–315.

Bruner, J. (1996). *Culture of education.* Boston, MA: Harvard University Press.

Bruner, J. S. (1966). *Toward a theory of instruction.* Cambridge, MA: Belknap Press of Harvard University Press.

Bruner, J. S. (1990). *Acts of meaning.* Boston, MA: Harvard University Press.

Buckley, P. J., & Carter, M. J. (1999). Managing cross-border complementary knowledge: Conceptual developments in the business process approach to knowledge management in multinational firms. *International Studies of Management and Organisation*, *29*(1), 80–92.

Buehler, J. (2005). The power of questions and the possibilities of inquiry in English education. *English Education*, *37*(4), 280–287.

Bullas, J. (2010). *How Best Buy energized 170,000 employees with social media.* from http://www.jeffbullas.com/2010/05/26/how-best-buy-energized-170000-employees-with-social-media/.

Burch, R. (2001). Effective web design and core communication issues: The missing components in web-based distance education. *Journal of Educational Multimedia and Hypermedia*, *10*(4), 357–367.

Burge, E. J., & Polec, J. (2008). Transforming learning and teaching in practice: Where change and consistency interact. In Haughey, M., Evans, T., & Murphy, D. (Eds.), *International Handbook of Distance Education* (pp. 237–258). Bingley, UK: Emerald Group Publishing Ltd.

Burke, K. (1978). Questions and answers about the pentad. *College Composition and Communication*, *29*(4), 330–335. doi:10.2307/357013

Burke, K. (2006). *A grammar of motives.* Berkeley, CA: University of California Press.

Burnett, B., & Meadmore, P. (2002). Streaming lectures: Enhanced pedagogy or simply 'bells and whistles'? In *Proceedings of the International Education Research Conference.* Brisbane, Australia: Australian Association for Research in Education.

Burnett, R., Consalvo, M., & Ess, C. (2010). *The handbook of internet studies.* Malden, MA: John Wiley & Sons.

Burnham, B. (2005). *The adult learner and implications for the craft of instructional design.* Paper presented at the 9th Annual Global Conference on Computers in Chinese Education. Laie, HI.

Burt, R. (1992). *Structural holes: The social structure of competition.* Cambridge, MA: Harvard University Press.

Burt, R. (1997). The contingent value of social capital. *Administrative Science Quarterly*, *42*(2), 339–365. doi:10.2307/2393923

Burt, R. S. (2000). The network structure of social capital. *Research in Organizational Behavior*, *22*, 345–423. doi:10.1016/S0191-3085(00)22009-1

Burt, R. S. (2004). Structural holes and good ideas. *American Journal of Sociology*, *110*(2), 349–399. doi:10.1086/421787

Buzzo, B. (2007). *Governare la comunicazione d'impresa: Modelli, attori, tecniche, strumenti e strategie.* Milan, Italy: Franco Angeli.

Cabre Castellvi, M. T. (1997). Standardization and interference in terminology. In Labrum, M. B. (Ed.), *The Changing Scene in World Languages: Issues and Challenges* (pp. 49–64). Philadelphia, PA: John Benjamins Publishing Company.

Cain, J., & Fox, B. I. (1999). Web 2.0 and pharmacy education. *American Journal of Pharmaceutical Education, 73*(7), 120. Retrieved from http://www.ncbi.nlm.nih.gov/pmc/articles/PMC2779632/doi:10.5688/aj7307120

Campbell, A., McNamara, O., & Gilroy, P. (2004). *Practitioner research and professional development in education.* London, UK: Paul Chapman Publishing.

Canadian Health Services Research Foundation. (2003). *The theory and practice of knowledge brokering in Canada's health system.* Retrieved from http://www.sandy-campbell.com/sc/Knowledge_Translation_files/Theory_and_Practice_e.pdf.

Cantoni, L., & Piccini, C. (2004). *Il sito del vicino è sempre più verde: La comunicazione fra committenti e progettisti di siti Internet.* Milan, Italy: Franco Angeli.

Cantoni, L., & Tardini, S. (2010). The internet and the web. In Albertazzi, D., & Cobley, P. (Eds.), *Media: An Introduction* (pp. 220–232). Harlow, UK: Pearson Education Limited.

Carliner, S. (2004). *An overview of online learning.* Amherst, MA: HRD Press.

Carr, N. G. (2004). *Does IT matter? Information technology and the corrosion of competitive advantage.* Boston, MA: Harvard Business School Publishing Corporation.

Carroll, D. (2005). Learning through interactive talk: A school-based mentor teacher study group as a context for professional learning. *Teaching and Teacher Education, 21*(5), 457–473. doi:10.1016/j.tate.2005.03.005

Carter, K. (1990). Teachers' knowledge and learning to teach. In Houston, W. R. (Ed.), *Handbook of Research on Teacher Education: A Project of the Association of Teacher Educators* (pp. 291–310). London, UK: Collier Macmillan.

Casquero, O., Portillo, J., Ovelar, R., Benito, M., & Romo, J. (2010). iPLE network: An integrated eLearning 2.0 strategy from university's perspective. *Interactive Learning Environments, 18*(3), 293–308. doi:10.1080/10494820.2010.500553

Cassell, J., Steedman, M., Douville, B., Pelachaud, C., Achorn, B., & Prevost, S. … Stone, M. (1994). *Animated conversation: Rule-based generation of facial expression, gesture & spoken intonation for multiple conversational agents.* Philadelphia, PA: University of Pennsylvania. Retrieved from http://repository.upenn.edu/cgi/viewcontent.cgi?article=1342&context=cis_reports.

Castells, M. (2010). *The rise of the network society.* Chichester, UK: Blackwell Publishing.

Castillo, C., Donato, D., Gionis, A., & Mishne, G. (2008). Finding high-quality content in social media. In E. Agichtein (Ed.), *Proceedings of the 2008 International Conference on Web Search & Data Mining.* Palo Alto, CA: ACM Press.

Caverly, D. C., & Ward, A. (2008). Techtalk: Wikis and collaborative knowledge construction. *Journal of Developmental Education, 32*(2), 36–37.

CBS News. (2011, February 6). Did the internet kill privacy? Facebook photos lead to a teacher losing her job: What expectations of privacy exist in the digital era? *CBS News.* Retrieved March 4, 2011, from http://www.cbsnews.com/stories/2011/02/06/sunday/main7323148.shtml.

Cercone, J. (2009). We're smarter together: Building professional social networks in English education. *English Education, 41*(3), 199–206.

Chaddock, K. R., & Saltiel, I. M. (2004). *When faculty collaborations crumble: How to know if the benefits outweigh the costs.* Paper presented at the 29th Annual Conference of the Association for the Study of Higher Education. Kansas City, MO

Chalmers, L., & Keown, P. (2006). Communities of practice and professional development. *International Journal of Lifelong Education, 25*(2), 139–156. doi:10.1080/02601370500510793

Chan, T., Corlett, D., Sharples, M., Ting, J., & Westmancott, O. (2005). Developing interactive logbook: A personal learning environment. In *Proceedings of the IEEE International Workshop on Wireless and Mobile Technologies in Education (WMTE 2005)*, (pp 73–75). IEEE Computer Society Press.

Chan, K., & Liebowitz, J. (2006). The synergy of social network analysis and knowledge mapping: A case study. *International Journal of Management and Decision Making*, 7(1), 19–35. doi:10.1504/IJMDM.2006.008169

Chapel, E. (2008). Mobile technology: The foundation for an engaged and secure campus community. *Journal of Computing in Higher Education*, 20(2), 15–23. doi:10.1007/s12528-008-9002-3

Chatterjee, P., & Biswas, T. (2011). Blogs and twitter in medical publications - Too unreliable to quote, or a change waiting to happen? *South African Medical Journal*, 101(10), 712–714. Retrieved from http://samj.org.za/index.php/samj/article/view/5213

Chen, G. M. (2011). Tweet this: A uses and gratifications perspective on how active Twitter use gratifies a need to connect with others. *Computers in Human Behavior*, 27(2), 755–762. doi:10.1016/j.chb.2010.10.023

Chen, G., Gully, S. M., Whiteman, J.-A., & Kilcullen, R. N. (2000). Examination of relationships among trait-like individual differences, state-like individual difference, and learning performance. *The Journal of Applied Psychology*, 85(6), 835–847. doi:10.1037/0021-9010.85.6.835

Cheng, C. E., Kimball, A. B., & Van Cott, A. (2010). A survey of dermatology nurse practitioners: Work setting, training, and job satisfaction. *Journal of the Dermatology Nurses Association*, 2(1), 19–23.

Chickering, A. W., & Gamson, Z. F. (1991). Applying the seven principles for good practice in undergraduate education. In Chickering, A. W., & Gamson, Z. F. (Eds.), *New Directions for Teaching and Learning*. San Francisco, CA: Jossey Bass.

Ching-Yung, L., Ehrlich, K., Griffiths-Fisher, V., & Desforges, C. (2008). SmallBlue: People mining for expertise search. *IEEE MultiMedia*, 15(1), 78–84. doi:10.1109/MMUL.2008.17

Chini, T. C. (2004). *Effective knowledge transfer in multinational corporations*. Basingstoke, UK: Palgrave Macmillan. doi:10.1057/9780230005877

Chinn, S. J., & Williams, J. (2009). Using web 2.0 to support the active learning experience. *Journal of Information Systems Education*, 20(2), 165.

Cho, H., Gay, G., Davidson, B., & Ingraffe, A. (2007). Social networks, communication styles, and learning performance in a CSCL community. *Computers & Education*, 49, 309–329. doi:10.1016/j.compedu.2005.07.003

Chretien, K., Goldman, E., & Faselis, C. (2008). The reflective writing class blog: Using technology to promote reflection and professional development. *Journal of General Internal Medicine*, 23(12), 2066–2070. doi:10.1007/s11606-008-0796-5

Christakis, N., & Fowler, J. (2009). *Connected: The surprising power of our social networks and how they shape our lives*. New York, NY: Little, Brown & Co.

Chu, L., Young, C., Zamora, A., Kurup, V., & Macario, A. (2010a). Anesthesia 2.0: Internet-based information resources and web 2.0 applications in anesthesia education. *Current Opinion in Anaesthesiology*, 23(2), 218–227. doi:10.1097/ACO.0b013e328337339c

Chu, L., Zamora, A. K., Young, C., Kurup, V., & Macario, A. (2010b). The role of social networking applications in the medical academic environment. *International Anesthesiology Clinics*, 48(3), 61–82. doi:10.1097/AIA.0b013e3181e6e7d8

Cisco. (2011). *Cisco's internet postings policy*. Retrieved June 9, 2011, from http://blogs.cisco.com/news/ciscos_Internet_postings_policy/.

Claridge, T. (2004). *Social capital and natural resource management*. Unpublished Master Thesis. Brisbane, Australia: University of Queensland.

Clearswift Limited. (2010). *Web 2.0 in the workplace today*. Whitepaper. Retrieved March 4, 2011, from https://info.clearswift.com/express/clients/clearhq/papers/Web2_0_InTheWorkplaceToday.pdf.

Clincy, V. A., & Ozturk, C. (2009). *Technological advances to distance learning*. Retrieved from http://ww1.ucmss.com/books/LFS/CSREA2006/FEC5134.pdf.

Clough, G., Jones, A. C., McAndrew, P., & Scanlon, E. (2008). Informal learning with PDAs and smartphones. *Journal of Computer Assisted Learning, 24*(5), 359–371. doi:10.1111/j.1365-2729.2007.00268.x

Cobb, P. (1995). Continuing the conversation: A response to Smith. *Educational Researcher, 24*(6), 25–27.

Cochrane, T., & Bateman, R. (2010). Smartphones give you wings: Pedagogical affordances of mobile Web 2.0. *Australasian Journal of Educational Technology, 26*(1), 1–14.

Cochran-Smith, M., & Lytle, S. L. (1999a). Relationships of knowledge and practice: Teacher learning in communities. *Review of Research in Education, 24*, 249–305.

Cochran-Smith, M., & Lytle, S. L. (1999b). The teacher researcher movement: A decade later. *Educational Researcher, 28*(7), 15–25.

Cole, A. L., & Knowles, J. G. (1993). Teacher development partnership research: A focus on methods and issues. *American Educational Research Journal, 30*(3), 473–495.

Coleman, J. S. (1988). Social capital in the creation of human capital. *American Journal of Sociology, 94*, 95–120. doi:10.1086/228943

Collier, J., & Esteban, R. (1999). Governance in the participative organisation: Freedom, creativity and ethics. *Journal of Business Ethics, 21*(2/3), 173–188. doi:10.1023/A:1006250627410

Collier, K. G. (1980). Peer-group learning in higher education: The development of higher-order skills. *Studies in Higher Education, 5*(1), 55–62. doi:10.1080/030750 78012331377306

Collins, A., Brown, J. S., & Holum, A. (1991). Cognitive apprenticeship: Making thinking visible. *American Educator*. Retrieved from http://elc.fhda.edu/transform/resources/collins_brown_holum_1991.pdf.

Collison, G., Elbaum, B., Haavind, S., & Tinker, R. (2000). *Facilitating online learning: Effective strategies for moderators*. Madison, WI: Atwood Publishing.

Constant, D., Sproull, L., & Kiesler, S. (1996). The kindness of strangers: The usefulness of electronic weak ties for technical advice. *Organization Science, 7*(2), 119–135. doi:10.1287/orsc.7.2.119

Cooper, J. (1990). *Cooperative learning and college instruction*. Long Beach, CA: California State University.

Cooper, R. A. (2002). There's a shortage of specialists: Is anyone listening? *Academic Medicine, 77*(8), 761–766. doi:10.1097/00001888-200208000-00002

Cornelius, S., & Marston, P. (2009). Towards an understanding of the virtual context in mobile learning. *ALT-J, 17*(3), 161–172. doi:10.1080/09687760903247617

Coskun Samli, A. (2002). *In search of an equitable, sustainable globalization: The bittersweet dilemma*. Westport, CT: Quorum Books.

Cottrell, S. (2003). *Skills for success*. New York, NY: Palgrave.

Couros, A. (2008, February 25). *What does the network mean to you?* Retrieved from http://educationaltechnology.ca/couros/799.

Cox, E. J. (2009). The collaborative mind: Tools for 21st-century learning. *Multimedia & Internet@Schools, 16*(5), 10-14.

Cressey, D. (2011). Q & A: The virtual trainer. *Nature, 477*(7365), 406. doi:10.1038/477406a

Cross, J. (2007). *Informal learning: Rediscovering the natural pathways that inspire innovation and performance*. San Francisco, CA: Pfeiffer.

Crotty, M. (1998). *Foundations of social research: Meaning and perspective in the research process*. Thousand Oaks, CA: Sage.

Currie, G. (2007). Beyond our imagination: The voice of international students on the MBA. *Management Learning, 38*(5), 539–556. doi:10.1177/1350507607083206

Cutillo, L. A., Manulis, M., & Strufe, T. (2010). Security and privacy in online social networks. In Furht, B. (Ed.), *Handbook of Social Network Technologies and Applications*. New York, NY: Springer. doi:10.1007/978-1-4419-7142-5_23

Dainton, M., & Zelley, E. D. (2010). *Applying communication theory for professional life: A practical introduction*. Thousand Oaks, CA: SAGE Publications, Ltd.

Daniel, D. (2007). Five tips for bringing Web 2.0 into the enterprise. *CIO Magazine*. Retrieved from http://www.cio.com/article/115300/Five_Tips_for_Bringing_Web_2.0_Into_the_Enterprise.

Dann, S. (2010). Twitter content classification. *First Monday*, *15*(12). Retrieved from http://frodo.lib.uic.edu/ojsjournals/index.php/fm/article/view/2745/2681

Darling-Hammond, L. (2003). Keeping good teachers: Why it matters, what leaders can do. *Educational Leadership*, *60*(8), 6–13.

Darling-Hammond, L., & Bransford, J. (2005). *Preparing teachers for a changing world: What teachers should learn and be able to do*. San Francisco, CA: Jossey-Bass.

Darling-Hammond, L., & McLaughlin, M. W. (1995). Policies that support professional development in an era of reform. *Phi Delta Kappan*, *76*(8), 597–604.

Davenport, T., & Prusak, L. (1998). *Working knowledge: How organisations manage what they know*. Boston, MA: Harvard Business School Press.

Davydov, V. (1999). The content and unsolved problems of activity theory. In Engstrom, R. M. Y., Miettinen, R., & Punamaki, R.-L. (Eds.), *Perspectives on Activity Theory* (pp. 39–52). Cambridge, UK: Cambridge University Press.

Day, D., Dosa, M., & Jorgensen, C. (1995). The transfer of research information within and by multicultural teams. *Information Processing & Management*, *31*(1), 89–100.

De Choudhury, M., Sundaram, H., John, A., & Seligmann, D. D. (2010). Analyzing the dynamics of communication in online social networks. In Furht, B. (Ed.), *Handbook of Social Network Technologies and Applications* (pp. 59–94). New York, NY: Springer Science and Business Media, LLC. doi:10.1007/978-1-4419-7142-5_4

de Jong, T. (2010). *Linking social capital to knowledge productivity*. Master's Thesis. Retrieved from http://josephkessels.com/sites/default/files/thesis_t_de_jong.pdf.

de Moraes, R. C. C. (2010). Educação a distância e efeitos em cadeia. *Cadernos de Pesquisa*, *40*(140), 547–559. Retrieved from http://www.scielo.br/scielo.php?script=sci_arttext&pid=S0100-15742010000200012&lng=pt&nrm=isodoi:10.1590/S0100-15742010000200012

Degree, A. (2010). *25 CEO blogs every biz student should read*. Retrieved from http://www.accountingdegree.com/blog/2010/25-ceo-blogs-every-biz-student-should-read/.

Demetriou, H., Wilson, E., & Winterbottom, M. (2009). The role of emotion in teaching: Are there differences between male and female newly qualified teachers' approaches to teaching? *Educational Studies*, *35*(4), 449–473. doi:10.1080/03055690902876552

Demiris, G. (2006). The diffusion of virtual communities in health care: Concepts and challenges. *Patient Education and Counseling*, *62*(2), 178–188. doi:10.1016/j.pec.2005.10.003

Demski, J. (2010). Tweets for teachers. *Technological Horizons in Education Journal*, *37*(2), 16–18.

Dennen, V. P. (2011). *Conversations on the hashtag: Does conference Twitter use promote professional discourse?* Paper presented at the International Conference on the e-Society. Avila, Spain.

Dennen, V. P. (2011). Facilitator presence and identity in online discourse: Use of positioning theory as an analytic framework. *Instructional Science*, *39*(4), 527–541. doi:10.1007/s11251-010-9139-0

Denzin, N. (1970). *The research act in sociology*. London, UK: Butterworth.

Denzin, N. (1989). *Interpretive biography*. Thousand Oaks, CA: Sage.

Department of Justice. (2008). *Privacy and civil liberties policy development guide and implementation templates*. Retrieved June 9, 2011, from http://it.ojp.gov/documents/Privacy_Guide_Final.pdf.

Di Bari, R. (2010). *L'era della web communication: Il futuro è adesso*. Trento, Italy: Tangram Edizioni Scientifiche.

Dika, S. L., & Singh, K. (2002). Applications of social capital in educational literature: A critical synthesis. *Review of Educational Research*, *72*(1), 31–60. doi:10.3102/00346543072001031

Dillman, D. A. (2000). *Mail and internet surveys: The tailored method* (2nd ed.). New York, NY: Wiley & Sons.

Dillon, J. T. (1981). A norm against student questions. *Clearing House (Menasha, Wis.)*, *55*(3), 136–139.

DiMaggio, P. (2001). Introduction: Making sense of the contemporary firm and prefiguring its future. In DiMaggio, P. (Ed.), *The Twenty-First-Century Firm: Changing Economic Organization in International Perspective* (pp. 3–30). Princeton, NJ: Princeton University Press.

Doktorowicz, K. (2003). Społeczności wirtualne-cyberprzestrzeń w poszukiwaniu utraconych więzi. In Haber, L. W. (Ed.), *Społeczeństwo Informacyjne - Wizja Czy Rzeczywistość?* (pp. 59–66). Kraków, Poland: Uczelniane Wydawnictwa Naukowo Dydaktyczne.

Dolan, P. L. (2011). *Health care embraces the iPad: Doctors jump on new technology.* Retrieved from http://www.ama-assn.org/amednews/2011/02/07/bisa0207.htm.

Dolmans, D. H. J. M., & Schmidt, H. G. (2006). What do we know about cognitive and motivational effects of small group tutorials in problem-based learning? *Advances in Health Sciences Education: Theory and Practice, 11*(4), 321–336. doi:10.1007/s10459-006-9012-8

Dragoni, A. F. (2009). Stable communications and social networking for the netmedicine of tomorrow (or today). *AIM-Abridged Index Medicus, 17*(3), 161–164.

Dron, J. (2007). *Control and constraint in e-learning: Choosing when to choose* (1st ed.). Hershey, PA: IGI Global. doi:10.4018/978-1-59904-390-6

Duncan-Howell, J. (2010). Teachers making connections: Online communities as a source of professional learning. *British Journal of Educational Technology, 41*(2), 324–340. doi:10.1111/j.1467-8535.2009.00953.x

Durkin, K. (2008). The middle way: East Asian master's students' perceptions of critical argumentation in UK universities. *Journal of Studies in International Education, 12*(1), 38–55. doi:10.1177/1028315307302839

Durland, M. M., Fredericks, K. A., & American Evaluation Association. (2006). *Social network analysis in program evaluation.* San Francisco, CA: Jossey-Bass.

Eastmond, D. V. (1995). *Alone but together: Adult distance study through computer conferencing.* Cresskill, NJ: Hampton Press.

Ebner, M., Mühlburger, H., Schaffert, S., Schiefner, M., Reinhardt, W., & Wheeler, S. (2010). Getting granular on Twitter: Tweets from a conference and their limited usefulness for non-participants. In Reynolds, N., & Turcsányi-Szabó, M. (Eds.), *Key Competencies in the Knowledge Society* (*Vol. 324,* pp. 102–113). Boston, MA: Springer. doi:10.1007/978-3-642-15378-5_10

Economides, A. A. (2008). Culture-aware collaborative learning. *Multicultural Education & Technology Journal, 2*(4), 243–267. doi:10.1108/17504970810911052

Edelman, S. (2011, March 13). Facebook vent burns teacher. *New York Post.* Retrieved March 14, 2011, from http://www.nypost.com/p/news/local/brooklyn/facebook_vent_burns_teacher_JiHBB6wQwDIjiYVfcUiIpN#ixzz1GhODXHPx.

Educause Learning Initiative. (2005). *7 things you should know about social bookmarking.* Washington, DC: Educause.

edWeb.net. MCH, Inc., & MMS Education. (2009). *Preliminary findings: A survey of D-12 educators on social networking and content-sharing tools.* Retrieved from http://www.edweek.org/media/k-12socialnetworking.pdf.

Eedy, D. J., & Wootton, R. (2001). Teledermatology: A review. *The British Journal of Dermatology, 144*(4), 696–707. doi:10.1046/j.1365-2133.2001.04124.x

Egbert, J., & Thomas, M. (2001). The new frontier: A case study in applying instructional design for distance teacher education. *Journal of Technology and Teacher Education, 9*(3), 391–405.

Egege, S., & Kutieleh, S. (2004). Critical thinking: Teaching foreign notions to foreign students. *International Education Journal, 4*(4), 75-85. Retrieved from http://ehlt.flinders.edu.au/education/iej/articles/v4n4/Egege/paper.pdf.

Ehrlich, K., Lin, C.-Y., & Griffiths-Fisher, V. (2007). Searching for experts in the enterprise: Combining text and social network analysis. In *Proceedings of the 2007 International ACM Conference on Supporting Group Work.* ACM Press.

Eisen, M. J. (2001). Peer-based learning: A new-old alternative to professional development. *Adult Learning, 12*, (n.d),. Retrieved from http://www.questia.com/googleScholar.qst?docId=5000657294

Ellison, N., Lampe, C., & Steinfield, C. (2009). Social network sites and society: Current trends and future possibilities. *Interactions Magazine, 16*(1).

Ellison, N. B., Steinfield, C., & Lampe, C. (2007). The benefits of Facebook "friends": Social capital and college students' use of online social networking sites. *Journal of Computer-Mediated Communication, 12*(4). Retrieved from http://jcmc.indiana.edu/vol12/issue4/ellison.htmldoi:10.1111/j.1083-6101.2007.00367.x

Ellström, P. E. (2011). Informal learning at work: Conditions, processes and logics. In Malloch, M., Cairns, L., Evans, K., & O'Connor, B. N. (Eds.), *The SAGE Handbook of Workplace Learning* (pp. 105–119). London, UK: Sage Publications, Ltd.

Engeström, Y. (1993). Developmental studies of work as a testbench of activity theory: The case of primary care medical practice. In Chaiklin & Lave (Eds.), *Understanding Practice: Perspectives on Activity and Context,* (pp. 64-103). Cambridge, UK: Cambridge University Press.

Engeström, Y. (1987). *Learning by expanding: An activity-theoretical approach to developmental research.* Helsinki, Finland: Orieta-Konsultit.

Engeström, Y. (2001). Expansive learning at work: Toward an activity theoretical reconceptualization. *Journal of Education and Work, 14*(1), 133–156.

Engeström, Y., & Mittienen, R. (1999). Introduction. In Engeström, Y., Miettinen, R., & Punamaki, R. (Eds.), *Perspectives on Activity Theory* (pp. 1–16). Cambridge, UK: Cambridge University Press.

Erez, M., & Zidon, I. (1984). Effects of goal acceptance on the relationship of goal difficulty to performance. *The Journal of Applied Psychology, 69*, 69–78. doi:10.1037/0021-9010.69.1.69

Erickson, B. H. (2004). The distribution of gendered social capital in Canada. In Flap, H., & Volker, B. (Eds.), *Creation and Returns of Social Capital a New Research Program* (pp. 27–50). London, UK: Routledge.

Eyrich, N., Padman, M. L., & Sweetser, K. D. (2008). PR practitioners' use of social media tools and communication technology. *Public Relations Review, 34*, 412–414. Retrieved from http://uga.academia.edu/sweetser/Papers/121858/PR_practitioners_use_of_social_media_tools_and_communication_technologydoi:10.1016/j.pubrev.2008.09.010

Fang, Y. W. (2001). *Does technology hinder or enhance learning and teaching technology in language education: Meeting the challenges of research and practice.* Retrieved from http://www.sjsu.edu/people/waimei.fang/articles/hinder-enhance.pdf.

Fenstermacher, G. D. (1994). The knower and the known: The nature of knowledge in research on teaching. In Darling-Hammond, L. (Ed.), *Review of Research in Education* (pp. 3–56). Washington, DC: American Educational Research Association. doi:10.2307/1167381

Ferdig, R. (2007). Examining social software in teacher education. *Journal of Technology and Teacher Education, 15*(1), 5–10.

Fernandez, J. (2004). *Corporate communications: A 21st century primer.* New Delhi, India: Response Books.

Feser, J. (2010) *mLearning is not eLearning on a mobile device.* Retrieved from http://floatlearning.com/2010/04/mlearning-is-not-elearning-on-a-mobile-device/.

Fielding, N., Lee, R. M., & Blank, G. (2008). *The Sage handbook of online research methods.* Thousand Oaks, CA: Sage.

Field, K. (2011). Reflection at the heart of effective continuing professional development. *Professional Development in Education, 37*(2), 171–175. doi:10.1080/19415257.2011.559700

Fischer, M. A., Haley, H.-L., Saarinen, C. L., & Chretien, K. C. (2011). Comparison of blogged and written reflections in two medicine clerkships. *Medical Education, 45*(2), 166–175. doi:10.1111/j.1365-2923.2010.03814.x

Fiszer, E. P. (2004). *How teachers learn best: An ongoing professional development model.* Lanham, MD: Scarecrow Education.

Flynn, N. (2006). *Blog rules: A business guide to managing policy, public relations, and legal issues.* New York, NY: AMACON.

Foglio, A. (2010). *E-commerce e web marketing: Strategie di web markeing e tecniche di vendita in internet*. Milan, Italy: Franco Angeli.

Fok, A. W. P., & Ip, H. H. S. (2006). An agent-based framework for personalized learning in continuing professional development. *International Journal of Distance Education Technologies, 4*(3), 48–61. doi:10.4018/jdet.2006070105

Fontaine, G., & Chun, G. (2010). Presence in teleland. In Rudestam, K. E., & Schoenholtz-Read, J. (Eds.), *Handbook of Online Learning* (pp. 30–56). Thousand Oaks, CA: Sage Publications, Ltd.

Foreman, T. (2011, March 8). How much is Facebook really worth? *CNN*. Retrieved from http://edition.cnn.com/2011/TECH/social.media/03/08/facebook.overvalued/.

Foster, A. (2004). A nonlinear model of information-seeking behavior. *Journal of the American Society for Information Science and Technology, 55*(3), 228–237. doi:10.1002/asi.10359

Fox, F. F. (1992). Research, teaching, and publication productivity: Mutuality versus competition in academia. *Sociology of Education, 65*(4), 293–305. doi:10.2307/2112772

Fox, S. (1997). From management education and development to the study of management learning. In Burgoyne, J., & Reynolds, M. (Eds.), *Management Learning: Integrating Perspectives in Theory and Practice* (pp. 21–37). Thousand Oaks, CA: Sage.

Francis-Baldesari, C., & Pope, C. (2008). Syllabus selection: Innovative learning activity. *The Journal of Nursing Education, 47*(3), 143–144.

Frost, T. S., & Zhou, C. (2005). R&D co-practice and 'reverse' knowledge integration in multinational firms. *Journal of International Business Studies, 36*(6), 676–687. doi:10.1057/palgrave.jibs.8400168

Fullan, M. (1982). *The meaning of educational change*. New York, NY: Teachers College Press.

Fu, Y. (2005). Measuring personal networks with daily contacts: A single-item survey question and the contact diary. *Social Networks, 27*(3), 169–186. doi:10.1016/j.socnet.2005.01.008

Gandel, P. B., & Golden, C. (2004). Professional development in tough financial times. *EDUCAUSE Quarterly Magazine, 27*(1).

Gandhi, S. (2010, January 19). *IBM dives into Second Life*. Retrieved from http://www.ibm.com/developerworks/opensource/library/os-social-secondlife/?ca=drs-.

Gannon, M. J. (2008). *Paradoxes of culture and globalization*. Thousand Oaks, CA: SAGE.

GAO. (2010, November 28). *Information management: Challenges in federal agencies' use of web 2.0 technologies – GAO testimony before the subcommittee on information policy, census, and national archives, committee on oversight and government reform, US house of representatives*. Retrieved June 9, 2011, from http://www.whitehouse.gov/omb/circulars_a130_a130appendix_iii.

Garet, M. S., Porter, A. C., Desimone, L., Birman, B. F., & Yoon, K. S. (2001). What makes professional development effective? Results from a national sample of teachers. *American Educational Research Journal, 38*(4), 915–945. doi:10.3102/00028312038004915

Gargiulo, M. (2010). Lingua e Identitá. La politica nella rete di Facebook. In Cresti, E., & Korzen, I. (Eds.), *Language, Cognition and Identity. Extensions of the endocentric/exocentric language typology* (pp. 155–166). Florence: Firenze University Press.

Gargiulo, M., & Benassi, M. (2000). Trapped in your own net? Network cohesion, structural holes, and the adaptation of social capital. *Organization Science, 11*(2), 183–196. doi:10.1287/orsc.11.2.183.12514

Garrick, J. (1998). *Informal learning in the workplace: Unmasking human resource development*. New York, NY: Routledge.

Garton, L., & Wellman, B. (1999). Studying on-line social networks. *Doing Internet Research: Critical Issues and Methods for Examining the Net, 75*.

Gatti, B. A., Barreto, E. S. S., & André, M. D. A. (2011). *Políticas docentes no Brasil: Um estado da arte*. Rio de Janeiro, Brasília: UNESCO.

GDRC. (2011). *What is collaborative learning*. Retrieved from http://www.gdrc.org/kmgmt/c-learn/what-is-cl.html.

Geddes, S. J. (2004). Mobile learning in the 21st century: Benefit for learners. *The Knowledge Tree e-Journal, 6*. Retrieved from http://knowledgetree.flexiblelearning.net.au/edition06/download/geddes.pdf.

Geertz, C. (1973). Thick description: Towards an interpretive theory of culture. In Lincoln, Y., & Denzin, N. (Eds.), *Turning Points in Qualitative Research: Tying Knots in a Handkerchief* (pp. 143–168). Walnut Creek, CA: Altamira Press.

General Medical Council. (2009). *Tomorrow's doctors: Recommendations on undergraduate medical education.* Retrieved from http://www.gmc-uk.org/education/undergraduate/tomorrows_doctors_2009.asp.

George, D. R. (2011). Friending facebook? A minicourse on the use of social media by health professionals. *The Journal of Continuing Education in the Health Professions, 31*(3), 215–219. doi:10.1002/chp.20129

George, D., & Dellasega, C. (2011). Social media in medical education: Two innovative pilot studies. *Medical Education, 45*(11), 1158–1159. doi:10.1111/j.1365-2923.2011.04124.x

Gherardi, S., & Nicolini, D. (2000). The organizational learning of safety in communities of practice. *Journal of Management Inquiry, 9*(1), 7–18. doi:10.1177/105649260091002

Gibson, S. (2006, November 20). *Wikis are alive and kicking in the enterprise.* Retrieved from http://www.eweek.com/c/a/Messaging-and-Collaboration/Wikis-Are-Alive-and-Kicking-in-the-Enterprise/.

Gilbert, E., & Karahalios, K. (2009). Predicting tie strength with social media. In *Proceedings of the 27th International Conference on Human Factors in Computing Systems.* Boston, MA: ACM Press.

Giles, H., Coupland, N., & Coupland, J. (1991). Accommodation theory: Communication, context and consequence. In Giles, H., Coupland, J., & Coupland, N. (Eds.), *Contexts of Accommodation: Developments in Applied Sociolinguistics* (pp. 1–68). New York, NY: The Press Syndicate of the University of Cambridge. doi:10.1017/CBO9780511663673.001

Giles, H., & Ogay, T. (2009). Communication accommodation theory. In Whaley, B. B., & Samter, W. (Eds.), *Explaining Communication: Contemporary Theories and Exemplars* (pp. 325–344). Mahwah, NJ: Lawrence Erlbaum Associates, Inc.

Gilroy, K. (2001). Collaborative e-learning: The right approach. *ArsDigita Systems Journal.* Retrieved from http://www.eveandersson.com/arsdigita/asj/elearning/.

Glisby, M., & Holden, N. (2011). Mastering tacit corridors for competitive advantage: Cross-cultural knowledge creation and sharing at four international firms. *Global Business and Organisational Excellence, 30*(5), 64–77. doi:10.1002/joe.20396

Glowacki-Dudka, M., & Brown, M. P. (2007). Professional development through faculty learning communities. *New Horizons in Adult Education & Human Resource Development, 21*, 29–39.

Goh, D. H., Ang, R. P., Chua, A., & Lee, C. S. (2009). Why we share: A study of motivations for mobile media sharing. In *Proceedings of the Fifth International Conference on Active Media Technology (AMT 2009),* (pp. 195-206). Beijing, China: IEEE.

Golby, M. (1996). Teachers' emotions: An illustrated discussion. *Cambridge Journal of Education, 26*(3), 423–434. doi:10.1080/0305764960260310

Goldhaber, D., & Anthony, E. (2007). Can teacher quality be effectively assessed? National board certification as a signal of effective teaching. *The Review of Economics and Statistics, 89*(1), 134–150. doi:10.1162/rest.89.1.134

Goldhaber, D., & Brewer, D. (2001). Evaluating the evidence on teacher certification: A rejoinder. *Educational Evaluation and Policy Analysis, 23*(1), 79–86. doi:10.3102/01623737023001079

Goodsell, A. (1992). *Collaborative learning: A sourcebook for higher education.* University Park, PA: The Pennsylvania State University.

Google. (2010a). *For educators: Teach collaborative revision with Google Docs.* Retrieved from http://learn.googleapps.com/.

Google. (2010b). *Google Apps: Apps learning center for users.* Retrieved from http://www.google.com/a/help/intl/en/edu/customers.html.

Gorini, A., Gaggioli, A., Vigna, C., & Riva, G. (2008). A Second Life for eHealth: Prospects for the use of 3-D virtual worlds in clinical psychology. *Journal of Medical Internet Research, 10*(3). doi:10.2196/jmir.1029

Grabill, J. T., & Hicks, T. (2005). Multiliteracies meet methods: The case for digital writing in English education. *English Education, 37*(4), 301–311.

Graham, J. (2004, December 14). Google's library plan a huge help. *USA Today.* Retrieved March, 13, 2011, from http://www.usatoday.com/money/industries/technology/2004-12-14-google-usat_x.htm.

Granovetter, M. (1973). The strength of weak ties. *American Journal of Sociology, 78*(6), 1360–1380. doi:10.1086/225469

Granovetter, M. S. (1982). The strength of weak ties: A network theory revisited. In Mardsen, P. V., & Lin, N. (Eds.), *Social Structure and Network Analysis* (pp. 105–130). Thousand Oaks, CA: Sage Publications. doi:10.2307/202051

Gray, B. (2004). Informal learning in an online community of practice. *Journal of Distance Education, 19*(1), 20–35.

Grbich, C. (2007). *Qualitative data analysis: An introduction.* Thousand Oaks, CA: Sage.

Grebow, D. (2002). *At the water cooler of learning. Executive Briefing.* Arlington, VA: University of Virginia.

Gredler, M. E. (1997). *Learning and instruction: Theory into practice* (3rd ed.). Upper Saddle River, NJ: Prentice-Hall.

Greene, J. A., Choudhry, N. K., Kilabuk, E., & Shrank, W. H. (2010). Online social networking by patients with diabetes: A qualitative evaluation of communication with Facebook. *Journal of General Internal Medicine, 26*(3), 287–292. doi:10.1007/s11606-010-1526-3

Greenhow, C. (2011). Online social networks and learning. *Horizon, 19*(1), 4–12. doi:10.1108/10748121111107663

Greenhow, C., & Robelia, E. (2009). Old communication, new literacies: Social network sites as social learning resources. *Journal of Computer-Mediated Communication, 14*(4), 1130–1161. doi:10.1111/j.1083-6101.2009.01484.x

Greenhow, C., & Robelia, E. (2009b). Informal learning and identity formation in online social networks. *Learning, Media and Technology, 34*(2), 119–140. doi:10.1080/17439880902923580

Grisham, D., Bergeron, B., & Brink, B. (1999). Connecting communities of practice through professional development school activities. *Journal of Teacher Education, 50*(3), 182–191. doi:10.1177/002248719905000304

Gross, R., & Acquisti, A. (2005). *Information revelation and privacy in online social networks.* Paper presented at the Workshop on Privacy in the Electronic Society (WPES). Alexandria, VA.

Grossman, P., Wineburg, S., & Woolworth, S. (2001). *What makes teacher community different from a gathering of teachers.* Retrieved from http://depts.washington.edu/ctpmail/PDFs/Community-GWW-01-2001.pdf.

Grossman, P., Hammerness, K., & MacDonald, M. (2009). Redefining teaching, re-imaging teacher education. *Teachers and Teaching: Theory and Practice, 15*(2), 273–289. doi:10.1080/13540600902875340

Grossman, P., Wineburg, S., & Woolworth, S. (2001). Toward a theory of community. *Teachers College Record, 103*(6), 942–1012. doi:10.1111/0161-4681.00140

Guest, D. E. (2002). Perspectives on the study of work-life balance. *Social Sciences Information. Information Sur les Sciences Sociales, 41*, 255–279. doi:10.1177/0539018402041002005

Guffey, M. E. (2010). *Essentials of business communication.* Mason, OH: Cengage Learning.

Guha, S., Tang, K., & Francis, P. (2008). *NOYB: Privacy in online social networks.* Paper presented at the 1st ACM SIGCOMM Workshop on Online Social Networks (WOSN'08). Seattle, WA.

Gulati, R., & Gargiulo, M. (1999). Where do interorganizational networks come from? *American Journal of Sociology, 104*(5), 1439–1493. doi:10.1086/210179

Guskey, T. R. (1986). Staff development and the process of teacher change. *Educational Researcher, 15*(5), 5–12.

Hager, P., & Halliday, J. (2009). *Recovering informal learning: Wisdom, judgment and community.* Dordrecht, The Netherlands: Springer Science + Business Media.

Häkkinen, P., Arvaja, M., & Mäkitalo, K. (2004). Prerequisites for CSCL: Research approaches, methodological challenges and pedagogical development. In Littleton, K., Faulkner, D., & Miell, D. (Eds.), *Learning to Collaborate, Collaborating to Learn* (pp. 161–175). New York, NY: Nova Science Publishers, Inc.

Halx, M. D. (2010). Re-conceptualizing college and university teaching through the lens of adult education: Regarding undergraduates as adults. *Teaching in Higher Education*, *15*(5), 519–530. doi:10.1080/13562517.2010.491909

Hanley, M. (2009). Are you ready for informal learning? *Information Outlook*, *13*(7), 13–18.

Hargie, O. (2003). *Skilled interpersonal communication: Research, theory and practice*. Hove, UK: Routledge.

Hargreaves, A. (1998). The emotional practice of teaching. *Teaching and Teacher Education*, *14*(8), 835–854. doi:10.1016/S0742-051X(98)00025-0

Hargreaves, A. (2000). Mixed emotions: Teachers' perceptions of their interactions with students. *Teaching and Teacher Education*, *16*(8), 811–826. doi:10.1016/S0742-051X(00)00028-7

Harris, A. L., & Rea, A. (2009). Web 2.0 and virtual world technologies: A growing impact on IS education. *Journal of Information Systems Education*, *20*(2), 137–144. Retrieved from http://learningtechworld.com/Documents/Virtual%20World%20Technologies.pdf

Harrison, R., & Kessels, J. W. M. (2004). *Human resource development in a knowledge economy: An organizational view*. New York, NY: Palgrave Macmillan.

Hart, J. (2010, August 1). *The future of social media in the enterprise*. Retrieved from http://janeknight.typepad.com/socialmedia/2010/08/futureenterprise.html.

Hawn, C. (2009). Take two aspirin and tweet me in the morning: How Twitter, Facebook, and other social media are reshaping health care. *Health Affairs*, *28*(2), 361–368. doi:10.1377/hlthaff.28.2.361

Haythornthwaite, C. (1996). Social network analysis: An approach and technique for the study of information exchange. *Library & Information Science Research*, *18*(4), 323–342. doi:10.1016/S0740-8188(96)90003-1

Hedlund, G. (1994). A model of knowledge management and the N-form corporation. *Strategic Management Journal*, *15*, 73–90. doi:10.1002/smj.4250151006

Hellriegel, D., & Slocum, J. W. (2007). *Organizational behavior*. Mason, OH: Thompson Higher Education.

Helou, S. E., Li, N., & Gillet, D. (2010). *The 3A Interaction Model: Towards bridging the gap between formal and informal learning*. Paper presented at the Third International Conference on Advances in Computer-Human Interactions, Saint Maarten, Netherlands.

Hendery, S. (2009, July 9). Great gadget, stratospheric price. *New Zealand Herald*, p. B4. Retrieved 9 July 2009 from http://www.nzherald.co.nz/technology/news/article.cfm?c_id=5&objectid=10583290&pnum=0.

Hennemann, S., & Liefner, I. (2010). Employability of German geography graduates: The mismatch between knowledge acquired and competences required. *Journal of Geography in Higher Education*, *34*(2), 215–230. doi:10.1080/03098260903227400

Hertel, G., Konradt, U., & Orlikowski, B. (2004). Managing distance by interdependence: Goal setting, task interdependence and team-based rewards in virtual teams. *European Journal of Work and Organizational Psychology*, *13*(1), 1–28. doi:10.1080/13594320344000228

Hew, K. F., & Hara, N. (2007). Empirical study of motivators and barriers of teacher online knowledge sharing. *Educational Technology Research and Development*, *55*(6), 573–595. doi:10.1007/s11423-007-9049-2

Hicks, T. (2009). *The digital writing workshop*. Portsmouth, NH: Heinemann.

Hiebert, J., Gallimore, R., & Stigler, J. W. (2002). A knowledge base for the teaching profession: What would it look like and how can we get one? *Educational Researcher*, *31*(5), 3–15. doi:10.3102/0013189X031005003

Hill, H. C. (2007). Learning in the teaching workforce. *The Future of Children*, *17*(1), 111–127. doi:10.1353/foc.2007.0004

Hitchcock, M. A., Bland, C. J., Hekelman, F. P., & Blumenthal, M. G. (1995). Professional networks: The influence of colleagues on the academic success of faculty. *Academic Medicine: Journal of the Association of American Medical Colleges, 70*(12), 1108–1116. doi:10.1097/00001888-199512000-00014

Hoekstra, A., Beijaard, D., Brekelmans, M., & Korthagen, F. (2007). Experienced teachers' informal learning from classroom teaching. *Teachers and Teaching: Theory and Practice, 13*(2), 189–206.

Hoekstra, A., & Korthagen, F. (2011). Teacher learning in a context of educational change: Informal learning versus systematically supported learning. *Journal of Teacher Education, 62*(1), 76–92. doi:10.1177/0022487110382917

Hofstede, G. (1980). *Culture's consequences: International differences in work-related values.* Beverly Hills, CA: Sage Publications.

Hogan, B. (2008). Analyzing social networks via the Internet. In *The SAGE Handbook of Online Research Methods* (pp. 141–160). Thousand Oaks, CA: Sage.

Holt, R. (2004). *Dialogue on the internet: Language, civic identity, and computer-mediated communication.* Westport, CT: Greenwood Publishing Group.

Honey, C., & Herring, S. C. (2009). *Beyond microblogging: Conversation and collaboration via Twitter.* Paper presented at the 42nd Hawaii International Conference on System Sciences. Hawaii, HI.

Hoover, J. N. (2007, June 20). *Motorola's IT department takes on Enterprise 2.0.* Retrieved from http://www.informationweek.com/news/199905701.

Howard, C. (2007). *m-Learning: The latest trends, development and real-world applications.* Oakland, CA: Bersin Associates.

Howard, J. B. (2003). Universal design for learning: An essential concept for teacher education. *Journal of Computing in Teacher Education* Summer, *19*(4), 113-118.

HP. (2010). *HP TRIM software and Microsoft SharePoint HP.* Whitepaper. Retrieved March 4, 2011, from http://h20195.www2.hp.com/V2/GetPDF.aspx/4AA2-1196ENW.pdf.

Huberman, B. A., Romero, D. M., & Wu, F. (2009). Social networks that matter: Twitter under the microscope. *First Monday, 14*(1).

Hudson, B. (2010). Candlepower: The intimate flow of online collaborative learning. In Rudestam, K. E., & Schoenholtz-Read, J. (Eds.), *Handbook of Online Learning* (pp. 267–300). Thousand Oaks, CA: SAGE.

Huffaker, D. A., Swaab, R., & Diermeier, D. (2011). The language of coalition formation in online multiparty negotiations. *Journal of Language and Social Psychology, 30*(1), 66–81. doi:10.1177/0261927X10387102

Hunzicker, J. (2011, April 01). Effective professional development for teachers: A checklist. *Professional Development in Education, 37*(2), 177–179. doi:10.1080/19415257.2010.523955

Hur, J., & Brush, T. (2009). Teacher participation in online communities: Why do teachers want to participate in self-generated online communities of K-12 teachers? *Journal of Research on Technology in Education, 41*(3), 279–303.

Hur, J., & Hara, N. (2007). Factors cultivating sustainable online communities for K-12 teacher professional development. *Journal of Educational Computing Research, 36*(3), 245–268. doi:10.2190/37H8-7GU7-5704-K470

Hyman, J., Luks, H., & Sechrest, R. (2011). Online professional networks for physicians: Risk management. *Clinical Orthopaedics and Related Research.* Retrieved from http://www.springerlink.com/content/q353mj5425106452/fulltext.pdf.

IBM. (2011). *Customers on social business.* Retrieved from http://www-01.ibm.com/software/lotus/socialbusiness/customers.

Illich, I. D. (1970). *Deschooling society.* New York, NY: Harper & Row.

Ingersoll, R. M., & Strong, M. (2011). The impact of induction and mentoring programs for beginning teachers: A critical review of the research. *Review of Educational Research, 81*(2), 201–233. doi:10.3102/0034654311403323

InternetWorldStats.com. (2010). *Internet usage statistics.* Retrieved from http://internetworldstats.com/stats.htm.

Ira, K., & Berge, Z. (2009). Online learning's future in the workplace with augmented reality. In Cartelli, A., & Palma, M. (Eds.), *Encyclopedia of Information Communication Technology*. Hershey, PA: IGI Global.

ISPS. (2011). *ISPI code of ethics*. Retrieved June 9, 2011, from http://www.ispi.org/content.aspx?id=418.

Jain, S. H. (2009). Practicing medicine in the age of Facebook. *The New England Journal of Medicine, 361*, 649–651. doi:10.1056/NEJMp0901277

Jakes, D. (2007). Professional development and web 2.0. *Technology and Learning, 27*(9), 20.

Jex, S. M. (2002). *Organizational psychology: A scientist-practitioner approach*. New York, NY: John Wiley & Sons.

Johnson, D. W., & Johnson, R. T. (1989). *Cooperation and competition: Theory and research*. Edina, MN: Interaction Book Company.

Johnson, D. W., Johnson, R. T., & Smith, K. A. (1991). *Cooperative learning: Increasing college faculty instructional productivity. ASHE-FRIC Higher Education Report 4*. Washington, DC: George Washington University.

Johnson, L., Levine, A., Smith, R., & Stone, S. (2010). *The 2010 horizon report*. Austin, TX: The New Media Consortium.

Johnson, M., & Liber, O. (2008). The personal learning environment and the human condition: From theory to teaching practice. *Interactive Learning Environments, 16*, 3–15. doi:10.1080/10494820701772652

Johnson, R. (1998). *User-centered technology: A rhetorical theory for computers and other mundane artifacts*. Albany, NY: State University of New York.

Jonassen, D. H. (1994). Thinking technology: Toward a constructivist design model. *Educational Technology, 34*(4), 34–37.

Jonassen, D. H., & Hernandez-Serrano, J. (2002). Case-based reasoning and instructional design: Using stories to support problem solving. *Educational Technology Research and Development, 50*(2), 65–77. doi:10.1007/BF02504994

Jones, C. G., Eileen, A. S., & Patrick, M. (2009). Informal learning evidence in online communities of mobile device enthusiasts. In Ally, M. (Ed.), *Mobile Learning: Transforming the Delivery of Education and Training* (pp. 25–47). Edmonton, Canada: AU Press.

Jones, S. (2011). Refresh for success: Moonee Valley libraries online database training wiki. *Aplis, 24*(2), 91–93.

Jue, A. L., Marr, J. A., & Kassotakis, M. E. (2009). *Social media at work: How networking tools propel organizational performance*. San Francisco, CA: Josey-Bass.

Jung, B. (2010). *Wokół świata mediów ery Web 2.0*. Warsaw, Poland: WAIP.

Kahn, J. H., Schneider, K. T., Jenkins-Henkelman, T. M., & Moyle, L. L. (2006). Emotional social support and job burnout among high school teachers: Is it all due to dispositional affectivity? *Journal of Organizational Behavior, 27*(6), 793–807. doi:10.1002/job.397

Kajder, S. (2003). *The tech-savvy English classroom*. Portland, ME: Stenhouse.

Kaldoudi, E., Konstantinidis, S., & Bamidis, P. D. (2010). Web 2.0 approaches for active, collaborative learning in medicine and health. In Mohammed, S., & Fiaidhi, J. (Eds.), *Ubiquitous Health and Medical Informatics: Advancements in Web 2.0, Health 2.0, and Medicine 2.0* (pp. 127–149). Hershey, PA: IGI Global. doi:10.4018/978-1-61520-777-0.ch007

Kamel Boulos, M. N., & Wheeler, S. (2007). The emerging Web 2.0 social software: An enabling suite of sociable technologies in health and health care education. *Health Information and Libraries Journal, 24*(1), 2–23. doi:10.1111/j.1471-1842.2007.00701.x

Kamel Boulos, M., Hetherington, L., & Wheeler, S. (2007). Second Life: An overview of the potential of 3-D virtual worlds in medical and health education. *Health Information and Libraries Journal, 24*(4), 233–245. doi:10.1111/j.1471-1842.2007.00733.x

Kamel Boulos, M., Maramba, I., & Wheeler, S. (2006). Wikis, blogs and podcasts: A new generation of web-based tools for virtual collaborative clinical practice and education. *BMC Medical Education, 6*(41).

Kane, K., Robinson-Combre, J., & Berge, Z. L. (2010). Tapping into social networking: Collaborating enhances both knowledge management and e-learning. *Vine, 40*(1), 62–70. doi:10.1108/03055721011024928

Kaplan, A. M., & Haenlein, M. (2010). Users of the world, unite! The challenges and opportunities of social media. *Business Horizons, 53,* 59–60. doi:10.1016/j.bushor.2009.09.003

Karkalis, G. I., & Koutsouris, D. D. (2006). *E-health and the web 2.0.* Retrieved from http://medlab.cs.uoi.gr/itab2006/proceedings/eHealth/124.pdf.

Katz, R. N. (2008). The gathering cloud: Is this the end of the middle. In R. N. Katz (Ed.), *The Tower and the Cloud: Higher Education in the Age of Cloud Computing,* (pp. 2-42). Washington, DC: Educause. Retrieved from http://net.educause.edu/ir/library/pdf/PUB7202.pdf.

Kay, A., & Goldberg, A. (1981). Personal dynamic media. In Wasserman, A. I. (Ed.), *Software Development Environments.* New York, NY: IEEE Computer Society.

Kennedy, G., Krause, K.-L., Judd, T., Churchward, A., & Gray, K. (2006). *First year students' experiences with technology: Are they really digital natives?* Melbourne, Australia: University of Melbourne. Retrieved from http://www.ascilite.org.au/ajet/ajet24/kennedy.pdf.

Kern, R., Ware, P., & Warschauer, M. (2008). Network-based language teaching. In N. Van Deusen-Scholl & N. H. Hornberger (Eds.), *Encyclopedia of Language and Education,* (pp. 281-292). New York, NY: Springer Science+ Business Media LLC.

Kerpen, D. (2011). *Likeable social media: How to delight your customers, create an irresistible brand, and be generally amazing on Facebook (and other social networks).* Columbus, OH: McGraw-Hill.

Keskin, N. O., & Metcalf, D. (2011). The current perspectives, theories and practices of mobile learning. *Turkish Online Journal of Educational Technology, 10*(2), 202–208.

Ketter, P. (2010). Six trends that will change workplace learning forever. *ASTD Training and Development.* Retrieved from http://www.astd.org/TD/Archives/2010/Dec/Free/December+2010+2010+Trends.htm.

Kilduff, M., & Tsai, W. (2003). *Social networking in organizations.* London, UK: Sage.

Kimmerle, J., Moskaliuk, J., Cress, U., & Thiel, A. (2011). A systems theoretical approach to online knowledge building. *AI & Society, 26*(1), 49–60. doi:10.1007/s00146-010-0281-7

Kinneavy, J. E. (1969). The basic aims of discourse. *College Composition and Communication, 20*(5), 297–304. doi:10.2307/355033

Kinshuk. (2003). *Adaptive mobile learning technologies.* Retrieved from http://www.globaled.com/articles/Kinshuk2003.pdf.

Kirch, D. P., Tucker, M. L., & Kirch, C. E. (2001). The benefits of emotional intelligence in accounting firms. *The CPA Journal, 70*(8), 60–61.

Kitchenham, B. (2004). *Procedures for performing systematic reviews.* Technical Report TR/SE0401. Newcastle-under-Lyme, UK: Keele University.

Klamma, R., Chatti, M. A., Duval, E., Hummel, H., Hvannberg, E. H., & Kravcik, M. (2007). Social software for life-long learning. *Journal of Educational Technology & Society, 10*(3), 72–83.

Knowles, J. G., Cole, A. L., & Pressword, C. S. (2008). *Through preservice teachers' eyes: Exploring field experiences through narrative and inquiry.* Halifax, Canada: Backalong Books.

Knowles, M., Holton, E. F., & Swanson, R. A. (2005). *The adult learner: The definitive classic in adult education and human resource development* (6th ed.). Burlington, MA: Elsevier.

Kock, N. (2005). Media richness or media naturalness? The evolution of our biological communication apparatus and its influence on our behavior toward e-communication tools. *IEEE Transactions on Professional Communication, 48*(2), 117–130. doi:10.1109/TPC.2005.849649

Kock, N. (2007). Media naturalness and compensatory encoding: The burden of electronic media obstacles is on senders. *Decision Support Systems, 44*(1), 175–187. doi:10.1016/j.dss.2007.03.011

Kohn, A. (1986). *No contest: The case against competition.* Boston, MA: Houghton Mifflin.

Kojiri, T., Ogawa, Y., & Watanabe, T. (2001). Agent-oriented support environment in web-based collaborative learning. *Journal of Universal Computer Science*, 7(3), 226–239.

Konstantinidis, A., Tsiatsos, T., & Pomportsis, A. (2009). Collaborative virtual learning environments: Design and evaluation. *Multimedia Tools and Applications*, 44, 279–304. doi:10.1007/s11042-009-0289-5

Koole, M. L. (2009). A model for framing mobile learning. In Ally, M. (Ed.), *Mobile Learning: Transforming the Delivery of Education and Training* (pp. 25–47). Edmonton, Canada: AU Press.

Koole, M., McQuilkin, J., & Ally, M. (2010). Mobile learning in distance education: Utility or futility? *Journal of Distance Education*, 24(2), 59–82.

Koro-Ljungberg, M., Yendol-Hoppey, D., Smith, J. J., & Hayes, S. B. (2009). Epistemological awareness, instantiation of methods, and uninformed methodological ambiguity in qualitative research projects. *Educational Researcher*, 38(9), 687–699. doi:10.3102/0013189X09351980

Kostova, T., & Roth, K. (2002). Social capital in multinational corporations and a micro-macro model for its formation. *Academy of Management Review*, 28(2), 297–317.

Koszalka, T. A., & Ntloedibe-Kuswani, G. S. (2010). Literature on the safe and disruptive learning potential of mobile technologies. *Distance Education*, 31(2), 139–157. doi:10.1080/01587919.2010.498082

Kukla, A. (2000). *Social constructivism and the philosophy of science*. New York, NY: Routledge.

Kukulska-Hulme, A., & Pettit, J. (2008). Semi-formal learning communities for professional development in mobile learning. *Journal of Computing in Higher Education*, 20(2), 35–47. doi:10.1007/s12528-008-9006-z

Kuuti, K. (1996). Activity theory as a potential framework for human-computer interaction research. In Nardi, B. A. (Ed.), *Context and Consciousness: Activity Theory and Human-Computer Interaction* (pp. 17–44). Cambridge, MA: MIT Press.

Laboratory for Educational Technology. (2011). *Lecture recording and podcasting*. Retrieved from http://let.pitt.edu/ProjectsAndPrograms/podcast.html.

Lagioni, I. (2004). *CMI: Comunicazione di marketing integrate: Una nuova cultura della comunicazione d'impresa*. Milan, IT: Tecniche Nuove.

Lam, A. (2000). Tacit knowledge, organizational learning and societal institutions: An integrated framework. *Organization Studies*, 21(3), 487–513. doi:10.1177/0170840600213001

Lamont, M. (2009). *How professors think: Inside the curious world of academic judgment*. Boston, MA: Harvard University Press.

Lasky, S. (2000). The cultural and emotional politics of teacher-parent interactions. *Teaching and Teacher Education*, 16(8), 843–860. doi:10.1016/S0742-051X(00)00030-5

Latour, B. (1987). *Science in action*. Milton Keynes, UK: Open University Press.

Laurillard, D. (1993). *Rethinking university teaching: A framework for the effective use of educational technology*. London, UK: Routledge.

Lave, J., & Wenger, E. (1991). *Situated learning: Legitimate peripheral participation*. Cambridge, UK: Cambridge University Press.

Lemley, T., & Burnham, J. F. (2009). Web 2.0 tools in medical and nursing school curricula. *Journal of the Medical Library Association*, 97(1), 50–52. doi:10.3163/1536-5050.97.1.010

Lenhart, A., Horrigan, J. B., & Fallows, D. (2004). Content creation online. *Pew Internet & American Life Project*. Retrieved March 13, 2011 from http://www.pewinternet.org/Reports/2004/Content-Creation-Online.aspx.

Leont'ev, A. N. (1978). *Activity, consciousness, and personality*. Englewood Cliffs, NJ: Prentice-Hall.

Leont'ev, A. N. (1981). *Problems of the development of the mind*. Moscow, Russia: Progress Publishers.

Letierce, J., Passant, A., Decker, S., & Breslin, J. G. (2010). *Understanding how Twitter is used to spread scientific messages*. Paper presented at the Web Science Conference 2010. Raleigh, NC.

Libâneo, J. C. (2011). *O dualismo perverso da escola pública brasileira: Escola do conhecimento para os ricos, escola do acolhimento social para os pobres*. Educação e Pesquisa.

Lieberman, A., & Mace, D. P. (2010). Making practice public: Teacher learning in the 21st century. *Journal of Teacher Education, 61*(1-2), 77–88. doi:10.1177/0022487109347319

Lincoln, Y. S., & Guba, E. G. (1985). *Naturalistic inquiry*. London, UK: SAGE Publications.

Lindholm, M. (1999). Influence of nursing management education in changing organizations. *The Journal of Nursing Administration, 29*, 49–56. doi:10.1097/00005110-199910000-00010

Lindholm, M., Dejin-Karlsson, E., Östergren, P. O., & Udén, G. (2003). Nurse managers' professional networks, psychosocial resources and self-rated health. *Journal of Advanced Nursing, 42*(5), 506–515. doi:10.1046/j.1365-2648.2003.02650.x

Lin, N., Cook, K., & Burt, R. (2001). *Social capital: Theory and research*. New York, NY: Walter de Gruyter.

Lipsey, M. J., Fischer, R. R., & Poirier, K. L. (2007). *Systems for success: The complete guide to selling, leasing, presenting, negotiating & serving in commercial real estate*. Gretna, LA: Pelican Publishing Company.

Little, J. W. (2002). Locating learning in teachers communities of practice: Opening up problems of analysis in records of everyday work. *Teaching and Teacher Education, 18*(8), 917–946. doi:10.1016/S0742-051X(02)00052-5

Liu, A. (2004). *Transcendental data: Toward a cultural history and aesthetics of the new encoded discourse*. Chicago, IL: University of Chicago.

Livingstone, D. W. (1999). Exploring the icebergs of adult learning: Findings of the first Canadian survey of informal learning practices. *Canadian Journal for the Study of Adult Education, 13*(2), 49–72.

Lombardi, M. M., & Oblinger, D. G. (2007). Authentic learning for the 21st century: An overview. *EDUCAUSE Learning Initiative*. Retrieved from http://alicechristie.org/classes/530/EduCause.pdf.

Lom, E., & Sullenger, K. (2011). Informal spaces in collaborations: Exploring the edges/ boundaries of professional development. *Professional Development in Education, 37*(1), 55–74. doi:10.1080/19415257.2010.489811

Lomi, A., & Larsen, E. (1999). Learning without experience: Strategic implications of deregulation and competition in the electricity industry. *European Management Journal, 17*(2), 151–163. doi:10.1016/S0263-2373(98)00074-7

Lortie, D. (1975). *Schoolteacher: A sociological study*. Chicago, IL: University of Chicago Press.

Loucks-Horsely, S., Love, N., Stiles, K., Mundry, S., & Hewson, P. W. (2003). *Designing professional development for teachers of science and mathematics* (2nd ed.). Thousand Oaks, CA: Corwin Press.

Lowry, P. B., Curtis, A., & Lowry, M. R. (2004). Building a taxonomy and nomenclature of collaborative writing to improve interdisciplinary research and practice. *Journal of Business Communication, 41*(1), 66–99. doi:10.1177/0021943603259363

Luehmann, A. L. (2008). Blogging as support for teacher learning and development: A case-study. *Journal of the Learning Sciences, 17*(3), 287–337. doi:10.1080/10508400802192706

Luehmann, A. L., & Tinelli, L. (2008). Teacher professional identity development with social networking technologies: Learning reform through blogging. *Educational Media International, 45*(4), 323–333. doi:10.1080/09523980802573263

Lund, N. (2010, April 25). *The use of Web 2.0 technology for professional development in Australia information associations*. Retrieved from http://networkconference.netstudies.org/2010/04/the-use-of-web-2-0-technology-for-professional-development-in-australian-information-associations/.

Lurati, F., & Eppler, M. J. (2006). Communication and management: Researching corporate communication and knowledge communication in organizational settings. *Studies in Communication Sciences, 6*(2), 75–98.

Macdonald, I., & Chiu, J. (2011). Evaluating the viability of mobile learning to enhance management training. *Canadian Journal of Learning and Technology, 37*(1). Retrieved from http://www.cjlt.ca/index.php/cjlt/article/view/535

Mader, S. (2008). *Wikipatterns: A practical guide to improving productivity and collaboration in your organization.* Indianapolis, IN: Wiley Publishing, Inc.

Madge, C., Meek, J., Wellens, J., & Hooley, T. (2009). Facebook, social integration and informal learning at university: It is more for socialising and talking to friends about work than for actually doing work. *Learning, Media and Technology, 34*(2), 141–155. doi:10.1080/17439880902923606

Magala, S. (2003). Elective identities: Culture, identification and integration. In Zdanowski, J. (Ed.), *Globalizacja a Tożsamość* (pp. 135–151). Warsaw, Poland: Wydawnictwo Naukowe ASKON.

Mair, F., & Whitten, P. (2000). Systemic review of studies of patient satisfaction with telemedicine. *British Medical Journal, 320*(7248), 1517–1520. doi:10.1136/bmj.320.7248.1517

Major, E., & Cordey-Hayes, M. (2000). Knowledge translation: A new perspective on knowledge transfer and foresight. *The Journal of Future Studies. Strategic Thinking and Policy, 2*(4), 411–423. doi:10.1108/14636680010802762

Mantovani, G. (1995). Virtual reality as a communication environment: Consensual hallucination, fiction, and possible selves. *Human Relations, 48*(6), 669–683. doi:10.1177/001872679504800604

Marcelo Garcia, C. (2011). *Políticas de inserción en la docência: De eslabón perdido a puente para el desaroollo professional docente.* Retrieved from http://www.inet.edu.ar/programas/formacion_docente/biblioteca/formacion_docente/marcelo_garcia_politicas_insercion_docente.pdf.

Marcelo Garcia, C., & Vaillant, D. (2009). *Desarrollo professional docente: Cómo se aprende a esneñar?* Madrid, Spain: Narcea.

Marsick, V. J., & Volpe, M. (1999). The nature and need for informal learning. *Advances in Developing Human Resources, 1*, 1–9. doi:10.1177/152342239900100302

Marsick, V. J., & Watkins, K. (1990). *Informal and incidental learning in the workplace.* New York, NY: Routledge.

Martinez-Sarriegui, I., Garcia Saez, G., Hernando, M. E., Rigla, M., Brugues, E., de Leiva, A., & Gomez, E. J. (2008). Mobile telemedicine for diabetes care. In Xiao, Y., & Chen, H. (Eds.), *Mobile Telemedicine* (pp. 143–160). Boca Raton, FL: Auerbach Publications.

Mason, R., & Rennie, F. (2007). Using web 2.0 for learning in the community. *The Internet and Higher Education, 10*, 196–203. doi:10.1016/j.iheduc.2007.06.003

Matzler, K., & Mueller, J. (2011). Antecedents of knowledge sharing – Examining the influence of learning and performance orientation. *Journal of Economic Psychology, 32*(3), 317–329. doi:10.1016/j.joep.2010.12.006

Maudsley, G., & Strivens, J. (2000). Promoting professional knowledge, experimental learning and critical thinking for medical students. *Medical Education, 34*(7), 535–544. doi:10.1046/j.1365-2923.2000.00632.x

Ma, W. W. K., & Yuen, A. H. K. (2011). Understanding online knowledge sharing: An interpersonal relationship perspective. *Computers & Education, 56*, 210–221. doi:10.1016/j.compedu.2010.08.004

Maxl, E., & Tarkus, A. (2009). Definition of user requirements concerning mobile learning games within the mGBL Project. *Serious Game on the Move, 1*, 91–104. doi:10.1007/978-3-211-09418-1_6

Mayhew, D. (1999). *The usability engineering lifecycle: A practitioner's handbook for user interface design.* San Francisco, CA: Morgan Kaufmann.

Mazur, M., & Richards, L. (2011). Adolescents' and emerging adults' social networking online: Homophily or diversity? *Journal of Applied Developmental Psychology, 32*, 180–188. doi:10.1016/j.appdev.2011.03.001

McCann, T. M., Johannessen, L. R., & Ricca, B. P. (2005). *Supporting beginning English teachers: Research and implications for teacher induction.* Urbana, IL: National Council of Teachers of English.

McCormick, A. C., & Zhao, C. M. (2005). Rethinking and reframing the Carnegie classification. *Change, 9*(10), 51–57. doi:10.3200/CHNG.37.5.51-57

McGee, B., & Begg, M. (2008). What medical educators need to know about Web 2.0. *Medical Teacher, 30*(2), 164–169. doi:10.1080/01421590701881673

McGuire, D., & Gubbins, C. (2010). The slow death of formal learning: A polemic. *Human Resource Development Review, 9*(3), 249–265.

McGuire, J. M., Scott, S. S., & Shaw, S. F. (2006). Universal design and its applications in educational environments. *Remedial and Special Education, 27*(3), 166–175. doi:1 0.1177/07419325060270030501

McKeachie, W. J., Pintrich, P. R., Lin, Y.-G., & Smith, D. A. F. (1986). *Teaching and learning in the college classroom: A review of the research literature.* Ann Arbor, MI: University of Michigan.

McKenna, K. Y. A., Green, A. M., & Gleason, M. E. J. (2002). Relationship formation on the Internet: What's the big attraction? *The Journal of Social Issues, 58*(1), 9–31. doi:10.1111/1540-4560.00246

McKinsey Global Institute. (2011). An economy that works: Job creation and America's future. *McKinsey Global Institute Report.* Retrieved from http://www.mckinsey.com/~/media/McKinsey/dotcom/Insights%20and%20pubs/MGI/Research/Labor%20Markets/An%20economy%20that%20works%20Job%20creation%20and%20Americas%20future/MGI_US_job_creation_full_report.ashx.

McLaughlin, M., & Talbert, J. (2001). *Professional communities and the work of high school teaching.* Chicago, IL: University of Chicago Press.

McLoughlin, C., & Lee, M. J. W. (2008). Future learning landscapes: Transforming pedagogy through social software. *Innovate, 4*(5).

McLoughlin, C., & Lee, M. J. W. (2007). Social software and participatory learning: Pedagogical choices with technology affordances in the web 2.0 era. In *Proceedings Ascilite Singapore 2007* (pp. 664–675). Singapore, Singapore: Ascilite Singapore.

McPherson, M., Lovin, L. S., & Cook, J. M. (2001). Birds of a feather: Homophily in social networks. *Annual Review of Sociology, 27*, 415–444. doi:10.1146/annurev.soc.27.1.415

Meenan, C., King, A., Toland, C., Daly, M., & Nagy, P. (2010). Use of a wiki as a radiology department knowledge management system. *Journal of Digital Imaging, 23*(2), 142–151. doi:10.1007/s10278-009-9180-1

Mergel, I. A., Schweik, C. M., & Fountain, J. E. (2009). *The transformational effect of web 2.0 technologies on government.* Retrieved May 30, 2011, from http://ssrn.com/abstract=1412796.

Merisotis, J., & Phipps, R. (1999). *What's the difference? A review of contemporary research on the effectiveness of distance learning in higher education.* Retrieved from http://www.ihep.org/Publications/publications-detail.cfm?id=88.

Mesch, G., & Talmud, I. (2007). The quality of online and offline relationships: The role of multiplexity and duration of social relationships. *The Information Society, 22*(3), 137–148. doi:10.1080/01972240600677805

Metaxiotis, K., Psarras, J., & Papastefanatos, S. (2002). Knowledge and information management in e-learning environments: The user agent architecture. *Information Management & Computer Security, 10*(4), 165–170. doi:10.1108/09685220210436958

Metcalf, D. (2006). *mLearning: Mobile learning and performance in the palm of your hand.* Amherst, MA: HRD Press

Meyerson, M. (2010). *Success secrets of social media marketing superstars.* Irvine, CA: Entrepreneur Media.

Michailidou, A., & Economides, A. A. (2003). Elearn: Towards a collaborative educational virtual environment. *Journal of Information Technology Education, 2*, 131–152.

Michels, S. (2008, May 6). Teachers' virtual lives conflict with classroom: Teacher in training says she was denied credential for online photos. *ABC News.* Retrieved March 4, 2011, from http://abcnews.go.com/TheLaw/story?id=4791295andpage=1.

Microsoft Inc. (2010). *Introducing Kinect for Xbox 360.* Retrieved from http://www.xbox.com/en-US/kinect.

Mika, P. (2007). *Social networks and the semantic web.* Doctoral Dissertation. Retrieved from http://dare.ubvu.vu.nl/bitstream/1871/13263/5/7915.pdf.

Milroy, J., & Milroy, L. (1985). Linguistic change, social network and speaker innovation. *Journal of Linguistics, 21*(2), 339–384. doi:10.1017/S0022226700010306

Mishra, P., & Koehler, M. J. (2006). Technological pedagogical content knowledge: A framework for teacher knowledge. *Teachers College Record, 108*(6), 1017–1054. doi:10.1111/j.1467-9620.2006.00684.x

Mislove, A., Koppula, H., Gummadi, K. P., Druschel, P., & Bhattacharjee, B. (2008), *Growth of the Flickr social network*. Paper presented at the 1st ACM SIGCOMM Workshop on Social Networks (WOSN 2008). Seattle, WA.

Mislove, A., Marcon, M., Gummadi, K. P., Druschel, P., & Bhattacharjee, B. (2007). Measurement and analysis of online social networks. In *Proceedings of the 5th ACM/USENIX Internet Measurement Conference (IMC 2007)*. ACM Press. Retrieved October 3, 2011 from http://www.mpi-sws.org/~amislove/publications/SocialNetworks-IMC.pdf.

Missouri State Senate. (2011). *Bill 54*. Retrieved June 9, 2011, from http://www.senate.mo.gov/11info/BTS_Web/Bill.aspx?BillID=4066479&SessionType=R.

Mizukami, M. G. N., et al. (2010). *Escola e aprendizagem da docência: Processos de investigação e formação*. São Carlos, Spain: EDUFSCar.

Mizukami, M. G. N., Reali, A. M. M. R., & Tancredi, R. M. S. P. (2010). Elementary public school and university partnership: Promoting and analyzing development processes of school teachers. In Slater, J. J., & Ravid, R. (Eds.), *Collaboration in Education* (pp. 54–60). New York, NY: Routledge.

Moller, L. (1998). Designing communities of learners for synchronous distance education. *Educational Technology Research and Development, 46*(4), 115–122. doi:10.1007/BF02299678

Monge, P. R., & Contractor, N. (2003). *Theories of communication networks*. New York, NY: Oxford University Press.

Mooradian, T. A., Renzl, B., & Matzler, K. (2006). Who trusts? Personality, trust and knowledge sharing. *Management Learning, 37*(4), 523–540. doi:10.1177/1350507606073424

Moore, S. (2010). *Strategic project portfolio management: Enabling a productive organization*. Hoboken, NJ: John Wiley & Sons.

Morgan, D. L. (2002). Focus group interviewing. In Gubrium, J., & Holstein, J. (Eds.), *Handbook of Interview Research: Context & Method* (pp. 141–159). Thousand Oaks, CA: Sage.

Morris, M. (2003). Professional development that works: The power of two: Linking external with internal teachers' professional development. *Phi Delta Kappan, 84*(10), 764.

Motorola. (2011). *Corporate responsibility: Training and development*. Retrieved from http://responsibility.motorola.com/index.php/employees/trainingdevelop/.

Naaman, M., Boase, J., & Lai, C.-H. (2010). *Is it really about me? Message content in social awareness streams*. Paper presented at the 2010 ACM Conference on Computer Supported Cooperative Work. Savannah, GA.

Nahapiet, J., & Ghoshal, S. (1998). Social capital, intellectual capital and the organizational advantage. *Academy of Management Review, 23*(2), 242–266.

Nair, M., & Webster, P. (2010). Education for health professionals in the emerging market economies: A literature review. *Medical Education, 44*(9), 856–863. doi:10.1111/j.1365-2923.2010.03747.x

Naismith, L., & Corlett, D. (2006). *Reflections on success: A retrospective of the mLearn conference series 2002-2005*. Paper presented at the Fifth World Conference on mLearn 2006: Across Generations and Cultures. Banff, Canada.

Nardi, B. A. (1996). *Context and consciousness: Activity theory and human-computer interaction*. Cambridge, MA: The MIT Press.

National Center for Education Statistics. (2001). *Attrition of new teachers among recent college graduates: Comparing occupational stablity among 1992-93 graduates*. Washington, DC: NCES.

National Council of Teachers of English. (2006). *Guidelines for the preparation of teachers of English language arts*. Urbana, IL: NCTE. Retrieved from http://www1.ncte.org/library/files/Store/Books/Sample/Guidelines2006Chap1-6.pdf.

National Council of Teachers of English. (2007). *21ˢᵗ century literacies: A policy research brief.* Urbana, IL: NCTE. Retrieved from http://www.ncte.org/library/ NCTEFiles/Resources/PolicyResearch/21stCenturyRes earchBrief.pdf.

Nelkner, T., Magenheim, J., & Reinhard, W. (2009). PLME as a cognitive tool for knowledge achievement and informal learning. In Tatnall, A., & Jones, A. (Eds.), *WCCE 2009, IFIP AICT 302* (pp. 378–387). International Federation for Information Processing. doi:10.1007/978-3-642-03115-1_40

Nelson, E. (2010). Elements of problem-based learning: Suggestions for implementation in the asynchronous environment. *International Journal on E-Learning, 9*(1), 99–114.

Neuendorf, K. A. (2002). *The content analysis guidebook.* Thousand Oaks, CA: SAGE Publications.

Newell, S., & Swan, J. (2000). Trust and inter-organizational networking. *Human Relations, 53*(10), 1287–1328.

Newman, B. M., & Newman, P. R. (2009). *Development through life: A psychosocial approach.* Belmont, CA: Wadsworth Cengage Learning.

Nielsen Company. (2010, January 22). *Led by Facebook, Twitter, global time spent on social media sites up 82% year over year.* Retrieved from http://blog.nielsen.com/ nielsenwire/global/led-by-facebook-twitter-global-time-spent-on-social-media-sites-up-82-year-over-year/.

Nielsen, J. (2006). *Participation inequality: Encouraging more users to contribute.* Retrieved September 2, 2011, from http://www.useit.com/alertbox/participation_in-equality.html.

NIST. (1987). *Computer security act of 1987.* Retrieved June 9, 2011, from http://www.nist.gov/cfo/legislation/ Public%20Law%20100-235.pdf.

OECD. (2001). *The well-being of nation: The role of human and social capital.* Paris, France: OECD.

Oh, W., Choi, J. N., & Kim, K. (2006). Coauthorship dynamics and knowledge capital: The patterns of cross-disciplinary collaboration in information systems research. *Journal of Management Information Systems, 22*(3), 265–292. doi:10.2753/MIS0742-1222220309

Olaniran, B. (2007a). Challenges to implementing e-learning in lesser-developed countries. In Edmundson, A. (Ed.), *Globalized e-Learning Cultural Challenges* (pp. 18–34). Hershey, PA: IGI Global. doi:10.4018/978-1-59904-301-2.ch002

Olaniran, B. A. (2007b). Culture and communication challenges in virtual workspaces. In St-Amant, K. (Ed.), *Linguistic and Cultural Online Communication Issues in the Global Age* (pp. 79–92). Hershey, PA: IGI Global. doi:10.4018/978-1-59904-213-8.ch006

Olaniran, B. A. (2010). Challenges facing the semantic web and social software as communication technology agents in e-learning environments. *International Journal of Virtual and Personal Learning Environments, 1*(4), 18–30. doi:10.4018/jvple.2010100102

Olaniran, B. A., & Agnello, M. F. (2008). Globalization, educational hegemony, and higher education. *Journal of Multicultural Educational & Technology, 2*(2), 68–86. doi:10.1108/17504970810883351

Olaniran, B. A., & Williams, I. M. (2009). Web 2.0 and learning: A closer look at transactional control model in e-learning. In Lambropoulos, N., & Rodriga, M. (Eds.), *Educational Social Software for Context-Aware Learning: Collaborative Methods and Human Interaction* (pp. 23–37). Hershey, PA: IGI Global. doi:10.4018/978-1-60566-826-0.ch002

Oliver, R., & Herrington, J. (2000). Using situated learning as a design strategy for web-based learning. In Abbey, B. (Ed.), *Instructional and Cognitive Impacts of Web-Based Education* (pp. 178–191). Hershey, PA: IGI Global. doi:10.4018/978-1-878289-59-9.ch011

Olson, M. (1971). *The logic of collective action: Public goods and the theory of groups.* Boston, MA: Harvard University Press.

Online Marketing Trends. (2011). *The latest online media trends, analysis, news, research on online advertising, social media, search marketing and more.* Retrieved June 15, 2011 from http://www.onlinemarketing-trends. com/2011/03/twitter-statistics-on-its-5th.html.

Orkwis, R., & McLane, K. (1998). *A curriculum every student can use: Design principles for student access.* Retrieved from http://eric.ed.gov/PDFS/ED423654.pdf.

Otte, E., & Rousseau, R. (2002). Social network analysis: A powerful strategy, also for the information sciences. *Journal of Information Science, 28*(6), 441–453. doi:10.1177/016555150202800601

Ozgen, E., & Baron, R. A. (2007). Social sources of information in opportunity recognition: Effects of mentors, industry networks, and professional forums. *Journal of Business Venturing, 22*(2), 174–192. doi:10.1016/j.jbusvent.2005.12.001

Palloff, R., & Pratt, K. (1999). *Building learning communities in cyberspace: Effective strategies for the online classroom.* San Francisco, CA: Jossey-Bass.

Panteli, N. (2009). *Virtual social networks: Mediated, massive and multiplayer sites.* Basingstoke, UK: Palgrave Macmillan.

Papacharissi, Z. (2011). Conclusion: A networked self. In Papacharissi, Z. (Ed.), *A Networked Self: Identity, Community, and Culture on Social Network Sites* (pp. 304–318). Abingdon, UK: Routledge.

Papastergiadis, N. (2000). *The turbulence of migration: Globalization, deterritorialization, and hybridity.* Cambridge, UK: Polity Press.

Papi, S. O. G., & Martins, P. L. O. L. (2010). As pesquisas sobre professores iniciantes: Algumas aproximações. *Educational Review, 26*(3), 39–56. doi:10.1590/S0102-46982010000300003

Pastore, A., & Vernuccio, M. (2008). *Impresa e comunicazione: Principi e strumenti per il management.* Milan, Italy: Apogeo Editore.

Paton, C., Bamidis, P., Eysenbach, G., Hansen, M. M., & Cabrer, M. (2011). Experience in the use of social media in medical and health education. *Yearbook of Medical Informatics, 6*(1), 21–29. Retrieved from http://www.schattauer.de/en/magazine/subject-areas/journals-a-z/imia-yearbook/imia-yearbook-2011/issue/special/manuscript/16534.html

Patton, M. (2002). *Qualitative evaluation and research methods* (3rd ed.). Newbury Park, CA: Sage Publications.

Paulus, T., & Scherff, L. (2008). Can anyone offer any words of encouragement? Online dialogue as a support mechanism for preservice teachers. *Journal of Technology and Teacher Education, 16*(1), 113–136.

Paus-Hasebrink, I., Wijnen, C. W., & Jadin, T. (2010). Opportunities of web 2.0: Potentials of learning. *International Journal of Media and Cultural Politics, 6*(1), 45–62. doi:10.1386/macp.6.1.45/1

Pempek, T., Yermolayeva, Y., & Calvert, S. (2009). College students' social networking experiences on Facebook. *Journal of Applied Developmental Psychology, 30*(3), 227–238. doi:10.1016/j.appdev.2008.12.010

Pérez Gómez, A. (2010). Nuevas exigências y escenarios para la profesión docente em la era de la información y de la incertidumbre. *Revista Interuniversitaria de Formación del Professorado, 68*(24), 17–36.

Persichitte, K. (2000). A case study of lessons learned for the web-based educator. In Abbey, B. (Ed.), *Instructional and Cognitive Impacts of Web-Based Education* (pp. 192–199). Hershey, PA: IGI Global. doi:10.4018/978-1-878289-59-9.ch012

Peters, K. (2007). m-Learning: Positioning educators for a mobile, connected future. *International Journal of Research in Open and Distance Learning, 8*(2), 1–17.

Petrou, I. (2010, April 5). Feeling the impact: Shortage of dermatologists getting worse. *Modern Medicine: Dermatology Times.*

Pettenati, M. C., & Cigognini, E. (2007). Social networking theories and tools to support connectivist learning activities. *International Journal of Web-Based Learning and Teaching Technologies, 2*(3), 42–60. doi:10.4018/jwltt.2007070103

Pettenati, M., & Cigognini, M. (2007). Social networking theories and tools to support connectivist learning activities. *International Journal of Web-Based Learning and Teaching Technologies, 2*(3), 42–60. doi:10.4018/jwltt.2007070103

Pew Internet and American Life Project. (2011). *Who's online: Internet user demographics.* Retrieved from http://pewinternet.org/Trend-Data/Whos-Online.aspx.

Pfeffermann, N., & Hülsmann, M. (2011). Communication of innovation: Marketing, diffusion and frameworks. In Hülsmann, M., & Pfeffermann, N. (Eds.), *Strategies and Communications for Innovations: An Integrative Management View for Companies and Networks* (pp. 97–104). Berlin, Germany: Springer Verlag. doi:10.1007/978-3-642-17223-6_7

Pifarre, M., & Cobos, R. (2010). Promoting metacognitive skills through peer scaffolding in a CSCL environment. *Computer-Supported Collaborative Learning, 5*(2), 237–253. doi:10.1007/s11412-010-9084-6

Pitta, D. A., & Fowler, D. (2005). Internet community forums: An untapped resource for consumer marketers. *Journal of Consumer Marketing, 22*(5), 265–274. doi:10.1108/07363760510611699

Podcastfaq. (2011). *Mashups*. Retrieved from http://www.podcastfaq.com/glossary/blogging-and-podcasting-terms/.

Polanyi, M. (1966). *The tacit dimension*. New York, NY: Anchor Day Books.

Poonawalla, T., & Wagner, R. F. (2006). Assessment of a blog as a medium for dermatology education. *Dermatology Online Journal, 12*(1). Retrieved from http://dermatology.cdlib.org/121/commentary/blog/wagner.html

Pope, C., & Golub, J. (2000). Preparing tomorrow's English language arts teachers today: Principles and practices for infusing technology. *Contemporary Issues in Technology & Teacher Education, 1*(1), 89–97. Retrieved from http://www.citejournal.org/vol1/iss1/currentissues/english/article1.htm

Posteguillo, S. (2003). *Netlinguistics: An analytical framework to study language, discourse and ideology in internet*. Castelló de la Plana, Italy: Publicacions de la Universitat Jaume I.

Powazek, D. M. (2002). *Design for community: The art of connecting real people in virtual places*. Indianapolis, IN: New Riders Publishing.

Prasanna, P.M., Seagull, F., & Nagy, P. (2011). Online social networking: A primer for radiology. *Journal of Digital Imaging, 24*(5), 908–912. doi:10.1007/s10278-011-9371-4

Preece, J. (2000). *Online communities: Designing usability and supporting sociability*. New York, NY: John Wiley & Son.

Prensky, M. (2001). Digital natives, digital immigrants. *Horizon, 9*(5), 1–6. doi:10.1108/10748120110424816

Prince, M. J., Felder, R. M., & Brent, R. (2007). Does faculty research improve undergraduate teaching? An analysis of existing and potential synergies. *Journal of Engineering Education, 96*(4), 283–294.

Prunesti, A. (2010a). *Social media e comunicazione di marketing*. Milan, Italy: Franco Angeli.

Prunesti, A. (2010b). *Enterprise 2.0: Modelli organizzativi e gestione dei social media in azienda*. Milan, Italy: Franco Angeli.

Putnam, R. (2000). *Bowling alone: The collapse and revival of American community*. New York, NY: Simon and Schuster.

Putnam, R. D. (2000). *Bowling alone*. New York, NY: Simon & Schuster.

Putnam, R. T., & Borko, H. (1997). Teacher learning: Implications of new views of cognition. In Biddle, B. J., Good, T. L., & Goodson, I. F. (Eds.), *The International Handbook of Teachers and Teaching* (pp. 1223–1296). Dordrecht, The Netherlands: Kluwer.

Putnam, R., & Borko, H. (2000). What do new views of knowledge and thinking have to say about research on teacher learning? *Educational Researcher, 29*(1), 4–15.

Quinn, C. (2000). mLearning: Mobile, wireless, in-your-pocket learning. *LiNE Zine*. Retrieved from http://www.linezine.com/2.1/features/cqmmwiyp.htm.

Quinn, C. N. (2011). *Designing mLearning: Tapping into the mobile revolution for organizational performance*. San Francisco, CA: Pfeiffer.

Raelin, J. (2008). *Work-based learning: Bridging knowledge and action in the work place*. New York, NY: Wiley Publishers.

Rafaeli, S., Barak, M., Dan-Cur, Y., & Toch, E. (2004). QSIA – A web-based environment for learning, assessing and knowledge sharing in communities. *Computers & Education, 43*(3), 273–289. doi:10.1016/j.compedu.2003.10.008

Rainbird, H., Munro, A., & Holly, L. (2004). The employment relationship and workplace learning. In Rainbird, H., Munro, A., & Holly, L. (Eds.), *Workplace Learning in Context* (pp. 38–53). London, UK: Routledge.

Ramburuth, P., & Tani, M. (2009). The impact of culture on learning: Exploring student perceptions. *Multicultural Education & Technology Journal, 3*(3), 168–181. doi:10.1108/17504970910984862

Reagans, R., & Zuckerman, E. (2008). Why knowledge does not equal power: The network redundancy trade-off. *Industrial and Corporate Change, 17*(5), 903–944. doi:10.1093/icc/dtn036

Reali, A. M. M. R., Tancredi, R. M. S. P., & Mizukami, M. G. (2008). Programa de mentoria on-line: Espaço para o desenvolvimento profissional de professoras iniciantes e experientes. *Educação e Pesquisa, 34*(1), 77–96.

Reid, N., & Smith, B. W. (2009). Social network analysis. *Economic Development Journal, 8*(3), 48–55.

Reinhardt, W., Ebner, M., Beham, G., & Costa, C. (2009). How people are using Twitter during conferences. In Hornung-Prhauser, V., & Luckmann, M. (Eds.), *Creativity and Innovation Competencies on the Web* (pp. 145–156). Salzburg, Austria: EduMedia/Salzburg Research.

Reverin, S. (2008). Sustaining an online community of practice: A case study. *Journal of Distance Education, 22*(2), 45–58.

Reychav, I., & Te'eni, D. (2009). Knowledge exchange in the shrines of knowledge: The "how's" and "where's" of knowledge sharing processes. *Computers & Education, 53*(4), 1266–1277. doi:10.1016/j.compedu.2009.06.009

Richards, I. A., & Ogden, C. K. (1923). The meaning of meaning. In Bizzell, P., & Herzberg, B. (Eds.), *The Rhetorical Tradition: Readings From Classical Times to the Present* (pp. 1273–1280). New York, NY: St. Martin's Press.

Richter, D., Kunter, M., Klusmann, U., Ludtke, O., & Baumert, J. (2011). Professional development across the teaching career: Teachers' uptake of formal and informal learning opportunities. *Teaching and Teacher Education, 27*(1), 116–126. doi:10.1016/j.tate.2010.07.008

Richter, P., Meyer, J., & Sommer, F. (2006). Well-being and stress in mobile and virtual work. In Andriessen, J. H. E., & Vartiainen, M. (Eds.), *Mobile Virtual Work: A New Paradigm?* (pp. 231–252). Berlin, Germany: Springer. doi:10.1007/3-540-28365-X_10

Rid, T. (2007). *War and media operations: The US military and the press from Vietnam to Iraq.* New York, NY: Routledge.

Riel, M., & Fulton, K. (2001). The role of technology in supporting learning communities. *Phi Delta Kappan, 82*(7), 518–523.

Ritchie, J., & Lewis, J. (Eds.). (2003). *Qualitative research practice: A guide for social science students and researchers.* Thousand Oaks, CA: Sage.

Ritzer, G. (2010a). *Globalization: A basic text.* Chichester, UK: Blackwell Publishing.

Ritzer, G. (2010b). *Enchanting a disenchanted world: Continuity and change in the cathedrals of consumption.* Thousand Oaks, CA: Pine Forge Press.

Ritzer, G. (2011). *Globalization: The essentials.* Malden, MA: John Wiley & Sons.

Robinson, J. (2009, June 2). *The terminology of it all.* Retrieved from http://blog.joyrobinson.com/2009/06/the-terminology-of-it-all/.

Robinson, K. (Producer). (2010, October 14). *RSA animate: Changing educational paradigms.* Retrieved from http://www.youtube.com/watch?v=zDZFcDGpL4U&feature=player_embedded.

Robison, L. J., Schmid, A. A., & Siles, M. E. (2002). Is social capital really capital? *Review of Social Economy, 60*, 1–24. doi:10.1080/00346760110127074

Rogers, E. M. (1995). *Diffusion of innovations.* New York, NY: The Free Press.

Rogers, E. M., & Bhowmik, D. K. (1970). Homophily- heterophily: Relational concepts for communication research. *Public Opinion Quarterly, 34*(4), 523–538. doi:10.1086/267838

Rogers, P., Graham, C., & Mayes, C. (2007). Cultural competence and instructional design: Exploration research into the delivery of online instruction cross-culturally. *Educational Technology Research and Development, 55*(2), 197–217. doi:10.1007/s11423-007-9033-x

Roger, Y., Connelly, K., Hazlewood, W., & Tedesco, L. (2010). Enhancing learning: A study of how mobile devices can facilitate sensemaking. *Personal and Ubiquitous Computing, 14*(2), 111–124. doi:10.1007/s00779-009-0250-7

Rogoff, B. (1990). *Apprenticeship in thinking: Cognitive development in social context*. Oxford, UK: Oxford University Press.

Roine, R., Ohinmaa, A., & Hailey, D. (2001). Assessing telemedicine: A systemic review of the literature. *Canadian Medical Association Journal, 165*(6), 765–771.

Rollett, H., Lux, M., Strohmaier, M., Dosinger, G., & Tochtermann, K. (2007). The web 2.0 way of learning with technologies. *International Journal of Learning Technology, 3*(1), 87–108. doi:10.1504/IJLT.2007.012368

Rose, D. H., Harbour, W. S., Johnson, C. S., Daley, S. G., & Abarbanell, L. (2006). Universal design for learning in postsecondary education: Reflections on principles and their application. *Journal of Postsecondary Education and Disability, 19*(2), 135–151.

Rosencheck, M. M. (2010). Navigating the interactive workplace. *Chief Learning Officer*. Retrieved from http://www.cedma-europe.org/newsletter%20articles/Clomedia/Navigating%20the%20Interactive%20Workplace%20(May%202010).pdf.

Rosenoer, J., Amstrong, D., & Gates, J. R. (1999). *The clickable corporation: Successful strategies for capturing the Internet advantage*. New York, NY: The Free Press.

Ross, C., Terras, M., Warwick, C., & Welsh, A. (2011). Enabled backchannel: Conference Twitter use by digital humanists. *The Journal of Documentation, 67*(2), 214–237. doi:10.1108/00220411111109449

Rossett, A., & Hoffman, B. (2011). Informal learning. In Reiser, R. A., & Dempsey, J. V. (Eds.), *Trends and Issues in Instructional Design and Technology* (3rd ed., pp. 169–177). Upper Saddle River, NJ: Pearson Education.

Ross, M. B., & Welsh, M. P. (2007). Formative feedback to improve learning on a teacher education degree using a personal learning environment. *International Journal of Emerging Technologies in Learning, 2*(3), 1–7.

Rothman, D. (2011). *List of medical wikis*. Retrieved July 23, 2011 from http://davidrothman.net/list-of-medical-wikis/.

Rovai, A. P. (2001). Building classroom community at a distance: A case study. *Educational Technology Research and Development Journal, 49*(4), 33–48. doi:10.1007/BF02504946

Roy, J. (2001). From data fusion to situation analysis. In *Proceedings of the Fourth International Conference on Information*. Montreal, Canada.

Rozema, R., & Webb, A. (2008). *Literature and the web: Reading and responding with new technologies*. Portsmouth, NH: Heinemann.

Rubin, D. L., Rodriguez, C., Shah, P., & Beaulieu, C. (2008). Ipad: Semantic annotation and markup of radiological images. In *Proceedings of AMIA 2008 Symposium*, (pp. 626-630). Washington, DC: AMIA.

Salavuo, M. (2008). Social media as an opportunity for pedagogical change in music education. *Journal of Music, Technology and Education, 1*(2), 121-136. Retrieved from http://miikkasalavuo.fi/SalavuoSocialMedia.pdf.

Salpeter, M. (2011). *Social networking for career success*. New York, NY: Learning Express.

Samarawickrema, G., Benson, R., & Brack, C. (2010). Different spaces: Staff development for Web 2.0. *Australasian Journal of Educational Technology, 26*(1), 44–49.

Sandars, J., Homer, M., Pell, G., & Crocker, T. (2010). Web 2.0 and social software: The medical student way of e-learning. *Medical Teacher*. Retrieved from http://www.scribd.com/doc/47545552/Medical-Teacher-Web-2-0-and-Social-Software.

Sandars, J., & Schroter, S. (2007). Web 2.0 technologies for undergraduate and postgraduate medical education: An online survey. *Postgraduate Medical Journal, 83*, 759–762. doi:10.1136/pgmj.2007.063123

Savery, J. R., & Duffy, T. M. (2001). *Problem based learning: An instructional model and its constructivist framework.* Bloomington, IN: Center for Research on Learning and Technology.

Scardamalia, M., & Bereiter, C. (2003). Knowledge building. In Guthrie, J. (Ed.), *Encyclopedia of Education* (2nd ed.). New York, NY: Macmillan.

Scardamalia, M., & Bereiter, C. (2006). Knowledge building: Theory, pedagogy, and technology. In Sawyer, K. (Ed.), *Cambridge Handbook of the Learning Sciences* (pp. 97–118). Cambridge, UK: Cambridge University Press.

Schachter, S. (1959). *The psychology of affiliation: Experimental studies of the sources of gregariousness.* Stanford, CA: Stanford University Press.

Schaefer, D. R., Kornienko, O., & Fox, A. M. (2011). Misery does not love company: Network selection mechanisms and depression homophily. *American Sociological Review, 76*, 764–785. doi:10.1177/0003122411420813

Schaffers, H., Carver, L., Brodt, T., Fernando, T., & Slagter, R. (2006). Mobile workplaces and innovative business practice. In Andriessen, J. H. E., & Vartiainen, M. (Eds.), *Mobile Virtual Work: A New Paradigm?* (pp. 343–368). Berlin, Germany: Springer. doi:10.1007/3-540-28365-X_15

Schank, R. C. (1990). *Tell me a story: Narrative and intelligence.* Evanston, IL: Northwestern University Press.

Schank, R. C. (1999). *Dynamic memory revisited.* Cambridge, UK: Cambridge University Press. doi:10.1017/CBO9780511527920

Schepp, B., & Schepp, D. (2010). *How to find a job on LinkedIn, Facebook, Twitter, MySpace, and other social networks.* New York, NY: McGraw-Hill.

Scherff, L., & Paulus, T. (2006). Encouraging ownership of online spaces: Support for preservice English teachers through computer-mediated communication. *Contemporary Issues in Technology & Teacher Education, 6*(4), 354–373. Retrieved from http://www.citejournal.org/vol6/iss4/languagearts/article1.cfm

Schlager, M. S., Fusco, J., Schank, P., & Dwyer, N. (2009). Analyzing online teacher's networks. *Journal of Teacher Education, 60*(1), 86–100. doi:10.1177/0022487108328487

Schlager, M., & Fusco, J. (2003). Teacher professional development, technology, and communities of practice: Are we putting the cart before the horse? *The Information Society, 19*(3), 203–220. doi:10.1080/01972240309464

Schön, D. A. (1993). *The reflective practitioner: How professionals think in action.* New York, NY: Basic Books.

Schopf, T., Bolle, R., & Solvoll, T. (2010). The workload of web-based consultations with atopic eczema at home. *BMC Research Notes, 3*, 71. doi:10.1186/1756-0500-3-71

Schramm, W. (1965). How communication works. In Schramm, W. (Ed.), *The Process and Effects of Mass Communication* (6th ed., pp. 3–26). Urbana, IL: University of Illinois Press.

Scollon, R., & Wong Scollon, S. (2001). *Intercultural communication-A discourse approach.* Oxford, UK: Blackwell Publishers Ltd.

Scott, S. (2000). *Social network analysis: A handbook* (2nd ed.). Los Angeles, CA: Sage.

Scovic, S. (2008). *Lost in transition?* London, UK: University of the Arts.

Selwyn, N. (2007). Web 2.0 applications as alternative environments for informal learning - A critical review. In *Proceedings of the OECD-KERIS Expert Meeting.* OECD-KERIS. Retrieved from http://www.oecd.org/dataoecd/32/3/39458556.pdf.

Servon, L. J. (2002). *Bridging the digital divide: Technology, community, and public policy.* Oxford, UK: Blackwell Publishers Ltd. doi:10.1002/9780470773529

Severance, C., Hardin, J., & Whyte, A. (2008). The coming functionality mash-up in personal learning environments. *Interactive Learning Environments, 16*(1), 9–14. doi:10.1080/10494820701772694

Sharepoint. (2011). *Customer success stories.* Retrieved from http://sharepoint.microsoft.com/en-us/customers/.

Sharples, M., Milrad, M., Arnedillo, S. I., & Vavoula, G. (2007). *Mobile learning: Small devices, big issues*. Retrieved from http://www.lsri.nottingham.ac.uk/msh/Papers/Mobile%20learning%20-%20Small%20devices,%20Big%20Issues.pdf.

Shelly, G. B., & Vermaat, M. E. (2011). *Discovering computers 2011*. Boston, MA: Course Technology.

Shen, D., Nuankhieo, P., Huang, X., Amelung, C., & Laffey, J. (2008). Using social network analysis to understand sense of community in an online learning environment. *Journal of Educational Computing Research, 39*(1), 17–36. doi:10.2190/EC.39.1.b

Shex. (2011). *Collaborative learning technologies*. Retrieved from http://shex.org/wiki/Collaborative_learning_technologies.

Shieh, R. (2008). A case study of constructivist instructional strategies for adult online learning. *British Journal of Educational Technology, 41*(5), 706–720.

Shih, C. (2010). *The Facebook era: Tapping online social networks to market, sell, and innovate*. Boston, MA: Prentice Hall.

Shotter, J., & Cunliffe, A. L. (2002). Managers as practical authors: Everyday conversations for action. In Holman, D., & Thorpe, R. (Eds.), *Management and Language: The Manager as Practical Author* (pp. 15–37). London, UK: SAGE.

Shulman, L. S. (1987). Knowledge and teaching: Foundation of the new reform. *Harvard Educational Review, 57*(1), 1–22.

Siegle, D. (2010). Cloud computing: A free technology option to promote collaborative learning. *Gifted Child Today, 33*(4), 41–45.

Singer, N. R., & Zeni, J. (2004). Building bridges: Creating an online conversation community for preservice teachers. *English Education, 37*(1), 30–49.

Slabon, W. A. (2009). *Learning by restorying: A naturalistic case study of an instructional strategy in a master's level conflict management course*. Unpublished Doctoral Dissertation. Tallahassee, FL: Florida State University.

Slavin, R. E. (1983). When does cooperative learning increase student achievement? *Psychological Bulletin, 94*(3), 429–445. doi:10.1037/0033-2909.94.3.429

Slavin, R. F. (1980). Cooperative learning. *Review of Educational Research, 50*(2), 315–342.

Smagorinsky, P., & Whiting, M. E. (1995). *How English teachers get taught*. Urbana, IL: National Council of Teachers of English.

Smaldino, S., Donalsdson, J. A., & Herring, M. (2011). Professional ethics: Rules applied to practice. In Reiser, R. A., & Dempsey, J. V. (Eds.), *Trends and Issues in Instructional Design and Technology* (3rd ed., pp. 342–347). Upper Saddle River, NJ: Pearson Education.

Smith, A. (2011). *13% of online adults use Twitter*. Retrieved from http://pewinternet.org/Reports/2011/Twitter-Update-2011.aspx.

Smith, A., & Rainie, L. (2010). *8% of online Americans use Twitter*. Retrieved from http://pewinternet.org/Reports/2010/Twitter-update-2010.aspx.

Smith, B. L., & MacGregor, J. T. (1992). *What is collaborative learning?* Retrieved from http://www.evergreen.edu/washcenter/natlc/pdf/collab.pdf.

Smith, K. A. (1986). Cooperative learning groups. In Schmoberg, S. F. (Ed.), *Strategies for Active Teaching and Learning in University Classrooms*. Minneapolis, MN: University of Minnesota.

Social Bakers. (2011). *Heart of social media statistics*. Retrieved July 15, 2011 from http://www.socialbakers.com/.

Social Media Defined. (2007). *What is social media?* Retrieved from http://www.socialmediadefined.com/what-is-social-media/.

Soloway, E., Norris, C., Blumenfeld, P., Fishman, B., Krajcik, J., & Marx, R. (2001). Log on education: Handheld devices are ready-at-hand. *Communications of the ACM, 44*(6), 15–20. doi:10.1145/376134.376140

Spradley, J. P. (1980). *Participant observation*. New York, NY: Holt, Rinehart and Winston.

Squire, K., & Johnson, C. (2000). Supporting distributed communities of practice with interactive television. *Educational Technology Research and Development, 48*(1), 23–43. doi:10.1007/BF02313484

Srinivasan, M. (2009). Visualizing the future: Technology competency development in clinical medicine, and implications for medical education. *Academic Psychiatry, 30*(6), 480–490. doi:10.1176/appi.ap.30.6.480

Steeples, C., & Jones, C. (2002). Perspectives and issues in networked learning. In Steeples, C., & Jones, C. (Eds.), *Networked Learning: Perspectives and Issues* (pp. 1–14). New York, NY: Springer.

Steinbring, H. (2005). *The construction of new mathematical knowledge in classroom interaction: An epistemological perspective.* New York, NY: Springer.

Stein, M. K., Smith, M. S., & Silver, E. A. (1999). The development of professional developers: Learning to assist teachers in new settings in new ways. *Harvard Educational Review, 69*(3), 237–269.

Stevens, V. (2006). Revisiting multiliteracies in collaborative learning environments: Impact on teacher professional development. *TESL-EJ, 10*(2), 1-12. Retrieved from http://tesl-ej.org/pdf/ej38/int.pdf.

Stripling, J. (2010). Not so private professors. *Inside Higher Ed.* Retrieved March 4, 2011, from http://www.insidehighered.com/news/2010/03/02/facebook.

Stritzke, W. G. K., Nguyen, A., & Durkin, K. (2004). Shyness and computer-mediated communication: A self-presentational theory perspective. *Media Psychology, 6*, 1–22. doi:10.1207/s1532785xmep0601_1

Stuart, T., & Podolny, J. (1999). Positional consequences of strategic alliances in the semiconductor industry. In Knoke, D. (Ed.), *Research in the Sociology of Organizations* (pp. 161–182). Greenwich, CT: JAI Press.

Subramaniam, M., & Venkatraman, N. (2001). Determinants of transnational new product development capability: Testing the influence of transferring and deploying tacit overseas knowledge. *Strategic Management Journal, 22*(4), 359–378. doi:10.1002/smj.163

Suh, B., Hong, L., Convertino, G., & Chi, E. H. (2010). *Sensemaking with Tweeting: Exploiting microblogging for knowledge workers.* Paper presented at the ACM Conference on Human Factors in Computing Systems. Atlanta, GA.

Sundar, M. (2006, July 9). *Top 10 CEO blogs.* Retrieved from http://mariosundar.com/2006/07/09/top-10-ceo-blogs/.

Sutton, R. E., & Wheatley, K. F. (2003). Teachers' emotions and teaching: A review of the literature and directions for future research. *Educational Psychology Review, 15*(4), 327–358. doi:10.1023/A:1026131715856

Swenson, J. (2003). Transformative teacher networks, on-line professional development, and the write for your life project. *English Education, 35*(4), 262–321.

Swenson, J., Rozema, R., Young, C. A., McGrail, E., & Whitin, P. (2005). Beliefs about technology and the preparation of English teachers: Beginning the conversation. *Contemporary Issues in Technology & Teacher Education, 5*(3/4), 210–236. Retrieved from http://www.citejournal.org/vol5/iss3/languagearts/article1.cfm

Tancredi, R. M. S. P., & Reali, A. M. M. R. (2011). O que um mentor precisa saber: Ou: Sobre a necessidade de um mentor construir uma visão multifocal. *Exitus, 1*(1), 33–44.

Tanis, M. (2007). Online social support group. In Joinson, A., McKenna, K., Postmes, T., & Reips, U. D. (Eds.), *The Oxford Handbook of Internet Psychology* (pp. 139–154). Oxford, UK: Oxford University Press.

Tan, S. (2010). Modeling engagement in a web-based advertising campaign. *Visual Communication, 9*(1), 91–115. doi:10.1177/1470357209352949

Text, S. (2011). *Customer case studies.* Retrieved from http://www.socialtext.com/customers.

Thibodeau, P. (2009, March 3). *Best Buy getting results from social network.* Retrieved from http://www.computerworld.com/s/article/9128877/Best_Buy_getting_results_from_social_network_.

Tobin, K. G. (1990). Social constructivist perspectives on the reform of science education. *The Australian Science Teachers Journal, 36*(4), 29–35.

Tomei, L. A. (2010). *Lexicon of online and distance learning*. Plymouth, MA: Rowman and Littlefield Education.

Topol, E. (2010, February 2). *Eric Topol: The wireless future of medicine*. Retrieved from http://www.ted.com/talks/eric_topol_the_wireless_future_of_medicine.html.

Tosey, P. (1999). The peer learning community: A contextual design for learning? *Management Decision, 37*(5), 403–410. doi:10.1108/00251749910274171

Tosoni, S. (2008). *Identitá virtuali: Comunicazione mediata da computer e procesi di constuzione dell'identitápersonale*. Milan, Italy: Franco Angeli.

Tough, A. (1979). *The adult's learning projects: A fresh approach to theory and practice in adult learning*. Toronto, Canada: Ontario Institute for Studies in Education.

Tran, K., Ayad, M., Weinberg, J., Cherng, A., Chowdbury, M., & Monir, S. (2011). Mobile teledermatology in the developing world: Implications of feasibility study on 30 Egyptian patients with common skin diseases. *Journal of the American Academy of Dermatology, 64*(2), 302–309. doi:10.1016/j.jaad.2010.01.010

Traxler, J. (2007). Defining, discussing, and evaluating mobile learning: The moving finger writes and having writ. *International Review of Research in Open and Distance Learning, 8*(2), 1–12.

Tremblay, E. A. (2010). Educating the mobile generation: Using personal cell phones as audience response systems in post-secondary science teaching. *Journal of Computers in Mathematics and Science Teaching, 29*(2), 217–227.

Triandis, H. C. (1995). *Individualism and collectivism*. Boulder, CO: Westview Press.

Trinkle, C. (2009). Twitter as a professional learning community. *School Library Monthly, 26*(4), 22–23.

Tufte, E. (2001). *The visual display of quantitative information* (2nd ed.). Cheshire, CT: Graphics Press.

US Department of Justice. (2008). *Privacy and civil liberties development guide*. Retrieved June 9, 2011, from http://it.ojp.gov/documents/Privacy_Guide_Final.pdf.

Valente, T. W., Gallaher, P., & Mouttapa, M. (2004). Using social networks to understand and prevent substance use: A transdisciplinary perspective. *Substance Use & Misuse, 39*(10-12), 1685–1712. doi:10.1081/JA-200033210

Van Cleemput, K. (2010). I'll see you on IM, text, or call you: A social network approach of adolescents' use of communication media. *Bulletin of Science, Technology & Society, 30*(2), 75–85. doi:10.1177/0270467610363143

van Duijn, M. A. J., & Vermunt, J. K. (2006). What is special about social network analysis methodology. *European Journal of Research Methods for the Behavioral and Social Sciences, 2*(1), 2–6. doi:10.1027/1614-2241.2.1.2

Van, B. J., & Renaud, K. (2008). A qualitative study of the applicability of technology acceptance models to senior mobile phone users. In *Proceedings of the 27th International Conference on Conceptual Modeling*, (pp. 228-237). Springer.

Vavoula, G. (2004). *KLeOS: A knowledge and learning organisation system in support of lifelong learning*. Unpublished Doctoral Dissertation. Bringham, UK: University of Birmingham.

Vavoula, G., & Sharples, M. (2009). Lifelong learning organisers: Requirements for tools for supporting episodic and semantic learning. *Journal of Educational Technology & Society, 12*(3), 82–97.

Vera, E. R., & Schupp, T. (2006). Network analysis in comparative social sciences. *Comparative Education, 42*(3), 405–429. doi:10.1080/03050060600876723

Vergeer, M., Hermans, L., & Sams, S. (2011). Online social networks and micro-blogging in political campaigning: The exploration of a new campaign tool and a new campaign style. *Party Politics*, (n.d), 1–25.

Vine, B. (2004). *Getting things done at work: The discourse of power in workplace interaction*. Philadelphia, PA: John Benjamins.

Vogel, M. P. (2009). Exploring the conditions for academic teachers☐ informal collegial learning about teaching: A social network approach. *Educate, 9*(2), 18-36. Retrieved from http://www.educatejournal.org/index.php?journal=educate&page=article&op=viewFile&path%5B%5D=200&path%5B%5D=209.

von Krogh, G., Ichijo, K., & Nonaka, I. (2000). *Enabling knowledge creation: How to unlock the mystery of tacit knowledge and release the power of innovation*. Oxford, UK: Oxford University Press.

Vygotsky, L. (1987). *Mind and society*. Cambridge, MA: Harvard University Press.

Vygotsky, L. S. (1978). *Mind in society: The development of higher psychological processes*. Boston, MA: Harvard University Press.

Wagner, C., & Majchrzak, A. (2007). Enabling customer-centricity using wikis and the wiki way. *Journal of Management Information Systems, 23*(3), 17–43. doi:10.2753/MIS0742-1222230302

Wagner, E. (2008). Realizing the promises of mobile learning. *Journal of Computing in Higher Education, 20*(2), 4–14. doi:10.1007/s12528-008-9008-x

Wain, K. (2004). *The learning society in a postmodern world: The education crisis*. New York, NY: Peter Lang Publishing, Inc.

Wali, E., Winters, N., & Oliver, M. (2008). Maintaining, changing and crossing contexts: An activity theoretic reinterpretation of mobile learning. *ALT-J, 16*(1), 41–57. doi:10.1080/09687760701850190

Walker, G., Kogut, B., & Shan, W. (1997). Social capital, structural holes and the formation of an industry network. *Organization Science, 8*(2), 109–125. doi:10.1287/orsc.8.2.109

Walker, R., & Monin, N. (2001). The purpose of the picnic: Using Burke's dramatistic pentad to analyse a company event. *Journal of Organizational Change Management, 14*(3), 266–279. doi:10.1108/09534810110394886

Wallace, P. (2001). *The psychology of the internet*. Cambridge, UK: Cambridge University Press.

Walters, G. (2009, March 1). Learning integration: Can informal learning be formalized?. *Training Journal*, 51-54.

Wang, L., von Laszewski, G., Younge, A., He, X., Kunze, M., Tao, J., & Fu, C. (2008). Cloud computing: A perspective study. *New Generation Computing, 28*(2), 137–146. doi:10.1007/s00354-008-0081-5

Wang, X., Jiang, T., & Ma, F. (2010). Blog-supported scientific communication: An exploration analysis based on social hyperlinks in a Chinese blog community. *Journal of Information Science, 36*, 690–704. doi:10.1177/0165551510383189

Ward, V., Smith, S., Carruthers, S., Hamer, S., & House, A. (2010). *Knowledge brokering: Exploring the process of transferring knowledge into action*. Retrieved from http://www.leeds.ac.uk/lihs/psychiatry/research/TransferringKnowledgeIntoAction/documents/Knowledge%20Brokering%20Final%20report.pdf.

Warlick, D. (2009). Grow your own personal learning network: New technologies can keep you connected and help you manage information overload. *Learning and Leading with Technology, 36*(6), 12–16.

Warr, W. A. (2008). Social software: Fun and games, or business tools? *Journal of Information Science, 34*, 591–604. doi:10.1177/0165551508092259

Wasko, M. M., & Faraj, S. (2005). Why should I share? Examining social capital and knowledge contribution in electronic networks of practice. *Management Information Systems Quarterly, 29*(1), 35–57.

Wasserman, S., & Faust, K. (1994). *Social network analysis: Methods and applications*. Cambridge, UK: Cambridge University Press.

Waycott, J., Jones, A., & Scanlon, E. (2005). PDAs as lifelong learning tools: An activity theory based analysis. *Learning, Media and Technology, 30*(2), 107–130. doi:10.1080/17439880500093513

Webster-Wright, A. (2009). Reframing professional development through understanding authentic professional learning. *Review of Educational Research, 79*(2), 702–739. doi:10.3102/0034654308330970

Wellman, B. (1996). Are personal communities local? A dumptarian reconsideration. *Social Networks, 18*(3), 347–354. doi:10.1016/0378-8733(95)00282-0

Wellman, B. (2007). The network is personal: Introduction to a special issue of social networks. *Social Networks, 29*(3), 349–356. doi:10.1016/j.socnet.2007.01.006

Wenger, E. (2006). *Communities of practice: A brief introduction*. Retrieved from http://www.ewenger.com/theory/.

Wenger, E. (1998). *Communities of practice: Learning, meaning and identity*. Cambridge, UK: Cambridge University Press.

Wenger, E. (2000). Communities of practice and social learning systems. *Organization, 7*(2), 225–246. doi:10.1177/135050840072002

Wenger, E., McDermott, R., & Snyder, W. (2002). *Cultivating communities of practice: A guide to managing knowledge*. Boston, MA: Harvard Business School Press.

Wenger, E., & Snyder, W. (2000). Communities of practice: The organizational frontier. *Harvard Business Review, 78*(6), 139–146.

Wexler, S., Brown, J., Metcalf, D., Rogers, D., & Wagner, E. (2008). *eLearning guild research 360 report: Mobile learning*. Santa Rosa, CA: eLearning Guild.

White, D. (2007). *Results of the "online tool use survey" undertaken by the JISC funded SPIRE project*. Retrieved from http://www.scribd.com/doc/464744/Online-Tool-Use-Survey.

White, T. (2010). iPads to be distributed in incoming class by Stanford medical students. *Stanford School of Medicine*. Retrieved from http://med.stanford.edu/ism/2010/august/ipad.html.

Whitman, N. A. (1988). *Peer teaching: To teach is to learn twice*. Washington, DC: Association for the Study of Higher Education.

Whitten, P. S., Mair, F. S., Haycox, A., May, C. R., Williams, T. L., & Hellmich, S. (2002). Systemic review of cost effectiveness studies of telemedicine interventions. *British Medical Journal, 324*, 1434–1437. doi:10.1136/bmj.324.7351.1434

Williams, I. M., Warren, H. N., & Olaniran, B. A. (2009). Achieving cultural acquiescence through foreign language e-learning. In Chang, M., & Kuo, C. (Eds.), *Handbook of Research on Learning Culture and Language via ICTs: Methods for Enhanced Instruction* (pp. 88–102). Hershey, PA: IGI Global. doi:10.4018/978-1-60566-166-7.ch006

Williams, J. B., & Jacobs, J. (2004). Exploring the use of blogs as learning spaces in the higher education sector. *Australasian Journal of Educational Technology, 20*(2), 232–247.

Wilson, S., Liber, O., Johnson, M., Beauvoir, P., Sharples, P., & Milligan, C. (2007). Personal learning environments: Challenging the dominant design of educational systems. *Journal of e-Learning and Knowledge Society, 2*(3), 27–38. Retrieved from http://je-lks.maieutiche.economia.unitn.it/index.php/Je-LKS_EN/article/viewFile/247/229.

Wilson, S. (2008). Patterns of personal learning environments. *Learning Environments, 16*(1), 17–34. doi:10.1080/10494820701772660

Wilson, S. M., & Berne, J. (1999). Teacher learning and the acquisition of professional knowledge: An examination of research on contemporary professional development. *Review of Research in Education, 24*(6), 173–209.

Wilson, S., Floden, R., & Ferrini-Mundy, J. (2001). *Teacher preparation research: Current knowledge gaps and recommendations*. Seattle, WA: University of Washington.

Winter, F. I., Greene, J. A., & Costich, C. M. (2008). Self-regulation of learning within computer-based learning environments: A critical analysis. *Educational Psychology Review, 20*(4), 369–372.

Winters, N. (2007). periLEARN: Contextualised mobile learning in the era of Web 2.0. In *Proceedings of IADIS International Conference on Mobile Learning*. Lisbon, Portugal: IADIS.

Woodill, G. (2011). *The mobile learning edge: Tools and technologies for developing your teams*. New York, NY: McGraw-Hill.

Wootton, R. (2001). Recent advances: Telemedicine. *British Medical Journal, 323*(8), 557–560. doi:10.1136/bmj.323.7312.557

Wright, K. B. (2009). Increasing computer-mediated social support. In Parker, J. C., & Thorson, E. (Eds.), *Health Communication in the New Media Landscape* (pp. 243–265). New York, NY: Springer Pub.

Wright, K. B., & Bell, S. B. (2003). Health-related support groups on the internet: Linking empirical findings to social support and computer-mediated communication theory. *Journal of Health Psychology, 8*(1), 39–54. doi:10.1177/1359105303008001429

Xiang, Z., & Gretzel, U. (2009). Role of social media in online travel information search. *Tourism Management*, *31*(2), 179–188. doi:10.1016/j.tourman.2009.02.016

Yamazaki, Y., & Kayes, D. C. (2004). An experiential approach to cross-cultural learning: A review and integration of success factors in expatriate adaptation. *Academy of Management Learning & Education*, *3*(1), 4–16.

Yeh, Y.-C. (2010). Analyzing online behaviors, roles, and learning communities via online discussions. *Journal of Educational Technology & Society*, *13*(1), 140–151.

Youngblood, P., Harter, P. M., Srivastava, S., Moffett, S., Heinrichs, W. L., & Dev, P. (2008). Design, development, and evaluation of an online virtual emergency department for training trauma team. *Society for Simulation in Healthcare*, *3*(3), 146–153. doi:10.1097/SIH.0b013e31817bedf7

Young, C. A., & Bush, J. (2004). Teaching the English language arts with technology: A critical approach and pedagogical framework. *Contemporary Issues in Technology & Teacher Education*, *4*(1), 1–22. Retrieved from http://www.citejournal.org/vol4/iss1/languagearts/article1.cfm

Youn, T., & Price, T. (2009). Learning from the experience of others: The evolution of faculty tenure and promotion rules in comprehensive institutions. *The Journal of Higher of Higher Education*, *80*(2), 204–237. doi:10.1353/jhe.0.0041

Yuan, Y. C., & Gay, G. (2006). Homophily of network ties and bonding and bridging social capital in computer-mediated distributed teams. *Journal of Computer-Mediated Communication*, *11*, 1062–1084. doi:10.1111/j.1083-6101.2006.00308.x

Zembylas, M. (2002). Constructing genealogies of teachers' emotions in science teaching. *Journal of Research in Science Teaching*, *39*(1), 79–103. doi:10.1002/tea.10010

Zhu, C., Valcke, M., & Schellens, T. (2009). Cultural differences in the perception of a social-constructivist e-learning environment. *British Journal of Educational Technology*, *40*(1), 164–168. doi:10.1111/j.1467-8535.2008.00879.x

Zimmerman, D. H., & Wieder, D. L. (1977). The diary: Diary-interview method. *Journal of Contemporary Ethnography*, *5*(4), 479–498. doi:10.1177/089124167700500406

About the Contributors

Vanessa P. Dennen is an Associate Professor of Instructional Systems at Florida State University. She earned a Ph.D. in Instructional Systems Technology from Indiana University. Her research investigates the nexus of cognitive, motivational, and social elements in computer-mediated communication, concentrating on two major issues: learner participation in online activities, and interactions, norm development, and informal learning within online communities of practice. Vanessa's publications, which have been well cited, have appeared in *Instructional Science*; *Distance Education*; *Computers in Human Behavior*; *The Handbook of Distance Education*; *The Handbook of Research on Educational Communications and Technology*; and *The International Handbook of Collaborative Learning*, among others. Additionally, she recently co-edited (with Stefan Hrastinski) a special issue of *The Internet and Higher Education* on Social Media in Higher Education.

Jennifer B. Myers is the ASSIST Project Director and an instructional designer and consultant at Orangeburg-Calhoun Technical College in South Carolina. Additionally, she is a Ph.D. candidate at Florida State University in the Instructional Systems program under the College of Education. Previously, Myers worked as a middle school teacher in North Carolina and earned her Master's degree in Instructional Systems at the University of North Carolina at Charlotte. She has designed and developed a number of instructional courses and materials for a variety of organizations and audiences in the K-12, higher education, and non-profit sectors, and has taught graduate and undergraduate level courses in addition to her experiences teaching in K-12. She has presented her research at various professional conferences. Additionally, she is working on her dissertation examining self-regulated learning within an informal online community of practice. More broadly, her research interests surround informal learning, professional development, mentoring, self-regulated learning, social learning, knowledge brokering, and online communities of practice.

* * *

Magdalena Bielenia-Grajewska is an Assistant Professor at the University of Gdansk (Institute of English, Department of Translation Studies and Intercultural Communication) and a Postdoctoral Researcher at SISSA (La Scuola Internazionale Superiore di Studi Avanzati di Trieste). She is a linguist (M.A. in English Studies, Ph.D. in Humanities, University of Gdansk), an economist (MA in Economics, Gdańsk University of Technology), and a specialist in managing scientific projects (Postgraduate Studies, Technical University of Gdansk). Her Ph.D. thesis was of an interdisciplinary character, being devoted to intercultural communication, translation, and investment banking. She is a member of the

Editorial Board of *International Journal of Actor-Network Theory and Technological Innovation* (IJAN-TII) and serves as an ad hoc reviewer for several international journals. Her scientific interests include organizational discourse, online social networks, intercultural communication, sociolinguistics, ANT, and symbolism in management studies. She is an author of over 50 publications on corporate identity, business communication, and the communicative dimension of organizations that have been published in Polish, English, and German.

Curt Bonk is Professor of Instructional Systems Technology at Indiana University and President of CourseShare. Drawing on his background as a corporate controller, CPA, educational psychologist, and instructional technologist, Bonk offers unique insights into the intersection of business, education, psychology, and technology. He received the CyberStar Award from the Indiana Information Technology Association, the Most Outstanding Achievement Award from the U.S. Distance Learning Association, and the Most Innovative Teaching in a Distance Education Program Award from the State of Indiana. A well-known authority on emerging technologies for learning, Bonk reflects on his speaking experiences around the world in his popular blog, *TravelinEdMan*. He has coauthored several widely used technology books, including *The World is Open: How Web Technology is Revolutionizing Education* (2009), *Empowering Online Learning: 100+ Activities for Reading, Reflecting, Displaying, and Doing* (2008), *The Handbook of Blended Learning* (2006), and *Electronic Collaborators* (1998).

Richard Brandt is a Physician Assistant with over 12 years of clinical experience in medical and surgical dermatology. Over the course of his career, he has also served as a Sub-Investigator (Sub-I) on multiple clinical research studies, an adjunct faculty member in Physician Assistant Studies, a moderator for Dermatology PA meetings, and an educator, while performing peer-to-peer and student lecturing. Additionally, he is a doctoral student in Technical Communications and Rhetoric at Texas Tech University studying Mobile Learning (m-Learning) and the use of new media in medicine.

Thomas Brush is currently the Barbara B. Jacobs Chair in Education and Technology as well as the Associate Dean for Teacher Education at Indiana University in Bloomington, Indiana. His research interests include the use of technology to support inquiry-based learning in K-12 settings and examining the best methods for preparing current and future teachers to integrate technology to support teaching and learning.

Kerry J. Burner is a freelance academic and consultant who works for online M.A., Ed.D., and Ph.D. programs at both brick-and-mortar and fully online universities. She has taught at the undergraduate and graduate levels for over 15 years, designing and delivering courses ranging from Theories of Learning and Cognition in Instruction to Advanced Instructional Design and Applied Research Methods. She chairs Ed.D. and Ph.D. committees, and sits on Communications and Dissertation Review committees. Previously, she has served as the Project Director for the FSU-Teach Launch Project at the Florida State University, and she has consulted on instructional design programs for the State of Florida through FSU. Her last publication is a chapter ("Performance Analysis and Training Needs Assessment") in ISPI's (2009) *Handbook of Training and Improving Workplace Performance*. In addition to her work in Human Performance and Training, her research interests online and computer mediated learning, social learning, communities of practice, cognitive apprenticeship, the relationship between writing and assessment in online learning, and the role reflection and reflexivity play in learning and instruction. Her current research foci include social network analysis, specifically in discussions in online courses, and understanding the intersection of Web 2.0 social networking technologies and privacy.

Xiaojun Chen is a Ph.D. Candidate in Learning Design and Technology at Purdue University. After Xiaojun obtained her Master of Education in Communication, Education, and Technology from the University of Manchester, she worked in K-12 and higher education institutions in the U.K. and in China. Xiaojun's research is centered around the following themes: 1) interdisciplinary team learning, 2) technology integration in formal and informal learning; and 3) international development of instructional technology. She has worked in various research projects including National Science Foundation funded projects in undergraduate design teams in service learning, instructional design for K-12 subjects, international online collaboration for teacher preparation, and virtual universities in global context. She has presented in many national and international conferences. She also published in the *Journal of Engineering Education, Journal of Distance Education, Journal of Computing in Higher Education*, and *Journal of Educational Technology Development and Exchange*.

Jea H. Choi is a doctoral candidate at Learning Design and Technology program at Purdue University. Originally from South Korea, she had her Bachelor's degree in Educational Technology from Ewha Womens' University. She also got her Master's degree in Instructional Technology at the University of Georgia. Her research area is on improving student's motivation in online learning environment. She is specifically focusing on social presence, social network analysis, and Web 2.0-technology integration. Currently, Jea is working under VOSS project, which sees the trends of loose network forming to a stable organization in an interdisciplinary field.

Kyle M. Christensen is the Director of the Social Research Center at Columbus State University and an Assistant Professor in the Department of Political Science. Dr. Christensen earned his Ph.D. and M.A. in Political Science from West Virginia University and his B.A. in Political Science from Mercer University. Dr. Christensen's research interests include research in comparative public policy, European Union politics, and international security. His research principally focuses on military personnel policy and the diffusion of the all-volunteer force.

Joseph Rene Corbeil is an Associate Professor at The University of Texas at Brownsville, earned his Doctoral degree in Education-Curriculum and Instruction in Instructional Technology from the University of Houston, and a Master of Education in Educational Technology from The University of Texas-Brownsville. With over 28 years experience in education, he currently develops and teaches fully Web-based undergraduate and graduate courses in Educational Technology. He presents and publishes on his research interests, which include best practices in synchronous and asynchronous communication and enhancing social presence and teacher immediacy in e-Learning environments through Web 2.0 and social media tools. He has also won numerous awards, including the 2007 EDUCAUSE Quarterly Contribution of the Year and the 2010 International Association of Computer Information Systems (IACIS) Best Paper in Technology Award.

Maria Elena Corbeil is an Assistant Professor at The University of Texas at Brownsville, earned a graduate certificate in Online Teaching and Learning from the University of Florida, a Doctoral degree in Education in Curriculum and Instruction from the University of Houston, a Master's degree in Education from The University of Texas-Brownsville; and a Bachelors degree in English from Florida International University. For over 10 years, she has developed and taught fully online educational technology courses. She presents at conferences and has published in numerous journals, winning the EDUCAUSE Quarterly Contribution of the Year award in 2007 and the 2011 International Association of Computer Information Systems (IACIS) Ben Bauman Excellence Award.

Shuang Hao is currently a doctoral student in Instructional Systems at Florida State University. She received her Master's in Instructional Design and Technology from Western Illinois University and her Bachelor's in Information Management System from Tianjin University of Commerce, China. Her research interests include online and mobile learning communities, performance improvement technology, and supportive learning environments.

Jung Won Hur is an Assistant Professor in the department of Educational Foundations, Leadership, and Technology at Auburn University. Her research interests include online communities of teachers, technology integration in K-12 classrooms, supporting teacher professional development online, and use of emerging technology to assist English language learners' language proficiency. She is interested in designing learning environments where every student is encouraged to achieve his/her potential.

Wenting Jiang is currently a third year doctoral student from Instructional Systems program at Florida State University. Her research interest is in instructional design and development, social networks, online learning environments, professional development, and performance improvement. She received her Master's degree in Educational Technology from the University of Missouri-Columbia in 2009 and Bachelor's degree in Computer Science from the Beijing Normal University-Zhuhai in 2007. While attending Florida State University, she has held several positions; she has worked at the Center for Assessment and Testing as a consultant and at the Learning Systems Institute as an instructional designer. She is currently an intern in the Florida Department of Highway Safety and Motor Vehicle, helping to design and develop online training courses for State of Florida employees.

Yalin Kılıç Türel is an Assistant Professor in Firat University in Turkey. He holds a Ph.D. in Educational Sciences and a Master's degree in Computer Software from Firat University. He has taught a variety of courses such as introduction to computer sciences, operation systems and office applications, desktop publishing, web page design, programming languages in several vocational high schools in Turkey. He received a Fulbright Scholarship in 2007 and has worked as a visiting scholar at Florida State University. In 2011, he worked as a visiting post-doc researcher at Learning System Institute in Florida State University. His research focuses mainly on learning objects, interactive whiteboards, instructional design, Web 2.0 technologies, and technology integration to school settings.

Maria da Graça Nicoletti Mizukami is a category 1 Researcher, CNPq (National Counsel of Technological and Scientific Development, Brazil). Advisory Board Member, CNPq. Professor Mizukami holds a degree in Education from UNESP-São Paulo State University, an M.A. in Education from the

Catholic University of Rio de Janeiro, and a Ph.D. in Social Sciences from the Catholic University of Rio de Janeiro. From 1971-1974, Professor Mizukami was a graduate student in Curricula and Educational Technology at Karl Ruprecht Universität Heidelberg and Pädagogische Hochschule, Heidelberg, Germany. In 1993, she carried out postdoctoral research at Santa Clara University, California, USA. Professor Mizukami is a member of the faculty of the Federal University of São Carlos, São Paulo, Brazil, and of Mackenzie University's Graduate Program in Education, Art, and Cultural History. Her research's interests are knowledge base for teaching, professional development of teachers, professional learning of teachers, pedagogical practices, and teaching cases.

Bolanle A. Olaniran is a Professor in the Department of Communication Studies at Texas Tech University. His research includes communication technologies and computer-mediated communication, organization communication, cross-cultural communication, and crisis management. He has authored several journal articles and book chapters in national and international disciplinary and interdisciplinary publications.

Aline Maria de Medeiros Rodrigues Reali is a category 2 Researcher at CNPq (National Counsel of Technological and Scientific Development, Brazil). She is a graduate in Psychology (FFCL of Ribeirão Preto, São Paulo State University, 1979), M.A. in Special Education (Federal University of São Carlos -1984), and Ph.D. in Psychology (São Paulo State University, 1990). She is a Full Professor in the department of Pedagogical Theories and Practices Department and in the Graduate Education Program of the Education and Human Sciences Center at the Federal University of São Carlos, São Paulo, Brazil. Her research's interests are professional development of teachers, teacher continuing education, and online teacher education. Currently, she is Secretary of Distance Education of the Federal University of São Carlos.

Rich Rice is Associate Professor of English at Texas Tech University, where he specializes in Technical Communication and Rhetoric. He directs the Multiliteracy Lab, which explores intersections between new media composing and teaching, research, and service. He teaches online and face-to-face courses in new media and rhetoric, grant writing, multimodal composition, and technical communication. His most recent work explores intersections between m-learning and health, museums, computer-mediated communication, and study abroad.

Randy Richards is a Professor of Managerial Studies and the Co-Director of the Master of Organizational Leadership at St. Ambrose University. He is a second career academic having spent twenty years in management in both the public and private sectors. He earned a Ph.D. in Philosophy at University of Iowa. He is also a Visiting Professor at Zagreb School of Economics and Management in Zagreb, Croatia, and International Business School in Vilnius, Lithuania. Professor Richards is especially interested in issues in adult learning, leadership, conflict management, organizational development, and ethics. He has an active consulting practice working with a wide variety of both public and private organizations.

Luke Rodesiler is a former high school English teacher and is currently a Doctoral Fellow studying English Education in the School of Teaching and Learning at the University of Florida and a teacher-consultant of the Red Cedar Writing Project at Michigan State University. His work has appeared in various publications, including *English Journal, Classroom Notes Plus, Screen Education*, and *Computers and Composition Online*, and he has made contributions to multiple edited collections, including NCTE's *Lesson Plans for Developing Digital Literacies*. Rodesiler's scholarly interests include teacher education, self-directed professional learning, and the use of popular media and technology in the teaching of English.

Iris M. Saltiel is the Director of the Faculty Center for the Enhancement of Teaching and Learning at Columbus State University (CSU) and a Professor in the College of Education. She holds an Ed.D. degree from Fordham University, an M.Ed. from Rutgers University, and a B.S. from Trenton State College. As a scholar, her work has primarily been in the area of collaboration among adult learners, faculty, and various organizations (corporate, nonprofit, higher education). Her primary research interests have centered on adult learners and collaboration, partnerships in learning and cohort based programming. Prior to her appointment at CSU, she served at Troy University as Director of the Quality Enhancement Institute and a Professor in the College of Education. Previously, she worked at Synovus Service Corporation in Columbus, Georgia. Before Synovus, she served as the Director of Enrollment Services and Director of Corporate Programs at Thomas Edison State College in New Jersey.

Wayne Slabon is the Director of Distance Learning Design and Delivery at Columbus State University. He earned his M.S. in Instructional Technology and Telecommunications from Western Illinois University and a Ph.D. in Instructional Systems from Florida State University. He is an experienced instructional designer and technologist committed to the effective use of elearning technologies to promote learning and enhance real world performance. His research interests include story-based instruction, case study methods, collaborative learning, scaffolding techniques, and instructional sequencing strategies. He has presented at such conferences as AERA, AECT, and ED-Media.

Regina Maria Simões Puccinelli Tancredi is a graduate in Mathematics from UNESP-São Paulo State University. Masters in Education and Doctor in Education from the Federal University of São Carlos, Brazil. In basic education, she was a teacher of mathematics and school principal. She teaches in the Graduate Programs in Education of UFSCar and Education, Art, and Cultural History of UPM. She develops research and extension activities in different areas: teacher and other educational agents' development, teaching and learning processes, and educational public policy.

Joseph M. Terantino is an Assistant Professor of Spanish and Foreign Language Education at Kennesaw State University. He is a passionate user and researcher of instructional technology and social media who enjoys the challenge of tinkering with new technologies. In particular, his research interests relate to computer-assisted language learning, foreign language education, and the integration of technology in teaching. In February of 2011, his article "YouTube for Foreign Languages: You Have to See This Video" was published in the journal *Language Learning and Technology*, and in November of 2011, his article "Using Facebook in the Language Classroom as Part of the Net Generation Curriculum" was published in the *Language Educator Magazine*. Currently, he is researching the uses of Facebook and other social media applications for foreign language teaching and learning.

Lauren Tripp is a doctoral student at the University of Florida in the Curriculum, Teaching, and Teacher Education program. She is a former high school English teacher, and her research interests include English education, teacher professional development, culturally responsive pedagogy, and overcoming the achievement gap. She is currently developing her dissertation study on first-generation Black college students' perceptions of the school- and community-based factors that supported them in their academic achievement during the crucial period of middle and high school. Instead of continuing to identify the struggles that Black students face, she hopes that this study will contribute to an asset-based philosophy, one which teachers can use in their own professional development and which will support their efforts to help all their students succeed.

Mariliis Vahe is a doctoral candidate and an instructor at the Florida State University School of Communication. As a Fulbright scholar, she received a Master's degree in Media and Communication Studies from Florida State University in 2010. She also holds a Master's degree in Social Sciences from Tartu University in 2004. Her current research interests include health communication and education, especially the applications of ICT-based health interventions in less developed areas. Mariliis Vahe's research and teaching portfolio is accompanied by years of professional work experience in the field of public relations and communication.

Indi Marie Williams received her Master's in Communication Studies from Texas Technology University, Lubbock, Texas, and her Bachelor's in Sociology from the University of Texas at Austin. She is currently a doctoral student in Educational Technology at Arizona State University. Her research interests include virtual learning communities, Web 2.0, globalization, and online culture.

Hanna Yakavenka is a Principal Lecturer at the University of Greenwich Business School. Prior to this, she held associate teaching posts in International Business and Marketing at Manchester Metropolitan University Business School and a management position in the British heritage and museum industry. She graduated with a Ph.D. from Manchester Metropolitan University Business School in 2006. Her research interests lie in the field of international knowledge management and cross-cultural communications. She is passionate about teaching and has conducted extensive research in the field of business education. Her monograph on the "Role of Host Education in the Knowledge Management Transfer Process" was published in 2009, and she has presented her research findings on learning processes and skills development at various professional conferences.

Ji Hyun Yu is a Ph.D Candidate in Learning Design and Technology at Purdue University. She received a Master's degree in Educational Technology from Ewha Women University, South Korea. Prior to the Ph.D program, she worked as a HRD training consultant. Her research interests include collaborative learning, social media, personal epistemology, scientific research collaboration, and virtual organization. Her current projects are to design and analyze collaborative learning using the affordance of social media; and to develop the instrument of Engineering-specific Epistemological Beliefs. She has been working on several projects including National Science Foundation funded project about the evolution of virtual organization in the field of engineering education research, Web 2.0 supported collaborative learning for pre-service teachers, and competency modeling for teaching engineering in the K-6 contexts. She published the outcomes of those studies in *Educational Technology Research and Development*, *Internet and Higher Education*, and *International Journal of Engineering Education*.

Khawaja Zain-Ul-Abdin is a Fulbright scholar and a doctoral candidate at the Florida State University. He holds a Master's degree in Media and Communication Studies from Florida State University and an MBA from Lahore School of Economics. He has received consecutive international Fulbright scholarships for his Master's and Doctoral studies and has presented his research at academic conferences worldwide. His research interests focus on the use of technological innovations to mitigate effects of communication barriers in learning, the most recent manifestation being a research project that uses the Microsoft Kinect sensor in learning systems. Besides research and teaching experience, Khawaja Zain-Ul-Abdin has more than ten years experience in the media and marketing industry in Pakistan.

Index

V

W